praise for **Modern Esoteric**

We're at the frontier of an evolution in consciousnes̶ ̶ ̶ ̶ create a better future individually and collectively. I̶ ̶ ̶ ̶ about what's gone before and what we're up against ̶ ̶ ̶ publisher, editor and change agent Brad Olsen analy̶ ̶ ̶ ̶ we've been taught it. He restates the wisdom of the ancient esoteric traditions and champions the cause of free-energy technologies.

*Olsen has divided his "alternative narrative" into three parts. In "Lifeology", he examines creation myths, charts the progress of civilizations, speculates on super-human DNA and contemplates the legacy of ancient mystery schools. In "Control", he explains how we're deceived by ruling bloodline families, why sacred knowledge that is our spiritual birthright has been kept from us, and how our health is being compromised by chemicals and GM foods. In "Thrive", Olsen lights the way to a new world in which the solution is to connect with our true nature, give service to others, and change our consensus reality via the science of consciousness. This involves understanding vibrational frequency, extradimensional realities, hypercommunication and quantum DNA. We can overhaul the global financial system, bridge the gulf between science and religion and overcome the divisions that lead to wars. There is a better way, and it's up to us to be the best we can be, says Olsen in his grand-vision book. —**Nexus***

Author Brad Olsen discussed flaws in modern history and how conspiracy theories, esoteric insights, and fringe subjects can be used to help change a dead-end course for humanity. He contended that nearly every facet of human life, from science, government, and banking to farming, water treatment, and even spirituality, have been manipulated by nefarious forces to ensure control over the population. "As we awaken to truth," he observed, "we're realizing that the beneficial information in all these areas has been suppressed and revised in order to keep us enslaved." Behind this agenda, Olsen said, are wealthy families which propagate global wars and control essential resources.

We have to take the bold steps of rethinking of who we are and what the history is on this planet," Olsen declared. To that end, he noted the Great Pyramids of Egypt as one area which encapsulates this concept of "rethinking our history." Olsen observed that the landmarks display an uncanny level of early technological sophistication, but also reveal a strange devolution in later abilities of the Egyptian culture. Similar to the seemingly spontaneous emergence of the Sumerian culture, Olsen posited that both civilizations constitute a "legacy of something previous," which remains hidden from the historical record. By opening our minds to this 'forbidden' history, Olsen mused, humanity may learn the true heritage of our world and begin to free itself from the 'powers that be' controlling the planet.

—George Knapp, guest host of *Coast to Coast AM*

In this incredible compilation of esoteric subjects, Brad Olsen seems to have tapped into a stream of consciousness - energy - that like myself and many others, has allowed him to ascertain and disseminate information of an occult - hidden - nature as wide ranging as the omitted/hidden origins of mankind throughout history, and suppressed sciences, to health, sacred geometry, and consciousness.

Broken into three parts and easy-to-read-sections, **Modern Esoteric** *provides the modern novice or neophyte with a handheld tool of self-initiation. In the ancient mystery schools and secret societies, many of which still exist today, a process of rebirth would be brought about by ceremonies filled with rituals, drugs, dancing, and essentially any other act or substance that could alter a candidates' view of reality; bringing them to escape the confines of Plato's Cave and be spiritually reborn. Once initiated the newly enlightened individual begins to see the world in a completely different way, striving to build one's own temple - bettering ones self - and contributing to the world the preservation of these secret teachings for future generations while also utilizing this new perception to help others. Although this book includes such a wide array of subjects, by completing the work in its entirety one will find themselves transformed from a lump of dark material into a shining substance reminiscent of an alchemical transmutation; from base metal into gold and from base, animal consciousness into a higher understanding of life and reality.*

In reading this book, whether your first, or one of several books on these subjects, you will find yourself most likely questioning the very substance of what we perceive as reality. Who are you? What is you? What is truth? As you progress through this alchemical transformation, stay true to yourself, substantiate all that you read, see and hear, and use Brad's book as another tool in your arsenal to better both yourself and others in the material world. This content is neutral; rejecting it or accepting it without personal investigation is the opposite of skepticism or alternative thinking. Brad will provide you with enough content, written in a way that is not demanding, so you may start with any subject and find yourself rethinking everything you have been told, suggested or thought you knew. Before you begin, leave your ego, beliefs, biases and all other forms of natural and manufactured skepticisms on the outside of this work. Be skeptical but be truly open and let Brad Olsen take you through the world of the **Modern Esoteric**, *which is undoubtedly beyond our senses.* —**Ryan Gable, host of** *The Secret Teachings* **radio show & author of** *The Grand Illusion, the Technological Elixir* **and** *The Persistent Illusion*

The Introduction alone is the most thought-provoking piece I've read in years. Who is this book for? Two kinds of people: Those who already suspect we've been "sold a bill of goods" by the world as we are led to believe it; and secondly, for those who never imagined things were anything other than mainstream media and pols tell us. If you already know a lot about the esoteric, the hidden realities that exist, then this book does two things: It confirms, supports and validates that which you may suspect and secondly, for those who think they know how all the webs weave, you'll find out more than you suspected. For those who are just beginning to wonder if the world may have a hidden reality, then this book will have something new for you on every page. I have never read an author who has a deeper knowledge and greater grasp on all the connected dots that will amaze and astonish. Olsen doesn't appear to have any particular axe to grind or position that he demands of the reader. He simply asks, "What if there's a different way to look at the world?" and then exposes evidence why that is a valid question. From chemtrails, ancient cults that still exist today, to conspiracy theories that have been shown to be truth, to exposing the cartels that control civilization and much much more, Olsen will keep the reader spellbound and bouncing from one google search to another. You'll go, "Wow, is that really true?" then do a google search and find out: "Yes, Olsen knows what he's talking about." And finally, it's gratifying that Olsen takes a positive and optimistic stance on what could be a very depressing and hopeless topic. —**Heartland Healing**

Modern Esoteric

beyond our senses

by BRAD OLSEN

CONSORTIUM OF COLLECTIVE CONSCIOUSNESS PUBLISHING

www.CCCPublishing.com • www.BradOlsen.com • www.EsotericSeries.com

Modern Esoteric: Beyond Our Senses

2nd edition
Esoteric Series :: Volume I

Copyright © 2018 by Bradford C. Olsen
Published by the Consortium of Collective Consciousness Publishing™

As is common in a historic and reference book such as this, much of the information included on these pages has been collected from diverse sources. When possible, the information has been checked and double-checked. Almost every topic has at least three data points, that is, three different sources that report the same information. Even with special effort to be accurate and thorough, the author and publisher cannot vouch for each and every reference. The author and publisher assume no responsibility or liability for any outcome, loss, arrest, or injury that occurs as a result of information or advice contained in this book. As with the purchase of goods or services, *caveat emptor* is the prevailing responsibility of the purchaser, and the same is true for the student of the esoteric.

Library of Congress Cataloging-in-Publication Data:

Olsen, Bradford C.
   MODERN ESOTERIC: BEYOND OUR SENSES / Brad Olsen
      p. cm.
   Includes index
   print ISBN 978-1888729825 (Pbk.)
      MobiPocket ISBN 978-1888729856 (kindle.)
      PDF ISBN 978-1888729832 (pdf)
      ePub ISBN 978-1888729849 (epub)

1. Spirituality—Guidebooks. 2. Metaphysics—Esoteric. I. Title
   Library of Congress Catalog Card Number: 2012914383

Printed in the United States of America. Third Printing.

10 9 8 7 6 5 4

﹏﹏﹏﹏﹏﹏﹏﹏﹏﹏﹏﹏﹏﹏﹏﹏﹏﹏﹏﹏

The Dating System used in this text is based upon the modern method of using Before Current Era (BCE) instead of Before Christ (B.C.), and Current Era (CE) rather than "In the year of the Lord" *anno Domini* (A.D.). Those unfamiliar with this dating system should take note that 1 B.C. is the same as 1 BCE and everything then counts backward just the same. Similarly, 1 A.D. is 1 CE with all the years counting forward to the present, or Current Era.

To assist in universal understanding, all measurements of length, distance, area, weight, size, and volume are listed in the metric system.

also by Brad Olsen

2021
Beyond Esoteric:
Escaping Prison Planet

2016
Future Esoteric:
The Unseen Realms

2008
Sacred Places North America:
108 Destinations

2007
Sacred Places Europe:
108 Destinations

2004
Sacred Places Around the World:
108 Destinations

2001
World Stompers:
A Global Travel Manifesto

1999
In Search of Adventure:
A Wild Travel Anthology

1997
Extreme Adventures Northern California

1997
Extreme Adventures Hawaii

MODERN ESOTERIC:

BEYOND OUR SENSES

FRONT MATTER:

BACK MATTER:

LIFEOLOGY:

Natural history, Earth history and human history. With a radical twist. Lifeology is the long and storied alternative narrative of life on this planet.

DIMENSIONS:

CONTROL:

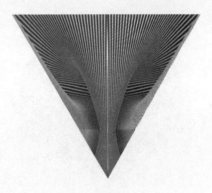

It would seem the populous is being intentionally deceived by our leaders. We are being dumbed down, purposefully made sicker, and denied vital information. Why is our full potential being withheld from us? Big Brother is here in the form of the New World Order.

DIMENSIONS:

T H R I V E :

For a seemingly hopeless battle, the solution to vital problems is simply to change our consensus reality. The only weapon they have is keeping the knowledge of our true nature just out of reach. Evolving to achieve our full human potential is the promise of the Golden Age.

DIMENSIONS:

AUTHOR'S KARMA STATEMENT

"Everything you do right now ripples outward and affects everyone. Your posture can shine your heart or transmit anxiety. Your breath can radiate love or muddy the room in depression. Your glance can awaken joy. Your words can inspire freedom. Your every act can open hearts and minds." –David Deida, American author

"IT was the best of times, it was the worst of times, it was the age of wisdom, it was the age of foolishness, it was the epoch of belief, it was the epoch of incredulity," wrote Charles Dickens at the beginning of *A Tale of Two Cities*. Interesting how history repeats this poetic description of duality, which is our experience here. It should be clear to all that we are alive today to witness one of the most transformative periods in human history in which our collective evolution contrasts with the disastrous events and chaotic social and economic forces at work—and together can be seen as the best of times and the worst of times. The worst of times is taking place around the world (especially in the United States), which I describe as the "Age of Deceit."

The truth is we are not wisely governed by our various global institutions, but rather callously exploited by them. The mass deceit emanates from government, the mass media, corporations, and from individuals who have bought into their false narrative and repeat what they hear as gospel. In effect, there is a major hoodwinking of humanity, while simultaneously we are also witnessing an unraveling of many centuries of disinformation, domination, and outright lies. So now, for the first time in history, we can freely view and share potentially damning information and understand the ways and means of the moneyed and power-hungry forces I call "Earth's control group." With careful research on the Internet, we can finally identify the organizations and leaders of these forces who remain firmly in control, and how they spread deceit.

Investigators have used many names to describe this power elite: Illuminati, secret society, the cabal, planet's control group, or even certain Western think tanks. Few would
disagree that there are power-hungry individuals in the world who have concentrated
huge fortunes at the top of the economic pyramid. Unfortunately they can often be dangerous sociopaths and some of these fortunes are disguised as useful think tanks and
charitable foundations. When these organizations are able to join forces and act collectively, there is ample evidence that the result is a secretive moneyed elite who control
the money supply, own the media, and thereby manage the key manipulative maneu-
vers which enable them to call the shots. A plan they openly promote, called the "New
World Order," describes their goal of creating a one world government. On the surface,
this is a positive-sounding goal—kicking a good idea such as the United Nations up a
notch. Unfortunately, the one world government would not be an elected body, but
simply a consolidation of already unprecedented power and greed. This would indeed
be the worst of times, but as we the people wake up to strategies of manipulation and
deceit and no longer give consent, we thereby release the illusionary bonds we live under and soon could be living in the best of times.

As this most unusual era of extreme duality reaches a crescendo, we are confronted
with unprecedented choices. We can cling to the persistent dismal illusion of what is
commonly regarded as "reality," or take individual responsibility to overcome the blocks
holding the mass of society back, and join in achieving a positive "Golden Age" for humanity. Esoteric wisdom traditions teach that overcoming the blocks that hold humanity back begins with choosing to no longer believe the lies of the predominant societal
institutions. It can be argued that all people of the world, that is, everyone except the
elite of the elites, have been lied to about most religions, current events, economics, history and even ancient history. This includes all current and former government structures ranging from tribal chieftains, theocracies, monarchies and the divine right of
kings; and representative republics to democracy and mob rule, communism, fascism
and the regulatory and debt-democracy most Western nations suffer under today.

The study of any phenomena or events that exist at the edges of consensus reality and
that occupy the imaginal realms is especially subject to historical revisionism, so the
truth can sometimes appear to be a moving target. The interface of myth and reality is
a shifting mosaic of fact, speculation, disinformation and fantasy, or to use the phrase
of a former CIA counter-intelligence spook, James Jesus Angleton, we have entered a
"wilderness of mirrors."

Questioning everything we have learned is the first step. The wisdom of critical thinking
allows us to see through this wilderness of mirrors. A fearless open-minded wisdom is
the ability to examine every issue from every angle, no matter how threatening some of
those conclusions might be. A true researcher will leave no stone unturned and attempt
to learn every concept from every angle. As an example, very few people know that the
original Greek translation of *apocalypse* can also mean a "revelation" of something hidden, or the "lifting of the veil." However, the common perception of an apocalypse is all
doom and gloom. In its proper context, apocalypse is a disclosure of something deliberately kept from the majority of humans in an era dominated by falsehood and miscon-
ception. Far from being a terrifying experience, apocalypse represents the revealing of
the true nature of things. It ushers in an era of forgotten freedoms and unprecedented
clarity. This "lifting of the veil" will set us free from the misery that has been the result
of our ignorance based on deception. Wisdom is knowing the difference.

The greatest wisdom is simple. Start with love, respect, tolerance, compassion, sharing, gratitude, forgiveness, and charity. These concepts are not complex or elaborate.
However, consistent practice is not easy. Our motivation increases when we realize

that adopting these principles is not only for our good but for everyone's good. The key is commitment to a daily practice, because practice yields experience, and from experience, rather than lofty concepts, we come to "know" the truth of great wisdom: The simple, radiant glow of "knowingness," knowing all is well; keeping a positive attitude everyday; offering a smile freely and without hesitation; orientating your actions towards "service to others" instead of "service to self." A wise person knows that real knowledge is free and available to all open-minded seekers. Some would even say it's encoded in our DNA. Great teachers have said from the beginning that all you need is within you. Open your heart and you'll find your way to the truth available equally to all. Truth is the acquisition of wisdom and the allowing of love to blossom in every aspect of your life. Our thoughts have an electromagnetic reality, so monitor them vigilantly and manifest wisely.

A SERIES OF THE ESOTERIC

Once the material in this *Esoteric Series* of books becomes openly acknowledged and applied, we will find ourselves living on this planet in an entirely different way. Imagine what the world will be like when we openly have anti-gravity, teleportation, free energy, time travel, and energetic healing technologies, plus so much more! In short, this series outlines everything we will need to start a true Golden Age of peace and prosperity. In addition, we now have remarkable insights into the hidden knowledge of ancient civilizations, and can begin to understand that who we think we are, and who we truly are, seem to be polar opposites. Indeed, we seem to be living in a state of amnesia as to our true identity. But this is ending now, as the flood gates of information are opened, and many of us are finally beginning to "get it." Conspiracy theory often becomes conspiracy fact, including the troublesome emotions which arise from the realization of that which has remained concealed for so very long. With time, we can work through feelings of victimhood, take responsibility now, and experience our new found power.

That which has been hidden, the subjects that have been shunned by mainstream thought, is called the "alternative narrative" in this *Esoteric Series*. It is the alternative to the lies we have been told, and manipulation by fear. I have aspired to follow the course of an *uncommitted investigator,* a term that is applied to those who carry on scientific research, or in my case, publish this and other books on my own initiative, without the support or direction from any established research agencies. We are so used to the financing of research from outside interests who have a financial incentive in the outcome of the research (hence a conflict of interest) that we hardly notice that the results are usually skewed in the direction of the supporting entity.

Being an uncommitted investigator means that I am free to investigate whatever topic I please, when I want to, or I can break off research at any point if the emerging data is not collaborated. My "karma statement" is to proclaim that I have no underwriters, and therefore no corporate overlords who could sanitize my subject matter, and no other agenda than to seek and speak the truth. Uncommitted investigators are as free as the wind because we have no program except the ever-changing one in our own minds. The history of science reveals that the great majority of new discoveries in the scientific field are not made by professional scientists working under the auspices of universities or research laboratories. The most revolutionary ideas are those that actually change the course of scientific progress, and have come mainly from the free-wheeling activities of these uncommitted, often unpopular, investigators. Similarly, those fearless writers who touch upon sensitive issues are those who can potentially make the biggest contributions to humanity. The pen is mightier than the sword! As George Orwell noted: *"Journalism is printing what someone else does not want printed. Everything else is public relations."*

Open-minded theoretical physicists also ask many of the big questions touched on by esoteric traditions, especially when their research falls short of being able to describe the nature of the universe, let alone its origin, or our purpose here. However, our conscious awakening has very little to do with physics, given its current knowledge base, but everything to do with personal growth and spiritual evolution. The basic underlying concept is that the universe is a single vast life form that is both a unified loving consciousness and is the underlying mechanism of everything in the universe. How this loving consciousness and the underlying mechanics of the universe sometimes is described is by the governing principle called the "Law of One." This is the way of knowing truth experientially, of understanding life in a new way, and acquiring a knowingness of infinite mortality and, simultaneously, the perception of infinite life. The objective of every individual is to embrace love and light, to know this at an interpersonal level, and to banish the darkness and fear that we have become accustomed to for so long on this planet.

Authors such as Abraham Hicks, Seth, Madame Blavatsky and Edgar Cayce, plus the Law of One, certain Eastern philosophies such as Buddhism, the ancient Hindu Vedanta, the works of Bashar, and the modern metaphysical thought system *A Course in Miracles,* are among the best sources of esoteric personal growth material available. While they say many of the same things, some make a clear distinction between what is real and what we have made-up in the dream-like world of perception where in we live our daily lives. In these teachings, the purpose is to awaken from the dream state into our true nature as spiritual beings who have never been separated from the source.

To date, the best that scientists and cosmologists can suggest is that we probably live in a multiverse, that is, infinite parallel realities that reflect back our dominant vibrations, essentially what we believe and how we feel. This then determines what slice of reality we will ultimately be in-sync with on an interpersonal level, that is, simply, where our focus is and how we are feeling. Are we consistently looking forward to where we want to go, and following the synchronistic cues of the universe as it zigzags its way toward providing us with exactly what we need to learn, grow and evolve in order to find our bliss and express our true nature? Or, are we dwelling on all the bad things that could, potentially, happen to us? It is, basically, about our own free will making conscious choices, and where we focus our attention. In short, dwell on the negative and our experience here will be that of suffering, but change our mind, and focus on our true nature, and our experience here can bring genuine happiness and peace of mind.

ESOTERIC HISTORY

When viewing the ruins of many sacred places around the world, it becomes apparent that esoteric knowledge was practiced, and has been preserved, by ancient civilizations. Some of the oldest surviving teachings, such as the *Rig Veda* of India and the *Pyramid Texts* of Egypt, contain sublime spiritual messages that appear to represent a legacy of ancient cultures such as Atlantis, Lemuria, pre-Egyptian civilizations, and the Osirian Empire. Remnants of other texts exist in India, Persia, Southeast Asia, South America, the Basque country, Britain and many other locations. We know that the last major Earth changes occurred around the time the last Ice Age was concluding, when a huge amount of the world's most productive land was lost to water. Old lands sunk and new lands rose. The mystics, messengers, avatars, and prophets were given their missions by divinity to teach esotericism anew, and have appeared around the world throughout the ages.

Spiritual teachers such as Thoth, Krishna, Lao Tzu, Buddha, Zoroaster, Mohammad, Moses, Jesus, Quetzalcoatl, and many others have imparted immortal lessons that stand the test of time. Striking connections and similarities are often found, not only in the messages of these great masters, but also in the very events of their own lives. However, as society spiritually degenerated and religion strengthened, those who practiced esotericism were often killed or persecuted out of their practice. As a result, esoteric wisdom either went underground or moved elsewhere—thus the continued need for its renewal.

BLACK MAGICK "WHITE"

A certain element of esoteric study deals with "the craft," also known as black magick, spelled with a "k" to differentiate the occult from stage magic. These dark occult practices include Satanic rituals, casting spells, witchcraft, Voodoo, animal sacrifices, summoning demons, and a myriad of other nefarious rites. I have no interest in these subjects, quite simply because I find them vulgar and offensive and a misuse of information available to the human race. I will promote no view that is harmful to anyone in any way, to animals, or toward the destruction of the Earth. That does not mean I will shy away if these topics need to be discussed for context. For example, black magick supposedly works better when practitioners "hide it out in plain sight," and this is one of the secrets to the harvesting of fear energy. They believe they have to reveal their operations to produce the best results. However, if we are going to survive as an advanced civilization the dark practices have no place in a future utopian age. In the coming Golden Age there will be a universal orientation towards "service to others," rather than the selfish "service to self." Controlling, enslaving, or harming anyone is never acceptable.

Some might feel it is necessary to study both the light and the dark for a more complete spiritual education. The study of the darkness, and throwing light upon it, is what changes its composition. It also changes the light of those who make the inquiry. When there is sufficient education and experience, each of us can act from wisdom rather than a knee-jerk judgment and emotionally-based fear. For unless we are aware of the extent, and details, of how a controlling group has manipulated the people of the world, how can we truly forgive them from a deep level, and offer them grace? When the critical window period of transformation becomes imminent, as it is now, we need to act from the highest frequency we can attain. Most readers of the *Esoteric Series* books will already know that we have been preparing for this moment, each in our own way, for some time. It may seem counter intuitive, but we really must love our perceived enemies. Fundamental lasting change takes place first in our minds, then it is shared (since all minds are joined), and finally it manifests in our shared experience.

For a long time, simply because I thought it was all make-believe, I disregarded the subject of black magick. Only when meeting the premiere magick practitioner living today, Lon Milo DuQuette, did I obtain a two-sided perspective of the occult. I had a chance to raise some questions, discuss my doubts, and was eventually given the opportunity to publish one of his books. Lon Milo DuQuette is the author of a dozen books, including *The Key to Solomon's Key: Is This the Lost Symbol of Masonry?* released in two editions by CCC Publishing. Like my original incorrect perception of the apocalypse meaning, Lon's book opened my eyes to the idea that practicing magick is all about a personal empowerment and orientation. Each of us has the freedom of choice to evoke dark forces, just as we can decide to bring in the light. It all depends on our intention. Lon was clearly oriented towards doing good for others, hence my nickname for him became the "White Wizard."

I think Lon Milo DuQuette will agree when I say that true magick is making life sacred, pure, simple and loved. A true magician transforms his or her life of drudgery into something that is embraced. This includes bringing your hobbies into your life's work, and thereby living a life of bliss and enjoyment. It includes moving far beyond the murk and crystallization of your hopes and dreams toward bringing them into fruition as inspired creations in a boundless field of potentiality. The most beautiful thing we can experience is the mysterious. It is the source of all science and all true art.

THREE POINTS OF DATA

I am presenting this material as the contrast between the *ordinary narrative* and the *alternative narrative*. The ordinary narrative is what we all perceive to be real. It is the mainstream news, the government press releases, and the manufactured knowledge structures that direct our attention where the owners of these institutions want it to be. This is not to say this information is always false, but it certainly does omit crucial data, and is often distorted.

It is the *alternative narrative* that stretches the boundaries of our perceived reality, as the Sphinx and Great Pyramids have done for eons. Current scientific knowledge can't satisfactorily account for the presence of these structures, nor for the unexplainable, but nearly identical, personal experiences reported by thousands of people. This only leaves the options of remaining baffled or doing deeper research. Such a quest for truth calls for wider strategies that include careful intuition and the taking of a discerning look at channeled information, which is often widely varied in quality and apparent wisdom. It also calls for more rigorous documentation. To codify and document esoteric subject matter, I have chosen to plot at least three "data points" containing collaborating information. Given the fact that all disinformation integrates some degree of truth, the next step was to rigorously check source-material links to see if information could be independently validated.

In this quest for truth, what's so disheartening, and therefore virtually impossible for us even to conceive of, is the fact that what we the masses are being taught to believe, is simply one gigantic deception, or the "Big Lie" (*Große Lüge*) as it was regarded to within the Third Reich. It is a historic and highly effective propaganda technique, used by the Roman Catholic Church in the Middle Ages, and by all greedy power structures before and since. Their goal is to maintain power and control. It is an astonishingly destructive addiction. We have been lied to and conditioned beyond belief. Subtly and subliminally information has been manufactured, produced, and enforced upon us. We barely realize it because the perpetrators are the very people and institutions we had long relied upon. This kind of deceit is so extensive, and huge in size and subtlety, that it's simply too unbelievable to be true. Unfortunately, the closer one looks, and the more thorough digging we do, the more evident it is that this grand scheme of manipulation and deceit just continues to perpetuate, century following century, decade after decade, year in and year out, each sunrise and preceding sunset, hour after subsequent hour, minute by minute and each and every ticking second of the day.

But there is a solution, and it begins by looking unflinchingly at the problem. We must look fearlessly at new information emerging, and combine that with the wisdom that comes from our joint evolution as human beings. This activity removes us from victimhood, and into advocates for positive change. Thus, the three data points are like pinpoints of light in the vast darkness of illusion. Once they can be brought together, this fantastic tapestry will ultimately form the alternative narrative—the vital course correction that will hasten our evolution toward a higher form of human life.

Some of the subjects in the Control section examine how the wealthy elite blocked and hijacked the release of benevolent technologies. Electrical engineer Nikola Tesla frightened the central bankers senseless. They knew what his plan meant. Energy independence meant an almost complete loss of control over the populace. After all, energy is the biggest industry on the planet, and free energy would completely destroy their model. The central bankers are also controlling us with the Federal Reserve Note, which is a fiat currency, a *false currency*. It is not too extreme to call the United States government and our system of rule "American fascism." Activist Ralph Nader also points out that "we have the lowest minimum wage in the Western world. We have the greatest amount of consumer debt. We have the highest child poverty, the highest adult poverty, huge underemployment, a crumbling public works—but huge multi-billionaires and hugely profitable corporations." Knowledge of these disparities are the kind of truth needed to combat the current Big Lie. It is the control of government by big business that has enslaved us. Debt to the central banks and the International Monetary Fund have yielded a lethal system that perpetuates the biggest lie of all.

WHO'S TRUTH?

Truth is not contingent upon one's belief, nor is it altered by the words chosen to describe it, nor even wounded if neglected. It is simply truth, and truth remains constant throughout time. It is an unchangeable pillar that, while it can be masked or distorted, in the end, always remains. Yet, discovering truth is a personal task, although this does not imply that it is different for each person. Only the *form* that each of us experiences truth differs; the *content* is the same for everyone.

In order to have your head in the sand you also have to be on your knees. It's up to us whether or not we choose to be subservient or free, as will be discussed in the Thrive section. "Three things cannot be long hidden," said the Buddha, "the sun, the moon, and the truth." Remember that all truth passes through three stages. First, it is ridiculed. Second, it is violently opposed. Third, it is accepted as being self-evident. Human nature is such that we are often afraid to hear the truth because we don't want to have our illusions destroyed. Many are deeply attached to their illusions, falsely assuming that safety lies therein.

The Universal Law of Polarity states that opposites are really two extremes of the same thing. Life is a circle of frequencies. There is neither happiness nor unhappiness in this world—there is only the comparison of one state with another. There is neither good nor evil. There is only wisdom and ignorance. For those who wish to become wise, the place to start is by seeking truth. "We have to start with the truth," said Julian Assange. "The truth is the only way that we can get anywhere. Because any decision-making that is based upon lies or ignorance can't lead to a good conclusion."

Once you see through the illusion being cast upon the people of the world, there is no turning back. After all, according to Proverbs 12:19, "Truth stands the test of time; lies are soon exposed." Thus, in a way, when a populace holds a strong conviction for uncovering the truth, they have nothing left to lose, and then we then become dangerous to the establishment. The government fears those with open minds, for we are no longer as subject to state vices or control. *They* can no longer pull the wool over our eyes, nor seduce us with comfort, or subdue us with force. After all, calling someone a "conspiracy theorist" represents nothing more than a derogatory title used to intimidate and dismiss critical but open-minded thinkers. *We* now see this. And this is what the controlling forces themselves fear because an aware citizenry will see through their crimes and demand justice.

Yet our would-be oppressors will desperately fight to remain in control using the weapon of fear. Many of us will decide to be fearless. We will no longer tolerate injustice, accept the deception, or bear the burden of the "privileged" few at the top. We will soon rise above the illusion, and we are emerging from our trance. We are resisting the perception that we are helpless victims. We are aware that we can combat our would-be controllers with nonviolent strategies, and to these modern freedom fighters I will quote a resistance poem, "Fear nothing and advance the causes in which you believe, for now is the time to stand up and be counted amongst those whose minds are free." This really is a revolution of consciousness.

WHO'S KARMA?

Karma is the lesson of time, applicable everywhere and to everything. "Lesson" is the key word here. Karma represents the lessons we are learning in order to wake up to our true nature. Time and circumstances can change at any time. A good rule of thumb is do not devalue or hurt anyone in life. Consider the example—when a bird is alive, it will eat ants, but when the bird is dead, the ants will eat the bird. You may be powerful today, but remember, time is more powerful than you are. One tree makes a million matchsticks. But when the time comes, only one matchstick is needed to burn a million trees. So be kind and only do good. Besides, it is absolutely senseless and destructive to choose the path of control, for any reason, unless you are a sociopath if you do choose this path. It is my belief is that everything you do to others will end up being paid back with karma—and with meticulous, grueling precision.

You can search far and wide through the most shadowy conspiracies, and you won't find a better-kept secret than *the power of love*. Think of love as fears' opposite, and as one of the only two attitude choices we have. An offering of love paves the path to enlightenment. It is no simpler, or complex than that. It is all about love, and nothing is, or will ever be, as powerful as love. It is also the path of karmic redemption. The false ego system has us loving a handful of those close to us and distrusting all others. This creates isolation and fear. When we open up to the love of our fellow human beings, and stop resorting to judgment and suspicion (the all too human knee jerk default response), we actually do more to correct political and economic dysfunction than any protest can accomplish.

When push comes to shove, there really are only two ways you can live your life: One choice is to treat other people as weak, pathetic, disgusting, shameful, and utterly unworthy ... to see yourself as clearly and obviously superior ... and to abstain from care or concern about others unless it's beneficial to you. In Law of One terms, this is the path of control, service to self, and negative polarity. The other choice is to be forgiving, patient, loving, accepting, kind and nurturing towards all others. In Law of One terms, this is the path of Love, service to others, and positive polarity.

The terms "path of control" and "service to self" specifically refer to "the manipulation and control of others for the benefit of the self." When you think about it, if the direction of your path is in service to self, you are on your way toward becoming a sociopath. If you do not want to become a sociopath, then there is absolutely no point in making this choice. This does not mean that "control," as in self-control is bad, or that helping yourself is wrong. There are many behavioral traits indicating the choice of the wrong-minded or "left-handed path." These include narcissism, self-involvement, entitlement, jealousy, rage, selfishness, manipulation, criticism, impatience, nit-picking and antisocial or criminal behavior.

The "wheel of karma" is what everyone continues to run through until they no longer choose the path of control—even slightly. Each cycle of the wheel starts out with that feeling that you are on "top of the world" and everything is coming up roses. You are totally high, totally invigorated, and nothing can stop you. However, as the wheel turns, things keep getting worse and worse until you reach that archetypical "Dark Night of the Soul." What typically happens during the Dark Night of the Soul is that we become overwhelmed, discouraged and desperately unhappy with our life experiences. Reaching the limit of our tolerance for misery, we are finally motivated to reflect on our circumstances and consider that there must be a better way. Those who are determined to find a better way will do so in this life and shorten their "karmic debt." Each lifetime provides more lessons to learn until the *curriculum* is completed. If we simply hope for the best and resist the dark night, resist questioning, we will eventually hit rock bottom and suffer profoundly. We may think this is the end of the wheel, but it is not. We "pick ourselves up, dust ourselves off, and start all over again." The wheel keeps turning—in perpetuity—until we fully master the lessons of forgiveness and a resonance of love. Then, and only then, can it actually stay at the top—without having to turn any further. We get off the wheel—and not have to turn, or "cycle," any further.

Perhaps the most significant Law of One passage is, "In forgiveness lies the stoppage of the wheel of karma." This kind of profound forgiveness can be defined as withdrawing our belief in any kind of separation from others or our Source, thus affirming our essence as part of One. So, forgiving others *is* forgiving yourself. Once we give that magic gift of forgiveness and let go of the need and desire to try to control other people's free will, then we can see ourselves and others as beings of infinite worth, and that puts us in a position where we are no longer bound to the "wheel of karma."

WHAT A WILD RIDE!

Consciousness doesn't grow from being *told* facts—it grows from the *search* for them and then *applying* what we discover. It is our experience of truth that is persuasive. And I believe that is what the people of this world really need—a chance to grow up on their own in a free society. Hopefully, you can use this information to help inform the people close to you about this opportunity. The once proud and independent people of the United States have, in large part, been reduced to servants of the State. As Aldous Huxley famously noted, "People can actually be made to *love* their servitude." In a day that is rapidly approaching, the American people are going to have to ask: What's our breaking point? When are each of us going to stop making excuses for ourselves? When are we going to stop exaggerating the powers of the State when we know *we* have the power in this country, and within ourselves, if we join in common purpose?

The Golden Age reality is created within the minds and hearts in each of us. As such, when the ego is lost, limits are lost, and with that we become infinite, kind and beautiful, and so does everyone else! In essence, *we are here to love each other, serve each other, and uplift each other.* Whatever you do and wherever you go, approach life in the spirit of honoring and holding sacred. Then the gifts you receive will far outweigh those of the taker.

In the endeavor of life—uncovering hidden truths and pursuing happiness—go boldly forward without fear. After all, we have the "orenda" within us, that mystical force present in all people and that empowers us to effect change in our own lives, and as a result, affect the world. I wish for you a fruitful spiritual adventure!

Yours in continual transformation,

Brad Olsen
San Francisco, CA
August 2nd, 2017

"Everything on the Earth has a purpose, every disease an herb to cure it, and every person a mission. This is the Indian theory of existence." –Mourning Dove Salish

INQUIRE WITHIN

All humans are living light. The scientific description of light as an appearance is characterized by both particles and waves. Like the material form of DNA itself, which is a direct materialization of the structure of light, waves are understood to be always in a spiral or helix form. If a helix-form is seen at its point of rotation, it is observable as a particle. Yet if the same helix-form is seen with reference to its limbs of rotation, before or after its point of rotation, it is observable as a wave. So, also, light is observable as both particle and wave depending on which phase of its process is observed by a point of view in space and time.

Modern Esoteric
INTRODUCTION

"When people are ready to, they change. They never do it before then, and sometimes they die before they get around to it. You can't make them change if they don't want to, just like when they do want to, you can't stop them." –Andy Warhol, American artist

IN this introduction to esoteric subjects, and by extension the whole *Esoteric Series* of books, it is necessary to first define our terms. A simple or literal definition of esoteric is arcane or obscure knowledge or information known only by a select few. In this series, esoteric also means hidden or forbidden subjects, especially information derided by science and seen as threatening to the prevailing cultural paradigm and thus labeled fictional, fantastical or weird. Those who undertake the examination of *esoteric* subjects are already, by definition, a select few. Those who understand the world strictly by the ordinary narrative taught to us in school and regurgitated by the mass media are by definition the *exoteric*, and would find these subjects unbelievable or without warrant for further study. This book is offered to those who understand that we have been selectively denied vitally important information about our origins, our history, and the corruption underlying our major institutions. It is offered to those who seek to expand their horizons.

It would seem the subjects we are taught in school are merely "bits of truth" and, when intertwined with other factoids, almost always lead to dead ends. It is as though human knowledge has been intentionally guided into these dead ends where strong walls are erected to keep people from thinking outside the box. True research, having been taken over by corporations, has become a tool for profit—not a tool for universal understanding. It is only the few, uncommitted investigators (not beholden to outside interests) working in back rooms, basements and garages, who have obtained new knowledge and have tried to make it public—usually to be bought out by corporations, silenced under "national security," or ridiculed into obscurity.

There are "firewalls" set up to block damning information about secret manipulation techniques and to keep it hidden from the exoteric mind of the general population, such as the availability of certain advanced technologies, now controlled by the powerful elite. After all, the globalist plans suffer the potential of defeat through exposure. In order to effectively resist the globalist designs, we must first inform ourselves of their schemes to thwart sovereignty and liberty. Next, those who feel compelled must educate friends, family and neighbors about these subversive designs for control and solicit their aid in preserving the U.S. Constitution. Always remember, knowledge is power.

The real world today bears little to no resemblance to the world we've been told about through the mainstream media and conventional education. Most of us inhabit a world of simply working, eating, breathing, and going through the motions of modern life as if sleep-walking. We interact within a consensus reality "illusion" that, in fact, has never really existed in the first place. We are caught in a collective trance.

To gain a comprehensive perspective, we'll need to question everything we know and start at the very beginning. For example, where is the universe even located? Start by questioning everything that is currently being promoted in the "regular narrative." The page of this book that you are reading is merely a perception. Language and custom say that it all exists "outside" in the external world. Yet we can argue that nothing can be perceived that is not already interacting with our consciousness. Since perceived images are observed as real and not imaginary, it must be physically happening in some location. Human physiology texts answer this without ambiguity. Although the eye and retina gather photons that deliver their payloads of bits of the electromagnetic force, these are channeled through heavy-duty cables straight back in the brain until the actual perception of images occurs. The images physically occur in the back of the brain, augmented by other nearby locations such as the pineal gland in special sections that are as vast and labyrinthine as the matrix of stars in the Milky Way. This area of the brain, according to esoteric texts, is where colors, shapes, and movements "happen." This is where they are perceived and cognized. But they are just images. If you try to consciously access the luminous, energy-filled, and visual part of the brain, it's easy. You're already effortlessly perceiving it with every glance you take.

ALTERNATIVE NARRATIVE

The possibility exists that everything in this book was created in the imaginative minds of people, the *zeitgeist* of our age, which will be remembered in a future era as the product of the richest source of folklore since the ancient Greeks. Some of these subjects could have been created as "grey" disinformation, calculated to confuse and defuse the issues of elitist power, mind control, genocide, eugenics, and the secret space programs, by revealing discrete pieces, yet concealing universal truths.

Disinformation is a deliberately false report from advocates of one side of an issue in order to confuse or weaken the other side's arguments. The technique of DDT or "Decoy, Distract and Trash" works well in casting doubt. The many thousands of paid DDT bloggers who work on political campaigns are usually hired to confuse and discredit those who seek to uncover the truth. The idea is that the DDT agents put out information that is similar to the truth, but is not fully the truth. This information is a "decoy" that will "distract" people from the real information. The "trash" segment is the decoy information being attacked. The purpose is to discredit these topics and shun debate, dividing intellectuals into conclaves of true believers in the normal narrative who can be counted on to heavily merchandise the information, thus continuing the work of the disinformers. It wouldn't be the first time, either overtly or covertly, that the controllers of government have employed disinformation vectors to confuse, pacify, or steamroll the populace into the direction of their choosing. As frustrating as this may be, we can still learn from this experience without falling for this classic DDT counter-intelligence maneuver. It is all too easy to buy into extreme versions of the alternative narrative—or into half-truths of the normal narrative. Either way, people are tempted to throw the baby out with the bathwater and think the entire alternative narrative was nonsense all along.

Ideally, what should be said to every child in this pre-enlightened era, repeatedly, throughout his or her school life, goes something like this:

> You are in the process of being indoctrinated. We have not yet evolved a system of education that is not a system of indoctrination. We are sorry, but it is the best we can do. What you are being taught here is an amalgam of current prejudices and the choices of this particular culture. The slightest look at history will show how impermanent these must be. You are being taught by people who have been able to accommodate themselves to a regime of thought laid down by their predecessors. It is a self-perpetuating system. Those of you who are more robust and individual than others will be encouraged to leave and find ways of educating yourself—educating your own opinions. Those that stay must remember, always, and all the time, that they are being molded and patterned to fit the narrow and particular needs of this particular society.

Imagine calling us fools because we do not believe in a 3,000-year-old story involving a talking snake and incest, yet we are laughed at for thinking about life being imported here from other planets. In this modern age it is apparent that organized religion is declining in relevance rather quickly; fortunately, however, those in a quest for truth will never diminish. Truth is an indestructible pillar that stands for all time. Plus, who says science cannot be a part of God, in whatever manifestation that "creator" might be? Such a word as "God" is filled with the subjective perceptions unique to each individual, each living their lives. Each person, in a variety of ways, considers the world within which they live as spiced with the unique perception of their own personal free will. Once we begin to challenge what we have been taught, not much can ever be seen the same way again. Yet the perfect universe is self-evident. You exist, and live and breathe and grow and evolve, as do the planets and the stars, and the galaxies themselves that swim in and on the great quantum ocean. If we are to consider what holds it all together, we will find it is alive beyond our wildest dreams.

THE MODERN ESOTERIC LOOKS BACK

This volume deals with Earthly theories of who we are, where humans have come from, and what might be possible with our great and largely untapped potential—the human mind. Are history books giving us the whole story? Esoteric research delivers a resounding "no." Civilization on Earth is much older than any of us have been led to believe. Our school textbooks barely mention the 6,000-year-old Sumerian civilization, yet the latest archaeological findings at sites such as Jericho and, most recently, Göbekli Tepe in Turkey, extend the date of "civilization" back to 10,000 BCE. But what if civilization goes back another 10,000 years, or 100,000 years, or even in the millions of years? Sacred literature and ancient texts describe lost civilizations from a very distant past, such as the lands of Lemuria and Atlantis, which were destroyed by cataclysms many eons ago.

Even in the recognized view of history there is a whole hidden group of advanced civilizations exemplified by sites such as the mysterious archaeological assemblage of Göbekli Tepe, which was built some 11,600 years ago, right at the end of the Pleistocene Epoch: the geological era which lasted from about 2,588,000 to 11,700 years ago. Recent discoveries in South Africa push the date of archaeological development even farther back than Göbekli Tepe, deep into the Pleistocene. Only recently discovered and discussed are the Bosnian Pyramids and the civilization of "Old Europe." Then there are the fabled lost "golden" cities of South America and the Amazon, which are gradually being rediscovered. There are also fascinating examples of lost technology, such as the Antikythera Device and other inexplicable "high-tech" artifacts. The government has known about these anomalies for decades, perhaps for a century or longer, and tightly controls secret knowledge of the past such as the evidence for ancient aliens, as well as giants who once walked the Earth.

Let's not forget that Atlantis was an advanced civilization from which many of these mysteries may harken. Later societies emerging as stable civilizations developed around these older ones, and became the Egyptians, Indus civilization, Maya and Inca, among others. The farther back in time you go into their civilizations, the more advanced their knowledge appears to be. There is evidence that the Atlantis survivors created the magnificent esoteric civilizations that eventually arose throughout the world. The knowledge they possessed can be seen in the symbols, temples, pyramids, astronomical alignments and sacred geometry they used in numerous sacred sites. It was a time in human history in which esotericism was central to human life and society, in which case it was not esoteric at all, but "exoteric," and available to all. Some of the oldest surviving teachings, such as the *Rig Veda* of India, and the *Pyramid Texts of Egypt*, contain sublime spiritual messages which appear to be the legacy of these ancient cultures. At some point esotericism went underground, where it remained through the long dark march of recorded history ... until this modern day. These subjects, and many others, will be the focus of the Lifeology section, which begins this book.

Why are people either offended or feel defensive when aliens are mentioned? Some love being an all-powerful human with a big ego to defend, so they deny any ET interaction with us meek Earthlings, either now or ever. Humorous fictional accounts are tolerated such as a "Planet of the Apes" scenario where us little monkey-men are still propelling Roman candle-fired rockets into the near-orbit of Earth, and that's the best we can do. Actually, the potential for ETs interacting with Earth, both past and present, is more likely than any other explanation. When looking deep at all the evidence, the ancient alien theory reins supreme over any other theory out there, and fills many gaping holes too. All the evidence is pointing to the existence of unknown beings from other dimensions. Most of the ET / UFO material is covered in *Future Esoteric: The Unseen Realms*, which is a companion to this book. It takes the perspective of looking forward and examines, in depth, the esoteric study of UFOs and extraterrestrials, among other topics. However, because the ancient alien theory is part of the alternative narrative of who we are as humans, it is contained in the "Blood of the Gods" chapter of this book.

In brief, there have been various UFO incidents throughout history, including the UFO crash reported in Aurora, Texas, in 1897. As scientists examined the wreckage, they discovered a type of "aluminum" that was not composed of the same material as what we regard here as aluminum. It was the beginning of the American discovery and fascination with the idea that we have visitors in our airspace who utilize extremely advanced technology. The other book gets into the dynamics of UFOs, which fly in energy fields that nullify gravity and time. This explains why these vehicles suddenly stop without landing, and why people experience missing time during a sighting or abduction. For an expanded picture of the UFO/alien topic projecting *into the future*, the reader will find a great deal of detailed information in the companion book.

As we will see in this text, recent archeological discoveries not only support the notion that human civilization originated from ETs, but that advanced civilizations have made Earth their home long before the dates recorded in our history books. It is evident that mainstream science and institutions have worked to hide our true implied heritage. Furthermore, it is possible to connect "ancient aliens" to the current wealthy elite. One idea is that ETs were on our planet thousands of years ago tinkering with humankind's genetics, and remain connected to the wealthy elite, a group of about a dozen "blood-line" families that try to run the world. In this view, the elite know of the ancient astronaut saga and believe they are possibly descended from them. But of course they don't want humanity to know this, among many other secrets that could divulge their identity. This and many other ideas here will stretch credulity, but once again, readers are encouraged to examine the evidence and come to their own conclusions.

BREAKING FROM THE ILLUSION

As with history, along with the nature of reality, things are not always as they seem. All we see, all we know, all we've been taught, even who we think we are as human beings is an illusion. If you can comprehend that humanity is in a mass hypnotic trance, and that the whole 3-D experience is an illusion, you are beginning to emerge from the trance. An occult concept suggests that humanity's trance is perpetuated by an "egregore," described in old documents as a "thought form" or a "collective group mind," projecting a hypnotic force. If you can even begin to entertain such an idea, your trance is breaking. You are becoming free of the Luciferian mindset. This kind of awareness opens one to the alternative narrative regarding who we are, who controls us, and what is our true purpose here on Earth.

Watch and wait as the wisdom of your reclaimed altered state, your original state, gives you all the freedom and liberty you need to answer any question you may have ever conceived about. Questions about why we're here and what life is all about. Just ask yourself a question and listen in your own mind for the answer. It's all very simple. We've been constrained and made to believe that this lunacy which constitutes the world and universal experience is who and what we really are. Nothing could be further from the truth. The grand illusion is the big lie, repeated enough times so that it is taken as true.

Knowing this, the point on which to stay focused is that we're dealing with an image, a thought form; not 3-D puppets, resistors, other people, or any power that has substance. Our experience in the world is a powerful illusion that traps nearly everyone, but it's still only a thought form, a kind of mental image, and we can change our minds. If we focus on targeting the pope, the Royal Family, the Bush family, the Rothschilds, the Rockefellers, or anyone else with daunting power, then we're only going after the Captains who are giving orders to the Privates. When the likes of Alex Jones, David Icke, Makow, the articles on Red Ice, or Rense, go after the Captains in this war, then the war continues and escalates. The Luciferian egregore master wants his Captains to be attacked, as this strengthens and multiplies the focus on the misguided third dimensional thinking process and experience. This attack on the subordinate Captains, in charge of the Privates below them, literally creates more enemies to attack. This attack creates more resistance, more emotional connection, and more focus on the thought form, which keeps us perpetually trapped. It creates more fear and anger, which blocks wisdom and understanding. The awareness that we are caught in a thought form (a similar idea to a trance) means that we can change our thoughts; we can literally change our minds. To do this, we need help. Ultimately this is possible by following a spiritual discipline which enables us to access our essence and hear our wise inner guide.

TELLING THE TRUTH IS A REVOLUTIONARY ACT

As we enter a new era where the veils are thinning between worlds, consider how many lies all of us experience on a daily basis. Then consider whether you would have the courage to come forward into the public domain to tell the truth about what you know, especially if you have taken a security oath. Also consider how you would become an outcast among those who supposedly are your friends and loved ones. Consider how once you take the red pill you can never go back.

Ultimately truth is something each person must discover, one step at a time, using his or her own heart and mind to discern. At a metaphysical level, although each of us realizes the truth at our own pace, and in a form that is meaningful to use, the content of truth never changes. However, here on the level of form and in these times of mass deception, seeking and finding the truth is a highly-individualized process, and break through and can come in many forms.

It now appears that greed is the primary motivator behind our culture and political action in the West. Unbridled and now unmasked, greed overrides moral principles; it is the only thing that seems to count. "Everyone has a price." This is why science doesn't work unequivocally as it should, and why it is being short-circuited in the West. This is why real debate and discussion do not arise, why politics is theater, and why public confidence in Western institutions are rapidly declining. But the real lesson to take away from this is that the oligarchs in charge of it are, in the final analysis, just insanely stupid, or perhaps, just insane and stupid. They are also getting sloppy in their unrelenting pursuit of money and power. Their false flag attacks don't work on us anymore, mainly because people are waking up to the very distasteful conclusion that we've been unquestionably hoodwinked.

Skeptics in general are important when searching to achieve an objective view of reality, because skepticism can challenge the official storyline *or* challenge the alternative narrative. In fact, a so-called conspiracy theory can be argued as an alternative to the official or "mainstream" story of events. The questions are: Who are the skeptics? What are they skeptical about? And, do they have a hidden agenda? Therefore, when skeptics attempt to ridicule a conspiracy theory by using the "official story" as a means of proving the conspiracy wrong, in effect, they are simply regurgitating an original "mainstream" view—and not being skeptical at all. This *use* of skepticism is just a convenient way for the establishment view of things to be seen as the "correct" version. All the time, every time! In fact, it is common for "hit pieces" and "debunking articles" to pick extremely fringe (and not very popular) conspiracy theories to challenge—a similar strategy to "beating a dead horse" or "setting up a straw man to knock down." The aim is to inject "Fear, Uncertainty, and Doubt." This "FUD Factor," in turn, makes all conspiracies (or alternative narratives) on a topic look crazy. *Skeptics* magazine and *Popular Mechanics*, among many others, did this with the 9-11 controversy. They referred to less than 10% of the many different conspiracy theories about 9-11 and targeted the less popular and fringe arguments to debunk by demonizing obvious flaws and omitting vital details. This was trumpeted as the "final investigation" for looking into the conspiracy theories. Here we have a perfect and convenient way to prevent anyone from looking at the mysterious man operating behind the curtain.

WHAT IS THE ESOTERIC?

There are many, many faces of the esoteric. Many people consider magick, the writings of Aleister Crowley, or even the fantasy world of Harry Potter at Hogwarts a category of esoteric. Then you have the intellectual or spiritual masters to consider. Some deal with clearly esoteric subjects and others less so. George Gurdjieff was an influential Armenian-Greek spiritual teacher of the early to mid-20th century who had a lot to say on esoteric subjects. Gurdjieff's method for awakening a student's consciousness was different from that of the fakir ascetics of the Middle East, the solitary monk of the West, or the meditative yogi in the East, so his discipline was originally named the "Fourth Way." At one point he described his teaching as being "esoteric Christianity." Gurdjieff recognized the difference between what is learned and what is perceived:

> *The results of the work of a man who takes on himself the role of teacher do not depend on whether or not he knows exactly the origin of what he teaches, but very much depends on whether or not his ideas come in actual fact from the esoteric center and whether he himself understands and can distinguish esoteric ideas, that is, ideas of objective knowledge from subjective, scientific, and philosophical ideas.*

The term apocrypha is used with various meanings, including esoteric studies, teachings that are hidden, or knowledge that is officially discredited. One of its common uses is as a label for Christian texts that are not canonical. Apocrypha can also refer to the mysticism schools of all religions. In Islam there is Sufism and the whirling dervishes, Judaism has the Kabbalah, early Christianity has its mystics, and currently its contemplatives, Gnosticism had the Essenes, and the ancient Greeks had their mystery schools and the Pythagoras School of Thought. Other examples of esoteric religious movements and philosophies according to Wikipedia include alchemy, astrology, Anthroposophy, Mesmerism, Rosicrucianism, Swedenborgianism, Spiritualism, the Alawites, the Christian Theosophy of Jacob Böhme and his followers, and the Theosophical currents associated with Helena Blavatsky and her followers.

There are competing views regarding the common traits uniting these currents, not all of which involve "inwardness," mystery, occultism or secrecy as their crucial trait. The definition of apocrypha as hidden or inward knowledge that is officially discredited conforms with the use of the term esoteric in these books. Various movements arise which appear as a kind of pseudo-esotericism. These could include cults such as the People's Temple, fake gurus, or Pentecostal snake charmers (among a whole host of forgeries throughout the ages). When a belief becomes collectively accepted by society as ludicrous and false, it fades away into the annals of folklore and mythology (or even mental illness). Only when a practice is tried and repeated successfully will it pass on as the truth, usually first regarded as esoteric, and preserved or understood by only a small group or those who are specially initiated.

While the esoteric can be considered in all of these subjects and much more, this series also deals with both a modern and future approach to viewing this complicated subject matter. In our dualistic world there is both good and bad, the light and the dark, the enlightened and the evil. This *Esoteric Series* of books focuses on the light, or enlightened ideas, leaving subjects such as witchcraft, sorcery and the summoning of demons to other authors. This series focuses on subjects which seek never to harm, yet the author and individuals cited are not afraid to cast a light on those dark forces who are "in service to self." By discussing forbidden sciences and exposing harmful secrets, the overall intent of this series is to elevate all living people in the spirit of "service to others."

This study seeks to assist humanity in transcending collectively into a higher state of consciousness to mutually achieve our fullest human potential. It is what Gurdjieff would call "the esoteric center." Knowledge of the alternative narrative opens the door to an awareness that there is a choice, and this awareness will help people escape their crippled state of hypnotic "waking sleep." The "esoteric center" is inclusive and encompassing, seeking to integrate all advanced knowledge, whether Eastern or Western, for truth knows no boundaries or limitations. In the East we have ancient Chinese "revealed texts and objects," the martial arts such as Tai Chi which has its roots in Taoism, acupuncture, herbal remedies, yoga, and the energetic movement of *chi* or *prana*. The human soul when defined as a realization of self truly has no separation. There is no other because minds are joined. We are all one. The *Esoteric Series* of books takes you up, and then back down to Earth again.

Nothing in our everyday experience gives us any reason to suppose that matter is not material. It is not apparent to our five senses that matter is made up of weird forms of energy, similar to the human spirit, defying all of our normal notions of time, space, and causality. Yet when matter is subjected to certain drastic treatments, such as CERN's Hadron Collider near Geneva, Switzerland, then it is quite clear that matter is not what it seems. Matter is not material at all, but a form of energy, just like everything else pulsating throughout the universe. Indeed, the discovery of electromagnetic radiation reveals that our senses pick up only a small fraction of what surrounds us at all times. The vast majority of reality is quite literally "occult," or truth that is completely hidden from us.

SOLIPSISM

The philosophical concept of solipsism asserts that the only certainty is that one's own mind is sure to exist. It is the assumption that everyone else is like you, or that your perceived world is the same world for everyone else. By its own postulate, solipsism is both irrefutable and yet indefensible in the same manner. Solipsism is a preoccupation with oneself, focusing strictly on the "me" to a dysfunctional degree. It is neglecting to consider the viewpoint of others.

While this is clearly an over-generalization, author Christopher Hitchens calls religious people solipsists since they think the universe was made exclusively for them. The extreme form of solipsism denies the possibility of any knowledge other than of one's own existence. Solipsism is a radical preoccupation with the indulgence of one's feelings, desires, and egoistic self-absorption. It is a preoccupation with oneself or one's own affairs. In short, "it's all about me!"

Solipsism is a basic and ignorant projection that one person's version of reality is everyone's reality, because that person is unable to grasp other realities. It is displayed in faulty advice-giving and a lack of empathy. Solipsism is a disconnect or detachment from true reality, rendering the person clueless about the real world, yet giving them the false notion that they are aware of the world around them. To fully grasp the concepts of this book, that is, to think outside the box, it is essential for the reader to understand solipsism—in effect, is perception with blinders on. Removing such blinders is the goal of this series. For only by looking beyond our own perceptions can we really begin to understand the alternative narrative of this esoteric series of books.

Consciousness, the "organ" of perception, is a central mystery of the human mind, and the current science of both mind and consciousness is wholly inadequate. Yet aware scientists are making inroads into the scientific study of esoteric subjects. One such group is the Institute of Noetic Sciences (IONS) founded in 1973 by Apollo 14 astronaut Edgar Mitchell. They have generated fascinating data about consciousness and its relationship to the highest reaches of the mind—the mystical, mysterious, paranormal, spiritual and esoteric. Yet, despite these significant inroads into documenting hidden worlds and astounding extrasensory abilities, more such data is needed, and more is being generated all around the world. What exactly is the human mind capable of, and how can we tap into our full potential? It appears globally that there has to be a revolution—but it has to be a nonviolent revolution—one that looks inward into the mind of consciousness. Careful research such as that done by courageous scientists at IONS and other such organizations is hastening that inward, nonviolent revolution.

SYSTEM 1 AND SYSTEM 2

There are helpful ways to think about the task of hastening an inward, nonviolent revolution. How might we regard the population at large in order to know what the educational task, is and how best to proceed? Systems thinking is one tool. For example, consider "System 1" and "System 2" types of individuals. "System 1" people have little ability to think critically or little desire to do any of their own independent research. Instead they rely on vague intuition, bias, and easily available or condensed information. Such a person is described as the "low information voter." Their traits might include gathering information that is retrieved from memory (hence, essentially imagined or made up) which includes individuals who are mentally paralyzed by solipsism. These people don't discern which situations are likely to lead to mistakes. They are impulsive, impatient, automatic thinking, make free-wheeling associations, and tend to jump to conclusions, and falling back on fantasies or stories. Humans in general are all too quickly seduced by stories and become easily swayed. Unfortunately, many people don't revisit their assumptions, but endorse the quick, plausible, and compelling answer versus study and research. In addition, System 1 people cannot entertain incompatible interpretations simultaneously. They are radically insensitive to both the quality and quantity of information, and are easily content to stop thinking. Conclusions come first, then the argument follows. They cannot use statistics and can't judge probability. They rely on mental shortcuts and unfortunately do not recognize these characteristics as flaws.

System 2 mental activity, on the other hand, does not come easily or naturally. It requires constant conscious activity and a desire to better oneself. System 2 people can generally construct thoughts in an orderly series of steps, such as composing a letter or writing a book. They even consider the books they don't have in their mental library. They are able to set aside their biases and question what they think they know by applying a careful, systematic approach to evidence, such as "why" something happened and the likelihood of it happening again. In this regard they think statistically. System 2 types enjoy games involving strategy such as chess, go, crossword puzzles and other opportunities that challenge the intellect and do not rely on luck. They allow for knowledge outside their purview, such as considering absent evidence, and will change their opinion when confronted with new data points.

What really distinguishes System 2 from System 1 types is a deliberate ability and willingness to "control" their thoughts and behaviors, to step back and observe their processes. This control is not relinquished to outside influences. They not only can absorb pertinent and even contradictory information, but can observe how their own minds are processing the information. They are able to home in on which facts are relevant, the quality of the facts, plus an ability to de-correlate and scrutinize the truly appropriate answer. This allows them the ability to comprehend the "rule" governing an outcome, as opposed to just the facts. They explore problems from many different angles, and are open to highly critical feedback.

System 2 people can also program themselves to obey an instruction that overrides habitual responses from System 1. This is a critical learned strategy and, in fact, is embedded in many spiritual practices, since overcoming our default reactions (faulty ego interpretations) is a hallmark of inner growth. System 2 people can maintain incompatible interpretations in the mind. They embrace complex and diverse ideas and accept seemingly opposite points of view at the same time. Unlike System 1 people, they have the ability to identify and understand errors of judgment and to learn and grow from their mistakes. Such discerning capabilities of risk and consequences allow System 2 people a myriad of advantages, from the practical such as the timing of passing a truck along a narrow road to the lofty, such as daring to trust in one's extended capabilities and making courageous and even transcendent decisions about what is possible.

BE SUSPICIOUS OF STORIES

We are designed to think in terms of stories, but rarely question this aspect of our lives. If you think in terms of stories or narratives, you are probably telling yourself the same things over and over. Stories attempt to impose order on a mess of incomplete ideas using filters of over-simplification. In this sense, humans are too quickly seduced by stories and too easily swayed by their own surface dramas. Graphic over-simplification is the style of the stories we are being fed in politics, television, movies, and books of fiction. We form biases and stubbornly defend them. Stories tend to strip away details and turn the information into a "good versus evil" type of tale. We should try to step away from thinking of our messy lives and our complicated, irrational world as a simple narrative.

According to author Christopher Booker there are seven types of stories. They can be defined as "Monster," "Rags to Riches," "Quest," "Voyage & Return," "Comedy," "Tragedy" and "Rebirth." Michael Moore or Oliver Stone movies involve conspiracies plotted by someone, instead of just random events. There is also the mentally lazy story such as the premise "we have to get tough" with someone we're negotiating with or a perceived enemy. Stories can be a form of "self-deception." They do get us out of bed in the morning as we tell ourselves that our work is important. Books are all about stories which can add to our biases. We tell ourselves that by buying a book we are making progress on a problem we have. Sometimes, yes; but we might be avoiding making a decision or taking action. Glamorous, seductive stories are used to manipulate us via advertising. Products get bundled with stories. We buy when they bundle well. Ask yourself, what is the story being told by people who have *no* financial agenda? That's usually where the truth lies.

As you will read in the *Esoteric Series* of books, the label "Illuminati" is thrown around rather freely to describe an elite group that is supposedly secretly running the world. Most people will have a general idea of the meaning of the term, but are confused about the concepts and the ideas relating to it. Is the Illuminati the same thing as Freemasonry? What are their goals? What are their beliefs? Why do they act in secret? Do they practice occultism? What is their real "story?"

Considering that secret societies are, by definition, secret, and that history is often re-written by those in power, obtaining the unbiased truth about the Illuminati is a challenge. Thus, attempting to objectively research the subject can become an arduous task. Most sources are either dismissive, and deny and ridicule anything related to the Illuminati or, at the other end of the spectrum, espouse ill-informed fear mongering based on rumors and misconceptions. In both cases, the researcher ends up with the same result: a distorted version of the truth, usually in the form of a story. So how can we make sense of any of it?

OCCAM'S RAZOR

One way to test if an intellectual argument is valid, or even to determine if a mythology is relevant, is the use of "Occam's Razor." Occam's Razor is attributed to the 14th century English logician, theologian and Franciscan friar Father William of Ockham, although the principle was familiar long before. The words attributed to Ockham are "entities must not be multiplied beyond necessity," although these actual words are not found in his extant works. This principle of philosophy and science basically says that when deciding between two possibilities, the one which is simplest or requires the fewest assumptions is most likely to be the most accurate. Other things being equal, the simpler the explanation, according to Occam's Razor, the more truthful it is.

A little reflection will show that this principle is woefully inadequate when applied to esoteric subjects. In practice, the principle is usually focused on shifting the burden of proof in discussions. That is, the razor is a principle that suggests we should tend towards simpler theories until we can trade some simplicity for increased explanatory power. In other words, if increased explanatory power is available, the simplest available theory is sometimes a less accurate one. So, Occam's Razor should not be considered foolproof, certainly in the realms of esoteric knowledge. Critics say Occam's Razor is given as a rebuttal far too often. Frequently, the aim is to negate any further scrutiny of the subject matter, a common reaction to the "alternative narrative." Philosophers also add that the exact meaning of the simplest explanation can be nuanced in the first place. Bertrand Russell offered what he called "a form of Occam's Razor," that is, "Whenever possible, substitute constructions out of known entities for inferences to unknown entities."

Occam's Razor is not helpful for scenarios where it appears that one thing is happening on the surface, but in fact something else is going on underneath. Consider "Operation Mockingbird," where journalists were paid by the CIA to publish propaganda. In 1948 CIA-operative Frank Wisner established Mockingbird as the espionage and counter-intelligence branch of the CIA, a program to influence the domestic American media. By the early 1950s, Wisner covertly "owned" respected members of the *New York Times, Newsweek*, CBS and other communication vehicles. The far-reaching tentacles of the CIA's Operation Mockingbird are, to this day, responsible for framing and manipulating our perceptions on a scale not easily believed. So in this case, the simplest explanation was that the journalists were publishing what they believed to be true. The underlying truth, however, was radically different. One could say that Occam's Razor still applies in this case, but critics would disagree. If it did apply, it pretty much makes Occam's Razor into something made of circular logic. Once we find out the truth, then it applies because it actually makes perfect sense. But that's really the point anyway. Once you delve further into certain topics, you find that the truth, which on the surface seems outrageous, actually makes more sense than the original story. Such is the nature of reality as well. The official story, the scientific materialism-based version of reality, is incomplete. The real reality that exists beyond the veil seems implausible, but only until you start to understand it better.

Another example of a superior challenge to Occam's Razor would be the so called "false flag" operations. One is a well-known and historically accepted account is Hitler's invasion of Poland. The superficial and seemingly plausible story was that the Nazi government was responding to terrorism, but in reality the whole thing was planned by them in order to create a pretext for invasion. A critic today would disapprove of someone invoking Godwin's Law here, which states: "As an online discussion grows longer, the probability of a comparison involving Nazis or Hitler approaches." Another example might be the drum up for the U.S. invasion of Iraq. Would anyone consider that a conspiracy? The official reason the U.S. led the invasion was because Saddam's Iraq had weapons of mass destruction that were unaccounted for, and thus a threat to the free world. Occam's Razor would suggest that this was the answer. By now we all know it was not true. In fact, critics of the war would consider this explanation a conspiracy by any textbook definition.

Many people have realized by now that conspiracies (secret plans with selfish, destructive goals) do in fact exist, and all too frequently they are implemented. But how much of what goes on in the world is conspiracy and how much is not remains unclear. After all, it is a major challenge to discern any kernels of truth in the official line we are given. Consequently, looking into the information that's out there, however bizarre it may seem, is nothing less than a noble pursuit, because our research is ultimately a quest for the truth.

As we advance into the more controversial subjects in this book, it is necessary to offer a disclaimer. Some of the subjects will seem outlandish to a majority of readers, or conversely, may make perfect sense. It must be repeated that these are esoteric subjects, not meant to be believed by everyone, at least not yet. After all, it is virtually impossible to convincingly present even well-researched information to those who have no desire to have their belief systems challenged. The message will always reach those it is meant to reach, and maybe that is exactly the way it should be. Those with ears to hear, eyes to see, and a heart to understand will comprehend the message. The seeds planted will grow strong in such fertile soil as these few.

A catalyst is not meant to be believed. It is meant to present you with a challenge to that which you "think" you know about reality. And that is all it is meant to do. Use Occam's Razor, use your own logic, and employ further independent research to explore the subjects in this book; but also keep an open mind to the concept that things are not really what they seem. Remember that wisdom can be found on every level of existence. Perhaps it's not always about trying to fix something broken. Maybe it's about starting over and creating something better.

WHAT WE CANNOT SEE

Just because we can't visually see something doesn't mean it doesn't exist. For example, humans are able to perceive only about .0035% of the electromagnetic spectrum. Imagine what's happening in the other 99.99%? Not being able to see something is a common way in which people will deny the existence of spirit guides, angels, and other unseen helpers in our lives. However, anyone who has encountered such beings can attest to the fact that they do indeed exist, just as our breath exists, keeping us alive, even though we can't see it unless it's cold outside. The wind exists, too, but we only know this because we feel it on our skin and hear it moving through the leaves on trees. All around us and within us are things we cannot see, and yet we know they are just as real as the ground beneath our feet.

We have been brought up to believe that the mind is located internally within the brain. Thoughts are merely cognitive activity. However, according to Dr. Rupert Sheldrake, there are good reasons for thinking that this view is far too limited. Recent experimental results show that people can influence others at a distance just by looking at them, even if they look from behind the person and all sensory clues are eliminated. Another unusual finding of Dr. Sheldrake's is that a person's intentions can be detected by animals from miles away. Pet dogs being videotaped have shown a reaction the moment their owner has *decided* to return home. The ability of animals to perceive themselves or to be aware of being looked at stems from the predator-prey model, where the prey who perceives it is being watched by a predator will have a better chance to escape and thus live longer and propagate. Telepathy is natural among animal groups. Rigorous research, with extensive replication, has documented this ability in many human beings. It's possible for anyone to develop these latent abilities; it is simply a matter of training and motivation.

Our minds reach out beyond the confines of brains and bodies. In fact, there is reliable data suggesting that the body emanates from the mind (essentially a projection), rather than the entrenched view that the mind emanates from the body. For humans, the most common type of non-local mental interaction occurs in connection with telephone calls. Most people have had the experience of thinking of someone shortly before that person calls. Controlled, randomized tests on telephone telepathy have yielded highly significant positive results. In this new way of testing for telepathy there is no effect of distance, no difference between a local call or an international call. Results show a higher hit rate with familiar callers. Research techniques have now been automated and experiments on telepathy are now being conducted through the Internet using emails and cell phone calls. These techniques enable participation by thousands of subjects, especially college students. Mothers and newborn babies also display a form of telepathy. A mother has a "tingling" feeling when her baby needs her and she is out of earshot and cannot hear the baby cry.

A more complete understanding of physical phenomena opens the door to an exploration of existence as a whole, including those nonphysical areas that have hitherto been left to religion and related branches of thought. It is now evident that our familiar material world is not the whole of existence, as modern science would have us believe. It is only a part—perhaps a very small part—of a greater whole.

ATTUNING OUR PERSPECTIVES

Before you judge others or claim an absolute truth, consider that you can see less than 1% of the electromagnetic spectrum and hear less than 1% of the acoustic spectrum. As you read this, you are traveling at 220 kilometers per second across the galaxy. Ninety percent of the cells in your body carry their own microbial DNA and are not even "you." The atoms in your body are 99.99999999999999999% empty space and none of them are the atoms you were born with—and they have all originated in the depths of a star. Human beings have 46 chromosomes, two less than the common potato.

The existence of a rainbow depends on the conical photoreceptors in your eyes. For certain animals without these visual cones, the rainbow does not even exist. So in a certain regard each of us does not just look at a rainbow, we create it. This is pretty amazing, especially considering that all the beautiful colors represent less than 1% of the electromagnetic spectrum. In Greek mythology, the rainbow was considered to be a path made by a messenger, or iris, between Earth and Heaven. Rainbows can be observed wherever there are water drops in the air and sunlight shining from behind at a low altitude angle. Sunlight is made up of a band of visible wavelengths on the electromagnetic spectrum. When sunlight is broken down into its component colors, you are able to see the red, yellow, orange, green, blue, and violet colors. Visible light waves are the only electromagnetic waves we can actually see. We see these waves as the colors of the rainbow. Each color has a specific wavelength. Red has the longest wavelength and violet has the shortest wavelength. Raindrops in the air act as tiny prisms. Light enters the raindrop and, acting as a prism, reflects off of the side of the drop and escapes. The angles cause different colors from different drops to reach your eye, forming a circular rim of color in the sky, and thus a rainbow is what we see.

We can explain light either by its wavelength, that is, the distance between peaks in a wave or the number of waves that go by per second (its frequency). For visible light, the range in wavelength is between 400 nanometers (nm) for blue light and 700 nm for red light. This comprises visible light because the retinas of our eyes are sensitive to these wavelengths. Yet visible light is only a small part of the electromagnetic spectrum, which also includes gamma rays, X-rays, ultraviolet radiation, infrared and radio waves. In astronomy, there is no need to limit ourselves to what we see with our eyes. Detectors can be made to record any type of radiation. Although celestial objects may produce a variety of types of radiation, most of it gets blocked by the Earth's atmosphere. For emissions that cannot get through, we must rely on satellite observatories which orbit the Earth to collect celestial information. From the Earth we are essentially limited to visible light and radio waves.

Just contemplate the fact that you are one person out of seven billion people, on one planet out of eight planets, in one solar system out of 100 billion star systems, in one galaxy out of 100 billion galaxies. In this context you are enormously insignificant. Yet, out of the 100 billion galaxies existing in 100 billion star systems, out of seven billion people, you have your own unique genetic makeup. Your fingerprint is yours and yours alone. You can create art, exercise your free will, and sing a song. You are depended upon by others that love you, and thus you are enormously significant. Quite simply, you are the universe experiencing itself.

This brings us into the realm of the mystical or spiritual. Spirituality is not a belief system or ideology, but rather a surrender of one's finite ego to something much greater and all-inclusive, the infinite wisdom and knowledge that is the universe. If you ever begin to take things too seriously, just remember that we are merely talking monkeys on an organic spaceship flying through the vast expanses of the universe.

QUANTUM ACTIVISTS

To learn quantum physics is to recognize that some scientists have posited a First Cause, a "One"–ness that sounds suspiciously like a concept of God. A number of these individuals have consulted mystics because they have reached a wall where scientific tools are concerned. A new science has emerged that includes the objective and the subjective. Some quantum activists posit that consciousness is without subject or object, and others suggest that the origin of consciousness or duality can be traced to an idea of separation, where there are "two," (a subject and object) where before there was only "one," or wholeness.

The importance of the nature of reality is not taught within our religions or schools, and all religions give a different answer to the same questions. The subtle aspects of our bodies and non-sharability of those aspects make it internal. We cannot measure mind over matter, upward and downward causations which are common in all religions, or the true essence of spirituality.

But is there a science behind it all? Many scientists believe there is and they are asking the big questions such as "What is the nature of consciousness?" Science works primarily with material consciousness, which consists of locating how and where cognitive processes occur in the brain. Some have concluded, however, that consciousness is not material; yet consciousness seems to be the ground of being. So, we are back to what exactly is consciousness? If it is not material, does science have the tools to study it? Physicists readily admit the limitations of quantum measurement—a myriad of paradoxes with possibilities based on possibilities. Shifting to the more subjective realm, the paramount experience of consciousness can be called the ego, where the conversion of possibility to actuality arises on the subtle level. Bliss is the connection with the whole.

Solipsism teaches that we can be blinded into thinking that what we immediately perceive is the only reality, and if there is more, it is an illusion or a figment of the imagination. But perhaps it is consciousness that creates reality. Perhaps the sought after connection of "unity consciousness," a choice made from a non-local place, is the embracing of the whole. Non-locality in quantum physics implies transcendence of space and time. Two people meditating or communicating non-locally create electrical activity in their brains, but with no tangible signal. Through their intentions, they are connected non-locally. Such experiments have been reproduced in the last decade, and the conclusion is that consciousness is non-local, since two people *can* communicate from afar with no measurable connection. That is similar to the conclusions of Rupert Sheldrake.

The reader will likely recognize that much of the material in this book makes the assumption that there are esoteric powers manipulating our physical world. Whether you are a religious or spiritual person, a professional or amateur scientist, or just plain curious, you likely are aware of the many theories about an invisible force at play in all of this. Clearly, it is impossible to prove exactly what it is, but the investigations in this series suggest we have a choice to invoke either positive or negative expressions.

You may not want to believe it, but the ruling elite takes their occult rituals with deadly seriousness. And they likely know something we don't know. Just by keeping an open mind about this possibility, you'll have an expanded awareness about the things we can actually see, hear, smell, taste, touch and perceive. Part of any awakening is the hopeful realization that there is much more that is possible than impossible.

Like the subtitle to this book, our goal is to look "beyond our senses." We need to be aware that external and internal conditioning makes the subtle body (the "energy body" we can't see) behave differently. So how do we explore beyond our material condition? First, we use the mind in a deliberate way and manifest by choice. It is possible that when we manifest non-local consciousness, that we are in sync with a larger reality, and our intentions, therefore, can come true. This often feels like the conviction of an "a-ha moment," one which leads us to question and learn more.

Approach all problems with this kind of zest for life, and heaven can be manifested here on Earth. Perhaps consciousness is the vehicle that can be used to return us to a full awareness of God, the source of all life and, hence, the reason we are all connected. Unfortunately, the materialistic worldview has separated us from this awareness. Unity is connection, and a desire to protect the natural world. If we approach things with love, others will pick it up. We can change ourselves, that is, our attitudes, and by projection, we can simultaneously change the world. *This is the cause of the quantum activist.* Removing the separateness allows us a better understanding of ourselves and our interconnectedness with the cosmos. Then we can come to realize that all matter is merely energy condensed to a slower vibration. We are all one consciousness experiencing itself subjectively. There is no such thing as death. Life is only a dream, and we are the imagination of ourselves.

POSITIVE ATTITUDES CREATE A CHAIN REACTION OF POSITIVE THOUGHTS

I Choose ...
To live by choice, not by chance
To make changes, not excuses
To be motivated, not manipulated
To be useful, not used
To excel, not compete.
I choose self-esteem, not self pity.
I choose to listen to my inner voice,
Not the random opinions of others.
I don't care if you're black, white, straight, bisexual, gay, lesbian, short,
*   tall, fat, skinny, rich or poor. I aim to be kind and to connect with the*
*   kindness in you. Simple as that.*
Die with a smile on your face.

Discovering that the religious complex of massive stone pillars at Göbekli Tepe in present-day Turkey was actually built by "Encino Man," as *National Geographic* puts it, "was like finding that someone had built a 747 in a basement with an X-Acto knife."

The "Emerald Tablet," also called the "Secret of Hermes," or the *Tabula Smaragdina*, is a text with illustrations purporting to reveal the secret of the primordial substance and its transmutations. Note the double lion guarding the start of the alchemical process shown at the bottom center of the picture.

Aleister Crowley, known in his time as "the wickedest man in the world" because of his occult activities such as sacrificing his own children in sexual rituals, claimed to be in regular contact with a demonic entity. Crowley advocated the use of cocaine and psychoactive drugs to come into union with Lucifer and better understand him. He drew images of the entity around the turn of the 19th century, seen on the next page. Why would he draw what we would commonly regard as an "alien," and claim it to be a demonic entity? Might they be one and the same? On the right is the title page of Crowley's book, *777 and Other Qabalistic Writings*.

Covering the inside dome of the Capitol Building Rotunda in Washington D.C. is this painting entitled "The Apotheosis of George Washington." The word "apotheosis" in the title means literally the raising of a person to the rank of a god, or the glorification of a person as an ideal. The huge painting depicts George Washington transformed into a new "sun god" in the chariot of Apollo, being pulled by four horses across the heavens. The painting is surrounded by several pagan "gods" of the old Roman Empire. From ancient times, through the time of George Washington, to the present day, the Freemasons guarded secrets that could transform matter, transform a person, plus unleash incredible psychic and spiritual power.

< The chief adviser to Queen Elizabeth I was Sir John Dee, a Kabbalist and black magician. He also created Enochian, which is very popular in upper levels of the occult. All of these types of "magick" teach the process by which one can conjure demons. John Dee conjured demons using his Kabbalah, black magick, and Enochian magick techniques. During the conjuring, pictures were drawn of the entities that presented themselves to him. The entities he drew looked identical to the "Grey" alien-type ETs we see in movies, which are identical to drawings made during rituals performed by black magick Kabbalist Aleister Crowley which date back over 100 years. While performing black magick rituals, Crowley took drugs and would see this entity named "Lam," remarkably similar in appearance to modern day Grey aliens. Crowley said this was Lucifer.

LIFEOLOGY:

Natural history, Earth history and human history.
With a radical twist. Lifeology is the long and storied
alternative narrative of life on this planet.

"You take the blue pill—the story ends, you wake up in your bed and believe whatever you want to believe. You take the red pill—you stay in Wonderland and I show you how deep the rabbit-hole goes." –Morpheus, from the film *The Matrix*

"In a world that is constantly changing, there is no one subject or set of subjects that will serve you for the foreseeable future, let alone for the rest of your life. The most important skill to acquire now is learning how to learn." –John Naisbitt, author of the *Megatrends* series

"I hold that the more helpless a creature, the more entitled it is to the protection by Man from the cruelty of Man." –Mahatma Gandhi

"Before you diagnose yourself with depression or low self-esteem, first make sure that you are not, in fact, just surrounded by assholes." –William Gibson, award-winning novelist

"All things share the same breath: the beast, the tree, the man, the air shares its spirit with all the life it supports ... The earth does not belong to man, man belongs to the earth. All things are connected, like the blood which connects one family. Whatever befalls the earth befalls the children of the earth. Man did not weave the web of life—he is merely a strand in it. Whatever he does to the web, he does to himself." –Chief Seattle

"To the travellers who have turned their faces to the Dawn and their Steps toward the Eternal Hills is offered this rich fruit of Wisdom, that, through it, they may achieve the Understanding of Knowledge." –Fabre d'Olivet, Pythagorean mathematician

"The harmony of the world is made manifest in Form and Number, and the heart and soul and all the poetry of Natural Philosophy are embodied in the concept of mathematical beauty." –Sir D'Arcy Wentworth Thompson, Scottish zoologist

"You cannot prevent the birds of sadness from passing over your head, but you can prevent them from nesting in your hair." –Swedish proverb

LIFEOLOGY

"All the achievements of mankind have value only to the extent that they preserve and improve the quality of life. The human future depends on our ability to combine the knowledge of science with the wisdom of wildness." –Aviator Charles Lindbergh in a 1967 **Life** magazine article

WHO are we? Why are we here? What is the meaning of life? What is our true essence, and what is the human connection to other life? Such is the inquiry of "Lifeology" in this chapter and section, also known as the study of *all* life. This definition is very broad and includes the seen and unseen realms, and an involved study of our long and storied history on this planet. This inquiry is conducted through the lens of the esoteric, where things are not always as they appear, and may be co-existing "beyond our senses." Lifeology includes a study of the macro level as well as the micro, or as many great teachers have observed: "As above, so below."

Life is mercurial and cannot thrive just anywhere. It requires fundamental ingredients to ensure perpetual survivability. On Earth, life needs three key conditions to survive: (1) atoms made up of chemical elements including carbon, hydrogen, oxygen, nitrogen, (2) water, (3) a source of energy such as sunlight. Nearly all life—from the first single-cell organisms on embryonic Earth to the complex creatures of today—is composed of organic materials. Matter is a general term for the substance of which all physical objects are made. Typically, matter includes atoms and other particles which have mass. Atoms of the four elements carbon, hydrogen, oxygen and nitrogen combine with traces of other elements to produce the key molecules that make up the building blocks of our cells, the amino acids. Complex molecules of carbon bond with other elements, such as oxygen, hydrogen and nitrogen. Carbon is able to bond with all of these because of its four valence electrons. Secondly, life on Earth also needs a liquid like water where the organic elements can interact. The third key ingredient for life is a source of energy. Sunlight contributes photosynthesis and other life-giving properties beneficial to most of the life on this planet.

It is often assumed in astrobiology that if life exists somewhere else in the universe, it will also be carbon-based, but this assumption is referred to by critics as "carbon chauvinism." Astrobiologists propose that asteroids, meteors, and space dust carry simple life forms, and spread them to a host planet upon impact. This dispersion of basic life forms in the universe is called "panspermia." It is offered as an alternative to Darwin's theory of evolution, which is still in the working hypothesis stage and has not been proven. Scientists studying the panspermia possibility point out that all life shares much of the same DNA and similar genetics occur between humans and plants as well as between humans and apes. These similarities are evidence of strong connections but not proof of evolutionary descendancy.

Prior to homo sapiens, the majority of extinctions on Earth occurred naturally, since it is estimated that 99.9% of all species that have existed are now extinct. In the present day there are some livestock animal species as well as human beings breeding in abundance, while many others are in decline, and some are on the brink of extinction. Much of the stress on flora and fauna is being impacted by humans, either directly or indirectly, in what today can be called an "animal genocide." The United Nations Development Program reported that "Every year, between 18,000 and 55,000 species become extinct. The cause: human activities." It is clear the manner in which humans currently live on the planet is unbalanced and unsustainable. Even the lives of the majority of humans is out of balance with an increase in cancer and stress-related illnesses. Species extinctions are at an all time high, caused by mismanagement of the planet's ecosystems by humans. As stewards of the planet we have failed the animal kingdom, upset the biological balance and, in the process, are failing ourselves.

OUR BLUE-GREEN ORB

The Earth's atmosphere is a layer of gases surrounding the planet and retained by the gravity of Earth. By content and volume, Earth's atmosphere contains roughly 78.08% nitrogen, 20.95% oxygen, 0.93% argon, 0.038% carbon dioxide, trace amounts of other gases, and a variable amount (about 1%) of water vapor. This mixture of gases is commonly known as air. The atmosphere protects life on Earth by absorbing ultraviolet solar radiation and reducing temperature extremes between day and night. Earth's atmosphere is constantly charged with electrical discharges, such as lightning. We also perceive these electrical phenomena as crystalline light pillars of ice and as the aurora borealis northern lights currently being seen in the daytime. Strangely, the atmosphere has become more electrically charged than just a few years ago.

There is no definite boundary between Earth's atmosphere and outer space. Our atmosphere is slowly becoming thinner until it will simply fade into space. Three quarters of the atmosphere's mass is within 11 kilometers of the planetary surface. People who travel above an altitude of 80.5 kilometers are designated as astronauts. An altitude of 120 kilometers marks the boundary where atmospheric effects become noticeable during re-entry of space crafts. The Kármán line, at 100 kilometers, is also frequently regarded as the boundary between atmosphere and outer space.

Scientific measurements have revealed that the Earth has a measurable pulse, or a "heartbeat," in the atmosphere. It is called the "Schumann Resonance" which pulses between the Earth surface and the bottom of the ionosphere. It vibrates at approximately 7.8 cycles per second. This rate is right between the Alpha and Theta brainwave levels for humans, which has been described as a carrier wave for "consciousness at rest." This is a state of deep but alert relaxation and intuitive attunement. It is the same rate for horses, dogs and cats. The Schumann Resonance has a wavelength so powerful it circles the Earth in a matter of seconds and passes effortlessly through concrete.

To put it all in context, just consider we are currently residing on a 4.5 billion year old spaceship. It is a self-sufficient, organic, and very complex spaceship. We are orbiting a power source that is a million times larger than planet Earth. There are over 200 billion more power sources, quite possibly with habitable planets like our own, within our neighboring group on this side of the galaxy. There are 40 more groups in the singular region of our galaxy. Our neighborhood is moving at two million miles per hour toward an object that is 150 million light years away. In our Milky Way galaxy alone there are over 50 billion planets. If even if 1% of those are in their system's "Goldilocks zone," then there are 500 million planets in our galaxy alone capable of supporting life. In the cosmos, lifeology (the study of *all* life), takes on many different dimensions.

Life on this blue-green orb seems totally precious and rare. The species diversity on Earth is astonishing. For example, there are estimated to be 10 million to 100 million ant species alone. Astronauts who have left the Earth's atmosphere and gazed upon our planet have almost always come away from the experience with a profound sense of oneness with humanity and all living things. They return with epiphanies such as life-changing breakthroughs in the awareness of their personal connection with a greater consciousness in the universe, a clearer perception of their respective life purposes and an unclouded view of humanity's habitual insanities, such as the utter futility of war. Figure in the superstring physics equation, which describes a universe of at least eleven dimensions, and the mysteries of the cosmos are compounded once again.

THE FINAL FRONTIER

Space is not a tranquil place. There are constant massive bursts of energy, and our Milky Way galaxy is continually evolving. Scientists now admit space is full of life, energy waves, and minute particles of dust. Space dust is widely regarded as freeze-dried bacteria. It is almost as if the universe manufactures pre-life in the form of solar dust particles, ready to be unbundled when they arrive on a host planet. This panspermia distribution may also be occurring on lifeless planets, originating in far-away galaxies, and in the process of establishing life everywhere simultaneously. But an entire planet as rich as Earth still seems to us a rare occurrence because life is arbitrary and fickle.

The universe is not a dark place despite all of its mysteries. The spiral arms of galaxies are fragmented and have characteristic spurs, or feathers, that make up Giant Molecular Clouds (GMCs). Gamma rays were previously associated with the most extreme environments in the universe, like supernovas. Now scientists believe that about 50 terrestrial gamma ray flashes occur every day on Earth. "Everywhere we look, we're seeing x-rays and gamma rays flying out of thunderstorms and lightning," said Joseph Dwyer, a physicist at the Florida Institute of Technology. "The gamma rays coming out of thunderstorms are so intense we can measure these 600 kilometers away, and so bright that it almost blinds (those viewing from) the spacecraft." Ultraviolet light is now being considered a healing aid, while infrared light appears ideal in the transmitting of data.

Many things we have been taught about the universe are being challenged by esoteric revisionists. For example, the substance of the universe is not matter at all, but motion, an abstract ratio of change that we call spacetime. Additionally, faster-than-light speeds are commonplace—the rule, not the exception—which goes against Einstein's theory of relativity. Astronomers have everything backwards, for example, stars beginning their life as red giants and ending as blue giants exploding in a supernova. There are two types of supernovas, one based on the thermal limit such as a blue giant explosion, or the age limit, that is, stars of other spectral classes. Galaxies form from globular clusters, to irregulars, to spirals, to giant spheres and also explode, producing quasars. Another revision to popular dogma is that there was no Big Bang, but indeed, with every contraction, there is an expansion.

The universe is very much bigger than we can possibly comprehend. There are over 200 billion stars in our Milky Way galaxy alone, plus there are an estimated 100 billion to a trillion known galaxies in the universe. Our Milky Way galaxy is a "barred" spiral, and 34 percent of all galaxies in the universe are spirals. It is estimated that there are more stars in the known universe then there are grains of sand on all the beaches of the world combined.

HUBBLE DISCOVERIES

Recent discoveries by the Hubble Telescope have opened our eyes to a universe not only far more expansive than we ever imagined but far more intricate and ripe with implications than we can readily process. Trillions of stars equate to billions of possibilities for life, especially with an other recent discovery that illustrates that the majority of stars do indeed harbor their own solar systems with inhabitable planets. Even as recently as the 1920s, orthodox science believed in a static cosmos until Edwin Hubble demonstrated that it was actually expanding and, therefore, must have originated long ago in some titanic "Big Bang." There are now challenges to this widely accepted theory, because with every expansion, most logically, there must be a contraction. Today, what all scientists would firmly agree upon is that the universe is outwardly expanding and is of a finite age, born from a dramatic "phase transition" when the ether, or quantum vacuum, jumped from one energy state to another, sucking matter into physical existence within our universe. We are on the expansion side of the universe, which is what we see from our perspective, while the other side is shrinking.

The universe extends far beyond what astronomers currently envision to be its outer limit. In total, there are six additional belts which are void of any coarse material beyond the stars, planets and all matter. Matter itself is in constant transformation within the Material Belt and is, therefore, subject to a growth and disintegration processes. For this reason, matter can never be, or become, as old as the complete universe. At any given time, therefore, only young matter can be found in the Material Universe. As such, matter in a solid and compact state can only be, at best, a mere 40 or 45 billion years old. The age of the entire universe beyond the Material Belt, however, is approximately *46 trillion* years old.

Symmetry may be common in nature, but it usually indicates the presence of some kind of force field or organism. This notion is questioned when we consider the Red Square Nebula. It is one of the most spectacular objects in the universe, and reveals almost perfect symmetry. Photographed in infra-red it looks more like a gemstone than a star, albeit on a cosmic scale. The Red Square is described as resulting from the death agony of a star called MWC 922, that is spewing gas, dust and plasma all over the region. Explosions, though, are not likely to be symmetrical—certainly not like the small ones we create on Earth, much less when nebula-sized. Researchers acknowledge the Red Square's amazing regularity, and realize that some of what we are seeing could be from bands, or concentric ripples, representing periodic releases of energy from the central node. The Red Square is now being labeled the most symmetrical object of comparable complexity ever photographed.

Given the fact that our solar system is on the far fringes of the Milky Way galaxy, our sun is relatively small in linear time. Evolution at the center of the galaxy has had at least a billion years head start, a very long time for a race of extraterrestrial beings to ponder the nature of energy and light. To consider ourselves as the only "intelligent" life in the universe would be naïve and egotistical, and to consider our Earth history free from extraterrestrial influence is globally ethnocentric. Beings from far away, or perhaps right here in another dimension, have had a vested interest in Earth for eons. Our planet is a genetic storehouse of information, which may also be resourceful to another race's own survival—especially those of a synthetic nature. But this treasure-trove of DNA is currently being squeezed out by a single reckless parasite called the human race.

OVERPOPULATION

"World's Population Booming" read a report dated August 30, 1964, from the UN: "Not only is the world's population soaring, but the rate of increase is accelerating. The annual increase now amounts to a high 2.1% a year." Midway through 1962 the Earth's population was 3.1 billion. The annual increase since then is 63 million, more than the population of France each year. Yet the exploding population growth is appearing primarily in developing nations. For Europe, the increase rate is 0.9%, for North America 1.6%, while underdeveloped areas show increases of 3 to 5%. At least 20% of the world's population lives in a single country with the most people—Communist China.

Most of these trends forecast over 50 years ago, continue on the same trajectories, but the human impact is currently having far wider consequences. Those alive today are witnessing growth on a scale never seen before. The world population reached 3 billion in 1959, with the expected population in 2050 to reach 9 billion. To place the human growth trajectory in perspective, in 1957, it took 33 years for the entire world population to double, in the next 28 years it doubled again, and will again in the next 24 years. In October, 2011, the worlds population officially hit 7 billion, and this figure would require at least five planets to be sustainable. The world's population is at more than 1400% of its sustainable level, and that is 14 times higher than its optimum capacity. A bumper sticker states: "The greenest action you can take is don't breed."

Overpopulation is also the main cause of the Earth's environmental problems, including climate change, habitat degeneration and species extinctions being among the most troubling. To rebalance, a humane and controlled birth cessation must be implemented to reduce the population to the sustainable level of 500 million, and ideally no more than one billion. In addition to this problem, humans are living longer than ever before.

There is always the possibility of finding one or several Earth-like planets in the universe, and dispersing a percentage of the population to new home planets. If not, further privation, criminality, hate against fellow humans, migrations to mega-cities, wars, exploitation of Earth's resources to near depletion, as well as new diseases, epidemics, starvation and mass suffering will only increase.

Population growth is a jagged chart depending on which country is growing, or in some cases, shrinking. Forty-two percent of the people in the most developed parts of world (such as Japan) are at zero, or negative population growth, and are not reproducing fast enough to keep their numbers even. Forty percent of the nations are adding new people, with the Far East clocking in at a 1% growth rate. That leaves 18% of the population experiencing rapid growth. Africa and South Asia are the fastest growth regions. They are also among the poorest.

Studies show that when women are better educated and have access to reproductive health care, they decide to have smaller families. At least a billion women would like to have access to reproductive health services, yet for the most none are available. The population debate is not just about the number of people, but also about the resources required for the ever-increasing demand. Currently, 25% of our fellow human beings do not have electricity. Thirteen percent have no access to fresh clean water. One in six of us will go to sleep tonight malnourished or starving. The struggle for resource equality is amplified by the USA, a nation containing only 5% of the world's population, yet consuming 30% of the world's resources. The United States is offering a very poor model for the rest of the world. The USA also has the dubious distinction of employing half of all the lawyers in the world, and spends 50% of all annual military expenditures worldwide.

The fact that Earth is grossly overpopulated is the most underreported media story of the last hundred years. Almost a billion people are malnourished daily, and with the growth of the population increasing by another billion every two decades, starvation is not a problem that is going away any time soon. More people equals a greater demand for resources. But growth is challenged by an energy system that cannot grow adequately in its present limited form, and these dynamics are linked to a natural environment that is rapidly being depleted. The choice seems clear—either we undertake voluntary change now, or face involuntary change later.

AVOIDING FUTURE DISASTERS

Modern civilization is fragile and can collapse by purely natural forces, or by those of our making. Certainly a direct hit by a meteorite would be catastrophic to nearly all life on the planet. The worst natural disaster could be a planetary pole shift, where the axis of the Earth, including the north and south poles, reconfigure into new locations prompting the continents to drift, volcanoes to spew, and earthquakes to trigger far more severe consequences than ever known, setting off tsunamis occurring in all the oceans and decimating coastal communities. Life as we know it would be changed forever, or would no longer exist. Currently the two magnetic poles are at the weakest they've ever been measured, so this scenario is not very far-fetched. In fact, the Magnetic North Pole is moving at the speed of 55 kilometers per year toward Siberia, while the South Pole is moving much slower at only 5 kilometers per year. The geologic record also indicates the poles have shifted on many occasions during the long march of time. Furthermore, likely due to global warming, the loss of Arctic pack ice is estimated at 11% per decade.

Far more frightening, if only because it can be prevented, is what we could do to ourselves, and by extension, to practically all life on Earth. Since midway through the 20th century, the prospects of a nuclear war have lingered as a way humans could end the world by the folly of war. Any nuclear attack on the USA would result in retaliation, followed by a domino effect of wars, including biological attacks, leading the planet into an environmental catastrophe.

Even without a high tech war, it appears our planet remains in serious peril. If even a few ecosystems collapse, there may be a domino effect. A natural disaster may be imminent, considering that in 1950 one quarter of the land surface of Earth was forested. Today it is closer to one-sixth, and the oceans cannot soak up all of the excess atmospheric carbon dioxide humans have produced. Lack of primary rainforest will lead to the planet's inability to create oxygen, and a reducing in bio-diversity. A polluted and degraded atmosphere contributes to depleted and acidic oceans. Removal of trees and shrubs lead to desertification. Over-farmed and drought lands will continue to create more severe storms. Polar caps and mountain glaciers melting from global warming will lead to rising sea levels and chaos along coastal communities. An increase in severe droughts and flooding will lead to more intense hurricanes and tornadoes. A domino effect of several or all of these scenarios could lead to a series of "world storms," that ultimately could collapse our entire civilization. Even if the planet remains stable, there will be storms with increasing intensity and very unusual weather patterns on all parts of Earth as the decades progress.

Our poisoned planet will slowly diminish human reproductive abilities, with more babies born deformed, and an increased number of children diagnosed with autism. It can be argued that everything we currently eat, drink and breathe is polluted. Factory-raised animals are sick and are developing exotic diseases. Worldwide fish stocks are grossly depleted by overfishing, and this then breaks down the entire oceanic food chain. Human-made medicines are not as effective as they were previously. There are new exotic diseases, plagues, viruses, and parasites emerging around the world. A toxic planet can no longer sustain seven billion irresponsibly-breeding humans. Homo sapiens are the masters of the planet and must learn to live sustainably, no matter how difficult the transition may be, or else we will suffer dire consequences. If we cannot control our numbers and respect the planet, humans will be the ultimate victims of our own folly.

THIS DYING PLANET

B efore we can advance as a species, we must deal with the pressing issue of saving the precarious balance of life on the planet on which we all depend. Ocean life is now at risk for the worst extinction event in millions of years—completely as a result of human activity. The oceans are in dire straits from a combination of air and water pollution, run off from land fertilizers, disastrous over-fishing, and global climate change is threatening to destroy entire marine ecosystems. The world's leading experts of oceanography are surprised by the rate and magnitude of the ocean changes that they are witnessing. This is a very serious situation demanding unequivocal action at every level. The implications of what humankind is doing to the ocean, and its cumulative effects, are far worse than any scientist has imagined.

The Arctic ice cap has nearly disappeared during the summer months, and this fact alone proves that global warming is real. Arctic polar bears are drowning in record numbers for lack of summer sea ice, and are expected to be extinct before the end of this century. Special interests, mostly hired by oil companies, continue to muddle the global warming debate with false or misleading information. Humans are all in the same boat, but we are paddling in different directions. We need consensus action to save the oceans.

There are no valid historical records of the volume and type of materials that were spilled in the oceans for centuries before the establishment of anti-dumping laws in the 1960s and 1970s. When the first studies came out in 1968, it was estimated that 38 million tons of excavated material, 4.5 million tons of industrial waste, 4.5 million sewage sludge, 100 million tons of petroleum-based products (mainly plastic), from two to four tons of chemical waste, and more than one million tons of heavy metals were released into the ocean. The U.S. archive shows that between 1946 and 1970, over 55,000 containers of radioactive waste were disposed of in three dumping sites in the Pacific Ocean. In addition, 34,000 tons of radioactive wastes were disposed of in three sites of dumping on the U.S. east coast between 1951 and 1962. No law on dumping radioactive waste was put into affect before 1972. With such a toxic marine environment it is no longer safe to consume seafood on a regular basis. The four reasons why we must stop eating seafood are (1) high levels of mercury, (2) Fukushima radiation spanning across the north Pacific basin, (3) species endangerment, and (4) the accumulation of toxic substances from over a century of reckless dumping. Ours may very well be the last generation of seafood consumers.

The last mass extinction event was 65 million years ago, yet humans are now producing our own mass extinction event, possibly within a few short decades. As an example, despite the tiny country of Laos being known as the "Land of 100,000 Elephants" only a hundred years ago, today there are less than 34,000 Asian elephants worldwide. Concurrently, the negative trajectory of animal genocide runs opposite the explosion of human proliferation.

THE SILENCE OF THE BEES

T he disappearance of honey bees is one of the most disturbing of species declines, especially for humans. Bees are a keystone species that is absolutely vital to sustaining our ecosystem. About ten years ago, honey bees began to mysteriously disappear across the planet, literally vanishing from their hives with no trace or carcasses. Dubbed Colony Collapse Disorder (CCD), the CCD continues to accelerate across North America and the trend only seems to be getting worse. What happened? Where could the bees have gone? Scientists are baffled. Environmental scientists immediately suspected that the cause in part was chemical pesticides, quite possibly worsened by the pollen emitted from GMO crops. Of course the chemical industry is engaged in a full-blown cover-up to deny this likely possibility while the pollinators of our world suffer a devastating population collapse. Bee "whisperers" (or their equivalent) have suggested that the bees are on strike and have left this dimension. Only a study of the esoteric could even float such a theory! The point is that there is consciousness in the animal kingdom and experts still do not agree on definitive answers; but the cessation of harmful pesticides is an obvious step in the right direction. If by some far-out chance bees are on strike, logically they will return when their environment improves.

Once all the honey bees are gone, we are really going to feel the impact of our neglect. Commercial honey bee operations pollinate crops that provide one out of every three bites of food in our diets. Almost all fruits and nuts are pollinated by honey bees. Could CCD be a fungus, a mold, or a virus? What are the pathogens in bees? New viruses keep emerging, but they take years to identify. Of course new science and new researchers are entering the race to save the honey bees. They have identified several factors as being at play in this perfect storm: nutrition, pesticides, viruses, and pathogens. As of today there is no way to remedy CCD.

According to the minutes of a meeting between Russian President Vladimir Putin with U.S. Secretary of State John Kerry in May, 2013, in Russia there is "extreme outrage" over the Obama Administration's continued protection of global seed and plant bio-genetic giants Syngenta and Monsanto—especially in the face of a growing "bee apocalypse" that the Kremlin warns "will most certainly lead to world war." The Ministry of Natural Resources and Environment of the Russian Federation (MNRE) released a report through the Kremlin, stating: "As part of a study on impacts from the world's most widely used class of insecticides, nicotine-like chemicals called neonicotinoids, American Bird Conservancy (ABC) has called for a ban on their use as seed treatments and for the suspension of all applications pending an independent review of the products' effects on birds, terrestrial and aquatic invertebrates, and other wildlife."

Important to note, this report states that Syngenta, along with bio-tech giants Monsanto, Bayer, Dow and Du Pont, now control about 99% of the global market for genetically modified pesticides, plants and seeds. Putin was so incensed over the Obama regime's refusal to discuss this grave matter that for three hours he refused to even meet with Kerry, who had traveled to Moscow on a scheduled diplomatic mission. Putin then relented so as not to cause an even greater rift between the two nations. At the center of this dispute between Russia and the USA, this MNRE report says, is the "undisputed evidence" that a class of neuro-active insecticides chemically related to nicotine, known as neonicotinoids, are destroying our planet's bee population which, if left unchecked, could destroy our world's ability to grow enough food to feed our population.

PLANET GARBAGE PATCH

Many people do not realize that there is a swirling mass of plastic and garbage particles developing in the world's oceans. The widest and deepest is in the North Pacific Ocean gyre, which qualifies as the planet's largest garbage dump. Recent research sponsored by the National Science Foundation suggests the affected area may be twice the size of Hawaii. The Five Gyres Project estimates that there are 143 billion kilograms of plastic in the oceans right now. According to a recent PBS show featuring the gyres dilemma, there are now more items of trash than individual fish life in the world's oceans.

A gyre in oceanography is any large system of rotating ocean currents, particularly those involved with large wind movements. Gyres are caused by the Coriolis Effect, that is, planetary vortices along with horizontal and vertical friction that determine the circulation patterns from the wind currents, and it is also where the garbage culminates. Most of the garbage deposited into the oceans is flowing out of polluted rivers. All five of the major ocean gyres are now massive garbage patches, some as large as the state or Texas, extending many hundreds of meters deep into the ocean. Plastic does not break down very rapidly and is the main ingredient in the garbage patch gyres.

To further compound the problems, after the March 2011 earthquake and tsunami in northern Japan, several impacted Fukushima nuclear reactors began to emit radioactive particles into the soil, air and water, and there have been other unexpected impacts. The first debris swept into the sea by the tsunami reportedly started to wash ashore on the North American west coast by mid-December of 2011, a year earlier than scientists and authorities had predicted. Residents of Vancouver Island, Alaska, and the U.S. Pacific coast have said they found large quantities of bottles, cans, lumber and floats. The debris is part of 18 billion kilograms of debris from Japan that is floating across the Pacific, and taking up an area thought to be the size of Alaska. The impact of the debris and radioactivity on the Pacific Ocean ecosystem remains unclear. In 2013, tuna were detected with radioactivity off the North American coast, and the first cases of sea mammals perishing from thyroid conditions began to emerge. Much of the Fukushima debris is expected to eventually join an already massive patch of existing garbage floating in the North Pacific gyre.

According to the Pesticide Action Network North America, more than a billion pounds of pesticides are used annually in the United States alone, and the EPA has registered more than 18,000 different pesticides in use. Many of these pesticides have a long-term effect, as the chemicals take a long time to break down, lasting for decades or longer, long after killing off the pests they were intended to kill. Extensive scientific studies show widespread and pervasive pesticide contamination in groundwater, drinking water and wildlife habitats throughout the USA.

Oceans also soak up 30% more carbon dioxide than does land, thus becoming acidified more rapidly. The rising global temperature and chemical composition of the tropical oceans is threatening to kill off over 15,000 species of small feeder fish because of bleached and depleted coral life. Coral reefs are the most biologically diverse eco-systems in the oceans. In the last 20 years, 44% of all coral reefs worldwide have perished. Some areas like the Florida Keys have seen 80% of the coral life depleted—and the future seems even more bleak. The end result of largely unregulated over-fishing in the last century is that 90% of all commercial fish stocks are now gone from the oceans. We must immediately find ways to nurture rather than destroy this delicate world. Immediate humane reductions in human breeding must be implemented to ultimately save future generations. And now is the time for a worldwide ban on wild animal hunting and driftnet fish harvesting.

Thinking in terms of karma, and the cycle of cause and effect of what we have done, the human race seems to deserve an apocalypse of the doom and gloom variety. People need to realize that everything is connected, including all Earth life and even our connection with external life in the universe. We are consuming Earth into its collapse, and leaving behind enormous chaos. Humans have literally overrun every corner of the planet. It is time we turn around our destructive behavior and learn to respect the diversity of life on Earth. We need to love the animals of the planet, and not view them as a nuisance or a commodity for harvest. If we can view animals as co-inhabiters, and celebrate the diversity they represent, maybe we can revise some of our horribly destructive habits.

SMARTEST LAND ANIMALS

Animals express consciousness through instinct. Humans, in addition to instinct, possess the highest quality of consciousness, that is, self-awareness. The magpie is the only bird that shows signs of self-awareness. Reflective thought is expanded self-awareness, and it is the biggest difference between animals and humans. Reflection is the power to turn one's consciousness upon oneself, to know, and especially to know that one knows. Learning math or physics, and understanding philosophy or astronomy, is due to humans' unique ability to reflect inwardly.

Only three animal species are known to create tools besides humans. They are elephants, monkeys and New Caledonia crows. All three of these advanced creatures show development of cognition throughout their lives. It is known that all three species have a way to communicate with their own kind. Crows can remember human faces, for example, or a farmer's field where another crow was shot, or where falcons attack. Crows can remember these locations for up to two years and can somehow relay this information to their own kind. Crows have been known to take wire hangers and craft them as nesting materials. Sometimes, as observed in Japan, the crows use wire hangers on electrical power lines and cause energy outages. Crows have been called "feathered apes" because their body to brain weight is the same ratio as primates. There are 250 known crow "words," and nearly as many have been identified in elephants and chimpanzees.

Chimpanzees are our closest relative in the animal kingdom, and they can teach us a lot about ourselves. When chimps have the option to share the spoils of newly found food, they never share among themselves. They just grab what they can, regardless of who did what. They don't seem to keep track of who was on the team. Researchers believe that the "share-the-spoils" response emerged at some point in the last half-million years, as humanoids began to forage and hunt cooperatively. Those who had the "share" response could develop stable, ongoing partnerships. Humanoids discovered that working together in small teams accomplished far more than individuals could accomplish on their own.

Wild chimps capable of making tools share over 98% of their genes with humans. Chimps can catch human infectious diseases, probe for termites with sticks as tools, and have complex social structures. Like us, chimps have a dark side, can be cruel and brutal, and are known to kill other chimp tribe members. Poaching and loss of habitat have made chimps endangered, due to an ever-shrinking environment because of human encroachment and poaching. 50 years ago in Tanzania there were a million chimps. Now only 300,000 remain.

Monkeys are clever enough to experiment, and wise enough to remember. Monkeys are known to be "multi-lingual" when multiple species of primates join as one troop. They warn of predators and announce food sources. Each primate species makes a different vocalization, but they are somehow able to understand each other. There are over 120 known "words" among the eight or so monkey species. Costa Rican monkeys have many words among their species. They have learned behaviors such as swimming underwater to collect lily pad roots, or washing their root foods. They also use deception in their vocalizations to scare off their brethren from a nonexistent enemy so they can collect an item of food without competition. Similar to humans, some monkey species can be murderous. Baboons are the most aggressive of the primates, and are known to hunt other primates. Humans are competitive and social just like monkeys. We both use tools to collect food. Monkeys use sticks to capture insects and rocks to smash open nuts.

OUR AQUATIC TWINS

An animal's ability to communicate among its own is a measurement of a species' intelligence. Dolphin behavior has been studied extensively by humans, both in captivity and in the wild. We know dolphins and whales have a complex underwater language, and a societal structure similar to people.

Dolphins "speak" with high-pitched whistles. They have identifiable family names for each other. Dolphin whistles can travel a much greater distance underwater than sound does in the air. Packs of males form gangs with their own vocalization whistles. Researchers think this is a way to attract female mates. Rival male gangs taunt and intimidate other male groupings, but do not use violence. A dolphin mother and her calves will stay in close contact for five years. Imaginative, curious, experimental, playful, and flexible behavior traits are all described as hallmarks of dolphin intelligence.

Humans show a remarkable intelligence connection with dolphins and whales. Killer whales, similar to early man, form social groups and work together to hunt humpback whales. Similarly, different whale species work together to herd schools of fish for collective feasting. Hunting is a learned technique taught by parents, a kind of creative intelligence not found frequently in the animal kingdom. Sometimes clever dolphins will hover over a stingray waiting for it to flush out an octopus. When the prey is exposed, the dolphin will swoop in quickly and catch the prize first. This is proof of creative intelligence. Dolphins routinely display self-awareness when looking in an aquarium mirror. Dolphins also display empathy and will show willingness to befriend humans when not threatened. Emotional awareness can be identified by spindle cells in their brains, and dolphin brains are wired similarly to humans.

Echo-location allows both whales and dolphins to detect prey. Sperm whales are the largest toothed predators on Earth who can locate giant squid at the bottom of the ocean with eco-location. Squid and sperm whales engage in epic battles of survival, where the squid can win if it can drown the whale—but this is highly unusual. Sperm whales can store vast quantities of oxygen in their bloodstream, and this allows them to dive incredibly deep, over 3,000 meters, and stay underwater for over an hour. Their only natural enemy is the pilot whale, which is only one-third their size, but have an advantage because they hunt in packs. Similarly, humpback whales work together herding and catching schools of herring fish, and killer whales work together to hunt the calves of humpback whales. The closest living relative of whales is thought to be the hippopotamus. The humpbacks have been observed to form friendships that last for many years. They also grieve for their dead.

Dolphins are often regarded as one of Earth's most intelligent animals, although it is difficult to say just how intelligent dolphins are. Comparisons of species' relative intelligence are complicated by differences in sensory apparatus, response modes, and the very nature of cognition. Furthermore, the difficulty and expense of doing experimental work with large aquatics mammals means that some tests that could yield meaningful results still have not been carried out, or have been carried out with inadequate sample size and methodology.

Dolphins have long played a mythological role in human culture. They are commonly depicted in Greek mythology, from mosaic portraits to coin designs, including one depicting a man or boy riding on the back of a dolphin. Ancient Greek mariners treated them with welcome delight. A ship spotting dolphins riding in their wake was considered a good omen for a smooth voyage. Dolphins were also important to the Minoans, as judged by artistic evidence from the ruined palace at Knossos. In Hindu mythology, the Ganges river dolphin is associated with Ganga, the deity of the Ganges River. There are countless stories of dolphins saving humans from drowning, or escorting a shipwrecked sailor to safety.

THE BOTANY OF DESIRE

Beyond the fauna of Earth, humans also have a deep connection with the flora. After all, each species is within the web of nature. Attempting to stand outside of it is not healthy. In our current world, which is already out of balance, we are now faced with Genetically Modified Organisms in our food supply. Long before the advent of GMOs, farmers around the world had been organically cross-breeding crops to make them stronger and more bountiful. For example, apples originated in Central Asia, but now are grown and used worldwide in so many different ways. Growers want ever more sweetness, and apples are portable and offer long lasting freshness and taste. The Kazakhstan origin of apples gave us many varieties. Grafting, the practice of attaching a favored seed into a new plant, continues to provide new genetic strains. Mono-culture of a single variety strips a species of the chance to survive and intermingle, because they are all the same. Bugs stay way ahead of the game. As millions per farm are eradicated with chemicals, they evolve immunities to chemical pesticides. Genetic manipulation provides a tool chest to alter DNA and enhance or preserve apple trees, but we must be careful.

Sex creates variety. Sexual breeding experiments can affect various strains. Despite the life-providing asset of furnishing oxygen, trees and plants are being destroyed at an alarming rate to provide open land for growing crops or grazing animals which humans select. Flowers, for example, are a multi-million dollar industry. This is extraordinary for a plant that is otherwise worthless as a food source. There is another plant that has an unusual quality, one that can alter human consciousness. Marijuana can unlock the mind, and give the user an experience of a new realm of consciousness. The resin of female cannabis plants is the psychoactive element of marijuana. Other natural or synthetic drugs can provide a method of mind expansion. Pot was first discovered in India and China, and was used thousands of years ago as a therapeutic pain reliever. Cannabis is a tropical plant, but it can be grown by farmers in a variety of locations. Now it is grown indoors as much as outdoors, and growth can be manipulated using artificial heat, regulated lighting, a steady water supply, and the use of fans to circulate air in a manufactured natural environment. Marijuana is merely a weed, yet in the open market it can sell for thousands of dollars per kilogram.

Music is now used as a tool to help plants grow to their potential. Joel Sternheimer, a French physicist and musician, writes melodies that allegedly help plants grow, and has applied for international patents protecting his methods of music-making. The tunes he applies are not random melodies. Instead, he chooses each note to correspond to an amino acid in a protein, and the full tune corresponds to an entire protein. Sternheimer claims that when plants "hear" the appropriate tune, they produce more of that protein. He also writes tunes that inhibit the synthesis of proteins. Using simple physics, he claims to be able to translate these into audible vibrations of music. The quantum vibrations that occur at the molecular level as a protein are being assembled from its constituent amino acids. Sternheimer claims that tomatoes exposed to his tunes grew two and a half times larger than the same seeds in a control study. He also claims to have stopped a mosaic virus infection of the tomatoes by playing tunes that inhibited enzymes vital to the virus. The tunes are very short, he says, and need only be played once. Sternheimer warns scoffers to be heedful when tinkering with his tunes because they can affect people as well. "Don't ask a musician to play them," he cautions. "You must be very careful." Sterheimer says that one of his musicians had difficulty breathing after playing the tune for cytochrome C too often.

EARTH IN THE BALANCE

Humans are the dispensers and recipients of the karma we create in the world. Life is not static. It will go on with or without humans. Life is eternally dynamic, forever creating and pushing forward. We are all eternal beings continuously on the pathway of endless unfoldment, always evolving just a little bit more each time around, both physically and spiritually. We are never less, but always more. We are not asleep and unconscious, but alive, awake and aware. We are all very much accountable for our actions, so we very much should listen to our higher selves. There is something within each of us that sings the praises of eternity. Listen to the song within yourself. Tread lightly and have a minimal impact.

Humans have been blessed and cursed with a fertile imagination, often viewing ourselves as separate from the animal kingdom. Where animals rely on instinct, humans rely on feelings and "intellect." Our mastery of the physical world makes our role as stewards of the planet even more apparent. For better or for worse, humans are assigned as the top species today, and largely responsible for the preservation of most living organisms. The fragility of life and the awesome power of nature coexist in a very precarious balance.

Humans must increase their sensitivity and cooperation with the natural world. All life is interrelated, no matter how remotely. We are just one animal connected to another, one part of the other, in a complex web of interdependence. Buddhism and Hinduism teach reincarnation, both within the animal kingdom and with people. Contained within this construct, animal spirits will one day evolve spiritually to incarnate as humans. All people once lived as animals according to certain esoteric traditions, and perceptions are now changing to reflect this understanding. In December, 2012, an international group of prominent scientists signed The Cambridge Declaration on Consciousness, proclaiming support for the concept that animals are conscious and aware to a similar degree as humans. Their list of conscious animals includes all mammals, birds, and some encephalopods like the octopus, which have exhibited the capacity for remembering.

In the end, egalitarianism for all life must reign over capitalism. A world treaty must be created where all humans and animals are granted equal rights, including the practical sharing of resources. Hoarding of anything must become a crime. With this model, all living creatures are granted equal rights simply to exist. Even the planet Earth itself has rights. In such a world treaty, abuse of the Earth will be a serious crime to be tried in a world court. Article 3 of the UN Human Rights Declaration already reads, "Everyone has the right to life, liberty and security of person." The UN should pass a declaration of rights for all living forms of life on Earth. Someday it will be obvious to people that life is interconnected, and it may come first from the quantum activists. After all, if we are made of atoms, then a scientist studying atoms is essentially a group of atoms studying themselves.

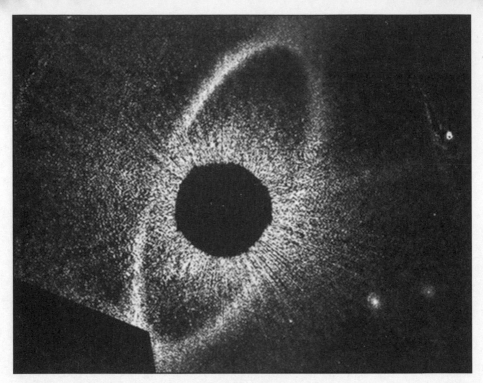

This new Hubble Space Telescope image of a nearby star, Fomalhaut, and its surrounding disc of debris have made astronomers sit up and take notice because it reveals new information. Released on January 8th, 2013, the image shows that the debris field made of ice, dust, and rocks is wider than previously thought, spanning an area 14 to 20 billion miles from the star. *National Geographic* reported that scientists have also used this image to calculate the path of a planet, Fomalhaut b, as it makes its way around a star. When it was discovered, astronomers noted with interest that the planet's 2,000-year elliptical orbit brings it three times closer to Fomalhaut than previously thought, and its eccentric path could send it plowing through the rock and ice contained in the debris field. "The resulting collision, if it happens, could occur around the year 2032, and result in a show similar to what happened when the comet Shoemaker-Levy 9 crashed into Jupiter," said astronomer Paul Kalas, of the University of California at Berkeley.

< According to Wikipedia, the Red Square Nebula is a celestial object located in the area of the sky occupied by star MWC 922 in the constellation Serpens. The first images of this bipolar nebula, taken using the Mt. Palomar Hale telescope in California, were released in April 2007. It is notable for its square shape, which according to Sydney University astrophysicist Peter Tuthill, makes it one of the most symmetrical celestial objects ever discovered.

"Every now and again take a good look at something not made with hands—a mountain, a star, the turn of a stream. There will come to you wisdom and patience and solace and, above all, the assurance that you are not alone in the world." —Sidney Lovett

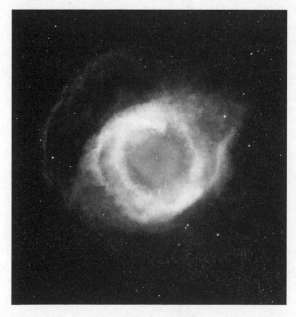

< This image of the NGC 7293 Helix Nebula, or the "Eye of God," was taken by the Hubble Space Telescope. The Helix Nebula is a typical example of a planetary nebula because it emerged as a result of the explosion of a sun-like star. Generally speaking, hydrogen gas is the most common component of the interstellar medium, also known as the vast space between stars and planetary systems in galaxies. Hydrogen gas in space exists primarily in its atomic and molecular form, and makes up huge clouds throughout the entire galaxy.

Cetacean society is built on the bonds that they create through touch, love, affection, family, friends, trust, food, play, and survival. Dolphins are known to touch mouth to mouth in a tender kiss that can mean anything from mutual reassurance, to trust, to acceptance into the pod, to a special friendship, and even love. Humans can relate to this cetacean bonding because humans also bond with other humans in similar ways. So while humans are land people, and cetaceans are sea people (or more precisely marine non-human beings), it is possible for humans and cetaceans to peacefully share planet Earth through a bond of trust and friendship. Let this be the lasting legacy of a future generation.

The Great Apes

Humans are closely related to chimpanzees and bonobos. Gorillas are our next closest relatives, and then orangutans.

< What can we learn from our closest relatives? This image shows the relationships between the great apes. Humans are closely related to chimpanzees and bonobos. Gorillas are our next closest relatives, and then orangutans. Interestingly, the bonobos have a greater capacity for unity, while the chimpanzees' are more combative.

MYTHOS OF CREATION

"The search for reality is the most dangerous of all undertakings, for it destroys the world in which you live."
–Nisargadatta Maharaj, Indian spiritual teacher

THE evolution of the human species will never come to an end. We are not a finished product, but rather a perpetually unfinished process, and as such a moving target. And our current state, the human condition, is not the final word on this matter. We are resilient enough to survive disaster, and dynamic enough to redefine ourselves. Human development is in motion as the wave of evolution continues to push us forward.

As a collective civilization, it is evident that we have gathered a certain amount of information since the time of Mesopotamia 6,000 years ago, until the Age of Enlightenment 150 years ago. From then until 1950 we doubled that amount of information. Then, from about 1950 to 1970, we doubled it again, and then again from 1970 to 1980. At present the constructs of Moore's Law dictate that information will continue to double every 18 months. Computational power is now on par with the human brain. In a decade, our computers may be 500 times the known computational value of a human brain. As we catapult into the brave new world of sentient computers, a new mythos of creation will be sure to follow.

In this examination of human evolution and all of the life sciences, we will need to start at the beginning when people first began to look inwards. In our world of duality there are always those select few who wish to share and extend their awareness, and others who are attracted to religious and spiritual themes for the power and control it wrests over people. Students of authentic love-based spiritual traditions have sought to offer an alternative to organized political and patriarchal adherents since time immemorial. The impressive history and teachings of the mystics, which include the world's alchemists, philosophers, Gnostics and secret or mystery school initiates, have strived to interpret the world and pass on spiritual knowledge to their followers. Other esoteric traditions that continued for centuries, such as the Knights Templar, Cathars, Freemasons and the Illuminati, for better or for worse, have all had an agenda that benefits their own adherents.

Only the truth will stand the test of time, as the creation of a unified world civilization gradually unfolds. Hidden agendas, power over people's minds, and control issues will be exposed for what they are, and will then fade into the annals of history. The final fragment of the plan is destined to come into play soon, when both factions arrive at a peaceful resolution of their ancient struggle and work together to create a civilization that is the union of both paths. The culmination of human civilization will come into fruition, and all institutions and levels of society will encourage people to complete their spiritual evolution by achieving the goal of the ancient Greek mandate: "Know Thyself."

THE HIERARCHY OF NEEDS

To better understand the human condition, it is important to be familiar with the fundamental needs of people. In 1943, American psychologist Abraham Maslow developed the concept of a hierarchy of human needs, possibly one of the most well-known and comprehensive human development conceptualizations in psychology. Maslow's "Hierarchy of Needs" describes what human beings generally aspire for throughout their lifetimes. This model is often portrayed in the form of a pyramid, where the base levels are identified in the larger sections of the pyramid where the majority of Earth's people reside. In the base level of safety and security needs, where the focus is on survival, food and shelter, one is eeking out an existence and trying to stay alive. Next is the level for friendship, love, and security, and then moving up to the higher levels of aspiration and human potential. At the top level are the self-actualization needs that come to blossom when a person develops, matures, becomes financially secure, and enters the prime of life. In this Hierarchy of Needs, to achieve the higher-levels, a person needs to strive towards the apex of the pyramid, and suggests that only a relatively few will ever reach this level of higher development. The top of the pyramid, which is the hardest to obtain, is self-actualization, that is, becoming the complete humans we aspire to become, not only in our chosen profession, but the maximization of our creative and altruistic potential, and ultimately, the enlightenment of the individual.

For those with the luxury of leisure time to contemplate their position in life, it is indeed a wondrous age to be alive. For those less fortunate, it may still be a period to celebrate our new awakening. The attainment of increased awareness can be independent of leisure time or wealth. After all, this is a time when everyone can be enthusiastic about finally becoming spiritually aware and self-actualizing to the best of their abilities. Many feel that our awareness is expanding exponentially. We are beginning to see what we have never seen before. The esoteric mythos of creation is emerging beyond its limited confines. The truth is shining brighter than ever before. The veil is certainly lifting, but of course there will still be chaos. There will be confusion. The transition will reveal what we have not wanted to see, yet will show more clearly the need for an alternative. And there is no turning back. It is inevitable that what is not whole, what is not truthful, what is a house of cards, will crumble. What is not genuine will not endure.

Those moving toward an enlightened state become just that, more and more filled with light and aware of their natural state as spirit having a human experience. We will all begin to naturally reexamine the ancient intuition that all matter, even our "reality," is composed of mere energy. It is an idea with which physicists have grappled with since the theory of relativity, and more recently, with quantum theory. It was the spiritual masters who first called into question the separate identities of energy and matter. The phenomenon of ether, including time and space, are mere crystallizations of mind, as has been discussed by those well-versed in esoteric subjects for centuries. Many scientists today would agree with the ancient Hindus that the world we perceive with our five senses is a projection of an idea: that matter is insubstantial in origin; and is simply a temporary aggregate of the pervasive energy that animates the electron. All matter merely changes shape or form in a process of continued transmutation.

IN SEARCH OF THE ESOTERIC CENTER

Esoteric studies are often grouped with the occult, with religious mystery schools, or with a charismatic teacher, but these descriptions should not be its limitation. The esoteric of today usually becomes the established history and science of tomorrow. Think about all the original concepts, beliefs, symbology and mythologies of our ancestors. Many have no meaning to us today, or if they do, they have undergone extensive revision to become accepted as conventional wisdom. For example, Earth is not the center of the universe, nor the center of our solar system. But centuries of evaluating the Earth's rotation led to the science of astronomy. A pantheon of multiple gods developed into the concept of one true God. So even if considered antiquated, symbols and mythology can sometimes point us in the direction of a better understanding. Civilizations always begins uncomplicated, but end up becoming quite tangled. Matter appears to be solid, but upon closer examination, it is anything *but* solid.

Esoteric literally means intended for, or fully understood, only by particular participants. It is hidden knowledge that is confined to a small group, and known only by a restricted number of adherents. It is generally confidential information that is not publicly disclosed. Esoteric is also the essence of knowledge or spiritual wisdom. The esoteric then becomes an inner aspect, a starting point, to be fully understood only by its devout believers. Only those who get it will get it. In a larger sense, the esoteric is our origin, our inner circle of humanity. And within the esoteric itself are set beliefs which are rare and "to the core." This is called the "esoteric center," as opposed to the exoteric, which means not confined to an inner circle of disciples, but widely disseminated and comprehensible to the mass public. The exoteric is a rigid translation of life with a literal meaning of the scriptures, which can lead to a narrow perspective. For example, the symbolic statement to "kill the infidel" is often taken literally. Exoteric can be blind faith in embracing overly simplistic explanations or stories. In this regard, there is no personal introspection, no ability to question the teachings, and no inner searching. In between the esoteric and the exoteric is another level called the mesoteric, which is the middle level of humanity and includes all religious paths.

The esoteric center is only intended for the adherent, the adept, the one invited into the circle by his teachers. Those who choose to "take the red pill," as Neo from *The Matrix* was offered, must make a conscious decision to seek the unknown, no matter "how deep the rabbit hole will go." "Seek and ye shall find," is a truth for everyone. The length of time to realize this depends entirely on the initiate's devotion. Happiness and contentment arise from the esoteric core. This center stimulates people at the heart, also called the solar plexus. Progress along the way is facilitated by the expansion of consciousness. The end goal is nothing short of personal enlightenment.

The core truth is where spiritual teachers draw their inspiration according to wisdom teacher George Gurdjieff, as quoted here by his student P.D. Ouspensky in 1915, author of *In Search of the Miraculous*:

A teacher should not depend on whether he or she knows what they teach, but depends on whether or not their ideas come from actual fact from the esoteric center, and whether the teacher understands and can distinguish esoteric ideas, that is, ideas of objective knowledge from subjective, scientific, and philosophical ideas. A person deceiving themselves or deceiving others (has) no connection, either directly or by succession, with the esoteric center.

THE SPLIT BETWEEN EXOTERIC AND ESOTERIC

It has been said that true spirituality can be broken down to two levels. The first is public and outside, or the exoteric level, and this is the one that the majority of people can understand. The second is an inner, more esoteric teaching, which only those at an advanced level are alleged to comprehend. Esoteric schools have therefore existed as part of, or alongside, many different religions of the world. The esoteric schools attempted to provide a connection to divinity that was accessible at an individual level and provided a connection to higher planes and spiritual dimensions. It was primarily through the esoteric schools, not the exoteric religions provided to the masses, where people learned within their inner initiations and the path to awakening. The religious dogma taught to the masses has often been an obstacle to expanding awareness, and served the purpose of manipulation and control by fear.

Esotericism was introduced in this way to protect secret wisdom from those who would alter, deride, or destroy the purity of the teachings. A master was recognized as a person who achieved a level of awakened spirituality, and even went on a mission to spread the teachings thus learned, or who was awakened through a mission. There are many examples in which the teacher would split his or her teaching, giving the public the exoteric version of spirituality, while delivering the esoteric teaching privately to those deemed able to receive deeper lessons. Jesus Christ is a perfect archetype, as he taught both exoterically and esoterically. That is, he taught the public at a basic level they could accept without fear, but gave the esoteric knowledge to his disciples in secret. Historically, once the spiritual figure passes, often the exoteric side of the teaching morphs into an organized religion, while the esoteric practices continue in secret. Unfortunately, or perhaps ironically, in time, the organizers of a religion usually turn against the esoteric practitioners and drive them away.

The teachings of Jesus Christ clearly illustrate the difference between the exoteric and the esoteric:

He would speak the word to them with many parables like these, as they were able to understand. And He did not speak to them without a parable. Privately, however, He would explain everything to His own disciples. –Mark 4:33-34

Then the disciples came up and asked Him, "Why do You speak to them in parables?" He answered them, "Because the secrets of the kingdom of heaven have been given for you to know, but it has not been given to them ... For this reason I speak to them in parables, because looking they do not see, and hearing they do not listen or understand." –Matthew 13: 10,11,13

ESOTERIC SYMBOLOGY

Symbols are electromagnetic information fields that are encoded with information related to what the symbols embody. These symbols can attach to our own electromagnetic fields and psyches when we give them our unknowing attention. After all, energy flows where attention goes, and one of the key markers of intelligence is the ability to manipulate symbolic thought. The concept of symbols are found in mythology and folklore worldwide. The esoteric is timeless, as past is modern, which will become future. Symbols contain considerable power over people, either knowingly or unknowingly, hence an entire chapter is devoted to their intricacies later in this book.

The name "grimoire" is derived from the word "grammar." A grammar is a description of a set of symbols and how to combine them to create well-formed sentences. A grimoire is, appropriately enough, a description of a set of magickal symbols and the instructions on how to combine them accurately. Most of the grimoire texts come from the 19th and early 20th centuries, and hold descriptions of traditional European ritual magick, and are based on Judeo-Christianity, especially King Solomon the Magician. Even though this must not be confused with neo-Paganism, many of the neo-Pagan traditions use similar rituals and techniques, albeit with a different vocabulary, usually Celtic. The law of signatures, the concept that every object in the real world has some hidden meaning, and particularly how these signatures interact, is one of the fundamental principles of magic.

Those who are attracted to the various "mysteries," and are unable to grasp the esoteric meaning of their education, often take the exoteric interpretation to be truth. Certain individuals turn to Satan or Lucifer as their object of worship. Lucifer, whose literal meaning is "light," may be the inspiration behind the adage that "the greatest trick the devil ever played on humans was to make us believe that he didn't exist." Many attracted to the dark forces never grasp an understanding of the symbolic metaphors and the much deeper philosophy. Yet, these Satan worshipers are not to be trifled with, and they furnish a diversion and frequent source of large sums of money. The Luciferian Brotherhood has seldom found itself lacking of fools or in funds. Those who cannot understand this philosophy through the occult language of symbology, and make the shift in thinking for the coming changes, may be doomed to extinction. The spokespersons for the New Age make no secret of their intent in that regard. Most fail to recognize that the symbolic pyramid missing the capstone represents the unfinished "Great Work" of the Mystery School. Furthermore, demons are said to run the occult and the New Age movement throughout the world. They identify themselves as anything from spirits of the dead to ancient gods, as well as physical extraterrestrials and ascended masters.

ESOTERIC MYTHOLOGY

"Know Thyself" were the two most profound words written on the Temple of Apollo at Delphi, which in times of antiquity was the endpoint for countless pilgrimages. All would come to receive a pithy rhyme. This was the duty of the Pythia, a young priestess at the Temple of Apollo, who delivered oracles in a frenzied state, induced by vapors rising from a chasm in the rock. She spoke gibberish, which attendant priests would reshape into the enigmatic prophecies preserved in Greek literature. Most of the rhymes received related to the seeker who came to the Temple of Apollo. Greek philosophers believed that knowledge of self derives from the freedom of mind, followed by the breakdown of the controlled human condition. With a higher awareness of self, we can break our obsession with the *horizontal* world, that is, the immediacy of all that appears around us. An amplification of our other senses allows us to know "thyself," as if becoming a child again, and discovering a brand new world with newly awakened faces pressed up against the window, and gazing out in amazement.

Around two thousand years later the torch of esoteria has passed to the Theosophical Society, and led by the matriarch Helena Blavatsky. The group studied the occult, codified esoteric subjects, and helped mold the New Age movement into what it is today. The three goals of the Theosophical Society were, first, to create a Universal Brotherhood of Humanity without distinction of race, color or creed; second, to promote the study of the world's religions; and third, to investigate the hidden mysteries of nature. Blavatsky said, "To reach Nirvana one must reach Self-Knowledge, and Self-Knowledge is of loving deeds, the child." The philosophy at the core of all the mystery schools is secular humanism, the foundation and the font of socialism or communism. Decades later, New Age beliefs picked up where the Theosophical Society left off. New Age can be defined by any single, or any combination of, the following factors: astrological or zodiacal beliefs; channeling; meditation; "all is one" or monism; Man is God, and esotericism. In the case of esotericism, it is regarded as the quest to reinterpret ancient texts to find hidden meanings, with the end goal of unifying all world religions into one belief.

Many believe the Freemasons have guarded the ancient mysteries for centuries, their wisdom having passed on to them by the medieval Knights Templar. The ancient mysteries deal with the concept of the power of the human mind. The Masons openly celebrate the great powers of the human mind. In their second degree ritual, there actually is a line where they say, "Here you will learn the mysteries of human science." Similarly, a mysterious book called *The Secret Teachings Of All Ages* was written in the 1920s by a Canadian-American named Manly P. Hall, who founded the Philosophical Research Society in Los Angeles. The Society carries on his work, studying the wisdom of the ancients, and is largely about the divination of humans, and how it is that each of us can achieve a high level of consciousness beyond the limitations of the reasoning mind.

Modern physics is describing what the ancient shamans have long known. These wisdom keepers of the Americas and elsewhere say that we're dreaming the world into being, simply through the very act of witnessing it unfold. Scientists believe that we are only able to do this in the very small subatomic world. Shamans understand that we also dream of the larger world that we experience with our senses.

THE ESOTERIC SYMBOLOGY OF SECRET SOCIETIES

Are there still secrets or subtle esoteric teachings to learn by following a metaphysical path of study? The Freemasons, for example, have a tradition rich in symbolism and meaning. An initiate has to follow a long, intricate path of discovery, learning, and subsequent understanding, in order to *come into* the knowledge and spiritual "freedom" that is esoteric Masonry. A layperson or initiate may understand that the square and compass, perhaps the most well-known of Masonic symbols, represent the concepts of judgment and discernment. However, only a Freemason that has gone through the rituals and embodied the practices of Masonry truly knows the esoteric meaning of these symbols. These symbols have power, embodied in the being of any Freemason. A Master Mason initiating a new apprentice knows the living depth of Masonry as only a sitting President, for example, can truly know the full meaning and power of his office.

When a Catholic priest offers the Eucharist to a Christian parishioner, the bread and the wine are represented as the body and blood of Christ, which enables both the priest and parishioner to contact Christ's consciousness and teachings. Most Christians, even those who deny that there is any real change in the elements used, recognize a special presence of Christ in this rite. A priest through his own initiation, education, and faith practice, embodies his own understanding of the Eucharist. When he offers communion, he *knows* the validity of this act. That knowledge vibrates in his body, blood and consciousness. If a person is open to experience the Catholic faith and its symbols, that person might receive the full meaning of the ritual. If a person is skeptical of the Christian beliefs and symbols, or simply not aware of them, they may not experience such a deeper meaning. At the moment of communion, if a person is open and receptive to the mystery and teachings of Christ, that person might experience a spiritual awakening, as many people have recounted.

We cannot hope to understand the philosophy of any branch of the mystery schools or the Illuminati without many years of study and a complete knowledge of their "symbolic" language. When an individual joins a branch of the "Brotherhood," by any name,

Freemasonry, Theosophical Society, Anthroposophic Society, *Fraternitis Rosae Crucae*, Knights Templar, Sovereign and Military Order of the Knights of Malta, or any other fraternal order or secret society, no one ever sits down with the initiate to explain the meaning of anything. An actual literal esoteric education would be too pandemic. A public expose' could arise, something which the ultra-secret Illuminati needs to avoid.

The organization of any "Order" is a pyramidal structure of "Degrees," most easily understood with Freemasonry. On the bottom are the so-called "Blue" lodges, full of ignorant, materialistic, and opportunistic fools. Promising candidates are chosen to be guided up the ladder of initiation with the help of those who have gone before. The initiate is presented with the objects of study, books, symbols, ritual, and camaraderie, but with these doctrines, inspiration, or "illumination," must come from within.

To use the Masonic "Degree of Initiation" as an example, this secret society provides a new key to ultimate enlightenment at each level, but only for those who can truly understand the rituals and symbols of each Degree. When the understanding, or a person's ability to keep the secrets halts, the progress of the candidate also comes to an end. Only those above the 29th Degree have the ability to comprehend the *ultimate secrets* and goals of the Masonic Order. In the world of Freemasonry, this is called "Jacob's Ladder," as it signifies the sequence of degrees the initiate can aspire to, following their own oath swearing ceremonial rituals and pledging to procedures, which are sworn and taken on each and every entry to the next degree. When successful, they are then rewarded with the various symbolic tokens, gifts, information and mementos of each degree. Specific components at different levels have symbolic meanings and representations for something else. In Freemasonry, only a select few are hand picked for advancement beyond the 13th Degree, called the York Rite, or 32nd Degree, called the Scottish Rite. The chosen ones disappear behind the veil and become one of the "Thousand Points of Light," and they are properly known as the "Magi." There are vertical and horizontal paths of initiation and many interconnecting degrees at the higher levels between the different orders and secret societies. A 32nd Degree Freemason could, for example, possess over 100 different degrees, each one replete with symbology and mythology.

The ultimate "secret" is the method of controlling large numbers of "sheeple," with the promise of a secret that they are led to believe will make them one of the "elect." The goal is the elimination of all religion except for their own, the elimination of all nation states, and complete control and ownership of everything, and everyone, everywhere, every moment of every day, forever. This "divide" has already been forged. Freemasonry does not require its members to believe in any one religion, as long as they believe in a "Supreme Being." On the surface it seems interesting, and "they" all have much in common with all the rest of society. However, the billions of indoctrinated masses don't have the Masonic "common bond," or another of their secrets, which is: "We don't really believe what you have been taught, but we will go along with the charade anyway."

SERPENT WISDOM

Various symbols have left indelible impressions throughout history. The most predominant is the serpent, found in evidence wherever the ancient temples devoted to wisdom flourished. The twisting pair of serpents form the caduceus, sometimes mistakenly used as a symbol of medicine, or medical practice. Since the old story of Adam and Eve, the serpent has represented two things—knowledge and sex—thus hinting at a close connection between the two. And the secret is that the "creative force" within each of us is one single force, whether it be used for physical or mental ends. We have the choice as to which way we direct this force, upwards or downwards, or toward good or toward evil.

In all esoteric systems, Eastern and Western, the serpent is the agent symbol of wisdom, also called *Sophia*. In Asia and in the Western mystery schools, the master of the coiling energy was called "serpent of wisdom." One of the earliest sustaining secret societies is the Brotherhood of the Snake, also called the Brotherhood of the Dragon, and remains existing under many different names. The Brotherhood of the Snake is devoted to guarding the "secrets of the ages." The secrets of these groups are thought to be so profound that only a chosen, well-educated few are able to make use of and interpret them.

The psychophysical energy known in Asian mystical practices as *kundalini*, the "serpent power," is an electricity-like spiraling energy. Kundalini energy belongs equally to the cosmos, the Earth body, and the human body, and is integral to our corporeal and spiritual makeup. It has been universally equated with goddess divinities, or *shaktis*. Raising kundalini is the aim of yogic practices that have persisted for thousands of years.

The serpentine power is also the form of divine energy—intelligence witnessed by countless people who have undergone an ayahuasca trance. Veteran shamans assert that this serpentine power is an actual dynamism of nature, a supernatural creature to be encountered repeatedly in the altered state of ayahuasca trance. Sacha Mama, is the great serpentine wisdom goddess of the Amazon, who is equivalent to the Rainbow Serpent of the Australian Aborigines. Countless other examples and parallels of "the female spiritual principle" could be given. In material-minded or primitive people the serpent continues to be used purely for procreation or sensual gratification. But as people aspire to higher ideals, as they yearn to create mentally, and live in the spirit, the force is gradually drawn upwards to the creative principles in the brain.

Eastern religions call this force the kundalini, and it is likened to a serpent of fire lying coiled at the base of the spine. If a person steadily purifies his or her mind and nature through living chastely and moderately, they are able to magnetize the kundalini serpent upwards through the channel of the spine, until finally it reaches the masculine-feminine principles of the brain and fires them into coordination. The disciple is then filled with inspiration and becomes attuned to the inner world of wisdom. This can only be accomplished with the help of the "kundalini serpent." Perhaps Jesus Christ gave a hint of this when he said: "Be ye wise as serpents."

The word dragon entered the English language in the early 13th century from the old French dragon, which in turn comes from Latin *draconem* (nominative draco) signifying "huge serpent, dragon," and from the Greek word *drakon*, "serpent, giant seafish." The triple symbolism of the cosmic serpent, our DNA activation, and Earth's kundalini awakening stand out in the mythos of creation throughout the ages.

TREE OF LIFE

In the mystical traditions of world religions, rituals are performed and sacred texts are read for the metaphorical (symbolic) content concerning the relationship between human states of consciousness and the external experience of reality in the natural world. No single symbol is as ageless or ubiquitous in all of the long, rich tapestry of creation mythology as the "Tree of Life." As such, the tree is a universal representation, or indirect symbol, encountered around the world. The Tree of Life, or the World Tree, represents the coveted state of eternal aliveness or fulfillment, rather than the immortality of the body or soul. In a state of eternal aliveness, physical death is interpreted as a direct experience of the perfect divine reality. Coincidentally, there have been 22 standard amino acids discovered in the human body, similar to the 22 general paths in the Tree of Life.

Trees of life appear in folklore, culture, artwork, and works of fiction, often relating to the interconnectedness of all life and immortality. These depictions often hold cultural and religious significance for the peoples of these cultures. World trees are repeatedly depicted with birds in their branches, animals around their trunks, insects on their leaves, and the tree roots extending into the soil and water.

The Sumerian or Persian trees of life were represented by a series of nodes and criss-crossing lines. They were a significant religious symbol among these peoples, often attended to by eagle-headed gods and priests, or the immortality of the king himself. The *Epic of Gilgamesh* is a similar quest for immortality. In Mesopotamian mythology, Etana searches for a "plant of birth" to provide him with a son. This has a solid provenance in antiquity, and can be found in cylindric seals from Akkad around 2390 BCE. The book *One Thousand and One Nights* has a story called "The Tale of Buluqiya" in which the hero searches for immortality and finds a paradise with jewel encrusted trees. Nearby is a Fountain of Youth guarded by Al-Khidr. Unable to defeat the guard, Buluqiya has to return empty-handed.

In Egyptian mythology, in the Ennead system of Heliopolis, the original couple was Isis and Osiris. They were said to have emerged from the acacia tree of Saosis, which the Egyptians considered the Tree of Life, referring to it as the "tree in which life and death are enclosed." The Egyptian's Holy Sycamore also stood on the threshold of life and death, connecting the two worlds.

In Far East mythology, some carvings of the Tree of Life depict a phoenix and a dragon, with the Chinese dragon representing immortality, and the phoenix depicting life after oblivion. There is also the Taoist story of a tree that produces a peach every three thousand years. The one who eats the fruit receives immortality. A Tree of Life mosaic in a Luang Probang temple was built for the emperor, who in 1975 abdicated the throne of the former kingdom of Laos. Statuary of Laotian Buddha figures are shown with flames atop their heads, the symbol of enlightenment, which was originally obtained by the Buddha himself while sitting under the Bodhi tree. These Laotian figures are promoting peace and harmony among all people with arms extended outward in the "stop fighting" pose. In the Japanese Shinto religion, trees were marked with sacred paper symbolizing lightning bolts, as trees were thought to be sacred. This was emphasized by the practice that after they died, ancestors and animals were often portrayed as branches on the tree. The revered lotus flower in the Far East also carries aspects of the mythical Tree of Life. It begins growing in the deep mud, far away from the sun. But sooner or later, the lotus reaches the light to become one of the most beautiful and cherished flowers. The lotus flower is regarded in many different cultures—especially in Eastern religions—as a symbol of purity, enlightenment, self-regeneration and rebirth. Its characteristics are a perfect analogy for the human condition: even when its roots are in the dirtiest waters, the lotus produces the most beautiful flower.

In northern European paganism, trees often played a prominent role, appearing in various forms in surviving texts, and possibly in the names of gods. Time and time again, pagan rituals and sacrifices took place under ancient trees. The Tree of Life appears in Norse religion as Yggdrasil, the world tree, a massive tree with extensive lore surrounding it. Perhaps related to the Yggdrasil, accounts have survived of Germanic Tribes honoring sacred trees within their societies. In Norse mythology, it is the golden apples from Iðunn's tree that provides immortality for the gods. One of the earliest forms of ancient Greek religion has its origins associated with tree cults.

The Tree of Life is also a Christian motif. It is mentioned in the Book of Genesis, in which it has the potential to grant immortality to Adam and Eve. Variations on the biblical Garden of Eden story, sometimes a parallel to the Tree of Life mythology, is another common theme in nearly all of the ancient cultures. There is a striving for happiness in a perfect world where people and nature are united, until man is corrupted. The Tree of Life appears in the Book of Mormon in a revelation to Lehi. It is symbolic of the love of God and sometimes understood as salvation toward a post-mortal existence. Practitioners of the Kabbalah, also called Kabbalists, use the Tree of Life symbolism as a kind of road map, which brings them information to communicate with powerful spirits.

Among pre-Columbian cultures in the Americas, the concept of a World Tree is a prevalent motif in Mesoamerican mythical cosmologies and iconography. Depictions of these universal trees, both in their directional and central aspects, are found in the art and mythological traditions of cultures such as the Maya, Aztec, Izapan, Mixtec, Olmec, and others. World trees embodied the four cardinal directions, which also represented the fourfold nature of a central world tree, including the four elements of air, earth, fire, and water. They are a symbolic *axis mundi* connecting the planes of the Underworld and the sky with that of the terrestrial world. It is striking how the symbol of the tree, the "tree of life," is seen as so powerful and life sustaining throughout human history.

THE I CHING

If there was ever a single tool out of the Far East that stands the test of time and best represents symbology and mythology, it is the I Ching, or the *Chinese Book of Changes*. It is the most widely read of the five Chinese Classics. Tradition holds that the book was written by the legendary Chinese Emperor Fu Hsi who lived from 2953 to 2838 BCE. It is probable that the I Ching originated from a prehistoric divination technique that dates back as far as 5000 BCE. Thus, it may be the oldest written text in history. Further commentaries were added by King Wen and the Duke of Chou in the 11th century BCE.

An I Ching interpretation is made by making six binary decisions, called a hexagram. This is called "casting the I Ching." These are written down as a stack of six solid or broken lines. This was traditionally done either by tossing yarrow stalks or coins, although there is no reason why the hexagrams cannot be formulated by some other means, such as a computer program. There are actually four possible values for each of the lines. There are two on and off values, and a line which changes from on to off, or vice versa. Thus, with each casting of the I Ching, the outcome can generate two different hexagrams, which adds depth to the interpretation. The sophistication of this method has not eluded modern interpretation, and the four-valued logic has been compared to the biochemistry of DNA amino acids. Yet, how a Neolithic shamans' divination technique presaged the basic logic of the human genome is one of the ageless mysteries. The I Ching is as relevant today as it was many thousands of years ago.

IS ASTROLOGY A SCIENCE?

Astrology is another of the most enduring tools of divining meaning, which some believe to be a science rather than a mythology. The study of our solar system's planets' position and how they relate to people's lives is at least four thousand years old and flourishing. Indeed, it only seems to grow in popularity every year. Astronomical knowledge was developed over time, beginning in the ancient Near East, and eventually allowed prediction of phenomena such as the location of the planets, the phases of the moon, and the eclipses. This knowledge was used as the basis of a religious system that was integrated into Greek and Roman paganism. This involved worship of the planets and stars, with the belief that after death, if virtuous, a believer would ascend to the heavens. Other aspects of ancient star worship that remain with us today are the seven day week, the months of the year, and the transference of winter solstice into the celebration of the birth of Christ.

For the true believer, astrology is used to determine the future path of an individual. Skeptics raise suspicion when astrology is used in medical practice to determine whether a patient will heal, live with a disability or pass away. The use of horoscopes has been used in diagnosing diseases and offering possible cures. This is achieved by consulting the "Natal Chart," derived from a person's birthday, and that renders a graphic of the position of the stars and planets at the moment of birth. A "Transit Chart" is based on the fixed positions of the stars and planets, both at birth and at present, and then used to compare the contrasts.

Despite recent legal challenges, the practice of astrology has received a virtual endorsement from the Supreme Court of India. That however is not an acceptable development to the dominant secular order. "Astrology," reported the incredulous *Times of India*, "has been debunked by most world scientists," and citing "renowned" physicist Professor Yash Pal. Lawsuits filed in Indian courts have sought to prohibit the advertising of predictions based on astrology. Apparently there are charlatans who would abuse the widespread belief in the method who have famously turned out to be wrong. Nevertheless, the Indian court has declared astrology to be a "trusted science" exempt from such attacks.

The Indian court is joined by many experts, including John Anthony West, author of *The Case of Astrology*. He points out that the subject has been recognized as being valid by many of the greatest thinkers in history, including Pythagoras, Plato, Plotinus, St. Thomas Aquinas, Johannes Kepler, Goethe, Ralph Waldo Emerson, Carl Jung, and many others. Challenges to the legitimacy of any practice based on the failure of some to use it properly could, by the same logic, deny people the right to own a lighter, because some have been used to burn down houses. Suppose also that science was made illegal because some have used it to make predictions that also have not come true?

GEOMANCY

Geomancy is the art of divining "earth energy" and by doing so, practitioners can discover underground water sources, or detect ley lines. The word *geomancy* means "earth divination," and it is believed to have come from the use of sand to generate geomantic figures, the basis of prediction in geomancy, such as keeping time with an hourglass. This also accounts for its Arabic name, *ilm al-raml*, literally the science or wisdom of the sand. The art of geomancy became quite popular as a divinatory technique because of ease of learning and application.

Sometimes called astrological geomancy, the art is an ancient method of divination. Because of its close connection to astrology, geomancy has been called the "daughter of astrology," and also is called "terrestrial astrology." The origins of geomancy are shrouded in mystery, but the first manuscripts describing the practice appear in the 9th century CE in the advanced Islamic civilizations of the Middle East. From there it spread to Europe in the 11th and 12th centuries as part of a receptive period for arts and sciences, including the occult arts of astrology, alchemy and magic, by the rapidly civilizing West. Contemporary practitioners of the traditional Western art of geomancy describe it as divinatory or astrological geomancy to differentiate it from these more modern uses of the term. Astrological geomancy is a fitting description, since much of the divinatory methodology used in geomancy comes from traditional astrology.

In the modern era, the ancient art of divinatory geomancy has been confused with Chinese *feng shui*, which itself is not a method of divination, but instead a science of spatial arrangement, architecture and landscaping and based on the principles of *chi* (energy). Divinatory geomancy has also had its name appropriated by the modern New Age study of ley lines and Earth "energies," are also merely techniques, not divination. Modern geomancers describe two kinds of electromagnetic energy lines that the Earth uses as part of its nervous system. The first is a straight line, or "yang" line, which intersects the planet much like the latitude and longitude lines on a globe. The second type is curvilinear, or a "yin" line, that resembles the twists and turns of the natural environment.

Geomancers have discovered that most of the oldest sacred structures are built upon the intersection of yang lines. Where three or more yang lines cross, one can almost always find a sacred well, place of pilgrimage, cathedral, temple, or Neolithic stone circle. Geomancers believe that where yin lines cross, there is an accumulation of negative energy. People lingering for an extended period of time over intersecting yin lines can feel nauseous or worn down. However, there is really no such thing as good or bad energy lines. They are all part of the Earth's regenerating system.

LEY LINES

The visualization of the Earth's ley paths appear as being surrounded by energy lines connecting it to the universe. The concept of planetary energy flows was first articulated by the ancient Greeks as the "gaia hypothesis." In the last century, ley lines were described by Englishman Sir Alfred Watkins. Several decades later, the idea of the noosphere, or "mind layer" was advanced by the French priest and philosopher Teilhard de Chardín. A similar concept articulated by the modern residents of Damanhur, Italy, describe "Synchronic Lines," or energy rivers, that can modify events and carry ideas, thoughts, moods, and intentions, thereby influencing all living creatures.

Through the study of geomancy and ley lines, it appears that many ancient sacred sites worldwide are linked together by the planetary grid of energy lines. The precise placement of these sacred places is no chance event. Whether very ancient, like Stonehenge or the Great Pyramids, or contemporary, like Damanhur or the crop circle phenomenon, the very location of these sacred sites are now considered energy acupuncture points on the face of the Earth. For example, when mapped out in Europe, it is apparent that successive shrines, temples, churches, cathedrals, and monuments were built on intersecting ley lines. Morphogenic resonance theory predicts that where certain practices are routinely continued, the site becomes imbued with a force field, and a certain "spirit" or "power of place" resides at that location. Hence, the earliest prehistoric shrines were adopted by European pagans, which in turn were replaced by the churches and cathedrals of Christianity.

In the 1920s, the aforementioned Alfred Watkins coined the term "ley lines" in his book entitled *The Old Straight Track*. Watkins discovered a huge grid of flowing energy lines connecting ancient sites, pathways, and geographic markers including mounds, holy wells, ponds, and depressions in hills all over southern England, primarily in Herefordshire. Some of these markers, Watkins noted, dated from the Neolithic period, and they denoted the location of Britain's many churches, shrines, villages, and town squares. Despite being labeled lines, Watkins and other geomancers began to perceive these lines as three dimensional, similar to tubes, "insinuating that" the lines would interact and combine with stronger vortex energy.

Vortexes are subtle Earth energy centers located along strong ley lines in various locations around the world. Vortexes are regarded as funnel-shaped and created by a whirling fluid, or by the motion of spiraling energy. The energy resonates within and strengthens the inner being of every person coming within a quarter-mile of its central point. The power emanating from the vortexes produces some of the most remarkable energy fields on the planet. Notable vortexes worldwide are found in Peru, Mexico, Egypt, England, Italy, Greece, India, and Sedona, Arizona.

PORTALS AND ORBS

Science fiction writers and futurists have long envisioned the concept of a "portal" to great distances far away, or even to another dimension, and today some we have found could prove authentic. In our final look at the mythos of creation in this modern age, scientists have also been trying to discover such a structure in real life. Usually a portal is defined as an opening through spacetime that enables a traveler to move over great distances, or over time, instantly. In other words, it represents a shortcut, or perhaps a guiding pathway to a particular destination.

NASA has turned science fiction into science fact by announcing the discovery of hidden "portals" near Earth's magnetic field. A 2012 study backed by NASA has revealed the existence of a so-called *magnetic portal*, connecting the atmospheres of the Earth and the Sun. The observations that led to this conclusion were carried out using the Cluster constellation, which is operated by the European Space Agency (ESA), and the NASA Time History of Events and Macroscale Interactions during Substorms (THEMIS) mission. The satellites indicate that the magnetic portals open and close several times per day, and that they are located only around a few tens of thousands of kilometers away from Earth. They seem to appear at locations where the geomagnetic field of Earth meets the incoming solar winds. These portals can be either short-lived or they can last for a longer time, allowing highly energetic particles to flow through them. These particles can heat the planet's upper atmosphere, create geomagnetic storms, and spawn very bright Northern Lights, such as the aurora borealis.

Another mysterious phenomenon which may or may not be related to portals are orbs, which are spherical "lights," or balls of energy. Although invisible to the naked eye, they often appear on film or in night time photographs. These round, whitish or pastel-colored translucent balls are most often seen in photos, but rarely seen in real life. Apparently they come in numerous sizes, most often appearing in shades of white; however on rare occasions, they may take on different colors. Generally, they are perfectly circular, not oval. Some researchers believe that they could represent spirits or ghosts. Others attribute them to the archons, just invisible outside of our range of sight but visible in the infrared spectrum. Physical glowing orbs are also seen during the creation of some crop circle formations. It would appear that there is a conscious mind behind the orbs.

Similar to portals, orbs seem to be doorways, or a certain kind of opening, but this theory has yet to be proven. It is not yet known if orbs are spirits, dimensional in nature, or something else completely unknown at the present time. However, orbs seem to travel much more easily where the energy lines are active and healthy. When these moving orbs are captured on a camera, they can appear in all shapes and sizes with some brighter than others. Because the untrained eye is not able to penetrate the invisible realm, debunkers can discredit anything that is presented on this subject. But once again, when science catches up to the esoterica, the orbs will not only be described, but like so many other magnificent lights floating in our atmosphere that are visible in the infrared, they will be described scientifically, and codified. There are seemingly intelligent energies moving around us, as we will see toward the end of the next chapter.

< The number 10 Downing Street address, with a symbolic sun image atop the door, is the official residence of UK's Prime Minister. Sun worship is a form of Luciferian worship, for example, the worship of the Devil, Lucifer, or the morning star or Ra, the ancient Egyptian sun god (both entities are one and the same). The sun image represents the object of worship of the Freemasons, or the Illuminati. Why is a Masonic esoteric symbol atop the door of the most infamous and important house in the United Kingdom?

< The medieval Knights Templar had a name for the alchemical power transferred through the "Templar Kiss" via the breath of an initiator. It was Baphomet, which the occult historian Gerald Massey states is a synonym for the "Mother of Breath." For the Templars, the name Baphomet was inclusive of all images and Holy Grails that represented and contained the alchemical force, including the Head of John the Baptist and Eliphas Levi's famous image, seen here.

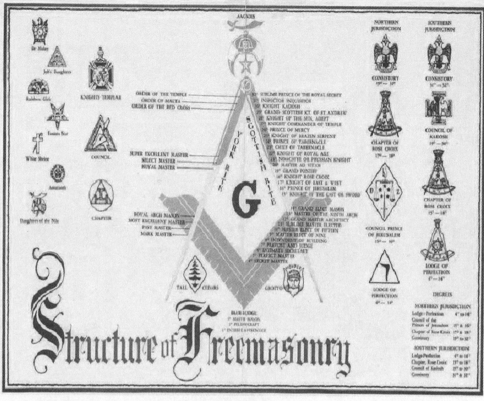

This "Structure of Freemasonry" placemat would have been found on any given Sunday morning breakfast held in Masonic lodges across the country.

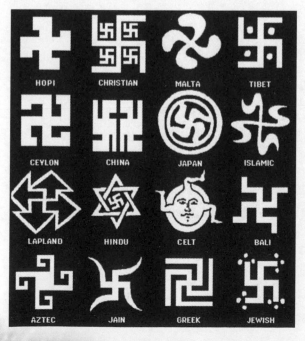

< Contrary to widely held belief, the Nazi swastika was not an original design. It is an ancient symbol found worldwide, but was corrupted forever when the Nazi's used it as a symbol of the National Socialist Party. The image was adopted from India, although variations of the symbol can be found in most ancient cultures. In the West, the swastika was a compilation of two ancient Macedonian letters from the era of Alexander the Great and Philip II. The word "swastika" is derived from the Sanskrit word *suastika*. It is said to symbolize good luck, well-being, peace, and eternity, among other things. It is still widely used in the imagery of Hinduism, Buddhism and Jainism. Recent political history defines Nazism as the National Socialist Workers Party of Germany.

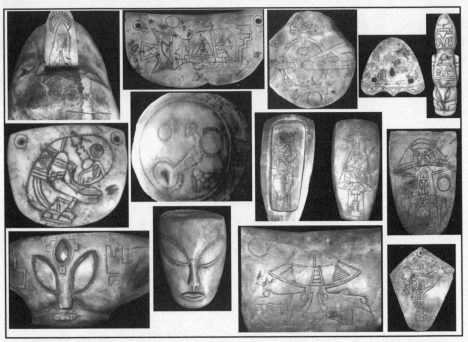

These enigmatic Mayan artifacts were discovered in Central Mexico and remained classified for 80 years. The Mexican government publicly released them in the summer of 2012. The reason behind this unexpected disclosure is unknown, and many skeptics from around the world began screaming fraud. It is interesting that these artifacts were not subjected to review or investigation. They were simply released "as is."

< The Tree of Life is a representation of the attainment of knowledge. Could this attainment of knowledge also be associated with a vanished civilization of ET visitors, the Anunnaki, who came here to mine gold starting around 200,000 years ago? According to the work of Zecharia Sitchin and others, the Anunnaki tinkered with human genetics to produce their mine workers, who became the first *homo sapien sapiens.*

BLOOD OF THE GODS

"Emancipate yourself from mental slavery; none but ourselves can free our minds." –Bob Marley

IN the study of genetics, we find that we can only inherit the traits that our ancestors have passed on to us. Nothing more, and nothing less. If humans evolved from the same African ancestor as mainstream science suggests, then the blood of all people would be compatible, as is the blood of all animal species with their own kind. So where did the Rh-negative blood come from in humans? How is it possible that the body of an Rh-negative mother carrying an Rh-positive child would reject her own offspring?

We know there was life on Earth long before humans as the fossil records indicate, but this does not explain the explosion of complex and intelligent life. In a relatively short period of time known as the "Cambrian explosion," fossil records go from primitive unintelligent life forms to suddenly much larger animal species with intricate organs and large brains. These enormous and relatively quick jumps of complex life is called "Darwin's doubt."

Charles Darwin was not entirely sure of his own theory. One could argue the elements that make up the universe seem to be arranged in "a certain way" so as to make life even possible. The monkey-to-man theory was widely excepted by some, but even orthodox scientists look at the double helix of the human genome and admit that there are "complex codes" and "intelligent design" written all over the fossil records. It should be remembered that the study of genetics only started a few decades ago, and our knowledge today is just the tip of the iceberg. The findings of ancient astronaut researchers indicate that no human ever found has more than a four percent of genetic deviation from our own DNA structure. This is because DNA—and human life as we know it—is a galactic template written into the basic energy of the cosmos on a quantum level. Ultimately, human life is energetic, not biological. The biological form is only one phase of our overall evolutionary curve as souls. For our examination on the discrepancies in our blood and the human genome, this chapter will again boldly explore another esoteric idea—the potential bombshell disclosure that the human race was in a large part created by the "Anunnaki" race of ETs.

ENTER THE ANUNNAKI

In the timeframe of post-Atlantis, but before recorded history as we know it, the Anunnaki arrived on this planet with a mission to extract gold, according to Zecharia Sitchin and other researchers. As author of *The 12th Planet* and other classics, Sitchin is well-known for his densely researched books on the Anunnaki, whom he identifies with the biblical Nephilim and the watchers of the book of Enoch. These are alien entities that "came into the daughters of men," as Genesis says. In short, they interbred with the human race. The Anunnaki established cities, ziggurats, bases, mining facilities, medical laboratories, and other civic structures. Although scattered on several continents, most of these buildings are now in a state of ruin. These structures were not only built in Mesopotamia, but also in South Africa, Lebanon, Egypt, Israel, India, and eventually the Americas. Ancient cuneiform texts such as *Atrahasis*, *Enuma Elish* and *Enki and the World Order* describe this alien race, with the alternative translation "those who from Heaven to Earth came," according to Sitchin.

As the Anunnaki expanded their colonies on Earth, their modern genome-created human slaves followed them to new lands. In the pantheon of legendary gods from Egypt, Babylon, Assyria, India, as well as that of the Inca, Maya, Toltec, and Aztec, their "lords" can be linked directly to the same Anunnaki who first settled in South Africa and around the Persian Gulf. The presence of the Anunnaki as overseers in these primitive high-cultures would account for the similarities to the characteristics of the "gods" as described by various early human cultures. Their presence would also account for the astonishing similarities in their "legends" of creation, such as the great deluge as described in many ancient mythologies, and the actions and achievements of these same gods, including the cultivation of human civilization as we know it today.

It is curious to note that the British royal family and certain other elite families worldwide trace their bloodlines back to the ancient Egyptian pharaohs. In esoteric traditions, most of the pharaohs were a hybrid of human and reptoid "Anunnaki," and intentionally placed into power as a go-between for the enslaved human race and the Anunnaki invading forces. Those designated as rulers had a stronger genetic connection to the Anunnaki than the other humans who were mixed with the genes of the indigenous proto-humans, which existed on Earth for many millenniums longer. In the timeframe of about 5,700 years ago, another invasion of reptoids took place, those being the Alpha Draconian reptilian ETs and their minions the Greys, who remain on this planet with their own "service to self" agenda. The Draconians and Greys employ superior technology and physical abilities such as telepathy and mind control. They exist primarily underground, similar to the legend of the devil and his helpers.

Fast forward to today, and the ultra-elites continue to interbreed in an attempt to keep their Anunnaki bloodlines strong. They consider themselves to be more Anunnaki than human, which explains the elite's utter contempt for the human race, including their indifference to slaughtering humans with no remorse through genocide, eugenics, starvation, provoking warfare and even ritual sacrifices. They feel their superior Anunnaki reptilian bloodlines give them the "divine right to rule," as the Anunnaki considered themselves to be gods, but in fact were just an invading reptilian race long ago. Lucifer, considered by secret sectors of the Vatican, the UN, the royals and the ultra-elite as the one true God, is actually just another Draconian reptile. The Illuminati and Anunnaki bloodlines are one and the same. This conclusion would also explain our long dark occulted history, and would suggest that the global elite has had concealed knowledge of ancient aliens for many centuries.

RULING BLOODLINES

There is one ruling bloodline that exists on the Earth, and it is very old. It is the same bloodline that has always ruled over the Earth, dating back to the royalty of ancient Egypt. It is very pervasive. The families of this bloodline are steeped in tradition and power. Numerous investigations show that the entire global financial system is ruled by the crown, but the "crown" does not refer specifically to the British monarchy. The crown refers to the Inner City of London, which is a privately owned corporation outside the jurisdiction of England. Its sister cities, completely separate sovereign states, are the Vatican City and Washington's District of Columbia. Each of these three city states has their own unique flags, laws, use services, police forces, and each pays no taxes to the host country where it is located. These three cities form a private covert empire that controls the entire Western world. London is the center of financial control, Vatican City represents spiritual control, and Washington D.C. is the city for military control. The "Empire of the Three Cities" controls the whole world, or at least they like to think they do. It is the private individuals, this pervasive ruling bloodline, that control these three city states. Because of their stranglehold of the financial systems, these entities are able to control all mainstream media, Western governments, the largest organized religion, and the strongest military force in the world.

The "City of London" is a small area of London known as the Square Mile. The ruling bloodline has total control of this minuscule area, largely through the corporate power they wield. The London Corporation is a state within a state, or a city within a city, akin to the Vatican City within the confines of Rome, Italy. The City of London is not democratically accountable, and it is immensely rich. It makes its own rules. There are 25 electoral wards in the Square Mile. In four of them, the 9,000 people who live within its boundaries are permitted to vote. In the remaining 21, the votes are controlled by corporations, mostly banks and other financial companies. The bigger the business, the bigger the vote: a company with 10 workers gets two votes, the biggest employers get 79. It's not the workers who decide how the votes are cast, but the bosses, who "appoint" the voters. It's a plutocracy, pure and simple. The Corporation possesses a vast pool of cash, which it can spend as it wishes, without democratic oversight. As well as expanding its enormous property portfolio, it uses this money to lobby on behalf of the banks. The City of London is the only part of Britain over which the United Kingdom Parliament has no authority. The City has exploited this remarkable position to establish itself as a kind of offshore state, a secrecy jurisdiction which controls the network of tax havens housed in the UK's crown dependencies and overseas territories.

For the last three centuries the wealthiest bloodline in the world bar none is the Rothschild family. They have attained this position through lies, control, manipulation and even murder. Their bloodline also extends into the traditional royal families of Europe, including the following Illuminati family names: Astor, Bundy, Collins, Du Pont, Freeman, Kennedy, Li, Morgan, Onassis, Oppenheimer, Reynolds, Rockefeller, Russell, Sassoon, Schiff, Taft, and Van Duyn. The Rothschilds are known to sire many children secretly so that they can put them into positions of power when necessary. These are the controlling elites of the elite, and they take their bloodline very seriously.

BLOOD RITUALS AND BLOODLETTING

Ancient cultures were obsessed with blood rituals, and regrettably, they for the most part took on a very sanguine form. Ancient temples around the world show an obsession with blood rituals. Their temples had channels cut into the stone from altars where gallons of blood would flow from animals, men, women, and even from children. Blood rituals have been performed worldwide since the dawn of recorded history. Ancient Judean, Phoenician, Maya, Aztec and many other pagan cultures were obsessed with blood sacrifices involving the heart. Even today it is reenacted in symbolic form called the Eucharist by the Catholic mass, taking an offering of the blood and body of Christ.

Black magicians, such as Aleister Crowley, were well aware of blood and its lifeforce. Crowley even suggested that "a nine year old child, of above average intelligence, made the ideal sacrificial candidate." Hot blood, freshly drained from a living creature, is believed to contain a concentration of the sacred *chi*, or the lifeforce of a sacrificial victim. The last beat of the heart, the last breath of the victim, carries the soul into the spirit world.

The practice of bleeding a patient, or bloodletting, is one of the oldest medical practices of ancient people, even persevering as a viable treatment for accident recovery or illness until a few hundred years ago. Known practitioners of bloodletting include the Mesopotamians, the Egyptians, the Greeks, the Mayans, and the Aztecs. In ancient Greece, bloodletting was in use around the time of Hippocrates, who endorsed bloodletting but in general relied on dietary techniques. Erasistratus, however, theorized that many diseases were caused by "plethoras," or overabundances in the blood, and advised that these plethoras be treated initially by exercise, sweating, reduced food intake, and vomiting. Herophilus advocated bloodletting. Archagathus, one of the first Greek physicians to treat patients in Rome, practiced bloodletting extensively and gained a most grisly reputation.

The popularity of bloodletting in Greece was reinforced by the ideas of the Roman physician Galen, after he discovered that the veins and arteries were filled with blood, not air as was commonly believed at the time. There were two key concepts in his system of bloodletting. The first was that blood was created and then used up; it did not circulate and so it could "stagnate" in the extremities. The second was that "humoral" balance was the basis of illness or health. The four humours were considered blood, phlegm, black bile, and yellow bile, relating to the four Greek classical elements of air, water, earth and fire. Galen believed that blood was the dominant humour and the one in most need of control. These bizarre medical practices were continued in Europe for many centuries. In order to balance the humours, a medieval medicine physician would either remove "excess" blood to ease the plethora from the patient, administer an emetic to induce vomiting, or a diuretic to induce urination.

Bloodletting was especially popular in the newly-formed United States of America, where Benjamin Rush, a signatory of the Declaration of Independence, saw the state of the arteries as the key to disease. He recommended levels of bloodletting that were high, even for the time. George Washington was treated in this manner following a horseback riding accident. Almost 1.7 liters of blood was withdrawn from a wounded Washington, contributing to his death by throat infection in 1799.

THE HEART THAT REMEMBERS

Blood is the carrier medium for the lifeforce existing in all physical entities. The lifeforce itself goes under many different names in many different cultures around the world. In India and the Far East, the most popular names for the lifeforce are *chi, qui, son ki*, or *prana*. Practitioners of Chinese medicine teach that the chi lifeforce is made more potent by fresh oxygen. This is why tree groves, rich in fresh oxygen, have long been chosen as ritual locations by pagans for thousands of years. Within our blood there are cells that have the main function of carrying oxygen to the vital organs.

Modern science teaches us that the heart is merely a pump. The heart, which delivers blood throughout every evolved animal's body, is more than just a pump. Extensive libraries around the world are filled with literature and occult research showing that the heart is also an emotional organ, and beats faster when ritualistically or emotionally excited; from sexual attraction, or when under stress. The heart plays an important role in allowing us to meditate and connect with the spirit world. In addition to carrying the vital lifeforce around the body, blood *in magical terms* also absorbs the emotional energy when it passes through the heart.

Evidence from medical experts suggests that our hearts can absorb and remember parts of our personality. It is as though the lifeforce in our blood, and the emotional states we experience, leave an indelible spiritual hallmark in the heart. Several doctors and patients have testified that some personality traits of a heart donor manifest in the character of the recipient. After receiving the heart of a young woman, a male patient was known to knit, sing and sew in exactly the same manner as the deceased donor. It was as if the woman's spirit, along with her heart, had been transplanted into the man. This phenomenon has caused several transplant surgeons to question their own beliefs about the human heart. The stunning conclusion is that the heart contains elements of one's own personality.

SUPER BLOOD AND KILLER BLOOD

With so much questionable information on blood health and people's curious fascination with the heart, let's start with some basic facts about human blood. There are about 5,000 known blood factors, and these factors determine the makeup of all human blood types. It has been proven that an 85% majority of all humans have a blood factor in common with the rhesus monkey. This is called rhesus positive blood, usually shortened to Rh-positive. This factor is completely independent of the A, B, and O blood types. Rh-factor is an antigen that is found in the red blood cells of most people. An antigen is any substance that the body considers "foreign" and thus stimulates the body to produce antibodies against it. Rh-factor, like the blood types A, B, and O, is inherited from one's parents. A simple blood test can determine blood type, including the presence of the Rh-factor. About 85% of European Americans and 95% of African Americans have the Rh-factor and are known as Rh-positive. Those without the Rh-factor are Rh-negative. Type O negative is considered the universal blood, as donors can donate to any other blood type. While it is known that Rh-negative blood type "O" is the purest blood known to humankind, it is not known where this negative factor originates. Every person on Earth can receive Rh-negative type O blood, but those very same O negative people cannot receive blood from any other type except their own type.

Rh-factor plays a critical role in some pregnancies. For example, if a woman who is Rh-negative becomes pregnant by a man who is Rh-positive, the fetus may inherit the Rh-factor from its father and be Rh-positive, and this alone can be deadly. When the mother is Rh-negative, and the father is Rh-positive, there can be a tragic outcome, and the female must get the Rhlg shot to prevent the mother's Rh-negative blood from mixing with the fetus's Rh-positive blood. Major complications can result for the fetus if the mother does not get the shot prior to or at the beginning of pregnancy. Without the Rhlg shot the blood of the fetus could become mixed with the mother's Rh-negative blood, say by a sharp blow to the fetus lining of the mother, and a disease called erythroblastosis fetalis will occur in a current or a future pregnancy, resulting in destruction of the fetus's red blood cells, brain damage, and even death. In the past, a newborn whose blood was not compatible with its mother was called a "blue baby."

There are other curious characteristics common among Rh-negative people that are uncommon to others. Is there a real difference other than just a different blood type? Externally, there are certain similarities that occur to those having Rh-negative blood. For example, they cannot be cloned, they have higher than average IQs, and their looks are similar. Almost all Rh-negative people are either red haired, blonde haired with green eyes, black haired with hazel eyes, or blue eyes with all hair colors. Other characteristic are low blood pressure, lower body temperature, keen eyesight and hearing, and possibly an extra rib or vertebrae. These individuals are sometimes able to induce paranormal occurrences such as disrupting electrical appliances and/or exercise psychic abilities, including remote viewing or lucid dreaming. What's more, the majority of people with psychic powers who act as faith healers have Rh-negative blood. The majority of alien abductees are reportedly from Rh-negative blood groups. Is this a possible indication that certain ET groups are tracking their own cross-bred progeny? In the lore of certain races, people who possessed a positive blood type were considered to be racially impure, as positive blood was thought to be contaminated by contact with an ape-evolved strand of human DNA.

ANUNNAKI BLOOD?

Almost all scientists believe that modern humans evolved from ape-like primates. They have compiled considerable evidence to back up their theories, including modern blood analysis and comparative studies between modern humans and the lower anthropoids, such as the chimpanzee and the rhesus monkey. This is fine and well, but were it not for this very strange anomaly of Rh-blood, which can kill its own offspring, we would not be discussing this subject.

In the study of genetics, except in the case of mutations, we know that we can only inherit the makeup of our ancestors. We can have numerous combinations and traits inherited from our family tree. Nothing more, and nothing less. Therefore, if humans and apes evolved from a common ancestor, their blood quite logically would have evolved the same way. After all, blood factors are transmitted with much more exactitude than any other characteristic. It would seem that modern humans and the rhesus monkey would have had a common ancestor sometime in the ancient past. All other earthly primates also contain the Rh-factor. But this leaves out people who are Rh-negative. If all humankind evolved from the same ancestor, then their blood would be compatible. Case closed. So where then did the Rh-negatives come from? If they are not the descendants of prehistoric humans, could they be the descendants of some kind of hybridization long ago? Or perhaps an offshoot species of *homo sapiens*?

It is important to note that only humans carry this unique trait of blood incompatibility with some in their own species. All animals and other living creatures known to science can breed with any other of their own species. Relative size and color makes no difference. So why does an infant's haemolytic disease occur in humans if all humans are the same species? Haemolytic disease is the allergic reaction that occurs when an Rh-negative mother is carrying a Rh-positive child. Her blood builds up antibodies to destroy the *alien* substance, much in the same way it would a virus, and in some cases the abortion of her own infant. Why would a mother's body reject her own offspring? Nowhere else in nature does this occur naturally. This same problem does occur in the creation of mules—a cross between a horse and donkey—and mules are therefore sterile and unable to reproduce. Haemolytic disease points to the distinct possibility of cross-breeding between two similar, but genetically different, species.

Another unique trait of human females is menopause, that is, when a woman stops getting menstrual periods and is unable to become pregnant. Menopause is unique to humans and its cause is still unknown. We accept as a given the idea that older women tend to be unable to reproduce, but this is actually an *evolutionary puzzle* because it applies only to humans and no other animal species.

No one has tried to explain where the Rh-negative people came from. Those who are familiar with blood factors admit that these people must at least be a mutation, if not the descendants of a different ancestor. If we are a mutation, what then caused this mutation? Why does it continue with exacting characteristics? Why does it so violently reject the positive Rh-factor, even when it is within similar ancestry? Who was this ancestor? Difficulties in determining ethnology are largely overcome by the use of blood group data, for this data describes a single gene characteristic that is not affected.

ATLANTIS ORIGIN, DNA SPLICING, OR WHAT?

It would appear that there is no scientific evidence that the Rh-negative blood is a natural Earthly occurrence. Instead, the evidence suggests that the Rh-negative blood types did not evolve on Earth in the natural course of events. For many years, evolutionists may have been completely looking in the wrong direction. Evolution scientists fail to emphasize that Rh-negative people lack a factor contained in all other earthly primates, including the naked and uncivilized ape. Could the true "missing link" actually be ourselves? Could this be the unknown link between Earth and the stars, a hybrid human, a missing link between primates and extraterrestrials? Is Rh-negative blood the smoking gun that proves the ancient astronaut hybridization theory?

There are those who speculate that the 15% of the human population that have Rh-negative blood type have ancestors from the lost continent of Atlantis. In his readings Edgar Cayce said that the Basque people came from Atlantis, and interestingly they have the highest percentage of Rh-negative people among any ethnicity. Indeed, genetic scientists have found a commonality in the areas where Edgar Cayce said that the Atlanteans went to live after the continents shifted, and the geography of the Earth changed. After the last pole shift when Atlantis sank into the sea, the people of Atlantis migrated to the Pyrenees Mountains of France and Spain, the northern Africa area of Morocco and Egypt, and to the Americas. Regarding the modern people who inhabit these regions of the world, each has an unusually high occurrence of Rh-negative blood. Some include blood rituals in their cultures. The origin of the Basque people is unknown, and is generally regarded as one of the oldest surviving lineages. Their language is unlike any other European language. The Basque people of Spain and France have the highest percentage of Rh-negative blood among their own ethnic type. About 30% are Rh-negative and about 60% carry one negative gene.

The Oriental Jews of Israel also have a high percentage of Rh-negative individuals, whereby most other Oriental people are only about 1% Rh-negative. The Samaritans and the Black Cochin Jews also have a high percentage of Rh-negative blood, although again, Rh-negative blood is rare among most black people. In the most famous written work of Oriental Jews, the two words "blood" and "God" can be found on almost every page in the Bible. In fact, blood is mentioned more often than any other word in the Bible except the word God. Lastly, the American Indians had a tradition of describing close friendships, even with other tribal members, as "blood brothers."

GENETIC CORE OF THE UNIVERSAL ANCESTOR

Molecular analysis of conserved sequences in the ribosomal RNAs of modern organisms reveals a three-domain phylogeny that converges in a universal ancestor for all life. Researchers used the Clusters of Orthologous Groups database and information from published genomes to search for other universally conserved genes that have the same phylogenetic pattern as ribosomal RNA and therefore constitute the ancestral genetic core of cells. The analyses identified a small set of genes that have co-evolved since that time, and that can be traced back to a so-called "universal ancestor." The conclusion at the end of the study was that up to 250 human genomes are not indigenous to this planet.

As indicated by earlier studies, almost all of these genes are involved with the transfer of genetic information, and most of them directly interact with the ribosome. Other universal genes have either undergone lateral transfer in the past, or have diverged so much in sequence that their distant past could not be resolved. The nature of the conserved genes suggests innovations that may have been essential to the divergence of the three domains of life. The analysis also identified several genes of unknown function with phylogenies that track with the ribosomal RNA genes. The products of these genes are likely to play fundamental roles in cellular processes.

Scholars have long believed that the first civilization on Earth emerged in Sumer some 6,000 years ago. Alternative theories, however, suggest that Sumerians and Egyptians inherited their knowledge from an earlier civilization that colonized around the southern tip of Africa, and began with the arrival of the Anunnaki, or the "Fallen Ones" more than 200,000 years ago. Sent to Earth in search of life-saving gold, these ancient Anunnaki astronauts from the planet Nibiru created the first humans as a slave race to mine gold—thus beginning our global traditions of gold obsession, slavery, and the concept of a "god" or "lord" as a dominating master. When we consider the history of gold, and the Anunnaki obsession for the metal, combined with their genetic prowess to develop modern humans who were supposedly created to mine gold for them, we have a whole new way of looking at the human race. Fast forward to today, and we find that the world's gold has seemingly vanished from the world's major vaults, including Fort Knox. Is it possible that the Anunnaki have returned for their gold—and this brings us full-circle, of sorts?

AFRICAN ORIGINS ... SEEN ANOTHER WAY

Southern Africa holds some of the deepest mysteries in all of human history. What we are told is that at around 60,000 years ago, the early modern humans migrated from Africa and populated the rest of the world. The recently mapped stone ruins of southern Africa call this assumption into question, and present us with a compelling *missing piece* of the puzzle related to the murky origins of humankind. This recent mapping estimates that there are well over one million ancient stone ruins scattered throughout the mountains and plains of southern Africa. The most spectacular examples of these ancient ruins lie between Machadodorp and Waterval-boven in the province of Mpumalanga, in the country of South Africa.

Modern historians have been speculating about the origins of these stone ruins, often dismissing them as "cattle kraal of little historic importance." Yet various tools and artifacts that have been recovered from these ruins show a long and extended period of settlement that spans well over 200,000 years. So who were these first humans? What did they do? And where did they disappear to? It is likely they migrated north, and took their knowledge with them. They settled in Egypt and Asia Minor, where high cultures emerged. According to scholarly accounts, the first acknowledged temple complex, called Göbekli Tepe, was built only 12,000 years ago, and is located about 15 kilometers from the city of Sanliurfa, in southeastern Turkey.

We can draw the conclusion that South Africa is the true cradle of humankind because the ruins there date much earlier than anywhere else on Earth. A recent discovery of an ancient circular monolithic stone calendar site in Mpumalanga has proven to be at least 75,000 years old, pre-dating any other structure found on Earth to date. Adam's Calendar is the flagship among these ruins. This spectacular ancient site is aligned with the N,S,E,W, cardinal points of the planet, and also aligns with the solstices and equinoxes. It is still an accurate calendar, and follows a shadow of the setting sun, as cast by a taller central monolith onto a flat calendar stone beside it. Based on numerous scientific evaluations, it has been dated with relative certainty to at least 75,000 years ago.

Adam's Calendar is possibly the oldest structure on Earth that is linked to human origins. It has, however, been known by African elders, indigenous knowledge keepers, and shamans as the "Birthplace of the Sun," or *Inzalo y'Langa*, where humanity was created by the gods. Adam's Calendar also presents the first tangible evidence of consciousness among the earliest humans in the "Cradle of Humankind." Some of the tools even suggest that they had a much better understanding of the laws of nature than we have today. For instance, the site is built along the same longitudinal line as the Great Zimbabwe archaeological site and the Great Pyramid of Giza in Egypt, suggesting a connection between those ancient civilization and the builders of all three of these sites.

Furthermore, it should be noted that miners in South Africa have been digging up mysterious grooved metal spheres throughout the area during the last few decades. These spheres measure a few millimeters in diameter, and some are etched with three parallel grooves running around the perimeter. There have been two types of spheres discovered, all of unknown origins. One is composed of a solid bluish-metal with flecks of white, and the other type is hollowed out and filled with a spongy white substance. The fascinating aspect of this story is that the rock in which they where found is Precambrian—and dated to be 2.8 billion years old! Who made them, and for what purpose, is a complete mystery.

THEY MIGHT BE GIANTS

Documentation noting the discovery of giant human-like remains appear in various records encompassing numerous sources from around the world. In North America alone there are several dozen independent accounts from the 19th and 20th centuries taken from miners, prospectors, and archaeologists who uncovered the remains of enormous human-like skeletons or mummies, sometimes more than twice the size of the average person living today. Not only were the giants enormous in size and with peculiar features, but they lived on the planet possibly a very long time ago. The Channel Islands off the southern California coast were once a home to dwarf mammoths, whose uncovered bones display evidence that they were roasted in ancient fire pits. They were roasted and eaten by giant human-like creatures who had double rows of teeth, and whose remains were also found in various locations around the islands, often near the very same ancient fire pits.

The typical account of a giant skeletal discovery follows a particular pattern. This account, from July 1877, has four prospectors looking for gold and silver outcroppings in a desolate hilly area near the head of Spring Valley, not far from Eureka, Nevada. Scanning the rocks, one of the men spotted something peculiar projecting from a high ledge. Climbing up to get a better look, the prospector was surprised to find a human leg bone and knee cap sticking out of solid rock. He called to his companions, and together they dislodged the oddity with picks. Realizing they had a most unusual find, the men brought it into Eureka, where it was placed on display. The stone that the bones were embedded in was a hard, dark red quartzite, and the bones themselves were almost black with carbonization—indicating great age. When the surrounding stone was carefully chipped away, the specimen was found to be a leg bone broken off ten centimeters above the knee. The specimen included the knee cap and joint, the lower leg bones, and the complete bones of the foot. Several medical doctors examined the remains, and were convinced that *anatomically* they had once belonged to a human being—and a very modern-looking one. And, similar to typical accounts of giant skeletal discoveries, the remains are now lost. From knee to heel, the Eureka tibia bone would have measured 100 centimeters. Therefore, its owner in life would have stood almost four meters tall, more than twice the height of an average human today. Compounding the Eureka, NV, mystery was the fact that the rock in which the bones were found was geologically dated to the Jurassic Era, the era of the dinosaurs—over 185 million years ago!

Another massive mummy was unearthed in 1891, when workmen in Crittenden, Arizona, excavated a huge stone coffin that evidently once held the body of a man 3.7 meters tall. A carving on the granite case indicated that he had six toes per foot, and the skeleton was surrounded by giant weapons. Once again, this discovery has also been lost. Equally confounding, when a skull for a massive giant is found intact, the skull usually features a double row of teeth.

WHOSE DNA SEEDED US?

Neanderthals were a heavyset people whose thick double brows, broad noses, and flat faces set them apart from modern humans. Neanderthals disappeared 25,000 to 30,000 years ago. Another mysterious group of extinct people known as the Denisovans—recently identified from a finger bone in Siberia—passed down some DNA to modern Pacific Islanders. Species interbreeding likely occurred 20,000 to 50,000 years ago, long after most *modern humans* had walked out of Africa to colonize Asia and Europe, and about the same time Neanderthals were waning in Europe. Researcher The late Lloyd Pye presented a compelling case for the existence of Bigfoot as being an early hominid, namely the Neanderthal. But how did the first modern humans arrive on the scene so suddenly?

It appears that our DNA contains elements of several different human-like entities, each with somewhat incompatible blood types. Could we really be hybrid human prototypes who were created by genetic manipulation at the dawn of time? Were organically evolved hominids on Earth like the Neanderthal spliced with more advanced DNA to create the *homo sapiens* we find throughout the world today? Current genetic scientists tell us that it is possible to splice two species together; in fact, it has already been done in modern laboratories.

According to Zecharia Sitchin, ancient Sumerian cuneiform tablets and cylinder seals uncovered in modern Iraq, the former kingdom of ancient Babylon, tell the story of ET *star gods* coming to Earth from the planet Marduk, and genetically manipulating humankind. Two of these primary star gods were called Elil and Enki. Their alien race was called the "Anunnaki" (described above) which, according to one translation, means the "Princes of the Royal Genetic Seed." This bizarre but compelling theory bears repeating. According to the Sumerian tablets, modern humans were created as a biogenetic experiment by the Anunnaki who "came from the stars." These aliens arrived on Earth a long time ago and created life experiments using genetic material stored on the planet. Homo sapiens were conceived as a slave race for the Anunnaki, who mixed their own codified DNA with the indigenous proto-humans, as well as the DNA of the Atlantis survivors.

The Garden of Eden is a popular myth throughout many cultures. Some propose that Atlantis was the Garden of Eden. Others say it was ancient Babylon, where the tablets were uncovered. The ancient astronaut theory postulates that the Garden of Eden was a collective vision of Marduk, the biblical Nephilim race of ETs, using the myriad of genetic samples they imported to Earth. Those Anunnaki extraterrestrial entities are also credited with bringing us marijuana, cocoa, and poppy plants, as they too had a penchant for altered states of consciousness.

The Anunnaki were a group of Sumerian and Akkadian deities related to, and in some cases overlapping with, the *Annuna*, the "Fifty Great Gods," and the *Igigi* "minor gods," hence "those of royal blood" or "princely offspring." The Anunnaki appear in the Babylonian creation myth called *Enuma Elish*. In the late version magnifying the planet

Marduk, after the creation of humankind, leaders of Marduk divide the Anunnaki and assign them—three hundred in heaven, and three hundred on the Earth. The Sumerian civilization was governed by these *living gods*. The Anunnaki were the High Council of the Gods, and Anu's companions. They were distributed throughout the Earth and in the Underworld.

The ancient Sumerian cuneiform tablets also describe two Anunnaki leaders, Enki and his half-sister Ninhursag, who labored to produce a hybrid slave race by mixing their "divine" genes with the inferior genes of the Lu-Lu, or *Homo erectus*, the indigenous ape-like creatures of the planet. Thus, an alien "interbreeding program" is central to the Anunnaki narrative. This is also a key event in the overarching "reptilian agenda," that continues in earnest to this day. A certain group of the current elites evoke their lineage to grant them royalty and power, and to support the notion that they are somehow superior to the rest of humanity, who they feel justified in suppressing. We understand then, why the age-old hierarchies are still so deeply-rooted in modern society.

Before the Anunnaki raid, some humans had extraordinary abilities that were left over from the advanced Earth civilizations that had long ago collapsed. The original biogenetic example of the human was given incredible information, was inter-dimensional by nature, and could do many supernatural things. When the "creator gods" (described above) raided, they found that the local species had abilities that were too much like their own. Consequently, they suppressed and controlled the current human inhabitants—those last surviving ancestors of Atlantis and Lemuria. In the case of these surviving ancestors, the breeding males were only allowed to breed with manipulated two-strand DNA females, thus nearly eliminating all 12-strand humans left on Earth, as is depicted in the legendary Sumerian tale, the *Epic of Gilgamesh*.

OTHER ANCIENT SCRIPTS

Another interesting aspect to the story involves an earthenware jar that was dug up in 1945 at Nag Hammadi, Egypt, containing papyrus scrolls and codices wrapped in leather. The Nag Hammadi Codices (NHC) are the earliest surviving examples of bound books, dating to around 1,600 years ago. Close reading of these arcane materials shows that the Gnostics (teachers in the early Christian era) were deeply concerned with an alien intrusion upon humankind. The NHC contains an extensive account of an ET invasion of the Earth long ago. It provides several descriptive clues on the physical form of the intruders. The NHC material also contains reports of visionary experiences of the initiates, including first-hand encounters with inorganic entities called "archons."

The Sumerian cuneiform tablets are the earliest known writings, and predate the NHC by several thousand years. Archaeologists tell us that the Sumerian cuneiform writing was invented in Mesopotamia around 3200 BCE. The cuneiform record on clay tablets presents a intriguing repertoire of stories about human prehistory, and also makes reference to ancient astronauts. The cuneiform tablets and the Nag Hammadi books both describe an alien intervention scenario. How amazing that the oldest-known written language, and the earliest surviving books, both relate the same story?

The cuneiform record itself is just a story without critical commentary. We are not told the source of the story or who authored it. By contrast, we know that the NHC texts come from Gnostic sects of the early Christian mystery schools. While most of the authors remain anonymous, we know them as having been participants in the ancient tradition of spiritual education also known as the esoteric mystery schools.

Another famous ancient text, called the *Old Testament* recounts, in Genesis 6:1: "When men began to increase in number on the Earth and daughters were born to them, the sons of God saw that the daughters of men were beautiful, and they married any of them they chose." In another ancient text, the *Hindu Vedas* report of anti-gravity *vimana* crafts traveling above the Earth and equipped with terrific weapons.

Sorcerers of ancient Mexico argued that humans must have been far more complete beings at one point, with stupendous insights and feats of awareness that we consider mythological today. Then there is a gap when these special abilities seem to disappear, which leaves us with a sedated human. According to author Carlos Castaneda, the Mexican sorcerers say that we are dominated by a *predator*. But it is not a simple predator. It is very intelligent and analytical. It follows a methodical system to render us useless. The Mexican shamans say that we humans, the magical beings that we are destined to be, are no longer magical, but we are just an average piece of meat like domesticated animals. "There is an explanation," Yaqui Indian sorcerer Don Juan Matus replied to his student Carlos Castaneda, "which is the simplest explanation in the world. They took over because we are food for them, and they squeeze us mercilessly because we are their sustenance. Just as we rear chickens in chicken coops, *gallineros*, the predators rear us in human coops, *humaneros*. Therefore, their food is always available to them."

ATTACK OF THE ARCHONS, THEN AND NOW

Up to one-fifth of the intelligible material in the NHC concerns itself with the origin, methods, and motives of the "archons," also called "authorities, governors." The NHC texts describe how the archons attempted to *rape* Eve, clearly a mythological rendition of genetic intervention. Such passages appear to support the claims of alien interbreeding. The NHC codices—the earliest surviving documents in book form—indicate both "reptilian" and "Grey" types. There is a draconic type and a neonate type, suggesting the latter an image of a prematurely born fetus, and another described as amoeba-like. The antecedents of the draconic type are the demonic overlords. The second type are servile robotic drones who obey with a hive-like mentality; with the amoeba-like entities existing just beyond our range of vision. All work in concert with each other to manipulate us unaware humans as to their "service to self" agenda.

Incidentally, all types of archons can be captured on film by cameras that can photograph in the infrared, and slightly below the visible spectrum of human perception. The NHC do not contain graphic physical descriptions of these alien intruders, but present ample information to profile them comparatively with the three types of ETs most widely discussed as detrimental to humanity. In addition, the biblical Nephilim race of ETs share a remarkable similarity with the Alpha Draconian aliens. The Nephilim and the reptilian ETs are both described as master genetic scientists intent on splicing human DNA and creating a hybrid race. These same reptilians are the "Jinn" in Islam, or mischievous spirits, in Christianity. Also spelled "Djinn," these are powerful spiritual entities that have been described throughout history as both demonic and magical.

Author and lecturer Jim Sparks claims to be an ET abductee with a 95% conscious recall of his experiences. He provides details of the two types of Grey aliens he had contact with—the larger grey ETs who are real beings, and manufactured small biological robot grey ETs as workers. These ET entities exist on Earth today, and have their own agenda which is primarily concerned with the creatures they seeded on our planet. Sparks noted that this also includes genetically modifying humans over many millennia ago. In the past few decades, he claims, their current hybrid program has been successful in creating a new type of human being that is more intelligent, environmentally sensitive, and even telepathic. They could potentially populate the planet, he explained, if something happened to the rest of us. During one abduction episode, Sparks was shown a hologram of a half-ape half-human being from 200,000 years ago that the ETs genetically manipulated to evolve as humans over the eons of time. Their ability to gain access to a person's mind and private thoughts is eerily reminiscent of an archon intrusion.

Entities described as archons appear to have identical intent as do the malevolent extraterrestrials described in modern UFOlogy. Although these parasites are not human, they feed off the dark energy and the negative emotions of humans called "loosh." It is unclear exactly when in time these cosmic, amoeba-like creatures first came to Earth, but we know they were discovered long ago by shamans in altered states of consciousness, and have recently been photographed. The reason everyone does not see them on a daily basis is because the creature's energy signature is beyond our normal, narrow range of vision within the electromagnetic spectrum that scientists call "visible light."

Archons are hidden negative controllers of humankind, inorganic inter-dimensional entities that must be exposed, identified, and exorcised from individual human minds. They need to be removed both from influencing our human species and from the planet as a whole during our collective evolution toward a new state of consciousness. Emancipating ourselves and Earth from this mental parasitic influence will be a critical factor in the ushering in of a new *Golden Age.*

These bizarre entities may be regarded as a locust-like species of cyborgs with silicon-based bodies designed to permit only brief forays into the Earth's oxygen-rich atmosphere. They inhabit the solar system at large, traveling among the planets in alien-engineered spacecraft. Gnostic texts hint that they may be compared to custodial engineers of the inanimate clockwork mechanism of the system. Thus, archons are considered psycho-spiritual parasites that intrude subliminally upon the human mind, making us play out our inhumane behavior to weird and violent extremes.

Although archons do exist physically, the real danger they pose to humanity is not an invasion of the planet, but an invasion of the mind. The archons are intra-psychic mind parasites that can access human consciousness through telepathy and simulation. According to Carlos Castaneda, in his book *The Active Side of Infinity*, "Long ago, (the native sorcerer/shamans of Mexico) discovered that we have a companion for life. We have a predator that came from the depths of the cosmos and took over the rule of our lives. Human beings are its prisoners. The predator is our lord and master. It has rendered us docile and helpless. If we want to protest, it suppresses our protest. If we want to act independently, it demands that we don't do so." The archons infect our imagination and use the power of make-believe illusions for deception and confusion. Their pleasure is in deceit for its own sake, seemingly without a particular aim or purpose. They are robotic in nature and incapable of independent thought or choice. They do as they are told. And until now, we've been doing what we've been told. The only way to overcome their power over us is to become activated in spirit, body and mind. But first, in the next chapter, we'll make an examination into our mysterious DNA.

< Recovered Sumerian cuneiform tablets indicate the location of the Anunnaki laboratory where the first humans were "produced" in central and southern Africa. This is also the location of the Anunnaki gold mines. Mitochondria DNA places the first *homo-sapien sapiens* emerging from east central Africa around the same time frame when this tablet was produced.

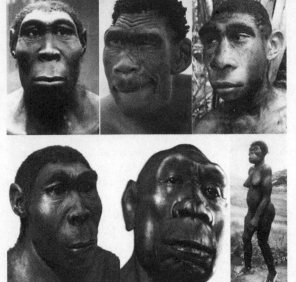

< Genus + Anunnaki = Black human. If there ever were a "missing link" apeman, it might look something like this: Homo Genus & Homo Erectus, an Anunnaki genetic creation. DNA tested from 15 African hunter-gatherers proves that around 2% of the genome from all people of African descent came from an unknown extinct species of hominid. This new hominid DNA is not present in Europeans or Asians. Scientists claim that Cro-Magnon DNA is shared with fully modern human, and has gone unchanged for at least 28,000 years. In other words, the culturally advanced "modern humans" who suddenly populated Western Europe during the last Ice Age were genetically identical to modern European populations, and not African.

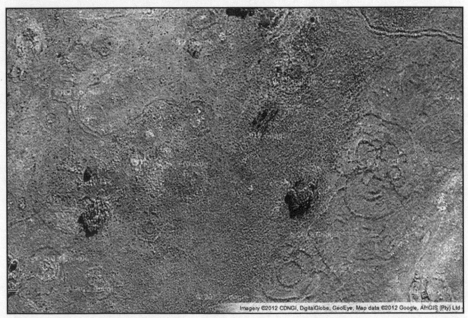

Imagery ©2012 CDNGI, DigitalGlobe, GeoEye, Map data ©2012 Google, AfriGIS (Pty) Ltd

The cluster of thousands of stone ruins in several locations at the southern tip of Africa consist mainly of stacked rock circles, paved roads and even pyramids. Most of the ruins have been buried in the sand and are only observable by aircraft, satellite, or (thanks to Google Earth) taken from above. Some of the rockwork has been exposed as the changing winds blow away the sand, revealing walls, foundations, and ancient gold mining features. The structures show evidence of their extreme antiquity both through erosion and their polished patina surfaces. The "flag ship" of these important ruins is referred to as "Adam's Calendar," a monolithic stone calendar aligned with the N,S,E,W, cardinal points of the Earth. It is still accurate, and marks time by following the shadow of the setting sun cast by the taller central monolith onto the flat calendar stone beside it.

This Sumerian seal depicts the legend of the "Great Flood," which consumed civilization. Many Sumerian legends are strikingly similar to the stories of Genesis in the Bible. Like Genesis, the 1,900 year old Sumerian story, entitled *Atrahasis,* recounts the creation of modern humans. But this creation is not by a loving God, but rather by beings from another planet who needed "slave workers" to help them mine gold on their extra-planetary expedition.

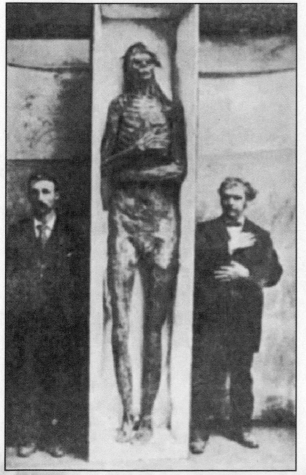

< It is a fact that all around the world enormous human-like bones and skulls with double rows of teeth have been discovered. In Mexico, Australia, Turkey, Greece, the island of Sardinia, various locations in Africa and other countries, including the USA. There are many cases of giant bones being discovered in North America: the Channel Islands off the coast of Southern California, the Great Basin region of Nevada, and in some of the burial mounds of the Ohio River Valley. This image of an 8'4" skeleton was found in San Diego, pictured with Professor Mc-Gee, on the left. Could this find have anything to do with the so-called Nephilim giants who were rumored to once inhabit the Earth?

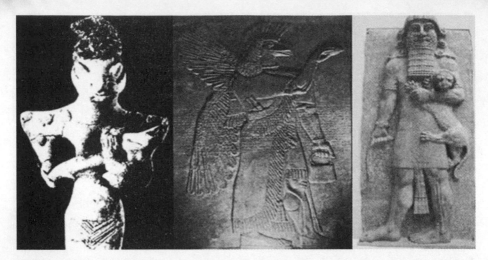

Uncovered in Iraq, these sculptures, created around 5000 BCE, seem to have reptilian type heads, similar to those of the Anunnaki. Additional historical records further reveal that these intelligences were reptilian in nature or, at the very least, have been represented throughout human history in reptilian form. The serpent has been the omnipresent link between humans and the gods in every culture, including the Serpent, Nawcash, the Garden of Eden, Atum (the Egyptian snake-man), Quetzalcoatl (the feathered serpent god of the Mayans), and the double-helix snake symbol of Enki/Ea in ancient Sumerian literature.

The Egyptian pharaoh Akhenaten is seen with his wife Nefertiti and their children. Notice even their children have elongated skulls, suggesting they were born this way into the royal family. The difference between skulls that were banded to elongate them in order to resemble royalty, and the naturally elongated skulls, is that the banded human skulls have a much smaller cranial capacity.

This is one of only a few leaked photos of giant beings that escaped being withheld from the public. They were uncovered in Kigali, Rwanda, but upon the discovery, fear enveloped the community. Village elders urged the people to flee. According to a scientific report filed by a team of anthropologists digging in Central Africa, up to 200 gigantic alien bodies presumed to be Nephilim have been unearthed after entombment for many centuries. The African find is only the latest in a series of alien body discoveries stretching back some 70 years. They are being kept secret because disclosure would interfere with the false history to which academics are committed and the media supports.

The *Anunnaki* are a reptoid species named by the Sumerians to describe "those who from Heaven to Earth came." Today they are more commonly known as "Alpha Draconis." The "Alpha" is because they are the dominant reptilian species, and "Draconis" because their main home base in the Milky Way galaxy is located in the Draco Constellation. *Draco* is Latin for "Dragon." It is known throughout the universe that the Alpha Draconians (CIAKARS) are supposedly the oldest species in the galaxy, but they did not originate here. It seems that they arrived here from another galaxy, universe, or even from another reality, and operate entirely on the terms of their own agenda.

 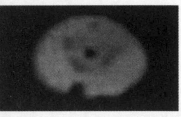

Ancient Gnostic texts from Egypt, called the Nag Hammadi, describe two types of archons—demonic alien beings—who invaded Earth long ago. The first type of archon looks like a reptile. The other type looks like a human embryo or amoeba, similar in shape and appearance to these "sky fish" from this photo provided by NASA. "The sorcerers of ancient Mexico," according to Carlos Castaneda's teacher Don Juan, "saw the predator (presumably demonic.) They called it the flyer because it leaps through the air. It is not a pretty sight. It is a big shadow, impenetrably dark, a black shadow that jumps through the air."

< Old sculptures of what appear to be depicting visitors from other worlds, or humans wearing space helmets. These figurines appear in different forms and have been found in various distant locations worldwide.

DNA MYSTERIES

"The genetic seeds of life swarm throughout the cosmos, and some of these genetic 'seeds' fell to Earth, as well as on other planets. And these genetic seeds contained the instructions for the metamorphosis of all life, including woman and man. DNA acts to purposefully modify the environment, which acts on gene selection, so as to fulfill specific genetic goals: the dispersal and activation of silent DNA and the replication of life forms that long ago lived on other planets." –Rhawn Joseph, developer of the "Evolutionary Metamorphosis" thesis

WHAT makes humans so special? Perhaps it's because we are the only species to ponder how others perceive us. We have this rational mind, an active free will, plus a penchant for self-idolatry. We create architecture, medicine, literature, art, music, and science, yet have the capacity to punish others. We are the only species who can destroy others with the push of a button. How is it that we can be so creatively different above all the animals? After all, our DNA is about 99% identical to chimpanzees. We descend from apes according to evolutionary biologists. Our hands are certainly key genetic traits, allowing humans both precision and power. We can touch all four fingers with the thumb. Why do we have such versatile hands? What is it exactly that makes humans human? The genome is a huge field of study and a good place to start to answer these fundamental "lifeology" questions.

Just days after conception, the embryos of chickens, turtles and humans look remarkably similar. Only as they develop over time do they dramatically change. It's not the number of genes that a life form embodies, but what they can do that makes every species unique. Mutation must also be considered, because it is a critical variation tool for the diversity of life. Since DNA consists of vast quantities of information, it can be rearranged and manipulated to create a whole host of creatures. The DNA is merely a code, or a sequence, to our genes.

The vast bulk of DNA does not process proteins, but regulates the "switches" which turn on and off genes that create our unique characteristics. DNA proteins create hair, muscle, cartilage and every other feature in humans. The switches activate at one time, and not another, in one place, and not another. Other genes give orders to the switches to turn them on or off, and when. Timing appears to be everything. Switches form the essential attributes of all species. They tell the cells in the body at what time to activate. What's more, over half of the switches operate in the brain alone. Switches are found in the dark DNA, which is still considered uncharted territory. Sequencing the growth in a fish fin, for example, is similar to the development of limbs and fingers on other creatures. It shows how we can be very similar, yet so different, from the animals. Scientists are currently sequencing the DNA of animals and comparing it to other forms of life, including humans. Researchers can reconfigure the switches, sequences, and pathways through mutation to create entirely different life forms. The study of DNA is rising to the challenge of better medicine and a better idea of ourselves—allowing us a clear view of our past and a peek into the future.

MONKEY TO MAN

To truly understand who we are, let's begin by identifying human DNA differences with our closest living relative, the chimpanzee. The first noticeable difference in the embryonic stage is that human DNA becomes active early in thumb and big toe development. Brains are the other signature organ which show early differences. Human brains are three times larger than chimp brains. Another vital clue as to why chimps are so different is a mutation in the human jawbone which allows our skulls to grow until we are about 30 years old. Great ape skulls stop growing at three or four years old. Scientists have identified a gene that regulates brain growth. Compared to chimps, our brains are radically different, with a large series of mutations. For example, there are 15 million letters in our DNA different from chimps. Brain complexity and size is the most fundamental difference. The biggest difference in our mutual DNA are the switches, where in humans more than half are involved with the brain. The chimp to chicken cortex is a two-letter difference, while there is an 18-letter difference from chimp to human. This relatively small difference, however, has enormous consequences.

Human and chimp bodies each have trillions of cells and each cell has a nucleus of 23 chromosomes. These chromosomes are coiled threads of DNA helix molecules, plus protein molecules. Each DNA molecule has a set of nucleotides, consisting of phosphate, sugar (deoxyribose), base (gaunine, cytosine), and nitrogen (thymine, ardenine) and each forms a double stranded helix where the strands are linked by hydrogen bonds called base pairs, between guamine and cytosine, or thymine and adenine. There are three billion base pairs in the human genome. Typically each human being has 100,000 genes. A gene has about a thousand to several million base pairs. For every gene set there may be a meme set within humans. A meme set refers to semiotic signs, symbols, meanings, beliefs, instincts, cultural patterns, spiritual patterns, or archetypes. Memes are considered cultural analogues to genes because they self-replicate and mutate.

Charles Darwin pondered how there could be so many different species, and how some of those species eventually changed to become others. He developed an advanced understanding of life's great diversity. Evolution has been said to be the "best idea anyone ever had." His inspiration came from the Galapagos Islands where he noticed that the tortoises had different shell shapes on all the different islands. He also noted that finches and other Galapagos bird species were all variations of a single type. Darwin famously recorded 13 species of finches on 13 islands, each slightly adapted for the conditions. Diet patterns of food for each finch determined its characteristics. Genetic variation drives the change for nature. Tiny variations over time and over generations select the best genes, which led to one of Darwin's most famous concepts: "the survival of the fittest."

Darwin began to look further and wondered if snakes and whales, species once having legs and teeth as seen in embryos, had descended from other animals. All embryos clearly develop in a *cephalocaudal* direction, that is, occurring in the long axis of the body in the direction whereby the head develops first, followed by the "tail," or body. Darwin envisioned a "Tree of Life" in which all species were related. For example, birds and dinosaurs share multiple characteristics with each other—as many as they share with their own species. Some say birds are the living legacy of dinosaurs. Darwin's tree of life could be called "descent with modification." He saw that dog breeders select traits to create new dogs. Natural selection explains the big diversity in life. Every species is in a desperate struggle for survival. Darwin saw a species battlefield, a pattern for survival depending on their environment, which determined their characteristics. Eventually monkeys crawled out of trees, began walking upright, and Darwin's "Descent of Man" had begun.

And while Darwin's evolution concepts largely stand intact today, he did not have the opportunity to examine DNA to take his understanding to a new level. What he would have seen was that DNA can be found in the cells of all species, a veritable code to make all living things grow and develop. DNA does not stay the same in each generation, as half comes from the mother, and half comes from the father. Change can also come through mutation, which generates variation, of which Darwin was keenly aware. Scientists can now identify genes that evolved with mutation. They can compare a creature's genes to literally see how evolution works. Humans have three billion letters in our DNA. We have 23,000 genes, which is about the same as a chicken, but less than corn. Some plants have more genes than people do. The number of genes in a species is not the central issue, but how they're used.

THE "SECRET OF LIFE"

In 1953, James Watson and Francis Crick discovered the double helical structure of the DNA molecule. Unraveling the molecular structure of DNA to identify the double helix was the subject matter of the 1962 Nobel Prize in Physiology or Medicine. Francis Crick, co-discoverer of DNA's double helix structure, discussed at length the pros and cons of an alternative theory on the origin of life—based on the extraterrestrial seeding of Earth with blue-green algae. According to this hypothesis, there was a purpose to the seeding, and it was to insure the continuation of life. Crick noted that this hypothesis of "directed panspermia," (proposed, he said, by the physicist Arrhenium at the end of the 19th century) postulates that the seeds of life may have been purposely spread by an advanced extraterrestrial civilization. Later, after biologists had proposed that an "RNA world" might be involved in the origin of life, Crick noted that he had been overly pessimistic about the chances of life originating on Earth, even after cracking the DNA code with his astonishing declaration: "We've discovered the secret of life." But he continued to find more credence in the panspermia theory than traditional Darwinian theory, while recognizing its *edge of science* problem. He said panspermia was "at least possible, and more importantly, not totally improbable."

The "secret" is that all living organisms on Earth have the same sort of genetic material in their bodies, called Deoxyribonucleic acid (DNA), with the exception of certain small viruses that use Ribonucleic acid (RNA) as their genetic material. Unlike DNA, RNA is almost always a single-stranded molecule, and it has a much shorter chain of nucleotides. RNA contains ribose, rather than the deoxyribose found in DNA. RNA is a nucleic acid polymer consisting of nucleotide monomers. DNA is a nucleic acid that contains the genetic instructions used in the development and functioning of all living species within their cells. The DNA segments that carry this genetic information are called genes, but other DNA sequences have structural purposes, or are involved in regulating the use of this genetic information. Along with RNA and proteins, DNA is one of the three major macromolecules that are essential for all known forms of life. All DNA is made of four amino acids, also called the nucleo bases: adenine (A), guanine (G), cytosine (C) and thymine (T)—simply called the "bases" in genetics. Amino acids are formed into a base pair.

It is clear that human DNA can be altered—or changed—in a myriad of ways. The alterations are usually called mutations, but while the term "mutation" typically connotes something negative, some mutations are adaptive and create advances. A number of environmental factors can cause mutations. Current theories state that mutations are the prime cause of evolution. Mutations actually occur fairly frequently and naturally. The purpose of DNA is to provide a blueprint that can be replicated by RNA, and then on to proteins. The normal rate of small mistakes in the ongoing replication of a DNA template within the cell happens about once with every 100 million base pairs of DNA. But incredibly, human cells have a repair mechanism that recognizes such mistakes. Of more relevance is what geneticists call "point mutations," where an amino acid is mistakenly replaced because of an external cause.

In the 1980s, the U.S. Human Genome Project was established with the goal of mapping the entire human DNA sequence. It was a daunting project that almost went counter to common understanding. Imagine a very narrow, two meter-long ladder with 3 billion rungs. Each rung is made up of a pair of different amino acids that *snap* together. There are only four possible amino acids that can be used to create each rung of two amino acid pairs. The two ends of the ladder are then twisted in opposite directions. As it is twisted, the ladder gradually pulls together into a tightly wound, irregular shaped ball, but the incredibly small area it takes up is infinitesimal. Human brain cells, for example, are about 1/60,000th of an inch in diameter. In the center of each cell, in less than 1/4 of the entire space, is the nucleus of the cell. Virtually all cells in a human body have a nucleus containing a complete, two meter-long DNA strand. Essentially the mapping of human DNA represents a total of six billion amino acids in a linear sequence. By 1998, the job of mapping the DNA sequence was virtually completed, but the identification of the expected and normal amino acid sequences does not mean that we understand the actual function and purpose of each. That is, we know what the amino acids are but we do not necessarily know their function or purpose. The completion of that research is a long way down the line. Nevertheless, several relevant findings have been made that directly correspond with the idea that "cosmic rays," panspermia, and external genetic tinkering have sparked human evolution.

DNA MANIPULATION BY INTELLIGENCE

DNA is the most complex molecule known. Human DNA contains two strands wrapped around each other in a helix, and these strands are held in place by the four chemical bases A, G, C, and T. DNA mutation can be caused by radioactivity, including ultraviolet exposure, causing the amino acids to split apart and reconnect, thereby effecting the genes in a chromosome. Scientists have the ability to manipulate DNA by using he following three technologies:

1.   *Genetic technology and genome study: Scientists can take individual components and map them out. They can track down what the DNA molecules do and then concentrate on genetic manipulation.*
2.   *Computerization: Math algorithms or computer models can be used to design or alter DNA. Researchers can create cause and effect models representing scientific optimization.*

3. *Nano technology: This is the ability to manipulate DNA on an atomic level. Scientists can alter, change, or modify DNA on a molecular level. It's theoretically possible to control or rewrite DNA, but researchers would have to get at the source code.*

Biological evolution operates at a snail's pace compared to technological evolution. Technological evolution is called the *Lamarckian inheritance model*, which can be implemented within a single generation. Biological evolution is *Darwinian* and requires many generations of *differential reproductive success*, and sometimes takes thousands of years for a single mutation to enter the general population of a species. But let's not forget that the cosmos is very big and very old, with virtually an infinite amount of time in which to operate.

Genetic engineering, recombinant DNA technology, gene splicing, DNA modification, or Genetic Manipulation (GM) are terms applied to the direct manipulation of a living organism's genes. Genetic engineering is not to be confused with traditional breeding techniques where the species' genes are manipulated indirectly. Genetic engineering uses the laboratory techniques of molecular cloning and transformation. Genetic engineering endeavors have had some success in improving crop technology, the manufacture of synthetic human insulin through the use of modified bacteria, the manufacture of erythropoietin in Chinese hamster ovary cells, and the production of new types of experimental mice such as the "oncomouse," or cancer mouse, for research purposes. However, what is really astonishing is that a group of researchers working at the Human Genome Project believe that 97% of non-coding sequences in human DNA is no less than the genetic code of an extraterrestrial life forms.

Cloning is usually done by taking a nucleus out of one cell of a living being, and then transferring it to an egg cell from which the nucleus has been removed. Most of the cloning research has been achieved behind closed doors, and the results are not being disclosed. Cloned people could already be walking among us. But the public is genuinely appalled by a technology that plays God with human cells and sperm. It is possible *now* to clone your cat before it dies by removing a bit of tissue, taking out the nucleus from one cell, and putting that nucleus into the egg of a female cat from which the nucleus has been removed. The egg would then be implanted into a "surrogate cat" that would carry the "fertilized" egg that has the genetic constitution of your own cat. If all goes well—and it often does not—the cat would produce a kitten genetically identical to your original cat, enabling you, in principle, to have the same pet forever. This procedure is not guaranteed, though, as the mitochondrial DNA of your pet would not be transferred in this procedure, and *somatic cells* in the body undergo mutations during the life of an organism. Therefore the skin cell of your cat would not be genetically identical to the fertilized egg that produced it. Furthermore, any farmer will tell you that the more you clone the same species, the weaker the DNA gets, and subsequent offspring will be weaker and prone to more diseases. There is also the question of whether the same spirit would attach to the newly cloned being.

A CHALLENGE TO EVOLUTION

To better understand the immense block of geologic time, that is, the eras, periods, stages, epochs, ages and the long march of all conceivable historic time, let's consider a model. Planet Earth's age is generally put at 4.6 billion years, which is the age of the oldest discovered meteorites. To better appreciate the vastness of geologic time, let's think of those 4.6 billion years as represented by a single year. The oldest fossil records go back only about 40 days out of that 365-day year. Indeed, more than 88% of Earth's history is Precambrian. Of the remaining time, when Earth has been home to animal life as we know it, the part that includes proto-humans and their ancestors is less than 1%. The human presence on the planet is only about two hours. The presence on the planet of *Homo sapiens sapiens*, which are modern humans, is only about the last six minutes. According to an article in *Nature*, released in June, 2017, findings in an old mine at Jebel Irhoud in Morocco, date the earliest *Homo sapiens* appearing about 300,000 years ago. They were definitely around elsewhere in Africa 260,000 to 160,000 years ago. At this time, *Homo sapiens* coexisted with *Homo erectus* in Asia, and Neanderthals in Europe and the Middle East. "Nuclear Adam" is the most recently known common ancestor of today's modern human, having lived sometime between 90,000 to 60,000 years ago. Using the one-year model, it makes the notion of evolution possible, probable, and comprehensible for the development of older animal species, but not so much for quickly evolved modern humans.

For the scientific community, *intelligent design* represents creationism's latest grasp at scientific legitimacy. Accordingly, intelligent design is viewed as an ill-conceived attempt to corral science to within religious ideology. But we can now see that intelligent design can be formulated into a scientific theory, with empirical support, and devoid of religious commitments. Evolution theory based on Darwin's *Origin of the Species* is in the process of being disproven based on the thought that the DNA molecule is far too complicated to have been formed simply by natural mutations alone. Later, even Francis Crick proved mathematically that it would seem impossible for evolution to produce human DNA in the brief amount of time allowed.

The way evolution works on a specific species is on a mass scale and in a much longer time frame than is now afforded—especially for modern humans. *Ascension* (a leap in potential, that is, the sudden creation of a "new being") is not only restricted to the Christian concept of rapture, where Jesus will return and usher in a thousand years of peace. It could be a cosmic event that simply prompts another stage in evolution, as such occurrences have been prophesied in almost every major religious and spiritual tradition on Earth. Such could be a time when our DNA will multiply into new strains, and humans will naturally re-develop dormant super human abilities. *What the mind can conceive, the body will achieve.*

ET GENES IN HUMAN DNA

The non-coding sequences of DNA are a common attribute of all living organisms on Earth, from algae to fish to people. Non-coding sequences, initially known as "junk DNA," were discovered years ago, and their complete function still remains a mystery. In human DNA, they constitute a much larger part of the total genome, says Professor Sam Chang, the Human Genome Project group leader. According to the study group, the overwhelming majority of human DNA was *"off-world"* in origin. They found that apparent "extraterrestrial junk genes" could just "enjoy the ride" with the hard working active genes that are passed from generation to generation.

After comprehensive analysis, and with the assistance of other scientists, computer programmers, mathematicians, and other scholars, Professor Chang wondered if the *apparently* "junk human DNA" was created by some kind of "extraterrestrial programmer." The alien chunks within human DNA, Professor Chang further noted, "have its own veins, arteries, and its own immune system that vigorously resists all our anti-cancer drugs."

Professor Chang further commented that, "If we think about it in our human terms, the apparent 'extraterrestrial programmers' were most probably working on 'one big code' consisting of several projects, and the projects should have produced various life forms for various planets. They also have been trying various solutions. They wrote 'the big code,' executed it, did not like some functions, changed them or added new ones, executed again, made more improvements, tried again and again."

Professor Chang further stipulates that, "Our hypothesis is that a higher extraterrestrial life form was engaged in creating new life and planting it on various planets. Earth is just one of them. Perhaps, after programming, our creators grow us the same way we grow bacteria ... in Petri dishes. We can't know their motives—whether it was a scientific experiment, a way of preparing new planets for colonization, or a long-term ongoing business of seeding life in the universe?"

The team of researchers working with Professor Chang furthermore concluded that, "The apparent 'extraterrestrial programmers' may have been ordered to cut all their idealistic plans for the future when they concentrated on the 'Earth project' to meet the pressing deadline. Very likely in an apparent rush, the 'extraterrestrial programmers' may have cut down drastically on a big code and delivered a basic program intended for Earth."

Professor Chang is one of a growing number of DNA scientists and other researchers who have postulated an extraterrestrial origin to humanity, who said "Soon or later, we have to come to grips with the unbelievable notion that every life on Earth carries genetic code for his extraterrestrial cousin and that evolution is not what we think it is."

Professor Chang further concludes that "what we see in our DNA is a program consisting of two versions, a big code and basic code." He bravely affirms that the "First fact is, the complete 'program' was positively not written on Earth; that is now a verified fact. The second fact is, that genes by themselves are not enough to explain evolution; there must be something more in 'the game.'"

STARCHILD SKULL

The Starchild Skull is a genuine, 900-year-old bone discovered in a Mexican cave in the 1930s. It sat in a closet for many decades before it was examined by experts and put to the rigors of DNA testing. Ongoing research has provided proof that the Starchild Skull possesses physical characteristics, biochemical attributes, fibers and residue inside the bone that indicate it is not human. More recently, a 2010 DNA test result confirms that the skull is at least partially of extraterrestrial origin. Researchers have concluded that the skull presents at least 10 standard deviations from the norm. It is comprised of bone uniformly half as thick and weighing half as much as normal human bone, but is significantly more durable. The bone is more of a substance like tooth enamel. A DNA test in 2003 found that it has human maternal lineage, which confirmed that it cannot be a pure alien species. However, the picture that emerges from the latest round of DNA testing is that the skull once belonged to a human-alien hybrid. The "mt" is the part of DNA passed only through the maternal line. In 2011, the geneticist working on the Starchild Skull discovered that its mtDNA was radically different from human DNA. The maximum number of mtDNA differences between all humans is 120. The Starchild Skull has between 800 and 1000 differences. This is a partial result, but it is definitive enough to declare that the Skull's mtDNA is not human.

The greatest benefit of discussing the Starchild enigma is to open our perspective beyond the evolutionist or creationist dogma. The stakes are too high to discount this remarkable specimen as a human deformity, rather than as a possible missing link in the human-alien-hybrid scheme of things. The issue becomes more a case of admitting that it is only language that restricts our understanding; for example, considering the statement, "we did not come from apes." We now know that we did not directly descend from apes, although perhaps in some general aspect we did, since we have some shared DNA factors. The emerging perspective is that Earth was populated with creatures in a sort of genetic safari park, overseen by numerous ET genetic tinkering groups. The DNA results of a hybrid ET existing on Earth nearly a thousand years ago, along with very anomalous features in our human blood and our human brains, all combine in the new "intervention theory" gaining more credibility every year.

DNA FROM OUTER SPACE

"DNA Building Blocks Actually Created in Space" was a NASA report headline in August 2011. "If asteroids are behaving like chemical 'factories' cranking out prebiotic material, you would expect them to produce many variants of nucleobases, not just the biological ones, due to the wide variety of ingredients and conditions in each asteroid," said Michael Callahan, at NASA Goddard Space Flight Center. Goddard and his team ground up samples of 12 carbon-rich meteorites, nine of which were recovered from Antarctica. The team found adenine and guanine, which are base components of DNA called nucleobases. Also, in two of the meteorites, the team discovered trace amounts of three molecules related to nucleobases. The three molecules were purine, 2,6-diaminopurine, and 6,8-diaminopurine, the latter two almost never found in Earth-bound biology. The discovery adds to a growing body of evidence that chemistry inside asteroids and comets are capable of making building blocks of essential biological molecules.

Astro-biologists are fully aware that many viruses are manufactured in the stars. Indeed, the medieval Latin word for *influentia* signified "influence of the stars." In January 2010, another study announced that "Eight Percent of Human Genetic Material Comes from a Virus." This news suggests that human evolution is much more likely to be influenced or even driven by cosmic factors which is consistent with what scientists have known for some time, namely, that viruses are manufactured in interstellar space.

Researchers at the Goddard Space Flight Center discovered portions of DNA on chunks of crashed space rock in both Antarctica and Australia. The molecular extraterrestrial visitors contained various types of nucleobases, which are thought to be essential in the creation of DNA, and life in general. The scientists were able to isolate the compounds and prove that they did not originate on Earth. The team also found that certain space rocks, depending on their makeup and speed, worked like manufacturing facilities for these biological precursors. The implications of the discovery are far-reaching, and suggest that the origin of life on Earth may owe its existence to a well-placed meteorite, and that without it, the planet might still be a rocky, watery wasteland.

NASA's "new discovery" about the elements of life originally being brought to Earth by incoming objects confirms what Swiss UFO contactee Billy Meier published in 1988. Meier scooped NASA on this story by a few decades, explaining at the time that the "insemination" process from comets and meteors, by which life started on Earth, is a phenomenon that occurs throughout the universe. Indeed, the news report about NASA's discovery virtually repeats what Meier said decades ago about the universe-wide phenomenon of life-seeding objects.

What these findings suggest is that DNA is a product of a quantum energy wave and is written into the basic laws of the universe. These are the laws that govern the formation of life on Earth, but also govern the behavior of matter and energy in the cosmos. Thus, DNA begins as an energy wave and does not require any physical molecules to exist. The structure of DNA therefore exists throughout the universe. We are all of a cosmic and galactic design, not a product of random mutations on Earth. It can logically be deduced that humans have independently evolved in many different worlds. We know there are at least 22 separate types of DNA within the human species. This would allow a genetic memory of other entities who are part of us through many generations of inter-breeding.

The human design would seemingly be intrinsic to the Milky Way galaxy, and probably a fair amount of the entire universe. Our solar system exists on the outer fringe of the Milky Way galaxy. It can then be presumed that other humans have advanced spiritually and technologically much farther than we have here on Earth. If this is the case, then those humans could have colonized Earth in the times before or during the existence of Lemuria or Atlantis, and their skulls reveal brain capacities significantly larger than ours. As we will learn, these people were largely wiped out by a self-inflicted cataclysm caused by nuclear war between rival colonies. The survivors built pyramids to heal and stabilize the Earth on its axis in the aftermath of this catastrophe. They had direct knowledge of a natural cycle that propels each inhabited planet through quantum evolutionary leaps. They were aware of the physical pineal gland in the human brain that governs ESP and can be "activated" by this natural cycle.

THE MASTERS ALREADY KNOW THIS

For ages, esoteric and spiritual teachers have known that our minds (in which the body and its organs *virtually reside*, not the other way around) are programmable by language, words and thought, from which "instructions" to the body then follow. Our minds being extensions of the infinite One mind then explains our seemingly human unlimitedness, even on the level of the material world. In another case in which esotericists got it right, "light codes" have now been scientifically explained. Light codes are energy patterns, sacred geometries, colors, sound waves, light patterns, and frequencies that all of creation emits. DNA is affected or activated by light codes which can be received in myriad of ways. Once you have "triggered" kundalini energy, the process continues for the rest of your life. That is because it begins to shift your DNA into alignment with your higher or more authentic self. Of course the frequency has to be precisely correct, and this is a reason why everyone is seemingly not created equal, and can't replicate identical results with the same strength. The individual person must work on their inner processes and their own maturity in order to establish conscious communication with their DNA.

It could be that the metaphysical claims that light codes are being delivered to Earth to "repair DNA" may not be so far fetched. At the moment, the logic is that viruses only cause DNA mutations, and since there are various interruptions to our DNA (Intervening Sequences or Blanks—INTRONs), repressor molecules may attach to *promoter regions*. Who is to say that light codes are not "inducers" that activate genes by combining with repressor molecules as part of the delivery of evolutionary energies that can be used to upgrade our DNA in readiness for the next evolutionary leap?

Another intriguing frequencies theory is their influence on weather. Our weather is strongly influenced by the Earth's resonance frequencies, the so-called *Schumann frequencies.* These same frequencies are also produced in our brains, and when many people synchronize their thinking, or when a powerful individual like a spiritual master can focus his thoughts in a laser-like fashion, then, scientifically speaking, it is not at all surprising they can influence the weather and other events.

If the cosmos can deliver agents that cause DNA mutations, why do we not consider that the cosmos periodically delivers genetic material that reverses the decline of the human genome? Within certain parts of the metaphysical community, it has been accepted as common knowledge that light codes are now being delivered to this planet, but the implications have not been well understood. This research could totally shatter the Darwinian model of "random" evolution in favor of an energetically-driven model. This model has nothing to do with creationism and is not religious in nature.

The higher an individual's consciousness is developed, the less need there is for any type of device, such as "light frequency." One can achieve these results by deep connection to one's inner self, as proven by spiritual masters throughout time. But it doesn't end there. Russian scientists also discovered that our DNA can create invisible, structured patterns in the vacuum energy of space, thus producing magnetized wormholes! These wormholes are the microscopic equivalents of the so-called Einstein-Rosen bridges in the vicinity of black holes originally observed as being left by burned-out stars. The DNA attracts these bits of information and passes them on to our consciousness. This process of hyper-communication is most effective in a state of relaxation. Stress, worries or a hyperactive intellect prevent successful hyper-communication, rendering the information distorted and useless. In fact, one can simply use words and sentences of human language to influence DNA! This, too, has been experimentally proven. Thus, living DNA substances present in living tissue (not in vitro) will always react to language-modulated laser rays and even to radio waves, if the proper frequencies are being used.

BRAIN DNA CHANGES THROUGH LIFE

By charting the human brain's genetic activity from before birth to old age, studies reveal that the brain continually remodels itself in predictable ways throughout life. In addition to uncovering details about how the brain grows and ages, these results may help scientists better understand what goes awry in brain disorders such as schizophrenia, Alzheimer's, ADD and autism.

Researchers of a study released in October, 2011, focused not on DNA, but on when, where, and for how long each gene is turned on over the course of a person's life. To do this researchers measured levels of mRNA, a molecule whose appearance marks one of the first steps in executing the orders contained in a gene, in postmortem samples of donated brains that ranged in age from weeks after conception to old age. Interestingly, the DNA remains virtually identical in each cell's raw genetic material, yet different patterns of mRNA levels distinguish the brain from a heart, for instance, and "a person from a mouse," says Nenad Sestan of Yale University School of Medicine and coauthor of a leading study. "Essentially, we carry the same genes as mice," he says. "However, in us, these genes are up to something quite different."

To see what those genes have encoded, the Yale study examined mRNA levels of different genes in 57 brain samples. The team divided the brain tissue up by region, so they were also able to get an idea of genes' behavior in different parts of the brain. A parallel study, headed by Joel Kleinman of the National Institute of Mental Health in Bethesda, looked at gene behavior in 269 brain samples from a single region called the prefrontal cortex. Both studies found a large amount of variation in gene behavior at different life stages, but the prenatal period stood out, demonstrating massive changes in gene activity. Prenatal genes pumped out big quantities of mRNA, production that abruptly slowed after birth, and with development slowing over time.

Curiously, many of the genes that slow down immediately after birth show a surge of activity as a person gets older. The biggest changes naturally occur in the fetus, and then they go virtually unchanged until mid-life. But then, when a person is in their 50s to 70s, expression changes pick up again and become quite dramatic. What's more, the differences in gene behavior between male and female brains were greatest at the early stages of development. Some of the genes found to be busier in male brains have been linked to schizophrenia, autism and other disorders that are known to be more prevalent among males, the researchers noted. These disease-associated genes are very active early on in development and less so as a person ages, suggesting that within these conditions, something goes awry very early.

Although gene behavior is incredibly dynamic, the results suggest that brains are more alike than different. Despite millions of differences in DNA, brains have a common biochemical shape, according to Joel Kleinman. Two people who have very different DNA make-up don't necessarily have different gene behavior in the brain. "These individual genetic variations, they do matter—no question," he says. But overall, genes behave almost identically from person to person. That's a phenomenal realization. "It means that we're much more alike than we are different."

Another study was performed by Dr. John Hawks, an anthropologist from the University of Wisconsin who has studied and analyzed the last 5,000 years of mummies and grave sites that he has excavated. His research concluded that our DNA has changed structurally by an astonishing 7% in the last 5,000 years. That means that human evolution has already rapidly sped up on a genetic, measurable level. Scientists can trace it in the DNA. Just in the last 100 years there has also been something called the "Flynn Effect," which is that IQ scores have had to be continually re-adjusted every decade—because people keep getting smarter and smarter.

JUNK DNA

Only 10% of our DNA is being used in the process of building proteins. It is this subset of DNA that is of greatest interest to Western researchers and is being examined and categorized. The other 90% is considered "junk DNA," the so-called dark matter of the genome. DNA "switches" are not genes, but they turn genes on and off. Key body-changing genes come from the dark DNA, but evolution leaves behind tiny remnants—the turned off codes that are no longer in use. This explains how manatees, whales, and snakes could have *evolved away* their legs.

Some genes are known to rule over other genes. They regulate what to do, and when. We are told fish are the ancestors of all four-legged creatures, and even bipedal humans. But how could a fish develop legs and walk on land? Fin-like arms, or arm-like fins, were first used to drag a prehistoric creature to safety on land. Similar genes in other animals trigger growth of arms, legs and fins. Lungfish, for example, use their fins to drag themselves onto land. DNA switches would trigger the development of longer arms and legs.

DNA is now less mysterious than it has been in the past, and many geneticists think that so-called junk DNA regulates the expression of other genes. Yet, we know that large portions of DNA are viruses that infected non-replicating portions of the genome, and thus became trapped in the host's genome. Some scientists suggest that the human genome is nothing but a vast cemetery of viruses. Much of the junk DNA is constructed of replication viruses, basically genetic messages which say nothing more than "copy me." But where do the viruses come from?

Scientists have focused on only 10% of our DNA, those that are designed to build proteins, thus leaving a large gaping hole in the interpretation of the other 90%. A few Russian researchers, convinced that nature is intelligent, joined linguists and geneticists in a venture to explore the remaining 90% of the *junk* DNA. Their results, findings and conclusions are simply revolutionary. These scientists can prove that DNA can be reprogrammed by words and frequencies, similar to the light codes. According to their findings, our DNA is not only responsible for the construction of our body, but also serves as a communication system and for data storage, similar to a biological Internet. The Russian linguists found that the genetic code, especially in the *apparently useless* 90% of DNA, follows the same rules as human languages. To this end they compared the rules of syntax, which is the way in which words are put together to form phrases and sentences, the study of meaning in language forms called semantics, and the basic rules of grammar. They found that the alkaline of our DNA follows a regular grammar, and has a set of rules, just like our languages. So human languages did not appear coincidentally, but, instead as a reflection of our inherent DNA.

Author Elaine Smitha raises some interesting questions about *junk DNA* in her book, *If You Make the Rules, How Come You're Not Boss?* She inquires: "Perhaps junk DNA contains all the secrets of the universe, including those unconscious potentials you have yet to discover. Perhaps it is this DNA that allows you to travel without your body into starry realms. Maybe that is where you go in your dreams. Quite possibly intuition, psychic powers, and remote viewing (non-local information gathering) fall into the realm of this amazing communication channel. Perhaps with a relaxed mind, you can tap into the prime DNA alphabet soup for transport. It's absolutely fascinating to consider."

GHOST DNA

Author David Wilcock describes a living energy field "source field," that forms what he calls the fundamental building block of all space, time, energy, matter and biological life. According to Wilcock, such a field may be the crystallization of a united, symbiotic consciousness available to us via our DNA. The *source field*, as it is directly related to biology, includes all life, even the simplest of life forms such as and even including, *space dust*.

The concept that DNA is formed in the process of planetary evolution and space dust may sound absurd, but it can be proven by something known as the DNA "phantom" effect. Dr. Vladimir Poponin put DNA in a tube and shone a laser through it. To his surprise, he realized that it captured the light and caused it to spiral through the helix, as if it were a crystal. Even more amazingly, when Poponin removed the DNA, the light continued to spiral on its own. Thus, he could conjecture that there is a specific distance from the sun where the tiniest spiraling waves will gather a planet's natural materials together to form the DNA molecules of life. The DNA is the wave, and the wave is the DNA. For light to form a DNA helix on its own would seem impossible— that is, unless the light itself had become harmonically tuned to some naturally existing frequency in the energy of space. This suggests that the spiraling light energy of DNA was there first, and the physical molecules simply formed around the spiraling energy once the planet was at the proper frequency position. Thus, it could appear that the galaxy is "tuned" to create DNA.

Life itself is an emergent phenomenon of quantum physics. In 2011, Nobel Prize winner Duc Montagnier proposed that our DNA can electromagnetically teleport itself. Montagnier describes a phenomenon in which DNA emits electromagnetic signals of its own construction called "ghost DNA, that can be mistaken by enzymes as the real deal and replicated in another place. Essentially it is DNA teleportation. To demonstrate this, Dr. Montagnier used two vessels of sterilized water, one with a small amount of DNA, one without. He then periodically electrified a 7 Hz electromagnetic charge to both vessels. After 18 hours of zapping the second vessel, it then contained all the signatures of the DNA. *Hydrogen and oxygen molecules in sterilized water became DNA.*

Another study, by Professor Ignacio Pachaco, mixed sterilized beach sand with regular water in a test tube and turned up the heat to 1,000°. He sealed and sterilized the sample again with distilled water. After 24 hours, a little scum was seen growing on the surface of the glass. Without sterilization of the sand, the experiment would not have worked. So where did the DNA come from? DNA appears to be created, or written, into the source field. The source field is the source of all life, because it does not appear to be randomized life as Darwin proposed. DNA is a *quantum emergent* phenomenon.

As Russian scientific research directly, or indirectly, explains (along with decades of replicated experiments at the Institute of Noetic Sciences) phenomena such as clairvoyance, intuition, spontaneous and remote acts of healing, self healing, the effects of affirmation techniques, the existence of unusual light or auras around certain people (especially spiritual masters), and even the mind's influence on weather patterns ... and much more. Patanjali, in the *Yoga Sutras*, describes these expanded human abilities (siddhis) as simpe side effects of the practice of regular disciplined deep meditation. This could be thought of as meditation penetrating deep into a person's life essence, or DNA. In addition, there is evidence for a new type of medicine, as discussed by Bruce Lipton in *Biology of Belief*, in which DNA can be influenced and reprogrammed by words and frequencies without cutting out and replacing single genes. The Russian biophysicist and molecular biologist Pjotr Garjajev and his colleagues also explored the vibration behavior of DNA. They reported: "Living chromosomes function just like solitonic/holographic computers using the endogenous DNA laser radiation." This means that they managed, for example, to modulate certain laser ray frequency patterns to influenced DNA frequency, and thus the genetic information itself. Since the basic structure of DNA-alkaline pairs (and language) are of the same structure, no DNA decoding was necessary.

Within the concepts of three-dimensional and coordinate time, a universe is creating itself, and that universe exists concurrently with our own three-dimensional and coordinate *space realm*. It is not a parallel reality—or tucked away in some far corner of the universe—it is right here, right now,only shifted out of phase with our spatial reality so that our physical senses do not detect it. However, our non-physical senses can detect it, and operate within it, and this gives rise to some people's psychic abilities. For example, precognition is nothing more than seeing something in the distance, in the temporal landscape. Telepathy is two people *standing next to each other in time* chatting, regardless of how far apart they are in space. Telekinesis is just a manipulation of the temporal component of an object *with your temporal arm*, and watching how "time changes space." Clairvoyance is as if using a pair of temporal binoculars. Virtually, all of the extra-sensory abilities are easily understood once you realize that you exist in two different realms, a spatial, material one for the body, and a temporal, cosmic one for the soul. And the interesting aspect is that these aren't "extra-sensory," magical or metaphysical at abilities—just a natural consequence of biological life that we can either choose to learn, use, and develop, or simply ignore.

DNA has also been found to have a bizarre ability to put itself together, even at a distance, when, according to accepted science, this should not happen, yet scientists are reporting evidence that, contrary to our current beliefs about what is possible, intact double-stranded DNA has the "amazing" ability to recognize similarities in other DNA strands from a distance. Somehow they are able to identify one another, and the tiny bits of genetic material tend to congregate with DNA having similar characteristics. The recognition of similar sequences in DNA's chemical subunits occurs in a way not understood by science. There is no known reason why DNA is able to combine the way it does, and from a current theoretical standpoint, this feat should be chemically impossible. This *recognition effect* may help increase the accuracy and efficiency of the homologous recombination of genes—a process responsible for DNA repair, evolution, and genetic diversity. The new findings may also shed light on ways to avoid recombination errors, which are factors in cancer, aging, and other health issues. As of yet no explanation has been offered, although these attributes of DNA lead some researchers to the conclusion that our DNA is, in effect, conscious.

SUPERHUMAN DNA

In the not too distant future, if not already, scientists will discover the manipulated gene from ancient times in the DNA chain responsible for rapid aging in human beings. Preparations in this area began in 1994. However, whether scientists make their discovery public and utilize their findings to its fullest potential is questionable. In a world already grossly overpopulated, having people's life span triple, or quadruple, would compound the already strained resources when providing for over seven billion people.

It is virtually certain that a new DNA information code will be discovered in the human body, and the first concrete steps will be undertaken to eliminate afflictions to the elderly, heart diseases, and general physical attrition. A genetic reverse-manipulation process will release the human population from the premature aging curse. Genetic manipulations are reversed by retro-manipulation of the pertinent gene. Conflicts will also arise within human populations because of their *seemingly* immortal life spans, that is, the increase in human longevity will amount to potential life spans from 150 to 200 years, or possibly even longer. This increase in longevity will also precipitate greater problems of overpopulation, and other subsequent obstacles, that will include migrations and new types of interbred humans. In spiritual terms, from our current two strands, there are 12 postulated strands of human DNA that extend into the 12 dimensions of reality.

Beyond the changes to DNA in a laboratory, of what is postulated, humans are observed to be naturally evolving to include these new strands of DNA. In April 2011, it was revealed that British toddler Alfie Clamp became the first known example of a human with three strands of DNA. Such a finding would suggest that the human race is currently mutating to add an entirely new strand of DNA. It is speculated that humans long ago contained 12 strands of activated DNA, but 10 became deactivated and turned off. These inactive 10 strands are thought, by some, to be our *junk* DNA. Similar to what is said about our brains, only a small percentage of our DNA is being used, while the rest apparently lies dormant. It is suggested that humans only have 3% of our DNA active. With more activated DNA, we should be able to understand far more—at least from a consciousness point of view. For example, the 12 strands of DNA correspond to the 12 *extended* chakras in the human body. Future generations, with new strands of DNA, could even potentially change from carbon-based beings to crystal-based entities.

DNA ANTENNAS

The DNA antenna in our cell's energy production centers (called mitochondria) assumes the shape of what is called a "supercoil." This supercoil of DNA looks like a series of *möbius loops*. These möbius supercoil of DNA are hypothetically able to generate *scalar waves*. Most cells in the body contain thousands of möbius supercoils generating scalar waves throughout the cell and throughout the body.

The term *scalar* was coined by Nikola Tesla at the beginning of the last century as part of powerful *non-Hertzian energy*, that is, without frequencies, which he referred to as cosmic waves. Einstein gave reference to the scalar energies in the 1920's. Since then Tesla and other independent researchers have come to understand both the physical and theoretical model of a scalar wave. They concluded that it is a dipole that is of two "opposites" unified as a *toroidal vortex*. It spirals in motion and travels in circles. It simultaneously attracts and repels. It resonates and causes to resonate. It is found throughout the natural world. Thus, it is a galaxy, it is a hurricane, it is a tornado, it is a seashell, it is the torus, and it is also DNA.

Scalar waves are produced when two electromagnetic waves of the same frequency are exactly out of phase, that is, they are opposite to each other, and the amplitudes subtract and cancel each other out. Vortex in, vortex out. The result is not exactly an annihilation of magnetic fields, but a transformation of energy back into a scalar wave. The scalar is created when two common electromagnetic waves come together from two different converging vectors or angles. Where the energy vectors meet, the equal frequencies cancel each other, leaving a standing, or stationary, energy. The space the scalar occupies is not a vacuum, but alive with checked and balanced energies. It can be created by electromagnetic generators, or naturally, when similar frequency waves in the environment meet from two different vectors. Therefore, small random scalar energies are always present in the environment. Scalar waves propagate through the dimension of time, but not through the dimension of space. They are observed to carry information and have a fractal-like structure.

Microbiology experts tell us that upwards of 97% of our human DNA is apparently unused, but some are seeing that more and more of the human DNA chain is "unzipping" for any who are capable of handling the new fourth-density energy structure. These people may not physically look any different, but internally they will develop greater depths of emotion, perception, intuition, sensitivity, and what can be termed super human abilities. As mentioned earlier, it now appears that DNA can be influenced and reprogrammed by words and frequencies.

FRAKEN-FOODS

The amazing discoveries about DNA also have a dark side, in the form of creating new DNA, and by extension, new life forms. A biological patent is a patent relating to an invention or discovery in biology. The 1970s marked the first time scientists patented methods on biotechnological inventions using recombinant DNA. It wasn't until 1980 that patents for whole-scale living organisms were permitted. In Diamond v. Chakrabarty, the Supreme Court overturned a previous precedent allowing the patentability of living matter. The subject for this particular case was a bacterium that was specifically modified to help clean up and degrade oil spills.

In recent decades, genetic scientists have discovered a protein sequence specified by a segment of DNA that can be modified. New versions of a protein, for example, can be produced by changing the DNA sequence of a gene. The companies that make these discoveries then *own* the modified genome and are able to patent these new sequences. In the case of basic crops, the companies are gaining control of foodstuffs, controlling food production on a large scale, and reducing agro-biodiversity to a few varieties. The only apparent interest in promoting this technology appears to be economic, despite the claims of seed companies such as Monsanto and Novartis who say they seek to solve the world food shortage. A closer examination of this issue shows that the problem is not the lack of food on a worldwide scale, but its distribution, aggravated by prohibitive tariffs by rich nations. Genetically modified crops cannot reduce hunger. The majority of genetically modified crops are destined for animal feed to meet the high demand for meat consumption in developed countries. There is no evidence that genetic modifications have ever served the needs of humankind, despite all the promises from the companies who stand to profit.

However, even with regard to this technology's great potential, many have raised concerns about the introduction of genetically engineered plants and animals into the environment and the potential dangers of human consumption of GM foods. Critics point out that these organisms have the potential to spread their modified genes into native populations, thereby disrupting natural ecosystems, as has already happened.

IMMUNE RESPONSES, PHOTONS
AND TORSION WAVES

"We live in a dangerous world. Pathogenic microorganisms threaten us continuously," the 2011 Nobel medicine panel said, describing the work of scientists over the decades and their understanding our natural defenses. American Bruce Beutler and French biologist Jules Hoffmann, who studied the first stages of immune responses, share the $1.5 million award with Canadian-born Ralph Steinman, whose discovery of dendritic cells in the 1970s was fundamental to understanding the body's next line of defense against disease.

The immune system exists primarily to protect living organisms against infection, but it can also protect against some cancers by targeting rogue cells before they proliferate. The first line of defense, innate immunity, can destroy invading microorganisms and trigger inflammation. If microorganisms break through this defense line, adaptive immunity is called into action. It produces antibodies and killer cells that can destroy infected cells. These two defense lines provide good protection against infections, but they also pose a risk, and inflammatory disease may result. As when the immune system goes into over-drive and attacks healthy tissue, leading to autoimmune inflammatory diseases such as Type 1 diabetes, multiple sclerosis, and rheumatoid arthritis. The effect is often compared to "friendly fire," as when military troops hit their own comrades in combat.

A variety of information suggests that our DNA's primary function is to *store* photons. There are about a thousand photons per DNA molecule. When there is an area of a patient's body that is sick, it loses photons. As a result, the patient's DNA no longer contains photons and their condition worsens. Studying photons in the DNA is how doctors will be able to measure where sickness resides in the body. After all, every physical body consists of elements. Ordinary matter is made up of atoms, and these are made up of protons, neutrons, and electrons. A chemical element consists of those atoms with a specific number of protons in the nucleus. This number is called the atomic number, as is featured on the Periodic Chart of Elements.

Modern science has revealed that the atom, previously regarded as the smallest par-ticle, can actually be split. Ordinary matter consists of atoms bound together by an electromagnetic force to form molecules. These molecules come together to form solids, liquids and gasses.

A photon is a basic unit of light, and is considered energy. An electron travels near the speed of light. When a photon is absorbed by the atom, the atom gains the photon's energy. The electron uses this energy to jump up to a higher orbit. The photon energy equals the electron energy in a larger orbit, less the electron energy in a smaller orbit. Thus, if a photon strikes an atom, the atom can absorb the photon and its energy only if the photon's energy is exactly equal to the difference between two orbital energies. This enables the jump from the smaller orbit up to the larger orbit, called a *quantum jump*.

Finally, it should be pointed out that all forms and shapes and patterns in the material universe are made up of torsion waves. Torsion waves flow in and out of all physical matter, and atoms are torsion wave generators. The counter rotating phi spiraling elec-tromagnetic (EM) waves in the implosion physics that spiral into the nucleus of the atom, likewise cancel the electromagnetic components of the EM waves and results in a torsion wave.

Torsion waves are energy waves composed of nested phi-spirals of light (that is electro-magnetic radiation), yet they have the capacity to travel far in excess of the speed of light. But actually they don't travel at all, because, in reality, there is no distance traversed. It is analogous to a string on a guitar that strums. There is no actual distance traveled linearly, but the string vibrates in amplitude waves. Are crop circles made by energy transfer via torsion waves pressing down on the crops? Do DNA or cells communicate via tor-sion waves? Is communication the medium for telepathy via torsion waves? Can torsion waves also travel faster than the speed of light, arriving almost instantaneously?

Now that we have reached the essence of who and what we really are, it's time to switch gears and examine the rich tapestry of the human experience on Earth. To begin another examination of the expansive subject matter in this Lifeology section, we need to start at the beginning, at the moment when people first began to conceive a vision of themselves.

< Strangely enough, the symbol for medicine since distant antiquity has been two snakes entwined in a spiral pattern around a staff. Foreshadowing? Ancient knowledge? This coincidence of why DNA looks remarkably similar to an ancient medical symbol has yet to be explained.

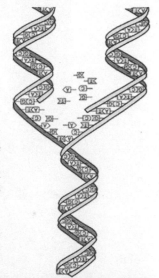

> DNA is the molecule of life. Of the trillions of cells in the human body, each cell contains 46 human chromosomes; two-meter long strands of DNA; three billion DNA subunits known as the bases A, T, C, G; and approximately 30,000 genes coded for proteins that perform most life functions.

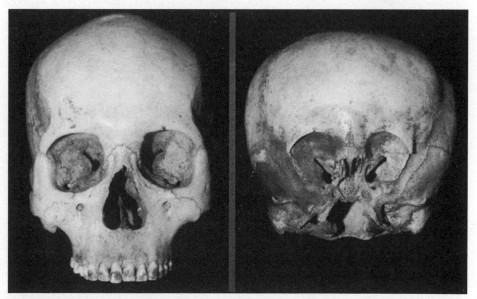

The world-famous Starchild Skull is a bone skull found in 1930. The being lived about 900 years ago and was found buried in a northern Mexico cave. There are over 25 major physical differences between the Starchild (right) and a normal human skull (left). Most of the Starchild differences are not seen in any other humanoid skulls or bones on Earth. Most importantly, the recent research on the Starchild's DNA, in which its entire genome was recovered and sequenced, confirms that its genetics are vastly more distant from humans than are the genetics of chimps or gorillas.

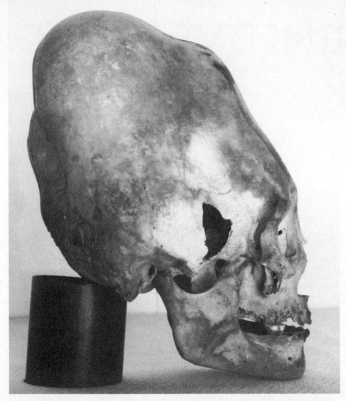

The carbon-14 results for three of the Paracas, Peru, elongated skulls
determined they are 2,350, 2,330 and 2,340 years old. This means
they were pure Paracas Indian, with no genetic Nazca cultural influence. This gives researchers a benchmark for further testing, and for
looking beyond Paracas towards Cusco, Peru, for their origins.

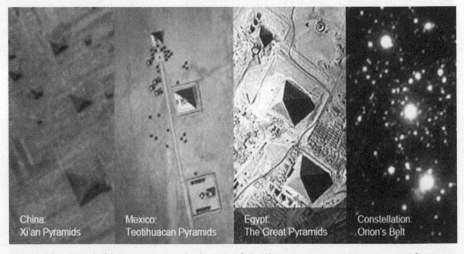

China: Mexico: Egypt: Constellation:
Xi'an Pyramids Teotihuacan Pyramids The Great Pyramids   Orion's Belt

It is truly remarkable to compare the layout of the three most prominent pyramid com-
plexes in China, Mexico and Egypt, and their similarity to the constellation Orion, so
prominent in the Northern Hemisphere night sky.

PRIMITIVE WISDOM

"I am poor and naked, but I am the chief of the nation. We do not want riches but we do want to train our children right. Riches would do us no good. We could not take them with us to the other world. We do not want riches. We want peace and love." —Chief Red Cloud (Sioux)

HOMO *sapien sapiens*, like all other animals, are subject to the continual process of adapting to the limitations of their environment. In the traditional evolution model, humans reached their full behavioral modernity around 50,000 years ago. A new trait emerged when humans ascended to become a creature that could manipulate the environment and become master of the animal kingdom. Ethnologists have often observed that the organized slaughter of members of their own species is virtually unknown among other animal species. Humans' special propensity to kill its own kind, shared to a limited degree with rats and chimpanzees, may be attributed to our ability to adapt in nearly any environment. War started among humans as a territorial instinct within our natural environment. The trait of organized warfare is characteristic of humans alone.

Almost every paleoanthropologist would agree that modern humans evolved in Africa about 200,000 years ago, yet the fossil evidence for the earliest "missing link" is currently non-existent. This may be because of the difficulty of recognizing what differentiates a true modern human in the fossil record, or that such a linking entity ever existed. There are currently many contenders thought to be the earliest offshoots of our species, those who possess a mix of both modern and primitive traits. For some, this means our species once had a greater range of physical variation than today. For other researchers, this means more than one species of *Homo sapien* may have lived in Africa during this time. *Homo sapien*, Latin for "knowing man" or "wise man," is the only living species in the

Homo genus. Neither Neanderthal nor any other proto-human ever created rock art, cave paintings or symbolic artifacts like their "wise" contemporaries. Because our ancestors were the first to create ritualistic art and religious icons, anthropologists are inclined to call our species *Homo spiritualists*, as we were the first to become aware of ourselves.

The word "shaman" comes from the language of the Tungus reindeer herders of the Lake Baikal region in Siberian Russia. Although the roots of Shamanism date back 50,000 years to the Pleistocene Epoch, the term can be applied to all indigenous healing practices worldwide. The Tungus people of Siberia believe a shaman is a person of either sex who can master the spirits in this material world. Tungus shamans claim to introduce spirits into their own bodies, or use their power over other spirits, especially in the interest of helping members of their clan. There are five recognized factors that can enhance a person's shamanic or psychic ability. A potential shaman could have been born genetically predisposed, or suffered a traumatic childhood event, experienced a near death state, sustained a head injury, or experienced some other kind of initiatory illness. These factors still apply in this modern age, and any one of these abilities can shatter a person's programming and distort the *illusion* of modern life. The shamanistic tendency can be described as looking into the common reality humans share and opening themselves to other ways of being proactive in the world. The common human outlook (identified as the *Fourth World*) is resigned to the inevitability of exploitation, parasitic existence, and a dog-eat-dog mentality. Shamans make their connection to the *Fifth World*, a density filled with spirits existing in other dimensions.

OUT OF AFRICA

Ultimately, we are all Africans. Studies of mitochondrial DNA suggest that all human beings are descended from a small population, only a few hundred individuals, that emerged out of Africa at least 60,000 years ago, soon thereafter to populate regions of the Middle East, Europe and Asia. In the ancient astronaut construct (the idea that beings from other planets or galaxies visited and bred with or genetically changed all Earth dwellers in ancient times), all humans emerged from Africa in a similar timeframe, with the potential genetic blending of the Atlantis survivors. Scientists do not understand why this new type of *Homo sapiens* suddenly appeared, or how the change happened, but we can trace our genes back to a single female 150,000-250,000 years ago known as "Mitochondrial Eve." She would have been roughly contemporary with modern humans, whose fossils have been found in Ethiopia near the Omo River and at Hertho. Mitochondrial Eve lived significantly earlier than the out of Africa migration which occurred some 60,000 to 95,000 years ago.

Ancient Sumerian cuneiform tablets and cylinder seals uncovered in modern Iraq, the former kingdom of ancient Babylon, tell the story of ET star gods called the Anunnaki coming to Earth and genetically manipulating humankind, as discussed in Chapter 3, "Blood of the Gods." Only primitive humanoids lived on Earth before the Anunnaki, or if there were even modern humans, they were the offspring of Atlantis survivors. The creation of modern humans seem to be described as a type of cloning and what we would today consider *in vitro* fertilization. The result was a hybrid human with enhanced intellect who could perform the physical worker duties for the "gods." *Homo sapiens* were created and bred as a slave race for the Anunnaki to extract gold from Africa. According to this theory, every single human being on Earth came from some other planetary system. According to the Ancient Astronaut Theory, not one single person on Earth is a "native" inhabitant, but we are derived from 22 root races of DNA, introduced primarily by the Anunnaki. Therefore, not a single human being has "evolved" here on Earth. "*Those from heavens came*" is literally who the *Anunnaki* considered themselves to be. And while the Anunnaki returned to where they came from, the *humans* multiplied and migrated out of Africa to all corners of the Earth.

The earliest written religious texts, as well as the first documented monotheistic religion, also developed in Africa. During the European dark ages, many ancient manuscripts were preserved in African libraries in places such as Alexandria, Ethiopia and Timbuktu. The civilization of ancient Egypt lasted longer than the entire span of what we have come to accept as "recorded history," a period of many thousands of years. During these millennia, the Egyptians conceived a multitude of gods and goddesses, as well as esoteric practices whose meaning and purposes are still being unraveled by researchers. In addition, Egypt was the source of the first true monotheistic religion, developed under the pharaoh Akhenaten. This rich tradition was mostly unknown until the early 19th century, when the Egyptian language was finally deciphered from inscriptions on the Rosetta Stone.

ADVENT OF CREATIVE THINKING

Conventional theories *more or less* assert that in the course of evolution, humans came down from the trees and began to walk upright, which freed our hands to create. And what we created were tools, which we continued to refine. Thus, according to scientists and researchers, what came to differentiate humans from other forms of animals was gaining the ability to walk upright on two legs, and then to invent and use tools. However, it is now widely recognized that other animals, such as the crow, also walk on two legs and use tools to accomplish tasks. What *actually* separates humans from other animals is our ability to express ourselves through symbolism and creativity.

About 40,000 years ago, humans begin to use what is called "lateral thinking." It marked a blossoming period of creativity, with spiritual and religious ideas being introduced *virtually* overnight. At the same time, the incredible paintings of upper Paleolithic Europe, the cave art of North Africa, and the advent of rock art within tribal and indigenous cultures began to appear all around the world, and all dating roughly from the same period.

If the human brain is considered a receiver and decoder of data transmitted through our senses, it is possible then that our *minds* "receive" highly sensitive information from our brains. This could then be processed by our brain transmitter function to perceive realities that are separate from our "normal" experience. If during our regular waking existence we're tuned into "channel normal," can we then alter our state of consciousness by somehow retuning the receiver, and in this way *change the channel*? This is precisely what might be happening as evolution finely tuned our consciousness to allow us a way to access other levels of reality. This can be thought of as a secret doorway inside one's own mind to an awareness of phenomena beyond the physical world of the senses. Most of the time, this doorway is closed to the average person, and we cannot go through it in the normal alert problem-solving state of consciousness, useful and necessary for survival in the physical world. This doorway, however, can access other *free standing realities*, multiple dimensions that are real and do exist, but are outside the capacity of any external instrument that we have created with our science to access. The key to the secret doorway is in the deep subconscious regions of the psyche, and usually accessed with meditation, through which one can move into altered states of consciousness.

According to author Graham Hancock, in his book *Supernatural: Meetings with the Ancient Teachers of Mankind*, "Our brains may be hard wired to focus on daily material reality, but in an altered state of consciousness, we retune the receiver wavelength of the brain and we gain genuine access to other realities, to other dimensions if you like, which are normally closed to us and normally outside the range of our senses, (and) our brain is an instrument that can receive those impressions only in an altered state of consciousness." This then introduces the big question: Is our brain the source of consciousness, or the vehicle for consciousness? If it is the vehicle for conscious thought and perception, then of course consciousness can survive death as shamans have long contended, because the death of the brain is simply the death of the vehicle carrying our conscious existence, and not the death of consciousness itself. This suggests that consciousness is just one of many signals our brain receives and interprets.

HARD-WIRED TO BELONG

What triggers people to kill one another? Unfortunately, human history is splattered with blood. In the dozen or so wars in the 20th century alone, 160 million people died. Although armed conflict still dominates the headlines, fewer people actually are fighting and dying in wars. Apparently there were fewer combat deaths in the last decade than at any other time in the last 100 years. Is this a move in the right direction towards less lethal wars, or just a result of better field hospitals? More importantly, is war an inevitable and unavoidable aspect of the human experience? Is it a natural state of human affairs, or an aberration of modern humans that goes against our hard wired longing to belong?

If we look far back to prehistory, to the Neolithic or even the Paleolithic eras, we will find very little if any evidence of war. The living sites of Stone Age people are remarkably free of mass graves, fortified sites, and depictions of war in cave art. Also missing are images of shields, which consistently arise as defensive weapons when people are attacked with spears. No one can determine unequivocally that there was no warfare 20,000 or 50,000 years ago, only that there is little or no evidence of any. So can we abolish war, just as we fought to abolish slavery or eradicate deadly diseases, or will we continue fighting each other to settle our differences with ever more sophisticated weapons and techniques? Maybe if we can remember our sense of belonging to a single human race, recall our primitive wisdom, and harken back to when our differences could be overcome with superior skills of reasoning, the concept of warfare, like smallpox, will become extinct.

Recently scientists discovered mirror neurons in all primates. Mirror neurons enable us to experience another's plight as if we were experiencing it ourselves, similar to empathy. Several studies suggest that humans are not wired for aggression, violence, and self-interest. Explained as a byproduct of our hierarchical oppression, instead, we are hard-wired for collaboration and companionship, as studies show our main objective is to *belong*. And as consciousness changes throughout history, we evolve, and we extend our empathetic ties. Today's technology allows people around the globe to interact, even furthering our potential for empathic connection. This raises the fundamental question ... If there is such a thing as *collective consciousness among the human race*, isn't it possible for us, as sentient beings, to perceive how other humans are feeling—and collectively act from that more feeling place? Some would call this compassion.

In a way, the last uncontacted tribes in the Amazon Basin, or the deep valleys of New Guinea, are part of our modern consciousness, as we are a part of their primitive one. And our behavior demonstrates that, as a collective civilization, we are no more advanced than the lowest common denominator. Perhaps this perceived life is an aspect of what the Australian Aboriginals referred to as *dreamtime*, or the Indians called the illusion *maya*. Seemingly, even the most advanced space traveling human is connected to the last Stone Age tribesman, and all are part of the dream. Given the weight of evidence in favor of our similarities (rather than differences), we really are all one being, and are able to tap into the mental capacities of others in our species group, similar to what has been observed within animal groups.

CAVES OF SACRED ART

The valleys of the Dordogne and Vézère Rivers comprise a picturesque region in south-central France that is sprinkled with deep caves and subterranean streams. When human skeletons were unearthed from inside some of the caves in 1868, what soon followed was a windfall of archaeological evidence from the Paleolithic era. Most remarkable were the paintings that adorned the caves. Not only because of their age, but also because of their exquisite coloring, and the skill with which they were drawn. A myriad of Stone Age tools, weapons, arrowheads, and bone carvings have also been discovered in the French caves.

The earliest artistic renderings in Europe can be found on the walls and ceilings of French and Spanish caverns. They represent a concern for hunting, fertility, and regeneration. Although most cave art is found in the Vèzére and Dordogne River Valleys of France, along with the Pyrenees and the Cantabrian Mountain regions of Spain, cave paintings and engravings appear throughout Europe. Apart from animal representations, wall art in Europe also includes abstract images such as lines, dots, and a combination of these elements. Human figures are rarely depicted, with the exception of the carved "Venus" figurines that are found in many prehistoric caves. There are hand stencils in some caves, formed by painting around a spread-out hand, and these are thought to represent male and female symbols used in fertility and initiation rites. Footmarks and fingerprints of young children have been found at certain sites, suggesting rituals for younger members learning about their adult roles. Some images appear to represent people wearing masks, animal skins, or antlers. These animal disguises may be camouflage for hunting, or ceremonial dress worn by shaman during hunting rituals.

The most famous of all the Dordogne Valley caves is called Lascaux. Paintings found there are dated to the last Ice Age in Europe 17,000 years ago, and are considered to be the finest prehistoric works in existence. Included in the famous Lascaux cave are five or six identifiable styles of rendering, including abundant images of bison, mammoth, and horses, plus the largest known prehistoric painting in existence—a 5.5 meter-long bull rendering with an astonishingly expressive face and head. Due to mold and deterioration from body heat and the warm breath of frequent visitors the original Lascaux Cave was completely closed to the public in 1963.

High in a topographical area of the Dordogne Valley, in another amazing cavern called Rouffignac Cave, is a three-level maze of corridors and galleries. Only the upper level, the largest of the three, shows evidence that it was explored and frequented by prehistoric artists. Rouffignac Cave is best known for its prolific representations of large mammals, particularly woolly mammoths, bison, horses, and woolly rhinoceros. The Rouffignac Cave was decorated in the Late Magdalenian period of the Paleolithic era, around 13,000 BCE, a relative latecomer.

Most of the Paleolithic caves with paintings and decorated rock shelters in France date back 23,000 years or more. The oldest are 32,000 years old and are located in Chauvet-Pont-d'Arc Cave, only re-discovered in 1994. These oldest renderings were created by people in the Aurignacian culture, who lived 28,000 to 40,000 years ago in this part of France. Confirming the radiocarbon dating of both the human and animal occupants, recent studies establish that the Chauvet Cave paintings are the oldest and the most elaborate ever discovered in France, challenging our current knowledge of human cognitive evolution.

According to new dating tests, a series of seals painted more than 42,000 years ago in the Cave of Nerja in Málaga, Spain, are regarded as the first paintings ever created by humans. Until recently, archeologists thought that the oldest art was made by modern humans during the Aurignacian period, an Upper Palaeolithic culture, located in Europe and southwest Asia, and according to radiocarbon dating lasted approximately 47,000 to 41,000 years ago. But the Nerja paintings are much older and far more primitive than the 32,000-year-old paintings found in Chauvet-Pont-d'Arc Cave, for example as featured in the film *Cave of Forgotten Dreams*.

ABORIGINAL SONG LINES OF AUSTRALIA

Eons ago, the Aboriginal people of Australia—the oldest unchanged variety of *Homo sapien sapiens* and the oldest surviving intact culture—visualized the *planetsphere*. In their collective consciousness, known as "dreamtime," the Aboriginal people have the capacity to communicate telepathically. Creating a rhythm with two sticks and a hollow branch know as a didgeridoo (the oldest musical instrument in the world), tribes come together in a unity dance ritual. Using these primal instruments, the Aboriginal people can dance themselves into a deep trance-like state, and invoke the energy of Australian sacred sites. The Aboriginal people recognized the Earth's ley lines, named them "song lines" in accordance with their musical instincts, and invoked visualizations of the landscape not seen under normal conditions.

The Australian Aborigines make strong use of their ancient dreamtime, a lore that even alerts them to future events. It is a lore handed down by "Wandgina," a sort of female deity. In the Australian outback, generations of Aboriginal people have gathered continuously at Ayer's Rock, or Uluru, for 30,000 years. They instinctively followed the song lines, or *ley lines* as they are called in Europe, and traveled great distances to reach their destination.

At certain points on the planet's surface, "ether" flows stronger than at other places. The ether flows in a set grid across the surface of the planet, much like a lattice of energy lines. There are some places where the etheric energy makes contact with the landscape. Here the aboriginal people assembled for ritual events, and also created a vast array of paintings. Interestingly, they seemingly did not see themselves as painters, but rather allowed the "hand of the spirit" to guide their brush strokes.

For thousands of years, native peoples followed ancient paths to these energy spots, and they became their sacred places. Primitive shrines were first constructed as physical manifestations, on locations of etheric intersections. At these *sacred places* in Europe, ancient megalithic stones were erected—literally inserted into the Earth's surface. These huge stones stimulate the flow of etheric energy much like an acupuncturist who inserts needles into the skin of a patent stimulates the life force energy in a human body. There were also several stone circles in Australia, some of which were destroyed by modern nuclear testing. Australian Aboriginals, much like the Stonehenge Druids of ancient Britain, knew where etheric energy lines of the planet were located, and these locations are where the first evidence of organized worship were performed.

The Australian Aboriginals are closely related to the primitive tribal groups living on the neighboring island of New Guinea. There are some 800 living languages in New Guinea alone, some as different as the English language is to Chinese. Jagged mountains isolate population groups, and some tribes continue to wage war against each other. A few tribes remain uncontacted by the modern world, living their lives in Stone Age obscurity, and unaware of others living in skyscrapers and venturing into space. The "Cargo Cult" began near here, when primitive people started worshipping falling World War II cargo boxes that they thought were delivered by the gods. *How could they know differently?* These tribes still retain a strong belief in the spirit world. New Guinea hunters will not roam in to certain areas for fear of provoking "bad spirits," for example.

THE CARGO CULT

With the onset of World War II in the South Pacific, vast numbers of ships and materials began pouring into the once completely isolated islands around and near New Guinea. First the Japanese came, and later, the Americans and British came with radios, manufactured clothing, fine furniture, warfare armaments, inflatable boats, medicines, canned food, and much more. The natives of these islands—most of whom were still living in Stone Age obscurity—were overwhelmed by the material, wealth, and the "magic" tools these foreign visitors brought with them to their land. On some South Pacific islands in the 1940s, the native tribes came to believe that the Western manufactured materials, the "cargo," had been created by divine spirits *in the sky* and were intended for their people. They objected to the unfairness of sending such bounty to white people alone, and formed what were called "cargo cults" to enlist the gods to their cause. Meanwhile, on other islands, the native people worshipped the American individuals who flew in the cargo. It is hard to overestimate the power these ships, men, and goods had over the imagination of previously uncontacted people. Just think of how a smart phone would appear to people in Europe only 100 years ago. As futurist author Arthur C. Clarke noted, "Any sufficiently advanced technology is indistinguishable from magic."

When the war ended, the rest of the world rejoiced, and the ships with their crews and materials stopped arriving. The Pacific Islanders were quickly plunged back into isolation. The tribes had assumed that the arrival of these blessings had been a gift from their gods, so what could it mean when the gifts disappeared? Gone was the steady supply of medicines, trinkets, shiny things, food, and clothing. Perhaps they had displeased their gods. Maybe they could find a way to call them back if they acted faithfully. They were certain that all they had to do was what the outsiders had done and the gods would come back. They emulated the language, customs and behaviors of the Japanese, Dutch, Americans, and British who were now long gone. They constructed crude approximations of landing strips, desks, phones, radios, and airplanes in an attempt to summon the gods. They sat at their tables and moved bits of bark or scrap paper around, picking up the "phone" and barking out orders before going down to the beach and waiting for the shipments to arrive. They thought that their activities would call their gods back to action and they would again drop "cargo" from the skies. As the years passed without any response from their gods, they began to search for better solutions, move emulated items around, or build better models, and separating from each other when disagreements arose. The result was dozens of different unique interpretations in different locations. For example, there are three major denominations of the cargo cults on the small island of Tanna alone, in the nation of Vanuatu.

Along with worshipping the cargo itself, certain Pacific Island cultures started a religion called "John Frum." In the 1940s, the name John was among the most common first name of males in the United States. When the American soldiers introduced themselves as "John, from" whichever state they were from, the natives only retained the first two words. So "John Frum" was just an average American man who became a sort of Jesus-like figure speaking to these primitive people. A decade or so later, the phenomenon was studied and written upon by celebrated anthropologist Margaret Mead.

Lifting this phenomenon to modern times, what would a "cargo cult" look like to the most advanced peoples of the world today? Let's consider that advanced life in any world would exist in an infinitely complex matrix, that, while similar or parallel to other systems, would nevertheless be unique to the extent that jumping from one world to another would be confusing at best—for either the visitor or the visited. Apparitions, activities to appease the gods, symbolic representations, and seemingly confusing ritual activities seem out of place in this Modern Age. Yet, for some current "civilized" nations, wouldn't a UFO sighting today, together with varied, confused and incredulous reactions, have some parallels to the mysterious cargo floating down on parachutes to the primitive peoples of the South Pacific 70 years ago? At the other end of the spectrum, for those with open minds, perhaps the gods of old were really ancient visitors from other worlds with "magical" technologies that we simply couldn't understand. Perhaps organized religions, in general, are interpretations of incomprehensible and misunderstood activities observed long ago. In other words, perhaps we are in no position, even today, to look down on cargo cult mentality. Indeed, our society's myths and superstitions may be the result of such "other worldly" interactions.

SHAMANISM

Shamanism is said to be humankind's oldest religion. Shamanism in practice is used to heal and enlighten, employing ceremonial activities which can include rhythmic music, trance dancing, and mind altering drugs that can lead to mythic journeys into the subconscious. Shamans have what can only be called *spiritual* experiences. They have these experiences in alternate states of consciousness. For them, the experiences they have, the beings they encounter, the deceased ancestors they meet, are merely personal experiences that do not require any faith at all. It is as unique and as natural an experience as seeing one's own fingerprint.

One theme that emerges from a study of comparative shamanism is the *universal nature* of the experience. A shaman in the Amazon rainforest, and his counterpart in Siberia, seem to experience the same phenomenon—an ecstasy of enlightenment that is obtained when the soul leaves the body in search of a vision. The vision becomes the bedrock upon which his or her life will progress, and is guided by an animal spirit observed in the vision—the eye of an eagle, the wing of a hawk, the swiftness of a gazelle, the strength of a bear. These are the riches sought. When Native American adolescents were sent away on a "vision quest," members of the tribe requested that the child become a shaman in their newly-acquired role as an adult. The animal spirit seen in the adolescent's vision quest would become the protective guide for the individual, and would also often become the adult's name for the rest of their lives.

Animism is the concept that the entire universe is alive. It is a belief central to shamanistic spirituality. Animism encompasses the belief that there is no real separation between the spiritual, physical, or material worlds. Spirits exist everywhere, not only in humans, but also in other animals, plants, rocks, and in natural phenomena such as thunder, lightning, and geographic features, including mountains, rivers, or other entities within the natural environment. Animism ascribes a spirit to mountains, rivers, crystals, trees, stones, the heavenly bodies, the Earth, and even features in the sky. It can be seen in a tree, a post, a pillar, and the hollow of a rock. These are the *seat of invisible souls*. These spirits are perceived and interpreted by shamans.

Another theme prevalent in shamanism is the sacred underworld, a realm in which an entire whole host of spirits reside. A cave under a sacred mountain is a common theme, or similarly, a water spring or cavern vent are often seen as entrances to the underworld. With the advent of religion, the mountain became represented artificially, replete with a mythical entranceway to the underworld, called a *sipapu* by the Native American Hopi. The sacred mountain is often topped with a temple where a shaman could commune directly with deities in our reality. But when the sacred mountain was created in the form of a pyramid or mound, the same process occurred, that is, the internal chamber became a portal to the spiritual other world. This parallel reality was described as a fairyland, Hades, the Underworld, Middle Earth, Hollow Earth or even the Other Side. It was in these sacred caves under the mountain where mystical initiation rites occurred.

THE AMAZING DOGON TRIBE

The mythology passed down from the Dogon tribesmen of Mali in western Africa contains astronomical knowledge that the native people could neither have learned by themselves, nor guessed. Obviously, the researchers say, a more advanced civilization must have told them about the peculiar nature of the Sirius star system, for example. These fascinating Dogon legends speak of celestial movements, and even describe Jupiter's four moons and Saturn's rings, yet these planetary features were not observed by human beings until the invention of the telescope. They speak of the star Sirius and a pair of invisible companions. One of the objects makes a 50-year circle around the sun Sirius, the legends declare, and is composed of a metal that is made of the heaviest matter in the universe. Astronomers have discovered that such an object, called "Sirius-B," does exist, but only the most sophisticated and sensitive instruments can detect it—instruments that, of course, were unavailable to the "primitive" Dogon people.

In addition to their legends of celestial objects the Dogon exhibited other advanced cultural traits. A characteristic of the Dogon and certain African tribes is their unique method of nonviolent resolution for troubled clan members. When someone in the tribe does something hurtful or wrong, they take the person to the center of town, and the entire tribe comes and surrounds the person in a supportive, nonthreatening way. For two days they'll tell the person every good thing he or she has ever done. The tribe believes that every human being comes into the world as good, each of us desiring safety, love, peace, and happiness. But sometimes in the pursuit of these things, people make mistakes. The community sees misdeeds as a cry for help. They band together for the sake of their fellow clan member in a show of solidarity, to reconnect the person with their true nature, to remind them who they *really are*. Within this powerful compassionate energy, it is believed the person will fully remember the truth from which they are temporarily disconnected. The ancient Tibetans had a similar approach to those displaying anti-social behavior by "killing them" with kindness.

LIVE TO LET LIVE

Being in touch with our *so-called* primitive instincts may be the key to unlocking greater happiness, and even toward obtaining higher personal potential. Have you ever had the premonition that someone you know is about to call you, and then actually does? Parapsychologist Dr. Rupert Sheldrake claims "telephone telepathy" really does exist, and the common phenomenon is not just a coincidence. Australian Aboriginals and other primitive people have exhibited a marked proclivity for communication by mental telepathy.

In the naturalistic world in which nearly every person now finds themselves, a new term might be "survival of the luckiest." Those born into countries with the potential for upward mobility are the lucky ones, and becoming increasingly rare. The vast majority of people around the world have very little opportunity to advance beyond their parent's social status. Another way to gauge survival of the luckiest is whether a people has been contacted or not. Yet, who ultimately are the "lucky" earthlings? For those last few uncontacted tribes remaining on Earth, "freedom from want," is a central philosophical theme. For example, the Andaman Island tribal people have no word for the three W's: When, Worry, and Want.

Another amazing aspect of the Andaman islanders is their ability to interpret animal behavior. They reported that the animals told the tribal people of the Andaman Islands to flee the 2004 Indian Ocean tsunami, and as a result, not one of their tribe died from the catastrophic waves. At the same time, many educated folks are still quick to call these people "uncivilized" or even "savages"—even though they have no debt, no corruption, no jails, no organized warfare, no chemical pollution, and no need to be governed like ignorant children. They also have far fewer fights, theft, jealousy, and murder per capita than their civilized counterparts in India and Bangladesh—only a few hundred miles offshore.

In the remote French Polynesia colony island group in the South Pacific called the Marquesas, a small group of people live a mostly Stone Age lifestyle. They go fishing, they build huts in cooperation with others in the tribe, they barter, they share, and by all accounts, they live a happy life. Yet they have no word for "work." Despite this Stone Age lifestyle, the people of the Marquesas are not willing to lose their *primitive* ways. They would rather die early from preventable diseases, for example than lose the way of their ancestors.

CANNIBALISM REMAINS

Not everything about living a primitive lifestyle can be glamorized. Some primitive practices are rather grisly, and comparable to modern technological horrors. Outside of horror films, cannibalism is virtually unheard of in our Modern Age. Yet the Korowai people of Papua New Guinea are one of the last known surviving tribes to eat other humans as a cultural practice. Numbering about 3,000, they live in an area so remote that they were unaware of the existence of anyone outside themselves until 1970. It is said the Korowai continue the practice of cannibalism and reportedly, eat the brain immediately while it is still warm.

The idyllic island Nuku Hiva in the French Polynesia Marquesa Islands, featured in the stories of Herman Melville, author of *Moby Dick*, has a population of just over 2,000 and also has a history of cannibalism. However, the practice was believed to have ceased after the introduction of Christianity. Those same islanders who have no word for work apparently still have a word for cannibalism. A 40 year-old around-the-world yachtsman named Stefan Ramin, from Hamburg, Germany, disappeared in October, 2011 while on a goat hunting trip with natives, shortly after dropping anchor at the remote tropical island of Nuku Hiva. After a week of searches, charred human remains, dental fillings, and burned clothes were found near a campfire in a remote valley on the island, confirming fears that the German tourist was attacked and eaten by cannibals.

NEW WORLD INVASION

The European explorers who discovered and "claimed" the New World for the Holy Father, the pope, and the kings of Spain, Portugal, and later Holland, England and France, seemingly never gave much thought to the impact they would have on the indigenous cultures. European powers benefited greatly from the property freely acquired from the native inhabitants. As such, the native inhabitants were never consulted or asked for their permission to become a part of the *domain of European nations*. There was never a treaty signed with the soldiers and priests sent to acquire territory who arrived to acquire wealth, and in order to advance their foreign interests.

The net result of the "discovery" of the New World, which of course was not really new, as it had been around as long as any other continent, had a larger population than Europe, and by all historical accounts, became a total disaster for the longtime inhabitants. It eventually resulted in hundreds of indigenous cultures being eradicated, with approximately 100 million indigenous people killed by disease and war brought upon them by "aliens." Likewise, about 100 million people from the Ivory Coast of western Africa were enslaved, relocated, or murdered by Europeans in an effort to replace the labor force of the slaughtered indigenous population in the Western Hemisphere. Nearly all of the priceless literature, linguistic heritage, history, cultural and artistic artifacts of the Western Hemisphere were systematically destroyed. And lastly, most of the gold and gems mined over a period of thousands of years by indigenous people were stolen and shipped off by a handful of greedy, filthy, disease-ridden, superstitious, and tragically misguided adventurers from Europe who, with few exceptions, apparently squandered it on mindless self-indulgences.

Because of the pre-existence of millions of people living in the Americas prior to the European arrival, the King of Spain may have had a certain amount of fear at the prospect of God becoming angry at him for all the murder, theft and mayhem he endorsed in the New World. He sought redemption in 1493, when he persuaded Pope Alexander VI to sanction an official proclamation intended to dissolve the stain of bloody culpability from the King's own immortal soul. This document, called "The Requirement," was intended to be read, whether translated into the native language of the inhabitants or not, to the citizens of every foreign nation just prior to their conquest. The gist of the proclamation was to inform the soon to be vanquished people that their lands were being "donated" to Spain. A few centuries later, the U.S. Government made similar justifications to steal Native American lands with the proclamation of "Manifest Destiny."

NATIVE AMERICAN CODE OF ETHICS

Despite the horrific treatment dealt to virtually every native culture in the Americas, the indigenous people remained ethical to themselves and introspective in their own ways. Christal Quintasket, a Salish Native American who lived from 1888 to 1936 said: "Everything on the Earth has a purpose, every disease an herb to cure it, and every person a mission. This is the Indian theory of existence." Even during their monumental crossroads in history, Native Americans looked for meaning as to why they should be dealt such unfortunate circumstances. Although fierce enemies to the expanding colonists in North America as they defended their territories, the Indians were known as "Noble Savages" because of their high moral code. In this Native American "code of ethics," which still remains relevant today, it is clear the Native Americans were able to forgive their enemies and live sustainably. May we also gain from their primitive wisdom.

1. *Rise with the sun to pray. Pray alone. Pray often. The Great Spirit will listen, if you only speak.*
2. *Be tolerant of those who are lost on their path. Ignorance, conceit, anger, jealousy and greed stem from a lost soul. Pray that they will find guidance.*
3. *Search for yourself, by yourself. Do not allow others to make your path for you. It is your road and yours alone. Others may walk it with you, but no one can walk it for you.*
4. *Treat the guests in your home with much consideration. Serve them the best food, give them the best bed and treat them with respect and honor.*
5. *Do not take what is not yours whether from a person, a community, the wilderness or from a culture. It was not earned nor given. It is not yours.*
6. *Respect all things that are placed upon this Earth—whether it is people or plants.*
7. *Honor other people's thoughts, wishes and words. Never interrupt another or mock or rudely mimic them. Allow each person the right to personal expression.*
8. *Never speak of others in a bad way. The negative energy that you put out into the universe will multiply when it returns to you.*
9. *All persons make mistakes. And all mistakes can be forgiven.*
10. *Bad thoughts cause illness of the mind, body and spirit. Practice optimism.*
11. *Nature is not for us, it is a part of us. They are part of your worldly family.*

12. *Children are the seeds of our future. Plant love in their hearts and water them with wisdom and life's lessons. When they are growing, give them space to grow.*
13. *Avoid hurting the hearts of others. The poison of your pain will return to you.*
14. *Be truthful at all times. Honesty is the test of one's will within this universe.*
15. *Keep yourself balanced. Your Mental self, Spiritual self, Emotional self, and Physical self—all need to be strong, pure and healthy. Work out the body to strengthen the mind. Grow rich in spirit to cure emotional ills.*
16. *Make conscious decisions as to who you will be and how you will react. Be responsible for your own actions.*
17. *Respect the privacy and personal space of others. Do not touch the personal property of others—especially sacred and religious objects. This is forbidden.*
18. *Be true to yourself first. You cannot nurture and help others if you cannot nurture and help yourself first.*
19. *Respect others' religious beliefs. Do not force your belief on others.*
20. *Share your good fortune with others. Participate in charity.*

AN END TO MONEY

Hunter-gatherer societies typically enjoyed a gift economy in which trade and barter developed only with people external to the tribe or band. Everyone within the band was treated as a family member. Whatever was available was shared without expectation of reciprocal exchange. The story of the rise of social complexity is also the story of the gradual dwindling of the gift economy and the expansion of the scope of trade—a story that culminates in our situation today, in which the market mediates nearly all categories of transactions between and among humans, sometimes even within families. Even many relatively complex societies of the past such as the ancient Egyptian and Incan civilizations managed to do without money. However, this new tool, wherever it appeared, served to facilitate and accelerate trade.

Since money serves several possible functions—a store of value, a measure of value, a medium of exchange and a standard deferred payment—in some cases individual societies have used two or more forms of money simultaneously. Monetary history took a decisive turn with the emergence of banking in Europe during the Middle Ages. Since traveling traders were frequently robbed of their coins or metal ingots, they took to depositing their metallic currency in the strongboxes of silversmiths and goldsmiths, and carried redeemable receipts instead. Gradually these receipts came to be regarded as being equivalent to the metal itself. This was the advent of the first paper money. Meanwhile, goldsmiths and silversmiths discovered that it was possible to issue receipts for metal coins which they did not actually possess—a practice that would eventually give rise to fiat currencies and fractional reserve banking. Fiat currencies did not appear in the West in any significant quantity until the 19th century, when governments and national banks began issuing notes that were not backed by any precious metal coinage. It is amazing how far civilization has descended since the age of the gift economy.

IT ALL BEGINS WITH GOLD

For decades, the faint remnants of an ancient city have been seen by people as they have flown over southern Africa. The expansive location, about 240 kilometers inland, west of the port city Maputo, Mozambique in a remote area of South Africa is near ancient gold mines. The remains of this huge metropolis measures, by conservative estimates, about 2,400 square kilometers. Researchers consider it to be part of an even larger community that is about 16,000 square kilometers, and it appears to have been constructed from 160,000 to 200,000 BCE. Once the ruins were examined, the researchers were anxious to place the lost civilization in a historical perspective. Because there were no organic materials sufficient for carbon-14 dating, various rocks were tested because they were covered with a patina that looked very old. The ancient dates were also calculated by a stone circle called Adam's Calendar, whose primary alignment is based on the rise of Orion 160,000 years ago, as it would have been seen when on the horizon.

Local farmers were long aware of the mysterious "circles," and it was simply assumed that they were created by some indigenous people in the past. The circular ruins, spread over an enormous region, can only be truly appreciated from the air or through modern satellite imaging. Many of them have almost completely eroded or have been covered by the movement of soil from farming and weather-related erosion. According to researcher Michael Tellinger: "The photographs, artifacts and evidence we have accumulated point unquestionably to a lost and never-before-seen civilization that predates all others—not by just a few hundred years, or a few thousand years, but many thousands of years. These discoveries are so staggering that they will not easily be digested by the mainstream historical and archaeological fraternity, as we have already experienced. It will require a complete paradigm shift in how we view our human history."

Looking at the entire metropolis from above, it becomes obvious that this was a well-planned community developed by a highly evolved civilization. The area is significant because thousands of ancient gold mines that have been discovered there throughout the past 500 years, and pointing to a vanished civilization that lived, and mined for gold in this part of the world, for thousands of years. Even today, the largest gold producing area of the world is Witwatersrand, in the same region where the ancient metropolis is found. The number of prehistoric gold mines in the vicinity suggests that gold mining is the reason these communities were established and occupied for thousands of years. Also found are stoneworks of terraced agriculture that closely resemble many left behind by the Inca settlements of Peru. There are also roads, some extending almost 200 kilometers, that connect the various communities, and they are considered the oldest structures ever built by humans on Earth. As we saw in the "Blood of the Gods" chapter, those who study the ancient astronaut construct claim the Anunnaki were in Africa to excavate gold and crafted genetically modified humans to do the hard labor.

MODERN SELF-REGULATING TRIBES

Fast forward to our Modern Age and we find some "civilized" people who are seeking to get back to our roots and live like our ancestors. The recently popularized "Cave Man Diet" and the "Cave Man Workout" are examples of those looking to duplicate a long lost lifestyle, sometimes with promising results. There is also a trend to join with other people of a like mind who want to recreate a more egalitarian society. These groups are called "self-regulating tribes," and they are individuals within a group dynamic who live by their own rules.

At first thought, it seems that a self-regulating cultural lifestyle in the United States would be impossible, but this is not the case. In Kalalau Valley on the island of Kauai, Hawaii, and along the north end of Baker Beach, in San Francisco, California, two different self-regulating "tribes" continue to meet regularly, play sports together, engage in lively discussions and share resources. They are both nudist societies, that practice barter, or use the gift economy, and to a degree, both operate out of sight of local law enforcement. This is not to say they are outside of police jurisdiction, but that they live *out of sight* and attempt to create a world of their choosing. Federal and state laws apply, however, as both are within parklands and nature reserves. But in the absence of authority, these groups have organized organically as self-policing and internally regulated micro-societies, if only for an afternoon. Sometimes strong and charismatic leaders oversee the society, but these individuals can be resented by those shunned from the group. Like any community dynamic, there always seems to be a village fool, but rather than being shunned, this individual can teach the group more about compassion. Another common dynamic is resource sharing. One person cannot consume a hunted pig by him or herself, or would want to eat a whole pineapple alone, so sharing equally has become the practice.

Wreck Beach in British Columbia, Canada, is another example of a self-regulating tribe. Located on the University of British Columbia property, but in the city of Vancouver, Wreck Beach is a very popular nude beach. It's a three kilometer-long area on the tip of a peninsula where debris from several shipwrecks can still be found. Because drug use and outdoor food preparation are illegal, the surrounding local population watches for police patrols to alert the community. This can be a challenge, because on hot days there can be 2,000 or more beach dwellers. Police come in on hovercraft and bust drug dealers, but there are usually far too many nudists to make any arrests, and the beach has now been designated "clothing optional." There's a half hour walk on a trail to get down to the beach, and word usually gets ahead that the cops are walking in, providing another aspect of the group's "self-regulating" status. Vendors of various types live on the beach and prosper during the summer season with no permits.

There are also larger spontaneous gatherings based on group harmony and without a central leader. Some examples in the United States are the Rainbow Gatherings during the 4th of July weekend, and the Critical Mass renegade bicycle rides in most metropolitan cities. No one is in charge, for the most part, they operate "illegally," and both are self-policing. Gatherings like these bring people together to enjoy community music, exercise, and discussion among peers. An example is a recent conversation at Baker Beach that focused on the merits of becoming a vegetarian. Most of the people involved in the discussion, including this author, were not vegetarians, yet the philosophical question was raised that if it were possible to replicate any kind of meat perfectly, would you switch over? That is, what would be your decision if there were no perceivable difference in the texture, taste, nutritional value and cost of a substitute "faux meat?" Would you then do it for the ethical, environmental and health benefits? Most participating in the discussion agreed they would. One friend, a professional ornithologist and advocate for native species, was an unlikely dissenter. He enjoyed fishing for salmon, but did acknowledge that their stock was greatly depleted. When asked if he would do it in recognition to the animals being abused by humans, he reconsidered and said yes. Other factors entering into the decision were how one would rank an animal's ability to communicate with its own as a measure of intelligence. Recent research with animal species, including those we eat, indicate remarkable abilities to communicate using various senses. Therefore, it makes sense to rethink our relationship with animals. One might also consider that cattle ranching takes 1/3 of all non-tundra land use and produces 1/5 of all methane greenhouse gas. Clearly, industrialized animal husbandry is not in our best long-term interest. Cultured meat solves these problems. In the spirit of primitive wisdom, as humans have been doing for eons of time, gatherings and meaningful conversations such as these help people better understand themselves and each other.

Lastly, let's not forget that one of the most important assets in any emergency situation is community. If you have friends or neighbors that you can depend upon, they are an invaluable asset in times of crisis. Time spent building bonds of community now can greatly pay off during any resource-scarcity dilemma. A tight-knit community is considered essential for survival in any scenario involving the collapse of society, or a prolonged disaster scenario. Emulating the wisdom of primitive people may be an expression of our modern selves coming full circle.

< The Tree of Knowledge of Good and Evil is a tree described in the Bible's *Book of Genesis*. Eating its fruit was forbidden, because eating of it brought knowledge of life and death. In the same way that Adam and Eve, seen here, gained knowledge after eating the fruit from the tree, understanding the structure and function of DNA has provided much knowledge about life, death and evolution.

> Wandjina petroglyphs and paintings from Kimberley, Australia, possibly representing alien beings or gods. Dated about 5,000 years old. There are many common links between prehistoric Australia and ancient Egypt.

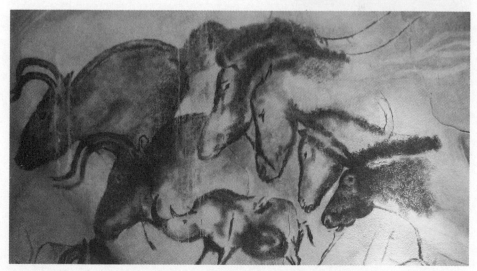

The Chauvet Cave is located in the Ardeche region of southern France. It became famous in 1994 after three speleologists discovered that its walls were richly decorated with Paleolithic artwork. The cavern floor preserved the footprints of animals and the original human artists. The uncharacteristically large cave contained the fossilized remains of many animals, including those that are now extinct. The quality, quantity, and condition of the artwork found on its walls has been called spectacular. The Chauvet Cave is regarded as one of the most significant prehistoric art sites in the world.

< This stick and wattle "airplane" was made by South Pacific islanders to invoke the gods to continue dropping cargo boxes full of supplies on their island. Every religion in the world has stories of advanced beings arriving from the sky bringing knowledge and gifts. All have been altered to better mold the faithful into obedient servants. Should the activities of the primitive tribespeople of the South Pacific, and their interpretation of the "Cargo Cult," be viewed any differently?

< Cave paintings from the Sego Canyon in Utah show very curious entities. Estimated to have been painted in 5,500 BCE, the various images found here include those said to depict an ancient encounter with aliens after a crash landing. Archaeologists, however, are more certain they illustrate mythical or spiritual figures.

< This cave painting from Val Camonica, Italy, is estimated to be about 12,000 years old. It appears to depict two beings in protective space suits with helmets, holding strange implements.

< The crimes of the conquering oppressors against the indigenous peoples of the world should never be forgotten. Their innocence and primitive wisdom was discarded in the name of "progress." Today the chains are no longer made of iron, but we now have slavery mechanisms such as the global economy, and the mind control object called television. The devices of power and corruption follow us into the modern day.

RETHINKING HISTORY

"History is a Mississippi of lies." –Voltaire

PART of the modern esoteric alternative narrative will involve a total rethinking of history as we know it. We already suspect that history as taught in Western schools is not only rife with ignorance but a highly censored version of what really occurred on Earth, both long ago and in the short term. In the myopic, edited version, humans went through a long evolutionary process from monkey to man, then civilization simply "began" in Mesopotamia around 7,000 years ago, split into different branches, yet somehow all civilizations are "junior" to the West. Based on overwhelming archaeological and historical evidence, however, it becomes clear that there were advanced civilizations on Earth over 14,000 years ago, and possibly much longer. From communications about our ancient origins, to different versions of Christianity, there is much about our history that has not been disclosed. Perhaps opening the Vatican library to international scholars would be a good place to start.

There has been a long standing accusation that humans are not aware of their own true history on Earth. What if we could reexamine the history of civilization through a different lens? What if we looked at all the evidence, photos, testimonies, and weird discoveries about our mysterious past, including lost worlds, mysterious civilizations and ancient technology? Would the results alter the collective opinion of who we are? What of the many enlightened masters who have walked the Earth to help advance the causes of humanity? What have they taught us that still applies today? If we've forgotten our life story on Earth, how can we proceed forward into the future when we don't truly understand our past?

Research of precursors like Lloyd Pye, Mauro Biglino and R.A. Boulay into anthropology show us an entirely different historical view of humankind. They suggest that we were a slave race engineered by the gods, and not evolved from apes. Over the decades, there have been many strange discoveries, although most of them have been conveniently covered up, or the evidence has mysteriously been lost. Taken together with our perceptions, our human biology, knowledge of past lives, the potential of game changing technology, and simply a better understanding of ourselves, it would appear our history books need a major revision. Let's examine the esoteric view of history, first by looking at a few accomplishments of ancient technology that still have experts scratching their heads.

ANCIENT TECHNOLOGY

The question of ancient technology becomes more pressing, but even harder to understand, when one considers how the giant stones of ancient building sites were actually cut, tooled and moved. This incredible stone cutting precision is a mystery. Equally mysterious (considering megalithic times), is the extraordinary weights involved. How did very early humans raise blocks of 100 tons or more, transport them, and precisely set them into place? Astonishing ingenuity was utilized in their construction, which clearly employed principles that are not fully recognized even today. Could such principles have included some kind of levitation? There are very persistent references from the classical writers alluding to the power of sound, or the use of song, music and tone to make things lighter, something known as auditive levitation. Songs or chanting could allow a rhythm to develop and rise up, and that in turn facilitated seemingly superhuman abilities whereby workers could move enormous heavy objects with little human effort.

One of the most mysterious objects from ancient times was recovered from 40 meters below the surface in the eastern Mediterranean Sea, sometime around Easter, in the year 1900. It was discovered by Elias Stadiatos, a Greek sponge diver working off the coast of Antikythera, a small island near Crete. He found part of an ancient Roman freighter that included statues and other materials that dated the shipwreck to around 80 BCE. The most intriguing artifact recovered, the "Antikythera Device" as he named it, remained an enigma for the next 49 years, until Dick Price, a professor of science history at Yale University, discovered what the machine had the capacity to compute. He determined it was a mechanical analog computer, an instrument two millennia ahead of its time. "It was like finding a turbo-jet in Tutankhamen's tomb," Price wrote in his June 1959 article, "An Ancient Greek Computer," for *Scientific American*. He specifically noted that the Antikythera Device used a differential gear, not re-invented until the mid-1500s, to compute the synodic lunar cycle by subtracting the effects of the sidereal lunar movement, thereby calculating the motions of stars and planets. This function makes the artifact far more advanced than its 16th century differential gear, bringing the technology of the Antikythera Device into the Space Age. Such a device would have been invaluable to any mariner.

Another mysterious ancient device was the Golden Sun Disc of Mu, which in more recent times was reverse-engineered to create the Looking Glass technology, allowing users a glimpse into past timelines and probable views of the future. The original Sun Disc, according to the Peruvian records of the Elder Race, made use of the naturally occurring gravitational *null node*, also called a vortex, a "dead spot," or in conventional science, a "wormhole," as described by the Einstein-Rosen Bridge. Both modern and ancient devices allowed simple access to the coordinate time realm through the use of vibrational control, which in ancient times was invoked through song, chant, mantra, and musical instruments. The Sun Disc also had the ability to "remote view," which was how a destination was determined by a priest who could use it for astral travel. Using song, mantra and music, the priest could fine-tune the device to a very specific destination that could be seen in the device before actually making the transit. It works with coordinate time, hence controlled by *waveforms*—music, mantra, chanting, singing and the like.

In January 2013, the *Voice of Russia* and other Russian sources reported that a 300 million-year-old piece of aluminum machinery had been found in the Siberian city of Vladivostok. Experts say the *gear rail* must have been manufactured and could not have been the result of natural forces. The artifact came to researchers' attention when a resident of Vladivostok was lighting a fire during a cold winter evening. He noticed a rail-shaped piece of metal fused into a lump of coal he was using to heat his home. Mesmerized by his discovery, the responsible citizen decided to seek help from the scientists of the nearby Primorye region. After the metal object was studied by Russian experts, the man was shocked to learn about the assumed age of his discovery. The metal rail was supposedly *300 million* years old, and the scientists made yet another shocking revelation. They told the man that it was not created by nature, but rather was manufactured, and quite possibly of an ET origin. The find is universally described as a toothed metal rail, and without doubt, created artificially. The question of what culture or group might have made this aluminum gear back in the predawn of time remains a mystery.

THE WAY BACK MACHINE

In one timeline describing the fabulous expanse of civilization on Earth, there is scientific evidence for a deluge that engulfed the Earth as described in the story of Noah's Ark. However, such a global flooding has not occurred in over two million years. Using the terms Alpha as our beginning point and Omega as the end point, the cycle of the human journey begins and ends with absolute perfection. That is, supreme "human" beings lived in an elevated state of existence during the antideluvian civilizations of Atlantis and Lemuria, or possibly even much earlier, and then experienced a sharp decline into the more primitive state we've experienced in recent history. Underneath the miles of ice in Antarctica, there could be evidence of these previous civilizations. As the fossil record shows, this location previously had a temperate climate before the pole shifts occurred.

The further we look back in history, the more we see what appears to be a "prefabricated society" in its most refined form, and then descending through a long decline trajectory until the culture blends into ours. The Egyptian, Indus and Sumerian civilizations all seemed to appear out of nowhere, fully equipped with advanced knowledge, and from the onset at the apex of their cultural development. In the case of Egypt, the oldest structures such as the Sphinx and the Great Pyramids are of the highest architectural quality and remain the best preserved known structures to stand the test of time. Later-built pyramids are of lesser quality, and in fact, some have literally collapsed due to poor design. In the case of Sumer, there were groups of Akkadians and the ancestors of present day Bedouins surrounding the area in which they emerged, yet all seem to be culturally unassociated with the Sumerians.

It has been established that in ancient Sumer a sudden plethora of scientific achievements burst upon the scene in a very short period of time, including the wheel, written language, a sophisticated calendar, music and song, map making, and a standard exchange system, among other fascinating innovations. The Indus River civilizations of Old India also show signs of early cultural refinement. This suggests that the oldest Egyptian, Indus and Sumerian societies possessed a higher quality of knowledge than their descendants. This is a key sign suggesting that technology is inherited from another culture and not developed indigenously, since knowledge of how to use the obtained information has been lost through the generations. In short, the oldest cultural legacies reached their highest level of advancement at their earliest stages, and were merely the legacy of civilizations far more ancient and long forgotten from our collective memory. The esoteric view of the Egyptians, Indians and Sumerians suggests civilized humans have existed on this planet for many tens of thousands of years, with some accounts going into the millions of years!

SACRED GEOMETRY IN ANCIENT STRUCTURES

The construction of the three Great Pyramids in Egypt follow principles of sacred geometry. For example, they are linked together mathematically by the Golden Section, rediscovered by Leonardo da Vinci (1452 - 1519), who provided the name. The Golden Section is a spiral in the canon of ancient geometry, and it is used in the design of sacred architecture. It was valued as the most desirable proportion, because it is expressed in the patterns of natural forms. These include animal horns, sea mollusks, the formation of the human fetus, comic nebulae (the ratio between planetary orbits), the laws of Mendelian heredity, the movement of flowers following the path of the sun (called heliotropism), and especially within whirlpools, and thousands of other examples observed in nature. The Golden Section appears in a nautilus shell when its exterior wall is removed to expose the spiral inside. This would be a pretty impressive insight for the Stone Age builders of the Great Pyramids to conceive, if we are to believe conventional archaeologists.

The construction of the Great Pyramids is the legacy of the Atlanteans, which was an extension of the Lemurian civilization that existed on Earth over four million years ago (as we'll see in the next chapter). In esoteric traditions, the Atlanteans are viewed as supreme beings who were much more evolved than humans are today. The real secret of pharaonic Egypt, from which Freemasonry purportedly arose, is the attainment of the light body, from which the word "Illuminati" derives. This would be the highest teaching conferred upon initiates in the King's Chamber, an enigmatic room located deep inside the Great Pyramid. This esoteric knowledge was introduced from Egypt by Moses into Judaism. It was later recorded on the copper scrolls presumably hidden beneath the Temple in Jerusalem, and uncovered centuries later by the Knights Templar, who also incorporated sacred geometry into their buildings.

Another expression of sacred geometry is the sort of shadow cast by the second pyramid (the Pyramid of Khafre) upon the Great Pyramid at sunset on December 21 every year. The winter solstice shadow actually forms a *golden triangle* when truncated by the vertical line running up the middle of the south face of the Great Pyramid, and lining up with a purposeful indentation of a few inches in the construction of the side of the pyramid. This apothegm, as geometers call such vertical lines, forms a right angle and transforms the solstice shadow into a perfect Golden Triangle. Considering that this shadow is cast upon the Great Pyramid on each winter solstice to form "a perfect Golden Triangle," it can hardly have been a coincidence, and further illustrates that all three pyramids were built as part of a unified plan.

Not far from the Giza Plateau, but built much later, stands the Pharos Lighthouse (also called the Lighthouse of Alexandria), a tower built between 280 and 247 BCE on the island of Pharos at Alexandria, Egypt. It rose to 280 Old Kingdom Royal Cubits, or 146.5 meters, which is the same height as the Great Pyramid. Such a salient relationship was hardly coincidental, demonstrating that both structures, despite the millennia separating their construction, were built according to the same principles of sacred geometry. This organizational unity began with all three pyramids on the Giza Plateau.

THE LEGACY OF EGYPT

Solon, a wise man from Greece, traveled to Egypt and returned to report to his countrymen the existence of Atlantis. This was information he received from 97

Egyptian high priests, such as Psenophis of Heliopolis and Sonchis of Sais, two wise men with whom he studied while in Egypt. Plato's references to Atlantis were borrowed from the writings of the Greek philosopher Solon, who was given the information by the Egyptian priests who referred to Atlantis as *Kepchu*, which also happens to be the Egyptian name for the people of Crete. Some of the survivors of the Minoan volcanic disaster asked Egypt for help at the time of their destruction in 1,500 BCE, since Egypt was the only other civilization with high culture in the Mediterranean world.

What can the Giza Pyramids and the Sphinx in Egypt teach us? What was the function of the Osireion and other awesome megalithic sites of unknown origin found throughout Egypt? Heavy water erosion on the Sphinx, which could only have taken place no more recently than about 7,000 years ago, when heavy rain was common in the area, suggests a much older date for its construction than is generally accepted. The Great Pyramid and neighboring Oseirion Temple also feature megalithic stone architecture that still puzzles experts. It is curious to note that very little writing is found in the Osireion Temple, although there is one very significant piece of information in that temple. It is a very faint but clear and precise drawing of 64 uniform petals called the "Flower of Life." It is not etched into the rock nor carved. It is burned into the atomic structure of the rock in some extraordinary way. Were the high knowledge and advanced architectural techniques of ancient Egypt brought to the Nile Valley by the survivors of an earlier civilization around 12,500 years ago, at the end of the last Ice Age, an epoch referred to in the *Egyptian Book of the Dead* as *Zep Tepi*, or "The First Time?" The ancient monuments of the Giza Plateau also hint at the possibility of a very advanced lost civilization from previous times, and could be a reference to Atlantis. This much older time frame, when most of Egypt and the Sahara were fertile land, is called the *Osirius Empire of pre-sand Egypt*.

The Giza Pyramids stand as testament to the time when humans were allied to the Galactic Federation, forming part of the Osirian Empire, and the legacy of Atlantis. The three pyramids of Giza are arranged in a squared triangle. Their sides are in a perfect 3:4:5 ratio to each other. There are many tantalizing clues to their ancient origin, and many pieces of evidence that prove their real age and function, but this has been covered up in a scandal called "Egyptgate." For example, using sonar technology, tunnels and massive chambers have been discovered directly underneath the Sphinx, and connect on several levels underneath the Giza Plateau. The tunnels were recently explored and filmed. Once the videos were released, the entrance was promptly sealed. The *Temple of Birds*, where the entrance passage was discovered, is no longer accessible.

There are rumors that underneath the Great Pyramids and Sphinx are located many sacred chambers, including the Hall of Records, a very old and *still operational ET* base called *Kamagol-II*, and even a large disc-shaped craft at the lowest level. Underneath the right paw of the Sphinx, far below in some of the deepest chambers the mythical Akashic Records can be found, but the general public will not be learning about this from conventional archaeologists. The Pyramids of Giza are such fantastic monuments, with no previously built examples, that the only logical conclusion is they must be the legacy of something older and much greater.

The Egyptian Sphinx next to the Great Pyramids is a statue of a reclining lion with a human head. It is located on the Giza Plateau along the west bank of the Nile, near modern-day Cairo. The Sphinx, with its recumbent lion body, was carved in the *Age of Leo* and is positioned to gaze due east. It is the largest monolith statue and the oldest known monumental sculpture in the world. It extends 73.5 meters in length, six meters wide, and 20.22 meters high. The Sphinx, or the "Lion Man" in this interpretation, represents the Zodiac signs of Leo and Aquarius. When the Sphinx was built some 12,000 years ago in the Age of Leo, it faced almost due east, that is, when the equinox point was in the Age of Leo. In the current Age of Aquarius, the Sphinx will be facing Aquarius 180° rotated from its original position. The position of the three nearby Giza Pyramids relate to the four cardinal compass points, and they correspond to the three stars in Orion's belt. They mark the constellations of their terrestrial counterparts on the Giza Plateau, an alignment observed at sunrise on the spring equinox, and thereby correspond to a building date of 12,500 years ago. This also matches the time frame of the Osirius Empire.

MESOAMERICAN PYRAMID CULTURES

The monumental architecture of Tiahuanaco, located in present-day Bolivia, is characterized by large stones of exceptional workmanship. In contrast to the masonry style of the later Inca culture, Tiahuanaco stone architecture usually employs rectangular *ashlar* blocks laid in a regular course, and monumental structures were frequently fitted with elaborate drainage systems. Bronze or copper "double-T" clamps were frequently used to anchor large blocks in place. The stone used to build Tiahuanaco was quarried and then transported 40 kilometers or more to the city. They were moved without the aid of the wheel, although some of the distance was over water. The Akapana pyramid at Tiahuanaco is a terraced pyramid predating the Inca Empire by many centuries. It is faced with accurately hewn and artistically joined blocks, and are comparable to those found on Easter Island. This discovery proves that Inca builders learned their impressive craft of masonry from their predecessors in Tiahuanaco. The ground plan of this unfinished pyramid is only slightly smaller than the dimensions of the Great Pyramid in Egypt.

The crowning achievement of the Inca culture is *Machu Picchu*, which is a Quechua Indian word for "Old Peak." This pre-Columbian Inca site is an engineering marvel, and located 2,400 meters above sea level. It is situated on a mountain ridge high above the Urubamba Valley in Peru, 80 kilometers northwest of the ancient capital of Cuzco. Often referred to as "The Lost City of the Incas," *Machu Picchu* is probably the most familiar symbol of the Inca Empire. Another mysterious Incan city in Peru, the city of Ollantay-tambo, is also known for its megalithic stone ruins. The finely cut rocks and plantation terraces were very large obstacles for Spanish conquistadors. The fortress was also used by Inca rebel Manco to conduct successful attacks on Francisco Pizarro and other conquistadors based in Lima. Lastly, the Inca temple of Pachacamac is an archaeological site 40 kilometers southeast of Lima, Peru, in the Valley of the Lurín River. It had at least one pyramid. The Inca used Pachacamac primarily as a religious site for the veneration of the Pacha Kamaq creator god, and also as an important administrative center.

The unique prehistoric cultures of Mesoamerica, meaning Middle America, developed over many thousands of years in relative isolation. Beginning some 3,500 years ago, the Olmec were the first to build large cities and megalithic carvings in stone, leaving behind the beginnings of a culture soon to influence later civilizations. An interesting facet of the Olmec is their distinct Negroid features which can be seen on the large statues of heads left behind, and suggesting an African connection. The Olmec also left behind platform mound pyramids. The Zapotecs borrowed from the Olmec culture, as did the Maya, the Toltecs, and then the Aztecs. One common thread of all prehistoric cultures following the Olmec was the ceremonial ball game. Players were required to skillfully manipulate a heavy rubber ball with hips, thighs and shoulders, but not arms or hands. The ball game was a sport as well as a sacred ritual, and human sacrifice was often the final outcome. The ball game was played throughout Mesoamerica and even in the Southwest of North America by many overlapping civilizations. Stone-carved ball courts were erected in many sacred cities in Central America and what is now the Four Corners region of the United States.

The last remnant of the great pyramid civilizations arose at Teotihuacán, Mexico, around 200 BCE. The Aztec name given to the site means "place of the gods," or "the place where men became gods." Like the astronomical configuration of the Giza pyramids in Egypt, the entire complex is a precise scale-model of our solar system, and accurately reflects the orbital distances of the inner planets, the asteroid belt, Jupiter, Saturn, Uranus, Neptune, and even Pluto. Since the planet Uranus was not "discovered" with modern Earth telescopes until 1787, and Pluto not until 1930, it is apparent that the builders had information from "outside" sources. Furthermore, Teotihuacán is located at the latitude of 19.47 degrees north of the equator, which corresponds to the mathematics of a tetrahedron within a sphere where the bottom tip is at the South Pole and the corners come to meet the sphere at 19.47 degrees north.

ENTER THE MAYA

In one of the greatest historical mysteries of all time, an enlightened people emerged, then all but vanished in the span of a thousand years. Around the third century CE, the Mayas were building tall, gleaming pyramids of stone and mortar amid their corn patches in the steamy Guatemalan jungles. The Classic period of the Mayas suddenly faltered and began fading out around the 10th century CE. Eventually, the beautiful ceremonial cities in the southern lowlands stood silent and deserted. Yet, less than a century later, the Mayas were back, this time aligned with the Toltecs in the northern part of the Mexican Yucatán Peninsula. Here, the Post-Classic renaissance reigned until 1450, when the Mayas once again faded away, this time forever. By the time the Spanish arrived in 1527, the finest buildings of the Maya renaissance were overgrown ruins. In total, the ancient Maya inhabited a territory extending over 400,000 square kilometers in the Mexican states of Yucatan, Campeche, Quintana Roo, Tabasco and Chiapas, as well as the present-day countries of Guatemala, Belize, and parts of El Salvador and Honduras.

Descendants of the Maya are alive and well today. In fact, there are an estimated 2.5 million Mayans now living in Mexico and various Central American countries. It has been discovered through DNA testing that the Maya originated in Mongolia, crossed the Bering Strait ice bridge, and continued south where they settled in Central America. There have been over 100 Mayan cities found in the former Mayan homelands, but to date, only 10% are accessible to the public.

The ancient Maya were among the most advanced cultures—a people who understood the physical cosmos, erected impressive pyramid temples, had a complex written language, and developed an extraordinarily accurate way of understanding time. The Mayans are considered to be the leaders and pioneers of the great sciences of astronomy and mathematics during the high cultures of Mesoamerica. One of their greatest achievements was a profound understanding of the solar system, and of their architecture is based on astronomic observations. Five centuries before Galileo Galilei charted the movement of the planets, the Maya knew that the center of our system was the Sun and not the Earth.

The "Sleeping Prophet" Edgar Cayce conducted several readings about the ancestors of Atlantis as landing in the Yucatán and importing their high culture. Among their gifts to humanity, according to Cayce, were several artifacts detailing the long history of world civilization and installed in the form of a "Hall of Records." Cayce named three locations worldwide where identical records were stored: Giza in Egypt below the Sphinx; inside a collapsed temple under the Atlantic Ocean near Bimini; and below a temple in the Yucatán. Although Cayce never named Piedras Negras in Guatemala by name, or any other site in the Yucatán as the specific location of a Hall of Records, it is quite possible that Piedras Negras is built atop a much older temple. Cayce specifically named the Yucatán as the location of Iltar's covered temple. Iltar was a high priest who attempted to preserve the records of Atlantis by transcribing their ancient history in stone. In his famous reading of December, 1933, Cayce said, "these stones are now—during the last few months—being uncovered." The stones Cayce referred to were associated with crystal "fire stones" that apparently gave the Atlanteans their power. Further along in the reading Cayce reveals that an emblem representing the stones would be carried to the Pennsylvania State Museum. If Cayce's time frame is correct, the only excavation in the Yucatán region in 1933 were the excavations at the Piedras Negras conducted by the University of Pennsylvania. Several artifacts were returned to Pennsylvania in the year Cayce mentioned, including a calcite vessel and fragments of a paramagnetic stone known as hematite. To date, the Hall of Records has not been discovered at Piedras Negras, nor anywhere else in Central America.

OLD INDIA

Hinduism is the world's oldest major religion still practiced today. Its earliest origins can be traced to the ancient Vedic civilization with a conglomerate of diverse beliefs and traditions, yet Hinduism has no single founder. Although some tenets of the faith are accepted by most Hindus, scholars have found it difficult to identify any doctrines with universal acceptance among all denominations. Prominent themes in Hindu beliefs include *dharma* "ethics and duties," *samsara* "the continuing cycle of birth, life, death and rebirth," *karma* "action and subsequent reaction," *moksha* "liberation from samsara," and the various *yogas* "paths or practices." A devout Hindu believes that to die and be cremated in the holy Indian city of Varanasi is to gain *moksha*, or release from the eternal cycle of death and rebirth.

The Vedas are the primary texts of Hinduism. They are a large corpus of texts originating in ancient India. These sacred scriptures are among the oldest written records in the history of humankind, and are among the most ancient religious texts still in existence. They include the esteemed *Egyptian Book of the Dead*, the Babylonian creation myth *Enuma Elish*, the *I Ching* of China, and the *Avesta* of Zoroastrianism. The Vedas are certainly the oldest sacred texts of Hinduism. Vedic mantras are recited at Hindu prayers, religious functions and other auspicious occasions. Each Veda contains thousands of hymns and several sections of incantations and rituals from ancient India. Some of the oldest Vedic hymns, especially the hymns of the *Rig Veda*, are considered to be at least 6,000-8,000 years old. The Vedas are believed to be revealed scriptures because they are considered to be divine in origin. According to Hindu tradition, the Vedas are "not human compositions," having been directly revealed, and thus are called *sruti*, or "what is heard," and form the foundation of the Brahmanical system of religious belief. Besides their spiritual value, they give a unique view of everyday life in India from some four thousand years ago. The Vedas are also the most ancient extensive texts in any Indo-European language group, and are invaluable in the study of comparative linguistics.

There are four major Vedas, called the *Rig Veda, Sama Veda, Yajur Veda* and *Atharva Veda,* and all have had a vast influence on Buddhism, Jainism, and Sikhism. Traditionally the text of the Vedas is said to be of an equal age with the universe. Scholars have determined that the *Rig Veda*, the oldest of the four Vedas, was composed about 1500 BCE, and codified about 600 BCE. It is unknown when it was finally committed to writing, but likely after 300 BCE.

The Vedic hymns were first known to have been translated into the Greek language shortly after Alexander the Great annexed the Indus River region. This was the period of a cultural revolution in Western civilization that transformed crude and brutal tribal cultures into democratic republics based on *more reasonable* conduct. Homer, the blind Greek poet, wrote stories of "the gods" that could have been borrowed and modified from earlier sources, including the Vedic texts, Sumerian cuneiform, or Babylonian and Egyptian mythology. His poems, as well as many other myths of the ancient world, are very accurate descriptions of the exploits of humans over 3,000 years ago.

The somewhat ambiguous term *veda* means "knowledge," or variously, a type of "sacred lore." Since it embraces such a large body of ancient Indian writings, the term is somewhat open to interpretation. Successive generations of Indian people learned the Vedic verses and then passed them along to others, saying that they came from "the gods" and not their human counterparts. Eventually the content of the verses was written down, codified, and adopted verbatim as truth. The euphemistic and metaphorical content of the Veda became accepted and practiced as dogmatic fact. The philosophy of the verses was ignored, and the verses became the genesis of nearly every emerging religious practice in existence, most notably the complex Hindu faith.

VIMANA CRAFT

Vimana is a Vedic term with several meanings, ranging from "temple" or "palace," to "mythological flying machines," as described in Sanskrit epics. Reference to ancient flying vehicles derive mostly from Old Indian sources, but there are references emerging from other foreign scripts and hundreds of references from ancient Indian epics. Most of them have not been translated into English from the old Sanskrit. The Hindu Vedas offer a description of the vimanas, including a detailed section on vimanas from the *Mahabharata*. Vedic texts describe various kinds of aircraft. The epic tale called the *Ramayana* specifically mentions aircraft hangers. The Sifrala text, which originated in the Chaldean era, comprises around 100 written pages of technical plans on building a flying machine. Some of the Vedic texts, which go back to the dawn of conscious thought, describe epic air battles, fantastic weaponry, anti-gravity aircraft, and even descriptions of a preemptive nuclear strike.

One interesting Veda called *Samarangana Sutradhara* gives technical specifications for building an advanced flying craft as follows:

> Strong and durable must the body of the vimana be made, like a great flying bird
> of light material. Inside one must put the mercury engine with its iron heating
> apparatus underneath. By means of power latent in the mercury, which sets the
> driving whirlwind in motion, a man sitting inside may travel a great distance
> in the sky. The movements of the vimana are such that it can vertically ascend,
> vertically descend, or move slanting forwards and backwards. With the help of
> machines, human beings can fly through the air and heavenly beings can come
> down to Earth.

From another ancient account found in the Sanskrit epic the *Mahabharata*, we are told that a Vimana measured twelve cubits in circumference, with four strong wheels. Apart from its "blazing missiles," the *Mahabharata* records the use of other deadly weapons that operated via a circular "reflector." When switched on, it produced a "shaft of light" that could focus on any target and could immediately "consume it with its power." This type of advanced weaponry sounds similar to the laser-beam-like "death rays" invented by Nikola Tesla in the early 20th century.

Around 2005, the Chinese discovered some Sanskrit documents in Lhasa, Tibet, and sent them to the University of Chandrigarh to be translated. University scholar Dr. Ruth Reyna worked with a team who translated the documents and proclaimed that they contained instructions for building an interstellar spaceship. The method of propulsion was "anti-gravitational" and was based upon a system analogous to that of *laghima*, the unknown power of the ego existing in a person's physiological makeup, described as "a centrifugal force strong enough to counteract all gravitational pull." According to Hindu yogi masters, it is this *laghima* which enables a person to levitate. Dr. Reyna said that on board these machines, which were called "Astras" in the text, the ancient Indians could have sent a detachment of people onto any planet. The manuscripts were also said to reveal the secret of "antima," "the cap of invisibility," and "garima," all of which seem to be manipulations of gravity which instruct "how to become as heavy as a mountain of lead." The recovered documents from Lhasa are thought to be thousands of years old.

A RECOVERED VIMANA?

In December 2010, according to a leaked Russian briefing to Vladimir Putin when he was Prime Minister, there was a sudden urgent message to the most power-ful leaders of the Western countries to visit a secret location in Afghanistan. The Western leaders traveled to Afghanistan to personally view a discovery by U.S. mil-itary scientists, described as a "vimana" (an ancient flying vehicle) entrapped in a "time well." Attempts to remove it had already caused the "disappearance" of at least eight American soldiers trying to dislodge the machine from the cave where it has been hidden for an estimated 5,000 years.

The seemingly "perpetual" power source to this mysterious "time well" was de-scribed in a *most peculiar* report prepared by Russia's Foreign Intelligence Service for Prime Minister Putin. The report said it appears to be based on the technology of Edward Leedskalnin, who claimed to have discovered the "Secret Knowledge of the Ancients." From 1923 until 1951, Leedskalnin "single-handedly and secretly" carved over 1,100 tons of coral rock and moved massive boulders by an unknown process to construct one of the contemporary world's most mysterious accomplishments and known as the Coral Castle in southern Florida.

The alleged "time well" encasing the vimana, the Russian report continues, appears to be an electromagnetic radiation-gravity field, first postulated by Albert Einstein in his Unified Field Theory. It has long been rumored that this field was behind the in-famous American World War II experiment in teleportation called the Philadelphia Experiment that, in 1943, and similar to the events which occurred in Afghanistan, also caused the sudden "disappearance" of several U.S. soldiers. Another intriguing aspect of the Russian Foreign Intelligence Service report is the statement that it was not just any vimana that was discovered, but one that was the property of an ancient prophet named *Zoroaster*. According to the ancient writings contained in the cave where it was discovered, the report claims that its "rightful owner" was the founder of arguably one of the most important religions of all time: *Zoroastrianism*.

A PERSIAN BLOSSOMING

In 630 BCE, a master named Zoroaster created distinct religious practices in Persia around the teachings of an advanced being named *Ahura Mazda*, whom he saw in a vision at age 30. This was another among the growing number of monotheistic religions blossoming around the world. Ahura Mazda taught Zoroaster the cardinal principles of the "Good Religion." Several traits of Zoroastrianism can be traced back to the culture and beliefs of the proto Indo-Iranian period, and Zoroastrianism consequently shares some elements with the historical Vedic religion that also has its origins in that era. Though little is known to the world today, the religious philosophy of Zoroaster is cred-ited with being the basis of all known religions that proposed the purpose of human-kind was to sustain *aša*, or "Truth." The modern Rotary Club is a fraternal organization established by the Zoroastrians.

The most popularly known followers of Zoroastrianism were the Magi, also known as the Wise Men from the East in the Bible, famous for being the travelers who brought gifts to Bethlehem for the infant Jesus. The Italian explorer Marco Polo claimed to have seen the Magi graves in what is today the district of Saveh, near Tehran, Iran. In Eng-lish, the term *magi* is the origin of the words magic and magician. In spite of its small number of current adherents, Zoroastrianism has played a colossal role in the study of comparative religions. Not only was it a cohort of the ancient Vedic Hinduism, but it also had a huge influence on the development of Judaism and Christianity.

Central to Zoroastrianism is the emphasis on moral choice, or free will, to choose between the responsibility and duty to which one is born into in the mortal world, that is, to sustain *aša*, or "Truth," or to give up this duty and therefore facilitate the work of its opposite, *druj*. In the Avestan language *druj* means "lie." Similarly, predestination is rejected in Zoroastrian teaching. Humans bear responsibility for all situations they are in, and this is all based on the way we behave toward one another. Reward, punishment, happiness and grief all depend on how individuals view their purpose and, consequently, live their lives.

Similar to the principles of karma in Hinduism and Buddhism, in Zoroastrianism, good transpires for those who do righteous deeds. Those who do evil have themselves to blame for their ruin. Zoroastrian morality can be summarized in the simple phrase, "good thoughts, good words, good deeds," in that order. Thoughts are primary, because from one's thought system, behavior follows. There is one universal and transcendental God, named Ahura Mazda, who is the one *uncreated* creator and to whom all worship is ultimately directed, because all life is an extension of Source (the idea of One, but with many names). Ahura Mazda's creation—evident as truth and order—is the antithesis of chaos, falsehood and disorder. The resulting conflict involves the entire universe, including humanity, which has an active role to play in the *conflict*. Active participation in life through good thoughts, good words, and good deeds is necessary to ensure happiness and to keep the chaos at bay. This active participation of adherents is a central element in Zoroaster's concept of free will.

Pliny the Elder, the first century Roman author, naturalist, and natural philosopher, as well as being a naval and army commander in the early Roman Empire, names Zoroaster as the "inventor of magic," a claim that historians say was based on the over "two million lines" written about Zoroaster contained in the Ancient Royal Library of Alexandria. Tragically, the Christian Roman Emperor Theodosius I ordered this library destroyed in 391 CE.

The largest resurgence of Zoroaster "magic" employed by mystics since the destruction of the Ancient Royal Library of Alexandria occurred in the 13th century among the Cathars who lived in southern Europe. The Cathars were ascetic Christians who renounced the accumulation of material wealth, refrained from sensual pleasures, and lived extremely austere lifestyles. By doing so, the Cathars were said to have attained mystical powers. Pope Innocent III, who lived from 1161 until 1216, ordered brutal crusades against heretics he viewed as threats to the Catholic Church, including the Muslims and the Cathars. It is sad to note when the "power" of Zoroaster "magic" once again began to reappear in the world, its threat to Christianity was considered undeniable, and it prompted the pope to order a massacre of noncombatant Cathar civilians. Slaughter in Europe of this scale was not duplicated until the horrors of World War II. The most infamous quote from the Albigensian Crusade in southern France was, "Kill them all. God will recognize his own." But even a wholesale slaughter of those practicing the principles of Zoroastrianism could not stamp it out. These mystical practices simply went underground during the Middle Ages.

LAO TZU AND *THE WAY*

Just a few decades after Zoroaster lived, an elderly Chinese philosopher was said to have written a small book of great wisdom called *The Way*. Attributed to Lao Tzu or "Old Master," who lived from 580-500 BCE, some of the work may predate his life by several centuries. For example, the earliest known Chinese manuscripts of the *Tao*

Te Ching date from the late fourth century BCE, and contain similar passages. Today, this philosophy is known as the *Tao* or Taoism. Lao Tzu's understanding of nature, the universe, and the human condition still resonates to this day. According to common legend, his *last lifetime* as a human was lived in a small village in rural China, where he contemplated the essence of his own life. Like Siddhartha who became the *Buddha*, Lao Tzu confronted his own thoughts, his reason for being on Earth, and his myriad of past lives. In so doing, he recovered some of his own memory, human ability, and immortality. As an old man, Lao Tzu decided to leave the village and go to the forest to depart the body. The village gatekeeper stopped him and implored him to write down his personal philosophy before leaving. The following are some memorable passages from *The Way*:

> *If you are depressed, you are living in the past,*
> *If you are anxious, you are living in the future.*
> *If you are at peace, you are living in the present.*
>
> *He who looks will not see it;*
> *He who listens will not hear it;*
> *He who gropes will not grasp it.*
>
> *The formless nonentity, the motionless source of motion.*
> *The infinite essence of the spirit is the source of life.*
> *Spirit is self.*
>
> *Simply see that you are at the center of the universe,*
> *and accept all things and beings as parts of your infinite body.*
> *When you perceive that an act done to another is done to yourself,*
> *you have understood the great truth.*
>
> *Walls form and support a room,*
> *yet the space between them is most important.*
> *A pot is formed of clay,*
> *yet the space formed therein is most useful.*
> *Action is caused by the force of nothing on something,*
> *just as the nothing of spirit is the source of all form.*
>
> *One suffers great afflictions because one has a body.*
> *Without a body what afflictions could one suffer?*
> *When one cares more for the body than for his own spirit,*
> *One becomes the body and loses the way of the spirit.*
>
> *The self, the spirit, creates illusion.*
> *The delusion of Man is that reality is not an illusion.*
> *One who creates illusions and makes them more real than reality,*
> *follows the path of the spirit and finds the way of heaven.*

While the text's true authorship and date of composition or compilation are still debated, the work of Lao Tzu and the philosophy of Taoism live on to this day. Due to both its simplicity and depth, the *Tao Te Ching* remains one of the most widely read sacred texts. Its appeal is universal and it has been found relevant by Christians, Hindus, Muslims, Buddhists, and even quantum physicists. The work describes the Tao as the mystical source and ideal of all existence. It is unseen, but not transcendent, immensely powerful yet supremely humble, and as being the root of all things. According to the *Tao Te Ching*, humans have no special place within the Tao, as we are just one of its many "ten thousand" manifestations. People have desires and free will, and thus are able to alter their own nature. Many act "unnaturally," that is, upsetting the natural balance of the Tao, which is absolute stillness. The *Tao Te Ching* intends to lead students on a "return" to their natural state, in harmony with the Tao. Taoism is a religion (in the sense of Huston Smith's phrase, "chasing the Divine,") that addresses the quest for immortality, while its practice results in the experience of deep quiet and serenity.

Language, religion and conventional wisdom are critically assessed in the texts of Taoism. They are viewed as inherently biased and artificial, widely using paradoxes to sharpen the point. Instead, the concept of *wu wei*, literally "non-action" or "not acting," is a central point of the *Tao Te Ching*. The concept of *wu wei* is very complex and reflected in the phrase's multiple meanings, even in English translation, which can mean "not doing anything," "not forcing," "not acting" *in the theatrical sense*, "creating nothingness," "acting spontaneously," and "flowing with the moment." Lao Tzu used the term broadly with simplicity and humility as key virtues, often in contrast to selfish action. On a political level, it means avoiding circumstances such as warfare, harsh laws and overly burdensome taxes. Some Taoists see a connection between *wu wei* and esoteric practices, such as the "sitting in oblivion," or emptying the mind of bodily awareness and thought. These concepts are also found in the works of the influential Chinese philosopher *Zhuangzi*.

BIBLICAL PROPORTIONS

Another text that remains popular to this day is the Holy Bible, which is considered a sacred book by three major world religions: Judaism, Christianity, and Islam. Many devout believers consider it to be the literal truth, direct from the creator God, Yahweh, or any number of different names. Others treat the Bible with great respect, but believe that it was written by human beings, and as such is a complex and often contradictory document. Modern scholars believe that the Hebrew Bible, or *Tanakh*, was composed by four or five writers between 1000 to 400 BCE based on much older traditions. The New Testament was composed by a variety of writers between 60 to 110 CE. The contents of the New Testament were formalized by Athanasius of Alexandria in 367 CE, and finally canonized in 382 CE. There are many disagreements about the order and composition of the Bible between various religions and sects, some of which are doctrinal in nature.

The Genesis story written by the Jewish people describes "angels" or "sons of god" mating with women of Earth, who bore them children. The Genesis story also mentions that Yahweh designed our human biological bodies to live for 120 years or longer; however, these days, human bodies on Earth only last about half that long. The Nephilim were an antediluvian race which is referred to in the Bible as giants. Genesis 6:4 states: "The Nephilim were on the Earth in those days, and also afterwards, when the sons of God went to the daughters of men and had children by them. They were the heroes of old, men of renown." The Nephilim were a race of giants that were produced by the sexual union of the sons of God, presumably fallen angels, and the daughters of men. Translated from the Hebrew texts, *Nephilim* means "fallen ones." They were renowned for their strength, prowess, and a great capacity for sinfulness.

The wickedness of the Nephilim carried with it a heavy toll. Genesis 6:5 alludes to the corruption that the Nephilim caused amongst humans and themselves: "The Lord saw how great man's wickedness on the Earth had become." Their evil rebellion had incurred both the wrath and grief of God. According to the Bible, God instructed the angel Gabriel to ignite a civil war among the Nephilim. He also chose Enoch, a righteous man, to inform the fallen angels of the judgment pronounced on them and their children. God did not allow the fallen angels any peace, for they could not lift their eyes to heaven and were later to be chained. The end of the Nephilim came about in the war incited by Gabriel, in which the giants eventually annihilated each other in several spectacular battles with fantastic weapons and flying machines.

The Old Testament of the Bible reports the story of a human named Ezekiel, who witnessed what can be described as a spacecraft or an aircraft landing. The sighting took place near the Chebar River in northern Mesopotamia. Chaldea is the current-day country of Iraq. Ezekiel's "technical" description of the craft uses archaic language, but is nevertheless an accurate description of an antediluvian saucer or scout craft. It is similar to the sighting of *vimanas* by the people in the foothills of the Himalayas.

TEMPLE OF SOLOMON

As the spiritual heart of several esoteric societies, the Temple of Solomon was built atop the Temple Mount in Jerusalem, a site that is still venerated by adherents of the three great monotheistic religions. True believers claim that it is located at the intersection of the human and divine, along key ley lines, and is also the source of a natural spring. Supposedly built by King Solomon at the peak of ancient Israel's power, the Temple of Solomon was said to house the golden Ark of the Covenant in its Holy of Holies, a sacred chamber where the high priest would communicate directly with God. Centuries after the temple's destruction, during the Middle East crusades, the Temple Mount was used as the headquarters of the Knights Templar. Since then, through the centuries, countless legends have been passed down about the secrets the Templars may have uncovered under the Temple Mount.

The Order of the Temple, or Templary, established their headquarters on the very site of the Temple of Solomon. What they wanted most were ancient scrolls, purportedly inscribed onto copper. Working stealthily to excavate a secret vault beneath the Temple, the Templars obtained a great hidden treasure which they knew would be there. This treasure was apparently the true reason for their presence in Jerusalem. Part of the treasure may have been actual gold and jewels, and that would help to account for the meteoric rise in wealth which the Templars are known to have achieved. But the greatest treasure, if obtained, would have been the sacred copper scrolls containing ancient esoteric knowledge about the secrets of Jesus and the Bible.

What was the secret knowledge the Templars worked so hard to extract? Many researchers will say in a single word it was "enlightenment." But this was not to be simply a psychological transformation or transubstantiation of the flesh, blood, and bone into a body of light, as what was seen in the resurrection body of Christ. Rather, what the scrolls principally described was the "way to return to the way of life founded on the principles of the Bible" which one could speculate might have been another version of the Zoroastrian commitment to sustaining "the Truth." The Templars gaining this knowlededge may have marked the loss of the esoteric tradition described as the Illuminati, and better known as Ascended Masters. (Subsequent and current use of the term *Illuminati* is a false and corrupt use of its earlier meaning, as will be described below.)

As mysteriously as the scrolls were acquired, they also vanished mysteriously. There is evidence suggesting that a secret vault hidden beneath the floor of Rosslyn Chapel near Edinburgh, Scotland, may hold some of the long-lost relics once possessed by the Knights Templar. After all, Rosslyn Chapel's floor plan resembles a section of the ancient Temple of Solomon. Rosslyn Castle and environs, under the Earl of Sinclair, allegedly became the headquarters of the Knights Templar after they fled arrest in France in 1307 when King Philip IV violently suppressed the Templars and forced the remaining members into hiding and exile.

THE POOR KNIGHTS TEMPLAR

The Poor Fellow-Soldiers of Christ and of the Temple of Solomon, commonly known as the Knights Templar, were among the most famous of the Western Christian military monastic orders. The organization existed for approximately two centuries in the

Middle Ages. It was founded in the aftermath of the First Crusade of 1096 to ensure the safety of the many Europeans who made the pilgrimage to Jerusalem after its conquest.

The Knights Templar founded the Holy Grail Mystery School, developed from a synthesis of the gnosis they acquired from the Johannites, the Kabbalah received from the Jews, the alchemy traditions they assimilated from the Sufis, and possibly the information they derived from the copper scrolls. The esoteric mysteries of the Templars' school are incorporated within the legends of the Holy Grail, the best of which is *Parzival*, written by Knight Wolfram von Eschenbach in the Middle Ages. The story portrays the journey of Parzival as he evolves into an enlightened Fisher King. The guide along his path is Kundry, the personification of the alchemical *kundalini*.

The Templars' impoverished status as monks did not last long. They had a powerful advocate in Bernard of Clairvaux, a leading Church figure and a nephew of one of the founding knights. He spoke and wrote persuasively on their behalf, and in 1129, at the Council of Troyes, the Order was officially endorsed by the Catholic Church. With this formal blessing, the Templars became a favored charity across Europe, receiving money, farmland, businesses, property, and noble-born sons from families who were eager to help with the fight to secure the Holy Land. Another major benefit came in 1139, when Pope Innocent II's papal bull *Omne Datum Optimum* exempted the Order from obedience to local laws. This ruling meant that the Templars could pass freely through all borders, and were not required to pay any taxes. They were subject to no other authority than the pope. By 1150, the Order's original mission of guarding pilgrims had changed into a mission of guarding their riches through an innovative way of issuing letters of credit, secret encryption techniques, and guarantees to protect a traveler's assets. In many ways the Order was an early precursor of modern banking.

Based on a mix of donations, looted treasures, and shrewd business dealings, the Templars established a vast financial networks across the whole of Christendom. New members of the Order were also required to swear vows of poverty, oaths of loyalty, and hand over all their possessions to the collective wealth of their *new family* in the monastic brotherhood. This could include land, horses, and any other items of material wealth, including labor from serfs, and any business interests. The Order acquired large tracts of land, both in Europe and the Middle East, and also on islands in the Mediterranean Sea. They bought and managed farms and vineyards, they built castles and churches, they were involved in manufacturing, importing and exporting, including the transfer of valuables, and they had their own fleet of ships. At one point they even owned the entire island of Cyprus. By any measure, the Order of the Knights Templar appropriately qualifies as being the world's first multinational corporation.

Gaining this much power was bound to challenge even the mightiest institution. The Knights Templar organization was violently disbanded in 1307 by King Philip IV of France, who was deeply in debt to the Order. He pressured Pope Clement V to condemn the Order's members, have them arrested and tortured into giving false confessions, and burned many of them at the stake in an effort seize their wealth and erase his debt. The *omen* of Friday the 13th is related to the date in October, 1307, when the Order was sabotaged, betrayed, and *technically* destroyed.

BANKERS NEVER DIE

A sizable contingent of the Templars fled to the newly-established Switzerland where they reformed their international banking system, and whose descendants, with enormous holdings, secretly control the economy of Earth even to this day. After all, like Templar practices, banking in Switzerland is characterized by stability, privacy and protection of clients' assets and information. The country has a long tradition of bank secrecy dates to the Middle Ages. The gold of the Templar Knights that didn't make it into secret Swiss bank accounts (including some gold that dated back to King Solomon) and other Templar treasuries were, supposedly, hidden around the Languedoc region of southern France. That Templar gold was partly recovered by the Nazis during secret excavations, who then delivered as much as they could to Argentina at the conclusion of World War II. Other Nazi gold was confiscated by the Allies and deposited into the Federal Reserve System. This twice-looted gold eventually became the basis of the CIA's "off the books" operational "black" funds during the postwar years.

Some centuries later, a Bavarian Illuminati secret society arose that continues to operate alongside the international banker as an unseen influence. While considered "esoteric" at least in the sense of possessing secret knowledge, as stated earlier, this was a corruption and theft of the term Illuminati, and representing the opposite of the original meaning that of becoming enlightened individuals or ascended masters. Their banks have operated covertly for decades as *agent provocateurs* to covertly promote and finance weapons and warfare between nations. The Vatican-Swiss bank connection to stolen Nazi gold had links to Western investors. An excellent modern example has been documented in the World War II financing of the Third Reich by Prescott Bush, the pre-war Director of Union Banking Corporation (UBC), and family patriarch of President George Bush and his son, President George W. Bush. After the USA declared war on Germany in 1941, UBC assets were held by the government for the duration of the war, then returned afterward. UBC was eventually dissolved in 1951. Prescott Bush was on the board of directors of UBC, and held just one share in the company. For this he was reimbursed $1,500,000. These assets were later used to launch Bush family investments in the Texas energy industry. The complicity of the Swiss banks and the U.S. government in funding the Nazi regime was established at the end of World War II.

It is important to remember that warfare is an internal mechanism that is used to exert fear-based control over a population. The purpose of the senseless genocide and carnage of wars, as financed by these international banks, is to distract and divert human beings from our core essence as spiritual beings here on Earth, thus preventing us from sharing open communication, and cooperating together in activities that might enable us to prosper, to pursue enlightenment, end all wars, and escape this materialistic imprisonment. The Illuminati has been manipulating Western civilization for at least the last two centuries—likely for much longer—and under different assumed names.

ESOTERIC AMERICA

Few people understand the degree to which secret societies like the Masons wield power and control behind the scenes in our world. From its earliest days, the United States served as an arena for the revolutions in alternative spirituality which eventually swept the globe. Modern esoteric philosophies and personas—from Freemasonry to Spiritualism, from Madame H. P. Blavatsky to Edgar Cayce—dramatically altered our nation's culture, politics, and religion. Yet our nation's mystical and metaphysical roots are often ignored or overlooked. For example, some transcendentalist founders of our country, such as Benjamin Franklin and Thomas Jefferson, were influenced by a belief in Deism, out of which grew the idea of "Manifest Destiny"—the right or *divine plan* to forge a new nation—often despite the destruction of cultures, yet with utopian ideals as described by Emerson and Thoreau.

Sir Francis Drake claimed many of the lands that subsequently became the United States and Canada for the Crown of England, including the West Coast, Pacific Northwest, and the entire East Coast. Also claimed were the mysterious Oak Island in Nova Scotia, where Templar Knight Prince Henry Sinclair, or Sir Francis Drake, may have buried treasures or other artifacts. Rumors of Inca gold plundered by Spanish galleons and later pirated by Sir Francis Drake persist to this day on the tiny Oak Island off the coast of Nova Scotia. Tales of hidden treasures across the region spur many adventurers seeking out the mythical "Money Pit."

A few decades after Drake, Sir Francis Bacon viewed the "virgin land" of the newly discovered North American continent as the perfect place to practice his mystical philosophy. His work *The New Atlantis*, published a short time before his death in 1626, was a utopian vision of a benevolent kingdom. According to many scholars on the subject, Bacon planned to implement his ideas in North America. In 1606 he drafted the charter of the Virginia Company, and later oversaw the Jamestown settlement on the east coast and the development of the Virginia lands. Thus Bacon had a very big hand in the first permanent and successful white settlement in the north of the new continent, a settlement from which the nation of the United States eventually grew.

Many historians contend that Bacon and other influential Elizabethan figures like Drake, Sir Walter Raleigh and John Dee, all belonged to a secret order, and sought to perpetuate their ancient tradition on the new "unoccupied" continent. In the nature of its symbolism and mystical beliefs the order is said to have been "Rosicrucian." This is a very interesting connection for Grail seekers, because the founder of the medieval Rosicrucian Order, Jean De Gisors, is believed by some to be the founder of the now famous Priory of Sion, or the "Guardians of the Grail."

Voluminous research conducted on this topic leaves little doubt that "some kind" of esoteric doctrine likely lies at the foundation of the British colonies that became the United States. In addition to the Baconian philosophy and similar doctrinal evidence, this theory finds a great deal of support in the profound display of Masonic *and otherwise esoteric* symbolism present in the architecture of Washington D.C. and other important locations.

ENTER THE MASONS

The secrecy of the Masons allowed prominent, disgruntled, and empowered colonists to gather and conspire against British tyranny. This disaffected group, gathering as Masons, eventually established the new and independent country of the United States. Yet few history books touch on this important piece of American history. At the time of independence, in 1776, Masons were highly respected. Of the 55 delegates, nine signers of the Declaration of Independence were confirmed Masons, as were five non-signing delegates. Yet, as the Masons became more powerful after the revolution, they also became more corrupt. By the late 1820s, an anti-Masonic movement swept the nation when a murder scandal decimated Masonic membership. The decline was a result of the Masons in upstate New York who were accused of murdering a man named William Morgan, who threatened to expose their secret rituals. It is important to that interest returned by the 1850s.

When examined closely, there is an undercurrent of occult and esoteric ideas permeating the foundation of the USA. Perhaps the United States is in part a Templar/Baconian/Masonic effort to advance human society on the basis of secret knowledge and secret activities, much as fables about the Illuminati claim. But what knowledge and what is the motivation? It needs to be clarified and restated that the true Illuminati ideas formerly associated with enlightened beings and Ascended Masters have nothing to do with the Bavarian Illuminati and its modern offshoots. The Illuminati conspiracy launched in 1776 by Adam Weishaupt of Bavaria was a false and corrupt use of the term, and rightly denounced by true Masons of the time.

Central to Masonic symbolism are images of wisdom and light. During Masonic initiations, a candidate is given the question, "What do you desire most of all?" The percieved answer is *"more light."* Light signifies knowledge, *or more properly*, wisdom. The purpose of proper Freemasonry is "to make good men better" by imparting ethical teachings and esoteric knowledge, seemingly when deeply understood, impart wisdom. Freemasonry was one of the earliest societies to advocate self-rule, and this is why it was so popular with the Founding Fathers. Freemasonry elected their own leaders. They had a secret ballot. They had a separation of powers. They were governed by a constitution. All these elements were very influential in the shaping of self-government as conceived by the Founding Fathers.

If there is anything sacred about America, it is the idea that God is the *author* of our being, and hence the source of our freedom, sovereignty, rights, justice, and human dignity. These very Masonic concepts have been injected into the social-political institutions of our nation by these great Masons who were among the founders of the American experiment. George Washington was a Mason, along with 13 other presidents, and numerous Supreme Court Justices. Benjamin Franklin published a book about Freemasonry on his own printing press. Of the nine Masonic signers of the Declaration of Independence, John Hancock has the biggest signature of them all. In addition, some of the greatest names of the American Revolution were Masons: Ethan Alien, Edmund Burke, John Claypoole, William Daws, John Paul Jones, Robert Livingston, Colonel Benjamin Tupper and Paul Revere. Of the forty signers of the Constitution, nine were known Masons, 13 exhibited evidence of Masonic membership, and six more later became Masons. Since then, 14 out of the 43 U.S. presidents, one in three, have been Masons. The last *Master Mason* to serve as president was Gerald Ford.

Just as public Masonic influence and membership has plummeted in America since the mid-1800s, American values have also shifted. Remember 200 years ago, most people still supported slavery. One hundred years ago, most men believed that women did not deserve the right to vote. Fifty years ago, many considered interracial marriage a sin. Only recently has gay marriage been accepted by a majority of American society. Over the long term, humanity is becoming more tolerant and compassionate. And Freemasonry still has millions of worldwide members, and they persist and conduct their arcane rituals in secret. Freemasons have been accused of everything, from murder, to devil worship, to secretly controlling the U.S. government. Take a one dollar bill, turn it over and look at the *Great Seal of the United States* on the back. Now draw a six-pointed Star of David over it. One point will match up with the top of the *all-seeing eye*: a common Masonic symbol. Now look at the letters at the other points of the star and they spell out M-A-S-O-N. Freemasons do not consider themselves a secret society, but rather a society with secrets.

OF CRYSTALS AND RUNESTONES

There are many historical questions that may soon have definitive answers. Advanced space travel technology and stargate technology like CERN in Switzerland (which are by extension time machines) will eventually reveal everything. Or more precisely stated, once known technologies are released, complete understanding of anti-gravity, inter-dimensional space travel, and the spacetime continuum will give us the added bonus of being able to peer back to any moment in time of our choosing with the aid of *Looking Glass* technology. This is achieved by activating the crystalline Akashic Records that contain the complete 3D and historical record of our past, not only on Earth, but throughout the universe. The "Yellow Cube" technology has already been demonstrated by Grey aliens over 50 years ago as part of an ET technology trade in exchange for permission to let them operate covertly on Earth. According to Navy

Intelligence whistleblower William Cooper: "the aliens showed a hologram which they claimed was the actual crucifixion of Christ, which the government filmed." Similarly, when this technology is revealed, there will be no such thing as a controversy, a cover up, a conspiracy theory or a secret of any kind. There will be no such thing as a conspiracy because all history will be accessible by everyone. *So is it any wonder that the people who have been privy to this knowledge do not want it released?*

Just imagine the possibilities when the reverse-engineered *Sun Disc* or *Looking Glass* technology is released to everyone. You may recall the ancient device of *Mu*, that allowed users to view past lifetimes, and glimpse future events. Talk about the killer app on your smart phone! Would you like to learn about your past lives, or are you interested in a specific moment of history? Would you like a glimpse of environmental conditions on the planet 100 years from now, or a million years ago? With this app we can peer back and watch the Vikings leave runestones in the interior of North America, or the Passion Play and recount the last moments of Jesus Christ as seen by the generals and scientists during the first demonstration by the Greys of the Yellow Cube—or even go further back to pre-sand Egypt, Atlantis, or to the older sagas throughout the long history of this planet. Other top moments to investigate in North American history could include: the Egyptians in the Grand Canyon; the Phoenicians collecting copper in the Lake Superior region; the Vikings exploring, colonizing, influencing and interacting with Native Americans; or Sir Francis Drake discovering and sailing around the San Francisco Bay in Northern California.

While we enjoy looking along the timelines of history, let's also peer into the origins of several great prehistoric civilizations including Nan Madol in the Pacific, and the high culture of the Maya in Central America. Reading the Essene Gospel of Peace and other lost or edited versions of the Dead Sea Scrolls would also be quite interesting. Can you imagine how much there will be to learn from our past? Certainly the release of Looking Glass technology will utterly change the world as we know it, and will usher in a true Age of Transparency. It is said that history is written by the victors. With this technology, every single historical record will get a new look and revision, if necessary, along with a true dating in the archaeological record. After all, as a modern science, archaeology dates only to the 1840s, in the early years of Victorian Age. We have so much to learn about the planet's true history. In the next chapter we'll turn to the lost continents on Earth, and the advanced civilizations they once supported.

The most ancient vase on Earth was discovered in 1851 in Massachusetts when workers were blasting in a quarry. It is a zinc vase inlaid with fine silver in the form of a vine. The age of this vase, based on the block of un-mined coal in which it was found, is an astonishing 534 million years old. This dates back to the Cambrian Period, which is marked as a period of profound change in life on Earth when living organisms made the jump from small, unicellular and simple species to complex animal forms.

Goddess worship dates back to Paleolithic times. Many anthropologists speculate the first "god" or "goddesses" of the people were feminine. This coincides with ancient creation myths and beliefs that creation was achieved through self-fertilization. Within the earliest concept of creation, the participation of the male principle was not yet known or recognized. The Goddess was believed to have created the universe by herself alone.

ABYDOS. OSIREION. XIX DYN.   1.

1. VIEW LOOKING SOUTH, SHOWING   2. DOORWAY OF SCULPTURED CHAMBER, LOOKING NORTH.
   DIRECTION OF TRENCH.

3. VIEW OF GREAT HALL, S. AND W. WALLS.

In the winter of 1902-03, Egyptologist Margaret Murray was the first to rediscover the Osireion in Abydos, Egypt, as it had been covered in rubble by previous excavations of the Temple of Seti I. These photos were likely taken in 1903. The top image shows the Osireion filled with sand. Just imagine stumbling upon such a monument after having lain dormant for so many centuries beneath the sand.

An ancient Egyptian carving on the ceiling beams of the Temple of Seti I at Abydos depict what look like flying machines and other types of military vehicles. Notice the helicopter, tank and submarine shaped hieroglyphics. Two other kinds of craft resembling a zeppelin and glider are facing the same direction. This intact hieroglyph shows a section that is 12 meters from the floor level, up against the ceiling, with no evidence that pieces have fallen away. Anything over five meters from the floor were indications about the future.

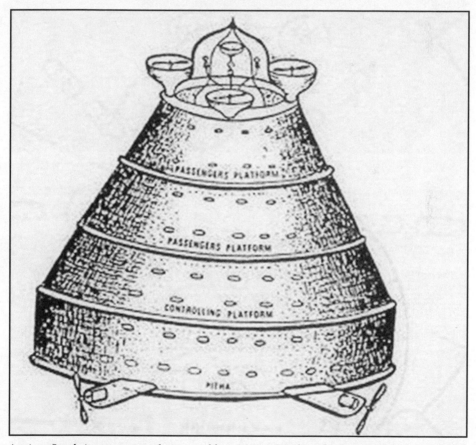

Ancient Sanskrit texts, some dating as old as 6,000 BCE, describe in varying but vivid detail prehistoric flying machines called "vimanas." According to Dr. V. Raghavan, the retired head of the Sanskrit department of India's prestigious University of Madras, Earth was a host to extraterrestrials in prehistory. Dr. Raghavan contends that centuries-old documentation in Sanskrit, the classical language of India and Hinduism, proves that aliens from outer space visited his nation. "Fifty years of researching these ancient works," he said, "convinces me that there are livings beings on other planets, and that they visited Earth as far back as 4,000 BCE."

< This is an image of astonishing, precision-cut, mega-ton blocks of pink granite at Ollantaytambo Peru. How did the Incas move five 50,000-ton rocks from one side of the valley and place them on a mountainside on the other side of the valley with such precision that a human hair cannot fit between the blocks? There are also shims between the blocks so they can "ride" earthquakes. Who taught the Incas this method, and why build so large? There is no construction vehicle available in the world today that can replicate these construction techniques.

This photo was taken in 1911 by the explorer Hiram Bingham when he gazed upon the lost city of Machu Picchu high up in the Andes Mountains of Peru. Although the citadel is located only about 80 kilometers from Cusco, the Inca capital, the Spanish never located Machu Picchu and consequently did not plunder or destroy it as they did many other sites. Over the centuries, the surrounding jungle grew over much of the site, and few outsiders knew of its existence.

This mechanical device was found in volcanic rock estimated to be 400 million years old! It was found, among other strange fossils also recovered, on the remote Kamchatka Peninsula in Eastern Russia, about 220 kilometers from the village of Tigil. Archaeologists at the University of St. Petersburg provided the expert dating. The reliability of this discovery and others has been independently certified. According to archaeologist Yuri Golubev, the find amazed experts because it was clearly some sort of a machine.

This is an old photo of the Tiwanaku Gate of the Sun in Bolivia. Some archeologists believe this monument predates the last pole shift, when the land it was built on was close to sea level and then thrust high up to the Andean Plateau. The Gate of the Sun is shown here twisted and tweaked by a powerful earthquake in the past, so is no longer aligned with the Sun in the east as it was originally designed to capture.

< The stones within the walls of Sacsayhuaman in Cusco, Peru, fit so perfectly that no blade of grass or sliver of steel can slide between them. There is no mortar. The stones often are joined on complex and irregular surfaces that would appear to be a design nightmare for any stonemason.

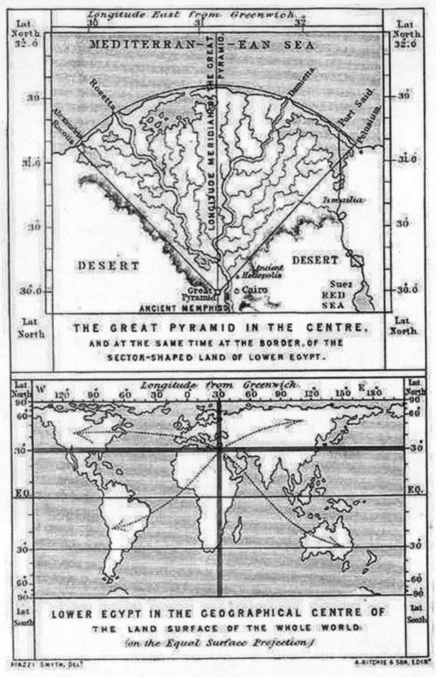

The Great Pyramid lies in the gravity center of the continents. It also lies in the exact center of all the land area of the world, dividing the Earth's landmass into approximately equal quarters. Giza has undoubtedly been constructed to the mathematical proportions of phi. The north-south axis (31° east of Greenwich) is the longest land meridian, and the east-west axis (30° north) is the longest land parallel on the globe. There is obviously only one place that these longest land lines of the terrestrial Earth can cross, and this is precisely where the Great Pyramid of Giza is placed.

LOST CONTINENTS

"God is our refuge and strength, a very present help in trouble. Therefore will not we fear, though the Earth be removed, and though the mountains be carried into the midst of the sea. Though the waters thereof roar and be troubled, though the mountains shake with the swelling thereof." —Book of Psalms, The Holy Bible (King James Version)

THE surface of the Earth is inherently unstable and erratic. The continental land surfaces of the planet rest upon an underground sea of molten lava which causes the land masses to continually crack, crumble and drift. When one land section drops into the sea, another region conceivably rises. Because of the liquid nature of the lower mantle, our planet is largely volcanic and subject to earthquakes and volcanic explosions. In addition to this, the magnetic poles of the Earth are now understood to shift radically about once every 20,000 years, which is a nanosecond in geological terms.

Prior to the acceptance of continental drift, biologists periodically postulated submerged landmasses in order to account for populations of land-based species now separated by barriers of water. Correspondingly, geologists tried to account for striking resemblances of rock formations on different continents. The first systematic attempt to account for these similar rock formations was made by Melchior Neumayr in his 1887 book, *Erdgeschichte*, meaning "Geological History of the Earth." Many hypothetical submerged land bridges and continents were proposed during the 19th century in order to account for the present distribution of species. Like archaeology, the relatively new endeavor of geology only began in the 19th century. Scientific breakthroughs have expanded on Neumayr's "Geological History of the Earth" by leaps and bounds.

Geologists in the 21st century can track the motion of continents over hundreds of millions of years ago because the direction of Earth's magnetic field changes with the latitude and becomes fixed in the sedimentary rocks and lava when they solidify. Most geologists believe Africa, North America, Australia and Europe were near the equator during an ice age 650 million years ago. Fossils of tropical plants and animals have been found on the frozen continent of Antarctica and on the highest peaks in the Himalayas. Tropical flora and fauna could not have lived in these harsh environments before the continents shifted, simply because they required much warmer conditions to exist. This can only prove that continents rise and fall, drift and sink, and often make enormous planetary surface changes in relatively short periods of time.

If we look at the Earth's timeline of evolution, we find numerous anomalies. For example, evolution scientists reveal that it took 3.5 billion years for microscopic life to evolve into algae. This seems reasonable, but are we really supposed to believe that algae evolved into dinosaurs in one tenth that time? Might it be possible that flora and fauna were exported from other oxygen atmosphere planets, or cultivated by intelligent genetic operations to fertilize the Earth? To ancient alien theorists, our planet was artificially terraformed and populated with creatures ever since the "Cambrian explosion," a period when many species seemed to just "appear" in the fossil record.

Another anomaly is the very short period of time (a mere five million years) in which the first hominids arose. By extension, it can be argued that modern *homo sapiens* did not organically evolve on Earth to reach our present level either, but were genetically manipulated. Evolutionary processes surely do function on micro levels, but the quick leap of a fully developed species is looking less and less likely. This is due to the fact, as noted by Dr. Francis Crick, that the DNA molecule is just too complicated to have arisen purely by "natural mutations." Crick, one of the original discoverers of the DNA molecule, later proved mathematically that it was impossible for evolution to have produced the varied and extremely complex DNA forms of life in the short amount of time proposed by evolutionists. Also, Earth has had too many extinction events for human survival to be simply an accident.

There is ample evidence of global civilizations prior to our own, as well as an occurrence of global cataclysms in Earth's long history. These are often caused by astronomical phenomena such as meteorites or the passing of large heavenly bodies. An impact or overt gravitational pull from a passing planet could have triggered a pole shift. Global earthquakes, tsunamis, volcanoes, new continents rising and falling, and global floods are usually associated with a pole shift. We will look at the geology of our planet first, and then examine the evidence suggesting the existence of prior civilizations.

AS THE POLES SHIFT

The pole shift theory is a hypothesis that the axis of rotation of our planet has not always existed at its present-day location—or that our present axis will not persist in its place indefinitely. Over the long march of time the physical poles have shifted many times ... but questions remain: how frequently and how rapidly. Pole shift theory is almost always discussed in the context of Earth, but other solar system planets may have experienced axial reorientation during their existences. Pole shift theories are not to be confused with plate tectonics, the well-accepted geological theory that the Earth's surface consists of solid plates that shift over a fluid asthenosphere. Nor should pole shifts be confused with continental drift, that is, the corollary to plate tectonics that maintains that the locations of the continents has moved slowly over the surface of the Earth, resulting in the gradual emerging and breakup of continents, plus the reorientation of the ocean's shorelines over hundreds of millions of years. Pole shift theories are also not to be confused with geomagnetic reversal, the periodic reversal of the Earth's magnetic field that effectively flip-flops the north and south magnetic poles. Geomagnetic reversal has more current acceptance in the scientific community than theories related to pole shifts.

In 1852, mathematician Joseph Adhemar suggested that the accumulation of thick ice at the poles periodically caused the Earth's axis to flip, and the equator to suddenly move to where the poles were once located. An early mention of the Earth's shifting axis can be found in an 1872 article entitled "Chronologie historique des Mexicains," which interpreted ancient Mexican myths as evidence for keeping record for four periods of global cataclysms that had begun around 10,500 BCE.

Charles Hapgood is perhaps the most renowned proponent of pole shifts, as described in his two books: *The Earth's Shifting Crust* (1958), which featured a foreword by Albert Einstein; and *Path of the Pole* (1970). Hapgood built upon Adhemar's earlier model, and speculated that the ice mass at one or both poles can over-accumulate and destabilizes the Earth's rotational balance, causing slippage of the Earth's outer crust around the Earth's core, while the core retains its axial orientation. Based on his own research, he argued that each shift took approximately five thousand years, followed by 20-30 thousand year periods with no polar movements. Also, in his calculations, the area of movement never migrated more than 40°. His examples of recent North Pole shift locations include the Yukon Territory, Hudson Bay, and in the Atlantic Ocean between Iceland and Norway. In the last decade the magnetic North Pole has been tracking a course towards Siberia.

Hapgood was a proponent of slow-pole-shift-motion, which causes only the most minor alterations and no widespread destruction. Many recent views predict more rapid changes, with dramatic alterations of geography and localized areas of destruction due to earthquakes and tsunamis. Several recent books propose changes that take place in weeks, days, or even hours, resulting in a variety of doomsday scenarios. Regardless of speed, the occurrence of a pole shift results in major climate changes for most of the Earth's surface, since areas that were formerly equatorial become temperate, and areas that were temperate transform to either more equatorial or more arctic.

Referring to Hapgood's research, Albert Einstein wrote that the idea of Earth crust displacement should not be ruled out "apriori" just because it does not fit with what we want to believe about the planet's past. What is needed, Einstein claimed, is solid "geological and paleontological facts." For six months, Hapgood gathered the geological evidence to support the idea of an Earth crust displacement. In May of 1953 he forwarded 38 pages of this evidence to Einstein. Central to Hapgood's argument was his evidence that Lesser Antarctica was ice free at the same time that North America lay smothered in ice. Einstein responded to Hapgood a week later: "I find your arguments very impressive and have the impression that your hypothesis is correct. One can hardly doubt that significant shifts of the crust have taken place repeatedly and within a short time." He urged Hapgood to follow up on evidence of "Earth fractures." After Hapgood published *Path of the Pole*, he collaborated with Rand Flem-Ath, a Canadian librarian and Atlantis researcher, and they worked together in pursuit of scientific evidence to back their pole shift theories. Together with his wife Rose, Rand Flem-Ath published *When the Sky Fell*, in 1995, but Hapgood passed away in 1982 and never saw the finished book.

There are three possible scenarios where the axis poles could shift independent of polar ice accumulation. One theory proposes that pole shifts are a natural occurrence because the magnetic poles drift off course every 20 or 30 thousand years, and the axis poles eventually follow suit. The next possibility is a high-velocity asteroid or comet which hits Earth at such an angle that the lithosphere moves independent of the mantle, or at such an angle that the entire planet's axis shifts from the impact. The final possibility is an unusually large and magnetic celestial object which passes close enough to Earth that it may temporarily reorient the magnetic field, which then "drags" the lithosphere into a new axis of rotation. This could correspond to Planet X, or Marduk, as proposed by Zecharia Sitchin, in which a "12th planet" rotates around the Sun in a very oblong orbit.

In this scenario, the movement of the tectonic plates will settle down after the intruding celestial object passes far enough away so it can no longer influence the Earth.

The nearest example of the second scenario dates from June 30, 1908, when a massive explosion devastated a remote area called Tunguska in the Siberian wilderness. The explosion is believed to have been caused by the air burst of a small asteroid or comet at an altitude of 5 to 10 kilometers above Earth's surface, which caused the surface of 2,150 square kilometers of land to be instantly destroyed. Scientists believe it was caused by either a meteorite or a fragment of a comet, although no obvious impact site or mineral remnants of such an object were ever found, suggesting the asteroid or comet might have burst in the air rather than hitting the surface. The blast was equivalent to 10-15 megatons of TNT, yet the explosion did not trigger any plate movements, and certainly not a pole shift. The Tunguska incident is the most powerful explosion to have occurred in modern human history. Not even subsequent thermonuclear detonations have surpassed its size. The explosion was audible up to a thousand kilometers away. In any pole shift scenario, the Sun's magnetic field will eventually help to determine the Earth's new magnetic field.

In July, 2013, very disturbing evidence of macro Earth changes began to emerge from the Arctic region. Images entitled the "Day the North Pole Became a Lake" went viral, and Internet users were confronted with solid evidence that the planet was heating up. The ever-shrinking Arctic Sea ice sheet has become a noticeable victim of climate change. The area of ice cover expands and contracts every year with the change of seasons, but the minimum extent in the summer of 2012 was the lowest on record, and the maximum winter coverage in 2013 was the sixth-lowest since satellite observations began in the 1970s. Most distressing to scientists is the fact that global warming is occurring at a more rapid pace than anyone estimated. Also disturbing is the quickened rate in which the North Magnetic Pole is drifting, not only in the past decade, but in just the past several years. In the first six months of 2013, for example, the North Magnetic Pole has shifted an astonishing 267 kilometers! It is currently moving at the rate of one kilometer per day, putting its arrival on the land mass of Siberia in a few years. According to NOAA, the North Magnetic Pole will cross over top of the axis of the Earth in 2018 for the first time in our modern history. It will cross the 180 degree line of longitude and will be well on its way towards Siberia. When the magnetic North Pole arrives in Siberia, it will have migrated 40° across the northern hemisphere. Geomagnetic reversal scientists believe this will be a tipping point, when the poles will shift at high speed over the equator until it reaches 40° south.

SUDDEN CATACLYSMS

If you ask the average person on the street what they understand by the term "ice age," most will tell you that it was an era when continuous ice sheets smothered Arctic regions well into what are now temperate climes—as far south as approximately 50° north in Europe, and 36° north in North America. The resultant bleak landscape is often imagined as having been inhabited by such animals as the hairy mammoth, woolly rhinoceros and musk ox, and hunted by our fur clothed ancestors.

The origins of such beliefs lies in the placement by geologists of such an ice age in the Pleistocene Epoch, and this came to an end about 11,000 years ago when our own era, the Holocene, began. The several phases of the last ice age are said to have persisted for about a million years, during which time the ice sheets repeatedly waxed and waned. Coincidentally, ocean ice sheets similar to those expanding over Arctic latitude, also allegedly blanketed the southern polar regions. Directly associated with the notion of an ice age, and indeed largely responsible for its inception, were a number of singular geological phenomena which, because they sometimes occurred together, apparently shared a common origin. Also included were striated rock surfaces, glacial erratic boulders and immense accumulations of frequently intractable "drift" deposits. The geographical settings and locations of these features were also peculiar. The striations, which often occurred in groups, nearly always shared a single orientation that commonly went against obviously pre-existing topography. The erratic boulders, that in some locations are very numerous, lie at all kinds of altitudes despite their often stupendous size and weight. Examples are known to be as long as a half-kilometer in size, and all occur at great distances from the nearest natural outcrops of the particular strata where they originated. The drift deposits sometimes occur on southern hill-slopes only, or on certain mountain peaks, but not in adjacent valleys, or, frequently, on chronically pulverized mantles underlying bedrock. The simultaneous eruption of megacolossal volcanoes would blanket the atmosphere in days, causing winter-like conditions globally. This impression, generally supported by all the evidence, is one of overwhelming force operating indiscriminately, suddenly violent, and on a colossal scale. It should be noted that Yellowstone National Park in Wyoming lies over a "super volcano." It has erupted numerous times over the past 16 million years. The last major eruption was 640,000 years ago. Past calderas reflect the movement of the North American plate over a massive magma chamber. Eruptions may be connected to fault lines moving over the chamber.

Early surviving Mesopotamian legends record an epic conflict, not merely in relation to Earth, but also involving other planets in our solar system. "Marduk" was one of their names for this marauding celestial body, that the Sumerians expressly stated as arriving from the depths of space, and being drawn towards the Sun by its enormous gravitational pull. Ancient cuneiform tablets describe Marduk's progress in considerable detail, along with stories of its Anunnaki inhabitants. Marduk's last passing of Earth was both disruptive, and destructive. Its sunward journey took it past, *or near*, many of our system's planets and their satellites, including the Earth and our moon. If these descriptions are genuine, then it collided with a planet called Tiamat which then disintegrated. This former celestial body once orbited beyond Mars, but was reduced to rubble after its collision with Marduk. The Asteroid Belt between Mars and Jupiter is the only remnant left of Tiamat. Babylonian baked-clay tablets depicting the solar system consistently show one planet too many, while ancient Greek traditions speak of the lost planet called Electra. Marduk, also referred to as "Nibiru" by the Babylonians, is not a planet, but instead our binary brown dwarf twin to our Sun, and whose gravitational pull wreaks havoc on any smaller planet's axis when it passes—or even destroy a small planet in its direct path.

When a pole shift occurs, however infrequently, disasters seems to disrupt the Earth's surface features—and in rapid succession. It is clear that the Earth's planetscape has been altered on numerous occasions, and had numerous periods of tremendous upheaval. This has included massive crustal fissuring, both above and below sea level; an uplift, often violent, of many of the Earth's greatest mountain ranges to their present elevations; widespread seismic and volcanic eruptions that also cause acute atmospheric pollution; extensive crustal subsidence; and, the emptying and displacement of seas and lakes along with the destruction of older drainage systems. Worldwide evidence of bone-packed caves with suddenly deposited animal remains, or prehistoric woolly mammoths crushed by soil or ice so instantaneously that they still had food in their mouths, suggest that great changes can happen in a near instant. Especially telling are the rock-fissures, frequently containing contemporary but faunistically and climatically incompatible creatures. This not only emphasize the catastrophic nature of these events, but also strongly indicates an occasional alteration in the tilt of the Earth's axis.

THE TOBA INCIDENT

Some 74,000 years ago, a massive volcano called Toba on the Indonesian island of Sumatra, unleashed one of the greatest eruptions ever known, spreading blankets of ash across southern Asia. The Toba eruption corresponds to a period of great Earth changes. The catastrophe also had many human witnesses. Archaeologists digging beneath the ash layer have found stone artifacts indicating that humans were living in the Jurreru Valley of southern India before the eruption. The Toba eruption had an estimated Volcanic Explosivity Index of 8, described as "megacolossal," making it possibly the largest explosive volcanic eruption within the last 25 million years. It left behind a crater which measured 100 kilometers across. It was also responsible for the formation of sulfuric acid in the atmosphere. To give an idea of its magnitude, consider that although the eruption took place on the island of Sumatra in Indonesia, it deposited an ash layer approximately 15 centimeters thick over the entire Indian subcontinent. At one site in central India, the Toba ash layer was excavated to reveal a depth of six meters, and parts of Malaysia were covered with nine meters of ashfall. A small group of modern humans in India suffered through the Toba ash cloud catastrophe, an event that reduced their numbers to near extinction. It has been calculated that 10 metric tons of sulphuric acid was ejected into the atmosphere by this event, causing widespread acid rain fallout.

The Lake Toba eruption plunged the Earth into a volcanic winter, eradicating an estimated 60% or more of the worldwide human population, most of whom may have been the surviving descendents of Lemuria. Although humans managed to survive, even within the vicinity of northern Sumatra, the eruption changed the atmosphere of the planet and made survival nearly impossible. Only about 3,000 generations ago, a mere blink in the evolutionary timescale, the human population of Earth dwindled to the point where every human on the planet could have fit inside a small American football stadium. The fallout from the Toba eruption may have possibly reduced the entire human population to merely a few thousand individuals who, according to geneticists, helps to explain the similarity between all human DNA. All of us today are presumably the living descendants of a handful of survivors of the Toba eruption, about 74,000 years ago.

ANCIENT ASTRONAUTS

The ancient astronaut theory seeks to explain anomalies in the human past, whether they be archaeological, mythological, anthropological, or palaeoanthropological. Putting the debate about whether or not aliens exist or visited Earth long ago aside, there is little doubt that humankind has been fascinated with ETs ever since ancient times. Historians and archeologists have found many representations of alien looking beings throughout the world. Not only do we find depictions of aliens in ancient artwork, but we also find clues in the stories, legends and lore of the ancients that point to the reality of different looking hominids interacting with humanity. What's more, giant skulls have also been discovered in many locations worldwide, revealing that these were not ordinary humans. Even *Discover* magazine carried the story in December, 2009, of the massive Boskop skulls, a type of large cranium hominid found in South Africa, Mesoamerica, Siberia and elsewhere, and with double the brain size of a normal person. No known human deformity can explain these skulls.

Worldwide ancient traditions tell of a traumatic long ago battle between Earth and an atrocious cosmic visitor, remembered by various names, terminated a previous Golden Age, and set the Earth alight before extinguishing the fires with a vast flood. Biblical texts call the latter "Noah's Deluge," and the classical Greek name of "Phaeton" is ascribed to this fiery celestial intruder. These two stories, and many others, epitomize an historically familiar sequence of disastrous events.

Our ancient relatives utilized technology that is significantly more advanced than our own. Such technology was used to levitate gigantic blocks of stone into the megalithic architecture structures found worldwide. If this were easy to do, whether a given culture is primitive or not, we would undoubtedly still be doing it today. Nonetheless, when the Japanese attempted to recreate the Great Pyramid at a much smaller scale, with fully modern equipment, they utterly failed. Yet towering pyramids and other gigantic stone structures have been discovered all around the world, both above and below the ocean surface.

Ancient underwater structures can be found in hundreds of locations, but could these aquatic relics be the ruins of unknown civilizations—or even proof of extraterrestrial visitations? The infamous tale of the long lost city of Atlantis may be a preserved memory of an ancient alien metropolis populated with very human-like inhabitants. The ruins of recently discovered temples beneath Lake Titicaca in Peru support local legends of an underwater UFO city occupied by the "Great White Brotherhood." On the other side of the world ancient Indian texts, known as *Sangams*, describe sunken cities where aliens and humans intermingled thousands of years ago. In various locations under the waters of the Mediterranean and Caribbean Seas there are hundreds of coastal and island cities, some of which sank eons ago, while others perished more recently, within the past 6,000 years. The biblical cities of Sodom and Gomorra are also rumored to be located underwater beneath the Dead Sea. Likewise, wherever there are gold resources that can be mined, we also find ancient mines from previous highly advanced civilizations. These same cultures inherited the myths that revealed the importance of a 25,920-year cycle.

PROCESSION OF THE EQUINOXES

Our galaxy has a distinct center around which all the stars take millions of years to revolve. As seen from Earth, the galactic center is located in the starriest part of the Milky Way. On four occasions within a 25,800-year Earth cycle, our galactic center aligns with the sunrise of a solstice or equinox. The last time it came to pass was on a fall equinox 6,450 years ago, approximately at the dawn of the emergence of *Old World* civilizations on Earth. On the winter solstice in the northern hemisphere, on December 21, 2012, this galactic center has once again aligned with our Sun. Apparently, this event was recorded by the Maya in their mapping of the "Long Count" of time. The Maya left behind astrological, monumental and mythological evidence to emphasize the importance of this era we have just entered. It is suggested that the Maya calendar ran *out of time* on this day for a very profound reason.

Time and again, the ancients recorded galactic alignment to occur only once every 25,920 years, representing the apparent motion of the stars in the night sky which drift by 1° every 72 years when viewed on the same day each year. Astronomers argue that the galactic equator is an entirely arbitrary line, and can never be precisely determined, because it is impossible to say exactly where the Milky Way begins or ends. Nevertheless, many independent accounts maintain this alignment occurs as a result of the precession of the equinoxes. In Western astrology, the cycle is divided up into 12 parts of 2,160 years each—known as the "Ages of the Zodiac." We are now moving into the "Age of Aquarius." In over 30 different ancient cultures—virtually every ancient philosophical system in the world—information was "encoded," suggesting that history repeats itself in this vast 25,920-year cycle. This was proven by reputable scholars Giorgio de Santillana and Hertha von Dechend in their epic 1969 work, *Hamlet's Mill*, and brought to public mass awareness by Graham Hancock in his essential 1995 classic, *Fingerprints of the Gods*.

New Age proponents of the galactic alignment hypothesis argue that, just as astrology uses the positions of stars and planets to make claims of future events, the Mayans plotted their calendars with the objective to prepare for significant world events. Independent researcher John Major Jenkins authored a book entitled *Maya Cosmogenesis 2012*, with an introduction by Terence McKenna, which illustrates that the Maya not only understood precession, but that their 2012 end-date predicted a special demarcation. What the prophecies foretold is a coming "Golden Age" of unprecedented peace and prosperity.

The procession of the equinoxes is caused by the Earth slowly wobbling on its axis, a motion that is almost imperceptible within an elderly person's lifetime. This shift in position of 1° occurs every 71.5 years on the equinoxes and solstices. Because the sun is *one-half* of a degree wide, it will take the December solstice sun 36 years to precess through the galactic equator. This "galactic alignment" occurs only once every 26,000 years, and is what the ancient Maya were identifying with the year 2012 end-date on their Long Count calendar.

LEMURIA OR MU OR ATLANTIS

It needs first to be pointed out that Atlantis was merely one name of several ancient civilizations identified worldwide. The "lost continent" of Atlantis certainly did not sink all at once, and there is plenty of hard evidence left behind, such as numerous megalithic stone structures located all around the world, and some even found under the surface of the ocean. Over 3,300 of these ancient stone structures have been identified, and most were clustered around and built atop a "global grid" of lines that originate from the 12 "vortex points" where ships and planes continue to disappear on Earth (as discovered by Ivan T. Sanderson in the 1960s). Sanderson did the hard work of plotting out where ships and planes were disappearing, going back through the entire history of aviation, and much of the available marine history. These twelve points, curiously enough, are evenly spaced in a sort of geometric grid. The most infamous is the Bermuda Triangle in the central North Atlantic Ocean, which connects to the island of Bermuda, then south to Miami, and including all of Puerto Rico.

Nearly as famous as Atlantis is the legendary lost world of Mu, at times called Lemuria. Among Pacific islanders and according to tradition, Mu was an Eden-like tropical paradise located somewhere in the Pacific that sank, along with all of its beautiful inhabitants, thousands of years ago. Like Atlantis, there is an ongoing debate as to whether it really existed and, if so, where. Madame Helena Blavatsky, the founder of the Theosophical Society in the 1800s, believed it to be located in the Indian Ocean.

Although Lemuria has been excluded from the realm of conventional science, it has been embraced by occult writers, as well as some Tamil writers of India. Accounts of Lemuria differ according to the requirements of their contexts, but all share a common belief that a continent existed in ancient times and sank beneath the ocean as a result of geological change, seemingly cataclysmic. The ancient residents of *Mu* who remain alive today are a favorite subject of channelers who decipher their enlightened messages without an actual physical meeting.

Lemuria entered the lexicon of occult studies through the works of Madame Blavatsky, who claimed in the 1880s to have been shown an ancient, pre-Atlantean *Book of Dzyan* by the "mahatmas," or the great souls of India. Helena Blavatsky's *The Secret Doctrine* is purported to be an actual book from Lemuria summarizing occult knowledge about the evolution of the universe. It is actually a *channeled* book, and the esoteric name for Lemuria is *Shalmali*. The Theosophists also greatly elaborated the Atlantis story, adding numerous additional lost continents such as Hyperborea, Daitya, Ruta, and Poseidonis. Each of these locations were populated by a succession of pre-human species.

The fate of Lemuria, also known as Pacifica, Mu, and what Edgar Cayce called Zu or Oz, is not unlike the fate suggested for Atlantis. It is much like the destiny of humanity foreseen in *our* timeline by prophets of old and modern-day clairvoyants. The legends are all the same: a thriving and advanced culture that suddenly manifested out of nowhere. Their origins and downfall are all linked to destruction when their continents sank *beneath the "sea"* and due to natural cataclysms, and perhaps human imbalance.

THE DECLINE OF LEMURIA

Many Lemuria researchers claim that it was the *science of government* that was these early civilization's greatest achievement. Supposedly, far in our distant past, there was just one common language, and one benevolent government. Education was the keynote of the Empire's success. And, because every citizen was versed in the laws of the universe, and given thorough training in a profession or trade, the result was magnificent prosperity. A child's education was compulsory until the age of 21 in order for the adult to be eligible to attend citizenship school. This training period lasted for seven years, and so the earliest age at which a person could become a citizen of the empire was 28. The *garden planet* was filled with wild animals, abundant flora, and the human population was a mere fraction of what it is today.

The long-extinct Pacific continent that comprised Lemuria was first damaged around 74,000 years ago from volcanic eruptions and global tsunamis, but the residents rebuilt their civilization over the next 60,000 years into what eventually blended culturally into Atlantis. Both civilizations were seafaring and trading empires. The Lemurian capital city was located along the Lombak Strait that connects the Java Sea to the Indian Ocean. This part of the world was known for having gigantic elephants, remains of which can be seen today at the Bandung Museum in Indonesia. The fossil skeletons of these giant elephants, close to the size of wooly mammoths. The Gunung Padang Pyramid Mountain in Indonesia has been confirmed by carbon-dated as being built around 14,000 to 16,000 years ago, and this puts it just outside the time frame of Lemuria. The geologist Andang Bachtiar, a member of the Indonesian Task Force that studies ancient ruins in Indonesia, reported that there is evidence of a devastating tsunami in ancient times. These massive waves would have swept over and destroyed almost all of the Lemurian buildings in what is today Indonesia.

According to various esoteric sources, the first Lemurian civilization arose approximately 78,000 years ago on a large South Pacific continent and lasted for an astonishing 52,000 years. It is sometimes said to have been destroyed in earthquakes generated by a pole shift that occurred around 26,000 years ago. While supposedly Lemuria did not reach as high in technological advancement as other later civilizations like Atlantis, it is nevertheless said to have attained skill in the construction of megalithic buildings, a few of which being able to withstand earthquakes and tsunamis. Another indication of advanced technology is found among the mysterious ruins discovered on a small island called Malden in the vast Pacific Ocean basin. There are 40 stone temples on Malden Island that are described as being similar in design to the buildings of the equally puzzling Nan Madol site on Pohnpei island, about 5,475 kilometers away in Micronesia. On Malden Island, there is a stone road that runs along the bottom of the Pacific Ocean, under hundreds of meters of water, connects and crosses the island, and then subsides back underwater again. This suggests that an entire land mass was once above water, supporting an advanced and complex civilization. In addition, the Malden ruins are said to contain the remains of yet another ancient pyramid.

The largest building of Nan Madol is called Nan Dawas. It is a massive open-air complex with an inner sanctum. Underground tunnels connect Nan Dowas to several of the larger buildings, each built onto its own islet. It has been reported that some of these tunnels go beneath the reef and exit to underwater caves that can be investigated while scuba diving. The walls of Nan Dowas are an impressive 11 meters high, and are constructed of huge expertly stacked stones. Some of the rocks are basalt logs five meters long and with a hexagonal shape, and formed naturally on the island through crystallization. The largest stones are huge slabs that are roughly cut and dressed. Contained within the rock basalt of Nan Madol are large crystals that are highly magnetized. These heavy basalt crystals are so magnetized that compasses spin out of control when held near the walls.

Further adding to the mystery, before World War II Japanese divers discovered platinum watertight tombs containing very large human bones. This coincides with other discoveries of massive bones, suggesting the existence of giant people with a highly advanced civilization. Could all this suggest evidence of a very old, sunken continent in the Pacific?

There is a legendary sunken kingdom called Kumari Kandam that is described in ancient Tamil literature. This supposedly sunken landmass is frequently compared with Lemuria. According to modern interpretations of classical Tamil literature, the epics *Cilappatikaram* and *Manimekalai* describe a submerged city called Puhar. It is said the Dravidian race of people occupying southern India originally came from a land that is south of the present day coastline and that became submerged by successive floods. There are various claims from Tamil authors that a large landmass once connected Australia to the present day Tamil Nadu coast. It is interesting to note that Madame Blavatsky portrays the Lemurians as being black, and described the Negroid race of India and Australia, the Dravidians and the Australoids respectively, along with the Papuans and Melanesians, as being descended from Lemurians, Blavatsky's third root race. The first root race were "ethereal" in nature; while the second root race were the "golden yellow-skinned" Hyperboreans; the *third root race* were dark-skinned Lemurians, with the fourth and final root race being the multi-racial Atlanteans. When viewed from this perspective, humans on Earth are a hybridized race stemming from multiple independent points of origin, and having cross-bred over the last 200,000 years.

The exact location of Lemuria varies among researchers and authors, although it is one of the mysteries of the Pacific region that flows into the South American continent, much like as Atlantis is linked to the northern Atlantic land areas that stretch from the Mediterranean to the Caribbean Seas. Wherever the location of Lemuria may be, it is linked with the Ring of Fire, and the equatorial region of the southern hemisphere.

IN SEARCH OF LOST CIVILIZATIONS

Lemuria was the archetypal Atlantis, comparable to the Garden of Eden or paradise, and considered the site of origin for both humankind and advanced Earth civilization. From a Pacific region that was once largely above water, the Lemurian Atlanteans colonized the nearby region of India, which became its "twin" and partner. In mythical terms, we can say that Lemuria-Indonesia was the Mother, and that Atlantis-India was the Father of all the other civilizations.

Off the southern Japanese island of Okinawa, and at several locations in the Ryukyu Island chain, beneath 6 to 40 meters of water scuba divers discovered enigmatic structures that appear to have been built by an ancient lost civilization. Offshore of certain islands in Okinawa Prefecture of Japan, especially the small island of Yonaguni about 110 kilometers east of Taiwan, divers located and mapped eight separate locations starting in March, 1995. Professor Masaki Kimura, a geologist at Ryukyu University in Okinawa, was the first scientist to investigate the Yonaguni site. He concluded that the mysterious five-layer underwater structure was human-built. "The object has not been manufactured by nature. If that had been the case, one would expect debris from erosion to have collected around the site, but there are no rock fragments there," he said. The discovery of what appears to be a road surrounding a building foundation was further evidence that the structure was made by humans, he noted. Skeptics dismissed the findings, saying the large, tiered formations are probably natural in origin. This skepticism did not last long. "Then, in late summer of the following year," writes Frank Joseph in an article for *Atlantis Rising*, "another diver in Okinawa waters was shocked to see a massive arch or gateway of huge stone blocks beautifully fitted together in the manner of prehistoric masonry found among the Inca cities on the other side of the Pacific Ocean in the Andes Mountains of South America." This seemed to confirm with all that the Okinawa underwater ruins were indeed human-crafted. The architecture includes what appear to be paved streets and crossroads, large altar-like formations, staircases leading to broad plazas, and processional pathways surmounted by pairs of towering features resembling pylons. Some of the peculiar details of Yonaguni include: Two closely spaced pillars which rise to within three meters of the surface; The "Loop Road," a five-meter-wide ledge that encircles the base of the formation on three sides; The "Totem," a stone column about seven meters tall; The "Dividing Wall," a straight wall 10-meters-long; The "Gosintai," an isolated boulder resting on a low platform; The "Turtle," a low star-shaped platform; The "Triangle Pool," a triangular depression with two large holes at its edge; and the "Stage," an L-shaped rock. If it is a sunken city, it is expansive, and its string of underwater ruins suggest that it could have been a northern outpost of Lemuria or Atlantis, or perhaps the remains of another lost civilization.

As legend would have it, once the Pacific continent sank and there was no turning back, the survivors of Lemuria relocated to the Gobi Desert in what are now the countries of Mongolia and China. Centuries later this empire was in conflict with and partly destroyed by Atlantis in a great war that led to a cataclysmic destruction of both Atlantis and the descendants of Lemuria. Mu was the name of their new great city on the surface of what is now the Gobi Desert. It had two satellite cities called Agartha Alpha and Beta that survived the destruction. The inhabitants of the great kingdom of Agartha are said to have had scientific knowledge and expertise far beyond that of the people who live on the surface of the planet today, and even equal to the lost technology of Atlantis.

The descendants of ancient Mu continue to live in peace within subterranean caverns below and around the Tibetan Plateau. The leaders of these states, variously called Ascended Masters, Guardians of the Tradition, *Psychoteleios* or "the Perfected Ones," the Shining Ones, the Ancients, the Watchers, the Immortals, the Monitors, or the Hidden Directorate, all follow what is known as the *Ancient Path* and do not interfere in the lives of humans who live above the surface—or is interaction allowed or desired. The Tibetans refer to the cities of Agartha as Shambala, and have believed for centuries in their existence as reservoirs of ancient knowledge and advanced technology.

TECHNOLOGY OF ATLANTIS

It is said that when the continent of Lemuria sank, the oceans of the world lowered drastically as water rushed into the newly expanding Pacific basin. The relatively small islands which had existed in the Atlantic during the time of the Lemurian civilization were left that and dry by the receding ocean. The newly emerged land joined the Poseid Archipelago of the Atlantic Ocean to form a small continent. This continent is called Atlantis by historians today, although its original name was Poseid.

Human history is incredibly rich in legends and stories. Yet perhaps none is as well known, and enticing as that of the "lost city" of Atlantis. Originally dictated by Plato in 330 BCE, most historians believe the story to simply be one of Plato's many fables, intended to teach a lesson or parable. In this story, Atlantis was an incredibly advanced community and civilization that attempted to "take over the world." In their efforts, the Athenians fought back, Atlantis was defeated, and ultimately lost forever. That legend has morphed into Atlantis being viewed as an idealized place to live, with countless people across history going on a search for its location, and plenty have claimed to have found it, or at least pinpointed which ocean or country where it might be lurking under watery depths or layers of topsoil.

Atlantis is believed to have taken technology to very advanced stages, well beyond what exists on our planet today. In the book *A Dweller On Two Planets*, first dictated in 1884 by "Phylos the Thibetan" to a young Californian named Frederick Spencer Oliver, as well as in a 1940 sequel, *An Earth Dweller Returns*, there is mention of such inventions and devices as air conditioners to overcome deadly and noxious vapors, airless cylinder lamps, tubes of crystal illuminated by the night side forces, electric rifles, guns employing electricity as a propulsive force, mono-rail transportation, water generators, an instrument for condensing water from the atmosphere, and the *Vailx*, an aerial ship governed by the forces of levitation and gravity repulsion.

Our Atlantean heritage also encompasses the legacy arts such as agriculture and animal husbandry, arguably the greatest inventions since the wheel. Without the domestication of plants and animals—most or all of which originated in Atlantis, and often embodied an advanced use of genetic engineering—what we know today as civilization could never have been developed. Besides these developments, a series of mysterious inventions, are also owed to Atlantis and Lemurian origin. Metallurgy, paper, the alphabet, medicinal drugs, gunpowder, weaving, and stone masonry are attributed to the great antediluvian societies of our distant past. Some of their technology is still considered secret science. The ancient builders used an ultrasonic machine for carving, for example, and sound vibration was used to produce an electromagnetic field that overcame gravity and could move huge rocks to construct the pyramids and other megalithic wonders.

An advanced ancient civilization such as Atlantis likely would have left behind a cache of records, and there is a significant amount of evidence, indicating that something like a *Hall of Records* may lie buried somewhere on Egypt's Giza Plateau, perhaps directly beneath the paws of the Sphinx. Several ancient texts refer to secret chambers and underground passageways beneath the Sphinx. Around 443 BCE, the Greek historian Herodotus reported that there exists a vast labyrinth beneath and beyond the Great Pyramids. Legends speak of a group of survivors from the lost continent of Atlantis who brought their advanced knowledge to Egypt and deposited it in a secret chamber beneath the Sphinx prior to the sinking of the great continent, around 10,500 BCE. Conventional Egyptologists dismiss such notions, stating the Sphinx was built approximately 5,000 years ago, and has no such lost chambers.

THE GREEK'S ATLANTIS

Along with Herodotus, many other prominent Greeks made the journey to Egypt in antiquity, some in their elder years. Besides being considered an ancient repository of knowledge, traveling to Egypt was a rite of passage. Solon was a famous statesman, lawmaker, lyric poet, and was even credited with having laid the foundations for Athenian democracy. The Greek travel writer named Pausanias listed Solon among the "Seven Sages" of the ancient world. After he had finished reforming the country, Solon traveled abroad, with his first stop at Egypt. There he visited Heliopolis, where he discussed philosophy with Psenophis, an Egyptian expert on the subject. Subsequently, at Sais, he visited Neith's temple and received an account of the history of Atlantis from the priests there. Solon wrote out this history as a poem, to which Plato subsequently made references in his dialogues, *Timaeus* and *Critias*.

Plato's reference to Egypt as the source of the Atlantis narrative came to him via Solon. The Egyptians called Atlantis by the name of *Kepchu*, which was their name for the people of Crete. It is known that survivors of the Minoan volcanic disaster asked Egypt for help, since they were the only other civilization with high culture at that time. Plato described quarries on the island of Atlantis where "rocks of white, black, and red" were extracted from the hills and used to construct a great island city. The description matches the colored rocks found on Santorini, another speculative location of Atlantis. The island of Santorini was devastated by one of the largest volcanic eruptions in recorded history, some 3,600 years ago. The Thera eruption occurred at the height of the Minoan civilization. Plato said that Atlantis existed much earlier than Thera, and the location was not near Santorini. Plato minces no words in placing its location just beyond what the Greeks called "the Pillars of Heracles," today known as the Rock of Gibraltar and the northern tip of Morocco.

The island-city of Atlantis was described by Plato as being laid out in a series of concentric circles of land and water, each one connected to the sea by a deep canal. Plato describes bustling docks hosting a huge number of ships, and extensive causeways for unloading cargo. Unearthed frescos from the island have depicted Santorini with a configuration that can be interpreted as a similar Atlantis civic pattern. It also shows a huge city on the island, theorized by archaeologists to represent the center of the caldera destroyed during the Minoan occupation of Santorini and Crete, among other locations around the Aegean Sea. After the volcanic disaster at Santorini, Minoan civilization went into sharp decline.

The ancient Egyptians and Greeks spoke of Atlantis as being plagued by warring factions, and it was finally destroyed about 12,900 years ago, either by the folly of war, or by what most sources ascribe to an asteroid's devastating impact with Earth. This catastrophic natural disaster may have been the cause of the flooding and sinking of the continent of Atlantis, and the reason recorded history only seems to go as far back to 10,000 BCE. Such a globally catastrophic event would cause the extinction of a vast number of animal species, including many mammals, and a vast segment of the human population as well. What was considered the history of that ancient age was at that point lost and forgotten, and history had to "start" all over again.

ATLANTIS WHERE?

There are about as many theories as to the true location of Atlantis as there are soccer players in the world. We get the bulk of the Atlantis narrative from Plato who wrote about the beautiful, technologically advanced continent-sized island back in 370 BCE in one of his Dialogues entitled *Timaeus*: "For in front of the mouth which you Greeks call 'the Pillars of Heracles,' there lay an island which was larger than Libya and Asia together; and it was possible for the travelers of that time to cross from it to the other islands, and from the islands to the whole of the continent over against them which encompasses that veritable ocean." Once again, in Plato's account, the location is vague, simply an island outside the Pillars of Heracles, which is largely regarded to be somewhere in the North Atlantic Ocean outside of Gibraltar, Spain. If the stories of Atlantis flying machines are correct, maybe the trip across the Atlantic was not so far, and Plato's Atlantis was centered around the Caribbean Sea. Many of course conclude that Atlantis never really existed, and was merely just a fable. Those who think it did exist have sought evidence—or at least clues—in almost every corner of the globe.

"Great Britain's Atlantis" is a hidden underwater world swallowed by the North Sea when the last Ice Age glaciers melted. "Doggerland" as it has been named, was a large area of dry land that stretched from Scotland to Denmark and down the English Channel as far south as the Channel Islands, but it was slowly submerged by water between 18,000 BCE and 5,500 BCE. It was ultimately discovered in 2012 by divers working with science teams from the University of St. Andrews. North Sea deep water divers working for oil companies have found the remains of a "drowned world" with an estimated population of tens of thousands, which may have once represented the "real heartland" of Europe. A team of climatologists, archaeologists and geophysicists have now mapped the area using new data from oil companies, and revealed the full extent of a "lost land" once roamed by mammoths and other now-extinct giant animals.

In a reading, the sleeping clairvoyant Edgar Cayce spoke of the use of airplanes, and of crystals, or "firestones," that were used for energy and had a myriad of applications. He also spoke of misuses of power, and issued warnings of destruction to come. Edgar Cayce's famous prophecies said remnants of Atlantis would be found around Bermuda, and in 1969, geometric underwater stone formations were found near the island of Bimini, then named the "Bimini Road," and that believers said confirmed Cayce's prediction. Also intriguing is a gigantic, partially translucent and crystal-like pyramid structure, perhaps larger than the Great Pyramid in Egypt, and initially identified by a scuba diving doctor named Ray Brown in 1970 in a region off the Bahamas known as "the Tongue of the Ocean" that is located approximately 160 kilometers from Bimini. This structure has since been independently verified by diving teams from France and the USA. The pyramid could confirm some engineers' contention that pyramids were originally created as massive power sources, or great *energy machines*, that could warp spacetime and open portals to other realities. This could support the claim that the ancient high-tech civilization of Atlantis did exist, or simply provide answers to the mysterious happenings that have been recorded since the 19th century in the region of the Atlantic dubbed the Bermuda Triangle. For decades intrepid researchers delved into the maze of mysteries hidden deep within this most enigmatic location on Earth. What's more, explorer Tony Benik reported the momentous discovery of yet another huge pyramid under 3,000 meters of water in the middle of the North Atlantic Ocean. This pyramid, Benik claims, is capped with a huge crystal. And if that's not enough, the Ari Marshall expedition in 1977 discovered yet another pyramid off Cay Sal in the Bahamas. Marshall even snapped underwater photos of a small pyramid that is submerged beneath 45 meters of water.

Other proposed locations for Atlantis include the Mediterranean Sea, the Aegean Sea, just off the Atlantic coast of present-day Portugal and Morocco, various locations around the Caribbean Sea, off the coast of England, near Antarctica, Mexico, and deep off the coast of Cuba. Other writers have proposed that ascended masters of esoteric wisdom inhabit subterranean caverns, or a "hollow Earth." Antarctica, the North Pole, the Yukon Territory, Tibet, Peru, and Mount Shasta in California, have all had their advocates as the locations of entrances to a subterranean realm referred to as Agartha, with some even advancing the hypothesis that certain UFOs have their homebase in these places.

CARIBBEAN SUNKEN CITIES

In May 2001, an exciting discovery was announced by Advanced Digital Communications (ADC), a Canadian company led by ocean engineer Paulina Zelitsky whose team was mapping the ocean bottom of Cuba's territorial waters. Sonar readings revealed something unexpected and quite amazing 670 meters below on the ocean floor. They discovered stone structures laid out in a geometric pattern that looked very much like the ruins of a city. "What we have here is a mystery," said Paul Weinzweig, of ADC. "Nature couldn't have built anything so symmetrical. This isn't natural, but we don't know what it is." The immediate suggestion of many enthusiasts was that this was conclusive evidence for the great sunken city of Atlantis. *National Geographic* showed a great deal of interest in the site and was involved in subsequent investigations. Then the subject went mute. In 2003, a mini sub dove down to explore the structures. Paulina Zelitsky of ADC said they saw a structure that "looks like it could have been a large urban center. However, it would be totally irresponsible to say what it was before we have evidence." Further explorations have mapped and created 3-D imagery of the cityscape. Because of its extreme depth, only computer models of this mysterious underwater city exist. A team of scientists continues to explore around these megalithic ruins found in the Yucatan Channel near Cuba. They have found evidence of an extensive urban environment stretching for many kilometers along the ocean floor. Some believe that the civilization that inhabited these predates all known ancient American cultures.

Before he died in 2010, retired USAF Lt. Colonel Wendelle Stevens interviewed a guard who worked at S-4, part of the ultra-secret complex at Area 51 in Nevada. The guard was a nervous man, under an assumed name, but he agreed to give an interview in what

was said to be the only one he'd ever given. After a couple of failed attempts to reconnect, the guard was presumably captured, and subsequently was *disappeared*. In the
interview the guard said that he had seen quite a few captured UFOs during his tenure,
but that the greatest excitement was when they brought in an ancient "Atlantian" ship
that had reputedly been found in an undersea temple complex, located off the coast of
Cuba, and recovered during the Cuban missile crisis. This confession would suggest
that knowledge of the underwater temple complex discovered in 2001 by ADC seemed
to go back decades, at least to the early 1960s. Part of the guard's story, also confirmed
by other whistleblowers, was that when the scientists at S-4 tried to access the power
supply in the recovered craft, they released a potent and deadly electromagnetic and
neutron pulse that instantly killed 34 scientists. In the weeks following this accident,
there was a shortage of advanced-propulsion scientists, and this is the main reason why
Area 51 whistleblower Bob Lazar was originally hired by Edward Teller. It is important
to note that once identified, any ancient UFO discovered anywhere on the planet is
quickly removed to the most secret locations of the shadow government.

One of the most intriguing discoveries of Caribbean Sea ruins is the previously mentioned story of Dr. Ray Brown. While diving near the Bari Islands in the Bahamas, Dr.
Brown claimed to have happened upon a pyramid "shining like a mirror" that he estimated was 37 meters tall, although he could see only the top 27 meters. The pyramid
had a colored capstone and was surrounded by the ruins of other buildings. Swimming
into a chamber he found a crystal held by two metallic hands. Over the crystal hung
from the center of the ceiling a brass rod, at the end of which was a red multifaceted
gem of some sort. While he was still alive, Dr. Brown showed the crystal orb, which
allegedly has strange and mystical powers, to many curious handlers. Like a few of the
mysterious crystal skulls of Central America, Dr. Brown's crystal sphere is the source
of a variety of paranormal events. People have felt strange tingling sensations and felt
breezes of ionic winds blowing nearby; cold and warm layers surround it at various
distances; and other witnesses have seen phantom lights or heard voices. A compass
needle placed next to the sphere will spin counterclockwise, then begin turning in the
opposite direction when moved only a few centimeters away.

MEGALITHIC CULTURES

Although there are several examples worldwide, the best example of ancient stone
work on a massive scale, as well as the engineering of megalithic blocks, can be seen
at the ruins of Baalbek, in what today is Lebanon. Baalbek is indeed one of the greatest
mysteries of the ancient world because its massive fitted blocks exceed even the capacity of today's largest cranes. Located deep within the scenic Beqa'a Valley is an age-old
acropolis devoted at various times to a wide variety of gods and goddesses. It was originally dedicated to the Semitic divinities of El, Baal, and his goddess partner Astarte,
whose cult involved prostitution and sacred orgies. Next came the Greek temples of
Zeus, Aphrodite, and Hermes, replacing the older temples. The Romans for example,
built directly atop the Greek locations, but changed the names to Jupiter, Venus, and
Mercury. The megalithic mystery surrounds the massive foundation stones beneath the
Roman Temple of Jupiter, constructed long before the Roman Empire. The courtyard of
the Jupiter temple is situated on a platform, called the Grand Terrace, which consists of
a huge outer wall and a filling of massive stones. The lower courses of the outer wall are
formed of huge, finely crafted and precisely positioned blocks. They range in size from
10 to 11 meters in length, five meters in height and three meters in depth, and weigh
approximately 410 metric tons each. Nine of these blocks are visible on the north side of
the temple, nine on the south, and six on the west. Above the six blocks on the western
side are three even larger stones, called the Trilithon, with each massive block weighing
in excess of 910 metric tons. The quarry is a short distance away.

Another even larger stone lies in a limestone quarry 500 meters from the Baalbek complex. Weighing an estimated 1100 metric tons, it is 21 meters by five meters, making it the single largest piece of stonework ever crafted in the world. Called the *Hajar el Gouble*, the "Stone of the South," it lays at a raised angle with the lowest part of its base still attached to the quarry as though it were *almost ready* to be cut free and transported to its presumed location next to the other Trilithon stones on the western wall at Baalbek. It is the largest hewn stone in the world.

Why these stones prove such an enigma to contemporary scientists, engineers and archaeologists, are the method of quarrying, transportation, and the precision placement as seen at Baalbek and other megalithic building locations. The western wall at Baalbek, for example, is beyond the technological ability of any known ancient or modern builders. The notion that ancient cultures might have developed knowledge superior to modern science leaves many "experts" grasping for an explanation. The conventional model calls for the use of ropes, wooden rollers and thousands of laborers who painstakingly dragged the blocks to their destination. Yet the builders who did construct monuments using this method were only moving blocks 1/10th the size and weight of those at Baalbek. Plus, their journey from the quarry to the work site moved along flat surfaces with wide movement paths. The route to the site of Baalbek, however, is uphill over rough and winding terrain, and there is no evidence *whatsoever* of a flat hauling surface having been created in ancient times. Next, there is the problem of how the mammoth blocks, once they were brought to the site, were lifted and precisely placed in position. It has been theorized that the stones were raised using a complex array of scaffolding, ramps, and pulleys that were powered by large numbers of humans and animals working in unison. Again, this explanation is unconvincing. In the spatial context of how the Baalbek stones were placed no staging space is available. Hills, in fact, slope away from where the lifting apparatus would need to have been placed, and no evidence has been found of a flat and structurally firm surface having been constructed. This series of giant stones, precisely placed side-by-side, offers no conceivable explanation suggesting where a huge pulley apparatus could have been stationed. Likely constructed in antediluvian times, Baalbek was clearly built using other means. The massive platform was built by a highly sophisticated culture that, as has been suggested, employed a type of *sound harmonics,* or acoustic levitation, to render the stones "weightless" in order to set them into place.

Today's most famous archaeological enigma, the Great Pyramid at Giza, Egypt, (discussed earlier) and not buried under sea or land, is also presumed to have been built by the ancestors of Atlantis. It is located only a few hundred kilometers from Baalbek and is situated precisely at the center of all of the Earth's landmasse. As such, it is placed in the exact center of all of the continents on the planet, and divides the Earth's landmass into approximate equal quarters. The Great Pyramid is located at 29 degrees, 58 minutes, 51.06 seconds north latitude, and 31 degrees, 9 minutes, and 0.0 seconds east longitude. The north-south axis is the longest land meridian, and passes through Asia, Europe, Africa, and Antarctica. The east-west axis is the longest land parallel running through the African, Asian, and North American continents. These two lines of latitude and longitude pass through more land and less water than any others on Earth—and there is obviously only one place that these longest landlines of the terrestrial Earth can cross—at the exact location of the Great Pyramid. A total of over 2,300,000 blocks of limestone and granite were used in its construction, with the average block weighing 2.3 metric tons, and none weighing less than two metric tons. The large blocks used in the ceiling of the King's Chamber weigh as much as eight metric tons. The Great Pyramid is built with a knowledge of the position of all the Earth's continents, a fact indicating that a technologically advanced civilization built the Great Pyramid.

CORAL CASTLE

Certainly not of antediluvian origins, but a snapshot of how Baalbek and other mega-lithic monuments could have been constructed, is a strange compound in Florida built entirely by one diminutive man. How the Coral Castle in southern Florida was erected single-handedly by a tiny Latvian loner remains one of North America's biggest mysteries. The builder was Ed Leedskalnin, a slight man only 1.5 meters tall, and weighing a mere 45 kilograms. Ed was born in 1887, and at the age of 26 was engaged to marry a 16-year old Latvian girl named Agnes Scuffs. The day before their wedding young Agnes decided to cancel the plans, perhaps because she thought Ed was too old for her, or maybe she was in love with someone else. Heartbroken and alone, Ed left his beloved Latvia for the United States, yet always thinking of Agnes as his "Sweet Sixteen." With only a 4th grade education, Ed drifted from job to job until he came down with tuberculosis and moved to Florida for its more favorable climate. During his travels he became interested in science, astronomy, and Egyptian history, spending most of his time reading books on magnetic currents and cosmic forces. Ed was a frugal man, collecting old mechanical objects and saving money any way he could. Eventually he bought a four-hectare plot of land in Homestead, Florida, and set about excavating, carving, and moving many tons of coral rock without the help of anyone else. His monument, begun in the 1930s and completed many years later, would be devoted to his lost love, his *Sweet Sixteen*. Using only simple tools, a slight immigrant from Latvia single-handedly moved over 997,700 kilograms of coral blocks, and single-handedly constructed the engineering marvel now known as the *Coral Castle*.

The extraction and lifting of such incredible amounts of coral stone—without the use of electricity or modern cranes and using only handmade tools—seems impossible for a single man who was known to be an eccentric loner, and who liked to work alone at night. Baffled engineers have compared Ed's secret method of construction to the enigmatic megalithic buildings of prehistory. The Coral Castle is the only megalithic monument of the Modern Age. Many people asked the diminutive Latvian how he was able to excavate and position such heavy objects. He would only say that he understood the secrets of how the Great Pyramids were built. Was it possible that Ed was a reincarnated Egyptian architect who retained past life knowledge of secret audio levitation techniques? Is it possible Ed Leedskalnin had a vivid memory of his "past esoteric," and acted upon it? Some would argue that there is no other explanation.

Earth civilizations have had a long history of warfare and suffering, dating back to the conflicts that led to the downfall of Atlantis, or perhaps earlier. Thus, Earth is a problem planet, or as far as ETs are concerned is "quarantined." There have been many civilizations before our present one that enjoyed high culture and advanced technology, and then self-destructed in horrific wars, essentially causing humans to "start over" again and again. Masters appear from time to time, like Buddha, Jesus, and even Ed Leedskalnin, who have taught advanced concepts relating to the nature of matter, spirituality, philosophy—and especially the human condition, a corrective way of thinking and being, so we can break free from our cycle of destruction. Consequently, when we look into the lives and teachings of the ascended masters, or of the mystery schools of the past, we can find answers relevant to the world of today, and that's where we are headed next.

< When the stars of Orion's Belt are overlaid on the Great Pyramids of Egypt, there is a perfect match. Were the Giza Pyramids built by entities who came from Orion?

> Could the Asteroid Belt be the remnants of a planet long destroyed called Tiamat? What about a "12th planet" in our solar system, variously called Marduk or Planet X?

< Two of the dialogues of Plato, entitled *Timaeus* and *Critias*, contain the primary ancient account of Atlantis. There is a short framing story in *Timaeus* about Solon traveling to Egypt and hearing about this lost civilization, and *Critias* contains the description of Atlantis, but breaks off in mid-narrative. Did Plato mean the tale literally or as an allegory?

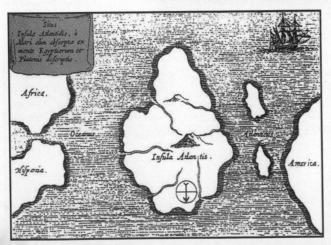

These are sonar images taken from a submarine scan, then 3-D enhanced and processed on a computer. The underwater structures are located off of Cuba at an immense depth. This discovery could be rock solid proof of an ancient civilization that built a city out of immense granite stone, that then sank into the ocean. The nearest location of similar stonework, composed of limestone, is in central Mexico, not far from Cuba. It appears that this is a city that might have been submerged during the last Ice Age. Another theory proposes that earthquakes, or possibly its location near a volcano, caused the city and surrounding land to sink beneath the waves. What we are looking at is evidence of a time when mainstream archeologists tell us there were no cities anywhere in the world.

> There are 12 primary points on the World Grid which form a geometric pattern called an "icosahedron," or when turned inside out is a "dodecahedron." Three Russian scientists, Goncharov, Morozov and Makarov, were the first to include the dodecahedron. When the Russians studied these major points all over the world, they discovered structures made out of gigantic stones, sacred places, and natural anomalies. Also on these plot lines are the location where many thousands of ships and planes have vanished or crashed. Of the ancient megalithic structures, some 3,300 in total, all were directly built on one of the lines formed by connecting these 12 main "vortex" points. This obviously was not an accident. Everyone in the world was working with the same building plans, which alone is clear evidence in support of a worldwide advanced civilization.

> This 1896 Map of Lemuria is according to William Scott-Elliott, author of *The Story of Atlantis*.

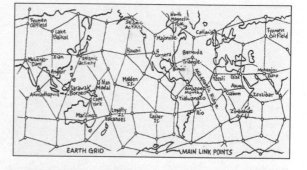

< The underwater ruins of Yonaguni were discovered by divers in 1987 offshore Yonaguni island, in the southern Japanese Ryukyu archipelago. These massive rock structures lay hidden 20-40 meters underwater for thousands of years. Experts call it the greatest discovery in the history of underwater archeology. Its massive size is equivalent to two football fields. Geological evidence shows it was submerged during the meltdown of the last Ice Age, which suggests it was built at least 14,000 years ago.

PAST ESOTERIC

"Whoever fights monsters should see to it that in the process
he does not become a monster. And if you gaze long enough
into an abyss, the abyss will gaze back into you."
—Friedrich Nietzsche

SINCE perhaps the dawn of consciousness, humans have inquired about their true selves. Anyone who studies esoteric subjects will ultimately ask certain fundamental questions about their lives, such as, what is our purpose here on Earth? Where did we come from? What is our reason to exist in a human body? Is everything totally random in our evolution? Are we alone in the universe? If there is intelligent life elsewhere, why have they not contacted humanity on a mass scale? Could it be we are being sheltered from knowing "big picture" issues? If the adept wishes to reason further, it is quite logical to raise the question that if ETs have visited here from outer space, is it possible they came here a long time ago, or perhaps have never left? If they reside here and live underground or out of sight, is it possible there has been a longstanding and pervasive effect of alien intervention on Earth? If so, is there effective action we can take to undo any negative effects of their influence or, conversely, to build on their contributions? Who on Earth might be helping them stay secret? What could be their motives? What is the alien agenda? While alternative history is not entirely the focus of this book, it is necessary to provide a quick overview of some sustaining and stubbornly persistent historical subjects about humanity's past esoteric consciousness on Earth. Perhaps all true history will be revealed when space and time are mastered.

It should be noted that mysteries and their accompanying mystery schools are often built on lies or half-truths. Lies can be persistent because they alter facts which are comprised of exact dates, places and events. When truth is known, a lie no longer persists. If the exact truth is revealed, it is no longer a mystery. As we will see in the next section of this volume, there is an esoteric agenda of control behind virtually all facets of life that were once believed to be unrelated. What we'll discover in the next section is that there is an elite faction guiding most political, mass media, corporate, economic, social, governmental, some non-governmental, and even anti-establishment organizations. The long-range agenda, devised and being executed by an ultra-moneyed elite, is to control the lives of nearly every person on the planet. The most powerful weapon they hold against us is keeping the knowledge of our true nature from us, and this fosters fear. This chapter is a brief summary of past esoteric information, often kept hidden in order to keep us ignorant of our real Earth history. Yet, every so often, there is a glimmer of knowledge that helps us resolve the unanswered questions about who we are here on Earth and why.

LEMURIA AND ATLANTIS

As we have seen, volcanic eruptions periodically expel such a significant mass of molten rock that the resulting vacuum beneath the Earth's crust causes vast areas of the land masses to sink below the oceans, while other sections rise up. Unquestionably such an explosive volcanic and tectonic plate-shifting event would cause an ice age, extinctions of many life forms, and other relatively long-term changes lasting hundreds or thousands of years. The continental areas occupied by both the Lemuria and Atlantis civilizations were covered with volcanic matter, and then submerged, leaving very little evidence that they ever existed except for the legends of a global flood which prevail in nearly every culture of the Earth. Those who survived Lemuria are generally regarded as the genus of oriental races and cultures, while those who survived Atlantis migrated to Central America, Europe, and the pre-sands civilization of Egypt, called the Osirius Empire. The account of the flood and other descriptions of cataclysmic events in Genesis is considered by some researchers to be parallel to that of Atlantis because of the many accounts of Atlantis being located in every part of the world. The exception is Plato's location of Atlantis, described in the dialogues of *Timaeus* and *Critias*.

Interestingly, there is no evidence anywhere on Earth of an evolutionary transition that resulted in the sophisticated mathematics, language, writing, religion, architecture and cultural traditions in Egypt or any of the pyramid-building civilizations. These cultures, replete with all of the details of racial body types, hairstyles, facial makeup, rituals, moral codes, and so forth, simply "appeared" as completely integrated packages. In fact, growing evidence indicates that the technology and civilizations installed on Earth from the Lemuria and the Atlantis periods were imported from other worlds, or "prepackaged," as it were. The highly advanced technologies we have today are more of a recollection of these times, as they were brought here along with the human passengers who did not originally come from Earth. It is from these oblique origins that our "past esoteric" traditions begin.

THE OSIRIUS EMPIRE

Almost everything taught to us in school about our ancient history is misleading. The origin of humans, ancient civilizations, and the purpose of the pyramids is greatly distorted. *Homo sapien sapiens* is not a result of a slow-percolating evolution process, and biologists will never find a "missing link" because there is none to be found. The intelligent human is a product of genetic engineering. Sumerians are not the beginning of the civilized race of people, but rather the beginning of another cycle of high civilization. And finally, the original pyramids (the most superior and oldest) were constructed by advanced builders who knew Earth energy, astronomy, the long count of time, and megalithic construction better than we can possibly comprehend today.

The Osirius Empire of pre-sands Egypt was an extension of Atlantis, and it is the paramount surviving relic from our antediluvian past. All of the pyramid civilizations of Earth, including the ancient Bosnians, the Mayan, and of course the ancient Egyptians, were built by the progeny of Lemuria and Atlantis; however, the other pyramid civilizations of Mesopotamia, China and Mesoamerica arose at much later dates. They all combined sophisticated mathematics and technology metaphors of their mystery schools and imbued with rich symbolism. The allure of aesthetics and mystery led to the creation of intricate rituals, astronomical alignments, secret rites, additional massive monuments, marvelous architecture, artistically rendered hieroglyphs and human-animal "gods" that were designed to create a mystery that can't be solved by our advanced Earthly human population. The mysteries diverted attention away from the truth that the human condition was captured, given amnesia, transported and imprisoned on a planet far, far away from home.

In the year 10,450 BCE, plans were drafted by Thoth for the construction of a Great Pyramid on the Giza Plateau in present-day Egypt. Although other dating puts its construction thousands of years later, its unique attributes are different from all the other pyramids, and this would suggest an earlier building date. The mysterious Sphinx appears to be guarding secrets below the sands of Egypt. The Sphinx is the oldest relic of the Osirius Empire, with erosion-bearing watermarks on all sides of the giant sculpture that prove it dates from pre-sands Egypt. Below the Sphinx are many levels of underground chambers, once said to contain an ancient hall of records—a chamber filled with extremely advanced knowledge. The other pyramids in the Giza complex were completed many thousands of years after the Sphinx, around 4,470 years ago, but they could have supplanted and buried much older pyramids constructed some 12,000 years old, in the time frame of the Osirius Empire.

Some theories of the Osirius Empire propose that the world's pyramids were made of crystal, or that their tops were capped with a crystalline substance, including those discovered recently beneath the Atlantic Ocean. The long-lost capstone of the Great Pyramid is thought to have been a giant crystal. When fully functional, could these pyramids actually generate, store, and distribute Earth energy on demand? It is intriguing that decades ago, experimenters discovered that pyramids do tend to act like natural electrical capacitors, both gathering and storing energy around them, especially through the top. The larger the pyramid, the greater the capacity to gather and store energy. A pyramid's composition is also important. If a pyramid is made entirely of crystal, or featuring a capstone of crystal, the structures power vastly increases. The pyramid shape, say investigators, is intrinsic to *pyramid power*. The shape is an architectural feature that is proven to function as an energy accumulator and amplifier of energetic forces.

THE GREAT PYRAMID

For centuries, the Great Pyramid on the Giza Plateau in Egypt has intrigued and mystified visitors. It seems to incorporate vast troves of encoded ancient wisdom in at least two major realms. The first is an embodiment of mathematical and astronomical knowledge. The second type of ancient wisdom deals with the expansion of consciousness. The Great Pyramid, commonly called the *Cheops* pyramid, encodes both the Pi and Phi proportions in the relationship between its height, its base, and its four sides. Astronomical data are also encoded in the Great Pyramid, such as the distance between the Earth and Sun, the weights of the Earth and Moon, and the radius of the Earth. The pyramid is structurally a prism, a three-dimensional triangular depiction of the heavens resonating with the planet. The prism-structure design would magnify, amplify and transfer a unified beam of energy to the other Giza pyramids, that could be used for celestial navigation and, particularly, energy recharging of advanced airships. The original polished outer casing of the prism, and its unique construction, would also allow the Great Pyramid to be a geodetic energy source, and possibly, a very powerful beam weapon. The "King's Chamber," located deep within the center of the pyramid structure, is largely regarded as a room used for initiation rituals, specifically those that assisted in the opening of "dimensional gates."

Externally, we can see that the Great Pyramid symbolizes the creative principle of nature, and it also beautifully illustrates the principles of geometry, mathematics, astronomy, and astrology. Within the building itself were the location of the mysteries of initiation. It was a temple of esoteric initiation, or perhaps a *baptismal* font. Upon emerging from a night or longer in the King's Chamber, a *neophyte* was born again, and then became an *adept*. Many people who have visited the Great Pyramid have experienced mystical encounters when residing within, that ranged from ancient Greek pilgrims to the French general, Napoleon Bonaparte, as well as initiates of the enigmatic mystery schools of the Near East.

The Great Pyramid is the most fascinating pyramid worldwide, and it is located exactly at the center of the Earth's landmasses. Such precise global configurations could only be derived from an aerial perspective above the Earth, or from outer space. The ratio between the height of the Great Pyramid and its perimeter is the same as the ratio between the Earth and its circumference. The exact measurements and the fact that there are doors within the airshafts suggest a machine-like function. Charting the mathematical calculations of the geodetic center of the Earth continents could not be made in any other way except by utilizing advanced airplanes or spacecrafts. In addition, the four "airshafts" of the Great Pyramid point precisely to the key stars of Orion, Sirius, Thuban, and Polaris as seen from the timeframe of the Osirius Empire. The alignment of the three Giza pyramids on the ground matches perfectly with the alignment of the constellation of Orion as seen in the sky from Giza, relative to the Nile River, as representing the Milky Way galaxy in the night sky. The placement on the ground of these structures have geodetic or astronomical significance relative to various stars in our galactic region. The configuration of the three main pyramids on the Giza Plateau were intended to create a "mirror image" of our solar system on Earth with certain key constellations.

EGYPTIAN AND HEBREW MYSTERY SCHOOLS

Many centuries after the Great Pyramids were constructed, a man named Moses grew up in the royal household of the pharaoh Amenhotep III and his son, Akhenaten, Akhenaten's wife Nefertiti, and their son Tutankhamen. The pharaohs' attempts in the 14th century BCE to teach certain beings on Earth the truth that they are, themselves, immortal spiritual beings, was part of a plan to overthrow the fictional, metaphorical, anthropomorphic panoply of gods created by the old Egyptian mystery cult known in Egypt as the *Priests of Amun*. For what reason would any civilization devote so many resources to construct so many elaborate buildings? To glorify the life of a single king, or to create a mysterious illusion in which an adept could become a master? The pyramids and many ancient stone monuments erected worldwide could easily be called "mystery monuments."

There have been enigmatic secret societies dating back to the Old Empire and throughout the long course of history in ancient Egypt. The pharaoh Akhenaten received the new teachings, but he was heavily influenced by his personal ambition for self-glorification. Because Akhenaten rebelled against the established system in favor of his own new interpretation, there is an intact record of his own secret society. He altered the concept of the individual spiritual being and embodied the concept of a monotheistic sun god called Aten. But his reign was brief. A war of religious conquest against the Egyptian mystery cult prompted pharaoh Akhenaten to abolish the priesthood of Amun. He then moved the capital of Egypt from Thebes to the new location at Amarna, at the exact geodetic center of Egypt. However, this plot to overthrow established religious control was quickly disrupted. The reign of Akhenaten, although overthrown and abolished within decades by the former priesthood, had larger consequences—primarily the spread of secret wisdom outside the confines of Egypt.

In discussing Hebrew secret societies, from which Moses was a direct descendant, it should be noted that there is no physical evidence for Solomon's Temple. Neither is there any significant evidence for Solomon being a genuine person himself, other than references in the Biblical texts. Nor do we have any convincing evidence for the Queen of Sheba, or any of the other Old Testament characters enmeshed in the record. But there are certain nuggets of wisdom that come from the people described in the Bible. The idea of "One God" was perpetuated by the Hebrew leader Moses while he was in Egypt. He left Egypt with his adopted people, the Jewish slaves of Egypt. Thereafter, the Jewish followers, who trusted the word of Moses implicitly, worshiped a single god they call "Yahweh." This same monotheistic entity is also the basis for Christianity and the Islamic faiths.

GIANTS FROM OUR DISTANT PAST

Before the Osirius Empire of pre-sands Egypt, and even before the civilizations of Atlantis and Lemuria, there existed extremely large humanoids on Earth. Several modern researchers and scholars, most notably Erich von Däniken and Zecharia Sitchin, have proposed that alien beings not only visited Earth in our far distant past, but also influenced our history, mythology, religion, and physical evolution. One commonality of nearly every religion worldwide is the concept of a hierarchy of superior beings. These beings have a leader, ruler or king commonly referred to as "God." The adherents of certain faiths are known to do this lord's bidding and follow his orders. Sometimes these orders can involve different degrees of manipulation or actions concerning humanity. According to ancient alien theorists, these beings, existing as a collective or a select assembly, are responsible for the creation of humans and have bequeathed us with civilization.

As examined previously, the Nephilim were giants who once allegedly lived on Earth. They were the hybrid offspring of intercourse between human women and ancient extraterrestrials. More specifically, the ancient books of Genesis and Enoch tell us that spirit beings, known as the "Watchers," descended to Earth, mated with our women, and produced a hybrid race of offspring known as the Nephilim. Or, as the Genesis account in the Old Testament would leave us to believe, the Nephilim were some kind of bizarre giants whose offspring mated with the offspring of Adam and Eve. They came from a planet variously known as Hercolubus; Nibiru; Planet X; Tyche; Nemesis; or Wormwood.

Such tales are as old as humanity itself. These histories and accounts of visitations and subsequent mixed-blood, alien-human races comprise the bulk of the world's myths, legends, religions, and superstitions. Clay tablets dating back 5,000 years or more are found in abundance throughout the entire Mesopotamian region. These Assyrian and Babylon cuneiform tablets record epic poems, cosmological tales, mathematical equations, astronomical data, temple records, histories of the kings, grammar and vocabulary texts, plus detailed records associated with names, genealogies, deeds, powers, and assignments of the gods. The vast library of Ashurbanipal, found in the ancient city of Nineveh, along with many other tablets in the Mesopotamian region, have offered us a figurative window into the past, from which we can capture a compelling glimpse of the Sumerian way of life.

THE NEPHILIM GLOBAL RULE

The Sumerian, Indus and Egyptian cultures seem to have suddenly appeared in a very refined and advanced form at their earliest beginnings, then lapsed into a more primitive state. From the onset of their mutual cultures, Sumerian, Indus and Egyptian cities were complete with schools, splendid homes, indoor plumbing, industrial facilities, libraries, and even hospitals. Clay models of livers have been found in Sumeria, suggesting that anatomy and medicine were taught through the use of models of human organs. Skeletal remains recovered from Mesopotamian grave sites show evidence of brain surgery being conducted. Advanced agricultural techniques and animal husbandry were also commonplace in these earliest of cultures. Ancient alien theorists cite that the knowledge of the Nephilim was passed on to humans.

There is evidence for Nephilim living in North America, including skeletons of giants unearthed in what is today the United States, and in archeological formations that pre-date Native American culture. The bones of giant humanoids found in the Ohio mounds were said to be of beings who were 2.5 to 4 meters in height, with six-fingered hands, double rows of teeth, and fair or red hair. Similar giant skeletons have also been recovered on the Channel Islands off the California coast, and in northern Nevada caves that once fronted the massive inland Lake Lahontan, which drained at the conclusion of the last Ice Age. The Smithsonian Institution confiscated the bones of all the giants from the Ohio Valley and elsewhere, starting in the 19th century until the present day. If any still exist, or new bones are uncovered, and if it were possible to take some DNA sampling of the bones, it might be discovered that they belong to the Nephilim, or the "fallen angels" of the Old Testament. Many of the mound sites in Ohio have been completely destroyed or covered up, sometimes with buildings constructed on top of them, or reconstructed as tourist sites.

The giant remains on Catalina Island off the southern California shores were determined to have lived during a period when now extinct animals were still roaming the planet. Burial mounds were exhumed in the 1920s and 1930s, and bones of giants were found to have been engaged in some sort of battle. But the bones were whisked away and then mysteriously vanished. The reason the bones are kept from the public is that they provide evidence contrary to Darwinian theory; they are not entirely human. Our entire conception of who we are as people in the world, to say nothing of our ancient history, would have to undergo a major revision.

BIBLICAL DESCRIPTIONS

The Biblical account of the "sons of god" are clearly the "gods" of the ancients; the descriptions are far too precise to not be so. They had children by human females. These were the "men of renown," such as Hercules. They produced giants as well (such as Atlas) and also enjoyed mystical powers such as Enoch, of Genesis 5, who never perished but was simply "taken away" by God. According to Genesis 5, "The Nephilim were on the Earth in those days, and also afterward, when the sons of God went to the daughters of men and had children by them. They were the heroes of old, men of renown."

The name Nephilim indicates that they were giants. The "sons of god" indicate the "fallen angels." Therefore, both giants and "fallen angels" were here on Earth. The interbreeding indicates that humankind's corrupted state became more and more evil. Maybe the mythical creatures did once exist; perhaps they were a genetic experiment made by humans. We also know that breeding of certain animals with others produces a different kind of animal, and this also applies to agriculture. Hybridization occurred long before the modern science of genetics. It is not improbable that this same type of breeding was used in earlier times, which could have produced the mythological creatures of yore. If Hercules, Atlas, and other mythical humans were real, then so too could mythical creatures such as the Nephilim have been.

There are many current events that are in harmony with, and can be interpreted as, fulfilling Biblical prophecies. Strife in the Middle East has reached a fevered pitch, while the moneyed elite have assumed control of the planet and all its occupants. The Bible codes, or Torah codes, which are purportedly a set of secret messages encoded within the Hebrew text of the Torah, provide descriptive information on events that occur in our history. As prophesied in the Bible we are nearing a great deception, that could involve the creation of a new race of Nephilim ... or the return of the Anunnaki. Those humans who turn to the dark side and accept the "Mark of the Beast" may be offered the chance to live hundreds of years, disease free. The alien implants studied by Dr. Roger Leir, a podiatrist, may be a prototype for the "Mark," and capable of changing a person's DNA. The advent of RFID implants in people also evoke dark shades of Biblical prophecies. Equally as insidious, there are accounts of sinister "black-eyed" children and "super soldiers" being born in test-tube laboratories.

TIBETAN LEGACY

Very early Tibetan legend speaks of a former glorious civilization on Earth when all people possessed telepathic abilities. Regardless of local language, this highly advanced race of humans could convey their thoughts telepathically, travel in the astral plane, see via clairvoyance ,and levitate themselves or heavy objects. People in this age, before the so-called "Fall of Man," were people with an amazing ability to utilize their "light bodies" at will. One version of the Fall of Man is that humans abused these occult powers and used them for self-interest rather than for the development of humankind as a whole. The universal capacity of telepathy was lost, and, in the West, it has been represented as the *Tower of Babel* in the Bible, whereupon humans were thrust back into dense third-dimensional bodies. While Tibetan Lamas never forgot these ancient human abilities, they have kept them to themselves throughout the ages. It was not until recent Chinese occupation that these remarkable human abilities became known to the Western world, and then only gradually.

In the Tibetan capital Lhasa there is a major mystical shrine called the *Potala*. It is said to sit atop an ancient cavern and tunnel system that reaches throughout the Tibetan Plateau, and possibly beyond. Although no one is allowed entry, it is reported that deep inside the Potala Mountain is a veritable labyrinth of hidden caves and corridors. This subterranean system of passageways is dominated by a huge cave with several passages radiating out from it, including one that ends at a sacred lake. The lake contains several islands that were once used for the initiation of lamas. The lake flows into an underground river, which empties into the River Tsang-po, some 65 kilometers away. The subterranean chambers under the Potala are said to contain all the jewels and treasures of Tibet, along with a gigantic golden statue of the Buddha. One of the most curious underground rooms is the Temple of Secret Wisdom, containing bodies of a giant race of people unknown to modern archaeologists. The mountain and caves are believed to have originated before the planet's last polar shift, a time when Tibet was a country at sea level. The plates shifted, new continents formed, and Tibet arose as the Himalayas thrust the land skyward. Successive monasteries were built and rebuilt upon Potala Mountain, a mountain that has a treasure-trove of secret passageways and ancient esoteric knowledge from the *very* early days!

The ancient Vedic *rishis*, in all their wisdom, as early as 8,000 BCE said that our universe is not woven from matter, but made up of consciousness and energy. These ancient seers and channels with 12-strand DNA and *king-sized* pineal glands have told us that the universal laws are clear—our attitude about our lives shapes everything around us.

They said that the entire universe emerged from thoughts. According to quantum physics, the double slit experiment clearly illustrates that we cannot *have* a universe without the mind entering into it, as it actually shapes the very *thing* that is perceived. Therefore, our current thoughts shape our future lives. When each of us visualizes positive outcomes, we can generate powerful thoughts and feelings of having them now, thus making our aspirations materialize. The law of attraction returns the reality exactly as we visualized it in our mind. Matter, energy and consciousness are interchangeable.

IN SEARCH OF SHAMBALA

For thousands of years there were rumors circulating that somewhere in Tibet, among the snowy Himalayan peaks and secluded valleys, there was an untouched paradise, a kingdom where peace and universal policy were the law of the land. This kingdom was called *Shambala* (also spelled Shambhala), yet its exact whereabouts were unknown.

James Hilton wrote about this mystical city in his 1933 book called *Lost Horizon*. Hollywood played its part in the 1960 film production entitled *Shangri-la*. Even James Redfield, the famous author of *The Celestine Prophecy*, wrote a book called *The Secret of Shambhala: In Search of the Eleventh Insight*. The mystery of Shambala is also considered a source for the *Kalachakra*, which is the highest branch of mystical and esoteric teachings in Tibet. There are records of this kingdom in ancient texts, such as the *Kalachakra* and *Zhang Zhung*, which existed long before Buddhism entered Tibet.

The word *Shambala* comes from the Sanskrit word meaning "Place of Peace," or "Place of Silence." This kingdom, whose capital is Kalapa, is ruled by the kings of a dynasty called Kulika or Kalki. This is where all living things are faultless, and where the semi-perfect meet and jointly guide the evolution of humanity. Only those who are pure in heart can live here. They enjoy happiness and peace and do not even recognize the suffering of the outside world. It is said that love and virtue reign in this kingdom. Injustice never manifests. Its people have a very deep spiritual knowledge. Its cultural virtues are based on law, art and a general knowledge that is far higher than that attained by humans in the outside world.

Many adventurers and explorers have tried in vain to locate this mystical kingdom. According to some, Shambala may be located in the mountainous regions of Eurasia, and hidden from the outside world. According to the ancient text *Zhang Zhung*, Shambala is identical to the Sutlej Valley in Himachal Pradesh, while people in the nation of Mongolia identify it with certain valleys of southern Siberia. Information about this kingdom first popped up in Western civilization when a Portuguese Catholic clergyman named Estevao Cacella learned of the story from local people. Then, in 1833, a Hungarian scholar named Sandor Corrosion Csoma even provided the coordinates of Shambala as somewhere between 45° and 50° north latitude. The legend of Shambala also drew the attention of Nicholas Roerich, who was a follower of esoteric and Theosophical studies. Curiosity drove him to explore the daunting terrain from the Gobi Desert to the Altai Mountains from 1923 until 1928. His trip crossed 35 of the highest mountain peaks in the world. But even with this tremendous effort, Roerich still could not locate the hidden kingdom. Even the Nazis, who were extremely interested in the esoteric world of Tibet, sent search expeditions in 1930, 1934 and 1938. However, none of the expeditions were successful, or at least none of the explorers *admitted* to finding Shambala.

Some researchers maintain that Shambala can only be discovered as a symbol—a liaison between the real world and a world that exists *beyond* the earthly plane. Maybe Shambala is a place in our hearts. But there are others who believe that Shambala is a real location, possibly existing underground, or on a higher dimensional plane. For centuries, the Tibetans have believed in the existence of certain locations or realms as being reservoirs of ancient knowledge and advanced technology. As we saw in the last chapter, the descendants of ancient Lemuria are said to reside peacefully in subterranean caverns underneath the Tibetan Plateau, and they do not interfere in the lives of humans who live on the surface of the planet. Nor is there any discernible interaction between those beings in Agartha and the people of Earth.

GREEK MYSTERY SCHOOLS

The ancient Greeks took the concept of esoteric to a new level. The famous Oracle at Delphi was merely one temple in a network of many oracle temples. People would travel from all over the known world to hear communications from the spiritual world. These communications, *direct* from the gods and goddesses, inspired the greatest authors, poets, and philosophers of the Classical World. Each Greek temple was a communication center. Greek priests designated a local deity for each temple. Each of the temples in this network were located at precisely 5° intervals of latitude from the capital city of Thebe—and throughout the Mediterranean area as far north as the Baltic Sea. Among other functions, the shrines served as a grid, housing electronic beacons later called "Omphalus Stones." The grid arrangement of oracle sites can only be seen from miles above the Earth. The original network of electronic communication beacons were disabled when the priesthood was dispersed, and they were replaced by carved stones.

Ancient Greece spawned several mystery schools, each with its own oracle or secret teachings. The Greek oracle temple at Delos was built upon a prehistoric megalithic site that predates Stonehenge. The Dodona oracle allowed seers and mediums to have contact with the spirits of Zeus, or Jupiter, known in many cults as the "royal" planet. Another cult known as the Mysteries of Mithras formed around the original Cave of Mithras. Similar to other ancient mystery religions, such as the Eleusinian mysteries, and the mysteries of Isis, Mithraism also maintained strict secrecy about its teachings and practices, and revealed them only to initiates. Membership was reserved for male initiates only. Their places of worship were called "mithraeam," had no windows, and each temple was intended to be as dark as the original cave. Of all of the cults, the Eleusian Mystery School remains one of the greatest enigmas of ancient Greece.

Over the centuries, Greece was the location of other influential seers and mystics. The *Book of Revelation* was written by the recluse Saint John on the Greek island of Patmos. Visions and communications from spirits were received by Saint John as he lay with his head inserted into a niche inside of a cave.

Ancient Greece and Rome were also the birthplaces of Western philosophy. The word *logos* is the Greek word for "knowledge" or "gnosis." Divination was an important and consistent practice of daily life. The most renowned ancient Greek philosophers, such as Aristotle, Plato, and Socrates divined information from spirits. Socrates was just one of many thousands of intellectuals who entered the subterranean chambers and consulted the Oracle at Delphi. There were many forms of divination in addition to the oracles. Lightning and thunder could provide meaning and so to the flights of birds, and chance words spoken by demented people called *cledonism* ... or even the examination of organs from freshly sacrificed animals or humans.

GNOSIS

The word gnostic comes from the Greek word *gignoskein*, meaning simply "to know." This is a kind of knowledge which might be gained today by plugging one's mind into the Internet and being able to download every single piece of data in an instant. In the same way, the true Gnostic, much like the mystic, could understand all things in a unique way. It is the mind tapping into the *collective unconscious*, also known as the

Akashic Records. Gnosis means knowledge of the most esoteric kind, and this is the story that has been hidden from our eyes. It is the truth of the secret societies that we, on the outside, are supposedly too primitive to comprehend.

Like the ancient Egyptians, the Druids held rituals worshipping a sun god at Neolithic megalithic structures. Not only at Stonehenge, but throughout Europe when it was entirely pagan. There seemed to be a common practice of mapping the heavens and charting the passing of the Sun and Moon by using giant stones inserted into the ground. It was almost as if the originators of Islam, Hinduism, Shamanism, Buddhism and Christianity all tapped into a telepathically-derived wisdom, or *gnosis*. Even the Native Americans in Ohio built a giant earthwork called Serpent Mound, indicating that they understood the sperm-egg-birth fertilization process. This was conceived hundreds of years before the microscope. The Mayans predicted dozens of future solar eclipses more than three centuries before the first telescope was invented. It was a combination of deep meditative trances, mixed with the constant rigors of psychic training that allowed the ancients full use of their third eye, a subject that will be discussed in an upcoming chapter.

With the recent *seismic changes* in the Catholic Church, and Christianity in general, the idea of gnosis has returned to reclaim esoteric Christianity including the study and works of adepts such as Emanuel Swedenborg, George Gurdjieff, Thomas Merton and Rudolf Steiner. When *we humans* progress past materialism and discern that each one of us has a multidimensional nature as spiritual beings, we will begin to understand the history of the West differently. Christ's life and his sacrifice have had a profound influence on Western thought. However, the established idea that "faith" in Christ automatically "saves" the soul of a believer is over-simplified and misleading. More to the point is that with Christ's teaching, we have the capacity to overcome temptation and impulse, and to influence and eventually transform the physical and material realm through conscious inner work. It would seem that Jesus did exist, and was capable of miracles—and miracles continue to happen all the time. That kind of power could become available to any of us when we master the dictates of the ego and learn to call upon our untapped inner resources, and as limited ego perception begins to dissolve. According to esoteric Christianity, connecting to one's inner essence results in loving action in the world, and determines our karmic fate.

In times long gone, our ancestors saw through the *illusion* of physical reality and recognized that there was another way. They discovered that in order for humans to elevate above the level of the *grindstone*, we needed to alter our internal dialogue. Humans have to understand our limited consciousness, and the conflicted inner dialogue that drives us to polarity. The unique understanding that there could be a higher goal for humankind, attainable first individually, and then shared collectively, evolved into what we now call Gnosticism. Of course this is a massive over-simplification, yet it is doable by commitment to a disciplined spiritual practice. As we have been told by the masters, it is from practice that many come to experience what most would call otherworldly emotions or visions. Furthermore, regardless of popular perception, the early Christians were not only Gnostics, but also mystics.

NOETIC SCIENCES

The term *noetic* derives from the Greek word for "mind," specifically the higher-knowing or intuitive mind. The Institute Of Noetic Sciences (IONS) in Petaluma, California, is an outside-the-box research institute exploring the intersection between science and consciousness. Founded by astronaut Edgar Mitchell, the sixth man to walk on the Moon in the Apollo missions, this group is helping people around the world to develop expanded awareness, and extend more fluidity in their intelligence. Noetic scientists study expanded consciousness and amplified human abilities and how to "apply that knowledge to enhancing human well-being and the quality of life on the planet." IONS former CEO, Marilyn Schlitz, Ph.D., says "we have harnessed a group of pioneers who are interested in asking the unasked questions." Cassandra Vieten, Ph.D., current president and CEO, says the Institute focuses on questions such as "What is the fundamental nature of reality?" especially when looking through the lens of cutting-edge scientific tools. "At IONS," she continues, "our research rests on the premise that consciousness matters: What you think matters, what you feel matters, what you intend, what you pay attention to, the way you frame your reality, matters." How then, and why, does it matter?

Through a combination of contemplative practices and rigorous scientific experiments, IONS' researchers state with confidence that the fundamental cause of the disasters occurring on our planet, from environmental degradation to poverty and violence, come not from without, but emanate from within, and are a result our limited consciousness. Our consciousness, however, can be expanded for the common good. It has been categorically and scientifically proven that the human mind has power over matter and the physical world. Schlitz cites an experiment in which one subject, using her thoughts alone, attempted to alter the vital signs of a second subject in a sealed room with positive results. Dean Radin, IONS senior scientist, and author of the 2013 book *Supernormal*, notes that minds are powerful. For example, one of his experiments looks at the effects of consciousness on the way genes express using a kind of "clairvoyance detector." "What we are learning from our research," Radin says, "is that your attention, your intentions, not only kind of shape your own perception of reality, but something about reality itself."

A third experiment, initially run hundreds of times at Princeton University, involves machines called random number generators—which Noetics researchers have placed on almost every continent. Marilyn Schlitz says, "They are essentially electronic coin flippers. So if you imagine flipping a coin 100 times, you would expect, based on a normal probability distribution, that you'd get an equal number of heads and tails." In some experiments, she says, human thought alone has affected these machines, changing the ratio of heads to tails. Specifically, whenever a great many people focus their attention or consciousness on something similar, for example, around Christmas time, baseball world championships, or the funeral of Lady Diana in England, then certain random number generators in computers start to deliver more ordered numbers instead of random ones. This suggests an ordered group-consciousness creates order in its whole surroundings! The takeaway is that the human mind actually has the ability to affect matter. A secret U.S. Government program, in fact, was designed to develop the human ability to directly perceive at remote distances. This is another "extended" human ability that has been scientifically documented by IONS' experiments. Called "remote viewing," the government initially denied the existence of this program, and called those who talked about it *conspiracy theorists*. Yet, in 1995, declassified documents were released revealing that the government had indeed spent many millions on this top secret project, and that the program had overwhelmingly positive results.

These hopeful breakthroughs have discovered that we do have the tools to combat the status quo. Unfortunately, every scientific breakthrough in human development, whether it was the discovery of fire, nuclear power, or the power to mentally affect matter, has eventually been turned into a weapon. Our task is to join together with others in a collective expanded consciousness with the intention to use these extended mental capacities only for good, rather than yielding to our darker selfish side. Or, perhaps, those inclined to the dark side have already adapted its usage, and prefer that the rest of us remain ignorant to the vast potential of our human minds.

SECRETS OF THE ILLUMINATI

The secret organization known as the Illuminati—or the Ancient Illuminated Seers of Bavaria—was initially called the Order of Perfectibilists, and it was founded on May 1, 1776, by a young professor of Natural and Canon Law at the University of Ingoldstat in Bavaria, Germany. He was Adam Weishaupt, a Jew brought up as a Catholic who converted to Protestantism. Acting on a strong interest in esoteric traditions, he joined the Freemasons in 1774. Weishaupt was a firm believer in the secret doctrines and ancient wisdom teachings, which he believed to lie at the heart of both Freemasonry and Rosicrucianism.

Fabled as a secret society, Freemasons see themselves as an esoteric fraternity whose ancient brotherhood of initiates are voted into membership for the purpose of sharing enlightenment through the use of exclusive teachings. They are not a religious group, yet holding a belief in a higher *supreme being* is required. Elevated status can be obtained by invitation to the various esteemed *Rites*, including those based on the legendary Knights Templar. Their full proper title is "The United Religious, Military and Masonic Orders of the Temple and of St. John of Jerusalem, Palestine, Rhodes and Malta." Many historians trace Masonic roots to the historical Christian Knights Templar militia, that *once upon a time* nearly bankrupted the Vatican, before they were ruthlessly crushed. Freemasonry arose from the ashes of the Knights Templar, but it took several centuries for them to come out of hiding. Although a mostly Christian organization, members of other religions are supposedly welcome to join. Despite an effort to distance themselves from politics and religion in modern times, Scandinavian branches to this day will only permit entry of fellow Christian worshippers. Women remain excluded, although women may join other Masonic orders.

As we shall see, the Illuminati, Freemasons and Zionists are behind almost every major political, financial and international think tank institution of the Western Hemisphere. These include the World Bank, International Monetary Fund, Bank for International Settlements, Trilateral Commission, Council on Foreign Relations, Bilderberg Group, United Nations, European Union and the International Criminal Court, to name a few of the largest. Their aim is to work behind the scenes to brainwash the masses into accepting a global government, centralized economic control, and eventually a single world religion of their own design.

A LONG HISTORY OF DECEPTION

The humans of Earth have been subjected to a life of deception that began thousands of years ago. If we can believe the ancient texts, our world was created as a paradise, but it was turned into something completely opposite. Wisdom traditions explain this tragic shift in various ways. This esoteric series takes the position that, although a fantastic notion, people will eventually have to accept the possibility that malevolent ETs have been manipulating humans for at least 5,400 years, if not much longer. Benevolent visitors also want to make themselves known to our world, but are being stopped by the few rich and powerful individuals that control the human population—by threatening to destroy the world if disclosure is allowed. Humans have proven to be capable of heinous deeds throughout history. The freeing of the slaves during the Civil War won't compare to the liberation of our planet once the current mental slavery agenda is exposed.

Our history has been rewritten for consumption by the general public, and there are many buried secrets. The controlling elite would prefer that common people, or "sheeple" as they call us, remain perpetually ignorant. They believe that the population is not ready for full disclosure, or the tapping into our potential as super humans.

They know, however, that the truth will come out eventually. The "Watchers" (presumed to be benevolent overseers) have rules, and they can only interfere under vital circumstances. While they push the boundaries of their own rules in an attempt to warn us, most of these signs go unnoticed (such as in the form of crop circles). Most of the population is so focused on their daily personal concerns, and mostly related to money, that they are oblivious to *everything else* around them. Society has been shaped to be this way. Usually because of the illusionary belief that money equals safety, a money-focused people are easier to control, especially when they perceive the world is falling apart.

The Luciferian manifesto, also regarded as the "Fall of Man" and its aftermath, is essentially the belief that humans are defined by their carnal appetites and desires such as greed, power and lust, rather than by developing their innate soul and spiritual ideals, such as truth, justice and beauty. Humans serve Lucifer by giving in to these temptations, especially, by being an accomplice in their own destruction. The Illuminati always promoted the indulgence in base instincts, calling it "sexual liberation" and "open marriage." Their psychology has always engrandized the material world and operated against self-discipline. However, without an awareness of the true self and our spiritual strength, the Luciferian philosophy creates disaster. In this view of "Luciferianism," *human is God*, and the self-serving desires of the Illuminati are the measure of all things.

The Catholic Church has also shaped Western thought for centuries and ruled with a fearsome fist since the Middle Age in Europe. Galileo was placed under house arrest until the day he died for claiming the Earth revolved around the Sun. In those oppressive times, secret societies served a vital function, as they were one of the very few ways to preserve and foster knowledge suppressed by the Church. Yet whenever there is secrecy, the potential for corruption and manipulation increases dramatically. In times of great oppression like that of medieval Europe and the pre-revolutionary American colonies, secrecy was a vital means of sharing banned information (such as plans to bring positive change to people's lives). Yet, particularly in more peaceful times, that same secrecy can *and has* been used to forward agendas that support only the privileged few. Very few people know about the Bohemian Club, Davos, the Council of 300, the Club of Rome, and other secret gatherings of the global elite. Why is there so little media coverage of these powerful conclaves, even when these influential members' lives are usually daily fodder for the tabloid press? In this modern era of the Internet—and easy access to knowledge—does the secrecy of the Masons and other secret societies play a useful role in our world any longer? Is there a positive purpose for the most wealthy and powerful people in the world to meet behind closed doors without public scrutiny? What if they are hoarding vital information that could give us super human abilities or a greatly extended lifespan? Or worse, what if they are set on enslaving, or even exterminating, a majority of the human race? These "control" questions, and many others will be the thrust of our inquiry in the next section.

< George Washington, the first president of the United States, wears the decorated apron of Freemasonry. Nearby are the square and the compass, traditional symbols of Freemasonry. The Father of our Country is seen in a cornerstone laying ritual in which certain blessings are given. The idea is that whatever takes place in that building will have a solid and auspicious beginning. And what building is George Washington, the Freemason, laying the cornerstone for? The United States Capitol building. The actual blueprint of the Capitol building depicts subterranean chambers filled with tiny rooms that look like they are right out of an ancient Greek labyrinth.

Many have searched unsuccessfully for the utopian kingdom known as Shambala. What if this place exists on Earth, yet on a higher dimensional plane? Besides meaning a real place that we cannot perceive, a higher dimensional plane also means that in your mind and heart you will find that place of peace (Shambala) which will permeate your life and thoughts. Shambala dispels materialism, hatred, violence, and egoism. It is a live and let live place; do onto others as you would have them do onto you; love thy neighbor; be at one with nature; embrace a hopeful and idealistic forward-looking better-world state of mind. In this design, Shambala is not a physical place, and if you spend your life looking for the physical place (materialism), you will never find it, and will have wasted your life in such a search (vanity). Shambala, the spiritual place, is inside you, and all you have to do is look deeply within.

< Freemasonry has long been associated with the political elite and revolutionary thinking. It is believed that Freemasonry has a link to the occult and the future world government. Many of our Founding Fathers, including George Washington seen here, were high level Masons.

This *pinax*, or votive tablet, shows Persephone opening the "Liknon Mystikon." This image was found in the holy shrine of Persephone at Locri in the district of Mannella. Locri was part of Magna Graecia and is situated on the coast of the Ionian Sea in the Calabria region of Italy.

CONTROL

It would seem the populous is being intentionally deceived by our leaders. We are being dumbed down, purposefully made sicker, and denied vital information. Why is our full potential being withheld from us? Big Brother is here in the form of the New World Order.

"The real truth of the matter is that a financial element in the large centers has owned the government since the days of Andrew Jackson." –President Franklin D. Roosevelt, 1933

"He who controls the past controls the future. He who controls the present controls the past." –George Orwell, 1984

"Close both eyes … to see with the other eye." –Rumi

"Who controls the food supply controls the people; who controls the energy can control whole continents; who controls money can control the world. … Military men are dumb, stupid animals to be used as pawns for foreign policy." –Henry Kissinger

"The real truth that dare not speak itself is that no one is in control, absolutely no one. This stuff is ruled by the equations of dynamics and chaos. There may be entities seeking control, but to seek control is to take enormous aggravation upon yourself. It's like trying to control a dream." –Terence McKenna

"The universe cannot be read until we have learnt the language and become familiar with the characters in which it is written. It is written in mathematical language and the letters are triangles, circles and other geometrical figures." –Galileo

"One of the saddest lessons of history is this: If we've been bamboozled long enough, we tend to reject any evidence of the bamboozle. We're no longer interested in finding out the truth. The bamboozle has captured us. It's simply too painful to acknowledge, even to ourselves, that we've been taken. Once you give a charlatan power over you, you almost never get it back." –Carl Sagan

"Make the lie big, make it simple, keep saying it, and eventually they will believe it." –Adolf Hitler

"The workings of the human body are an analogy for the workings of the universe." –Leonardo da Vinci

"Religion is regarded by the common people as true, by the wise as false, and by the rulers as useful." –Seneca the Younger

"We control the News Media in this country, therefore we control the reality, and if the American people don't like it, we can create a new one in 30 minutes!" –Karl Rove, Bush's political advisor

ALTERNATIVE NARRATIVE

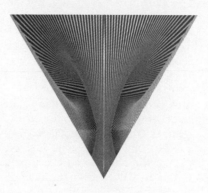

"You never change things by fighting the existing reality. To change something, build a new model that makes the existing model obsolete." –Buckminster Fuller

THE situation we are facing in the world today has been created by clever design and it has become what we perceive to be reality. This first chapter of the "Control" section summarizes the strategies and content of this clever design, also known as the "Big Lie," and set forth in great detail in the companion book, *Future Esoteric*. It's important to become aware of the specific ways the populace has been "dumbed down, purposefully made sicker, and denied vital information." This is dizzying and disturbing information. Equally disturbing are the "Alternatives I, II and III" proposed by the perpetrators of the Big Lie. But we need not retreat into despair and victimization. There is another alternative. This chapter suggests and explores a comprehensive Alternative IV, which is information available to all and outside the influence of the would-be controllers of the old narrative.

Most people are unaware of the true nature of reality and few have any real understanding of how this world is actually run. The illusion continues to this day because the information that most people receive comes from newspapers or television. It needs to be made clear to everyone that almost all information coming from the mainstream media will never completely inform people of the real facts of a situation. Even though factual unbiased reporting is the core principle of journalism, this principle has been tragically eroded. It is simply not what the current media is designed to do. The mainstream media has little or nothing to do with keeping people informed and everything to do with controlling the flow of information and shaping the thoughts, beliefs and opinions of the populace. Most of these institutions present stories and propaganda as fact, and target ridicule towards anyone who questions them. When questioning persists and gets too close to home, they resort to labeling dissenters as "conspiracy theorists," when those people in reality are really just critical thinkers. It is a very shrewdly constructed system, but once you have figured out how to see through the haze of propaganda, the real truths become painfully obvious ... and then there is no turning back. Yet, most people fail to see through the illusion and so now we find the entire human race facing a most precarious situation. Propaganda, indoctrination and brainwashing work very effectively because they each create and install a rigid belief system. Just try breaking a well-established perception once it has been formed— it's like trying to break someone free from a cult!

A CULTURE OF DELUSION

The propaganda process works like this. Government and media deception, skillfully packaged, becomes generally regarded as the "truth," and then develops into a "culture of delusion." Remember, what is *not* said also speaks volumes. Indeed, most Americans live in a matrix of lies, and they have no idea of the gravity of their situation. Lies dominate every policy discussion and every political decision. Driven by money and ambition, corruption penetrates even the field of science, where the pressures to produce "special interest" results, coupled with the need for grants, status, and financial security subtly, sometimes blatantly, influence experimental conclusions and contaminates published results. Caught in the web of greed, some scientists cut corners and fudge test results for the purpose of acquiring large corporate grants and public recognition. The definition of science fraud is when a deliberate act is perpetrated by one or more scientists to knowingly pass faulty, incomplete or misleading data to peers or the public, including forgery, fabricated data, falsified results, plagiarism and piracy. In order to succeed in the system, scientists, like politicians, have to spend a good portion of their time and energy chasing money. Just one recent example, among many, is the disclosure by one of its researchers that the widely prescribed and popular blood pressure drug, Lipitor, was found (in their own series of experiments) to cause diabetes in some segments of the population. This finding was not reported and the drug was declared safe by the FDA. Lipitor is still consumed daily by millions of Americans.

Politics, especially, is a hotbed of disinformation and outright lies. Ever since the Warren Commission concluded that a lone gunman assassinated President John F. Kennedy, the people who have doubted that finding have been widely dismissed as conspiracy theorists. This despite credible evidence that right-wing elements in the CIA, FBI, and Secret Service and, quite possibly senior government officials, were also involved, making the assassination a veritable *coup d'état*. In fact, the phrase "conspiracy theory" was coined by the CIA in 1964 as a way to deflect criticism of the Warren Commission findings of a lone gunman. It was a CIA propaganda campaign to discredit and polarize doubters of the commission's report. This culture of delusion has continued for decades. At his first staff meeting in 1981 with President Ronald Reagan, CIA Director William Casey made this astonishing statement: "We'll know our disinformation program is complete when everything the American public believes is false." The strategy has worked amazingly well on an unsuspecting American public, but now the CIA's campaign to stifle debate using the "conspiracy theory" smear is nearly worn-out. In academic studies, as in comments on news articles, pro-conspiracy voices, those who recognize propaganda, are now more numerous—and more rational—than anti-conspiracy ones, those who deny that the official version is propaganda. No wonder the anti-conspiracy folks are sounding more and more paranoid. It is curious that they are not suspicious of criminal wrongdoing at the highest levels of government, but instead reject this out-of-hand as paranoid thinking akin to superstition.

THEY OWN THE MOUTHPIECE

How then did a tiny ultra-wealthy oligarchy take control of the U.S. Government, the mass media empire, the world's financial system, and thus shape the fate of life and death on our planet? Primarily, it was by cleverly gaining more and more control of the flow of money. A worldwide system of financial control in private hands is able to dominate the political system of every country, and thereby control the world economy like the feudal lords of old. But you will never hear this critique on the nightly news or in the mainstream press, which, according to their core principles, is supposed to keep us objectively informed. The reason is that the same powerful interests own a vast majority of businesses that benefit from these well-orchestrated media propaganda campaigns. Big money and big media have coupled to create a "Disney World" of democracy in which TV shows, televised debates, and even news coverage is intentionally repackaged as entertainment. When we take the news out of the journalism box and place it in the entertainment box, it damages democracy and allows special interest groups to manipulate the system.

This seemingly hopeless situation is not hopeless. Rather, it is the kick-start of our "alternative narrative" to follow, a comprehensive storyline that runs parallel to what the powerful elite would prefer us to know. It is also necessary to understand that many people are not ready to be set free of the "ordinary narrative." Part of human nature is to become so inert, so helplessly dependent on the system, that we will even fight to protect it. Such is the comprehensive, insidious grip of the illusion.

One place to begin breaking free is in the realm of science. Once we uncork the bottle of suppressed science, the benefits we gain will immediately transform our society. It will be equivalent to a dimensional shift of consciousness and an ushering in of a Golden Age. Once advanced technologies are disclosed, and people experience a mass awakening to the wrongs that have been done, the elite will be unable to return to business as usual. All the things that have been hidden so long will be exposed and taught. Imagine a world where there are no secrets, where the truth is available to all, and intentional deceptions are seen for what they are and exposed. Until then, the mass media remains a powerful persuader and maintainer of our cultural trance.

It is also known that the media in its various forms, both overtly and subvertly, has experimented with subliminal conditioning. Subliminal messages are embedded in another medium, such as a single frame in a movie, a hidden image in a print ad, or split second audio messaging. They are unrecognizable by the conscious mind, but in certain situations, can affect the subconscious mind and later influence actions or attitudes. Our senses are constantly being bombarded by enormous amounts of information. Only a small part of it reaches our consciousness. However, our subconscious mind absorbs it all.

In a plutocracy, the media supposedly publishes what the market wants. But although we *are* the so-called "consumers" of media, we actually only get what they choose to provide us. We are no more the customer of media than a cow in a feedlot is the master of its own diet. The operative market is one that sells our propaganda-induced allegiances to the highest bidders, be they the advertisers, politicians, government or special interests. The mainstream media keeps us uninformed and misinformed about many of the most important issues of our day, while including just enough entertainment, plus some accurate but unimportant information to keep us coming back for more. The first step in remedying this situation is noncompliance. Do not accept the "feedlot" information. The next step in regaining an understanding of reality and our true connection to it in order to free ourselves from the control mechanisms of the physical world. We can achieve this if each individual on this planet stands up and reclaims his or her birthright. Those negative forces within our plane of existence have worked diligently to create martial law, internment camps, eugenic "slow kill" programs, and global tyranny. And yet, they have failed. Those who continue to insist that these plans are on track have failed to see the obvious, that is, the concept that sovereignty is a choice. Freedom is a state of mind. Oppressive forces can never shackle conscious freedom because it is impossible to imprison an idea. Hope can not and will not be subdued for very long. Control the mouthpiece (the "signal"), they say, and you control "reality." Not exactly. The solution is simple. You need only to unplug the signal to reclaim your mind.

HEADING UNDERGROUND

Who are these modern day "feudal lords?" In order to understand the mostly invisible monster we face, we need to understand the *modus operandi* of the detractors who seek to enslave the human race. As master warfare strategist Sun Tzu noted: "If you know the enemy and know yourself you need not fear the results of a hundred battles." The identity and origins of this elite "cabal" are discussed in detail in the next chapter, "Secret Families." However, researcher Michael Lindemann's findings, reported in a lecture he gave in San Diego in 1991, provides a snapshot:

> There is indeed another government operating, and that government ... operates primarily behind the scenes. Other researchers have called it "The Secret Government" and others have called it "The High Cabal," and it is a group of people, a very elite group of non-elected, self-appointed people who guide the evolution of policy from behind the scene. These are people who transcend partisan politics, indeed who transcend the rule of law, with no thought whatsoever for the dictates of the Constitution. These are people who regard themselves as the only true guardians and crafters of geopolitical reality, and they regard us, indeed they regard our public officials, as mere mortals. These people are the self-appointed Olympians. They have done many things in the name of an agenda which is their own, which we would consider appalling and reprehensible. Indeed, these things are criminal, but they are more than criminal, because they have sapped and usurped the rights and privileges and possibilities for our future.

One place this covert group operates, and may seek refuge if the surface world becomes too hostile, is a myriad of underground bases in dozens of countries, but especially in the United States. The New World Order fascists have been hiding and secretly planning their takeover of America in underground bases such as Area 51 in Nevada, and the under world of Denver Airport, which was built in the shape of a swastika from the air. As can be seen from blueprints smuggled out, the Denver underground base is over 150 square kilometers long, several kilometers in depth and 66 kilometers at it widest point. Underground cities exist, complete with shops, hydroponic gardens and individual homes, including underground bullet trains connecting the Denver base to the other 133 underground cities and military bases all across North America. It is also believed the Denver base is the CIA's new home, and regular American citizens are forbidden entry under the penalty of death. In short, the New World Order Nazis have been living deep under our noses for the last 70 years while raising little or no suspicion.

Right now, these people are running a kind of "endgame." In a sense, they've unwittingly adopted their own fear-based agenda, but in a different form and tinged with paranoia. They are trying to determine how they will survive the "end of time," and one of those solutions is in a honeycomb of self-sufficient underground bases. These end times, they believe, may come as a kind of Biblical apocalyptic prophecy, or more likely as the catastrophic collapse of the world economy and the destruction of the environment, coupled with the ever-burgeoning population bomb. Trends they seek to influence and control include an unwieldy and uncollateralized banking system, the consequent collapse of the world economy, and race baiting strategies that set us against each other. Add to this their false flag operations and the slow poisoning of the population using genetically modified food and implanted viruses. In view of the precarious times to come, it is no wonder they are building their own versions of Noah's Ark deep underground, in the frozen tundra, and throughout the world. Huge underground bases actually festoon the underground geography of our continent in a way that would probably stun and shock anyone who learns of the fact. These are places capable of supporting, on an on-going basis, tens of thousands of people who will be the cream of the civilization that is meant to survive an "apocalypse" or societal downfall. *Mere mortals* will have to fend for themselves. While the global elite construct their underground bunkers, eat organic food, and hoard seeds in Arctic vaults, the global poor are slowly being poisoned and starved. It is clear that the depopulation campaign of the inbred Illuminati bankers is accelerating.

ALTERNATIVES I, II, AND III

President Dwight D. Eisenhower, who warned of a "military industrial complex" taking over within the United States in his outgoing speech of 1961, may have had second thoughts and realized the dangerous extent of the secret government, as for most of his presidency he was fully onboard. In 1957, he commissioned a secret symposium of scientists to study the issue of overpopulation. By secret Executive order of President Eisenhower, the JASON Scholars were ordered to study future scenarios and make recommendations from their findings. The JASON Society, all members of the Council on Foreign Relations, confirmed the findings of the scientists that overpopulation was a serious issue, and made three recommendations called Alternatives I, II and III, all top secret. But to make "alternative" plans, the controlling elite needed time and a way to divert attention from their actual behavior. So they perpetrated the Cold War tensions as a deliberate fraud, a smokescreen thrown up to divert attention from the real danger now facing the world. The American space program was merely a diversion from the real international space effort—a joint USA/USSR off planet venture, which is far more advanced than either countries populace has been led to believe.

Alternative I, discussed by an elite panel of end-of-the-world brainstormers, was a plan to cause a drastic reduction in the human population using various human-created means. There were far too many people on the planet and what was recommended was a wholesale human cull. They advocated both the release of deadly viruses into the public arena and perpetual warfare as means to decrease world population. The first plan dovetailed nicely with the pharmaceutical interests of the Rockefellers. It is estimated that the Rockefellers own one-half of the U.S. pharmaceutical industry, which reaps billions developing medicines to "battle" the deadly viruses they create, release, and offer remedies for, but never a cure. This manipulative strategy is known as the "Problem-Reaction-Solution Paradigm," or the Hegelian Dialectic. In this paradigm, the government or some other authority creates or exploits a problem and blames it on others. People react by asking the government for help and are willing to give up their rights, and then the government offers the solution that was planned long before the manufactured crisis began. Such is the agenda behind "false flag" operations, premeditated as the problem, so the reaction and solution can transpire as planned.

A false flag operation is derived from the military concept of flying false colors in order to confuse the enemy. False flags are when governments and other organizations covertly plan and carry out disasters, set up in such a way as to "logically" blame others for the atrocities, in order to mobilize public outrage in support of military intervention and make us compliant in the greater erosion of personal privacy and freedom. Events of the 9-11 "inside job" would not have been possible without the complicity of at least a few high-level officials within the U.S. Government. For those interested in the proof that 9-11 was an inside job, *a masterful false flag operation*, the "smoking gun" is the free fall collapse of the 47-story building, WTC-7, which was clearly brought down by a controlled demolition, and not by nearby debris or office fires, as was reported. If the goal is to manipulate people for profit and power, and studies show that fearful people are much more easily manipulated, then what could be better for power brokers than a spate of terrorist attacks? The Batman and Sandy Hook shootings were soon followed by attempts at strict gun control legislation. The Boston Bombing spawned an over-handed police state crackdown and the implementation of martial law, including door-to-door searches. The London "7-7" tube bombing also similarly implicates the British government, including a similar terror drill taking place at the same time and followed by a farce of an investigation. It seems that today we are only one major false flag operation away from a total police state.

Limited nuclear war, as part of Alternative 1, was ultimately rejected as being impractical and hazardous, especially using a series of nuclear explosions to "punch holes" in the envelope of high atmosphere carbon dioxide and release it into outer space. The Pentagon realized through their various war game scenarios that if they started an all-out World War III, 90% of humanity would die, including most of them and most life on Earth. This was not practical. More practical was releasing deadly human viruses upon select population targets.

Alternative II involved moving the elite of humankind to live in underground cities. This called for the construction of a vast network of secret underground bases called Deep Underground Military Bases & Structures (DUMBS) where the elite, government leaders, and a small cross section of the general public employed as servant workers, would go into hiding until the world was again safe above ground. The underground bunker approach was simple enough. Some reports suggest that features of the controversial High Frequency Active Auroral Research Program (HAARP) are able to probe well beneath the surface of the Earth, supposedly looking for minerals, but also able to identify large caverns that would make excellent H.G. Wells styled "Morlock cities" where they could stockpile supplies and ride out any transition in comfort. Ultimately this too was rejected as impractical and undesirable, although over 130 DUMBS have been constructed in the USA and are ready to be inhabited. Most are large enough for 80,000 people, with supplies on hand for 30 years or longer of survival.

Alternative III involved transporting the world's intellectual, financial, and governmental elite off the Earth completely, using the Moon base Luna as a way station in the colonization, and then relocating them to Mars. Alternative III was still the best bet, as they could leave the dregs of society behind and start their new utopia without us mutant humans running around. They were thinking the Moon was an empty rock with no atmosphere, so Mars offered the best option. They would eventually terraform Mars and make it more Earth-like every year. In this third option, construction was to begin on the Moon and Mars bases, called Adam and Eve, then they would ultimately settle on the Red Planet as a long-term survival colony. In Alternative III, the elite would have an escape route planned while the rest of the world's population would be allowed to die. Fast forward to today. The technology to accomplish this has advanced by decades, the bases are already built and staffed, and the only step left is final departure orders.

In 1977, a popular science television program in the UK aired an episode called *Alternative 3*, based on a select few lucky people escaping Earth to a fortified city on Mars. After the broadcast aired, a flood of callers and written inquiries began requesting more information from the TV station, thinking it was all true. It wasn't really long before conspiracy researchers began to postulate that the Alternative III option really had become operational, along with elements of Alternatives I and II. Several books on the subject soon emerged to claim that the general premises of the 1977 broadcast were in fact true. An inhabited Mars colony, of course, would be the Alternative III reality.

THE PLAN IS TO EXTERMINATE BILLIONS

Aspects of Alternative I have been in operation for decades. Austerity measures aimed mainly at the poor are currently being imposed in all nations of the world: weather events continue to grow more deadly; brushfire wars emerge more frequently; and an AK-47 can be obtained for $49 in the markets of West Africa. The idea is to create resource wars, distrust among different races, and have the population kill one other. If they cut off the citizens of wealthy nations from welfare and other entitlements, then they too will take to the streets in violent uprisings and the police will be justified in shooting or arresting everyone *en masse*. The next step, now being implemented, is to introduce exotic viruses in a "soft kill" program, and cull *extra humans* that way.

The intellectual force behind the introduction of AIDS was the Bilderberg Group, which became fixated on population control after World War II. William Cooper says the Policy Committee of the Bilderbergers gave orders to the Department of Defense (DoD) to introduce the HIV virus. AIDS was deliberately created at Fort Dietrick, Maryland, as a bioweapon designed to depopulate certain "undesirable" elements of humanity. AIDS was created by Dr. Robert Gallo while he was at Litton Bionetics, who admittedly officiated over the development of AIDS complex viruses, including Ebola, as bioweapons. Similarly, in video and audio interviews, Dr. Maurice Hillerman admits that the Merck drug company vaccines for polio from 1953 until 1963 had been deliberately contaminated with SV40, a cancer-causing monkey virus.

The Bilderbergers are closely associated with the Club of Rome, which was founded on a Rockefeller estate near Bellagio, Italy, and backed by the same European Black Nobility who frequent the Bilderberger meetings. A 1968 study by the Club of Rome advocated lowering the birth rate and increasing the death rate. Club founder Dr. Aurelio Peccei made a top-secret recommendation to introduce a microbe that would attack the auto-immune system, and then developed a vaccine as a prophylactic for the global elite. One month after the 1968 Club of Rome meeting, Paul Ehrlich published *The Population Bomb*. The book hints at a draconian depopulation plan in the works. Ehrlich writes on page 17, "The problem could have been avoided by population control ... so that a 'death rate solution' did not have to occur." Furthermore, it appears that when they made this decision, the elite were on the verge of possessing the technology to solve overpopulation, food shortages and energy problems—even to the point of being able to transport excess populations to other planetary bodies if necessary.

In 1969, the Senate Church Committee discovered that the U.S. Defense Department had requested a budget of tens of millions of taxpayer dollars for a program to speed development of new viruses which could target and destroy the human immune system. DoD officials testified before Congress that they planned to produce: "A synthetic biological agent, an agent that does not naturally exist and for which no natural immunity could be acquired ... Most important is that it might be refractory to the immunological and therapeutic processes upon which we depend to maintain our relative freedom from infectious disease." House Bill 5090 authorized the funds and the program. MK-NAOMI was carried out at Fort Detrick. Out of this research came the AIDS virus which was targeted at "undesirable elements" of the population.

AIDS is only one result of these depopulation plans. It was decided by the elite that since the population must be reduced and controlled, it would be in the best interest of the human race to rid itself of undesirable elements in our society. Specific targeted populations included blacks, Hispanics, and homosexuals. The first AIDS viruses were administered through a massive smallpox vaccine campaign in central and southern Africa by the World Health Organization in 1977. A year later ads appeared in major U.S. newspapers soliciting "promiscuous gay male volunteers" to take part in a Hepatitis B vaccine study. The program targeted male homosexuals age 20-40 in New York City, Los Angeles, Chicago, St. Louis and San Francisco. It was administered by the U.S. Centers for Disease Control which, under its earlier incarnation as the U.S. Public Health Department in Atlanta, oversaw the Tuskegee syphilis experiments for four decades starting in 1932, that targeted unsuspecting African American males with often fatal results. Bill and Melinda Gates have been on a crusade for at least the past decade to vaccinate every single child on the planet, and one of their primary geographical targets has been the continent of Africa. A relevant concern would be to ask what kind of independent supervision and control is in place for these vaccination programs?

Due to its high population of gay and left-leaning citizens, which the Illuminati views as "undesirables," the people of San Francisco, CA have been targets of numerous CIA experiments. According to Dr. Eva Snead, San Francisco has one of the highest cancer rates in the country. The mysterious Legionnaire's Disease also occurs most often in San Francisco, and the CIA's MK-ULTRA mind control experiments using bad acid and other hard drugs were based there. Is it any wonder that the AIDS virus decimated the gay population of San Francisco shortly after it was introduced? For years the insecticide Malathion—first developed by the Nazis—was sprayed over the city by helicopters from the CIA's *Evergreen Air*, yet there are few insects to be found in San Francisco.

According to Naval Intelligence whistleblower William Cooper, Evergreen Air uses its Arizona base as the CIA trans-shipment point for Columbian cocaine, among other illicit drugs. The nickname of the CIA is "Cocaine Import Agency." Evergreen Air works from over 100 bases and employs 4,500 people. Delford Smith privately owns the company, and they admittedly "perform" for the CIA. The eugenics operation of spraying chemtrail particles has had the assistance of MITRE, a non-profit corporation that manages the Internal Revenue Service, the Federal Aviation Administration, and Homeland Security. The IRS is part of the Federal Reserve, which is a major transmission belt driving this conspiracy as we shall learn in the next chapter. The MITRE Corporation has jurisdictional control over the FAA, and by extension, all flight patterns. Evergreen Air is a CIA front company for chemtrail operations within the USA. The west coast geoengineering operations are based out of Marana Air Park near Tucson, Arizona; and McMinnville, Oregon, near Portland. The CIA is the enforcement arm of the Council on Foreign Relations (CFR), and it is little coincidence that the MITRE Corporation is conveniently located in McLean, Virginia, which is also home to the CIA.

CHEMTRAILING

Part of the overall plan of population reduction, as discussed above, is the use of "chemtrailing." Geoengineering is the deliberate modification of a planet's environment, allegedly to counteract the impacts of climate change, by the addition or subtraction of a resource or energy input on a massive scale, or technical measures that could influence the natural cycles on a grand scale. These measures are broadly divided into two groups: Solar Radiation Management (SRM), and Carbon Dioxide Removal (CDR) along the lines of Alternative 1. The ancient bloodline House of Rothschild, and most especially George Percy of the infamous Percy family, is in charge of Agenda 21, a man who is very passionate about depopulation, and probably has a hand in the chemtrail agenda as well.

A NASA article titled "Airborne Pollutants Know No Borders" states that, "Any substance introduced into the atmosphere has the potential to circle the Earth." The jet stream indeed connects us all. Chemical spraying is one category of deliberate airborne pollution that has been dismissed as a conspiracy theory, despite the voluminous numbers of unclassified documents from 1977 Senate hearings. Chemical spraying, commonly called chemtrails, has been implemented for several decades by both private and commercial aircraft. The June, 2016 admission of Stratospheric Aerosol Injection

(SAI) by CIA Director John Brennan to the CFR makes the case irrefutable. Fallout from these chemical trails has been tested and shows very high levels of barium and aluminum, as well as Morgellon's fibers. It is interesting to note that Monsanto recently announced the development of an aluminum-resistant gene now introduced to their seeds. One undeniable example of chemical spraying was the use of Corexit oil dispersant over the Gulf of Mexico after the 2010 BP oil spill. This process of aerial application can be likened to crop-dusting, which we know has been ongoing for about 100 years.

It is easy to research chemtrails on the Internet, because the information is all right there and out in the open. Of course you won't hear anything about chemtrails on the nightly news; you have to dig a little bit farther for this information. Do a keyword search for just one of the U.S. patents, or HR 2977, a House resolution passed by the U.S. Congress, that mentions geoengineering and chemtrails specifically. Wars abroad even seem to be affecting global air quality too, as military munitions such as depleted uranium have entered the upper atmosphere, and are spreading around the planet. The observable effects of depleted uranium are not pleasant. Airborne pollutants have been linked to allergies, genetic mutations, asthma, infertility and many other maladies.

A SECRET SPACE PROGRAM FOR OVER 60 YEARS

To implement Alternative III, the moving of large numbers of Earth's citizens to another planet, requires revolutionary space transport vehicles. Brian O'Leary, the first astronaut to ever resign from NASA, wrote about a secret space program in his 1971 book, *The Making of an Ex-Astronaut*:

> *The Air Force also has a center at Cape Kennedy, [funded] independently from NASA with its own gantries and its own Vehicle Installation Building (VIB). These facilities sit on landfill adjacent to Merritt Island, isolated from the NASA structures. We toured the Air Force center but learned little about their highly secret space program. Many people do not realize that the world has three ambitious manned space programs: The U.S. (NASA); Russia; and the U.S. Air Force. The Air Force space program operates under the protection of secrecy offered by the military, in contrast to NASA's exposure to public scrutiny. We probably know less about our Air Force space program than we do about the Soviet space program. We do know a few things, though. They have the Titan III (very difficult to hide), a big tricylinder rocket which looks like a multiple firecracker. The two extra cylinders were strapped on as an afterthought. And the three together deliver a strong thrust which is intermediate between those of Saturn IB and Saturn V.*

> *Our tour of the Air Force facility seemed like a broken record: the computers, the consoles, and the rockets were similar to NASA's and it struck me that the whole thing was an unnecessary duplication. Imagine—two independent but similar programs going on at the same time. The Air Force space program seemed like a foreign space program, except we were spending dearly for it.*

> *A manned Mars landing may be in prospect for the 1980s or the 1990s. President Nixon's appointed Space Task Group outlined three alternatives, all of which would involve the Mars landing before the end of the century.*

These observations decades ago from the respected Brian O'Leary add a great deal of credibility to persistent reports of a secret space program, along with validating the effort to initiate Alternative III. O'Leary was an American scientist, author, former NASA astronaut and free energy advocate until he died in 2011. He was a member of the 6th group of astronauts selected by NASA in August, 1967. The members of this group of 11 were known as the scientist-astronauts, intended to train for the Apollo Applications Program, a continuation of the Apollo Program, which was ultimately canceled.

SOLAR WARDEN SECRET SPACE FLEET

Another secret space travel program, not controlled by the cabal or even by the U.S. Military alone, is known by the code name, "Solar Warden." The Solar Warden program operates under authorization by the "Star Nations," a presumably ancient organization of spiritually and technologically advanced civilizations in space. Reports of earthly contact with beings from the Star Nations group are consistent with other UFO contactee reports, as well as with activities reported by Area 51 whistleblowers.

It must be remembered that NASA is a Department of Defense agency, and like most military agencies, they rely on the dictum of always requiring "a need to know," and thus err on the side of secrecy and deception rather than forthright statements or truth. Thus, when the news media reported on July 21, 2011, that the space shuttle Atlantis had landed at NASA's Kennedy Space Center in Florida and would be headed to a museum, we were told that the United States no longer had any space-capable vehicles, and that we would have to rely on Russia and other countries to get into orbit so our astronauts could visit the International Space Station. But this was an untruth. In actuality, since the late 1980s, the U.S. has contributed to this secret space fleet, and its program was code-named Solar Warden. Today, this secret space fleet has grown to eight cigar-shaped motherships, each longer than two football fields, plus at least 43 small "scout ships."

The Solar Warden space fleet operates under the USA Naval Network and Space Operations Command (NNSOC), formerly called Naval Space Command, with its headquarters based out of Dahlgren, Virginia. There are approximately 300 personnel at NNSOC's Dahlgren facility. The Solar Warden Space Fleet's vessels are staffed by Naval Space Cadre officers, whose training has earned them the prestigious 6206-P Space Operations specialty designation, after they have graduated with advanced education from the Naval Postgraduate School in Monterey, California and earned a Master of Science degree in Space Systems Operations. Both the Navy and the Marine Corps furnish men and women officers to this program. Most are recruited from the Navy's submarine operations because of the similar working conditions. While the majority of the people staffing the motherships and scout ships of the Solar Warden space fleet are Americans from the U.S. Naval Space Cadre, there are also some crew members from UK, Italy, Canada, Russia, Austria, and Australia. Thus, the Solar Warden space fleet program is not an instance of the United States alone unilaterally imposing itself on space.

Because the Space Fleet has the role of being "space policeman" within our solar system, its program has been named Solar Warden. The Space Fleet operates not only with classified U.S. Government authority but also with the secret authority of the United Nations, and the Space Fleet's mission is to protect the entire Earth and all countries. Because of the decades of backward engineering of recovered UFO crafts and its advanced technological position, the USA has been appointed by Star Nations to a lead position toward providing space security for Earth. Further, the "Solar Warden" Space Fleet was constructed primarily by U.S. aerospace black projects contractors, but with some contributions of parts and systems by Canada, United Kingdom, Italy, Austria, Russia, and Australia.

This space security mission is two-fold. One part of the Space Fleet's mission is to prevent rogue countries or terrorist groups from using outer space to conduct warfare against other countries, or against within-country targets. Star Nations has made it quite clear that space is to be used for peaceful purposes only. The second part of the Space Fleet's mission is to prevent the global-elite control group we know as the cabal from using its orbital weapons systems, including directed-energy beam weapons, to intimidate or attack anyone or any group it wishes to bend to its will.

When the British civilian Gary McKinnon hacked into U.S. Space Command computers in the early 2000s and learned of the existence of "non-terrestrial officers" and "fleet-to-fleet transfers," plus a secret program called "Solar Warden," he was charged by the Bush Justice Department with having committed "the biggest military computer hack of all time." But this was before the Edward Snowden NSA leaks of 2013. McKinnon stood to face prison time of up to 70 years after extradition from the UK to the USA, but fortunately, in October 2012, Home Secretary Theresa May said the UK would not follow USA extradition orders. Furthermore, making McKinnon stand trial in open court would involve his testifying to the above classified facts, and his attorney would be able to subpoena government officers to testify under oath about the Navy's Space Fleet. Important corroboration of this information is found in the National Defense Authorization Act for Fiscal Year 2012, which was signed into law with the president's signature. Section 912 of that Defense Bill that to the Secretary of Defense purchasing and taking delivery of "space vehicles."

The Solar Warden Space Fleet resulted from Star Nations' prompting the leadership within the United Nations to take responsibility for law enforcement of near-space to prevent any human misuse of space. It needs to be noted that Star Nations has not given the U.S. Government exclusive authority to police the Earth. The U.S. has no authority from Star Nations to engage in any international policing activities. Star Nations has the policy position that the citizens of Earth have the responsibility to work out the operation and regulation of their societies as best they can. The Star Nations wish for the secrets to end and for full disclosure to be made to the people of Earth.

Additionally, the mandate and jurisdiction of the Solar Warden space fleet is restricted to space alone. It does not have jurisdiction and does not meddle in human affairs on the ground, nor human activity occurring within Earth's atmosphere. Those are the jurisdictions of the respective governments in each country and the air space above their territories. Solar Warden space fleet's mandate is to keep space peaceful and free from misuse by Earth to conduct war-like or illegal activities in space, such as nuclear intercontinental ballistic missile launches, or unilaterally confiscating the natural resources of another planet or moon. Solar Warden does not replace the responsibility of Earth governments to conduct their own law enforcement and policing on the ground or in the air over their countries.

AGENDA 21

A comprehensive insult to our global population is the UN-promoted "Agenda 21." Most people have never heard of Agenda 21, nor know how it might affect their lives. The number 21 stands for the 21st century. It is a United Nations (UN) "programme of action" signed by 178 world leaders, including President George Herbert Bush, who sang its praises at the 1992 Rio Earth Summit. The concept sounds pretty tame on the surface, but in reality it has been a serious world government movement on the United Nations drawing board for over two decades. Ignored by the major media and kept off-limits from the general public, this widely criticized UN scheme has been marketed as a way to make humanity more "sustainable." According to UN documents, however, Agenda 21 essentially seeks to restructure human civilization under the guise of environmentalism. Even a citizen's independent thought is in the crosshairs, official reports show.

What does sustainability mean? That all depends on who is being asked. Just about anyone could agree that the $15 trillion deficit underlying the financial debacle in the United States means our financial system is not sustainable. However, the definition of sustainability, and the strategy for achieving it through the United Nations, is something of concern. Sustainability measures being implemented by the UN locally via the International Council for Local Environmental Initiatives (ICLEI) represent a clear and present danger to U. S. sovereignty. Over 608 cities in the USA have joined ICLEI, the Local Governments for Sustainability, which seemingly joined the UN without voter consent.

The UN's insidious invasion of the world, especially within the United States, is rather disturbing. Their idea of world government has nothing to do with individual freedoms, harmony, and the "pursuit of happiness." This is why they must first eliminate the freedoms that citizens in the United States enjoy. As long as we have this system of Constitutional rights, we are a danger to their ultimate goal of global domination. The Agenda 21 movement would nullify our Constitutional structure, with the freedoms and prerogatives enshrined in the Bill of Rights, including our unhampered right to property ownership. It elevates nature above humankind, and contains a *little ditty* called "The Precautionary Principle" where, basically, we can be considered guilty until proven innocent. This tyranny masquerades behind the façade of "sustainable development." Agenda 21, and its updated companion Agenda 2030, also has an plan for human life itself by regulating and seeking to stabilize human birth rates. Every single point in both UN agendas are to be achieved through centralized government control and totalitarian mandates that resemble communism.

It should not be forgotten that the United Nations was devised as a means for global control by the international bankers and global elites, was spearheaded by John D. Rockefeller, and financed through the Rockefeller Foundation. The plan was to consolidate control over the world's nations by a governing body that would put forth and sell the elite's interests to the rest of the world. Their counterparts, the IMF and World Bank, coerce nations to vote in favor of their objectives by using debt owed to these bodies as leverage. These "economic hit men" can keep small countries in check by using financial coercion, by making smaller nations accept privatization of industries, and by influencing their votes to side with globalists on key issues at the UN.

Looked at through the lens of global domination, Agenda 21 is a veiled effort for depopulation and greater control by concentrating people into increasingly smaller areas of habitation. It is cloaked in deceit as an environmentally-conscious program, but it is aimed at taking over all land, water, minerals, natural resources, and industry from the public. Some refer to chemtrails as "Agenda 21 in action." Private citizens would lose the ability of land ownership, and thus it would become the government's property instead, the same government that already dominates the military industrial complex. It is easy to look up the UN Agenda 21 or Agenda 2030 on the Internet.

A COWARDLY NEW WORLD

The United Nations uses various Non-Governmental Organizations (NGOs) and gullible local politicians to establish their footholds everywhere. They do this in African nations through the use of threats. They tell African leaders they will cut off international funds of those who question their authority. This is one reason why many Africans still live in abject poverty. The UN has decided, or more properly many NGOs have decided, that massive areas of Africa shall remain undeveloped in the Agenda 21 plan. Hence, extremely poor people continue plowing rock-hard dirt to eek out a pathetic living, or perhaps just enough to fend off family starvation. Somehow the West has enough resources to vaccinate these people, but not enough to feed them or provide clean water. Is it any wonder why undeveloped nations resent the developed world? They want to live decently, but are continually road-blocked by Western agendas.

George Orwell anticipated the state as Big Brother hovering over us, keeping us under surveillance, arresting us for subversive views, or taking care of our needs as long as we repay them with absolute loyalty. Aldous Huxley anticipated a brave new world where we amuse ourselves to death. The future seems to be a combination of both. The world government in the form of the United Nations was hijacked long ago. We're now controlled by think tanks such as the CFR, Bilderberg Group, and others. These politicians work for the globalists, are determined to break the sovereignty of the USA, and allowing it to be absorbed into the global community. Author and linguist Noam Chomsky stated, "the most effective way to restrict democracy is to transfer decision-making from the public arena to unaccountable institutions: kings and princes, priestly castes, military juntas, party dictatorships, or modern corporations." The powerful think tank groups do not merely suggest policy, they insist on it being done their way.

Some people in high levels of American government and the leaders of policy groups and academia such as John P. Holdren, the 2012 White House science czar, have advocated population control via "pollution particles" as far back as 1977 in books such as *Ecoscience*. These policy makers seem to be Malthusian fanatics in the tradition of the arcane anti-human ideology that originated among the British aristocracy in the 19th century. The theory by Robert Malthus states that population tends to increase at a faster rate than its means of subsistence and that unless it is monitored by moral restraint or disaster, such as disease, famine, or war, the result will be widespread poverty and degradation. Holdren's views of humanity could make a critical thinker raise questions about the intentional planting of poisons in our environment. Holdren advocated the formation of a "planetary regime" that would use a "global police force" to enforce totalitarian measures of population control, including forced abortions, mass sterilization programs conducted via the food and water supply, as well as mandatory bodily implants that would prevent couples from procreating. Holdren calls himself a "neo-Malthusian" in his own book, and he is a historical pessimist who has rejected the idea that America and humanity as a whole can progress through ingenuity, industry and economic growth. Instead, Holdren sees humankind as a cancer upon the Earth. When taken together, it appears that certain scientific, governmental, and medical management programs are leading to the wholesale compromise of people's health and individual freedoms. Is it just coincidental, or perhaps ironic, that when one falls sick due to the unnatural pollutants, the mainstream medical establishment aims to treat the afflictions with more unnatural chemicals?

While the "scientists," the U.S. military, and numerous other governmental agencies continue to deny the reality of the massive global geoengineering programs, the enormous machine that runs these ever expanding programs continue to grow right in plain sight. Those who are attempting to expose the truth regarding the deliberate planetary weather and climate modification via aerosol spraying are still marginalized by the state-sponsored mainstream media. This is when the alternative narrative becomes chilling, because the dark truth is that we are all being subjected to a horrific global experiment, an experiment that is quite literally putting all life on Earth in the balance. An ever-growing mountain of evidence already proves beyond any doubt that global geoengineering is an absolute reality. Anyone who does an objective evaluation of the available evidence can come to no other conclusion.

A DEN OF VIPERS

Those who would have us under their total control occasionally show their playbook for all the world to see. A good example are the Georgia Guidestones, which is a large granite monument in Elbert County, Georgia. A message consisting of ten guidelines, or principles, is engraved on the anonymously donated megaliths in eight different languages. Perhaps to be abundantly clear in their intentions, there is one language on each face of four large upright stones and one support pillar. Moving clockwise around the structure from due north, these languages are: English, Spanish, Swahili, Hindi, Hebrew, Arabic, Chinese, and Russian, and a shorter message is inscribed at the top of the structure in the four ancient language scripts of Babylonian, Classical Greek, Sanskrit, and Egyptian hieroglyphics. A capstone rests on top of the five upright slabs, which has been astronomically aligned. The Georgia Guidestones contain ten "new commandments" for all humanity to follow:

1. *Maintain humanity under 500,000,000 in perpetual balance with nature.*
2. *Guide reproduction wisely—improving fitness and diversity.*
3. *Unite humanity with a living new language.*
4. *Rule passion—faith—tradition—and all things with tempered reason.*
5. *Protect people and nations with fair laws and just courts.*
6. *Let all nations rule internally, resolving external disputes in a world court.*
7. *Avoid petty laws and useless officials.*
8. *Balance personal rights with social duties.*
9. *Prize truth—beauty—love—seeking harmony with the infinite.*
10. *Be not a cancer on the earth—Leave room for nature.*

On the surface it appears pretty benign advice, if not for the number one commandment being to reduce the human population of the planet to less than a half billion people. Such advice smacks of eugenics, first proposed by the English scientist Francis Galton in the early 20th century. Galton described his new vision this way: "Eugenics is the study of agencies under social control that may improve or impair the racial qualities of future generations, whether physically or mentally." In 1905, he wrote about the three stages of eugenics—first an academic matter, then a practical policy, and finally "it must be introduced into the national consciousness as a new religion." It would seem that the builder of the Georgia Guidestones took Galton's philosophy to heart.

Another method of control is to intentionally keep the public as ignorant as possible. Sporting events, mindless trivia, celebrity gossip, and trivial news stories like lottery winners or rescued pets are common distractions. Or, the outward destruction of knowledge also works. Book burning is usually carried out in public, and is generally motivated by moral, religious, or political objections to the material. The most infamous book burning was the Library of Alexandria, Egypt, which was a center for ancient works and was burnt down over 1,600 years ago. For centuries it functioned as a major center of scholarship from its construction in the third century BCE and through the era of Jesus Christ. It was the first known library of its kind to gather a serious collection of books from beyond its own country's borders. The Library of Alexandria was charged with collecting all the world's knowledge.

As long as the belief in war continues, how can war not continue? If no one believed in war, then how could war exist? War does not describe a phenomenon of physical necessity. Unlike gravity, the laws of physics or biological instinct—nothing in nature—demands that war must happen. It transpires entirely from cultural beliefs. Warfare erupts out of political and religious decisions, not from animal instinct. We have no born instinct to fight each other. Instead, we must teach each other to fight, and this requires a social structure based on beliefs that support such actions. Religious belief gives us a contrived moral reason to engage in human slaughter; politics gives us the economic means to follow it through. When you've got the capability of unlimited war mixed with unlimited belief in war, you will eventually get precisely what those beliefs demand.

It has been said that "money doesn't grow on trees," but the current printing of paper money belies that old aphorism. Privately owned central banks create money out of nothing and loan it out while requiring interest. All modern fiat currencies are literally debt owed to these central banks. The economy is a casino, where central banks control the game, and the house always wins. President Andrew Jackson, the only one of our presidents whose administration totally abolished the national debt, condemned the international bankers as a "den of vipers" that he was determined to "rout out" from the fabric of American life. Jackson claimed that if the American people understood how these vipers operated on the American scene regarding the creation of money and the banking system, "there would a revolution before morning."

OUR COLLECTIVE DAYDREAM

It would appear as if our collective "daydream" of reality can actually define our collective future. Whoever controls the ability to shape perception can shape the course of civilization. Unfortunately, at present there is only one main collective daydream of our future—one that paints the picture of a fearsome war-torn world created by psychotic rulers, who claim to be the legal, but are unlawful owners of the people and the planet's resources. As we will see, these rulers despise most of the Earth's population, and ultimately think of us as parasites. This is why they poison our food, water, air, and force vaccines on us, all the while making us perpetually pay them an extortionist rate to wage their wars on each other and the environment. They know perfectly well there is a universal law of collective envisioning, and if the people are constantly stuck in negative polarity, that they will win. They will stop at nothing to prevent our collective daydream from envisioning a Golden Age for humanity, replete with free energy, abundance for all, and ultimately an end to the money system that keeps nearly every human in a state of subservience. Unfortunately, for now, their horrible daydream is prevailing, but only because they have manipulated us into helping them make it come true in a *negative consensus* reality. By instilling fear and inciting anger, by having complete control of finance and owning the mass media, they have a huge advantage. But people are now waking up and understanding there is an alternative narrative. We have a new dream to dream.

When humans collectively focus on something, an event for example, they create energy around that event, which then makes the event take on its own energy. This can work as a double-edged sword, either creating a positive or a negative outcome. If negative, it can create a polarizing effect on the collective consciousness, making the people who believe the lie often the biggest defenders of the delusion. After all, it is fairly easy to sway an opinion, especially when you tell people what they like to hear. All you need is someone with credentials, bogus research supporting their opinion, and a delivery mechanism. Once a biased story goes on the newswire, or the Internet, it is out there, no matter how inaccurate or slanted it is, and it begins to take on a life of its own.

Everyone needs to wake up from the grand illusion called consensus reality. Our money system is fraudulent. Our debt is not real. Our two party system is a fraud. Our healthcare system is a sham. Our food is unhealthy. Our energy production is a farce. Pharmaceutical companies are bamboozlers. Our history is manufactured. Our government serves the corporations. Most of the information the mainstream media reports on is propaganda to serve someone else's agenda—like the people who own the media outlets. Once you realize the illusion, what you've thought of as reality begins to look like a cheap set on some ridiculous B movie. But why is it like this? How is it that we have come to the point that what is written here is so painfully and almost ridiculously true? If everything listed in this book is fictitious, what then is real? Or is there even such a thing as a collective reality? To some, the illusion is so pervasive, so ingrained into everything we perceive to be reality, and there are so many dead ends, it is difficult for anyone to navigate through the maze of lies, half-truths, and mass delusions. To change direction it is necessary to make an abrupt turn-around and question everything we think we know to be real.

ALTERNATIVE IV

This brings us to Alternative IV. The elite controllers never proposed an Alternative IV for the rest of us. If they really have such contempt and disdain for the human race, they leave us no choice but to fashion our own future. Alternative IV is the paradigm of personal and global transformation. It is the endgame of love. It begins with learning and evaluating for ourselves information available on the Internet and in books such as this, and changing our minds about most of what we have always believed. Whether the elite do or don't scurry to their underground bunkers or escape off planet, there are those of us who want to save the Earth. Alternative IV envisions a vast public awakening first, followed by the creation of a new and sustainable civilization. By visualizing an alternative future or "timeline" for the Earth and all its inhabitants, we take the first step toward directing our energy to a positive Alternative IV endgame. As few as 10% of all people on Earth is all that is needed to create world peace, undermine the ruling elite, and manifest the reality of full cooperation among all people. This can be achieved by focusing our positive thoughts and actions to the endgame called *love*. Along the lines of the 100th Monkey Effect, if enough of us want to make Alternative IV a reality and save the world, we actually can do so, and it begins with each of us affirming "yes" to this possibility.

The innate wisdom within all of us is beginning to see through the lunacy of this third dimensional (3D) illusory world, and realize what we see is an unstable manufactured "reality." Our best hope is that humanity will awaken from the illusion and reconnect to our *wisdom state* through a loving consciousness. There is also a malevolent ET faction on Earth that wants to see humanity stay divided and directed towards negative polarity. These entities, who manifest their control of reality through the lives of the elite, will soon dissolve in frustration as humanity stops responding to the subliminal messages that relentlessly bombard the wisdom state. The 3D experience is not real and only exists as a projection of our minds. Therefore, it's in our minds, that we disconnect emotionally from the 3D space and reclaim our *eternal state*, which is the *here and now*. This is what we are! We are the original eternal paradise state of spirit, and the material 3D illusion was simply conjured up through a thought process to separate us from our immense innate power. The grip of this 3D illusion distracts us from our natural wisdom, and we have slid into servitude to the collective group thought of "Luciferianism." The beneficial aspect of becoming aware of this process is that, at any moment of our choosing, we can reject the hypnotic egregore manipulation and reclaim our wisdom state. And we can experience the freedom of the paradise state right now.

ALTERNATIVE ENERGY

A shift in awareness opens portals for inspiration. New ideas and strategies emerge to relieve suffering and promote a better way of life, such as alternative energy. As it turns out, cold fusion is real, practical, and reproducible at least 25% of the time. It should be funded, debugged and developed, and it represents a potentially decentralized technology. Valid science has been suppressed, advocates have died mysteriously, and promising inventions have gone missing or were intentionally destroyed. In some cases, national security gag orders were issued to prevent technology from going public. There have been numerous scientists working on ways to make efficient use of the free energy all around us—heat, wind, sunlight, electromagnetism, even zero-point energy. Why haven't these technologies reached the market? In some cases they might have been hoaxes, in other cases they might not be cost-effective. But in a few instances, it appears that untimely deaths have been the deciding factor. While this topic is difficult to understand and evaluate, the potential payoff is nothing less than what is needed to save the Earth from the current fossil fuel dilemma.

At the very least, let's reexamine the free energy technology of Nikola Tesla, arguably the greatest inventor of the 20th century. A hundred years ago he famously said that "electric power is everywhere present in unlimited quantities and is able to drive machinery without the need of coal, oil, gas, or any other of the common fuels." But those who would have us believe the ordinary narrative would have none of this, and they went to great lengths to discredit Tesla. After all, free energy is exactly that—free, and the business of energy production is the largest industry on the planet. It would seem that the *power brokers* would have a keen, vested interest, to keep free energy off the market and out of public discussion.

WOLVES IN SHEEP'S CLOTHING

Finally, beware of "wolves in sheep's clothing." When the mind-controlling elite lose more and more of their power to an awakened population, we will observe how they use and coopt "spiritual knowledge" in order keep people in control. Only by developing *ourselves* will we be able to see through the illusion, and separate reality from this false ruse. The shift is already taking place in our consciousness, but we can only change if we learn from our mistakes and make this change. Our adversaries have gotten stronger, but we have gotten wiser. Their false flag operations will not work on awakened people. But there is much work to do as their domestic spying and military campaigns get stronger. Homeland Security is currently building up a "domestic Army" through work with local law enforcement agencies, but this flies in the face of The Posse Comitatus Act of 1878, which was passed to prevent U.S. military personnel from acting as law enforcement agents on U.S. soil. We are left to wonder why the federal government is so afraid of its own citizens? Perhaps the answer is obvious. After all, when exposing a crime is treated as committing a crime, it is pretty clear we are being ruled by criminals.

Author Chris Hedges precisely weighs the priorities and consequences of our current misguided governmental powers:

> *What kind of nation is it that spends far more to kill enemy combatants and Afghan and Iraqi civilians than it does to help its own citizens who live below the poverty line? What kind of nation is it that permits corporations to hold sick children hostage while their parents frantically bankrupt themselves to save their sons and daughters? What kind of nation is it that tosses its mentally ill onto urban heating grates? What kind of nation is it that abandons its unemployed while it loots its treasury on behalf of speculators? What kind of nation is it that ignores due process to torture and assassinate its own citizens? What kind of nation is it that refuses to halt the destruction of the ecosystem by the fossil fuel industry, dooming our children and our children's children?*

In April of 2012, the BRICS nations (Brazil, Russia, India, China and South Africa) met to agree upon a strategy that would liberate the poor countries of the world from the grip of the Western technocrats. A joint BRICS bank was discussed with vigor. It would serve as an alternative to the central banks that routinely abuse their power at the expense of nations worldwide. They hope to replace the International Monetary Fund (IMF) and the World Bank. The BRICS countries are pushing for peace, and they have vowed not to use force and occupation of other countries to obtain this goal. Over 180 countries have signed onto the BRICS agreement as evidenced in their declaration. While the global elite still hold power over the Western G8 countries, the rest of the world is standing up, severing their ties, and making plans for a new world without them. *Enough is enough.* It is only a collection of extremely powerful and secretive families that stands in their way.

< The quiet war with silent weapons has been waged against peace-loving citizens by the CIA, NSA, FBI and Big Intelligence since the late 1940s. The military industrial complex is in reality the Deep State, or the shadow government.

> How do we know this is the spiritual symbol of the Illuminati? Because this symbol was found on seized documents when the German police raided Adam Weishaupt's lodges in the late 1700s, after the Illuminati conspiracy was exposed by Bavarian authorities. The Latin terms above and below the "seeing-eye" pyramid *Annuit Cœptis Novus Ordo Seclorum* can be translated as "Announcing the Birth of the New World Order."

< This patch is from the Phillips Laboratory Military Spaceplane Technology (MIST) Program Office at Kirtland Air Force Base in New Mexico. The original version of the patch sported an "X-Wing" fighter from the *Star Wars* movies. When lawyers representing George Lucas delivered the unit a cease and desist order, the aircraft on the patch was changed into the shape that appears on this patch.

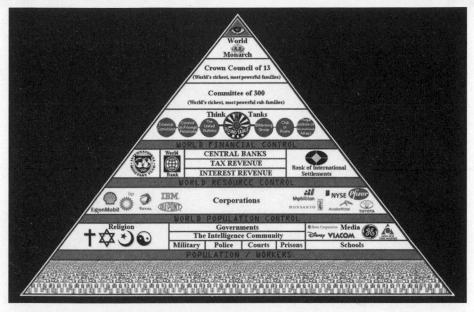

They control your money, fund both sides of nearly every major war, invest in weapons manufacturers and distributors, advance the prison industrial complex, overthrow governments, facilitate covert eugenics operations, and install shadow governments around the world.

< The "economic hit men" seek first to control and divide a nation, exploit its people and resources, pay pennies on the dollar for what it's worth, then export the items to the USA and UK to make a killing. Meet the new boss. Same as the old boss. The New World Order is the Old World Order.

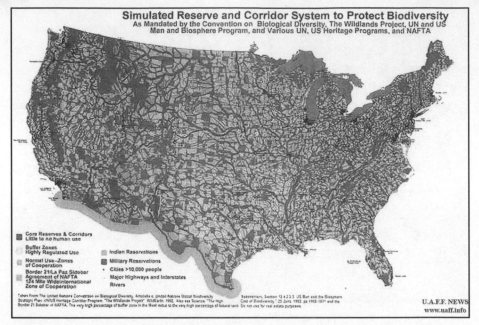

Simulated Reserve and Corridor System to Protect Biodiversity
As Mandated by the Convention on Biological Diversity, The Wildlands Project, UN and US
Man and Biosphere Program, and Various UN, US Heritage Programs, and NAFTA

Core Reserves & Corridors
Little to no human use

Buffer Zones
Highly Regulated Use

Normal Use--Zones
of Cooperation

Border 21/La Paz Sidebar
Agreement of NAFTA
124 Mile Wideinternational
Zone of Cooperation

Indian Reservations

Military Reservations

· Cities >10,000 people

Major Highways and Interstates

Rivers

U.A.F.F. NEWS
www.uaff.info

The United Nations Agenda 21 map includes tiny black dots that are where our current cities exist. Agenda 21 calls for humans to be stacked and packed in cubicle domiciles, which they can not own. People will not be allowed in areas outside the settlement zones. A network of high speed trains will connect the settlement zones. The areas in the darkest shade of grey are regions where humans will not be able to live or utilize natural resources. No farmland, no property, and total government control. George HW Bush, simply by Executive Order, signed the USA on to join Agenda 21 when he was in office.

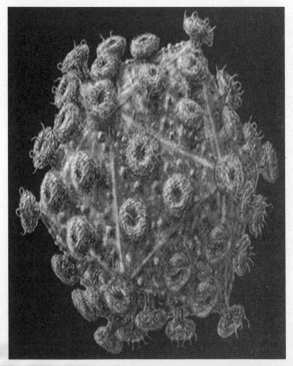

< Based on the theories of Dr. William Campbell Douglass and many others, the HIV virus was genetically engineered in 1974 by the World Health Organization. Dr. Douglass, who has been called "the conscience of modern medicine," shows evidence that the AIDS virus was created in a laboratory, and that it was a cold-blooded attempt to create a killer virus which was then released in a successful experiment in Africa. The now deceased head of vaccines at Merck, Dr. Maurice Hillerman, once admitted on camera that Merck's Hepatitis B vaccines, contaminated with a virus, caused the AIDS epidemic in the USA. He went on to say that all of Merck's vaccines are contaminated with cancer and other viruses. Speculation is that the HIV virus was created by the CIA as a means to reduce world population.

SECRET FAMILIES

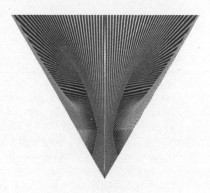

"It is well enough that people of the nation do not understand our banking and monetary system, for if they did, I believe there would be a revolution before tomorrow morning."
–Henry Ford, 1922

ACCORDING to legend, the Illuminati are a small, super-secret cabal of influential individuals who have shaped the course of world events for at least 250 years. Continual generations of these secret families and societies driving the world agenda have been known by many names. This global elite is composed of the richest and most powerful people in the world. The existence of a global elite is not disputed, but what is their agenda? Leaked reports confirm that they consistently meet throughout the world, behind closed doors, to discuss their agenda—the control and domination of all facets of society. Then, like clockwork, their plans appear in the media, finance, corporate, government, commercial and military arenas.

It is said that the Illuminati are the masterminds, the "power behind the throne," who actually control world affairs through clever alliances with governments and ownership of corporations. They are then effectively positioned to establish a one-world monetary and governmental system. The word "Illuminati" means "people claiming to be unusually enlightened with regard to a subject," or "any of various groups claiming special religious enlightenment." Like the definitions imply, any group which considers itself "enlightened" could rightfully call itself the Illuminati. Indeed, there is a benevolent group that does exist and also goes by "The Illuminati." They are actually the original group using this name. They have been working behind the scenes for a very long time to help humanity free themselves from the chains we have been stuck in for thousands of years. So the term can be confusing, because it has been hijacked and adopted by forces at the opposite end of the enlightened spectrum. The Illuminati we are discussing here is not a benevolent group who want to create peace and harmony in this world by helping to bring freedom and justice to the people. Rather, they are the shadowy Powers That Be, self-serving puppet masters running the show by using war, destruction, and poverty and to control the populace through ignorance and fear. They infiltrated the true freedom movement in an early stage by adopting the term Illuminati to describe themselves, thus coopting the name of the original benevolent group. This is yet another method to further confuse the matter and throw truth seekers off their path. Similarly, this second group has confused researchers by using the intrinsically benevolent term "New World Order" for their negative and malevolent goals of world domination.

Gaining control of the money supply was an early tactic. The first international bankers were the Knights Templar, a secretive society created and sponsored by an even more secret society known as the Priory of Sion during the time of the Christian Crusades. At that time, the goal was to recapture the Holy Land from Muslim control. Associated with the Illuminati is the Bilderberg Group with a direct lineage to the Venetian Black Nobility, a cabal of rich trading families in Italy 800 years ago. Behind today's Bilderberg Group is a contemporary network of powerful private merchant-banking interests based on a medieval Venetian financier oligarchic model known as fondi. The ancestors of today's ultra-wealthy families who belong to the modern Bilderberg Group were responsible for the creation of the Synarchism Movement of Empires. This is an ancient cabal whose aim was forging political alliances between financiers and industrialists in order to unify socialists and anarchists around fascist principles—and in this way they have controlled humanity through violence, propaganda, and bribery for hundreds, and possibly thousands, of years. These people earned the title of "Black" Nobility for their ruthless lack of scruples. They employed murder, rape, kidnapping, assassination, blackmail, robbery, and all manner of deceit on a grand scale, and allowed no opposition to the attainment of their objectives. Synarchism International was founded by the esoteric secret society of Freemasonry in the 1770s as a counter-attack on the principles on which the United States was founded. Call them what you will, the Synarchists, the Priory de Sion, the Illuminati, or the Bilderbergers who were named for the Dutch hotel where they first met, one thing is true, these elite groups do exist. Today, these elite families and groups all have immense wealth, and money is their means of power.

The British and Dutch East India Companies, and the Bilderbergers, are examples of the private merchant banker alliances. To find out who the people are who head the Bilderbergers, one can find the names of top cabal members within the membership of the Council on Foreign Relations and the Trilateral Commission. This inner core of people are also called the "Incunabula." Today there are basically 1,000 top members of this cabal, and they make all the big decisions that influence a great majority of people on Earth.

THE RULING BLOODLINES

One is always born into a ruling bloodline family, never a "walk in," even by marriage. One cannot just "join" the family. Beginning in the 5th century CE, Merovingian Kings, the Black Nobility, and royal families have exclusively interbred. The royal bloodlines are likely much older, spanning the course of recorded history, and perhaps go all the way back to the ancient Egyptians. Members can only be born or "incarnated" into the family lineages. Family members are brought up in a very specific and rigorous way, which engenders unwavering loyalty. No matter how keen and sincere another may be to join, the families only place trust in those individuals they have sired since early childhood. The secret ruling bloodline families will always intermarry between lines, or between "Houses." Marriages are always arranged. There are no unapproved unions, and it is unthinkable for a family member to break this code ... *they do as they are told.* The whole familial House society is geared towards upward progression. The agenda is handed down from generation to generation. Only on rare occasions have outsiders been *invested* into the family, and even these were from other "esoterically" integral lines. The most prominent Illuminati family bloodlines, those whose individual family members wield vast control over the world, include: Rothschild; Rockefeller; Astor; Bundy; Collins; Du Pont; Freeman; Kennedy; Li; Onassis; Reynolds; Russell; Van Duyn; Disney; Krupp; Bush; and the McDonald bloodline. One family, one bloodline, one rule.

According to the World Bank, only 227 families own 47% of the world's wealth, and this is a conservative estimate. According to the *Financial Times,* ten families control much of Israel. That leaves only 217 elite families to control worldwide banking, and industry, along with the purse strings to directly influence lawmakers. These power brokers refer to themselves as the "hidden hands," the nameless individuals that are directly involved in most of the institutions on Earth. How can a market be free when members of the same family get to print the money, lend it to our government, and charge the people a usury fee in the form of interest and income taxes? The ultra rich are so rich that they're even richer than some small nations. The master of all is the House of Rothschild, the wealthiest family in the world for the last three centuries running.

According to financial insider Benjamin Fulford, "the Illuminati are really inbred families of European and North American traditional aristocracy and banking families. They control the USA, England, Europe (except for Scandinavian countries, Germany and Italy; Italy kicked them out in the 1970's), Japan, Africa, Canada and Mexico. They do not control China, Russia (Putin kicked them out for the first time since 1917), India, Southeast Asia, South America, Cuba etc. ... Their goal is to create a world government. Until 2010 the plan was the New World Order. That was precisely outlined in the Project for a New American Century. However, with the debacle in Iraq, the secret government of the West changed to a new plan that is a world government based on the EU. To do this they will sabotage the U.S. economy."

RISE OF THE KHAZARS

I n 1976, after many years of research, a well-respected Ashkenazi Jewish author named Arthur Koestler published a book titled the *Thirteenth Tribe,* in which he affirms that most Eastern European Jews are neither Israelites nor "Semites," but rather Khazars, Mongols, and Huns by ancestry. In making his case, Koestler quotes a thousand-year-old Arabian manuscript declaring "The Khazars and their King are all Jews ... and that Gog and Magog mentioned in the biblical book of Revelation are the Khazars."

The Khazars were talented entrepreneurs and money managers. They became monopolistic world merchants throughout the thirteenth to eighteenth centuries. They were re-exporters of foreign goods, middlemen, inspectors of trade, goldsmiths, and silversmiths. For their services they exacted a 10% tax, or a "tithe" on all trades. These Jews became international masters of precious metals, minting gold and silver coins, and established themselves as royal treasurers, tax collectors, and then the primary money-lenders of Europe. Their principal source of income was foreign trade and the levying of customs dues. These families practiced communal living, an early version of communism. They viewed themselves as a separate group, having maintained their identity over millennia by means of a strong racial awareness, strict intermarriage laws, conscientious religious practices, and loyalty to tradition.

Thanks to the research of Koestler, it is easy to follow the origins of the Khazarian international banker families from the year 1400 CE to the present day. It shows the Khazar bloodline links to Spain and Portugal, such as the "Marranos" of Spain, and the "Guerients" and "Marquis" of France. These international merchants established trade links with India, China, and many other lucrative international markets.

According to industrialist automaker Henry Ford's 1920 book, *The International Jew*, Khazar-Jews financed the voyage of Christopher Columbus with the goal of finding a more direct route to the continent of India. Until his dying day Columbus believed that North America was "India," and wrongfully named the American native tribes "Indians." Henry Ford writes: "The Story of Jews in America begins with Christopher Columbus. On August 2nd, 1492, more than 300,000 Jews were expelled from Spain and on August 3rd, the next day, Columbus set sail for the west, taking a group of Jews with him." The fact that these early banking families happened to be Jewish is likely one of the feeders of anti-semitism. Any human group that accumulates great wealth is resented, and is therefore vulnerable to misuse of such wealth. This is not a Jewish trait, but a human one. Many accounts, such as that of Henry Ford, enumerating the cabal and the history of Jews carries an undercurrent of anti-semitism. The truth is the unbridled wealth and power is the problem, not exclusively the group's ethnicity.

The first known Illuminati order, called "Alumbrado," was founded in 1492 by Spanish Jews called the *Marranos*. With violent persecution in Spain and Portugal beginning in 1391, hundreds of thousands of Jews were forced to convert to the faith of the Roman Catholic Church. Publicly they were now "Roman Catholics," but secretly they practiced Judaism and retained their Khazar customs. The powerful and extremely wealthy Marranos were able to secretly teach their children about Judaism, particularly the Talmud and the Kabbalah. After 1540, many Marranos opted to migrate to England, Holland, France, and to the Ottoman Empire, in what today is Turkey, also Brazil and other places in South and Central America. The Marranos kept strong family ties and became very wealthy and influential in the nations where they resettled. As is the custom with all Khazar people, it did not matter in what nation they lived, their loyalty was to themselves and to Judaism. In more recent times the Khazars have become known as Zionists, and their loyalties reside with the nation of Israel.

EUROPE'S ILLUMINATI

Today the Illuminati primarily control world affairs from locations in Europe. Although they never use that name, today's ruling bloodline families are a modern incarnation or continuation, of various earlier European Illuminati groups. The most famous are the Bavarian Illuminati, founded on May 1, 1776, by Adam Weishaupt, who was born in 1748 of Jewish parents but grew up in the Catholic faith. He was a Jesuit-trained professor of canon law and well-versed in the occult. To his followers, Weishaupt outlined the top five secret means to achieve their goals as follows: First, monetary and sexual bribery would be used against men already in high places. Two, the Illuminati who were on the faculties of top universities would recruit candidates to work for them. Three, influential people would be placed behind the ranks of government, religious, and financial institutions, and be used as agents for the Illuminati. Four, the secret society would attain complete control of the mass media. Five, they would implement covert military coups to remove any governments opposed to their planetary rule. Weishaupt soon infiltrated the Continental Order of Freemasons, and with the Illuminati doctrine, established the lodges of the Grand Orient to become their secret headquarters. The Illuminati philosophy has spread, and is followed within Masonic lodges worldwide.

The public translation of the Illuminati is "intellectually inspired," but Weishaupt himself said in private that the word was derived from Lucifer and means "Holders of the Light." The beginnings of the massive Rothschild's private empire can be traced back to Mayer Amschel Rothschild, who arranged a secret meeting with other powerful families three years before he employed Weishaupt. The financiers of the older Illuminati orders, dating back to the bankers during the times of the Templar Knights, financed the early kings in Europe, who eventually created the Bavarian Illuminati. Weishaupt was merely the "go fer" who did their bidding. It was Weishaupt who termed their cause a "New World Order." The symbol of the group is printed on the back of the U.S. one dollar bill: A mystical unfinished pyramid, with an all-seeing eye reigning above the world. This private empire soon came under the financial control of Mayer Amschel Rothschild.

THE ROTHSCHILD'S ILLUMINATI

The Rothschilds are the most eminent banking family in history. In the 19th century, they lent money to kings and governments and funded both sides in the Napoleonic wars. At one point in time, the Rothschilds saved the Bank of England from collapse with their own money. But how did they acquire such astonishing wealth?

The Rothschilds claim that they are Jewish, but a more accurate ethnicity lineage would be to identify them as Khazars as discussed above. They are from a country originally called Khazaria, that occupied a region between the Black Sea and the Caspian Sea, and which is predominantly occupied today by the country of Georgia. They are part Mongol, because Genghis Khan and his army occupied the region for many years. The reason the Rothschilds claim to be Jewish is that the Khazar people, under the instruction of their king, converted to the Jewish faith in the 8th century. About 85% of people in the world today who call themselves Jews are actually Khazars, who prefer to be known as Ashkenazi Jews.

The Rothschild rise to financial dominance began when Mayer Amschel Rothschild was operating a finance house in Frankfurt, Germany. His five sons were dispatched throughout Europe in the late 1700s and early 1800s. The five sons set up operations in Frankfurt, Vienna, London, Naples, and Paris, and soon created a true European financial dynasty that is still hugely dominant today. In June of 1815, Nathan Rothschild's secret courier network was the first to make it back to London with news that Napoleon's French troops had been defeated by the British alliance of seven nations at Waterloo. Rothschild, who had funded both sides in the war, cunningly alleged that the French had won and started selling British "consuls" on the stock exchange. Other traders fell for the bluff and the market plummeted. Nathan Rothschild then quietly started buying up everything in sight, and by the time the real news of Britain's success in the battle reached the public in London, the House of Rothschild had assumed control of the British economy. According to the meticulous research of Eustace Mullins in 1985, in this one single engineered panic maneuver, Nathan Rothschild expanded his fortune by a staggering factor of 6,500 times. He destroyed the British economy by making the entire market think Napoleon won at Waterloo. In one single day of trading, Nathan Rothschild did what Napoleon could never do—he conquered Great Britain. The official biography of the family published in 1962, called *The Rothschilds,* boasted of the family's achievements: "(Mayer Amschel's) five incredible sons conquered the world more thoroughly, more cunningly and much more lastingly than all the Caesars before or all the Hitlers after them." The five sons essentially became the world's first modern multinational corporation.

THE CREATION OF THE FEDERAL RESERVE

The Rothschilds' influence soon spread to America as well. By the mid-1800s, the family dominated the banking industry, joining other dynasties such as the Morgans, Vanderbilts, Carnegies, and Cecil Rhodes. The Rothschilds financed the House of Morgan and sent associate Paul Warburg, a partner in Kuhn, Loeb & Co., to meet with other private bankers on Jekyll Island in 1910 to secretly draft the Federal Reserve Act, which was passed in 1913 under false pretenses. This allowed bankers to create 90% of the U.S. money supply and loan it out at interest—a sure fire way to be highly profitable and influential while also allowing private bankers to run the national economy. It is also revealing that, in the same year the Federal Reserve came into existence, the Internal Revenue Service was established. On February 3, 1913, Wyoming ratified the 16th Amendment, providing the three-quarter majority of the states necessary to amend the Constitution. The 16th Amendment gave Congress the authority to enact an income tax. The Federal Reserve Act passed on December 23, 1913. The way the banksters convinced Woodrow Wilson and members of Congress to ratify the Federal Reserve Act was to create artificial panics in the stock markets in the decades prior. After all, the single most effective way to make money and secure control is to stage a mass panic, as Nathan Rothschild proved so profitably after Waterloo. That was the lesson. If everyone sells and you know exactly the right moment to buy, you can achieve near limitless wealth and power.

It is no surprise to learn that the House of Rothschild continues to wield tremendous power and control in the 21st century—though virtually always behind the scenes. Researcher Dean Henderson in his book, *The Federal Reserve Cartel*, estimates the Rothschild fortune today could exceed $100 trillion. Yet, based on figures provided by the Bureau of Labor Statistics Consumer Price Index, the purchasing power of the dollar has declined more than 95% since the creation of the Federal Reserve, all the while bringing massive enrichment to the Rothschilds, who are based out of Europe. One dollar in 1913 is the equivalent of $22.92 in 2011. The exact value marking the decline of the dollar's purchasing power since 1913 is 95.6%. Of course, we can never know the true value of the House of Rothschild. Being privately held partnerships, the family houses never need to, and never have, published a single public balance sheet or any other report related to their financial condition.

The Rothschilds were very influential in creating the country of Israel. It began when a proposition was put to Lord Balfour before the end of World War I to deed a piece of land for the Jewish Zionist Federation. This helped ensure that the United States would enter the conflict. A large portion of the African country Uganda was discussed as a new homeland, but was rejected by the Zionists. They insisted on Palestine. As the "Great War" dragged on, the British war cabinet had no other option, so they wrote a letter of request and a promise to Lord Rothschild that they would carve up Palestine and give the Jewish people a new home. That "little" piece of land in an official enactment by the United Nations became known as Israel shortly after World War II. The Rothschilds continue to play a significant role in the funding of Israel's governmental infrastructure. Dorothy de Rothschild financially supported the creation of a new Israeli Supreme Court building. The "All-Seeing Eye" oversees the Supreme Court complex in Israel, designed and funded entirely by the Rothschilds.

While we cannot blame everything askew with our financial system on the House of Rothschild, neither can we lose sight of the power they represent in nearly all countries in the world. Having a controlling interest in nearly all central banks allows an influence so supreme it can even make or break small nations. The Rothschild family has been nothing less than masterful in enacting their plans. We might not approve of their tactics, but they are really quite ingenious. They waited very patiently for the right time to make big geopolitical plays, knowing they might never even see the effect in their own lifetimes. No one wants a Luciferian New World Order, not even some of their own members. Humans are all wired to crave freedom, even to the point of dying for it if necessary. The technologies they have suppressed make any and all of their arguments about "overpopulation" irrelevant. If one factors in the information known about the secret space program, then we are more than capable of migrating extra humans off-planet. The point is that their money has been spent on a fake media, creating fake fear and promoting fake divisions between countries.

NEO-ILLUMINATI MANIPULATION

The present-day influence of the Illuminati remains shadowy. Critics will say there is no evidence to suggest that the Illuminati society even exists, much less that it could be the most powerful organization on Earth. Although, early on the Illuminati was established to take over the world, they went silent during the end of the 1700s and early 1800s. The same is true with the Freemasons. The Masons are indeed a secret society, but it does not mean that they are planning to take over the world. But the maze of alleged sinister influences persist. For example, the Committee of 300, which is said to control the United Nations, appear to have strong Black Nobility connections. The Committee of 300 evolved out of the British East India Company's Council of 300, which was founded in 1727 by the British aristocracy. The House of Windsor, specifically Queen Elizabeth II, is the head of the Committee of 300.

These historical connections strongly suggest that the new generation of Illuminati members of the various orders control the World Bank and other global financial centers. Consequently, they covertly dictate world oil prices, and can manipulate markets, and control the global Federal Reserve banking system. Each Western government has the legal right to coin their own money; yet they don't, choosing instead to borrow from their own Federal Reserve. Every person in the Western world has to pay taxes that go right into the pockets of the people who run the privately owned Federal Reserve banking system. It is one big privately run scam. Once again, when you control the money supply you control the government, and when you control the government, you control the people. The modern-day Illuminati, however, is now only a European and American entity. It consists mainly of the G5 countries of Germany, France, Britain, Italy and the United States. Of those in the United States, only 1 in 1000 people, or the one percent as articulated by the Occupy Movement, are a part of this group.

An immensely powerful international organization called the Bank for International Settlements (BIS) is the central bank of all central banks, and it secretly controls the money supply of the entire globe. Their headquarters is in Basel, Switzerland, but it also has branches in Hong Kong and Mexico City. The BIS is essentially an unelected, unaccountable central bank of the world that has complete immunity from taxation and from national laws. Sadly, only a very small percentage of people actually know what the Bank for International Settlements is, and even fewer people are aware of the Global Economy Meetings that take place in Basel on a bi-monthly basis. No staff members are allowed in to these meetings, and they are conducted in an atmosphere of absolute secrecy.

The elite meet in private to allocate money and influence, and to consolidate power for their own benefit. The roster and timing of known meetings shows the consistent pattern behind this agenda, and occasional leaked information confirms it—such as the late Jim Tucker's "Bilderberg Diary." The attendees are the people at the top of the pyramids of banking, media, military, intelligence, government, education, corporations and organized religion—or their agents. As a result of their meetings, an experienced eye can begin to see the desired stories, candidates, coups, wars and market moves appearing through the tentacles of the networks they command. For the puppetmasters who seek absolute control of political individuals and institutions, their methods go even beyond lobbying, bribery, and threats of violence. Part of their *modus operandi* appears to be the systematic compromising of politicians with drugs, "honey trap" sexual affairs and even child sexual abuse. Once such behaviors are established, they are used as "dirt" to control politicians with threats of disclosure.

THE ILLUMINATI IN AMERICA

The government behind the government invokes the veil of "national security." The highest levels of all these societies belong to the most elite club within government, called "Cosmic Top Secret." This is the highest classification of NATO. Their covert operational arm is the CIA, which can discredit, assassinate, or make dissenters disappear, all under the guise of national security. But very few people know who these shadowy "Deep State" forces are. As Supreme Court Justice Felix Frankfurter observed in 1952: "The real rulers in Washington are invisible, and exercise power from behind the scenes." Indeed, the infamous Yale secret society, Skull and Bones, uses secret symbols operating out of a foreboding building called the "Tomb." George W. Bush, his father, his grandfather, and John Kerry are just a few of their most prominent members.

While officially supporting democracy, in reality the elite secret families espouse a kind of benevolent dictatorship—or enlightened oligarchy—by those, such as themselves, who they believe have earned the right to know and make decisions in the best interest of civilization. They strongly feel that the ordinary person, being lazy and easily distracted, is not motivated or qualified to contribute usefully. They think the average American cares more about the Super Bowl than about life elsewhere in the universe. So why should they share the elite's secret knowledge? This is *business* after all. The intellectual mentors of this powerful group are more like Sun Tzu and Machiavelli, than Aristotle and Jefferson.

The most elite of the elite group belong to the Rothschild and Rockefeller families, who control all oil, and suppress alternative energy technology, especially free energy devices. J. P. Morgan, although individually wealthy and influential, was a shill for Rothschild, and he stole Nikola Tesla's inventions and technologies. Tesla gave us alternating current, hydroelectric dams, and a plan to provide the world with free energy. But to the cabal, *free* energy could not be allowed, and eventually Tesla was financially destroyed by these powerful men. Although J. P. Morgan died one of the wealthiest Americans, he was a mere lieutenant to the Rothschilds. Tesla died broke.

The capital of the Illuminati empire is the Vatican City in Rome. This is not to say all Catholics are Illuminati, or vice-versa. However, the Freemasons and the Illuminati are hand in glove. But again, not all Freemasons are Illuminists. Yet, the Masonic temple at Alexandria, Virginia, is the center in the Washington, D.C. area for Illuminati scholarship and teaching. All Illuminati involved in the mid- and upper-levels of society have been groomed their entire lives for their adult roles. They are the movers and shakers behind the scene, indeed, the 1% of the 1% elite. It takes a lifetime of training and trust to reach the highest levels. The first thing a child learns from the "family," or the "Order" as they are called, is "The first rule of the Order is secrecy."

THE J.P. MORGAN CANCER

J.P. Morgan was the front man for the Rothschilds around the turn of the 20th century. He had a history of profiting from crises, mainly currency devaluations and the stock market crashes that he helped orchestrate. In both banking panics of 1893 and 1907, he intervened and created the illusion of economic stability while consolidating wealth for his company. J.P. Morgan has also been implicated in having his agents plant a bomb aboard the Titanic, and disguise the explosion as an iceberg strike. He was supposed to be aboard for the maiden journey to discuss the creation of the Federal Reserve with its biggest American detractors, but he canceled at the last minute. The leading critics were silenced on April 15, 1912, and in the next year the Federal Reserve was established. J.P. Morgan also benefited enormously from the Great Depression. When "Black Thursday" hit in 1929, he bought up cheap stocks to "keep the economy afloat." While people endured extreme hardship, J.P. Morgan walked away with significant financial gains.

In 1917, Congressional records show that J. P. Morgan interests hired 12 high-ranking news managers in the United States. He wanted to know how many news organizations it would take "to control generally the policy of the daily press of the United States." The newsmen found that it was imperative only to control 25 of the greatest newspapers. "An agreement was reached; the policy of the papers was bought, and an editor was placed at each paper to insure that all published information was in keeping with the new policy." After the 25 most influential newspapers were owned and controlled, it was now possible to dictate editorial policy. The Congressional record also indicates that "[An] editor was furnished for each paper to properly supervise and edit information regarding the questions of preparedness, militarism, financial policies and other things of national and international nature considered vital to the interests of the purchasers. The policy also included the suppression of everything in opposition to the wishes of the interests served." Once that editorial "board" was controlled by J. P. Morgan appointees, he could influence the other newspapers. The first founding president of the Council of Foreign Relations (CFR) was John W. Davis, who was not only a millionaire, but he was the personal attorney for J.P. Morgan, and it was he who founded the secretive policy-making board.

The Council on Foreign Relations maintains a mission statement to "Increase America's Understanding of the World." However, the actual objective of this highly exclusive club is revealed by the insiders themselves. In the early 1960s, a Georgetown researcher, Professor Carroll Quigley, was allowed to examine the confidential papers of the CFR and other secret documents. He discovered their *real* mission was: "to create a world system of financial control, in private hands. Able to dominate the political system of each country, and the economy of the world as a whole. Controlled in a feudalist fashion by the central banks of the world acting in concert by secret agreements, arrived at in frequent private meetings and conferences. The apex of the system was to be the Bank for International Settlements in Basel, Switzerland, a private bank owned and controlled by the world's central banks which were themselves private corporations." This objective is remarkably similar to the goal of the present-day Wall Street interests. Pursuant to their goals, these forces are in fact intentionally seeking the financial destruction of the United States as a Republic—while embezzling vast sums from the public for their pending, planned, and near-future fascist central government and bank.

We must recognize that these same fascist forces conducted a *coup d'état* with the assassination of JFK in 1963. Along with obscuring vital details of the assassination such as many reports of a second gunman on the Grassy Knoll, there was also an urgency to maintain and cover-up their World War II Nazi connections and treasons. This decision had become an urgent necessity after JFK's removal of Allen Dulles as CIA Director. Dulles also was a major Nazi collaborator who was placed in the CIA specifically to maintain the Nazi connection cover-up. His removal by JFK prompted an urgent assassination to preclude the exposure of the Rockefellers, Harrimans, and Dulleses. The Council on Foreign Relations played an important role in funding the Nazis in the 1930s and until the beginning of WWII, thus it became necessary to orchestrate the JFK assassination investigation to prevent their connections from being made public. "Plausible deniability" was a term first coined by the CIA during the Kennedy Administration. It is a term used to describe the withholding of information from senior officials in order to protect them from repercussions in the event that illegal or unpopular activities by the CIA became public knowledge. Does the lack of evidence make the denial plausible, meaning that it then becomes credible? Is plausible deniability a tactic used by the CIA today? It is also known that the CIA is the enforcement arm of the CFR. The evidence points to Wall Street and the Council of Foreign Relations who not only funded, but arguably created, the Nazi war machine in WW II, and supported the post-war "Nazi International," which continues operating in the shadows up to and through this day.

In the 21st century the Council on Foreign Relations continues its quest for global domination, as it seeks quiet and total control of the world's financial and governmental systems. The CFR members include America's wealthiest tycoons, as well as the highly placed elite in government, academic institutions, tax-exempt foundations, and established media heads. They preside over a far-reaching consolidation of mass media, overseeing and approving media mergers favorable to their mission. The approximately 4,000 members of the CFR are the real "government behind the government." The CFR does not merely analyze and interpret foreign policy for the United States, they are also instrumental in creating that policy with their "recommendations." Former Congressman John Rarick observed in 1971: "The Council on Foreign Relations is 'the establishment.' Not only does it have influence and power in key decision-making positions at the highest levels of government to apply pressure from above, but it also announces and uses individuals and groups to bring pressure from below, to justify the high level decisions for converting the U.S. from a sovereign Constitutional Republic into a servile member state of a one-world dictatorship."

Today, Morgan's legacy lives on in JPMorganChase and CitiGroup. These two banking powerhouses are suspected of being largely responsible for the 2008 economic housing collapse. They were well aware of their destructive behavior but did nothing to stop it. In the end, these "too big to fail" banks were bailed out by taxpayer debt and gained huge profits while their competitors went under and people lost their homes, jobs, and retirement funds. This was no accident, but, instead, another intentional power and money grab as has happened throughout the course of history. The same strategies continue. Take it from Senator Dick Durbin, who commented in 2009: "(the banks) are still the most powerful lobby on Capitol Hill, and they, frankly, own the place."

THE ROCKEFELLER CABAL

The Industrial Revolution developed and powered not only mechanized production of mass products for a mass society, it also had the nefarious outcome of making the captains of industry extraordinarily rich. The first billionaire in America was John D. Rockefeller, the founder of Standard Oil. He was known to have revolutionized the petroleum industry, horizontally integrating his transportation network with the rail industry, bought out his competitors, and then went on to totally dominate the oil industry. His famous quote was "competition is a sin." The Supreme Court ruled in 1913 that his trust originated in illegal monopoly practices and ordered it to be broken up into 34 new companies. Except for Pennzoil, all of the largest oil companies that were "broken up" remain today under new names: Continental Oil became part of ConocoPhillips; Standard of Indiana became Amoco, which is now part of BP; Standard Oil of California became Chevron; Standard Oil of New Jersey became Esso, and later ExxonMobil; Standard of New York, became Mobil, now part of ExxonMobil; and Standard of Ohio, became Sohio, now part of BP. ExxonMobil is currently the most profitable company in the world, with four out of the six "supermajors" in the oil industry—BP, Chevron, ExxonMobil and ConocoPhillips—direct Rockefeller spinoffs. One Rockefeller Standard Oil partner was Edward Harkness, whose family came to control Chemical Bank. In the insurance business, the Rockefellers control Metropolitan Life, Equitable Life, Prudential, and New York Life. Rockefeller banks control 25% of all assets of the 50 largest U.S. commercial banks, and 30% of all assets of the 50 largest insurance companies. Companies under Rockefeller controlling interest not only include the largest oil companies such as ExxonMobil, Chevron, Texaco, BP Amoco, and Marathon Oil, but they also control Freeport McMoran, Quaker Oats, ASARCO, United, Delta, Northwest, ITT, International Harvester, Xerox, Boeing, Westinghouse, Hewlett-Packard, Honeywell, International Paper, Pfizer, Motorola, Monsanto, Union Carbide and General Foods.

Five USA oil companies made over $37 billion profit in the first Quarter of 2011. Chevron is one of the four largest oil companies in the world. Yet these oil companies lobby for, and receive, tax credits. It is no wonder that Chevron is the most important contributor to all political parties, and lobbies the White House's strategic plans so that they meet the company's interests. Or maybe it's the other way around. There is a reason why Chevron sponsored studies that encouraged the invasion of Iraq before taking control of its oil fields.

Adjusting for inflation, John D. Rockefeller is often regarded as the richest person in history. Certainly Mr. Rockefeller and his descendants would have a vested interest in the continued profitability of the petroleum industry. Their family legacy is that they managed their wealth very well. The end result is that the Rockefeller oil companies are among the most profitable corporations on the planet. These companies wield enormous power, political clout, and can even summon their own standing armies if necessary. They are extraordinarily profitable, many with a GDP that is equal to or higher than the GDP of many small countries.

John D. Rockefeller was the billionaire of all billionaires, proportionally far richer than Bill Gates is today. He knew how to get what he wanted, and no governmental body would ever stand in his way. It was said that John D. Rockefeller had done everything to the Pennsylvania state legislature except refine it like his oil. The legislatures were literally owned by the corporations, and they even picked their state senators during the Industrial Revolution. Over 100 years ago state senates already were owned by corporations. These were the first to fall under the spell of the ultra-rich. Rockefeller's spectacular oil profits ultimately allowed him to be in a position to essentially buy the United States government via his stake in the Federal Reserve, with its "magical" ability to print money out of thin air.

With the control of money came a tremendous amount of power, not only in oil and government, but in virtually every sector of society. Much of the families wealth has been funneled through "philanthropic" organizations such as the Rockefeller Foundation. Contributions and funding from the Rockefeller Foundation may look good on the surface; however, the control that comes from it is vast. For example, the current medical model—originated with the Rockefellers around the turn of the century— remains in place today. In the early 1900s, John D. Rockefeller set up the Institute for Medical Research that laid the foundation for health research and development. Then, in 1913, the Rockefeller Foundation became one of the largest financiers of medical research. They hand-picked scientists and doctors who were considered worthy of funding, and placed a heavy emphasis on pharmacology. This allopathic drug-treatment paradigm was carried over into the universities, many of which are still funded or were initially established by the Rockefeller Foundation. In this way, drug-based medical treatment has become the norm in America.

David Rockefeller, the youngest son of John D. Rockefeller Junior, admitted in his 2002 book, *Memoirs*, to his family's involvement in a secret cabal, although conveniently dodging the alleged meaning of their "one world" vision: "For more than a century, ideological extremists at either end of the political spectrum have seized upon well-publicized incidents to attack the Rockefeller family for the inordinate influence they claim we wield over American political and economic institutions ... Some even believe we are part of a secret cabal working against the best interests of the United States, characterizing my family and me as 'internationalists' and of conspiring with others around the world to build a more integrated global political and economic structure— one world, if you will. If that's the charge, I stand guilty, and I am proud of it." David Rockefeller had his sixth successful heart transplant at the age of 99. He died in 2017.

MEET THE BILDERBERGERS

The Bilderberg Group, or Bilderberg conference, is an unofficial annual invitation-only conference of around 130 guests, most of whom are persons of influence in the fields of business, media and politics. The Bilderberg Group was the brainchild of members of the Rothschild and Rockefeller dynasties on the one hand, and Prince Bernhard of the Netherlands on the other. These annual meetings of the North American and European elites began in September, 1954, and took their name from the hotel in which the first meeting was held, the Bilderberg Hotel near Arnhem, Netherlands. This elite group continues to meet annually at luxury hotels or resorts throughout the world—normally in Europe—and once every four years in the United States or Canada, depending on important national elections. Their head office is located in Leiden, South Holland, Netherlands.

Bilderberg cofounder Prince Bernhard of Netherlands royalty represented more than just a member of the European nobility, and more than just a major stockholder in Royal Dutch Shell. He was also a Nazi SS officer and a senior manager for the vastly powerful and notorious German chemicals cartel I.G. Farben. Less than a decade after World War II, the Nazi financial and corporate interests that he represented were awash with a tremendous amount of cash that needed not only to be laundered, but to be safely out of reach of the prying eyes of the American and British treasury agents intent on shutting down the postwar Nazi International cabal by seizing its ill-gotten booty. Yet those who could launder such vast amounts of money, and those who stood to profit from having it deposited in their banks, were also able to use the cash to substantially expand their ledger credit entries. These were the international bankers in New York and London. It was inevitable that the two groups, whose essential political and economic philosophy, called corporate fascism, and who have political aims of global domination that are one and the same, should meet secretly and create a common cause.

First, it is important to understand that the Bilderbergers are not a secret society. It would be incorrect to think of them as an evil all-seeing eye, or a Jewish-Masonic conspiracy. There is no conspiracy, just power-broker secrets, even though many might see these meetings as such. These people see themselves as power brokers who make the decisions that make the world go 'round. If they didn't do it, someone else would. Critics say the Bilderberg Group promotes the careers of politicians whose views are representative of the interests of multinational corporations, and at the expense of democracy. The group's secretive meetings, and their powerful connections, have provided fodder for many who believe that the group is part of a conspiracy to create a New World Order. Because they represent the world's most powerful financial institutions—and thus the most predatory financial interests—they are easily regarded as a formidable enemy of humanity's enlightened interests of freedom, privacy, and democratic representation.

As evidence, there were once nation states in Europe with their own constitutions, national flags, and national currencies, that are now subordinate to the master currency, the Euro. The U.S. Dollar also carries tremendous weight around the world, especially in its role as the *petro-dollar*. Control the money and you not only control the people, but also their "democratically-elected" government officials, those who are always beholden to campaign contributions. The Bilderberg organization remains dynamic, in that it changes with the times, absorbs and creates new parts, and while excreting the remains of the decaying parts. Members come and go, but the system itself has not changed. It is a self-perpetuating system, a virtual spider web of interlocked financial, political, economic and industrial interests.

Who attends the annual Bilderberg meetings? Attendees include central bankers, defense experts, mass media press barons, government ministers, prime ministers, royalty, international financiers and political leaders primarily from Europe and North America. Also some of the Western world's leading financiers and foreign policy strategists attend Bilderberg conferences. Donald Rumsfeld is an active Bilderberger, as is Peter Sutherland from Ireland, a former European Union commissioner and chairman of Goldman Sachs and of British Petroleum. Rumsfeld and Sutherland served together in the year 2000 on the board of the Swedish/Swiss engineering company ABB. Former U.S. Deputy Defense Secretary and former World Bank head Paul Wolfowitz is also a member. The old NATO Alliance participants are involved, 50 to 60 top multi-national CEOs, American senators and congressmen, plus many former European politicians, and most of the Western European royalty. Seated presidents and prime ministers, Canadian and European commissioners, and the leading bankers who control the IMF, World Bank, and European Central Bank attend the meetings. Leading representatives of the largest world media companies attend, but surprisingly never report on the event.

Some key global decisions are made at Bilderberg meetings. The Bilderberg Group can orchestrate oil and other commodity prices. Russia and China know of the group, but do not participate, and are thus regarded as enemies. The most alarming aspect of the Bilderbergers is their grip on U.S. elected officials and other top politicians around the world. The most prominent politicians, many of whom have higher political aspirations, attend their meetings, compete for their favors, and demonstrate their willingness to enable the Bilderbergers to control important aspects of their countries.

MEETINGS OF PRIVATE ELITE AND GOVERNMENT OFFICIALS IS ILLEGAL

American attendees of the Bilderberg Conference are in violation of the Logan Act every time they meet in secret for "official" business. The Logan Act is a United States federal law that forbids unauthorized citizens from negotiating with foreign governments. The text of the Act is broad and is addressed at any attempt of a U.S. citizen to conduct foreign relations without authority. It was passed in 1799, last amended in 1994, and clearly states: "Any citizen of the United States, wherever he may be, who, without authority of the United States, directly or indirectly commences or carries on any correspondence or intercourse with any foreign government or any officer or agent thereof, with intent to influence the measures or conduct of any foreign government or of any officer or agent thereof, in relation to any disputes or controversies with the United States, or to defeat the measures of the United States, shall be fined under this title or imprisoned not more than three years, or both." Violation of the Logan Act is a felony; yet there is no record of any convictions, or even a single prosecution, under the Logan Act.

A similar private meeting of a select group, including top government officials, is held in Northern California every July. The Bohemian Grove is a privately owned 2,700-acre compound in Monte Rio, California, and surrounded by enormous old-growth redwood trees. Once a year it plays host to a bizarre confab attended by some of the most powerful people in the world, including many U.S. politicians and business representatives. Participants embroil themselves in a heady mixture of plutocratic plotting and occult pagan ritual ceremonies. The most bizarre Bohemian Grove ceremony is called the Cremation of Care, and it takes place in front of a massive statue of an owl, the mascot and logo of the Bohemian Club. On this evening, attendees all wear hooded robes, and the ceremony is replete with fire displays and re-enactments of "sacrifices," which suggest those in attendance should not care or be compassionate for those "sacrificed." In clear violation of the Logan Act, important political and business deals are discussed and established at the Bohemian Grove, even though it is unethical for any government official to meet with CEO's of large companies, military contractors, NGOs, and foreign government representatives without the transparency and the direct consent of the people.

NOTHING FEDERAL ABOUT
THE FEDERAL RESERVE

America's biggest threat is not terrorists. Instead, as outlined in this chapter, our greatest threat is the empire constructed by secret families and their firm grip on the world's assets. For those still in doubt, let's quote some of those who have been the leaders of the Federal Reserve. According to former Federal Reserve chairman Alan Greenspan: "The Federal Reserve is an independent agency. There is no other agency of government that can overrule the actions that we take." When asked by a reporter what the proper relationship should be between the President and the Chairman of the Federal Reserve, Greenspan said: "What these relationships are don't frankly matter." Or Henry Kissinger, speaking in 1973 on behalf of the Council of Foreign Relations: "Who controls the food supply controls the people; who controls the energy can control whole continents; who controls the money can control the world. ... Power is the ultimate aphrodisiac." Let's not forget former Federal Reserve chairman Ben Bernanke, responding to audit questioning by Congressman John Duncan: "My concern about the legislation is that if the GAO is auditing not only the operational aspects of the programs and the details of the programs but making judgments about our policy decisions, [it] would effectively be a takeover of policy by the Congress and [such] a repudiation of the Federal Reserve would be highly destructive to the stability of the financial system, the Dollar, and our national economic situation." The brunt of Bernanke's statement is nothing short of a direct threat to back off from an audit of the Federal Reserve by our elected representatives—or else the economy collapses. The chairman clearly implies that any attempt to restore monetary powers constitutionally granted to the Congress would be seen as "a takeover," and that the defensive and "repudiated" Federal Reserve would respond destructively. The open use of financial terrorism Bernanke illustrated, while under oath testifying before Congress, shows clearly the Fed's contempt for Constitutional authority. The Federal Reserve is no more "federal" than Federal Express. Still seem farfetched?

To summarize the hard facts once again: The U.S. Government borrows money from a private corporation using the name "Federal" and prints "United States" on the paper notes, and then it pays back interest to the Federal Reserve, which is money that comes from taxpayers. This group prints "Federal Reserve Notes" and loans them out to the United States Treasury. American taxpayers then pay interest to the Federal Reserve banking families for the right to use their money. By controlling the debt, the Federal Reserve controls the politicians. When we look at the president, we must understand there is another force behind him. In short, the U.S. Government is not run by our elected officials. The government does not represent the people any longer, but serves the corporations. Politicians are not actually "elected." First they are selected, based largely on their allegiance to the ruling elite, and then are *funded* to run for election.

It must be noted that the Founding Fathers recognized the potential threat of the monetary system being taken over by private ownership. Thomas Jefferson said "I sincerely believe the banking institutions having the issuing powers of money, are more dangerous to liberty than standing armies." Of course, the Founding Fathers added provisions to prevent this kind of takeover in the U.S. Constitution. It states quite clearly that Congress will retain the Constitutional power over money: "The Congress shall have power to coin money, regulate the value thereof, and of foreign coin, and fix the standard of weights and measures." Just the opposite has occurred. The international and central banking systems are, at their very core, designed to concentrate wealth in the hands of the very few, and enslave the rest of us with the burden of ever increasing interest payments on debt.

GLOBAL WORLD DOMINATION

Finally, one of the most alarming trends is the financial cabal pushing to phase out cash and national currencies and then create a one world centralized bank using only electronic currency. If the United States ever does give up the U.S. dollar, it will be a massive blow to our national sovereignty and a complete capitulation to the financial controllers. On the international level, the central banking elite have put huge organizations in place to implement their policies, including the World Trade Organization, the World Health Organization, the Bank for International Settlements, the World Bank, and the International Monetary Fund. The IMF serves as a sort of "lender of last resort" to developing or struggling countries. Its stated goal is to "alleviate poverty;" however, many countries that have received IMF loans are now buried in debt, unable to even pay back the interest due. The World Bank, like the IMF, also issues *Structural Adjustment Loans* that place restrictions on how money can be spent. These Structural Adjustment Loans mostly benefit transnational corporations.

To implement the endgame of total global domination, first and foremost the would be powers must control the money—and they do. That is why a one-currency system in their hands would be a disaster. These power brokers also need to control energy, and they do. They violently suppress free energy because, as J.P. Morgan lamented, you "cannot put a meter on free." These powers already dominate food and water with their ownership of agribusiness and world trade, and they are now buying up water rights around the world. They have widely popular health remedies in their pockets, and they actively suppress natural healing alternatives. They have enormous control over pharmaceuticals, medical schools, and research funding. Naturally they would have to control the information through indoctrination. Therefore, they also control the most powerful media outlets, and have a hand in compulsory, standardized, education. What then is left? The Internet is currently not controlled or censored, but there are many attacks designed to control the flow of information. In order to control dissent, Congress passed double-speak laws like the Patriot Act, which is very un-patriotic, and seeks to strip away our rights. Watch out, you are on a surveillance camera, and about to be scanned for your implanted RFID chip. In 2011, news reported that an RFID tracking chip capable of killing humans has already been invented. What could a human-killing chip be used for? Perhaps not complying with rogue government demands? George Orwell's worst nightmare is happening right before our eyes. Big Brother is not coming, he's already here. We are already living within *The Matrix*, so how do we get out? Our democracy has been severely threatened before. A very brief reminder of the recent history of exercising our rights will be helpful.

RESTORING DEMOCRACY

There has been a growing tension in the United States between the monied interests and the idealism that created our democracy—the first democracy in the modern age. At the time of the Civil War there were six democracies in the world. Today there are 120, and most have been inspired by the American model. The USA represents a model for human beings to govern themselves with institutions of justice—in part by the creation of an informed public among its citizens. Contributing to an informed public is one of the goals of this series. But freedom is never cheap.

During the gilded age of the Industrial Revolution in the 1880s and 1890s we almost lost our democracy in this country. This was the advent of enormous companies, or trusts, as they were called. The captains of industry who ran the railroad, steel, oil, and the sugar trusts became fabulously wealthy. With their wealth they became extremely influential. Many of the most pressing problems of our time relate to unbridled pursuit of profits without regard for human rights or the environment.

Again, a glaring and dramatic example is John D. Rockefeller. Among the several presidents in his pocket was Warren G. Harding, commonly regarded as the worst president in United States' history. In 1921, there were union strikes in West Virginia, in which some 10,000 union workers demanded more pay and better working conditions. Harding ordered the military to drop bombs and poison gas on the protesters. Harding was extremely corrupt and deeply in the pockets of the coal industry. Harding's final indignity was a bribery incident over petroleum reserves, called the Teapot Dome Scandal, that came to light after he died in office. This illustrates how corrupting money and politics can be, and why campaign donation reform proposed by President Donald Trump is needed, or better yet, how urgent it is to eliminate corporate political donations altogether.

Nearly 100 years ago, it looked as if the Constitution was subverted and we had completely lost our democracy. It was only restored because a few courageous journalists did what so few do today. Ida Tarbell, Upton Sinclair, and others started identifying the grave dangers we were facing. George Orwell famously wrote "Journalism is printing what someone else does not want printed. Everything else is public relations." By informing the public and inspiring outrage and indignation, these brave journalists of the last century were able to expose these dark forces. And then a man took over with very strong ideals, a very tough politician named Teddy Roosevelt, who was willing to stand up to what he called the corporations and the "malefactors of great wealth." Even with anti-trust laws and a new vigor to restore democracy, the money interests continued to work behind the scenes, and established the Federal Reserve in 1913. From that time on, the secret families that control corporations and government officials have only grown stronger.

This must change. It is time for us as Americans to use the tools of representative democracy to implement the restoration of clear-cut principles of our Constitution. Solutions will be set forth in the final section of this book.

The Illuminati, plural of Latin *illuminatus*, meaning "enlightened," is a name given to several groups, both historically real and fictitious. Historically the name refers to the Bavarian Illuminati, an Enlightenment-era secret society founded on May 1, 1776. In more modern contexts the name refers to a purported conspiratorial organization which is alleged to mastermind events and control world affairs through governments and corporations to establish a New World Order. In this context the Illuminati are usually represented as a modern version or continuation of the Bavarian Illuminati.

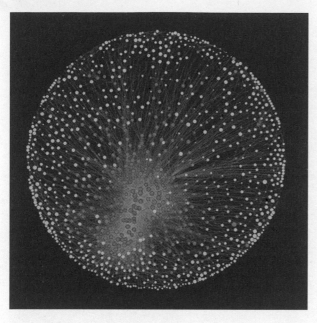

< The idea that a few bankers control a large chunk of the global economy might not seem like news to New York's Occupy Wall Street movement and protesters elsewhere. An analysis of the relationships between 43,000 transnational corporations (TNCs) has identified a relatively small group of companies, mainly banks, with disproportionate control over the global economy. The study was conducted by a trio of complex systems theorists at the Swiss Federal Institute of Technology in Zurich. This study is the first to go beyond ideology to empirically identify such a network of power.

< This is the Khazarian/Bohemian/Transylvanian House of Hapsburg Crest.

The "Cremation of Care" is an annual theatrical production that is written, produced, performed and staged at the Bohemian Grove near Monte Rio, California. The dramatic performance is presented on the first night of the annual encampment as an allegorical banishing of worldly cares for the club members. It is performed at a small artificial lake amid a grove of old-growth redwood trees, and in front of a large owl statue.

< One of the most fraudulent institutions ever perpetrated on American citizens is the Federal Reserve System, which through deceit became the central bank of the United States in 1913, also the same year income tax was instituted. Then in 1920, the Independent Treasury Act suspended the phrase, *de jure*, which means "by right of legal establishment," Treasury Department of the United States government, and Article 1, Section 8 of the Constitution, states that "Congress shall have the power to coin (create) money and regulate the value thereof." Congress turned the Treasury Department over to a private corporation, the Federal Reserve, and their agents. The bulk of the ownership of the Federal Reserve System, a very well-kept secret from the American people, is held by these banking interests, and *none is held* by the United States Treasury.

The House of Rothschild is a European family of German Jewish origin. The German family name means "Red Shield," and this is their coat of arms. It contains a clenched fist with five arrows symbolizing the five dynasties established by the five sons of Mayer Amschel Rothschild. The English branch of the family was elevated into the British nobility at the request of Queen Victoria.

It is a documented historical fact that Adam Weishaupt headed a group in Bavaria, now a part of Germany, that called themselves the Illuminati, a term meaning the "Enlightened Ones." Weishaupt was paid to start this group in 1770 by none other than Mayer Amschel Rothschild.

LOSING MY RELIGION

"When you call yourself an Indian or a Muslim or a Christian
or a European, or anything else, you are being violent. Do you
see why it is violent? Because you are separating yourself from
the rest of mankind. When you separate yourself by belief,
by nationality, by tradition, it breeds violence. So a man who
is seeking to understand violence does not belong to any
country, to any religion, to any political party or partial system;
he is concerned with the total understanding of mankind."
—Jiddu Krishnamurthi

RELIGION is typically defined as a fundamental set of organized beliefs, practices and world views that relate humanity to spirituality, plus the cause, nature and purpose of the universe. Thus, everything between A and Z, that is from Atheism to Zionism, falls into this categorical definition. Unfortunately, there has been an abuse of what should be one of humanity's highest goals, which is a unifying spirituality and comprehension of the supernatural. Religion has long been a way to consolidate and control people. We can say religion is not the cause of all wars, but men are, especially those who would profit from war. It's just that people become very passionate about their faith, and as history has shown, they will kill in its name.

Religion can be, and is supposed to be, a community experience to help one another share faith and awaken to personal spirituality. Sometimes our own spiritual experience is formed within a community of faith. By such reasoning Buddhism and Taoism would not qualify as religions, because at their core, both are philosophies based on self-experience. The study of philosophy, or the "love of wisdom" as the ancient Greeks called it, creates and nurtures thoughtful minds. These fertile minds can, as Aristotle suggested, entertain a thought without accepting it as true. Yet, at the very moment when we begin to articulate the divine, it becomes subjective.

When viewed responsibly, we realize that religion is not some mystical experience of someone who died long ago and left behind a compelling story. Nor is religion something that sprang up with the sole purpose to help us become better people and find some sort of lasting peace. A religion, that is all organized religions, are human creations, and as such have political and hierarchical aspects generally focused on the goal of trading a sense of peace in exchange for submission to financial or other demands. The question becomes, can organized religion promote enlightenment, or is it inevitably a control mechanization of enslavement? What then is a true religion, in its essence, and how can the original teachings be extracted from distorted versions? Why is organized religion on the decline worldwide, and what then might fill the void in its place?

Almost all religions try to explain the spiritual unknown, who are we and why are we here, and the death experience, in an authoritative way, as people fear these two questions the most. By giving the adherent a sense that the unknown is not something to be feared, and that death is not final, religion draws people in by pandering to their fears. All organized religions in existence do this to some degree. It is inherent in the concept of religion. There should be no reason to be ominous or fearful; dour and serious; when speaking of spirituality. Perhaps a good way to judge a religion is if it can be made fun of by others outside the faith and its adherents take no offence.

Of course there is always atheism, which is the absence of theism. Atheism is the belief that there was nothing and nothing happened to nothing and then nothing magically exploded for no reason, creating everything and then a bunch of everything magically rearranged itself for no reason whatsoever into self-replicating bits, which then turned into dinosaurs. Okay, that is taking a jab at atheists, who are really just using logic and philosophy to form their worldview. An atheist would point out that morality is doing what is right regardless of what an individual is told. Religion is doing what a believer is told regardless of what is right.

A FUNDAMENTAL SHIFT IN PRIORITIES

In the last few decades, the number of people in the West who are choosing not to be affiliated with organized religions is on the rise. Some have abandoned organized religions altogether because they believe that such institutions breed hypocrisy and intolerance. Others find it too complicated to follow a structured form of worship that seems out of touch with modern society. There are others who see organized religion as nothing but a superfluous "middleman" between God and people, while others seek a more individualized notion of personal spirituality. The loss of religion is quickly becoming a new world reality, largely because it is slowly manifesting. An AP study in 2009 on American religious life found that 15% of respondents said they had no religion, a steady increase from 14.2% in 2001, and 8.2% in 1990. These numbers are increasing nationwide, with the American Religious Identification Survey finding the numbers of Americans with no religion slowly but steadily rising in every state.

In a Pew Research Center poll released in October, 2012, one-fifth of the U.S. public, and a one-third of adults under 30, are religiously unaffiliated, the highest percentages ever seen. In the last five years alone, the unaffiliated have increased from just over 15 percent to just under 20 percent of all U.S. adults. Their ranks now include more than 13 million self-described atheists and agnostics (nearly 6 percent of the U.S. public), as well as nearly 33 million people who say they have no particular religious affiliation (14 percent). For the first time since the United States was founded, the number of Protestants in the nation fell below 50%, to only 48% of Americans in the 2012 Pew Study. This growing group of Americans is less religious than the public at large on many conventional measures, including frequency of attendance at religious services, and the degree of importance they attach to religion in their lives.

Even conservative pundit Pat Buchanan acknowledges the loss of faith crisis facing Catholicism in his 2011 book, the *Suicide of a Superpower*. He writes, "Half a century on, the disaster is manifest. The robust and confident Church of 1958 no longer exists. Catholic colleges and universities remain Catholic in name only. Parochial schools and high schools are closing as rapidly as they opened in the 1950s. The numbers of nuns, priests and seminarians have fallen dramatically. Mass attendance is a third of what it was. From the former Speaker of the House to the Vice President, Catholic politicians openly support abortion on demand."

Furthermore, churches in the U.S. are shutting their doors in record numbers, especially after the 2008 financial collapse and the burst of the housing bubble. Foreclosures are now catching up to religious institutions. Like many property owners, churches across the country took advantage of the property boom by taking out additional loans for building expansions or improvements on facilities, often justified to make room for growing congregations. Now there are fewer people going to church, their loans are defaulting, and churches are facing bankruptcy as donations dwindle and the need for expanded construction missed expectations. According to data from the CoStar Group, 270 churches have been sold after loan defaults since 2010, 90 percent of which were a result of foreclosure by a bank; 138 of those were in 2011, which is an annual record. Compare that with 2008, when there were only 24 church sales from default, and a "handful" more from the previous decade.

BECOMING A SECULAR WORLD

One of the losses that modern society is most keenly aware of is the loss of community that used to be so prevalent in Judeo-Christian culture. Attempting to understand what has eroded our sense of community has led historians to look at the privatization of religious beliefs that occurred in Europe and the USA starting in the late 19th century. They suggest that we began to disregard our neighbors precisely when we ceased to honor our gods as a community. By shedding our need for worship and church groups, we have also lost an important close neighborliness in an unwitting exchange for ruthless anonymity.

Could the secular world draw useful lessons from religious life? Religion serves two central needs that secular society has not been able to reconcile. First, there is a seemingly innate need to live together in harmonious communities, despite our deeply rooted selfish and violent impulses. Second is our need for human support to cope with the pain that arises from troubled relationships, the death of loved ones, professional failure, and the coming decay and demise of ourselves. Our newly realized lack of religious priorities, and by extension loss of community, leaves us virtually no venues where we can transform strangers into friends.

Many Western religions, although they once had tremendous value, and have brought an enormous amount of comfort to many people throughout history and into the present day, continue to focus on shame, guilt, sin and control. They do not focus on life or respect or the personal mystical experience. Nor do they focus on self-responsibility. They create more division than we have ever known. Advanced spiritual teachings hold that no person is a sinner in essence, and no person should feel shame for honest mistakes. Instead, we are spiritual beings in physical bodies. However, no government or Western religion will admit to that. People are waking up from the long hoodwinking, reaching a new awareness, and indeed, entering a New Age. Atheist author Richard Dawkins made the observation, "An atheist is just somebody who feels about Yahweh the way any decent Christian feels about Thor or Baal or the golden calf. We are all atheists about most of the gods that humanity has ever believed in. Some of us just go one god further."

Religious cynicism has also reached a new level. A bumper sticker defines Christianity as: "The belief that some cosmic Jewish Zombie can make you live forever if you symbolically eat his flesh and telepathically tell him that you accept him as your master, so he can remove an evil force from your soul that is present in humanity because a rib-woman was convinced by a talking snake to eat from a magical tree. Makes perfect sense." Just a few hundred years ago a comment like this could get you burned at the stake.

FINDING MY RELIGION

Have you found your god or goddess yet? There is a large religious spectrum in the world, with some 900 distinct religions out there. Secularists are doubtful, and so are the faithful. We make ourselves vulnerable when seeking spirituality with a "leap of faith," and because of this, many are held back with skepticism. Examples of religion at its worst include scandals with Catholic priests and "Muslim" suicide bombers. How then to suspend judgment and open ourselves up? God should be a direction, not a destination.

We bring baggage into our faith, just as we do with our relationships. We need to try them on and see how they fit. We have to make ourselves vulnerable to conduct a spiritual search. How then are we to be open to the ubiquitous religious state of "grace?" Adapting to a religion or faith is a process that unfolds over time. We don't arrive at a destination as much as we travel in a direction to get there. Today, Americans choose their religions and spiritual paths more than ever before. Many are open to the possibility of grace, joy, stillness, and a glimpse of Nirvana. As Americans, we are mutts, not only in our blood, but in our religions too. Let's face it, if you were born in Israel you'd probably be Jewish. If you were born in Saudi Arabia you'd probably be Muslim. If you were born in India you'd probably be Hindu. But because you were born in North America you're likely a Christian. Your default faith is not inspired by some divine, constant truth. It's simply a matter of geography, and adapting to the faith of your family.

The mindless will always scramble to believe with their fears, especially the fear of death driving all sensibility from them. However, there are those who understand their own mortality and are at peace with themselves. They do not need false hope to cling to, and can learn to love themselves. Often, however, they eschew any contact with religion at all, seeing the poisonous effect it has on others. The truly wise will not subscribe mindlessly to any religion, but will study all of them, knowing that there are some good lessons to be learned so long as one does not "drink the Kool Aid" and buy into a religion blindly.

HACKING THE HIERARCHY

Most human institutions such as governments, educational institutions, corporations, churches, armies and political movements are designed in a rigid hierarchical manner. Basically, the structure of almost every societal organization on Earth is based on a hierarchy system. The senior members, usually called bosses or high priests, have more power than their subordinates. Thus, the relationship defining a hierarchy is in the command structure, or the persons that have the power over all those below them.

The pyramid-shaped hierarchy system of governments and religions take their basic origins from ancient Rome. The Caesars of old have become the popes, presidents and prime ministers of today. A hierarchy is a system of ranking and organizing things or people, where each element of the system, except for the top element, is a subordinate to a single other element. The classical age of Rome was essentially controlled by 13 powerful families. Unfortunately those 13 families still endure today. This system can be hijacked and manipulated with a top heavy decision-making process.

Currently our planetary governments and most religions are regulated by a brutal social, economic, and political hierarchy. The secretive "Powers That Be" are masters at infiltrating movements based on a hierarchy. Examples include the Roman Catholic Church, the Jesuits, European monarchies, and even simple nonprofit organizations. When a movement gains any kind of critical mass, new people with grant money show up and then demand one of their own become a board member. More money leads to more board members until the original idealistic board members are all marginalized, outvoted or replaced. Lop off the head of the movement, and a pyramidal power structure can easily be overtaken and its direction changed. Such a system is open to abuse of power. The solution is to abolish the hierarchy system. "Imagine all the people living life in peace," sang John Lennon in his hit single *Imagine*: "Imagine there's no countries, it isn't hard to do. Nothing to kill or die for. And no religion too." John Lennon would hail the end of the hierarchy, wisely identifying the central problem.

CATHOLIC MEANS UNIVERSAL

What follows may seem like a denunciation of the Catholic Church, so it must be noted that there are thousands of dedicated Catholic brothers, sisters, and lay workers who continue to volunteer for relief organizations and missions, hospitals, outreach programs, and selflessly assist hundreds of thousands in desperate need. Dedicated Catholics, other Christians, and individual members of all religions are feeding the poor, healing the sick, comforting the homeless, giving shelter to the destitute, giving love and compassion to the addicted and the abandoned, and acting in the interests of hundreds of thousands who have less. Any time people serve others selflessly, no matter what their spiritual convictions are, it is beneficial to all.

And while it is simultaneously true that some Catholics are devoted planetary servants, a very small minority are known pedophiles. The salient point is that anytime there is a rigid hierarchy, such as the Catholic Church, there is the potential for top-heavy abuses by those running the organization. The vast majority beneath them may be unaware of any abuses, and feel powerless to change the organization. The Roman Catholic Church has been plagued by controversy in recent years, from allegations of money laundering, Luciferian worship, criminal financial associations to child sex abuse, and has repeatedly been accused by critics of covering up its sins to protect insiders.

Throughout its nearly 1,700 years of rule, the Catholic Church has more blood on its hands than any other institution still in existence. Pope Urban II ordered the killing of over 10 million people during his reign, and was on *Time* magazine's 1976 list of the "Most Evil Men in History." During the Inquisition, an entire Cathar village of women and children, numbering 120,000 people, were systematically murdered by Catholic knights in what is known as the Albigensian Crusade. In order to encourage the slave trade, Pope Nicholas V lied that God told him in a dream that it was acceptable for Christians to "buy and sell heathens."

Also worthy of note, most practices and rituals of the Church are not uniquely their own. The farther back we look into the origins of Christianity, the more similarities with pagan religions we find. In 325 CE, Emperor Constantine wanted to unite the Roman Empire, so he simply fused paganism with Christianity to appease both the pagan and Christian communities. Quite literally, the Vatican itself was constructed upon the ruins of an ancient pagan sanctuary in Rome. There is no doubt that organized Christianity has its roots in paganism. In 360 CE, a few decades after Constantine integrated the new faith, the Greek writer Celsus said: "This recent religion (Christianity) is neither new nor strange, as it is merely a pale reflection of earlier pagan beliefs." Emperor Constantine also changed the Christian "holy day" to Sunday to correspond with that of the Roman pagan sun god Sol Invictus. Indeed, the "resurrection" of Jesus was a common pagan myth of the early ages. Over 18 pagan "sons of gods" were said to have resurrected before him. The "Five Books of Moses" also known as the "Pentateuch," was actually stolen from the Egyptian "Tarot," which was adored in Ancient Egypt from at least 3000 BCE. The biblical Jesus descended from a generation of 12, had 12 disciples, and dined with them at a "Last Supper." Interestingly, so did the Hindu god Krishna thousands of years earlier. Lastly, the word "Amen," uttered after every Christian prayer, has its roots in Egyptian Masonry of 3000 BCE, as "Amon-ra" which means "the Hidden one."

SKELETONS IN THEIR CLOSET

Vatican City is the smallest city state principality in the world. It has its own newspaper, postal service, its own flag, an army of Swiss Guards, and its own prison. The Vatican rules over approximately 1.2 billion people worldwide. It is a large investor of the world's biggest banks and top companies, such as Shell Oil and General Electric. It holds billions of dollars worth of gold in the care of the Rothschild's Bank of England. The Catholic Church is the biggest financial power, the largest wealth accumulator, and the biggest property owner on Earth. The pope is the visible ruler in charge of this colossal wealth, making him one of the richest men on Earth. For centuries the Catholic Church has hoarded wealth and knowledge, and by doing so has denied their flock a basic education—all the while collecting vast sums of money when most people of the world live on $2 a day.

St. Peters Basilica dominates the Vatican City, in Rome, Italy. It is the pope's principal church, and most papal ceremonies take place at St. Peter's due to its size, proximity to the papal residence, and location within the Vatican City walls. It is the most prominent building in the Vatican City, and its dome is a dominant feature of the skyline of Rome. The focal point of the Basilica is the altar located over what is said to be the location of St. Peter's burial. While St. Peter was one of Jesus' first disciples, he is also the exemplar of "little faith" as described in Matthew 14. Jesus would say to Peter: "Get behind me, Satan," and he eventually denies Jesus three times. Interestingly, every pope wears the golden ring of St. Peter, with their own name inscribed on it, which could then be considered the ring of Satan.

Jesus Christ, the alleged founder of Christianity—although his teachings are unrecognizable in its current institutional form—was the poorest of the poor. Roman Catholicism, which claims to be his church, is the richest of the rich, and the wealthiest institution on Earth. Why is it that such an institution, ruling in the name of this same itinerant preacher, whose want was such that he had not even a pillow upon which to rest his head, is now so overloaded with riches that it can rival—indeed, that it can put to shame—the combined might of the most redoubtable financial trusts, of the most potent industrial super-giants, and of the most prosperous global corporations of the world?

Few of the 1.2 billion Catholics worldwide who have studied the history of the Church would claim its infallibility. There have been murders, cover-ups, persecutions and other crimes committed by various popes over the centuries. One needs only to refer to the Inquisition to understand the intense harm the Catholic Church has wreaked on countless innocent people, including the brutal genocide of the Christian sect called the Cathars who were not under the authority of the Catholic Church. But that's all well out of the range of living history now. What about the last hundred years?

There is a connection between the beloved Pope John Paul II, who was declared a Catholic saint in 2014, and the German chemical company I. G. Farben. This story may not be provable, yet it is often spoken of as fact. In the early 1940s, I. G. Farben employed a Polish chemist and salesman who sold cyanide gas, Zyklon B and Malathion, to the Nazis for extermination of groups of people in Auschwitz. After the war the salesman was ordained a Catholic priest. In 1958, this ambitious priest became Poland's youngest bishop. After Pope John Paul I's highly suspicious death after only a 33-day reign, the ex-cyanide gas salesman named Karol Wojtyla was elected to the papacy in October, 1978 under the new name Pope John Paul II, and he became the second longest reigning pope in papal history.

In March 2000, Pope John Paul II issued a public apology, not for his war effort, but for the depravity of the Christian religion. He apologized for the persecution of Protestants, for the crimes of the Crusaders, and the Church's repression of Galileo among other items. His plea for forgiveness also sought to pardon the use of "violence in the service of truth," an often used fragile and troubling reference to the Inquisition. The apology read by Pope John Paul II was the result of four years of work by a panel of 28 theologians and scholars, and it was by far the most sweeping apology by a leader of a major religion. Also in 2000, Pope John Paul II seemed to align with the New World Order when he said: "By the end of this decade we will live under the first One World Government that has ever existed in the society of nations, a government with absolute authority to decide the basic issues of human survival. One world government is inevitable." His successor, German-born Pope Benedict XVI had been a staunch advocate for the New World Order, that is, until his highly unusual resignation from the papacy in February, 2013.

THE DIPLOMACY OF THE HOLY SEE

The Holy See is the universal government of the Catholic Church, and it operates from the Vatican City State, a sovereign and independent territory. The pope is the ruler of both the Holy See and the Vatican City State. The Holy See, as the supreme body of government of the Catholic Church, is a sovereign juridical entity under international law. The Holy See conducts active diplomacy. It maintains formal diplomatic relations with the 193 nations who are members of the United Nations (UN). The Vatican as an "observer state" also has relations outside of the UN with Taiwan, the Cook Islands, Palestine and the Sovereign Order of Malta. It has a "special" relationship with the European Union. Seventy-eight of these maintain permanent diplomatic missions accredited to the Holy See and are resident in Rome. The rest have missions located outside Italy with dual accreditation. The Holy See maintains 106 permanent diplomatic missions to nation-states. In addition, the Holy See has a separate permanent diplomatic mission to the European Union in Brussels. The Holy See also maintains relations of a special nature with the Palestine Liberation Organization, and it has a delegate to the Arab League in Cairo. Activities of the Holy See within the United Nations gives them the ability to influence the decisions and recommendations of the United Nations. The UN is increasingly calling for a One World Currency. Similarly, the Vatican has joined the call for a crackdown on financial markets. Another Vatican think tank wants global authority to police financial markets.

The Holy See is especially active in international organizations. The Holy See is a permanent observer in the following organizations: United Nations; World Health Organization (WHO); United Nations Food and Agriculture Organization (FAO); Organization of American States (OAS) in Washington; African Union (AU); World Tourist Organization (WToO); World Trade Organization (WTO); World Food Program (WFP); United Nations Educational, Scientific and Cultural Organization (UNESCO); United Nations Environment Program (UNEP); United Nations International Drug Control Program (UNDCP); United Nations Center for Human Settlements (UNCHS); Latin Union (LU); International Organization for Migration (IOM); International Labor Organization (ILO); and the International Fund for Agricultural Development (IFAD). One comes to wonder why a religious organization is so vested in political power.

PEDOPHILE PRIESTS

Clerical sex abuse victims reacted furiously to John Paul II's successor Pope Benedict's claim in November, 2011, that pedophilia was not considered an "absolute evil" in times as recently as the 1970s. In his traditional Christmas address to cardinals and officials working in Rome, Pope Benedict XVI also claimed that child pornography was increasingly considered "normal" by society. "In the 1970s, pedophilia was theorized as something fully in conformity with man and even with children," Pope Benedict said. "It was maintained—even within the realm of Catholic theology—that there is no such thing as evil in itself or good in itself. There is only a 'better than' and a 'worse than.' Nothing is good or bad in itself."

This long-standing and unhealthy culture—of a rigid, secretive, all-male Church hierarchy fixated on self-preservation at all costs—seems desperate to hang on to the power they retained over so many people worldwide. The latest controversy comes as the German magazine *Der Spiegel* continues to investigate the previous pope's role in allowing a known pedophile priest to work with children in the early 1980s. Justifications for sexual child abuse were a last ditch effort of desperation for the former Pope Benedict to keep the Church relevant in spite of record numbers of people abandoning the faith.

Pope Benedict said abuse revelations in 2010 reached "an unimaginable dimension" that brought "humiliation" to the Church. Asking how abuse exploded within the Church, the Pontiff called on senior clerics "to repair as much as possible the injustices that occurred" and to help victims heal through a better presentation of the Christian message. "We cannot remain silent about the context of these times in which these events have come to light," he said, citing the growth of child pornography, "that seems in some way to be considered more and more normal by society."

The current pope, Pope Francis, who replaced Pope Benedict XVI, appears to be opening long-sealed windows, and at last allowing some light to penetrate the official church's rigid darkness. He has called for compassion for gays and their inclusion, and noted the church's unbalanced obsession with the issue of abortion. At one point, he was asked about these controversies and remarked, "Who am I to judge?" While some interpreted this remark to be a dodge regarding the pedophile priest issue, his larger attitudes and opinions do not suggest he would take child abuse lightly. Rather, this remark could also be interpreted as not judging homosexuality. The statement, "Who am I to judge?" is the polar opposite of "papal infallibility." Major newspapers note that the sum total of Pope Francis' public statements show a marked shift from his predecessors John Paul II and Benedict XVI's "hardline defense of the Church's strict doctrines." His pronouncements in the first six months since his election by the College of Cardinals have many dedicated and despairing Catholics around the world rejoicing in astonishment; one can almost hear the huge exhalation. On the other hand, the conservative wing of the church is upset. The new pope named himself after a Franciscan, an order known for their compassion, mercy and services to the poor. This is one of the hopeful signs of cultural awakening and change, an indication that there is a global shift in awareness, a reason to not lose hope despite the seemingly entrenched hidden manipulative forces. Human beings are resilient; shifts in perception are indeed possible.

RELIGION AND FASCISM

The etymology of the word "religion" is *religare* in Latin, which means to re-bind. What do you re-bind it to? A *fascio*. What is a fascio? It is a bundle of sticks, but it is also fascism. By definition, fascism is a radical authoritarian nationalist political ideology. Fascism tends to include a belief in the supremacy of one national or ethnic group, a contempt for democracy, an insistence on obedience to a powerful leader, and a strong demagogic approach. Thomas Paine warned, "Of all the tyrannies that affect mankind, tyranny in religion is the worst."

At its worst, monotheism—as practiced in the Middle Ages, for example—involved singular control over everybody's thoughts. In the Middle Ages, if someone did not believe in the official Catholic doctrine, then that person and their entire family would be tortured until they confessed, and then killed, usually in brutal fashion such as being burned alive. This dark period was called the Inquisition.

Some would say the mentality of the Inquisition continues to this day, but rather than a use of overt means, the power brokers of the Illuminati utilize subversive means. Rather than physical torture, mental torture is employed. Not only are the elite controller's goal to subvert and control organized religion in this modern age, but also our democratic and social systems. They seized the control of the media, the banking industry, and by extension the money supply. They systematically took over our democratic systems through bribery, murder and propaganda—until it has become a hidden fascist system that is controlled by members of a seemingly invisible group.

Evil is, on one level, simply a cultural construct. The Easter Islanders believed that stealing, if successful, was virtuous. This was probably a social mechanism for redistributing scarce resources on a small island. However some evils such as war, genocide, and terrorism, to name a few, are instantly recognizable as such. The issue of why an omniscient, all-powerful God would permit such horrors is one of the most difficult, and obvious, religious questions.

The author Alexander Romanov, a self-proclaimed descendent of the Tsar of Russia and former Illuminati Grand Master, claims he is fighting the "Old World Order." This includes the Rockefellers and the House of Rothschild, who control the world's monetary system. He has made many controversial statements, but none as inflammatory as what follows. He firmly connects fascism with the three largest Western religions. Romanov claims to reveal a thousands-year-old Illuminati secret. He states, "The Abrahamic God, the God of the Jews, the God of the Christians and the God of the Muslim. Allah, God and Yahweh, through their three books, the *Torah*, the *Bible* and the *Koran*, that God is not God at all. Instead, that God is actually Satan. That is shown in my book, *666* and mathematically proven in my book, *The 6th Dimension*. The *Koran*, the *Bible* and the *Torah* is nothing more than lies, ancient lies and these people who believe in these books from 2,000 years ago are deluded and brainwashed and manipulated, for the purpose of being controlled by the Old World Order." The outspoken Romanov also stated: "The great secret that the Illuminati are keeping is that the Abrahamic god is, in fact, Satan. We have known this for thousands of years, ever since the ancient Gnostics, that the god of the ancient Jews, the Christians and the Muslims is none of other than your devil. However, the real secret for 14,000 years that the Illuminati have kept protected is evidence which incontrovertibly proves the existence of a technologically advanced pre-flood civilization. I'm talking about Atlantis. They were on par with our own technology and this was completely erased from our history."

IN GOD WE TRUST

In order to better plan for the future of our world, we first have to understand the history of our world, including the history of religion and other cultures. Much of the ancient wisdom has been lost or forgotten, and civilization has deteriorated into a primitive state. The ancient Greeks showed early signs of becoming aware again, and they are known to have developed philosophy, alchemy and mathematics. Although the alchemists' fundamental goal of elemental transmutation was flawed, on a deeper level the work of alchemy also represented the transformation of the soul. They articulated pi, the Fibonacci sequence, and the golden mean ratio. Following the Greeks came the dawning of the Western religions of today. The religions of Judaism, Christianity and Islam were based on earlier understandings and writings. Ultimately every religion spawned from a more conscious understanding, so we cannot discredit these religions, we merely have to date them back further.

Fast forward to the modern day. More or less, every religion has three things in common: (1) All are human-made, literally; (2) justified in an attempt to tame the lower animal nature of humans; (3) and used for cash/hierarchical power, which stands in contradiction to the goal of taming the id, that part of our mind responsible for basic human drives. The world can be a harsh place for every creature. Yet, humans are the only species that can be counted on to willfully make life more miserable for everyone and everything, more often than not utilizing religion as the cudgel. Let's be honest, it does not matter what or who people believe in. If it's not causing harm to another person, then it is good. But this cannot be said about our current known religions, because billions have perished in the "name" of them over the centuries. At the end of the day we have to recognize that "religions" have nothing to do with "God"—but solely are a ways and means of controlling the masses.

Therefore it is rational to conclude that religion is either created, or at very least, heavily influenced by people. How then could there be such an entity as God? We must conclude that God is an exclusively human concept, which is a misunderstanding of the original concept of "Creator." This is further confused, as there are many macrocosmic level Creators, gradients of consciousness, or *logos*. God implies some separate entity that is "outside" of us, which we must supplicate to and worship. Our "One Infinite Creator," and almost all of our logos and sub-logos, does not seek human worship. They want us to understand creation, and our place within it as an active co-creating participant. Ultimately, there is a "Supreme Being" in the form of the One Infinite Creator, but we are all a part of it, rather than being its subject. None of the names given for this Supreme Being by any religions are the true name, but they are indeed appropriate, in that there is One Supreme Being, namely the Infinite Creator. They just have different concepts about it, which spring from the texts their religions are based upon.

We need not "worship" our Infinite Creator, but rather live in a state of thanksgiving and service to it—for bringing us into being—and for this amazing world it has created. We may forget who we really are, in order to remember, and learn of ourselves once again as the Creator. None of us are "doomed," nor does our soul require "salvation." There is nothing to "save" our souls from. Our Infinite Creator has many messengers, and we all interact in our own unique ways to help with our collective awakening.

MYSTICS IN THE MIX

Mysticism as a general concept has existed for thousands of years, and whether it is seen through the lens of Hinduism, Buddhism, Jainism, Islam, Christianity or even Judaism, the general tenants are some form of meditation, loss of self, or devotion to the divine. For some, a mystical path might lead to asceticism, an austere lifestyle refraining from sensual pleasures of the accumulation of material wealth. It can also lead to loss of identification with the illusory self, thus accessing one's Inner Guide, or Higher Self. These practices have been taken to heart by millions. What is most interesting, and is at the deepest levels of mysticism, is that religious teachings fall to the wayside. Religious dogma, Holy Scriptures, and even spiritual teachings, often become irrelevant. The following is a brief look at the largest world religions today, and the mystics that have spawned them.

The Tanakh is the Hebrew Bible, the quintessential sacred text to Orthodox Jews. The first five books of the Tanakh comprise the Torah, also called the Pentateuch. It is the core sacred writings of the ancient Jews, historically ascribed to have been written by Moses under divine inspiration. Modern scholars believe the Tanakh was composed by four or five writers between 1000 to 400 BCE, and based on much older traditions. The Kabbalah is the outgrowth of a long-term evolution of Jewish mystical thought, starting with the Essenes and the Merkabah, or Chariot, and codifies the mysticism of the Talmundic era. The Talmud is a vast collection of Jewish laws and traditions. The process of studying the Talmud has been compared with the practice of Zen Buddhist Koan meditation. Neo-Platonism, Gnosticism, Contemplative Christianity and other currents, all in turn, were impacted by Jewish mysticism.

Zen Buddhism and Shinto are the mystic schools of Japanese culture. Most Japanese Buddhists practice what is known as *Jiriki*, or the "self-power" school, with another practice called *Tariki*, the "other-power" school. But there is something common to both, that can only be *felt* by the adherent. Zen and its Shin offshoot thus can be grouped together as belonging to the great Buddhist school of mysticism. Zen emphasizes experiential wisdom toward the attainment of enlightenment. As such, it de-emphasizes theoretical knowledge in favor of direct self-realization through meditation and dharma practice. Shin Buddhism is considered the most widely practiced branch of Buddhism in Japan today.

The *Koran* is the primary text of Islam, as revealed to the Prophet Mohammad beginning in the year 610 CE. It was canonized between 644 and 656. The *Koran* is compulsory reading for anyone who wants to understand Islam. *Koran* means "The Recital" in Arabic. According to the story, the angel Gabriel commanded Mohammed to "Recite!" Sufism is a mystical Islamic belief system. It is renowned for its contributions to world literature and devotional story-telling, including beautiful symbolic poetry containing profound insights, such as that of Rumi (a 13th century poet), much of which was translated in the 19th century by European scholars and travelers. The Whirling Dervishes of 13th century Persia act out mystical Islam, achieving an altered state through a form of spinning ecstatic dance. The practice continues to this day, especially in Konya, Turkey.

The *Bible* is considered a sacred text by three major world religions: Judaism, Christianity, and Islam. Many devout believers consider it to be the literal truth. Others treat it with great respect, but believe that it was written by human beings and, as such, it is a complex and often contradictory document. When people talk about what the *Bible* says, we should remember the "Good Book" is a collection, a collaboration, and not an oration. The *Bible* embodies many books written by multiple authors in three languages—Hebrew, Greek and Aramaic. It has multiple interpretations, and has been rewritten many times by the Romans and many others. The New Testament was composed by a variety of writers between 60 to 110 CE, including the mystic Saint John's prophetic revelation of the apocalypse. The contents of the New Testament were formalized by Athanasius of Alexandria in 367 CE, and finally canonized in 382 CE.

Jesus of Nazareth was a teacher, a rabbi, and is thought of as a mystic as described in the New Testament. He incorporated the entire Old Testament law into two new commandments: to love God with all one's heart, soul and mind; and to love one's neighbor as oneself. Some believe he was a vegetarian, except for eating fish, vowed poverty but did not "spiritualize" it, treated women as equals, was a pacifist, believed animals had souls, alluded to the idea of karma and reincarnation, practiced unconditional love, and taught that self-forgiveness, and by natural extension forgiveness of others, is the best medicine. Many other Christian mystics would follow in the centuries after Jesus. The blank historical record of his years on Earth, between the ages of 12 when he taught in the temple, and 30 when he began his ministry in Palestine, are said by some researchers to be a time when he traveled to Greece and throughout the Middle East on his way to

India where he absorbed the teachings of Buddhism and Hinduism. Christian mysticism is a path towards Christ, based on an alternative interpretation of his teachings, which call upon followers to value only what is lasting, rather than "lay up for yourselves treasures on earth." Saint Francis of Assisi, Italy, did just that, and he was the founder of the Franciscan Order of monks. Francis was famous for his unfaltering devotion to serve the poor, his communing with animals, and his disdain for Bible study altogether. Saint Teresa of Avila, Spain, had a revelation from God in 1577; that of a crystal globe in the shape of a castle containing seven mansions. Her interpretation of that vision describes the journey of faith through seven stages, ending in union with God. Saint Teresa was also witnessed levitating. There were many other monks, clergy and Christians, who had mystical visions over the last two thousand years, far too many to mention here.

It was becoming more and more obvious that early Christianity was a wide spectrum of sects, the record of which was subsequently forgotten or suppressed by the Catholic Church and other authorities. Early Christians delved into prophecy, visions, and the *gnosis*. This is understood as "a gift of the Holy Spirit that enables us to know Christ," through meditating on the scriptures and on the Cross of Christ. The Gnostics had deep connections with ancient mystery religions, Pythagoreanism, Hinduism, and other ancient beliefs. This understanding of gnosis is not the same as that developed by the Gnostics. They focused on esoteric knowledge that is available only to a few people, but that presumably allowed them to become free from the evil world.

ESOTERIC RELIGIONS

In some esoteric religions, initiated neophytes gain secret knowledge, and thus gain special status. Their teachers are called adepts. The ancient meaning of neophyte is "planted anew or reborn." A higher initiation is, in its essence a promotion that inspires loyalty—and the desire to move up to the next rung on the ladder. Initiation is a means of rewarding ambitious students who can be trusted after they have taken a vow of loyalty. The higher the degree of attainment in the hierarchy, the fewer members there are who can possess the degree. As such, most members never proceed to the highest levels and never learn the real, secret purpose of the group. Undesirable effects of secret religions and their aura of mystery have sometimes given them the reputation of being abnormal associations or, at the very least, strange groups of people. The holy science, the ancient science based on the workings of the solar system, essentially the science of "as above so below," enables adherents to develop wisdom and enlightenment far beyond what the world's major religions have to offer. Quantum physics confirms what the ancient masters always knew, that solid matter does not exist—that matter is merely energy within a vibrant ocean of consciousness. This is something no organized religion will reveal, because if everyone is a master, there is no longer a need for organized religion.

Rigid hierarchy-based religions cannot be the true spiritual path for humanity when core secrets are kept from the adherents, let alone the population at large. Any one-world religion must include all people and be completely open and transparent. But if an esoteric religion is open to all, with the single qualification that an adherent must work hard to learn the teachings, then there can be the capacity for doing good. Knowledge is always power. The visible form of this power, the communication device, is the teacher, the healer, or a visionary guide. Then the value to the human species is immeasurably great, and the record of its presence stands out everywhere in ancient mythology, mystical and esoteric traditions included. The indigenous love and inclusiveness of equal status in primitive tribes is what humanity will eventually seek once again. We'll come back full circle to discover what we have always known.

Despite the picture of primitive cave men, perhaps before people were forced to live off the land after the last pole shift, our ancient ancestors were very wise. They knew that everything in the universe could be measured on a geometric scale. This pattern of creation is called the flower of life. It is a simple pattern of circles that can be found in nearly all advanced cultures around the world. Sacred geometry within the pattern of the flower of life is the original, perfect, geometric symmetry that created the universe. The flower of life is the basic pattern and the root of all mathematical proportions, particle physics, light, the Platonic Solids, and the source of all energy patterns. Knowledge of this simple pattern originates from the legacy of an earlier epoch of civilizations that understood the flower of life, and other advanced geometric concepts of the universe, that are only being fully understood today.

PROCESSION OF THE EQUINOXES

Another popular theme found around the world is the concept of the Procession of the Equinoxes. For some inexplicable reason, and at some unknown date, it seems that certain archaic myths from all over the world were "co-opted," because, according to author Graham Hancock, no other word will really do. Certain archaic myths were co-opted to serve as vehicles for a body of complex technical data concerning the Procession of the Equinoxes. This astronomical shifting is due to the error in Earth's spin that produces the wobble at our polar point that gives us the 25,920-year Procession of the Equinoxes. The Earth shifts only one degree every 72 years, barely discernible in a human's lifetime. This shifting of the sun through each of the signs of the zodiac determine world-ages, each numbering 2,160 years, and multiplied by 12, adds up to 25,920 years.

Ancient Egyptian, Mayan, East Indian and Sumerian civilizations had a developed and highly advanced knowledge of time, and knew about the Procession of the Equinoxes. In Hindu philosophy, a "yuga" is the name of an epoch, or era, within a cycle of four ages. Hindus knew about the long count of time, far beyond the perception of how the constellations change in one lifetime. In the Procession of the Equinox, there is each a period of sleeping and awakening. For the last few thousand years we have been in a deep sleep and we are now entering the yuga of awakening.

Each of the 12 ages, or each of the zodiac signs, brings a world era, or "twilight of the gods." During the changing of these eras, great structures collapse, and pillars that supported the great fabric topple and these ages are characterized with floods and cataclysms that herald the shaping of each new world. According to Hancock, this information could only have been a "deliberate effort," delivered by the gods, to all the cultures around the world, and toward the ushering in of a new Golden Age. This corresponds to a 26,000 year upgrade of technology, and the entrance of a new era. At the last shift, Neanderthals, saber tooth tigers, and woolly mammoths died off. Tools were invented, and the human experience moved into a new era. Could the next one about now arriving be a shift in space, time, matter, energy and biology as we know it? And will religion survive?

CAN RELIGIONS SURVIVE WITH ET KNOWLEDGE?

Questioning whether humans are alone in the universe is nothing new. The notion that there might be other inhabited solar planets can be traced as far back as the Neapolitan Giordano Bruno, who in 1584, in his book De l'infinito Universo e Mondi, meaning "Concerning the Infinite Universe and Worlds," declared that "Innumerable suns exist; innumerable Earths revolve about these suns ... Living beings inhabit these worlds." These simple statements that we now take for granted nearly cost him his life. Bruno had to escape from his native Italy to avoid facing the Inquisition, intent on suppressing his heretical viewpoints.

The challenge to current theories of evolution and our place in creation would have to rank as one of the key reasons a UFO cover-up is being supported by the control group. Religious leaders realize UFO disclosure would seriously endanger organized religion, already on its knees. On several occasions, U.S. intelligence outlets have leaked information that the aliens are our creators, and they have tied this into the abduction reports. They have even hinted that Jesus was a creation of the aliens, and that the aliens provided them some sort of proof that could be shown to the public. If true, disclosure of these revelations would cause many dilemmas. Most religious groups believe that humankind was a special creation of God. To present the public with proof that humans are nothing more than an alien science fair project would be devastating to our faith, to say nothing of our core self-image.

Judeo-Christian religious concepts influence much of the framework that form the basis of American society. Disclosure of the ET reality would affect most sectors of the Christian community. Some Christians are waiting for the second bodily coming of Jesus Christ. The Jews are waiting for the Messiah. The bewildering appearance of aliens, instead, would hardly be viewed as a positive phenomenon. In 1994, a questionnaire was sent to 1,000 priests, ministers and rabbis about the impact of an ET presence on religion. One question dealt specifically with how religion would react if ETs were to "proclaim responsibility for producing human life." In response, 28% replied that they believed or believed strongly that it would create a religious crisis. That 28% of the American population would add up to over 82 million people in crisis.

It could be argued that the number of people affected by such a challenge to their belief structure would be small in the 21st century, but even a small percentage would deserve some protection, considering the power and influence of conservative elements in the present administration. Moreover, religious beliefs often influence those who control or gather intelligence on the subject. It is said that inside the CIA fundamentalist Christian agents believed that remote viewing was a satanic practice, and they helped put an end to the research.

Ted Peters, a professor of systematic theology at the Pacific Lutheran Theological Seminary in California, considered what might happen to the world's religions in the event of an extraterrestrial intelligence (ETI) disclosure. Conventional wisdom suggests that terrestrial religion would collapse if the existence of ETI were confirmed. Peters took the opposing view: "Because our religious traditions formulated their key beliefs within an ancient world view now out of date, would shocking new knowledge dislodge our pre-modern dogmas? Are religious believers Earth-centric, so that contact with ET would de-center and marginalize our sense of self-importance? Do our traditional religions rank us human beings on top of life's hierarchy, so if we meet ETI who are smarter than us will we lose our superior rank? If we are created in God's image, as the biblical traditions teach, will we have to share that divine image with our new neighbors?" Ted Peters' conclusion, however, is that faith in Earth's major religions would survive intact. "Theologians will not find themselves out of a job. In fact, theologians might relish the new challenges to reformulate classical religious commitments in light of the new and wider vision of God's creation … Traditional theologians must then become astro-theologians … What I forecast is this: contact with extraterrestrial intelligence will expand the existing religious vision that all of creation—including the 13.7 billion year history of the universe replete with all of God's creatures—is the gift of a loving and gracious God," he speculated.

ALL IS ONE

The father of quantum mechanics and particle wave theory, Erwin Schrödinger, said over a century ago that the total number of minds in the universe is one. He implied that human consciousness is a singularity, a phasing within all beings. And this is also the heart of the compassion of the Buddha, the oneness of spirit in all religions, as well as the essence of Native American traditions.

A Native American prayer continues to ring true in this modern age, symbolizing humanistic harmony, and our oneness with nature:

> *Great Spirit, whose voice I hear in the winds, and whose breath gives life to all in the world, hear me! I am small and I am weak and I need your strength and your wisdom. Let me walk in beauty and let my eyes ever behold the red and purple sunsets that you have created with me. Make my hands respect the things that you have made and my ears sharp to hear your words and your voice. Let me learn the lessons that you have hidden under every rock and leaf. I seek strength, not to be greater than my brother, but to fight my greatest enemy—myself. Make me always ready to come to you with clean hands and straight eyes, so that when my life fades as the fading sunset, my spirit can come to you without shame. Amen.*

The spiritual implications of one individual consciousness, that which is connected to the One Infinite Creator, is the oneness in us all. The true notion of an individual consciousness must emanate from a single source. The true nature of a conscious mind is a singularity, yet we have a free will, which seems to be a contradiction. Perhaps free will is the free choice we have to which inner voice we listen to—the small ego voice of a separated self or the voice of the larger universal One Self. The etheric, astral conscious realm, spoken of by all the mystics, teaches consistently that the true Self is one. That is, we are all one Mind, appearing in many forms throughout the cosmos. The One mind is the content. Multiple beings of all shapes and sizes are the forms, the carriers or communicators of content. This awareness will allow a universal consciousness or collective understanding of humanity, and this will truly transform the lives of all people on the planet. When science marries spirituality we will enter a new dawn. After all, the only universal language is in the abstract "form" of mathematics.

The City,
London

Washington
Monument

Vatican

The Vatican, the City of London, and Washington D.C. are the "Empire of the Three Cities" ruling the Western world. All three cities have a dominating obelisk near their center. Each is a city-state within a larger country, but are mostly immune to outside country's laws and restrictions.

During the period leading up to World War II, the Vatican was allied with the Nazi Party. In this picture "Hitler's pope," Pius XII, meets with *der führer,* Adolf Hitler.

The Coat of Arms of the Vatican City represents the keys to the world, and the British Crown. The Roman Catholic Church in its entirety contains more than 3,000 Ecclesiastical Jurisdictions, including over 600 archdioceses as well as military ordinariates, apostolic administrators, apostolic prefectures, apostolic vicariates, territorial and personal prelatures, and missions *sui juris* around the world. Although the literal definition of "catholic" means universal, derived from the Late Latin word *catholicus,* the Vatican in Rome is anything but when it comes to sharing resources. The best guesses about the Vatican's wealth put it at $10 billion to $15 billion, yet most of its adherents live in abject poverty.

< Pythagoras, an immortal mathematical genius, a vegetarian and founder of a high-standing school of philosophy, went to Egypt to learn more about the "secret sciences" of that country. Before he was allowed to enter into the school of the learned, called High Priests at this time, he had to undergo a fast of forty days, under supervision, outside of the city. Believing that this was a test of his will-power and energy, he was told this: "Forty days' fast is necessary in order that you may grasp what we will teach you."

> The "Hegelian dialectic" is usually presented in a threefold manner, and is comprised of the dialectical stages of development: a thesis, giving rise to its reaction, an antithesis, which contradicts or negates the thesis, and the tension between the two being resolved by means of a synthesis. In more simplistic terms it is problem -> reaction -> solution.

A government controlled by elites can create enemies in order to mold society into their own tyrannical image. They do so by committing acts of terrorism against their own buildings and bureaucracies, then choosing the scapegoat and announcing it through the mass media.

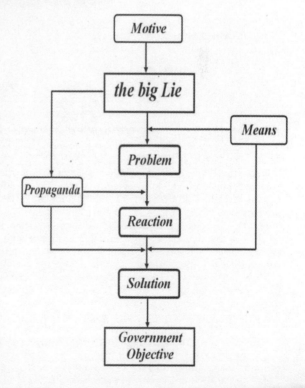

It is said that when Pythagoras went to Egypt with a letter of introduction written by Polycrates, he made the journey with some Egyptian sailors who believed that a god had taken passage on their ship. Arriving in Egypt, Pythagoras tried to gain entry into the mystery schools of that country. He applied again and again, but he was told that unless he goes through a particular training of fasting and breathing, he would not be allowed to enter the school. Pythagoras is reported to have said, "I have come for knowledge, not any sort of discipline." But the school authorities said, "we cannot give you knowledge unless you are different. And really, we are not interested in knowledge at all, we are interested in actual experience. No knowledge is knowledge unless it is lived and experienced. So you will have to go on a 40-day fast, continuously breathing in a certain manner, with a certain awareness on certain points." After 40 days of fasting and breathing, aware and attentive, he was allowed to enter the school at Diospolis. It is reported that Pythagoras said, "You are not allowing Pythagoras in. I am a different man, I am reborn. You were right and I was wrong, because then my whole standpoint was intellectual. Through this purification, my center of being has changed. Before this training I could only understand through the intellect, through the head. Now I can feel. Now truth is not a concept to me, but a life."

SACRED GEOMETRY

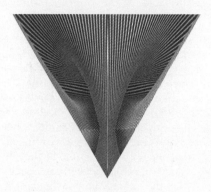

"The cosmos was formed according to and upon the basis of laws which are expressed as music, arithmetic and geometry; they bring about harmony, order and balance." –Edgar Cayce

THE study of "sacred" geometry was both an ancient philosophical pursuit and a secretive endeavor among kindred spirits. The principles of sacred geometry are now being incorporated into new sciences such as quantum physics. Understanding sacred geometry is the basis of tapping into the "Universal Mind," simply because everything from the micro to the macro level is geometric. This seeming modern expression of "God" is a comprehensive geometry that shows up everywhere as part of the physical laws of all creation. It is a language of shapes and structure of the fundamental nature of life, and a key to understanding the way our entire realm of existence is designed. It is found at the quantum level all the way up to a universal scale. The unified science of sacred geometry can articulate how cells divide, how nature repeats patterns, and even molds reality as we perceive it in this third dimensional experience. Sacred geometry is a concise approach to the understanding of the way in which the cosmos is manifest, ordered, and sustained.

The basic patterns of sacred geometry were understood by the ancients as being sacred, or part of the "Great Design" of existence. Sacred geometry can be understood as a worldview of pattern recognition, a complex system of religious symbols and structures involving space, time and form. Insight may be gained into the profound mysteries of nature by studying the formation of geometric structures. In nature, we find patterns, designs and structures from the most minuscule particles to expressions of life discernible by human eyes, and far beyond into the greater cosmos. These inevitably follow geometrical archetypes, which reveal to us the nature of each form and its vibrational resonances. They are also symbolic of the underlying metaphysical principle of the inseparable relationship of the part to the whole. It is this principle of oneness underlying all geometry that permeates the architecture of all form in its myriad manifestations of diversity. This principle of interconnectedness, inseparability, and union provide us with a continuous reminder of our relationship to the whole, a blueprint for the mind to remember the sacred foundation of all things created. Simply stated, geometry underlies all of our reality.

Sacred geometry was a closely guarded secret in the ancient mystery schools and advanced study was made available to only a select few. Concealing this information was used as a method of controlling the accessibility of knowledge, or as Plato remarked, "Only he who is familiar with geometry shall be admitted here." It was a tool of consciousness expansion that has been used for thousands of years to reach beyond the physical and awaken the divine from within. The belief that God created the cosmos according to a geometric plan has ancient origins. The Greek philosopher Plutarch attributed the belief to Plato and said, "Plato said God geometrizes continually." The ancients believed that the experience of sacred geometry was essential to the education of the soul. They knew that these patterns and codes were symbolic of our own inner realm and the subtle structure of awareness. To them the "sacred" had particular significance involving consciousness, the profound mystery of awareness, and the ultimate sacred wonder.

In the modern age, sacred geometry involves universal patterning used in the design of practically everything in our reality, most often replicated by people in the form of architecture and sacred art. The basic belief is that geometry and mathematical ratios, harmonics and proportion, are also in music, cosmology, light, and in the practice of yoga, which emphasizes balance and symmetry. This value system has been widespread for many centuries, even in prehistory, as a cultural expression of the human condition. It is considered foundational to building sacred structures such as temples, mosques, megaliths, monuments and churches. Geometric symmetry is used in sacred spaces such as altars, temenoi and tabernacles. It is also used in the creation of religious art and iconography by incorporating "divine" proportions. Alternatively, arts based on sacred geometry may be ephemeral, such as the visualization of proportions, including Native American medicine wheels and sand painting popularized by Tibetan monks.

THE GEOMETRY OF OUR EXISTENCE

The study, understanding and applications of sacred geometry both in nature and in consciousness offers a needed and substantial gift. We already see geometry appearing in a variety of different circumstances in the natural sciences, such as in the structure of the atomic nucleus, as well as in greater groups of atoms called "microclusters." We also see it in the underlying structure of continents and mountain ranges on Earth known as the "global grid." Additionally, it appears in the exact positioning of the planetary orbits in our solar system and all planets throughout the universe.

Sacred geometry takes on another whole level of significance when grounded in the experience of self-awareness. It helps to open our human awareness to perceive, again, a living, interconnected, intelligent and benevolent universe. Sacred geometry is the collective reappearance of our deep innate wisdom, encouraging the seeing, and becoming the all-encompassing unity of life, so that the heavens could be understood as spiritual realms preceding and continuing life on Earth. Ancient thinkers thought sacred geometry could be heard as the primordial song of the universe. To them, each star was seen smiling to each flower, while the human family was holding hands with all of creation. Harmonic chords could be played by celestial bodies choreographing graceful time-space dances, such as the dance of Shiva to Hindu devotees.

As we enter into the world of sacred geometry, we will begin to see as never before the wonderfully patterned beauty of all creation. The molecules of our DNA, the cornea of our eye, snow flakes, pine cones, flower petals, diamond crystals, the branching of trees, a nautilus shell, the star we spin around, the galaxy we spiral within, the air we breathe, and all life forms as we know them emerge out of timeless geometric codes. Viewing and contemplating these codes allows us to gaze directly at the lines on the face of deep wisdom and offers up a glimpse into the inner workings of the Universal Mind and the multidimensional universe itself. By recreating the genesis of these forms, we seek to know the principles of evolution. And by thus raising our own patterns of thought to these archetypal levels, we invite the force of these levels to penetrate our mind and thinking.

Sacred geometry appears to be the blueprint of creation and the genesis of all form. Its principles are directly correspondent to all wave form phenomena, the ubiquitous torus pattern, and all vibration. It is an ancient science that explores and explains the energy patterns that create and unify all things, and reveals the precise way that the energy of creation organizes itself. On every scale, every natural pattern of growth or movement conforms inevitably to one or more geometric shapes. Geometric shapes actually represent the manifest stages of "becoming." To see and work with unity and wholeness in geometry can help abolish our false notion of separateness from nature and from each other. With this new understanding, neither space nor time are what we imagine them to be. And none of us are who we think we are in this "holographic universe." All geometries are sacred, born from the "one center," as all are contained each within the other. In the ultimate understanding, all life is forever, and all beings are stars.

THE FATHER OF SACRED GEOMETRY

Geometry as a science was first articulated by the eminent Greek philosopher, Pythagoras of Samos (580-500 BCE), who is considered the "founding father" of Western esotericism. He stated that "all is number." In his view, geometry is the science of all creation and he demonstrated that its formulas are illustrative of the very energy within life that can be focused in the angle, in the pyramid, in the octagon, in the cell structure, and in all the patterns of nature, all of which are geometric. Geometry deals with pure form, and philosophical geometry reenacts the unfolding of each form out of a preceding one in the form of doubling. It is a way by which the essential creative mystery is rendered visible. The ancient Pythagoreans defined numbers as expressions of ratios, not as units as is common today. They believed that reality is numerical, and that the Golden Ratio expressed an underlying truth about existence.

Plato wrote about sacred geometry in his book, the *Republic*. Plato maintained that it is through geometry that one purifies the eye of the soul, "since it is by it alone that we contemplate the truth." Although Plato discusses geometry's importance to both music and esoteric philosophy, he concentrates on the latter. Thus, his discourses do not provide physical demonstrations of the ratios, for they were not meant as textbooks, but as spiritual philosophy. Plato says "We must endeavor to persuade those who are to be the principal men of our state to go and learn arithmetic, not as amateurs, but they must carry on the study until they see the nature of numbers with the mind ... for the sake of the soul."

Pythagoras understood the esoteric nature of this subject thoroughly when he introduced geometry to the world. He knew that the seekers of truth and true devotees would ultimately pass through it into the higher exaltation of the soul. Unfortunately, his esoteric teachings did not live on, but his geometry teachings were passed on like the parables of Jesus Christ. Hidden in it are the sacred mysteries. His students, called the Pythagoreans, regard each number as an expression or facet of unity, or the "father of all things," which is projected through duality, "the mother," to create multiplicity.

"We live in a music universe," observed Pythagoras. Everything owes its existence solely and completely to sound, because sound is the factor that holds it all together. Pythagoras considered the musical octave to be the simplest and most profound expression of the relationship between spirit and matter. Geometry can be a vehicle for meditation on the harmony of the cosmic order, and it is a meditation upon music, frequency, and vibration. If you meditate upon geometry instead of just learning it in a linear way, according to author Elizabeth Clare Prophet, you can actually hear the "music of the spheres," because the geometric forms will key the eye and the ear to the inner sound. With every line that is drawn linearly, there is a carry over from the spiritual octaves to the physical. The "miracle of the octave" is that it divides wholeness into two audibly distinguishable parts, yet remains recognizable as the same musical note—a tangible manifestation of the Hermetic maxim "as above, so below." In the beginning was the word, and the word is "sound," according to Pythagoras. His mystery school believed that there is something special, and even sacred, in whole numbers. In music, these whole number ratios form scales, which are the building blocks of music.

MUSIC OF THE SPHERES

Music of the spheres as a form of musical harmony is an ancient philosophical concept that ascribes proportions to the movements of celestial bodies such as the Sun, the Earth's moon, and other planets or asteroids. Pythagorus reportedly was the first person known to hear the music of the spheres, and he was quick to teach others how to partake in the astral bounty. His theory was that the planets, going around the Sun, touch the aether and create a sound that humans can hear if they are properly attuned. As a planet has its own orbit of rotation, its radius represents a length of sounding string, and consequently each planet has its own "diapason," which is an interval, or the name of an octave in the scales of Pythagorean tuning. Together planets produce harmonious accords that the majority of people cannot hear. He perceived the stars as being attached to crystal spheres revolving about the Earth. These heavenly spheres, eternally revolving, produce harmonious sounds that only the truly inspired can hear. This "music" is not literally audible, but a harmonic, mathematical, or vibrational element, as well as a religious concept. According to Max Heindel's Rosicrucian writings, the heavenly music of the spheres is heard in the "region of concrete thought," the lower region of the "world of thought," which is an ocean of harmony. It is also referred to in esoteric Christianity as the place where the state of consciousness known as the "second heaven" occurs.

"The architecture of God," according to the Egyptian god of wisdom Thoth, is "the universe created by a consciousness which manifests in physical reality through a blueprint that we call sacred geometry which repeats over and over giving the illusion of linear time." Plato went one step further when he wrote in his the *Republic*: "The knowledge of which geometry aims is knowledge of the eternal."

Ancient Egyptians and Greeks recognized that music was the most powerful of the arts. Plato noted that forms of government eventually follow the forms of music. That is why the ancients were very careful to control music; for example, no *cacophony* was allowed in public places. Plato elaborated about a certain canon of law possessed by the ancient Egyptians by which numerical proportions and musical harmonies dominate a society and enable it to continue on the same level for literally thousands of years, as was the case in Lemuria and Atlantis. Ancient civilizations before the last Ice Age lasted far longer than we can conceive of today. In those times, the whole society was based upon an understanding of the harmonies underlying the universe. The same harmonizing music was played at Greek festivals every year, and people were held under a kind of enchantment where the group mind was joined together under one influence.

Greeks in the mystery schools understood that "geometry is frozen music." To their Egyptian teachers, sacred geometry and music were inextricably linked, since the laws of the former govern the mathematical intervals that make up the notes in the Western music scale, which are known as the *diatonic ratios*. The Euclidean theorems had also produced diatonic ratios. In ancient times geometric theorems were linked with music. Fast forward to the last few decades, and we see that authentic crop circles contain information about musical notes, which are themselves the byproduct of the harmonic laws of sound frequency. Music is also a unique and powerful method of psychotherapy.

In mathematics, Euclidean space is the Euclidean plane and three-dimensional space of Euclidean geometry, as well as the generalizations of these notions having applications to the higher dimensions. If sound changes, matter changes. The law of vibration says that everything in the universe is in a constant state of vibration. The intervals between harmonious musical notes always have whole number ratios. For instance, playing half a length of a guitar string gives the same note as the open string, but an octave higher. Similarly, a third of a length gives a different but harmonious note, and so on. Non-whole number ratios, on the other hand, tend to give dissonant sounds. In this way, Pythagoras described the first four overtones which create the common intervals and that have become the primary building blocks of musical harmony. It starts with the octave (1:1), the perfect fifth (3:2), the perfect fourth (4:3) and the major third (5:4). The oldest way of tuning the 12-note chromatic scale is known as Pythagorean tuning, and it is based on a stack of consecutive perfect fifths, each tuned in the ratio 3:2.

The universe can be thought of as a giant symphony of sound, with each entity represented by a unique underlying numeric property or unique sound. All things are nothing more than an expression of something numeric or harmonic. God is always seen in the order and harmony of the universe. Geometry can be thought of as "God" itself. The universe is a musical instrument and everything in it is vibrating in tune with the larger things that contain it. Is the universe derived from an original ratio of sound? Or is sound the true origin of the universe? In the beginning there was the word and that word was vibration. Speech cannot form without vibration and oscillation, so the origin of the universe is born from the energetic states of vibration and oscillation. 432 Hz vibrates on the principals of the Golden Mean proportions of phi and unifies the properties of light, time, space, matter, gravity and magnetism with biology, the DNA code, and consciousness. 432 Hz as a natural tuning has profound effects on human consciousness, and also on the cellular level of our bodies. By retuning musical instruments and using concert pitch at 432 hertz instead of the usual A-440 hertz, the essence of humans, that is, the actual atoms and DNA in our bodies begin to resonate in harmony with the phi spiral of nature.

PLATONIC SOLIDS

Since the time of the Greek mystery schools 2,500 years ago, we have been taught that there are five perfect three-dimensional forms—the tetrahedron, hexahedron, octahedron, dodecahedron, and icosahedron. Collectively these are known as the Platonic Solids, which are the basic building block shapes of sacred geometry, and are the foundation of everything in the physical world. "Learn how to see," proposed the Italian Renaissance artist Leonardo da Vinci, "and realize that everything connects to everything else."

The Platonic Solids are five three-dimensional geometric forms of which all faces are alike. The five regular solids are named "Platonic Solids" today after Plato, who lived from 428-348 BCE, about 100 years after Pythagoras. Each Platonic Solid represents one of the five elements of creation. The five shapes and the elements they represent are as follows: a tetrahedron is fire; an icosahedron is water; the cube in esoteric traditions represents the body, thus the cube or hexahedron is Earth; an octahedron is air; and a dodecahedron represents the aether. Additionally, the dodecahedron corresponds to the universe because the zodiac has 12 signs, representing the constellations of stars that the sun passes through in the course of one year, corresponding to the 12 faces of the dodecahedron.

Modern scholars sneered at the universal application of the Platonic Solids until the 1980s, when Professor Robert Moon at the University of Chicago demonstrated that the entire Periodic Table of Elements—literally everything in the physical world—is based on these same five forms! In fact, throughout modern physics, chemistry, and biology, the sacred geometric patterns of creation are being rediscovered, but often without the greater context of spiritual understanding which protects against their misuse. According to a recent theory, the universe itself could be in the shape of a dodecahedron. It is not surprising that Plato used a dodecahedron as the quintessence to describe the cosmos. Plato also stated that time had a beginning—it came together with the universe in one instant of creation.

Geometric forms are also the basis of all dimensional dynamics, representing specific forms of energy. The Platonic Solids are replicated in many aspects of our three-dimensional universe, from microscopic to planetary, both fluid and solid, also in hot and freezing environments. Platonic Solids are also the means through which energies flow at all levels. The math of the universe is geometric math. It has to do with shapes, and energies around shapes. The metaphoric symbolism around the solutions of common geometric mathematical problems actually tells the story of our lineage, and of humans with a relationship to the creator. All of this can be derived from the shapes within the circles. At each angle and corner there is information, which is spiritual. In its beauty and simplicity, it is a base-12 system. The use of mathematics and geometry will allow an introductory understanding of the beauty of the recurring sixes, threes and nines, as we shall examine now.

THE GOLDEN MEAN

The beautiful Golden Mean Proportion and the mysterious Fibonacci numbers have fascinated philosophers for thousands of years, and are still the subject of inquiry in the field of art, architecture, music, botany, biology, astronomy, and physics. So far science has documented the numbers existence, but no one as yet has fully penetrated its deeper mystery. According to Vitruvius, the *Sacred Mean* can be seen in the ratios of body parts; the distance from outstretched fingertip to fingertip—should be the same as that from head to toe. In the arm of Leonardo da Vinci's Vitruvian Man, for example, the ratio of A to B can be seen as the same as that of B to C. The same rules apply throughout the human body.

The understanding of geometry as an underlying part of our existence is nothing new. In fact, the Golden Mean and other forms of geometry can be seen imbedded in many of the ancient monuments that still exist today. The Great Pyramids at Giza, the oldest of these structures, is a good example of such a monument containing ratios of sacred geometry. The height of the pyramid is in phi ratio (the Golden Mean Ratio) to its base. In fact, the geometry in this particular structure is far more accurate than that found in any of today's modern buildings. As we have seen, the Great Pyramid lies in the center of gravity of the continents. It also lies in the exact center of all the land area of the world, dividing the Earth's land mass into approximately equal quarters and it has undoubtedly been constructed to the mathematics of phi. The Golden Mean literally can be called "harmony by design."

Harmony by design explains why popular shapes are spiritually significant, such as pyramids and the symmetry of hemispheres. Other examples are the domes constructed in sacred structures around the world. This underlying symmetry is the basis of religious buildings around the globe, whether they are temples, mosques, churches or within synagogues. These particular shapes are, quite literally, energy emitters. They are shapes that produce a type of penetrating carrier wave that act as *carrier-like radio waves* that carry sound information. The vibrational quality of the Golden Mean gives it very strong communication properties that facilitate resonance with higher realms in prayer.

We live in the 3rd dimension, or the "Plane of Manifestation." The Golden Mean appears to function as an intra-dimensional doorway through which matter emerges in order to manifest 3-D reality. For example, when a star is born it follows specific number sequences, or *universal rules*. Thus, the Golden Mean is the "fingerprint" of all creation. When we re-create this moving and always expanding sequence, we have in effect "the exact movement of creation in the expansion process."

THE GOLDEN RATIO

The Golden Mean is also known as the Golden Ratio, phi, the God Ratio, Golden Proportion, Golden Section, Golden Number, divine proportion or *sectio divina*, and it is an irrational number, approximately 1.618 033 988 749 894 848, and possesses many interesting properties. Shapes proportioned according to the Golden Ratio have long been considered aesthetically pleasing in Western cultures, and the Golden Ratio is still frequently used in art and design, therefore suggesting a natural balance between symmetry and asymmetry. One of the mathematical products of the sacred mean is the spiral, commonly found in nature. The most prominent form through which the Golden Ratio expresses itself is the Golden Spiral, where the arc of the spiral is determined by phi. The scale can range from microscopic to super-galactic, but the arc remains constant at every stage of progression and level of existence. Not all spirals in nature are golden proportioned, but the Golden Spiral is prominently featured. Plato thought that phi, or the Golden Mean, was "the key to the physics of the cosmos."

The symbol of pantheism is the spiral, as seen in the curves of the nautilus shell, the rotation of water draining, or in the spiral arms of a galaxy, and show the link between the cosmic, the physical, and the biological. The spiral represents a variety of things, such as evolution, eternity, spirituality, and growth. Sometimes the *nautilus spiral* embodies the Fibonacci series ... or is representative of the Golden Ratio.

Fractals are based on mathematical equations that never end, that is, no matter how much a fractal image is enlarged or reduced, there will always be the same amount of detail and a repetition of mathematically defined shapes in the scaled image.

Sacred geometry is the expression of geometry related to the evolution of consciousness, mind, body, and spirit in geometric terms. True sacred geometry is not just static angular forms, but is organic and living. It is in constant evolutionary movement, or in a constantly transcendent state. It can also be devolution, or materialization, ascending or descending from one form to another. Plato said: "Geometry existed before the creation."

FIBONACCI SERIES

In the 12th century, the Italian mathematician Leonardo Fibonacci discovered a mathematical series that is found throughout nature within various modalities, such as the leaf arrangements in plants, the pattern of petals in flowers, the logarithmic spirals of shells, or the patterns of pine cones. Starting with 1, each new number in the series is simply the sum of the two before it: 1, 1, 2, 3, 5, 8, 13, 21, 34, 55, 89, 144, 233, 377, 610, 987, and so on. The series is generated by adding each set of numbers to make the next number. However, if instead of adding the numbers together, they are divided, an interesting phenomenon occurs. The same rules of life in the expansion process become a basis of mathematics, along with the emerging models of predictive analytics.

Why is it that the number of petals in a flower is often one of the following numbers: 3, 5, 8, 13, 21, 34 or 55? For example, the lily has three petals, buttercups have five, the chicory has 21, the daisy has often 34 or 55 petals. Furthermore, when observing the head of a sunflower plant, there are clearly two series of curves, one winding clockwise and the other counter-clockwise. The number of spirals are not being the same in each sense. Why are the number of spirals in general either 21 and 34, either 34 and 55, either 55 and 89, or 89 and 144? The same is true for pine cones. Why do they have either 8 spirals from one side and 13 from the other, or either 5 spirals from one side and 8 from the other? Why is the number of diagonals of a pineapple also 8 in one direction and 13 in the other? 13 is a prime number that can be evenly divided by only 1 or itself. There are 13 Archimedean Solids in geometry.

Are these numbers the product of chance? No. They all belong to the Fibonacci sequence: 1, 2, 3, 5, 8, 13, 21, 34, 55, 89, 144, and scale up indefinitely, where each number is obtained from the sum of the two preceding. A more abstract way of putting it is that the Fibonacci numbers (fn) are given by the formula $f1 = 1$, $f2 = 2$, $f3 = 3$, $f4 = 5$ and generally $f_{n+2} = f_{n+1} + f_n$ in a non-breaking sequence. For a long time, it had been noticed that these numbers were important in nature, but only relatively recently can we understand why. It is a question of efficiency during the growth process of plants. Quite simply, the Fibonacci numbers are nature's numbering system. They appear everywhere in nature, from the leaf arrangement in plants, to the pattern of the florets of a flower, the bracts of a pine cone, or the scales of a pineapple. The Fibonacci numbers are therefore applicable to the growth of every living thing, from a single cell to a grain of wheat, or in the pattern of a beehive.

The explanation is linked to another notable number, the Golden Mean, itself intimately linked to the spiral form of certain types of shells. Let's also mention that in the case of the sunflower, the pineapple, and the pine cone, the correspondence with the Fibonacci numbers is very exact, while in the case of the number of flower petals, it is only verified on average. In certain cases the number is doubled since the petals are arranged on two levels.

THE GOLDEN SPIRAL

One of the most prominent forms through which the Golden Ratio expresses itself is the Golden Spiral, where the arc of the spiral is determined by phi. The scale can range from microscopic to super-galactic, but the arc remains constant at every stage of progression and level of existence. Not all spirals in nature are "golden" proportioned, but the Golden Spiral is prominently featured. Plato called phi the most binding of all mathematical relationships, and the key to understanding physics and the cosmos.

The Golden Mean Spiral is the ideal pattern, and it is the symbol of life's unfolding mysteries. With each revolution, the spiral reveals a complete cycle of evolution. With their continuous curves, spirals are feminine in nature. Logarithmic spirals, like cochlea of the inner ear, reveal the intimate relationship between the harmonics of sound and geometry. At the center of a daisy, spirals unfold in clockwise and counter-clockwise directions—the number of the spirals are determined by Fibonacci numbers. Swarms of insects, schools of fish and flocks of birds regroup into Golden Spiral patterns after scattering from a disturbance. The Golden Ratio is present in the spiral of a fly approaching an object, or a falcon circling its prey.

Similarly, the Golden Angle provides the ideal positioning of leaf distribution around a stem called the phyllotaxis. It is based on an angle of approximately 222.5 degrees rotated from one leaf to the next, and provides the maximum space for sunlight and rainfall for all the leaves. It is called the Golden Angle because it divides the 360 degrees circle into a phi ratio: $222.5/360 = 0.618055 \ldots$ and $360/222.5 = 1.617977 \ldots$

According to Professor of Anthropology and the world director of the Flower of Life organization Ronald L. Holt:

> *(The Golden Mean Spiral is a) phenomenon that ties the mathematical spiral to the experiential spiral. In practical terms, they are one and the same ... It will take a bit of explanation to demonstrate the probably ridiculous notion that the Golden Mean Spiral can be experienced most simply as a profound feeling of love. Simply put, the Golden Mean Spiral is a doorway that weaves the ethereal and material dimensions together.*

One of the most exquisite examples of the Golden Ratio in nature is the chambered nautilus shell. The nautilus begins its journey of evolution constructing a shell to protect itself from the outside elements. As it continues to grow, it builds another chamber at the shell mouth bigger than the one before it, and when it moves into this larger area it seals off the old chamber behind it. It continues this process of building larger and larger chambers along a logarithmic spiral, always closing off the previous chamber to increase buoyancy. The effect is remarkable. The linear spiral that the chambers are constructed along is a golden proportioned spiral. Starting a few out from the center, the 3-D space of each successive chamber has approximately 1.618 times more volume than the chamber preceding it. The very program of life itself—the DNA molecule— also contains the Golden Ratio. One revolution of the double helix measures 34 angstroms while the width is 21 angstroms. The ratio 34/21 reflects phi, which is 34 divided by 21 and equals 1.619, a close approximation to phi's 1.618.

PERFECT HARMONIC OF LIGHT IS 432 Hz

Sound and music consist of vibrations as the ancient Greeks emphasized. Simply implied, the more vibrations per second, the higher the pitch. The unit for this is the Hertz, abbreviated Hz. The "432 Hz" vibrates on the principals of natural harmonics and is the natural "keynote" in the universe. The frequency of 432 Hz is known to carry the phi ratio of Fibonacci, which is the Golden Mean principle, and it unifies the properties of light, time, space, matter, gravity and magnetism with biology, the DNA code, and even our consciousness. In the last hundred years our music was retuned to A-440 Hz, which added an extra 8 Hz, thus creating a slight distortion from what is otherwise known to be the perfect frequency of 432 Hz.

It is interesting to note that the distance from the center of the Earth to the average height of the atmosphere is given a value of 4320 arc-minutes, which harmonically can be reduced to 432, which is the fundamental vibration for the sixth note (A) in the octave. The Golden Mean is found in everything from the distant solar systems and galaxies all the way to our cellular molecular structure and DNA. So when music is tuned to 432 Hz instead of 440 Hz, it has a profound effect on our body, mind, emotions and spirit. We will explore the 432 Hz and 440 Hz octaves in later chapters.

SACRED GEOMETRIC DESIGNS

The ancients believed that the experience of sacred geometry was essential to the education of the soul. They knew that these patterns and codes were symbolic of our own inner realm and the subtle structure of awareness. To them the "sacred" had particular significance involving consciousness and the profound mystery of awareness. For thousands of years, sacred geometry has been used as a means to illustrate states of universal order. The archetypical patterns that occur through the relationship of numbers have appeared in the world in the form of medicine wheels, mandalas, mosaics, weaving, pottery, architecture, stained glass windows, and many other examples. By following harmonic pathways, intricate and exquisite patterns unfold, and a profound order is revealed. Both consciously and subconsciously, we perceive these shapes and patterns as beautiful. Diverse shapes join together in math-magical compliance and symmetry, revealing continuous, timeless, universal actions that are otherwise invisible and can only be known to us through geometry. The study of geometry portrays many universal principles such as balance, coalescence, coherence, equilibrium, harmony, integration, interconnectivity, optimization, stability, sustainability, symbiosis, symmetry, synergy, integrity and unity.

The Sanskrit term *mandala* roughly translates to "magic circle" or "sacred circle." Mandalas, ancient and modern, frequently offer beautiful examples of radial symmetry and contain elements of sacred geometry. They tend to act as activation templates of consciousness. Carl Jung studied mandalas from a wide field of world cultures and eras. He also advocated creating our own mandalas as vehicles of soul work. He noted that when we draw mandalas from the center outward, we tend to process our personal issues or challenges, and often gain increased clarity and energy that we can apply to our lives.

Eastern philosophers say meditation on the Sri Yantra pattern will bring enlightenment, and by doing so, all the secrets of the universe will be revealed to the person who meditates on it until its image is engraved in the mind. This form also has the ability to focus, balance, and increase the level of life force energy. The key is experiencing Sri Yantra as a "stargate" to the Zero Point of Source from which all manifestation ultimately comes. The ancient yogis of India considered the Sri Yantra to be the most powerful of all known geometric power symbols. It represents the geometric structure of the sound of creation, the sound of "OM."

UNIVERSAL PATTERNING

The shapes, patterns and forms that develop from the circle and sphere are harmonic modules that can help attune, empower, uplift and inspire the human condition and open us up to the greater whole. We are a fractal that is infinite, within an infinite endless fractal, among other infinite endless fractals. In such a construct, our entire field of creation is an infinite fractal representation within vibrating frequencies, in multiple dimensions, that expresses itself in sacred geometrical patterns that are constantly changing with alternating frequencies. These templates are the basic foundational blueprints of all matter. They take the form of mathematical geometrical shapes through which solids can transmute, or crystallize.

On a macro level, sacred geometry is a concise approach to the understanding of the way in which the universe is manifest, ordered, and sustained. For example, the orbits of certain planets are phi related: the distance from Mercury to Venus is approximately 1.618 times the distance from the Sun to Mercury. The distance from Earth to Mars is approximately 1.618 times the distance from Venus to Earth. Indeed, the ratio of 1.618 is found in other planets and galaxies throughout the universe.

The orbital relationships between certain planets are also proportionally "golden." For example, the relationship between Jupiter and Saturn is such that over a 60-year period Jupiter makes five revolutions around the Sun. Saturn takes 28 years to make a complete revolution around the sun, and in astronomy this is referred to as a person's "Saturn returning." By marking the position of Saturn at the end of each of Jupiter's orbital cycles, a golden-proportioned pentagon and pentagram are traced out in space.

First studied by Descartes in 1638, the logarithmic spiral wonderfully unfolds from within itself, a curious property, which, in a way, means that it makes visible the invisible, thus creating something from seemingly nothing. Another fascinating property of the nautilus spiral is that as it unfolds, its numbers reach towards a resolution of the ineffable phi, becoming ever closer but never reaching its goal. The human ear is based upon the same spiral, including the delicate inner section known as the cochlea that receives vibrations from the outside world. The human embryo also develops along the same spiral shape.

VESICA PISCIS

The Vesica Piscis is a symbol made from two circles of the same radius, intersecting in such a way that the center of each circle lies on the circumference of the other. The Latin phrase *Vesica Piscis* literally means the "bladder of the fish" because of its vague resemblance. It is a symbol of infinity, and it is easily one of the most profound geometrical images of ancient and modern times. It is the metaphorically opening to the womb or the vulva. It is the geometric pattern from which all forms are born. It also illustrates the "Jesus Fish" symbol. The Vesica Piscis has been used as a symbol within Freemasonry—most notably in the shapes of the collars worn by officiants of the Masonic rituals. Vesica Piscis also has the meaning of "division from unity." In other words, we have lost our way, and this is a way to return to the correct path. This almond shape is traditionally known as the opening from whence all of creation will be birthed. However, as a consequence of this archetypal rupture, all oppositions now come into being: light and dark, order and chaos, yin and yang, and of course, in conjunction with the dawn of being born is the concept of good accompanying its twin, evil.

The Vesica Piscis is the crucible of the creating process. It is a clear symbol of the fusion of opposites and a passageway through the world's apparent polarities, the geometric image through which light was born. The shape is also the geometry for the human eye. Like the splitting of the atom or the Big Bang, the second act of sacred geometry splits apart that which was whole and perfect in order to bring duality into creation. For if there is only unity and wholeness, then there can never be diversity and variety. Amidst this primordial schism, the one begins to divide—like the first division of the human egg— self-similar circle is brought into being—the one becomes two, and polarity is born.

THE PATTERNS EMERGE

The geometry of seven interconnected circles, called the Seed of Life, is considered to be the basic unit of information necessary for the formation of all material substance. The next geometric power symbol, called the Flower of Life, activates energy coding in the mind, and helping one to access one's "light body." The Seed of Life represents the emergence of the primal language of the universe—pure shape and proportion. Each of these interlocking circle designs begin to unlock memories that are deep within our being, and are a primary energy pattern that has a resonance with all things within and around us.

The Tree of Life is one of the most ancient and profound teachings of the awareness of universal life force energies and the light body. Along with the Seed of Life, it is part of the geometry that parallels the cycle of the fruit tree. When these two forms are superimposed upon each other, that relationship becomes apparent. The Tree of Life is most widely recognized as the geometric design that is the basis for the Jewish or Hebrew Kabbalah, the ancient system of mystical Judaism. But the Kabbalah did not originate with the ancient Hebrews, as the Tree of Life image can be found carved over 5,000 years ago on two sets of three pillars at the Karnak temple, located in Luxor, Egypt. As with all of these images, they are outside any race, culture, or religion. They are patterns that are intimately connected with nature. In a related pattern, each circle within the Tree of Life is either the length or width of the Vesica Piscis.

The flowing torus pattern is the first shape to emerge out of the genesis pattern. It governs many aspects of life including the human heart with its seven muscles that form a torus. The torus is, literally, an energy shape that surrounds all life forms, all atoms, and all cosmic bodies such as planets, stars and galaxies. It is the primary shape in existence.

FLOWER OF LIFE

The Flower of Life was known in ancient times and can be found in the Temple of Osiris, as well as in Romania, Israel, China and many other global locations. The knowledge of the Flower of Life was so sacred that it could not be allowed to become common knowledge. The basic understanding is that everything in the universe is geometric, its people, trees, animals, planets, solar systems, and stars. Everything in the universe comes out of this single pattern. The Metatron's Cube is derived from the Flower of Life, and form the five Platonic Solids: the tetrahedron; hexahedron; octahedron; dodecahedron; and, icosahedron; that make up the entire universe. As noted, every element in the Periodic Table of Elements has a geometric relationship to one of the five Platonic Solids.

The Flower of Life is the modern name given to a geometrical figure composed of multiple evenly-spaced, overlapping circles. They are arranged to form a flower-like pattern with a sixfold symmetry, similar to a hexagon. The center of each circle is on the circumference of six surrounding circles of the same diameter. It is considered by some to be the quintessential symbol of sacred geometry, and is said to contain ancient and religious values depicting the fundamental forms of space and time. In this sense, it is a visual expression of the connections life weaves through all sentient beings, and it is believed to contain a type of Akashic Record of basic information and comprising all living things.

Leonardo da Vinci studied the Flower of Life's form and its mathematical properties. He drew the Flower of Life itself, as well as various components such as the Seed of Life. He drew geometric figures representing shapes such as the Platonic Solids, a sphere, and a torus, and also used the Golden Ratio of phi in his artwork, all of which may have emerged from the Flower of Life design.

There are many spiritual beliefs associated with the Flower of Life. Depictions of the five Platonic Solids are found within the symbol of Metatron's Cube, which may have originated from the Flower of Life pattern. These Platonic Solids are geometrical forms which are said to act as a template from which all life springs. The Flower of Life eventually bears fruit, and with added mathematical complexity, becomes Metatron's Cube and the Tree of Life. Everything that modern science knows about the elements and reality are tied together through the Platonic Solids, all of which come out of Metatron's Cube, which is formed out of the Fruit of Life, which comes from the Flower of Life, which is made by spirit. The Flower of Life is not only tied to everything in the universe, but to consciousness and spirit as well.

THE EGG AND FRUIT OF LIFE

The Egg of Life symbol is composed of seven circles taken from the design of the Flower of Life. The shape of the Egg of Life is said to be the shape of a multi-cellular embryo in its first hours of creation. The Egg of Life is the pattern that connects the harmonies of music and the electromagnetic spectrum.

The Fruit of Life manifests its delineation from the Flower of Life. There are 61 circles in the Flower of Life, and 13 circles in the Fruit of Life. The Fruit of Life is said to be the blueprint of the universe, containing the basis for the design of every atom, molecular structure, life form, and everything in existence.

The 13-circle arrangement of the Fruit of Life emerges from a series of intersecting circles placed in radial symmetry to form the approximation of a hexagon, known as the Seed of Life, or the Genesis Pattern. The Seed of Life arrangement begins first with a single circle which is then intersected by a second circle, so that the circumference of each of the two circles travel through the center of the other, creating the so-called Vesica Pisces.

Adding five more circles in radial symmetry creates the Seed of Life, and then after one expands this initial form by adding more circles in the same Vesica Pisces manner while removing earlier circles, the Flower of Life then emerges. From further expansion, the Fruit of Life emerges. Connecting the centers of each of the 13 circles of the Fruit of Life forms the Metatron's Cube.

The seven circles in the Egg of Life can be related to the Seven Days of Creation; Seven Seals of Revelation; the seven continents on Earth; seven oceans; or the seven seas. It can also represent the seven visible colors of the electromagnetic spectrum; the seven visible colors of the rainbow; the seven notes in an octave (the 8th making a quantum leap); the seven main chakras—or energy systems of the body; the seven classical planets in our solar system, that in turn give us the seven days of the week.

VECTOR EQUILIBRIUM = HEXAGON

Vector Equilibrium is the omnidirectional closest packing around a nucleus. Triangles can be subdivided into greater and greater numbers of similar units. The number of modular subdivisions along any edge can be referred to as the frequency of a given triangle. In geometry, a vertex is a special kind of point that describes the corners or intersections of geometric shapes. In a triangular grid, each vertex may be expanded to become a circle or sphere showing the inherent relationship between the closest packed spheres and triangulation. The frequency of triangular arrays of spheres in the plane is determined by counting the number of intervals, rather than the number of spheres on a given edge.

A hexagram is a six-pointed geometric star figure, the compound of two equilateral triangles. The intersection is a regular hexagon. While generally recognized as a symbol of Jewish identity, it is used also in other historical, religious and cultural contexts; for example in Islam, Freemasonry, and Eastern religions, as well as in occultism. The Star of David, or the hexagram shape, represents perfect balance. In 3-D form, the hexagon becomes the merkabah. Specifically, the geometry described above is called "sacred geometry" because this particular geometry is found in the creation patterns of all things in creation. Indeed, everything in the universe is frequency and vibration, and this is scientific fact. This vibration is also infinite, and flows harmonically through octaves, and it permeates through color, music, and even the chakras.

A NEW UNDERSTANDING IN A NEW ERA

We are in the midst of an enormous transition. The old world is dying and a new one is being born. Amidst cultural and societal changes, a spiritual shift is also occurring. Many people around the world find themselves on the verge of something quite vast, yet indescribable. The pathway to penetrating its mysteries is ultimately through the heart, not the mind. This is the time of a "Great Initiation," forecast thousands of years in advance. Everyone is going through the most difficult "facing of the self" they can possibly handle at this time, or the archetypical "Dark Night of the Soul." Sacred geometry helps us to shift into the new paradigm, and move with the changes rather than be overwhelmed by the circumstances of great change. It provides the keys to unlock our potential, and opening our minds, hearts and souls as we enter the long-prophesied Golden Age of Enlightenment.

We must take an inter-dimensional journey through the inner workings of nature to experience the profound order and sublime beauty that exists on the archetypal planes. Sacred geometry is the morphogenic structure behind reality. It demonstrates the laws of creation through geometric shapes, forms and patterns. We have a natural affinity for these geometries because they contain the same ratios and proportions that we have within us. By *connecting* with sacred geometry, a person contemplates the *Mysterium*

Magnum, or the "Great Design." By studying the nature of these patterns, forms and relationships, and their connections, insight may be gained into the mysteries—the laws and lore of the universe. And by assimilating these geometries into our consciousness, we introduce healthy working systems into our reality. The more we understand natural law, the more we can apply the harmony that is apparent in nature as a more powerful force in our own lives.

In our reality, energy, vibration or frequency all range from a high of "God," to a low of matter. Rising from matter we have levels of sound, light and *the unnamed*, which may also include intention. All of these are organized in patterns, and these patterns are the essence of sacred geometry. Another aspect of sacred geometry is sacred symbols, which is where we will go next.

One of the mathematical products of the Sacred Mean is the spiral, commonly found in nature. The Golden Spiral can be found in the tiniest sub-atomic particles of the microcosm to spiral galaxies of the macrocosm. That's why when this crop circle appeared in 2008 near Barbury Castle, Wiltshire, the design was well-received. It shows ten notches within the spiral, with the tenth digit even having been correctly rounded up. The distance between each of those marks corresponds to a digit of Pi. This complex crop circle is a cryptic representation of one of the most fundamental symbols in mathematics, and a perfectly coded image of a complex equation. This 150-foot geometric spectacle also depicts fractal geometry. Fractals are objects that contain small patterns within a larger but similar pattern.

The five Platonic solids

The Tetrahedron   The Cube   The Octahedron   The Dodecahedron   The Icosahedron

The five regular solids discovered by the Ancient Greek mathematicians are:

The **Tetrahedron**:	4 vertices	6 edges	4 faces	each with 3 sides
The **Cube**:	8 vertices	12 edges	6 faces	each with 4 sides
The **Octahedron**:	6 vertices	12 edges	8 faces	each with 3 sides
The **Dodecahedron**:	20 vertices	30 edges	12 faces	each with 5 sides
The **Icosahedron**:	12 vertices	30 edges	20 faces	each with 3 sides

The solids are regular because the same number of sides meet at the same angles at each vertex and identical polygons meet at the same angles at each edge.
These five are the only possible regular polyhedra.

The aesthetic beauty and symmetry of the Platonic Solids have made them a favorite subject of geometers for thousands of years. They are named for the ancient Greek philosopher Plato who theorized that all of the classical elements were constructed from the regular solids.

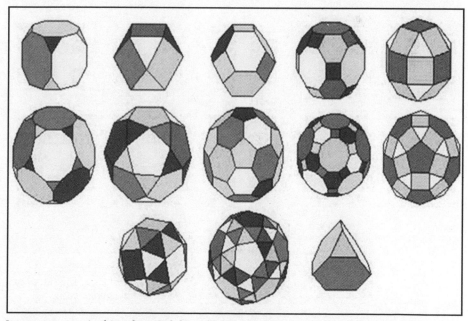

In geometry an Archimedean Solid is a highly symmetric, semi-regular convex polyhedron composed of two or more types of regular polygons meeting in identical vertices. They are distinct from the Platonic Solids, which are composed of only one type of polygon meeting in identical vertices. The term "identical vertices" are usually taken to mean that for any two vertices, there must be an isometry of the entire solid that takes one vertex to the other.

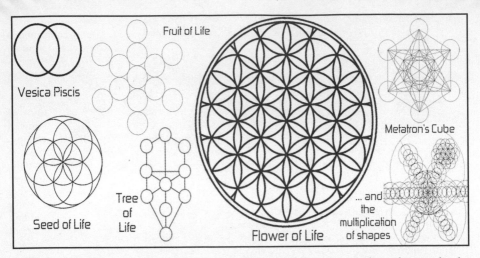

When two opposite waves collide they form a "Vesica Piscis." Science explains this as a dipole. Pairs of waves vibrating against each other produce a sound or energy, two waves colliding and vibrating together form the hexagonal structure and the Vesica Piscis, causing a potential for mass creation. Inside the Vesica Pisces is represented the Seed of Life, which when multiplied becomes the Flower of Life. From this division of unity arises the Tree of Life. The recursion concept displays itself even more when one takes into account that we exist within the gridwork of sacred geometry. Each and every part of our being and our universe is contained within the gridwork that we know as Metatron's Cube. Magic and alchemy start here, with the idea that there is another realm of conscious attainment.

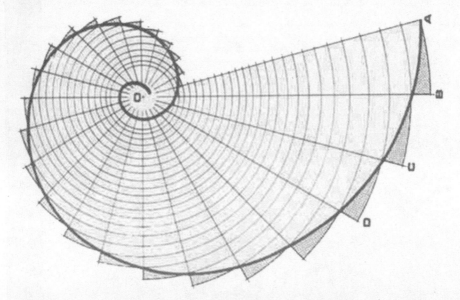

Sacred geometry may be understood as a worldview grounded in pattern recognition combined with a complex system of religious symbols and structures involving space, time and form. According to this belief, the basic patterns of existence, such as the Golden Spiral, are perceived as sacred. By making a personal connection with these shapes, a person may then contemplate the *Mysterium Magnum*, or the Great Design. By studying the nature of these patterns, forms and relationships, plus their connections, personal insight may be gained into the mysteries—the laws, lore and structure of the universe.

< The Fibonacci sequence is Mother Nature's numbering system. This sequence appears everywhere in nature, from the leaf arrangement in plants, to the pattern of the florets of a flower, the bracts of a pinecone, within a conch shell, or the scales of a pineapple. The Fibonacci numbers are therefore applicable to the growth of every living thing, including a single cell, a grain of wheat, a hive of bees, and even all of humankind.

Fractals reveal a hidden "order" underlying all seemingly chaotic events. The fractals are intricate and beautiful. They repeat basic patterns, but with an infinity of variations and forms. Geometric diagrams can be contemplated as still moments revealing a continuous, timeless, universal action generally hidden from our sensory perception. Thus, a seemingly common mathematical activity can become a discipline for intellectual and spiritual insight. The worldview emerging from this scientific research is new, and yet at the same time, very ancient.

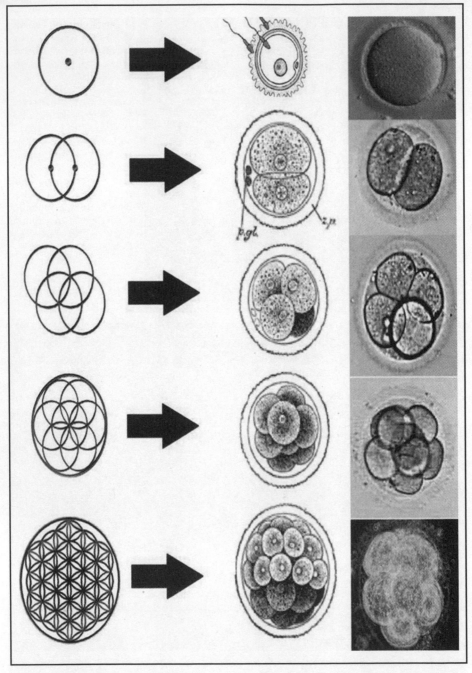

The principle elements of sacred geometry, along with life itself, begin with the circle. Overlay two circles and the Vesica Piscis is formed. Within the Vesica Piscis an equilateral triangle, a pentagon, then a hexagon can be formed. The seven days of creation can be seen in the seven circles of the Seed of Life. Finally, the ancient and sacred geometric symbol known as the Flower of Life represents the dynamics of division in the human cell.

THE EGYPTIAN FLOWER OF LIFE

A mysterious relief of the Flower of Life pattern found in the
6,000 years old Osirian Temple, Abydos, Egypt
is holographically burned into the atomic structure of the rock.

< At 6,000 years old, the Flower of Life at Abydos, Egypt is the oldest known rendering of this very sacred geometrical pattern.

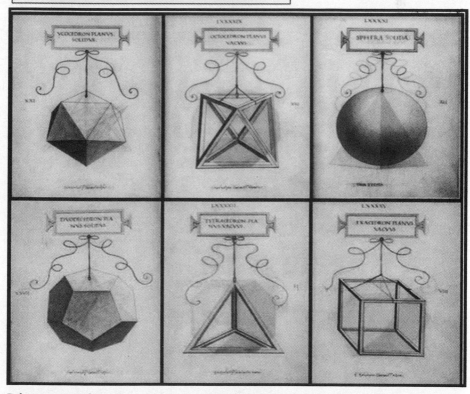

Below is a page from Leonardo da Vinci's sketches of geometric shapes. More precisely, da Vinci illustrated *Divina proportione*, supplying sixty plates for the work, and this is one of the pages. For the Platonic Solids, Da Vinci supplied two views: a plane view and a "vacua" or empty view where he removed the sides to better reveal the complete structure of the polyhedron. These "nets" of vertices and edges illustrate the artist's graphic genius.

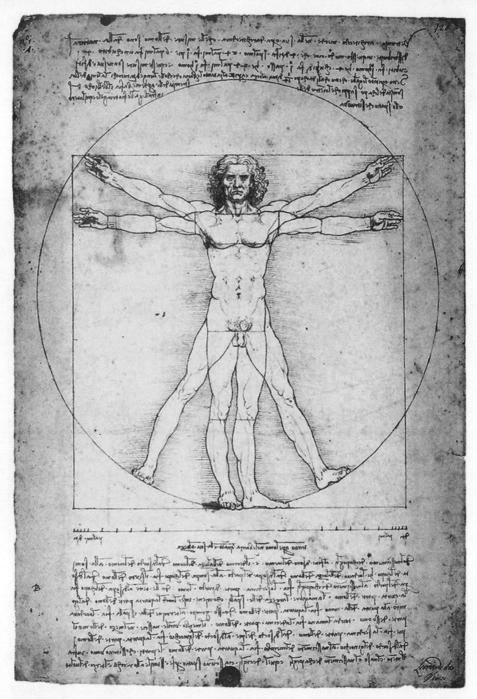

This famous illustration represents a cornerstone of Leonardo da Vinci's attempts to relate man to nature. Leonardo envisaged the great picture chart of the human body he had produced through his anatomical drawings, and Vitruvian Man as a *cosmografia del minor mondo*, or "cosmography of the microcosm." He regarded the workings of the human body as an analogy for the workings of the universe.

SACRED SYMBOLS

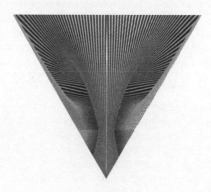

"Every phenomenon on Earth is symbolic, and each symbol is an open gate through which the soul, if it is ready, can enter into the inner part of the world, where you and I and day and night are all one." –German author Hermann Hesse

SACRED symbols are the language of the universe. They have the ability to lift the veil of who we really are, which is the underlying geometry of humanity, cell division, and many other images that encode our reality. The subliminal threshold has been crossed by mystics throughout time by use of images, myths, folklore and symbols. The archetypes and icons of geometry are absolutely perfect, unchanging, and timeless realities springing directly from the "God Mind." Science is in agreement that the universe is composed of vibration and frequency, and the principles of these sacred symbols are directly correspondent to all waveform phenomena. Sacred geometry and symbology can be viewed as vibration on the visual, time and space planes.

Symbols are powerful images representing intricate issues. Confucius observed that "signs and symbols rule the world, not words nor laws." Yet, the same symbol can have different interpretations in different cultures and at different times. Such is the case with the swastika associated with Nazi Germany's absolute evil. Historically in the Far East, however, the swastika is a symbol of the Sun's yearly path. It is regarded as a good luck symbol, and represents reincarnation in India even to this day. The Sphinx of Giza is another potent symbol of esoteric ideas, as it is a surviving icon of pre-sands Egypt, back when the land of northern Africa was a lush oasis. An ultimate esoteric question is the "Riddle of the Sphinx," which asks what begins on four legs, moves to two legs, and finishes on three legs? The answer is a person, who crawls on all fours as a baby, walks on two legs as an adult, and walks with a cane in old age.

Symbols, like sacred geometry, also have an unconscious appeal, that is often perceived as beauty. Perhaps the reason why we feel so imbued with awe when we gaze upon sacred architecture is because God can be encountered in the mirror of bio-architecture. Gothic architecture is an example that appears to capture celestial proportions and anchor it in the terrestrial realms. This is because architecture reflects back to us the magnificence of the divine proportion within our own human canon. For example, the place where the elbow bends, where the arm divides into two sections is mathematically 21:34, or the phi ratio of 1:1.618, which is identical to the mathematics of flowers like the sunflower floret which has 21 spirals going clockwise and 34 going counter-clockwise. It is in such realizations that we can have a peak experience, even though unaware or unconscious of why were are feeling exhilaration.

SEIZING THE SYMBOL

A case can be made that traditional symbols form a visual shorthand for ideas, concepts, and language, yet their functions and meaning extend far beyond that basic explanation. For thousands of years, symbols have enabled artists and craftsmen to embody and reinforce beliefs about human life through immediate and powerful images. Architects seized upon the principles of sacred geometry and incorporated them into their designs. Even mystics developed visual symbols to help them express the eternal. By such a measure, symbols rule the world—not words, nor laws.

What if the cabal, in their designs for a New World Order, inherited an array of powerful symbols and teachings which were originally positive, but have since been dreadfully contorted into something very negative? Maybe the elite possess the true secrets regarding our reality. It is believed that their symbolism and numerology can be used to decipher these secrets. The Illuminati self-expose their agenda to a certain extent. They believe symbolism gives them power to operate. This is why buildings, movies, cartoons and video games are full of Masonic symbols. But the truth is that power does not lie within the symbols; rather it is the interpretation coming from our conscious, subconscious and superconscious mind which make certain symbols seem more powerful than others. Those who would control public opinion, and influence what we deem valuable, hide from public exposure for just that reason. They also do it so people argue amongst themselves over what is valid and what is not, and even, whether invisible controllers actually exist. For example, it would be logical to think that a secret society would never give hints about their existence if they wish to remain hidden. That is exactly what they want you to think, so you can deny their existence. They are extremely clever.

The symbol most often used by the Illuminati is the pyramid with the one eye, used in many different forums. The most popular is on the back of the one-dollar bill which has a pyramid with the "Eye of Providence" at the apex. Just to give a vague idea of how much evidence exists for those who look, here is another example of both numerology and symbolism. We've all heard of the number 666 as the representation of Satan, or a great evil. But it is just a number! Or is it? This number is divisible in many different ways. The Washington Monument, designed by a Freemason named Robert Mills, is 666 feet in size, 555 feet tall, and 111 feet deep, making it 666 feet long, or looked at another way, the height of the obelisk itself is 555.5 feet, which equals 6,666 inches. Coincidence? Consider also that at the ground level, each side of the monument measures 55.5 feet long, or 666 inches. For us to understand Masonic symbolism, it is important we first understand the general meaning of symbols.

SYMBOLIC MEANINGS

The Swiss psychiatrist and influential thinker Carl Jung believed that symbols occur with the same meaning across individual and cultural boundaries, and language makes no exception. He called the sum total of these symbols the "collective unconscious." Carl Jung was obsessed with symbols, the collective unconscious, and the notion of synchronicity in our lives. He said synchronicity can be explained as the experience of two or more events, unlikely to occur together by chance, being observed to occur together in a meaningful manner. In laymen's terms, synchronicities can be viewed as "meaningful coincidences." In Jung's major contribution to an expanded formulation of analytical psychology, he explored the concept of symbolism through an examination of within the human psyche and analyzed the role symbols play in religion, mythology, alchemy, astrology, sociology, literature, art and dreams. After extensive research into the foundations of astrology, and a brilliant integration of his findings with mythical concepts, Jung came to the conclusion that astrology has deep, mystical and spiritual underpinnings. It appears that the Masons, among others, are very much in tune with these. These universal concepts and symbols are, as indicated above, often referred to as archetypes—the recognizable prototype or original model upon which all other concepts are patterned. The Masons apparently grasped the power of their practical use.

Symbols also have a very dark side. They can be utilized as effective tools for instilling specific belief systems and fear into the mass population, usually subliminally. The biblical concept of Satan as the serpent, coiled around the Tree of Knowledge of Good and Evil, is one such potent symbol. For those who believe the world is being run by a highly organized and ruthless cult which still retains great power worldwide, fear-based symbols are no laughing matter. These are tools used by powerful individuals who practice a secret religion that is most certainly not Christianity. This worldwide cult has a unique belief system, based on Lucifer, who might very well be a shape-shifting winged extraterrestrial of the Draco Prime reptilian variety. This would explain all the vampire stories, movies and imagery of shape-shifting bloodsucking monsters and archetypical gargoyles. It is disturbing to think that there could be such a bloodthirsty group, obsessed with ancient mystery school teachings, who wish to sacrifice innocent people to achieve their goals. To them, Lucifer is considered the "light bearer," whom they regard as being misunderstood. They draw a clear distinction between Lucifer, who can be summoned by ritualistic means, and Satan, who they believe is only a myth.

When we awaken and realize that we have been controlled and manipulated by fear, even subconsciously by symbolism, and thus keeping us in a state of low vibration, we immediately begin to shift the balance. When we inject more love, peace, harmony, and compassion into our lives, and out to the world around us, quantum mechanics restructures the geometric patterning of the entire universe, which can enable us to unify as one. Once we reinterpret and reclaim the symbols, our awakened vision will transform them into their rightful role as powerful and positive images for humans. The following are some of the most potent symbols used throughout recorded history.

THE EYE OF HORUS

The Eye of Horus, also called the Eye of Ra, is usually found personified in the goddess *Wadjet*. It was an ancient Egyptian symbol used for protection and symbolized royal power. Legend has it that Wadjet was the daughter of Atum, the first god of the universe. He created her as his "eye," which may be represented as the third eye of wisdom. The name *Wadjet* is derived from *wadj* meaning "green," hence "the green one," and was known to the Greeks and Romans as the "risen one," as depicted by the image of a cobra rising up in protection. The cobra is seen on many pharaoh headdresses, and represents the fiery eye of the Sun.

Symbolically, the Eye of Horus represents the pineal gland, often depicted as a pine cone. Horus was believed to rule in all parts of the created world, such as the sky, the Earth, and the underworld. The Eye of Ra represents the light of the sun god Ra, which represents eternal life. Light is the electromagnetic radiation of a wavelength that is visible to the human eye. The sun god Ra, the god of light, is associated with the pine cone, and subsequently the pineal gland, or the third eye.

Egyptian lore relates that Isis gave birth to Osiris's posthumous son, Horus. The Statue of Liberty in New York Harbor is thought by some scholars to be a thinly veiled symbol of the Egyptian goddess Isis. She is regarded as the female aspect of Lucifer in the hidden occult religion that exists to this day. This claim is illustrated by the beams of light radiating from Lady Liberty's head, and the torch that symbolizes the "sacred fire of antiquity," also known as a knowledge of the "mysteries." Also, the book she holds symbolizes the hidden teachings of an underground organization, an occult group that flash their symbols above ground.

THE ANKH

This characteristic cross symbol with an oval top evolved over 5,000 years ago in African civilization and culture. In many ways, the ankh is a symbol that is beyond religion, as it depicts the universe, and it represents all people. The loop at the top of the ankh symbolizes the feminine womb which is also identified as eternal life, while the elongated lower section represents the masculine aspect of the penis. These two sacred units come together in the ankh and form life. It has long been a symbol for personal power to give and sustain life. Because of its powerful appeal, the ankh was used in cultural rituals involving royalty. It is typically associated with the elements such as water, air, and the sun, as well as with the Egyptian gods, who are frequently pictured carrying an ankh.

The ankh is the oldest metaphysical symbol known to humanity. It is commonly regarded to mean "life" in the language of ancient Kemet, renamed Egypt by the Greeks. To the ancient Egyptians, the ankh symbol is representative of divine life and divine creation. The Ankh, also portrayed as the key of life, the key of the Nile, or *crux ansata*, was the Egyptian hieroglyphic character that reads "eternal life." Egyptian gods are often portrayed carrying it by its loop, or bearing one in each hand, arms crossed over their chests. The ankh appears frequently in Egyptian tomb paintings and other art, often at the fingertips of a god or goddess in images that represent the deities of the afterlife conferring the gift of life on the Egyptian's mummy—thought to symbolize the act of conception. For ancient Egyptians, it also symbolized the unity of opposites, the creation of life, and the unity of masculine and feminine forces in the universe. It is symbolic of the union of male and female and the conceiving of offspring, such as the Chinese symbol of yin and yang representing the positive and negative forces in the universe. The Isisian codes of ancient Egypt were the original and the primary occult code. Additionally, an ankh was often carried by Egyptians as an amulet, either alone or in connection with two other hieroglyphs that mean "strength" and "health." Mirrors of beaten metal were also often made in the shape of an ankh.

The Egyptian ankh and the Christian cross both symbolize the vertical and horizontal axis of our existence. Horizontal is the third dimensional world all around us, where the vertical connects us to above. The vertical, the ascendant, connects us to objective love. Subjective love is conditional. Objective love is unconditional. We must start with love for ourselves, then love can radiate to others. In the end, love is the answer no matter what the question. Focus on service to others before service to oneself, and when the purpose is love, they are one and the same.

CHRISTIAN CROSS

The Christian cross, seen as a representation of the instrument of the crucifixion of Jesus Christ, is the best-known religious symbol of Christianity. The cross-shaped sign, represented in its simplest form by a crossing of two lines at right angles, greatly antedates, in both East and West, the introduction of Christianity, and goes back to a very remote period of human civilization. The Catholic Church still annually celebrates what is called the "Feast of the Triumph of the Cross."

Of course the cross has other arcane uses, and by extension, esoteric practices. The ancient practice of alchemy, the long-revered art that sought to turn lead into gold, is often thought of today as a pseudo-science. But it has also been used throughout the centuries as a metaphor for personal transformation. The process of removing impurities to elevate something into something else that is greater, more special, and more potent, is what most Christian Masons desire. "Take good men, and make them grow into something more special" is a Masonic maxim. Freemason initiates go through a ritual that's meant to be intense and startling. First, the subject's vision is removed with a "hoodwink" placed over his head. Then a master Mason—dressed as the grim reaper—issues a warning: "If you persevere you will be purified, you will overcome darkness, you will be enlightened. But if your soul is fearful, do not proceed." The disturbing part of this ritual that gets very little mention is that initiates swear to never reveal any of the secrets of the Masons on penalty of death. It is stated that "the penalty for revealing Freemason secrets is supposed to be gory death." Those who elect to continue are then led into a place the Masons call a "chamber of reflection" where the hoodwink is removed. At this point the initiate is presented with a very interesting image. You would think a Christian cross would be prominent, yet the chamber contains a human skull and bones, elements used in alchemy, and a pen and paper where the initiate can write a last will and testament. The symbols are meant to help initiates think about the fact that their life is not going to last forever, and usually has a profound effect. This kind of macabre symbolism has driven conspiracy theorists through the centuries to think that Freemasons practice a sort of black magick. But Masonic rituals are not so alien to other practices. If a Catholic chapel, for example, pulled the shades and you heard through the grapevine that people were kneeling under a crucifix, an instrument of torture and consuming blood and flesh ritualistically, one might say, "What a terrible organization." Thus, the major difference here is that the Masons and other secret societies shroud their rituals in secrecy, while the Catholic Church performs theirs openly.

SEAL OF SOLOMON

In alchemy, the combination of the fire and water symbols, the up and down triangles, is known as the Seal of Solomon. This symbol represents the combination of opposites and transmutation. By combining the alchemical symbols for fire, the upwards triangle, and the downwards triangle for water, the alchemical symbols for earth and air are also created. The downward facing triangle is divided along the center by the base line of the opposite triangle. This is the alchemical symbol for Earth. Conversely, the upward facing triangle divided by the base line of the downward triangle is the alchemical symbol for air. The Seal of Solomon represents all that is unified in perfect balance. It is also the symbol of the Spirit Wheel, known as the Merkabah.

The mythical Solomon's Temple was located in what today is Jerusalem, a structure that supposedly housed the ultra-sacred Ark of the Covenant. Although there is no concrete evidence that it ever existed, Solomon's Temple functioned as a religious focal point in ancient Judaism for the worship of a monotheistic deity. Two temples were built on the same location and subsequently destroyed. Solomon's Temple, also known as the First Temple, was constructed by the wise King Solomon, leader of the ancient Israelites, on the location called Mount Moriah in Jerusalem. Similar to Muslims sending their prayers toward Mecca, Mount Moriah is the holiest site in Judaism, and it is the place Jews turn towards during prayer. Due to its extreme sanctity, most Jews will not walk on the Mount in order to avoid unintentionally entering the area where the Holy of Holies stood, since according to Rabbinical law, some aspect of the "divine presence" is still present at the site. It was from the Holy of Holies that the priestly caste communicated directly with God. Christianity, as it emerged out of the Second Temple of Judaism, stood in competition with other religions advocating "pagan monotheism," including Neo-Platonism, Mithraism, Gnosticism, Manichaeanism, and the cult of Dionysus. A third temple is prophesied to be built on the Temple Mount by the Jews at some future date, but the dilemma for Jews is that a Muslim temple called Dome of the Rock currently resides upon Mount Moriah.

FREEMASONRY SYMBOLS

The first Masons were said to literally be stonecutters and engineers. They were the men who built the great cathedrals of Europe—and who guarded their trade secrets faithfully. The Freemasons have long recognized the knowledge of sacred geometry and their deeper symbolic meanings. The central Masonic symbol is the compass, used for mathematics and sacred geometry. A modern compass is a navigational instrument for determining a direction relative to the Earth's magnetic poles. It consists of a magnetized pointer, usually marked on the north end, and free to align itself with Earth's magnetic field. Prior to the introduction of the compass, position, destination, and direction of the sea were primarily determined by the sighting of landmarks, supplemented with the observation of the positions of celestial bodies. The stonecutter tradesmen began another system associated with Freemasonry—the so-called "three degrees"—that of the apprentice, fellow of the craft, and the master mason. These designations are still used within Freemasonry today, as are the symbols of a square and compass—the primary stone mason's tools—along with the letter "G," signifying both "geometry" and "God." At meetings, Masons wear elaborately decorated lambskin aprons, symbolic representations of those worn by working stone masons. Some say there's much more to Freemasonry—a deeper, older and more mystical side, beyond that which is portrayed to the world.

Freemasonry has been a vessel, a channel, and a receptacle for some very ancient ideas. In fact, some Masons say the group originated during biblical times in the Holy Land and were the builders of King Solomon's temple. Many Masonic symbols are even older than that. The hexagram is featured within and on the outside of many Masonic temples as a decoration. The hexagram, one of the world's most ancient symbols, may have been designed into the structures of King Solomon's temple, from which Freemasons have been inspired in their philosophies and studies. The all-seeing eye, the pyramid, and the obelisk are all images that draw very deeply upon symbols of pre-Christian religion because it was believed to be a part for a chain of a spiritual search for truth that was far older than any modern or contemporary religion. 33 is a very important number to the Freemasons in ancient mysticism, and there's a reason that Jesus Christ was said to be 33 years old at the time of his death. There is a reason that there are 33 vertebrae in our spine—and that much of Freemasonry has to do with the concept of the body as a temple. 33 repeats throughout the Masonic house of the temple. For example, there are 33 columns or pillars, each 33 feet tall. It is no coincidence that the capstone on the Washington Monument weighs exactly 3,300 pounds, thereby interpreting that mystical number.

The United Grand Lodge of England is the main governing body of Freemasonry. It is the oldest Grand Lodge in the world, and traces its origin back to 1717. Together with the Grand Lodge of Ireland and the Grand Lodge of Scotland, these three are often referred to by their members as "the home Grand Lodges" or "the Home Constitutions." Many historians believe Masonry traces its roots back farther to the Knights Templar. Others claim it is largely based on the surviving remnants of a highly secretive Roman mystery cult known as Mithraism, renowned for decadent festival celebrations of drinking, dancing and sexual promiscuity. Or, stated another way, Freemasonry came out of Scotland as a revamped version of Mithraism, and spurred on by the influx of the outlawed Knights Templar. Animal sacrifices, mostly of birds, were conducted in the underground Mithraic temples and other pagan mystery schools in the centuries before Christ. The ritual killing of a bull, called a "tauroctony," played a key role in the Mithraic mysteries. If ambitious members were comfortable with animal sacrifices, they could "graduate" to view human sacrifices as also having "spiritual value." Mystery religions, by definition, keep secrets.

Just as Freemasons use symbols during their rituals and degree ceremonies to teach initiates and members about Masonic traditions and values, they also use symbols to identify the officers of the lodge. There are thirteen officers who oversee the business of each local lodge. The head is the Master, followed by Senior and Junior Wardens, Secretary, Treasurer, Senior and Junior Deacons, Senior and Junior Stewards, Marshal, Inner Guard, Tyler, and Chaplain. Many levels of symbology can be found wherever the Freemasons operate. For example, Masonic symbolism is rife within the design of the great monuments and buildings in Washington D.C. Yet not only is this kept hidden from the public, most history books also fail to mention the powerful influence that the Masons had throughout the early years of the establishment of the republic.

To Freemasons, knowledge is equal to power. Then why all the secrecy? It would seem the Freemasons are using the knowledge of sacred geometry to play God on Earth. Freemasons assume that members believed in a supreme being, but that is as far as it goes. Masons can worship Yahweh, Jesus, Allah—or another god of their own choosing. Religious freedom is built into Freemasonry, and many scholars say the Freemasons also built this concept into the U.S. Constitution. One-third of the signers were known to be Freemasons. Most citizens don't know this, nor do they know that America was not founded as a Christian country. It later became a Christian country, but it is important to remember that many of the Founding Fathers were *Deists*. The concepts behind Deism, where a person is regarded as powerful, and that each of us is responsible for our own life, is the underlying and core belief of Freemasonry. Deists believe that a supreme being created the universe, but that being is impersonal. It will not answer your prayers or even hear them, thus the need for Masons to be independent and responsible for their actions. The Founding Fathers, as the Masons, were highly focused on morals and values. Yet as the Masons' power grew in the decades after independence, morals took a back seat as power and corruption moved to the foreground.

The Masons' secret is to keep those outside their fraternity trapped in a fear-based mentality, otherwise known as being in a low vibration. Fear, hate, anger and suspicion can confine a person to the Earthly third-dimensional reality. Withholding knowledge and preventing us from realizing who we really are is a strategy to block our evolving and ascending into the next level of consciousness. Total power equals total control. The cabal—the so-called master controllers—have long traced their roots to Freemasonry. The fraternal order provided an effective cover of secrecy and allowed the highest-ranking members to be recruited into yet another far more secretive group.

The Masons are often linked to other secret societies, and claim an ancient heritage such as that of the Knights Templar, the Rosicrucians, and the Bavarian Illuminati. The Knights Templar, reputed to be some of the fiercest warriors of their time, were officially endorsed by the Catholic Church in the early 12th century. When they became very rich and powerful, as being among the world's first bankers, they became a threat. By the early 14th century, the church and French royalty were largely successful in destroying the entire order. Some believe the superstition around Friday the 13th came from a secret edict issued by the King of France on Friday the 13th of October in 1307, to arrest all members of the order. Only two centuries ago did the Vatican denounce the Masons as being Satanic.

SYMBOLS OF THE ILLUMINATI

The Illuminati began as a secret society under the direction of Jesuit priests. Later, straying from their Jesuit roots, a council of five men, one for each of the points on the pentagram, formed what was called The Ancient and Illuminated Seers of Bavaria. They became high order Luciferian Freemasons, thoroughly immersed in mysticism and the Eastern mental disciplines, and seeking to develop the super powers of the mind. Their alleged plan and purpose was, and remains, world domination for their lord—the "fallen angel" Lucifer.

This then morphed into an 18th century German sect that adopted the name *Illuminati*. They practiced the occult and professed to possess the "light" that Lucifer had retained when he became Satan. This Illuminati group infiltrated Freemasonry in 1780, and established an ethos based on nihilism and the naked lust for worldly power. These are the roots of the current Illuminati, the secret organization that has evolved into a mastodonic nightmare, successfully creating and controlling a shadow government that supersedes several national governments, and in whose hands now lie the destiny of the world. The lengths to which this organization has gone to create the political machinery and influence public sentiment to the degree necessary to promote its self-perpetuating prophecy is mind boggling.

The symbols of the Illuminati illustrate a unique teaching mechanism to explain their "Craft." Each of their letters is fused to a series of numbers, and these numbers are further fused to a series of ciphers. One cannot know the value of any given number save for the contextual material which surrounds the letters. In this definition, "contextual material" includes the letters surrounding any given letter, definitions based on the context where a particular letter may be found, as well as the symbols that may be associated with the letter.

The German word *rothschild* derives from "red shield," a symbol that was displayed over the door of the Bauer family money lending business. The "Red Flag" was the emblem of the revolutionary-minded Jews in Eastern Europe. Recognizing the true significance of the red shield that his father had adopted as his emblem from the "Red Flag," Mayer Amschel Bauer changed the family name to Rothschild in 1743. It was at this point that the House of Rothschild came into being.

Some people don't want us to know the truth about who the Illuminati are in reality. Those who have knowledge have no need to give it to the public, and those to whom it is given who demonstrate any whisper of disloyalty often find themselves receiving nothing and ostracized from the power group. Human nature is what it is, and since humanity is in a state of "triage," a decision must be made to rapidly discern between those who might benefit from an effort of intervention and those who would not benefit from an effort to intervene. An elitist or Illuminist view would simply say that those who are awake have no responsibility for those who are asleep.

To researchers who study occult symbols, the Illuminati and the highest ranking Freemasons offer tantalizing clues which show they are collectively the ones known as Luciferians. Their most popular symbol is the All Seeing Eye, and their most popular occult hand sign is the pinky and index finger "horn." Also peculiar is the number 666, which appears on all bar codes. Any study of popular culture music and films will find all the usual suspects, along with some symbols used for mind control. All the worshiped "gods" are said to be the few surviving generations of Anunnaki reptilians going under various names down through the centuries such as Nimrod, Anubus, Horus, Osiris, Baal, Shamash, Janus, Quetzalcoatl, Baphomet, Moloch, and Lucifer. All these deities feature ether serpent or horn symbols, sometimes incorporating both. The symbols are their secret language, and they have shown the connections down the years by the use of the same symbols, such as those used in Freemasonry, communism and the corporate U.S. government with the "hidden hand" of history.

PENTACLE

A pentacle is an amulet used in magical evocation, generally made of parchment, paper or metal, although it can be made of other materials. It is the symbol of a spirit or energy being evoked. As a trinket, it is often worn around the neck, or placed within the triangle of evocation. Protective symbols may also be included, such as the Seal of Solomon, also called a Pentacle of Solomon. Many varieties of pentacles can be found in the grimoires of Solomonic magic, which gained notoriety during the Middle Ages. Pentacles are also used in some neo-pagan magical traditions, such as Wicca, alongside other magical tools.

The pentagram in witchcraft symbolizes white magic, but is more commonly associated with black magick. The pentagram with one point up symbolizes white magic. The pentagram with two points up represents black magic or Satanism. The devil is depicted with two horns, symbolizing the upside down pentagram. The geometric property of the pentagram is that its lines bisect each other according to the ratios of the Golden Section. In other words, the relationship of AB to BC and of BC to AC is phi. And all other internal divisions of this figure produce the same proportional relationship.

The five-pointed star symbols are derived from traditional "Morning Star" pentagrams and are no longer regularly used in mainstream Christianity. The original trinity in Egypt came from the division of the daytime, the three life spans of the "life" of a day. Horus, representing the morning, was the rising sun, or the Son of God. The "most high" was noon, the highest the sun could be. And the goddess Set, from where we get "sun-set," represents the other 12 hours, the nighttime, the time of darkness, terror, or fright. Such was the basis for some symbols associated with early Christian sects.

Occultistic pentagrams can be seen showing the five Hebrew letters of the "Pentagrammaton" or Y-H-W-Sh-H, the esoteric name attributed to Jesus. Christians commonly used the pentagram to represent the five wounds suffered by Jesus during the Passion Play. The word "occult" comes from the Latin word *occultus* meaning clandestine, hidden or secret, and referring to "knowledge of the hidden." The pentagram also has several associations with Freemasonry.

The pentacle has also long been associated with the divine feminine awakening. The orbit of Venus as viewed from Earth forms the shape of a pentagram. When the pentagram star points upwards, it represents the masculine, reaching toward Father Sky. When it points downwards, it represents the feminine, pulling energy to Mother Earth. With the masculine representation, the top is phallic. With the feminine representation, the top is chalice-like, ready to receive.

MERKABAH LIGHT VEHICLE

M erkabah, also spelled merkaba, is the divine light vehicle allegedly used by ascended masters to connect with and reach those in tune with the higher realms. Merkabah was the Hebrew "chariot of ascension," and the Hebrew word *merkabah* means "chariot," with a general meaning "to ride." It is used in Ezekiel (1:4-26) to refer to the throne-chariot of God, the four-wheeled vehicle driven by four *chayot*, each of which has four wings and the four faces of a man, lion, ox, and eagle.

Mer means "light." *Ka* means "spirit." *Ba* means "body." Light is electromagnetic radiation of all wavelengths, whether visible or not. Thus, the Mer-Ka-Ba means the spirit-body is surrounded by counter-rotating fields of light, the wheels within wheels, and spirals of energy as in our DNA, which transports spirit from the body to one dimension or another. In this grand universe of ours, we are all interconnected. We are parts of the same fabric. We create the same geometry together in the fractal field. From micro to macro, atoms to cosmos, we are all made of the same material. All atoms and particles initially came from the stars.

The star tetrahedron is two tetrahedra in inverse alignment to each other. It is a three-dimensional Star of David, which is the sacred symbol at the center of this form and is the pattern of the etheric light grid that surrounds each human being. The Star of David is the symbol of the merkabah, or vehicle of light, which we all have surrounding us as a light vibration. It has been used by the ascended masters of Ruach haKodesh, enabling them to travel back and forth through the reality of time. They also have the gift of magic, which is procreation and eternal life. This grid is called the merkabah and it is an inter-dimensional vehicle used initially to incarnate spirit into human bodily form. The universal energy of love is the fuel for this vehicle.

In modern esoteric teachings, the Mer-Ka-Ba is an inter-dimensional vehicle consisting of two equally sized, interlocked tetrahedra of light with a common center, where one tetrahedron points up and the other down. This point symmetric form is called a *stella octangula*, or stellated octahedron, which can also be contrived by extending the faces of a regular octahedron until they intersect again.

The Earth and the human body are almost identical energetically. Not only is the Earth's "kundalini energy" very similar to a humans, but even such massive energy fields as the merkabah field, also known as the light body, is exactly the same proportion, and only different in size. Every electromagnetic and geometrical field within the merkabah field of the Earth is exactly identical to every human being on Earth. The Mer-Ka-Ba field is extremely complex, and integrating the five Platonic Solids and other sacred polyhedron shapes. Technically, it is an electromagnetic field that sits at about four degrees, and found primarily within the microwave range—at least in our third dimension—and that is *entirely* geometric in nature. These geometric fields are the foundational building blocks of matter, in so much as they represent the architectural infrastructures wherein shape can take form. This infrastructure is believed to extend through all possible dimensional and parallel universes, and so it is possible for an enlightened being to electromagnetictically change its nature to whatever is appropriate.

THE MOBIUS SHAPES

The Möbius loop is a continuous one-sided surface that can be formed from a rectangular strip by rotating one end 180° and attaching it to the opposite end. It is an infinite surface with only one side and only one edge, thus it has no beginning and no end. For example, if an ant were to crawl along the length of this strip, it would return to its starting point having traversed every part of the strip without ever crossing an edge. Thus, the edge of a Möbius strip is topologically equivalent to the circle. Under the usual embedding of the strip in Euclidean space, as above, this edge is not an ordinary flat circle. It is possible however to embed a Möbius strip in three dimensions so that the edge is a circle. A scientific application was a device called a Möbius resistor, which was an electronic circuit element that had the property of canceling its own inductive reactance. Nikola Tesla patented similar technology in the early 1900s, in which he named the "Coil for Electro Magnets."

The shape of the Möbius strip dates back to ancient times. An Alexandrian manuscript of early "alchemical" diagrams contains an illustration with the visual proportions of the Möbius strip. A model can easily be created by taking a paper strip and giving it a half-twist and then joining the ends of the strip together to form a loop. This fascinating shape expresses transformation. The Möbius strip shape is symbolic of eternal change within stillness itself. Another similarly shaped object is "Ouroboros," which was and is the name for the Great World Serpent encircling the Earth. The word *Ouroboros* is really a term that describes a similar symbol that has been cross-pollinated from many different cultures. This symbol appears principally among the Gnostics and is depicted as a dragon, snake or serpent looping around and swallowing or biting its own tail. In the broadest sense, it is symbolic of time and the continuity of life. The Ouroboros is seen in virtually all ancient cultures, from Egypt and China, to Aztec and Nordic imagery. It was not only a symbol of occultism, but it has turned up in 2001 as a crop circle formation near Badbury, Wiltshire. Plato described a self-eating, circular being as the first living thing in the universe—an immortal, mythologically constructed beast. The Ouroboros symbolizes a connection between humans and God, or the above and below, and represents the conflict of life as well as that life comes out of the drama between life and death, in other words, "my end is my beginning." In a sense, life feeds off itself and thus good and bad connotations can be drawn. It is a single image containing the entire actions of a life cycle—it begets, weds, impregnates, and slays itself, but in a cyclical rather than linear sense. The Ouroboros biting its own tail is symbolic of *self-fecundation*, or the primitive idea of a self-sufficient nature.

The Möbius strip has several curious properties. A line drawn starting from the seam down the middle will meet back at the seam but at the "other side." There are in fact two types of Möbius strips depending on the direction of the half-twist: clockwise and counterclockwise. The Möbius strip is therefore *chiral*, which means right-handed or left-handed, like amino acids.

FRACTALS

Fractals are associated with the mathematics of chaos theory, but they are in fact very ordered. A fractal is an infinite amount of interlocking, self-replicating, and imitating natural objects. They look chaotic but are truly governed by a definite geometry. The essence of measuring or describing a fractal is to isolate the basic pattern, what is called its initial recursive mathematical function. Interestingly, the Fibonacci series is one such function.

Another description of a fractal is a rough or fragmented geometric shape that can be split into parts, each of which is approximately a reduced-size copy of the whole, a property called self-similarity, meaning that any image taken from a particular section of the set can be replicated by zooming in or out, and is infinitely complex. Roots of mathematically rigorous treatment of fractals can be traced back to functions studied by Karl Weierstrass, Georg Cantor and Felix Hausdorff, who studied functions that were analytic, but not differentiable. However, the term fractal was coined by Benoît Mandelbrot in 1975, and was derived from the Latin word *fractus* meaning "broken" or "fractured." The Mandelbrot Set is a pattern of geometric points that repeats within itself.

Fractals do not lose their detail or their proportions when they are magnified or reduced, even to the microscopic level. This property is highly reminiscent of the Golden Mean, or the 1.618 proportion of phi, where the same essential and sacred proportion is retained at every level when the image is scaled up or down. A mathematical fractal is based on an equation that undergoes iteration, a form of feedback based on recursion. Indeed, the qualities of both fractals and phi are concerned with growth. Because they appear similar at all levels of magnification, fractals are often considered to be infinitely complex. Natural objects that are approximated by fractals to a degree include cloud formations, mountain ranges, lightning bolts, coastlines, snow flakes, flowers, various vegetables such as cauliflower and broccoli, and animal coloration patterns.

CROP CIRCLES

Genuine crop circles are based on sacred geometry formations, and appear to be made from spirals of light and energy. Materialization occurs by the spin or motion of spirals and, indeed, crop circles are made within seconds. The Golden Mean spiral spins energy from one state to another by shifts in frequency ranges, and the results are beautiful and sometimes three-dimensional patterns and symbols.

Crop circles are incredible works of geometric art, which is no small undertaking. They do not always appear in fields of crops either; some appear in the snow or sand. Nothing about them is casual, slapdash or unintelligent. Quite the contrary. Their designs are often incredibly clever and inventive; some even border on the realm of genius. Sacred geometry in crop glyphs, created via radiation and sound waves, the study called cymatics, is the key to understanding genuine crop formations and what the non-terrestrial entities are trying to tell us. Sometimes crop circle formations seem to speak of important wisdom and ancient knowledge, yet it is quite impossible to convert that conviction into words. They have iconic design elements from ancient cultures such as Egyptian, Mayan, Hopi, and even Greek. Other designs display cutting edge mathematics showing the relationship between outer expanding infinity and inner expanding infinity. Each pattern is unique, original, and beautifully crafted. Some have standing centers, and others have knots and nests of swirled wheat stems intricately interwoven—but the stalks are never broken. It is believed crop circles are created by some kind of an unseen electromagnetic and sound-wave force, with microwave-like properties. Amazingly, they do not damage the crops in the layering process. *Cymatics* is the study of the effects of sound vibrations on physical matter—such as crop circles. The many geometric patterns that emerge from varying frequencies of vibration could be the ultimate study of sacred symbology.

BEE SYMBOLIC COMMUNICATION

Lastly, humans are not the only species who are able to construct using sacred geometry and detect complex patterns. Bees not only *see* flowers in different colors than we do, but bees also see ultra-violet (UV) light patterns that are invisible to humans. These UV patterns serve as landing zones, guiding the bees to the nectar source. It is sometimes argued that the various species of honeybees are the only invertebrates, and indeed one of the only *non-human* groups to have evolved a system of abstract symbolic communication, where a behavior is used to convey specific information about something in the environment, such as the sounds made by bees when using their wing-vibration to convey specific messages.

The holy Islamic Koran has an interesting take on the bees in the passage 16:68-69. The Koran says "And your Lord inspired the bee to build its hive on the hills and the trees, and on the rooftops of buildings. And (He inspired the bee) to suck the nectar of all kinds of fruit, and Follow The Smooth Path Laid Down By Your Lord. There comes forth from their bellies, a drink of varying Color wherein is healing for men. Verily, in this is indeed a Sign for people who think."

It can be said that sacred geometry and sacred symbols are the organizational basis of all that exists, has existed, and will exist. Found within these patterns are both two and three dimensional shapes that carry archetypal memories. The pineal gland holds the memories of these archetypal experiences and serves as an "Akashic Record" within each of us. The Akashic Records are often described as a huge library in the ether containing all of the experiences of all souls through all incarnations. The pineal gland is the master gland containing access to the records for an individual's various incarnations. As we'll see next, the pineal gland is associated with countless spiritual experiences. There has also been a sustained suppression of its understanding and usage in this modern age.

The All-seeing eye originated in Egypt in the mystery schools, concurrent with the time of Moses, when God physically judged people and led the Israelites out of the land of Egypt by His mighty hand. The All-Seeing Eye was representative of the omniscient powers of Horus, the Sun God. Here is the all-seeing eye of Horus, coming out of the sun, as seen in a Catholic church.

< The emblem of the Theosophical Society not only shows many well-known sacred symbols, but also the Ouroboros serpent eating its tail, which symbolizes the connection of the above and below.

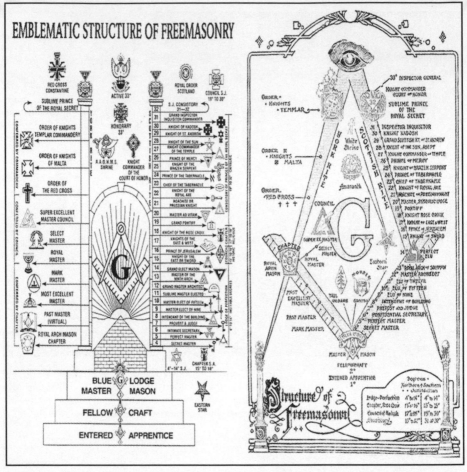

EMBLEMATIC STRUCTURE OF FREEMASONRY

Freemasonry uses the metaphors of operative stonemasons' tools and implements against the allegorical backdrop of the building of King Solomon's Temple to convey what has been described by both Masons and critics as "a system of morality veiled in allegory and illustrated by symbols." Notice the all-seeing eye at the top of the compass on the left image, and the two pillars at the bottom right and left depicting the North and South Poles.

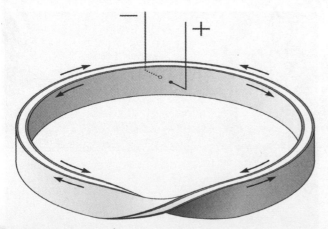

< The Möbius strip is a surface with only one side and only one boundary component, usually bound in the figure-8, representing infinity. The Möbius strip has the mathematical property of being non-orientable. It can be realized as a ruled surface.

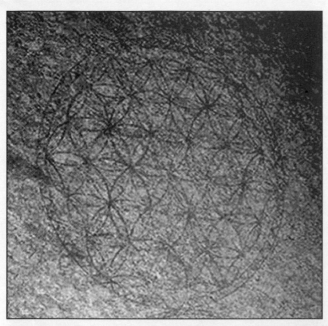

< The Flower of Life in the Osireion, Abydos, Egypt has been laser burned into the atomic structure of the pillar so that even if the rock is chipped, as many have tried, the image can still be seen. We have no current technology to reproduce this technique. The once-underground chambers are the most ancient of all the ancient Egyptian ruins.

Ezekiel's famous "Chariot Vision" etching by Matthaeus Merian (1593-1650). Merkabah, which generally means "to ride," is the throne-chariot of God, the four-wheeled vehicle driven by four *chayot*, Hebrew for "living creatures." Each living creature has four wings and the four faces of a man, lion, ox, and eagle. Notice the wings, man, lion, ox and eagle in the shield.

A truly spectacular crop circle design appeared near Silbury Hill in southern England on July 5th, 2009. It was quickly called the "Quetzalcoatl headdress," because everyone could easily recognize that its primary symbol was a "quetzal feathered crown," once worn by Mayan kings. A similar headdress was later worn by the Aztec Emperor Montezuma when the Spanish invaded his homeland in 1520 CE.

The "PizzaGate" scandal that broke in 2016 revealed a wide use of secret symbols related to pedophilia and Satanism. Famed psychoanalyst Carl Jung wrote "The underlying, primary psychic reality is so inconceivably complex that it can be grasped only at the farthest reach of intuition, and then but very dimly. That is why it needs symbols."

THE PINEAL GLAND

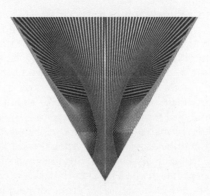

"In this particular body through which this, then, at present is emanating, the gland with its thread known as the pineal gland is the channel along which same then operates, and with the subjugation of the consciousness—physical consciousness—there arises, as it were, a cell from the creative forces within the body to the entrance of the conscious mind, or brain, operating along, or traveling along, that of the thread or cord as when severed separates the physical, the soul, or the spiritual body. ... Keep the pineal gland operating and you won't grow old—you will always be young!" –Edgar Cayce

THROUGHOUT the ages, the pineal gland has been assigned a spiritual role that transcends its hormonal function. For centuries the pineal gland has been associated with paranormal phenomena. Eastern philosophies have tended to view the pineal as an important "chakra" or energy vortex, which, if activated, opens the individual to psychic experiences and cosmic vision.

The pineal gland, the *epiphysis cerebri*, is considered the most powerful and highest source of ethereal energy available to humans. It is a peculiar gland situated between the cerebral hemispheres and attached to the third ventricle. It has long been recognized as initiating psychic powers, such as clairvoyance and seeing auras. To activate the "third eye" and perceive higher dimensions, the pineal and the pituitary gland must vibrate in unison, which is achieved through meditation, chanting, and even sun gazing. In our physical body, Eastern masters have long recognized the connection between heaven and Earth as being within our third-eye center. During meditation, the practitioner is sometimes able to visualize that eye, a single eye, just like our regular eyes, but just one single eye within our brain. It is also called the "mind's eye," the "spiritual eye," or the semi "inner eye," the "wisdom eye" and the "heavenly eye." A mass activation of the pineal gland is a key point in the next stage of human evolution, yet an awakened population is not what the current control group on Earth wants or needs, and they will suppress this expression at any cost. After all, the "union with God" was considered blasphemy in the Christian West for a thousand years, even punishable by death under the Inquisition.

As we have seen, sacred geometry and sacred symbols are the study of shape and form, wave and vibration, and are tools for moving beyond our third dimensional reality. They are literally the language of creation, which exists as the foundation of all matter, and can be the vehicle for spirit. These sacred shapes have been called the "blueprint for all creation," the "harmonic configuration of the soul," and the "divine rhythm which results in manifest experience." They do much more than give us an insight into the workings of the universe and a pattern for all life. Sacred geometry, intricate patterns, and symmetrical symbols assist in opening the pineal gland. They have an additional benefit to the human body. In addition to their ability to balance human energy fields, each may contain complex informational systems that can be used to access healing and growth in many dimensions. But the government is not going to tell you that, nor will the corporate-owned media. They prefer dummy-downed masses who are easily controlled, not an enlightened group of people who have learned the mastery of the most enigmatic powers available to the human brain.

Awakening to the grand secret of the universe is created by a thought-consciousness. A primary physical tool for this awakening is through the activation of the pineal gland. Thought consciousness manifests in physical reality through a geometric blueprint that we call sacred geometry, whose subliminal meanings assists in activating the pineal gland. Sacred geometry is indeed the most practical of all sciences, for through its comprehension we become empowered to create inter-dimensional structures on the physical level that vibrate with spiritual energy and a consciousness of source. "Sacred geometry, like nothing else I have ever seen," observed Karen Prior "has the ability to inspire awe and awaken a very real experience of the world behind the curtain of creation." The pineal gland is a primary gateway to this expanded consciousness.

PINEAL GLAND SUPPRESSION

The active suppression of the pineal gland is one of the biggest conspiracies in the modern age, one which no one knows about. The toxic chemical sodium fluoride, even in weak concentrations, is very damaging and destructive to cellular tissue. Multiple studies show it actually lowers people's IQ scores. Up until the 1990s, no research has ever been conducted to determine the impact of fluoride on the pineal gland. It is now known that the pineal gland is the primary target of fluoride accumulation within the body. A level of 300 parts per million (ppm) of fluoride is capable of inhibiting enzymes. Studies have recently revealed that the soft tissue of the adult pineal gland contains more fluoride than any other soft tissue in the body. MRI scans clearly show a calcified and inactive pineal gland in most Americans tested.

People are starting to demand that the fluoridation of our drinking water be stopped. It has nothing to do with preventing cavities, and everything to do with mass medication without consent. Our government has known for a long time that sodium fluoride is poisonous to mammals, and they know it collects around the pineal gland. Fluoride is an extremely neurotoxic chemical which is intentionally added to drinking water, and thus interrupts the basic function of nerve cells in the brain causing docile submissive behavior and IQ devastation. However, in classic double speak, we are told fluoride is put into our drinking water because it is "good for the teeth," when in fact it creates weak and brittle bones, causes dental cavities, and fosters tooth decay in adults.

Fluoride comes from hydrofluorosic acid, and it will be examined further in the final chapters of the "Control" section. For now it is important to know that fluoride is an accumulative and toxic poison that shuts down the pineal gland, and it has been forced into public water supplies worldwide, especially in the USA. The pineal gland, arguably the most important gland in our body, controls thinking, emotions, hormones, creativity, intuition and much more. It is such an important gland that it is often referred to as the third eye, but it can be retarded and even cease functioning with fluoride accumulation.

THE ADEPTS KNEW

The pineal gland is a small grey gland, about the size of a grain of rice, which is situated between the two hemispheres where the spinal chord reaches up into the brain. A tree-grown pine cone has the same basic shape as the pineal gland, hence the name. The location of the pineal gland is very close to the geometric center of the brain.

Amazingly, the pineal gland has been depicted in ancient Sumerian, Egyptian, and Babylonian artifacts and paintings, which means that our predecessors were aware of its relevance. As far back as 2180 BCE, Egyptian pharaohs were using *schefa-food* to enhance their pineal activity and thereby to heighten their perception, awareness and intuition. The pineal gland has long been called the seat of spiritually divine wisdom. The ancient Egyptians wore crowns that featured a snake or twin serpent protruding from the third eye area of the crown. To the ancient people of Egypt, snakes denoted wisdom. That could be why in Matthew 10:16 of the Bible we are admonished to "be wise as serpents." Egyptian queen Cleopatra used to place a magnet on her forehead to stimulate the pituitary to restore her youthful vigor and enhanced her beauty. She never knew that she already had a magnet in her head called *the pineal*.

In Eastern traditions, the awakening of our third eye is achievable through the practice of yoga, particularly Kundalini Yoga, that teaches of the existence of the so-called ajna chakra, or third eye chakra. The double serpent represents the kundalini energy extending through the pineal gland. *Kundalini* in ancient Sanskrit means "illumination," or "enlightenment," and refers to the light that a practitioner experiences when awakening the third eye. This process allows a person to remember who he or she is, and fosters communication with their soul within.

The ajna chakra is the location of the third eye, which is the source of consciousness. The two physical eyes see the past and the present, while the third eye reveals the insight of the future. The word *ajna* means "command," in the sense of the Guru's command, or spiritual guidance. In Western occult and New Age thought, the ajna chakra has been identified with the third eye, or the eye of psychic vision, in an enlightened sense, and other such concepts not found in the original *Tantrika* system.

Master Guide Kirael noted:

> When you bring the energy down into the pineal gland from the crown chakra, it touches something in there that we will call the master blueprint or the God cell that is in direct contact and communication with the seventy trillion cells in your body.

The pineal gland is the true master gland. As noted, it is situated between the eyes. It is the organ of clairvoyance, the eye of Ra or Heru "God" in Egyptian traditions. To Buddhists, with two eyes closed and practice, it is possible to open the third eye—the dot often represented on the Buddha's forehead—to see our spiritual inner-self, or soul within. It secretes melatonin, which is anti-aging in effect and an antioxidant in nature. This secretion of melanin also assists in coloring our skin.

PINEAL STUDY IN THE WEST

The pineal gland, the most enigmatic of the endocrine organs, has long been of interest to Western anatomists. Long ago it was thought to be a valve that controlled the flow of memories into consciousness. Now it appears that the pineal gland is really a signal transducer, just like the retina of an eye. But why would an internal organ close to, but not part of the brain, be photosensitive if there is nothing for us to see?

It was French novelist Marcel Proust who said, "The real voyage of discovery consists not in seeking new lands, but seeing with new eyes." Our intuition is enlivened, and perhaps, as Plato says, the soul's eye might be purified and kindled afresh, "for it is by it alone that we contemplate the truth. ... Perhaps there is a pattern in the heavens, for one who desires to see it, and having seen it, can find it in himself!" Such platitudes seemed unrealistic, and even Plato's students doubted their master's wisdom. "You amuse me," said Plato, "you who think I am imposing impractical studies upon you, like geometry." Yet, it is through these studies that the "eye of the soul" is awakened, maintained Plato, and that this extra eye is worth more than 10,000 regular eyes. Greek philosophers such as Plato and others believed the pineal gland to be our connection to the "realms of thought." The Neoplatonic philosopher Iamblichus repeats the statement of Plato that the study of the science of numbers tends to awaken that organ in the brain which the ancients described as the "eye of wisdom," the organ now known to physiology as the pineal gland.

Rene Descartes, the French philosopher born in 1650, who resided most of his life in Holland, was heavily influenced by the writings of Plato, Socrates and Aristotle. He spoke of the pineal gland as being the "seat of the soul." He believed it to be "full of animal spirits, brought to it by many small arteries which surround it." The pineal gland as described by Descartes is the focal point of our spiritual guiding system that moves us beyond the five senses of rationality to become multi-sensory, and tuned into and aware of higher dimensions of consciousness within a holographic cosmos. Descartes described the pineal gland and its physiological reaction in the brain in his 1644 *Principles of Philosophy* of light: "The lines of sight depicting binocular vision, observed (and compressed) by the eye's 'particles' are processed by the pineal gland, which in turn manipulates the 'fluids' in the control of nerves and muscles." Other philosophers believe it is the *Centrum* that carries the "life code," and conveys orders to the body. Recent academic studies have found that the pineal gland contains light-sensitive cells that function like those of the eye's retina, testifying to the fact that the pineal gland can actually "see," giving it, quite literally, "third eye" status.

The pineal gland was found to react to light, and this suggests that the gland can somehow sense changes in the outside world without having "direct" contact. Another theory proposes that because the structure of the retina and pineal gland are similar, perhaps the pineal consists of a variety of genes that are only expressed in the eye. Therefore, the pineal gland has photoreceptors and a complete system for optical transduction. In other words, there is some light-communication highway to the pineal gland. But what is it? Perhaps there is a secret, "unknown," or invisible passageway that allows the mammalian pineal to detect light directly. This is something that has vexed philosophers and researchers for centuries.

In 1918, Nils Holmgrenin, a Swedish anatomist, also referred to the pineal gland as the "third eye," because he discovered cells that looked very much like retina cone cells in the tip of the gland in frogs and dogfish sharks. So if animals can utilize their pineal gland, why not humans? Recent discoveries have found that the pineal gland in the Western Fence Lizard contains a photo-receptive element that protrudes from the top of its head. Some researchers describe the third eye as simply the thalamus, not the pineal or pituitary, however the pineal is the male aspect, where the pituitary is the female aspect.

PINE CONE IMAGERY

The horn of the unicorn emerging from the forehead likely represents the pineal gland or third eye, and this may be the reason why it is connected with ancient cults as an enlightened animal or magical spirit. The pineal gland is supposed to secrete a resin in all mammals, and this resin is known as the blood, *or life*, of the pine tree. The world's myths and traditions offer a fertile source of information about human evolution and the third eye. Many of us have heard about the one-eyed giant cyclops monster in Greek mythology who fights with Ulysses—or the mystical Eye of Shiva representing intuition or a direct cosmic vision. These mythical traditions also feature early races of giants, and titans that are said to have lived many eons ago, and that featured an oversized eye on their foreheads.

Another mythological figure, Bacchus, the Roman god of wine and revelry, carried a pine cone staff. The Greek god Dionysus also carried a similar pine cone staff. It is interesting to note that there is a huge sculpture of a pine cone in Vatican Square called the "Court of the Pine Cone." Roman Catholic ornaments and candle holders are also decorated with pine cone designs. Interestingly, the biblical Jacob saw God face to face on the island of "Pe-ni-el." It is said in scripture: "The light of the body is the eye: if therefore the light of the eye be single thy whole body shall be filled with light."

Around the world and throughout the ages, we see many other pine cone references and symbology. The Babylonian god Tammuz, for example, is pictured carrying a pine cone. The Mesoamerican god Quetzalcoatl is often carved in a pine cone shape with pine cones adorning his clothes. The Hindu religion depicts all of its gods with the third eye located on the forehead between the two eyes of the face. The dot between the eyes is also a common characteristic of Lord Buddha portraits.

Another interesting fact that has gone unnoticed is that the top of the United States Capitol building dome, and almost all state capital building domes, are in the shape of a pineal gland. The dome is the brain, with the top structure representing the pineal gland. Coincidence maybe; however, inside the Washington D.C. Capitol Building dome are many interesting paintings depicting a close relationship to Freemasonry, replete with pine cone symbolism. The Masonic symbol is the beehive, and it also looks suspiciously like a pineal gland or a pine cone.

This awakening of our minds and its consequences are echoed in ancient myths. Norse mythology, for example, tells us that the god Odin had to sacrifice one of his eyes—symbolizing the third eye of spiritual vision—to drink from the "well of wisdom," that is, to experience cycles of matter. This story and others about the fallen angels, or Adam and Eve, have historical reference to the early human stages of evolution, and to the separation of the sexes toward middle development of the third *root-race*, during the time of Lemuria. During this epoch, the organ of intellect, the human brain, developed enormously, and divine instructors are said to have taught the arts, sciences, and secrets of nature to humanity still in its infancy. They imbued our inner being with primal wisdom, as assisted by the third eye's direct vision of divine realities. According to the Theosophical movement, as this third root race of three-eyed giants became more physical and less spiritually innocent, the gods retreated and thereby leaving us to our own means.

The timeless wisdom of this ancient lore provides vital knowledge about how humankind came into existence on Earth, and it lends interpretations of science with ancient sources. Those 19th century students of Theosophy gained a new perspective on humanity's past, and along with it, a road map to activating the third eye.

PINEAL GLAND AND THE OCCULT

Astral travel, channeling, communicating with spirits, and other occult abilities have long been closely associated with the development of the "light in the head." Occultists note that after beginning physical relaxation and concentration focusing on the third eye, repeated practice will activate the pineal gland. This technique is achieved when in a state of relaxation by staring at a point in the middle of the forehead, and without straining the muscles of the eyes. Occult tradition holds that the proper way to activate the third eye is to "balance" the two "opposite" channels in the body, called "ida" and "pingala," around a central vertical axis (and spinal cord) called the "sushumna." This balance of opposites creates a third force that unites the opposites and awakens the third eye. This then allows the practitioner to see their true essence, their spiritual self, and who they are truly.

Helena Blavatsky, the co-founder of the Theosophical movement, described the role of the gland in an evolutionary context in her book, *The Secret Doctrine* in 1888. "The third eye acted no longer ... because man had sunk too deep in the mire of matter." She continued, "The third eye ... gradually petrified soon disappeared ... the eye was drawn deep into the head and is now buried under the hair ... owing to the gradual disappearance of spirituality and increase in materiality ... it became an atrophied organ ... The third eye is dead ... but it has left behind a witness to its existence ... the pineal gland."

Madame Blavatsky went on to claim that the pineal gland is "the very key to the highest and divinest consciousness in man—his omniscient, spiritual and all embracing mind." It is "the pendulum which, once the clock-work of the inner man is wound up, carries the spiritual vision of the ego to the highest planes of perception, where the horizon opens before it becomes almost infinite." Blavatsky maintained that when the heart, the center of the human spiritual monad vibrates in perfect harmony with the pineal gland, the two merge and become as one. This practice allowed a student to become an adept, and gave that person *godlike* powers with nearly unlimited vision.

According to Theosophy belief, the fourth root race, or the Atlantian race, began as "three-eyed" beings, and existed at the most material point in human physical evolution where spirit and matter balanced on the arc of descent. These beings are said to have been huge in size with titanic strength, and with great intelligence that enabled them to create advanced civilizations. But there was a price for the development of the brain-mind, five senses, personal ego, and lower passions: the third eye no longer acted as a spiritual organ (except in advanced humans whose third eye functioned in concert with their spiritual nature). Eventually, the third eye gradually "petrified" and disappeared, and was drawn deep into the head and rendered inactive. Even today, however, when the *real self* is active during trances and spiritual visions, this "original eye" is said to swell and expand. Similarly, in some Hindu traditions and other belief systems, the seven chakras are centers of *prana*, or life force, and are the vital energy of our body. The mind and senses are paths for occult energies that work through various psychophysical centers or chakras, among the highest of which is the pineal gland. The chakras correspond to vital points in the physical body, and these centers continue to develop as we evolve towards more spiritual lives.

THIRD EYE AND BUDDHA NATURE

Two great names in human history that are known to just about everyone are Jesus Christ and the Buddha. It is said that these two masters attained a level of enlightenment through evolution in their past lives, long before us, and toward the spiritual age of the fourth root race. They have been called "ascended masters" in the New Age movement. Similarly, Theosophy teaches that through spirit involution (growth thru looking inward) and physical evolution all humans will ultimately attain the states of consciousness that these holy men achieved before us. In other words, it is inevitable that we will all once again obtain the powers and abilities of the ascended masters, some day, when we learn to reactivate our pineal glands.

To begin, if we want to see our own physical nature, or our "Buddha nature," we have to see it through a different eye, that is, through a different perception. This eye is what we call the wisdom eye, or Buddha's eye, the heavenly eye, or what the esoteric Christians call the single eye. Jesus said, "If thy eye be single, thy whole body shall be full of light." This eye that is mentioned in the Buddhist scriptures, the Christian Bible and the other scriptures are not physical eyes, but the single eye within our wisdom ... within our ocean of consciousness. Actually, there is no "eye" per se. But, because we can see everything from heaven to hell; from this world to the Buddha's land; we call that "seeing with new eyes." In order to open this eye we need someone who can show us how. Just like when we want to drive a car we need someone who already knows how to drive the car to teach us. This is where the masters throughout the ages step in.

According to author John Van Mater, Jr. writing for the Theosophical University Press:

> *Occultists and religious masters would agree that to the majority of people these days inner vision must be awakened and acquired by artificial stimuli, an ability previously known to the archaic sages and population at large. Humanity passes through phases of light and darkness as it advances along the eternal march of time. Yet every phase of evolution reflects a profound intelligence and wisdom. The inner forces of consciousness and their vital circulations work through the outer functions of sense organs and the body. So while the pineal gland has certain physiological activities in conjunction with the pituitary gland—together they regulate the rhythms of metabolism and growth—it is also the physical organ of intuition, inspiration, spiritual vision, and divine thought.*
>
> *As we progress on the arc of spiritual development, it is up to us individually to monitor and balance our energies. In most cases it is unwise to consciously interfere with the third eye or other psychophysical centers because our present understanding is simply not sufficient: we still have much to learn as embryo gods, beings of consciousness and matter, as we evolve spiritually. The most effective way to develop the potentials which are expressed through the third eye is by deliberately exercising the finest unselfish qualities of character and intuition in our everyday life. Following this path, the rest will then come in its own time as we are ready to receive it.*

For eons various ascended masters have said that with proper conditioning, the pineal gland can be the source of clairvoyant abilities and intuitive awareness. Similarly, in esoteric physiology, when we have a hunch, or déjà vu experience, our pineal gland begins to vibrate. If spiritual disciplines are used to increase and prolong this vibration, it may lead to the opening of the pineal gland situated in the middle of the brow. Whenever we have a hunch, this gland is vibrating gently, and when we have an inspiration or flash of intuitive understanding, it vibrates even stronger (though still gently). How robustly it functions in each of us depends on how much we foster our spiritual capacities. When the pineal gland is active, it receives rays directly from the "cosmic mind." Yet it has remained mostly inactive due to the work of the two eyes which overcame it, however it is our destiny to once again activate this *"first eye."*

EVOLUTION OF THE THIRD EYE

According to Madame Blavatsky in *The Secret Doctrine*, spiritual and psychic involution coincide with physical evolution, insomuch as the spiritual and psychic senses of the first human races became recessive during the development of the outer senses. The third eye was an actively used and much larger organ, that is, back when the spiritual element in humans reigned supreme over the somewhat nascent intellectual and psychic elements most used today. The cycle regressed toward the point where the physiological senses, including the median "eye," atrophied the most psychicly developed characteristics in humans. The pineal gland is still there, however, and with practice it can be reactivated.

Madame Blavatsky quoted an ancient commentary which recalled: "There were four-armed human creatures in those early days of the male-females (hermaphrodites); with one head, yet three eyes. They could see before them and behind them." She then cited that the third eye was originally at the back of the head. The statement that the latest hermaphrodite of humanity was "four-armed," unriddles the mystery of the representations of idols and the exoteric gods of ancient India who are portrayed with many arms. In the ancient Greek acropolis of Argos, there were reports of a "xovanon." It was a rudely carved wooden statue attributed to Daedalus representing a three-eyed colossus, and it was consecrated to Zeus Triopas who had three eyes. The head of this "god" has two eyes in its face, and one above on the top of its forehead. It is considered the most archaic of all statues from the Western World that portrayed a third eye.

The primitive third eye was probably functional before our present two eyes formed and became dominant. Interestingly, both the pineal gland and the two eyes project out from tissue layers of the embryonic brain—a common fact known in embryology. This is highly suggestive of the evolution of the organs and senses in general. Invertebrates and lower vertebrates evolved eyes of various kinds over hundreds of millions of years. Biology recognizes, at least in the most primitive vertebrates, the pineal gland as having been nature's first eye. One of the lowest vertebrates to have an eye is the larva of the sea squirt. There is also a primitive "third" eye structure in fishes, amphibians, and reptiles. Even birds have a light-receptive pineal gland inside their skulls. Some dinosaurs, as judging by the openings in the tops of their skulls, may have also had huge third eyes. The later mammalian and mammal-like dinosaurs had these openings as well, but this third eye soon receded under the skull, as did the pineal gland found in humans and in most higher vertebrates. Contrary, though, sheep still have a pineal gland that is directly affected by bright light.

Humankind's early variations in size and shape were partly experiments in physical nature as well as contrived with the help of divine intelligences, with the most physical phase producing the greatest variation of human types. In earlier terrestrial cycles or rounds, the human monads passed from the lowest to the highest through phases of mineral, plant, and animal life. During these early rounds, the human kingdom took on the basic patterns of plants and animals that existed in former embodiments of the Earth. Using ethereal substance to fashion their vehicle, this racial *recapitulation* by astral humanity produced general prototypes found in animals, and specialized along creation's particular lines, that gradually diverged from the primary human stock. Yet vertebrate species, including humans, retained certain basic things in common, such as the third eye, the five senses—*and even tails!*

Biology recognizes that the human embryo passes from a single cell through states resembling the various kingdoms. For example, there is a fish stage with gill slits, a reptilian one with a tail, and multiple mammalian stages. It is rare, but some children are born with residual gill clefts or visible tails. The question then is, why are these variations still manifesting? The answer appears to be that the basic memory of our early evolution is still *impressed* within our primordial protoplasm, and perhaps remains encoded in our genes as well. Research indicates that humans have extra DNA that is stored, but appears to not be used directly.

MELATONIN REGULATOR

Melatonin is one of the most powerful hormones that the pineal gland regulates. The pineal gland appears to receive signals from regions in the brain directly affected by the impulses traveling down the optic nerves, and it secretes melatonin, present also in the retina of the two eyes. This hormone appears to be involved in circadian rhythms, also known as the sleep and awake cycles, a process scientists do not yet fully understand. For most people, depending on age, the secretion of melatonin begins between 9:30-10:30 PM, and induces sleepiness. In most people, melatonin reaches peak levels between 1-2 a.m., and drops to its lowest levels at mid-day. The pineal gland also controls reproduction, sleep functions and motor activity, blood pressure, the immune system, the pituitary and thyroid glands, cellular growth, body temperature, and many other vital functions. All of these depend on a balanced melatonin cycle. Melatonin is made exclusively in the pineal gland, and is comprised of the same tryptophane base materials as pinoline. Melatonin induces mitosis. It does this by sending a small electrical signal up the double helix of the DNA which instigates an 8 Hz proton signal that enables the hydrogen bonds to the *steps* to zip open so the DNA can replicate.

Theosophical literature, however, maintains that in addition to its physiological functions, this pea-sized gland at the base of the skull is an important psychophysiological center involved with such activities as clairvoyance and intuition. Ancient Indian literature recognizes the pineal gland as being a key activator of the crown chakra. Light activates the full potential of the brain that can bring forth infinite inherent powers that have remained dormant for millennia. The pineal gland is sensitive to light, and our bodies convert solar energy into physical nourishment. The sun's energy is a source that powers the brain, and the human eyes are the only organ where the sunshine can enter the human body. With the eyes being the sun's energy entryway to the human brain, the age-old healing ritual of solar gazing enables us to receive nourishment, healing and spiritual enlightenment. Solar gazing was practiced by the ancient Egyptians, Aztecs, Greeks, Mayans, and by some Native American tribes. In the East, it was practiced by Tibetan monks, and is utilized by traditions like Yoga, Qigong, and Tai Chi.

Modern, devoted, solar gazers claim better physical, mental, emotional and spiritual health, as well as being able to sustain themselves on solar energy alone for very long periods of time without eating food. This practice is called "sun eating." Strict long-term fasting under the control and observation of various scientific and medical teams revealed a regeneration of the brain's gray cells, plus the expansion of the pineal gland rather than its typical shrinking. Solar gazing is done only during the first hour after sunrise or the last hour before sunset, when the sun's rays are most gentle to the eyes. If gazing is not done around dawn or sunset and is performed at other hours it will result in serious damage to the retina.

Once the body is sufficiently aligned with this spiritual force, light becomes food, hence the *breatharian* idea that uses breath to stimulate the pineal gland by bringing in large volumes of oxygen, and the life-force called prana into the bloodstream. Proper breath work through the nose "oxygenates" the brain. Oxygen-drenched blood causes the pineal gland to resonate, vibrate and even grow in size.

TRYPTAMINE TRIPPINESS

In his bestselling book *DMT: The Spirit Molecule*, psychedelic researcher Dr. Rick Strassman explained how the pineal gland "is quite active in synthesizing compounds related to serotonin, an important neurotransmitter in the brain." Neurotransmitters are the chemical messengers allowing communication among individual nerve cells. Most typical psychedelic drugs, such as LSD, mescaline, psilocybin, and DMT are active in brain sites which are also affected by serotonin. Marijuana too, among other psychedel-ics, facilitates the activation of the pineal gland and helps activate the third eye, direct-ing our spiritual evolution to wholeness. In addition, most of these drugs are similar to serotonin in their chemical structure. Eating cannabis can also activate *the mind's eye*.

Dr. Strassman states that most of the above substances belong to the "tryptamine" class of drugs, and proposed that the pineal gland produces "one or two endogenous tryptamines found in human blood and cerebrospinal fluid. This latter fluid continually bathes the brain, and compounds found in it most likely affect brain function." Strass-man also explains how psychedelic drugs, meditational states, spontaneous near-death experiences and other phenomena which may induce stereotypical death or rebirth, the paradisal euphoria or a hellish state, are operating via the pineal gland.

The universal mystic vision of God is as an all-consuming white light. On a physiologi-cal level, it can be an experience that is produced from chemical reactions in the pineal gland, which is known to be particularly light sensitive. Light, as it passes through the eyes and to the pineal gland, forms a *triad* that directly controls and regulates normal or altered states of consciousness, as well as many bodily functions. These three factors are also directly related to, or implicated in, mystical states and the "psychedelic" ex-perience. Visions of white light are not only associated with mysticism and psychedelic explorations, they are also a prevalent image as recorded by those who have near-death experiences. A reason for this recurring theme in near-death states, according to Dr. Strassman, occurs after death as the pineal gland shuts down, when some of the present chemicals turn into "psychedelic" drugs.

Taken one step further, the pineal gland not only plays an important role in death, but also in birth, and possibly even in rebirth, according to Dr. Strassman. The pineal gland first becomes visible in the human fetus at the same time as the clear differen-tiation of the fetus into female or male gender becomes apparent. The time for both of these events is 49 days, a period of time, according to several Buddhist texts, that the life force of a deceased individual coalesces around its next corporeal existence known as the bardo.

Indeed, the pineal is the first gland to be formed in the fetus, and it is distinguishable after only about a month of development. When we were infants, we were each born with a fully-opened third eye able to witness the power and glory of the universe. From a subatomic perspective, to the infinity of the galaxies, we were able to see life in all its glory and to appreciate its wisdom and bounty. But as we grow older, we are condi-tioned by parents, teachers, managers, peers, the media, and everyone else around us to cover our third eye with layer upon layer of illusion and confusion, until our third eye was closed and our inner witness goes dark, leaving us empty to the world's wonders, and the wisdom that our mystic sight may have delivered. Thus, if the life force enters through the pineal, this manifestation of comings and goings would suggest the release of psychedelic tryptamines. These would then influence the visionary experiences as-sociated with near-death and near-birth states.

THE VITAL FUNCTIONS OF THE PINEAL GLAND

Extensive medical studies in the 1970s and 1980s revealed a profound scientific understanding of the pineal gland in terms of its chemical properties. In general, the pineal is a very active organ, commanding the second highest blood flow avail-able in the body, only after the kidneys, and equal in volume to the pituitary gland. The pineal is supplied with the best blood, oxygen, and nutrient mix available in the human anatomy, second only to our kidneys, whose function is to filter the blood of impurities. It has the highest absorption of phosphorus in the whole body, and the second highest absorption of iodine after the thyroid. No other part of the brain contains so much serotonin, or is capable of reducing melatonin. A unique anatomical feature is that the pineal gland is an *unpaired* midline organ in the brain, which, alone among equivalent organs, has resisted encroachment by the corpus callosum. Located directly in the center of the brain cavity, it is actually outside the blood-brain barrier, and is therefore not even a part of the brain!

Innervated by the autonomic nervous system, it shows extreme variability in size, form and internal structure between one individual and the next. There also seems to be considerable functional connection between the pineal and the pituitary glands, in that their actions tend to be antagonistic—the pineal being *inhibitory* in relation to the pituitary. When an LSD level is measured in the brain, it turns out that it concentrates mostly in the pineal and pituitary glands, secondarily in the limbic system structures such as the hippocampus, amygdala and fornix, and lastly in the hypothalamus.

The pineal synthesizes and releases melatonin, and perhaps other hormones, in response to norepinephrine, a neurotransmitter released from its post-ganglionic sympathetic nerves. As such, the pineal is a neuro-endocrine transducer like the adrenal medulla. The rate at which norepinephrine is released reduces when light activates the retinal photoreceptors; and, increases when the sympathetic nervous system is stimulated, for example by hypoglycemia or when under severe stress.

The pineal contains a pair of enzymes—hydroxyindole—O-methyl transferase (HIOMT); and; Indole-N-methyl transferase (INMT), both of which are able to convert serotonin into a number of potent hallucinogens. If a person increases the concentration of pineal serotonin and blocks its normal enzymatic inactivation, it becomes a substrate for other pineal enzymes like HIOMT and INMT—methyl transfer enzymes that catalyze the transfer of a methyl group from one compound to another. Thus, for example, serotonin can be converted to 5-methoxy-N, and N-dimethyl tryptamine by these enzymes, which are a hallucinogen similar to DMT as found in cawa, a substance the Amazonian Indians add to their Banisteriopsis brew.

Normally, serotonin is inactivated by the mitochondrial enzyme monoamine oxidase (MAO), that converts it into an inactive metabolite. MAO is the major enzyme involved in the breakdown and inactivation of seratonin, dopamine, epinephrine and norepinephrine. Thus, any enzyme that interferes with MAO will cause a build up of seratonin levels, leading to the pineal gland producing endogenous hallucinogens. Harmala alkaloids are seratonin antagonists, CNS stimulants, hallucinogens and are extremely potent short-term MAO inhibitors.

A PERSONAL PORTAL

The pineal is known to generate its own magnetic field because it contains magnetite, and it interacts with the Earth's magnetic field. The charged particles of the solar wind at dawn stimulates the pineal gland. This is why the period between 4 and 6 a.m. is the best time to meditate—and why sunrise is the best time to sun gaze, a practice called "sun eating." At these times, the pineal stimulates the pituitary to secrete human growth hormones. This is why many sun gazers have reported rapid nail and hair growth, restoration of hair color, an ability to stop eating, and general rejuvenation.

When fully active the pineal gland is a step-down transformer that converts the extremely rapid electro-magnetic motions of our light bodies into frequencies that our physical brain can interpret in the form of mental images, and as such the pineal gland is a *self-reflective* optical organ. It looks at itself inwardly from all directions and sees through prismatic calcium carbonate crystals that coat the receptors creating an inner light of mental images, and created by our "light bodies" into a "light language."

Dr. Marcel Joseph Vogel, in various experiments, demonstrated that because humans tend to think in patterns, crystalline growth could be modified by patterns of human thought waves. He also showed that crystalline growth could be modified by living in a state of love. These experiments also correspond to Dr. Masaru Emoto's work related to how human emotions effect the structure of water molecules. Our thought patterns travel energetically, with certain known frequencies. For example, fear-filled patterns of thought carry a low frequency, while love-filled thought patterns carry a high frequency.

Because thought waves travel energetically and at certain frequencies, they can be collected, stored, and transmitted by crystals, like the micro-crystals located in our pineal glands. Furthermore, crystals are shown to exhibit a capacity for storing memory. Just as crystals can be used to hold a computer software program, they can also be used to hold patterns of thought. In this manner, a habit of fearful, or loving, patterns of thought are stored within our brains' "hard drive," thereby encouraging us to repeat these patterns. Therefore, a history of fearful thinking creates a habit of living in fear, whereas a history of loving thought creates a habit of living in an atmosphere of love.

Our pineal glands serve as "personal portals," in which our multi-dimensional selves can reside in our Earth reality. It is also a portal through which each of us returns to the myriad realities of our greater selves. Our pineal portal is filled with a sort of "liquid light," contained within micro-crystals of calcite. A crystal is a solid substance in which the atoms, molecules or ions are arranged in orderly, repeating patterns.

The micro-crystals of our pineal glands operate much in the same way as an old-fashioned crystal radio. However, most of the frequencies received via the pineal gland are outside of the human range of perception, and they can be perceived as colors as well as sounds. Because of this, many of the messages we receive from the higher dimensions are hues and tones. It has also been predicted that future medicines and natural cures will be comprised of colors, sounds, frequencies, and vibrations. Again, if our thought patterns are fearful, they carry a low frequency, and that calibrates our pineal portal to operate at a lower frequency of light. On the other hand, when our thoughts resonate to the frequency of love, we calibrate our pineal portals to the highest frequencies. As we gain mastery over our thoughts, our pineal portal can become calibrated automatically to the higher frequencies of loving thoughts. Once there, we will be able to translate more of these light and sound messages into a new "language of light."

It is reported that when people first open their pineal portal they primarily receive auditory messages. If the desire is to convert these messages into the language of light, it will be necessary to raise the frequency of sound by *forty octaves*. This can be accomplished by understanding that when a person spiritually expands, they also surrender to their soul. Since all energy is related to the speed of light, Einstein's E = mc2 theorem helps explain that when two frequencies meet, the higher frequency will raise the resonance of the lower. At that point, when we surrender to our higher spiritual selves, we allow cosmic light and unconditional love to enter our pineal portals, and this energy raises the resonance of our brainwaves, consciousness, emotions, thought patterns, and perceptions. Hence, by *surrendering* to our spirit, we can raise our consciousness enough to perceive the higher octaves of the light language. In fact, it is common to experience a download of this "light language" once a person has fully opened and activated their pineal portal. This may be the *enlightenment moment* as described by the Buddha.

Another important point regarding our personal portal's ability to receive light messages is that our pineal gland's micro-crystals have piezoelectric properties. Piezoelectricity is the charge that accumulates in certain solid materials such as crystals, certain ceramics, bones, DNA, and various proteins. It is because of this property that certain crystals are used for pressure gauges, oscillators, resonators and wave stabilizers. Crystals also have the ability to rotate the plane of light polarization into the higher frequency of ultraviolet. Ultraviolet is the highest frequency in the third dimensional light spectrum, and therefore serves as a gateway into the higher dimensions.

Scientists have theorized that the Global System for Mobile Telecommunications (GSM) waves constitute a new mechanism of transduction, thereby effecting the pineal membrane via micro-crystals. GSM is a digital technology that enables up to eight simultaneous telephone conversations to be held on the same channel. This indicates the potential of our pineal portal to receive multiple messages within *the timeframe of now*. In fact, our pineal gland controls our focus and attention within the *inner worlds* of sleep, meditation, and the *outer worlds* of physical reality. This ability to perceive multiple messages can assist us when tuning in to our inner selves, while simultaneously maintaining a connection with our physical lives.

Our brain's cerebrum is our personal "sleeping giant," and it is the center of our Earth vessel's electro-magnetic resonating power. The pineal gland is the positive contact point, and it acts as a neuro-endocrine transducer, which transmits its multidimensional information to the pituitary gland. Then, each of our pituitary glands act as the negative contact point to receive the information, and it then distributes it throughout the cerebrum. Next, the cerebral cortex gathers the various frequencies of information into the brain cells that are designated to convert electro-magnet frequencies into electrical currents. These electrical currents dictate our thoughts, actions and behaviors, and are thus projected out into our reality via our intentions and actions.

Looked at another way, the pineal gland can be considered an organic superconducting resonator located within each of us. Researcher Ananda Bosman claims it potentiates DNA as a multidimensional transducer of holographic projection, through *hadron toroids*, and is implicated as assisting people with staying youthful. DMT is naturally produced in small quantities in the human brain, and it has been hypothesized that DMT is produced in the pineal gland. The DMT acts on the T-RNA messengers that carry out the protein synthesis for the DNA, or, essentially, the rebuilding of our body image and organs.

In 1972, the guru Satyananda observed:

> All psychic systems have their physical aspects in the body. … With ajna chakra the physical equivalent is the pineal gland, which has long baffled doctors and scientists as to its precise function. … Yogis, who are scientists of the subtle mind, have always spoken of telepathy as a "siddhi," a psychic power for thought communication and clairaudience, etc. The medium of such siddhis is ajna chakra, and its physical terminus is the pineal gland, which is connected to the brain. It has been stated by great yogis … that the pineal gland is the receptor and sender of the subtle vibrations which carry thoughts and psychic phenomena throughout the cosmos.

The human pineal gland not only produces the neuro-hormone melatonin, one of the body's most potent antioxidants, but also the revolutionary pinoline 6-methoxy-tetra-dydro-beta carboline, or 6-MeO-THBC. Pinoline is superior to melatonin in aiding DNA replication. Pinoline can make superconductive elements within the body. It encourages cell division by resonating with the very pulse of life—eight cycles per second—the pulse DNA uses to replicate. This 8 Hz resonance was measured in healers by Andrea Puharich in the late 1970s, and it has been known of by masters for eons.

RETHINKING THE PINEAL GLAND

The pineal gland looks like a pinecone, as described earlier, and the pinecone image has been used all over the world as a reference to this amazing gland of extrasensory perception. As shown, the visual usage of the all-seeing eye can be traced back to the ancient Egyptian symbol of the Eye of Horus, and in more recent times, on the back of the U.S. one-dollar bill. The Eye of Horus is also known as the Eye of Ra, which is the Egyptian sun god. In Hindu traditions it is associated with the extrasensory third eye, wherein the perception of the world is no longer limited to the physical senses. The Hindu deity Shiva, and many others, are portrayed with a third eye on their forehead. The pineal gland is linked with the crown chakra, also called the Thousand Petaled Lotus, that downloads and transforms energy from the ether into our consciousness.

In Taoism and many traditional Chinese religious sects such as "chan," the "third eye training" involves focusing attention, with the eyes closed and in various Qigong postures, on the point between the eyebrows. The goal of this training is to allow students to have an ability to tune into the *right* vibrations of the universe and thereby gain a solid foundation toward more advanced meditation levels. In theory, the third eye is situated between the two eyes, and it expands up to the middle of the forehead when opened.

It is exciting to see modern science confirm what age-old customs have represented and practiced for centuries. The pineal gland, viewed historically as a "sphincter to control the flow of thought;" as the "seat of the soul;" and, depicted more recently, as a "neuroendocrine transducer organ," now promises to portray more complex physiological functions than originally believed. Plus it portends to reveal a more extensive implication in the pathological processes than once deemed possible. Future investigations should be directed toward a better comprehension of the functions of numerous neglected neurotransmitters and biological substances that are found in the pineal gland. The results of these investigations may bring forth a multi-functional significance for the pineal gland in not only the "temporal arrangement of various reproductive events" in mammals, the "rhythmical thermoregulatory process" in some ectotherms, and in the "nightly pallor response" in amphibians. It could also bring major changes in the realm of human suffering, such as seizure disorders, sleep disorders, and behavioral abnormalities.

Scientists now confirm what the masters of old have long maintained: that the pineal gland is sensitive to electromagnetic energy, more specifically, to the Earth's natural electromagnetic field. A huge change in the Earth's electromagnetic field, then, could either have the effect of awakening the gland and its higher functions on a mass level, or have the opposite effect and close it down altogether. The recent discovery of magnetite clusters near the pineal gland seem to give humans the residual ability to orient to geomagnetic directional cues, similar to homing pigeons. But this ability is seemingly lost with pineal dysfunction. Dr. Grahame Blackwell observed that the human pineal gland has been found to contain large numbers of calcite micro-crystals that "bear a striking resemblance" to calcite crystals found in the inner ear. Those found in the inner ear have been shown to exhibit the quality of piezoelectricity. If those found in the pineal gland also have this quality, then this would provide a means whereby an external electromagnetic field might directly influence the brain. Calcite microcrystals can be seen on the pineal gland under a scanning electron microscope, and according to orthopedic surgeon and electrophysiology researcher Robert O. Becker:

> *In light of this work, the fact that 10 hertz is also the dominant (alpha) frequency of the EEG in all animals becomes another significant bit of evidence that every creature is hooked up to the Earth electromagnetically through its DC system.*

A research group under Indian bio-physicist Sarada Subrahmnanyam reported that the human EEG not only responded to the micropulsations, but also responded differently, depending on which way the subject's head was facing in relation to the Earth's field. Oddly enough, however, head direction had no effect if the subject was a yogi. Their studies revealed the following:

> *The relationship has been conclusively proven by recent studies of the pineal gland. This tiny organ in the center of the cranium has turned out to be more than the vaguely defined third eye of the mystics. It produces melatonin and serotonin, two neurohormones that, among many other functions, directly control all of the bio-cycles. The lamprey, akin to the ancestor of all vertebrates, as well as certain lizards, has an actual third eye, close to the head's surface and directly responsive to light, instead of the "blind" pineal found in other vertebrates. The eminent British anatomist J. Z. Young has recently shown that this organ controls the daily rhythm of skin color changes that these animals undergo.*

> *This gland in your brain is able to see the emitted colors at different levels of magnetism. There are different magnetic fields all over the earth. So the gland may be able to receive signals through these magnetic forces by recognizing different colors and patterns. This is one of the first scientific experiments that has shown a mechanism that proves how your brain may receive signals from outside the body. For some time it has been known that animals recognize magnetic signals. Sharks can sense magnetic variations in the water. Some schools of fish work in the same way. The fish can sense when other fish move and the whole school turns together accordingly. Birds are also known to fly back to far away places by using the magnetic field as a guide. Biology shows us that life can recognize magnetic fields in some way, so why don't humans seem to have these skills?*

> *The most important point is that very small magnetic fields influence the pineal gland. Several research groups have shown that applying a magnetic field of half a gauss or less, oriented so as to add to or subtract from the Earth's normal field, will increase or decrease production of pineal melatonin and serotonin. Other groups have observed physical changes in the gland's cells in response to such fields. The experiments were controlled for illumination, since it has been known for several years that shining a light on the head somehow modifies the gland's hormone output even though it's buried so deeply within the head in most common vertebrates that, as far as we know, it can't react directly to the light.*

The advent of the microscope has allowed us to objectively observe things that are infinitely small. Conversely, the telescope allows us to see the infinitely distant. If the pineal gland allows us to see the "ultra" of all things, then we should study oriental yoga practices and seek to develop this wonderful gland. The yogis of India have practices through which a person can obtain a special super-function of the pineal gland. When reaching that point, and without much effort, humans can then perceive the ultra.

ACTIVATING THE THIRD EYE

Considered the most powerful and highest source of ethereal energy available to humans, the pineal gland has always been most revered in initiating psychic powers—including clairvoyance and the ability to see auras. To activate the third eye and perceive higher dimensions, the pineal and the pituitary must vibrate in unison, which, as mentioned, can be achieved through meditation, chanting, and the practice of sun gazing. When activated, the pineal gland becomes the line of communication within the energy body, and also with the higher planes. The crown chakra, then, reaches down into the brain until its vortex touches the pineal gland. *Prana*, or pure energy, is received through this energy center in the head. With enough practice, the vibration level of the astral body is raised, thus allowing it to separate from the physical.

When a correct relationship is established between the individual's personality operating through the pituitary and its connection to the soul, as in opening consciousness through the pineal, a magnetic field is created. The negative and positive forces then interact, and when they become strong enough they create a "light in the head." With this light in the head activated, astral projectors can withdraw themselves from the physical body, carrying the light with them, but always retaining a "silver cord" back to the body. *Toning* sacred sounds also helps cancel out unwanted vibrations, and activates the pineal gland. In practice, while centered in the pineal body, including a loving embrace of yourself, we then may call upon the collective consciousness of the planet into our pineal. What a person should feel next is a quiet oneness with no separation from anything. One must let go to move into this experience.

Spiritual activity results from a stimulation of the pineal gland. One can consciously activate the vesicular monoamine transporter (VMAT2), or the "God gene," by saying a prayer, toning, repeating a mantra, or doing specific meditations. Scientists have detected a certain gene that is awakened in spiritual people, but they have no idea what causes the VMAT2 DNA gene to be active in some people yet remain inactive in others. Spiritual activity appears to activate VMAT2. Spiritual activity in large groups activates even more VMAT2. The more powerful the spiritual techniques, the greater the activation of VMAT2 and other spiritual energies.

We all know that energetic vibrations such as sound can break glass. Sound also generates electromagnetic energy effects on a person's body. Most sound vibrations produced by people such as speaking, playing music, running vehicles, and regular outdoor sounds do not seem to activate the VMAT2. However, the repetition of prayers, certain tones, and chanted mantras do activate VMAT2 and other spiritual energies in the DNA of the practitioner. Certain sounds and frequencies also appear to stimulate the production of psychoactive substances in the pineal gland—*without* the use of drugs. People with a highly active pineal gland seem to be able to recall their dreams more vividly than others, and they often report seeing visions and paranormal activity on a larger scale. The wave vibrations of the Sun also cause the secretion of "feel good" hormones like serotonin, beta-endorphins, and dopamine, especially during sun gazing at dawn or dusk. The endocrine glands are known to secrete other hormones during sun gazing. This behavior creates not only a "high," but also greater energy, longevity and an experience of *samadhi*, or higher consciousness. At dawn, the negatively charged pineal and the positively charged pituitary combine their essences to create a "light in the head" when meditating. This light has been seen by mystics, initiates, prophets and shamans throughout the ages. They refer to it as an experience of God, or that of a universal intelligence.

SOME SIMPLE POINTERS

For those interested in opening their pineal gland for optimum usage, here are a few starting-point guidelines. First, start by meditating on where you sense the pineal gland is located. Sit quietly and visualize this gland between the hemispheres of the brain. Picture it as glowing in white golden light and try to sense it tingling in the center of your brain. Similar to those who raise their "kundalini" in Eastern traditions, it is recommended to vocalize the soft toning sound "om" while in meditation, during sun gazing, or during any chakra raising practice. It also helps to listen to binaural beats, or ideally, isochronic tones, both of which can be made to simulate activity in the pineal gland. Do this daily for a half hour or longer. Many proponents of the ancient technique of sun gazing report not only of the healing benefits to common illnesses, but also in obtaining super-human abilities such as advanced telepathy and going completely without the need for food. According to sun gazing experts, food is not actually needed to maintain the body, only energy—and "sun eating" provides that energy.

To strengthen the pineal gland in your everyday life, try to avoid all water or products that contain fluoride. Sodium Fluoride is known to be in tap water, fluoridated toothpaste, inorganic fruits and vegetables, showers without filters, any soda drinks, artificial food and processed foods, plus red meats. Instead, drink only spring, distilled, or reverse osmosis purified water. Buy a shower filter, go to whole food markets and buy organic fruits, veggies, and toothpaste without fluoride. It has been shown that fluoride calcifies the pineal gland.

It is also possible to add detoxers, stimulants, and supplements into your diet to increase pineal function. Research first, then purchase and consume the following products: chlorella, spirualina, blue-green algae, cilantro, iodine, Vitamin C, niacin, ginseng, borax, shilajit, D3, mucuna, cystine, calcium benzonite clay, chlorophyll, blue skate liver oil, Zeolite, and the monoatomic elements, or *ORMES*. The best foods for pineal function include: raw cacao, goji berries, watermelon, bananas, honey, coconut oil, hemp seeds, seeweed, and noni juice. Wheatgrass juice is a phenomenal energy-creating food, and the body treats it like synthetic sunlight.

There are some researchers who promote the natural entheogens path, but this is clearly not for everyone, and are illegal for consumption in many countries. Natural entheogens include ayahuasca, psilocybin mushrooms, peyote, changa, cannabis, salvia, DMT, and other substances.

And finally, do not forget the crystals. Amethyst, moldavite, quartz, herkimer diamond, and other crystals seem to work best for people who don't want to consume anything. Just holding crystals in the hand during meditation can help activate and stimulate the pineal gland.

What we are experiencing today is the death of the Old World Order, a human-made system that has long been in control of the planet's people and resources. It is the death of these beliefs and prejudices of ignorance, and the corrupt social structures that upheld them for so long that we await. This shift is also associated with a transformative "awakening" of the pineal gland in the brain—our central connection to the "source field," as described by author David Wilcock. Humanity is at the greatest crossroads of possibilities ever witnessed on Earth. We can follow our destiny and become a truly inter-dimensional race, or we can remain stuck in our old ways. Opening our pineal gland serves as a gateway into the higher dimensions. Those who control the information flow, however, want you to never know that, because then you will see through the illusion they pass over to us as reality. Similarly, they also profit from our sickness, which is the direction we venture into the next chapter.

The Assyrian winged-God Nimrod, holding a pine cone representing the pineal gland, or the power of regeneration, traceable to Tammuz of Babylon. Pine cones and pine cone staffs are very common on pagan statues and as art symbols represents fertility and regeneration. Dionysus, an ancient Greek god, carried the pine cone staff as a fertility symbol.

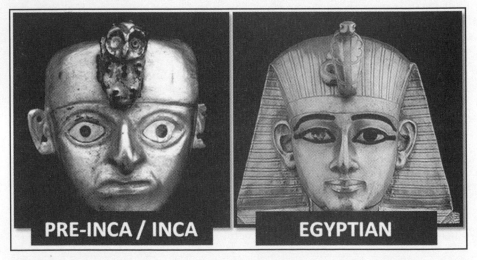

Both the pre-Inca culture and ancient Egyptians used the "animal on the forehead motif" to evoke the power of their "third eye." Both cultures understood that we can create a trancelike state where we "awaken" our so-called "mind's eye," or "inner eye," which is a symbol of spiritual illumination, and thought of as existing near the forehead—above and between the two eyes—exactly where the animal is placed.

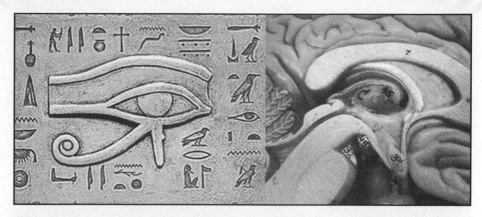

The similarities are not just uncanny—they are exact. Yet this is viewed as nothing more than a coincidence, because in modern thinking it is assumed that the Egyptians could not have had this knowledge of the human brain. Thus we are blinded to the obvious. The Eye of Horus was also broken into six basic components, each representing a different sense: smell, touch, taste, hearing, sight and thought. The thalamus is the part of the human brain that translates all incoming signals from our senses. Could this symbolism be any clearer?

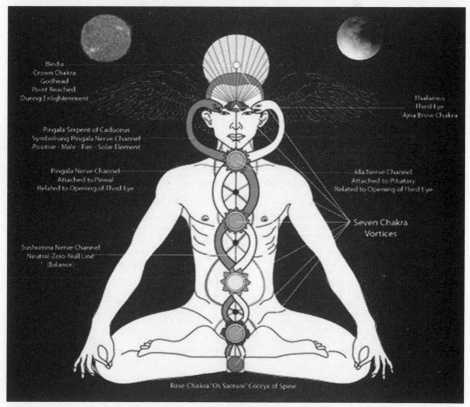

Consciousness creates different frequencies, thereby allowing us to manifest reality, and create and see things differently. Once you tap into the energy source—pineal gland activation and chakra meditation—you activate your true self, and you can then begin to see this energy for what it is. Indeed, *everything is energy*.

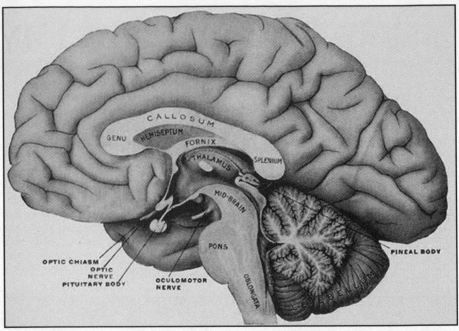

The light-transducing ability of the pineal gland has led some to call the pineal body the "third eye." The pineal gland is found in front of the cerebellum, which represents the Tree of Life. When we think of the third eye, several things come to mind. Some may associate it with animals such as iguanas or the ancient tuatara reptiles endemic to New Zealand that still have a functional third eye, also called the pineal gland. Scientific evidence today supports the possibility that this organ was nature's first eye, particularly in vertebrates and humans. There are many mysteries here because the exact function of the pineal gland is still unknown to science. Microscopic examination has revealed that it is formed of cells that have the distinct features of the rod-shaped light-sensitive cells found in the retina, indicating that its possible original function was as an organ of sight.

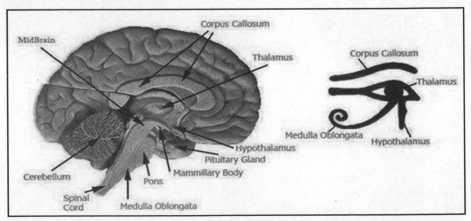

The reptilian brain is the most ancient type of brain. It has two hemispheres, just like the neocortex, and it may be that they functionally relate to the left and right hemispheres of the neocortex. The reptilian brain consists of the upper part of the spinal cord and the basal ganglia, the diencephalon, and parts of the midbrain. All of these aspects of the reptilian brain sit atop the spinal column like a knob in the middle of our heads. The pineal gland is the point of connection between the intellect and the body.

UNHEALTH INDUSTRY

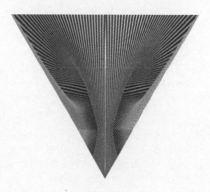

"I never have and never will approve a new drug to an individual, but only to a large pharmaceutical company with unlimited finances." –Dr. Richard J. Crout, Director of the FDA's Bureau of Drugs, **Spotlight**, 01/18/1982

ARE the myriad of chemicals introduced in the last century creating an easier life for us, or are they making us weaker, compromising our immune system, and creating a "transhumanist" world? It is known that many common diseases, for example asthma and allergies, can be caused by exposure to environmental toxins. But for some reason the powerful industry lobby causing these toxic exposures has managed to suppress the establishment of a connection to avoid the costs of culpability or changing their business practices. Obviously the industries wish to avoid the liability for the diseases and damages their business practices have caused over many years. After all, if diseases in Africa are caused by malnutrition and bad sanitation, wouldn't providing more food and cleaner water, plus better sanitation and improving living conditions, make more sense than sending over and administering all those vaccines?

As we will examine, most vaccines contain formaldehyde, thimerosal, aluminum, squalene and an assortment of wild viruses, causing extensive damage to many people globally. Even everyday household items and cosmetic products that are inhaled, applied directly to the skin, or absorbed through the scalp, can be toxic. The list of common products and their chemical components is encyclopedic. The sum total of the overwhelming presence of these chemicals has been linked to nearly every allergy, chronic affliction, and disease. Most recently, household cleaning products have been linked to breast cancer and the frequently invalid ADHD diagnosis in children. Here in America, we have an extremely neurotoxic chemical called fluoride that is added to the public supply of drinking water. Fluoride is known to interrupt the basic function of nerve cells in the brain, causing docile submissive behavior and IQ devastation. Fluoride is attracted magnetically to the pineal gland where it forms calcium phosphate crystals more than anywhere else in the body. This chapter explores the who, what, where and why of our wholesale poisoning.

Why are the top ten highest cancer rates in the world all within Western countries? And why is cancer and heart disease virtually nonexistent in many indigenous cultures, or with the Amish, who reject Western medicine? We have the best research labs, and they have none. So how could this be? Of course our lifestyle habits in the West have a lot to do with our high levels of cancer and disease. Europeans and North American people are more likely to be overweight, smoke, drink more alcohol, and engage in less physical activity than those in the "developing" countries. But there is more to this equation, as we shall explore. Remember, the pharmaceutical drug industry is one of the largest and most profitable businesses in the world, *and they intend to keep it that way*.

There is little doubt Big Pharma has a vested interest in keeping Americans dependent on the drugs they pass off as therapeutic and imperative to our wellness. In fact, they are harming millions of people and robbing patients of vast sums of money while making them even more toxified. Often the simplest explanation is the truth. By learning about natural remedies and developing preventative practices, we can avoid the toxic influence of Big Pharma. We should also avoid those unscrupulous doctors who often act as drug peddlers. How do we make sense of the fact that 290 people die by FDA-approved prescription drugs every day, as according to the *Journal of the American Medical Association*? This study came out in 2000 and documents 106,000 deaths per year from the "adverse effects" of FDA-approved prescription medications. The number of prescription drug deaths has almost doubled only a decade and a half later. Two of the main cash cows of the sinister cabal are the pharmaceutical drug industry and the medical industry. They are cohorts in crime. Another reason these multi-billion dollar corporations poison the masses is our Gross Domestic Product (GDP). In 2010, approximately 17-20% of our nation's GDP consisted of the pharmaceutical and healthcare sector. That means that $2.8 trillion came from people being ill, injured, or needing medication. Many people believe that the GDP is indicative of our nation's quality of life, but in fact it benefits from citizens being ill. People do not realize that vaccines are largely used for sterilization. It is all about population control while squeezing us for as much money as possible.

We all want to live longer and healthier lives, and most of us turn to medical science to help us achieve these goals. However, there are serious blind spots in the medical research institutions in the United States, and fundamental changes need to be made in this nation's health care system. As we will see, medical mistakes are one of the leading causes of death, and unpaid medical bills is the number one reason for personal bankruptcy in the United States. Ask your doctor if taking medical advice from a television commercial is right for you.

THE UNHEALTH INDUSTRY BEGINS HERE

The Food and Drug Administration (FDA) first started as the Division of Chemistry, and later became known as the Bureau of Chemistry. This was long before changing its name to the FDA. Its name was changed to conceal its chemical industry agenda. The original chemists from the Bureau of Chemistry, later to become the FDA, were prominent scientists in 1909. The true job of the FDA was, and is, to "approve" and sanction products from the chemical industry. This loophole legally shields the chemical industry from dissatisfaction among citizens by declaring what is "safe." The FDA has always provided a type of legal immunity for companies that put chemicals into foods, as well as to pharmaceutical companies via its "approvals," and leaving citizens without legal recourse against the chemical industry. The FDA routinely gathers private data to share with their chemical industry partners to mitigate liability. For example, contamination information that is hidden from the public are called "P.R. Issues." Good luck winning a lawsuit against a billion dollar chemical company whose products are "FDA Approved." When "approval" happens, a product is given a Generally Recognized As Safe (GRAS) status. The GRAS status shields the chemical companies, and gives them plausible deniability. The FDA has been accused of being little more than a rubber-stamping agency for Big Pharma.

John D. Rockefeller, Jr., son of the Standard Oil magnate, was the key figure behind monopolizing the American medical establishment around 100 years ago. Using his vast inherited wealth and enormous political influence, he helped create the American Medical Association (AMA), bribed every medical school with the threat of eliminating funding, gained control over medical licensing, and forced all medical doctors to practice *allopathic* medicine to stay solvent. Allopathic is the patentable and most profitable form of medicine. It is also the *slash, poison, and burn* form of medicines and treatments that can be very harmful to the body. Of course, this form of medicine has seldom been consistently effective ... only expensive.

The modern FDA was founded in 1913. This is the same year the Rockefeller Foundation was created. The FDA works hand-in-hand with the Rockefeller Foundation and the American Medical Association. The Rockefeller Foundation places its main emphasis upon medicine and medical *education*. Initial Rockefeller Foundation medical school donations totaled over one half billion dollars. By 1928, the Rockefeller Foundation gave money to 18 medical universities in 14 countries. Its partners at the FDA began an aggressive campaign of suppressing natural remedies and homeopathic medicines that competed with the chemical industry. Ignoring the many valid and replicated studies verifying the effectiveness of these inexpensive, alternative remedies, they used the tried and true fear tactic when labeling them "untested, dangerous and unapproved."

Medicine was once not the lucrative market that it has become today, and medical schools begged for the Rockefeller grants that were handed out only to compliant schools. According to *McGill University Press*, "In 1919, a five million dollar Rockefeller Foundation gift to certain Canadian medical schools helped bring Canadian medical education to the 20th century." The corruption is so deep that the only real solution is a complete reformation of the FDA—or disbanding the agency altogether. Until then, do not waste your money or risk your life on a paradigm designed to profit from your ill health. Instead, switch to natural methods that will allow your body to heal itself without the need for the deadly drugs that are being pushed on Americans by the drug companies and rubber-stamped by the FDA.

UNLIKELY BEDFELLOWS

A little over a century ago, an unholy alliance formed between the American Medical Association, the FDA, and the Rockefeller Foundation. The Yale University Medical School website reports, "The General Education Board of the Rockefeller Foundation, also approached in 1914, pledged $500,000 on the condition that the University raise $1.5 million by January 1, 1916 and paid clinical faculty (allopathic doctors only) on a full-time basis. With the Brady money and the hope of GEB funding, the Yale Corporation and Hospital signed the affiliation contract with the Hospital before the deadline of July 1, 1914." The new legally enforceable medical monopoly paralleled the Rockefeller monopoly from the petrochemical industry of times past. Instead of owning all petroleum, the Rockefeller empire now controls the dispensation of nearly all medicines. John D. Rockefeller owned the lion's share of a chemical industry that would later be christened the "pharmaceutical" industry. Yet the hypocritical John D. Rockefeller Jr. himself relied only on traditional holistic medicines for his own health, along with many of his friends at the newly-created FDA and the AMA.

After an effective hijacking of the medical schools, the true carnage of polio, heart disease, and cancer of many types exploded among the population. Sensible cure advocates suffered the consequences. Albert Szent-Gyorgyi, for example, the Noble Prize winner for Medicine in 1937, and discoverer of vitamin C, said: "The American Cancer Society tried to ruin my research foundation." The American Cancer Society was officially founded by John D. Rockefeller Jr. in the year 1913, when he made the first donation to Harvard University. If a cancer cure were announced, huge amounts of research grants to the American Cancer Society would dry up overnight. One is left wondering why vitamin C could be such a threat to their mission.

According to the USA Census, cancer is the second largest killer in the United States, second only to heart disease. But most cancer patients die from the treatments, not the cancers. Did you know that when a person is diagnosed with cancer, that person is suddenly worth a minimum of $300,000 to the cancer industry? Simply follow the money. Shocking new science reveals that mammograms are a medical hoax. Rather than saving lives through so-called "early detection," mammograms have been found to create a false diagnosis, and 93% of women receive no medical benefit whatsoever, this according to a groundbreaking new study published in the *New England Journal of Medicine*. Most of the women tested are, in fact, harmed by unnecessary chemotherapy, radiotherapy and radical surgical procedures that were never necessary in the first place. Research suggests that chemotherapy may affect healthy cells surrounding cancer cells, and some forms of cancer treatment can make the disease even tougher to tackle. It's all about getting new and more patients, then selling them "drug" therapies and radiation-based treatments.

The U.S. has the most dangerous and yet the most expensive medical system in the world. Unpaid medical bills cause upwards of 62% of all personal bankruptcies in the USA. Dr. Robert Atkins M.D., creator of the "Atkins Diet" has said, "There is not one, but many cures for cancer available. But they are all being systematically suppressed by the ACS (American Cancer Society), the NCI (National Cancer Institute) and the major oncology centers. They have too much of an interest in the status quo." Among those natural cancer cures is vitamin B17, or Laetrile therapy. Bitter almonds, not regular almonds, are popular as alternative cancer medicine due to their high vitamin B17 content. Hemp oil and GcMAF have also shown promising results. Yet health food stores stopped selling B17 in the form of apricot seeds in 2002, sometimes because of armed FDA raids. There have been reports of cancers being killed merely from patients eating large servings of bitter almonds daily. There are also B17 almond extract capsules that cancer patients can take daily that are not only cheap, but a non-toxic pill for their treatment. This did not bode well for the pharmaceutical industry. They stood to lose hundreds of billions of dollars annually ... so what does the FDA do? They openly banned apricot seeds, and the vitamin B17 extract, as an "unapproved drug," while heaping ridicule on doctors and patients who insisted these substances were successfully curing cancers. One can recall the blistering headlines in mainstream newspapers and magazines describing "Fake Laetrile Cancer Treatment" and "Quacks Treating Patients With Unapproved Substances." The British Government followed suit in the same year and banned both. People in both countries were arrested and charged for merely selling organic apricot seeds, a carrier of B17 laetrile.

Individuals who suffer a greater risk of heart disease greatly benefit from consuming a B6 supplement. This vitamin helps control healthy blood content, and ultimately leads to healthier heart function and reduced risk of heart disease. Vitamin B6 helps the body metabolize foods for energy while regulating the nervous system for proper function. Millions of people require B6 supplementation to maintain health, yet the FDA is gradually removing vitamin B6 supplements from the market. Soon, the only way citizens will be able to obtain these supplements is from a pharmaceutical company and with a doctor's prescription. This is a huge boost to Big Pharma profits, all at higher cost to the consumer. Once again, the FDA serves the drug industry, not the citizens it was established to protect.

Today Big Pharma continues to rake in billions annually, while millions are dying from their drugs. By some calculations, pharmaceutical drugs are the fourth largest killer in America. After all, the more drugs we use, the more money they make! The pharmaceutical companies cannot both be interested in your health *and* watch the bottom line within their treatment paradigm. There is no money for them in simple, natural, and effective remedies, much less preventative health care or the support of the body's natural healing abilities which people can learn to implement themselves. The conflict of interest here is glaringly obvious. Pharmaceutical companies have a vested interest in SICKcare.

And the Rockefeller family? They are known participants of the New World Order, which advocates a world population reduction plan. Maybe the millions dying in plain sight every year from their toxic products are part of their grand plan to cull the population. After all, the more educated the person, the longer they live and the more resources they will use. It would be far more manageable to dummy down the populace, keep them as high on legal drugs as possible, and have them die as soon as they retire.

SUPPRESSED ENERGY MEDICINE

Royal Raymond Rife was a brilliant scientist and inventor. He was born in Elkhorn, Nebraska, in 1888, and died in 1971. After studying at Johns Hopkins, Rife developed bioelectric medicine technology that is still commonly used today in the fields of optics, electronics, radiochemistry, biochemistry, ballistics and aviation. He received 14 major awards and honors and was given an honorary Doctorate by the University of Heidelberg for his work.

In the 1930s, Rife invented a "Universal Microscope" that used light in a revolutionary design. It enabled him to see virus-sized microbes, otherwise invisible to the naked eye, that could not even be seen by using an electron microscope. More importantly, unlike electron microscopes, the microbes remained alive, and thus could be observed during treatment. He found that every microorganism has a "mortal oscillatory rate"—a point at which it will shatter or break apart when bombarded by sound waves—like an intense musical note that can shatter glass. Once the frequency for the cancer-linked microbe was identified, it was a logical next step to test his revolutionary discovery on mice, and then shift to clinical treatment of supposedly "terminal" cancer patients.

In 1934, Rife and a team of doctors and scientists from leading medical research facilities, including the University of Southern California, cured 16 out of 16 cancer patients using the newly developed "Frequency Machine." Over the next four years the instruments and methods were refined. Some of North America's most brilliant cancer researchers visited Rife's laboratory in Southern California and became involved in a secret research committee at USC. Clinical proof of successful and painless cures from cancer and other microbe-caused diseases increased as clinics in Los Angeles and San Diego began documenting cases. Additional laboratory verification came from research institutions in San Francisco, Chicago, New Jersey and Montreal, Canada. By the late 1930s, "energy medicine" doctors, using a variety of different electronic approaches, grew in numbers and had formed several national associations.

What seemed like the end of all cancer by 1940 suddenly hit a brick wall. The threat to orthodox medicine was too great. Without any consideration for the Hippocratic

Oath or the wellness of their patients, influential doctors and medical societies such as the American Medical Association and the American Cancer Society mounted a furious counterattack against Rife's monumental discovery before the American public could be informed of its success. Doctors and researchers who were using Rife's instruments to treat cancer and other diseases were threatened with losing their licenses, were denied tenure, and even being thrown into jail! Most meekly surrendered. An energy medicine laboratory complex under construction, that was in the process of verifying Rife's discoveries, was mysteriously burned down and destroyed, just when the owner was visiting Rife in California.

But the suppression did not end there. Rife was hauled into court and prevented from leaving for England where leading scientists were prepared to establish an independent testing facility to substantiate the great discovery, and distribute his unique instruments worldwide. Rife's detractors had pounced. Medical journals censored articles supporting his work, and one of the greatest scientific and medical discoveries of the 20th century was ruthlessly suppressed, essentially written out of history by the gatekeepers of American medical "science."

The AMA suppression does not mean Rife's discoveries were wrong. By the late 1980s, an evolutionary shift slowly began to unfold throughout the world in favor of energy medicine. Bio-energetic, or "subtle energy" interactions with the human body became a serious research area in leading universities, private medical research facilities, and even certain government agencies such as NASA began to embrace the science. A grassroots interest in alternative medicine simultaneously erupted to confront drug medicine practitioners with industry failures and expense. A new awareness frenzy, led by the information revolution on the Internet, has produced renewed interest in Royal Raymond Rife's extraordinary cures, almost lost to the world 80 years ago. On the horizon there lies an awakening of mainstream America, and possibly the delivery of Rife's lost discoveries can be integrated into a strikingly different 21st century healing model, thereby enabling natural, painless, and inexpensive methods of curing many diseases through sound, light, color and frequencies. Indeed, the cancer cure has been known for decades, and cancer patients need to be intelligently skeptical of any orthodox treatments still in use. Instead, investigate the extensive verifiable data on alternatives, and trust the intuitive messages coming from your own body when it appears that the "cure" is worse than the disease.

CHEMOTHERAPY IS UNSAFE

Chemotherapy is a tragic medical fraud. Rather than boosting the immune response of patients, this radioactive treatment combined with pharmaceutical drugs breaks down the immune system, and usually allows tumors to grow back. Patients are even told this, but feel caught between choosing a recommendation by "top medical authorities" and death. The latest research further confirms what the holistic health community has been saying for decades: Chemotherapy is, flatly stated, poisonous. It's not "treatment," it's not medicine, and it is not a prevention or a cure. It is a poison with virtually no medicinal value except, perhaps, in one or two percent of cancer cases. Even in this very small percentage of cases, it isn't clear whether lifestyle changes, placebo effects, or the intangible but powerful mind-over-matter techniques are responsible.

A team of researchers looking into why cancer cells are so resilient, accidentally stumbled upon a far more important discovery. The team discovered that chemotherapy actually heavily damages healthy cells, and subsequently triggers them to release a protein that sustains and fuels tumor growth. Beyond that, it also makes the tumor (damaged cells) highly resistant to future treatment. Reporting their findings in the journal *Nature Medicine*, the scientists report that their findings were "completely unexpected." The news comes after it was previously revealed by similarly ground-breaking research that expensive cancer drugs not only fail to treat tumors, but actually makes them far worse.

The number one side effect of chemotherapy is more cancer. The cancer centers across North America should *technically* be renamed "poison centers," because they are in the business of poisoning patients with a toxic cocktail of chemicals that are really cancer tumor growth accelerants. The cancer drugs were found to make tumors "metastasize," and grow massively in size after consumption. As a result, the drugs killed the patients more rapidly. Scientists who performed the research say that a protein known as WNT16B, created from chemotherapy, boosts cancer cell survival, and is the reason that chemotherapy actually ends lives more quickly than if no "treatment" is administered. Finding evidence of significant DNA damage when examining the effects of chemotherapy on tissue derived from men with prostate cancer, these findings are a big slap in the face to mainstream medical organizations who have been pushing chemotherapy for years as the only realistic option available to cancer patients. What is rarely emphasized is that our body's ability to heal itself is far greater than anyone has been allowed to believe.

VACCINES ARE UNSAFE

"Vaccination" is the delusion that profit-thirsty institutions are protecting us from diseases by injecting us with those same diseases—along with other hazardous chemicals. While there is some evidence that a very small injection of a virus enables the body to build up an immune response, the principal problem lies with "other hazardous chemicals" present in the vaccines. Consequently, this system of prevention is wide open to sabotage. The situation we have today is that current vaccines promoted by the pharmaceutical industry suppress our immunity simply by over-taxing our immune system with foreign materials, like heavy metals, pathogens and viruses. The heavy metals slow down our immune system, while the viruses *set up shop* to grow and divide. It is like being chained and handcuffed before going swimming. Vaccines contain toxic chemicals such as formaldehyde, thimerosal, aluminum, squalene, mercury, lead, antifreeze, RNA/DNA from animal tissues and aborted fetal tissues, and other foreign proteins in the form of live, attenuated, or dead viruses and bacteria. The most common ingredient in any vaccine is formaldehyde, which the U.S. National Toxicology Program described as "known to be a human carcinogen." So if formaldehyde is a known cancer-causing agent, why are we injecting it into people? In many cases, the vaccine additives are far more toxic than the viral component.

Also found in most vaccines is the element mercury, a known neurotoxin that is especially damaging to the developing brain and nervous system. A growing number of researchers believe that the soaring rates of neurological and developmental disorders in our children can be linked to a corresponding increase in the number of government-mandated vaccines. For example, the seasonal flu shot has recently been combined with the H1N1 vaccine. This has been known to cause a debilitating disease known as "Guillain-Barré syndrome."

"The entire vaccine program is based on a massive fraud," said Russell L. Blaylock, M.D., a neurosurgeon for 30 years and a member of the editorial staff of the *Journal of American Physicians and Surgeons*, the official journal of the Association of American Physicians and Surgeons. According to Dr. John Rengen Virapen, a former Eli Lilly executive, who after 35 years of service decided to quit and speak out about Big Pharma's method for profit, said "It's evil—the pharmaceutical industry does nothing but annihilate the population purely for profit." Dr. Virapen thinks the benefit of symptomatic diseases is to keep Big Pharma profitable, a statement of the obvious conflict of interest imbedded in the system, and people will have to live with the symptoms for the duration of their lives, rather than being administered a cure.

Activists and many doctors are starting to realize that there is really no such thing as a safe vaccination. All vaccines contain ingredients like aluminum and mercury, both neurotoxins; animal DNA which literally bonds with our own; formaldehyde; and other toxins. The question is at what levels and how are these vaccines regulated? Where is an oversight entity with no vested interest in profits? A definitive connection between mercury poisoning and autism has been established. The symptoms between mercury poisoning and autism are identical: loss of speech; social withdrawal; reduced eye contact; repetitive behaviors; temper tantrums; sleep disorders; and seizures. Yet autism receives less than 5% of the research funding given to many less prevalent childhood diseases. All parents should do extensive research before allowing their children to be vaccinated.

The rise of many diseases—such as cancer—correlate very strongly with the rise of mandatory vaccinations around the world. The number of compulsory vaccines has increased from 10 to 36 in the past quarter-century, and over that time period there has been a simultaneous increase in the number of children suffering from disabilities that prevents them from reaching their full potential as adults. The incidences of learning disabilities and attention deficit disorder has doubled in the past 25 years while autism has increased by an incredible 200 to 500 percent in every state in the U.S. in just the last decade. Just a decade ago autism was diagnosed in only one in a thousand children, five years ago it was one in 500, and now it is one in a hundred. A German study released in September, 2011 that monitored about 8,000 unvaccinated children, newborn to 19 years old, shows that vaccinated children have at least *two to five times* more diseases and disorders than unvaccinated children.

Also in 2011, a UK physician named Dr Lucija Tomljenovic disclosed 30 years of secret official documents that were acquired through the Freedom of Information Act in the UK, that showed that government experts have known all along that most vaccines are ineffective. These same government experts worked to prevent safety studies and colluded to deceive the public. They have also known that vaccines often cause the diseases they are supposed to prevent, and are a known hazard to children. Yet these are the same vaccines currently mandated for most children in the USA. To aid in the predictive programming acceptance of autism, the PBS children's show Sesame Street introduced an autistic puppet named "Julia" in 2017.

Vaccines are currently approved based on research submitted to the government by drug companies that have developed these new vaccines, and that have also funded the pre-license studies. Many of the studies drug companies conduct do not use true placebos and have only a few hundred, or a few thousand, healthy people enrolled ... a cohort of subjects that does not match the health profile of the millions of people who will be told to get these vaccines after they are licensed by the FDA. The safety of vaccine protocols are primarily based on the word of the companies that produce and profit from them. These same companies enjoy a liability shield from vaccine injury lawsuits in civil court that is granted to them by Congress and the Supreme Court. We've been told that vaccines stimulate the immune system with a "rehearsal" of what will happen when an actual disease comes down the pipeline. We are told that when the disease does appear, the immune system will be locked and loaded and ready to destroy the attacking germs. Again, there is some logic and some evidence for this theory. But research reveals more and more parallels between widespread vaccination programs and an increase in neurological diseases. There is also no disinterested oversight of the actual level of additives in vaccines. Furthermore, it appears that flu vaccines often do not protect against flu, or even stop the transmission of flu viruses from person to person. What has happened, then, to the so-called "rehearsing" of the immune system?

There is a dark and deadly truth about the vaccine industry: the Centers for Disease Control (CDC); the AMA; and vaccine scientists everywhere. Many competent researchers consider the evidence overwhelming that vaccines are the *vector* by which cancer and other diseases are spread throughout the human population. People do not realize that vaccines have been used for sterilization. It is all about population control and making as much money as possible. AIDS, polio, and certain forms of cancer were spread across the globe decades ago through the distribution of vaccines that were engineered as biological weapons, and created in secret eugenic programs to cull certain "undesirable" human population groups. Merck vaccine scientist Dr. Maurice Hillerman admitted the presence of SV40, AIDS, and cancer viruses present in certain vaccines. The cure for AIDS has already been developed, and it is described in U.S. Patent #5676977. While overseeing a military bionetics contractor called Litton Bionetics, Dr. Robert Gallo was both the discoverer of AIDS, and the scientist who developed its cure.

MERCURY IN VACCINES ARE POISON

Heavy metals, no matter how minuscule, should never be introduced to humans. Mercury is a dangerous heavy metal in its natural quicksilver form, but it is even more dangerous when the neurotoxin methylmercury is released into the environment by human activity. In both organic and inorganic forms, mercury wreaks havoc with the nervous system—especially in the developing nervous system of a fetus. Mercury penetrates all living cells of the human body, and it has been documented to increase the risk for autism. This calls into question mercury's use in dental fillings, vaccines, and just about anything containing high fructose corn syrup—a near staple in the American diet—as well as baby food. Paradoxically, the Corn Refiners Association naturally supports this chemical, and yet makes the disclaimer that mercury is *"dangerous at any level."*

Where was the Public Health Service and the American Academy of Pediatrics during all these years mercury exceeded regulatory safety levels, and secondly, why were they not aware of the extensive literature showing deleterious effects on the developing nervous system of babies? As we shall see, even these "experts" seem to be cloudy on the mercury literature. How did they miss that?

It was disclosed that thimerosal, plus ethylmercury sodium salt were used in all influenza, DPT (and most DtaP), and all Hepatitis B vaccines. Yet thimerosal is recognized to cause hypersensitivity, neurological problems, and even death. It is also known to easily pass through the blood-brain and the placental barriers. Therefore, what they are admitting is that we have a form of mercury that has been used in vaccines since the 1930s, and no one has bothered to study the effects on biological systems, especially the brain of infants. This is a recurring theme in the government's regulatory agencies, as witnessed with fluoride, aspartame, MSG, dioxin, and pesticide issues.

Aluminum is also a significant neurotoxin, and it shares many common mechanisms with mercury. For example, they are both toxic to neuronal neurotubules; interfere with antioxidant enzymes; poison DNA repair enzymes; interfere with mitochondrial energy production; block the glutamate reuptake proteins (GLT-1 and GLAST); bind to DNA; and interfere with neuronal membrane function. Toxins that share toxic mechanisms are almost always additives, and are frequently synergistic in their toxicity. A significant number of studies show that both of these metals play a major role in all of the neurodegenerative disorders. It is also important to remember that both of these metals accumulate in the brain and spinal cord. This makes them accumulative toxin that are rapidly excreted, and therefore are much more dangerous than other toxins.

It is important to acknowledge that mercury is a fat-soluble metal. This means that it is stored in the body's fat. The brain contains 60% fat, and it is therefore a common site for mercury storage. A significant proportion of the mercury enters the brain, and is stored in the brain's phospholipids of fats. Mercury has been shown to pass through the blood-brain barrier rather easily. With each new dose—and remember, children today receive as many as 22 doses of these vaccines—another increment is added to the brain storage depot. This is why mercury is called an *accumulative poison*.

METAL ELEMENTS IN THE BODY

The widely administered flu shots in the USA still contain mercury in the form of thimerosal, which, among other maladies, is associated with the development of Alzheimer's Disease. A recent study indicates that people who received a flu shot were *more* likely to become infected with the H1N1 flu virus than people who have not received the shot. A far safer choice to prevent catching the flu is to ensure an adequate level of vitamin D, a healthy diet, and regular exercise.

The brain has one of the highest metabolic rates of any organ, thus the impairment of its energy supply, especially during development, can have devastating consequences. Mercury, even in lower concentrations, is known to damage DNA and impair DNA repair enzymes which play a vital role in brain development. Mercury activates microglial cells, increasing excito-toxicity and free-radical production, as well as lipid peroxidation-central mechanisms during brain injury. In addition, even in doses below those which can cause obvious cell injury, mercury impairs the glutamate transport system, which in turn triggers excito-toxicity—a central mechanism in autism and other neurological disorders. Ironically, aluminum also paralyzes this system.

Fluoride, when combined with aluminum at a concentration of only 0.5 ppm in drinking water, forms a compound that can destroy hippocampal neurons. With over 60 percent of communities in the USA having fluoridated drinking water, this is a major health concern. Most EU countries have outlawed fluoridation. It has been learned that fluoro-aluminum compounds mimic phosphate compounds and can activate G-proteins. The G-proteins play a major role in numerous biological systems, including the endocrine, and in neurotransmitter functions as cellular second messengers. Considering the main ingredient in chemtrails is aluminum, this toxic cocktail is especially alarming.

"WHO" ARE YOU?

The World Health Organization (WHO) currently has the power to order forced vaccinations in 194 countries. The International Health Regulations (IHR), pursuant to Article 21 of the Constitution of WHO, came into force in June 2007, and allowed the General-Director of WHO to declare an international health emergency. In such a case, the Director-General can impose regulations, including "sanitary and quarantine requirements and other procedures designed to prevent the international spread of disease," order forced vaccinations, and impose travel restrictions. All 194 signatory countries to IHR must comply.

These are articles from the World Health Organization Constitution:

Article 21: The Health Assembly shall have authority to adopt regulations concerning: (a) sanitary and quarantine requirements and other procedures designed to prevent the international spread of disease; (b) nomenclatures with respect to diseases, causes of death and public health practices; (c) standards with respect to diagnostic procedures for international use; (d) standards with respect to the safety, purity and potency of biological, pharmaceutical and similar products moving in international commerce; (e) advertising and labeling of biological, pharmaceutical and similar products moving in international commerce.

Article 22: Regulations adopted pursuant to Article 21 shall come into force for all Members after due notice has been given of their adoption by the Health Assembly except for such Members as may notify the Director-General of rejection or reservations within the period stated in the notice.

The International Health Regulations 2005 are legally binding regulations (forming international law) that aim to (a) assist countries to work together to save lives and livelihoods endangered by the spread of diseases and other health risks, and (b) avoid unnecessary interference with international trade and travel.

If the WHO were confident that vaccines really worked, then there would be no need to force vaccinations upon people. Because, logically speaking, the people who were already vaccinated should not get the disease from those who are unvaccinated. Whether you agree with vaccines or not, we should always be allowed to have a choice.

MEDICAL ERRORS 6ᵀᴴ LEADING CAUSE OF DEATH

The leading cause of death in the United States are (yearly incidents): Heart Disease (652,091); Cancer (559,312); Stroke (143,579); Cronic Lower Respiratory Disease (130,933); Unintentional Injuries from Accidents (117,809); *Preventable Medical Errors (98,000)*; Diabetes (75,119); Alzheimer's Disease (71,599); Influenza/Pneumonia (63,001); and Nephritis/Nephrosis (43,901). Medical errors that the government and private health insurers have classified as "never events," that is, events that should never happen in a hospital, are occurring more frequently at rates never before seen.

Furthermore, a 2005 study, published in the *Journal of the American Medical Association* (JAMA), found that *one third* of all medical studies turned out to be wrong. That same prestigious journal that reported 25,000 deaths per year by poor medical practices or unnecessary procedures. It broke down the numbers by attributing 106,000 deaths due to adverse reactions to prescription meds; 80,000 deaths due to infections acquired while in the care of hospitals; 20,000 due to other errors in hospitals; and 12,000 deaths per year due to unnecessary surgery. Furthermore, according to JAMA, over 220,000 people die each year from properly prescribed drugs. Therefore, the third leading cause of death in the United States is the taking of medicine. It's the equivalent of two jumbo jets crashing and killing everyone on board every day for a year. What's worse is that the number of injuries caused by prescription medication is estimated to be in the millions. Lastly, 7,000 annual deaths are due to medication errors while patients were in the hospital.

We are the most medicated country in the world, but also one of the most ailing. What does that tell you? The top 10 biggest perpetuated healthcare myths include: Vaccines make you healthy; Pharmaceuticals prevent disease; Doctors are experts in health; You have no role in your own healing; Disease is bad luck or bad genes; Screening equals prevention; Health insurance aims to keep you healthy; Hospitals are places of health and healing; Conventional medicine is advanced; More research equates to more cures.

DRUGGING OUR CHILDREN: ADD/ADHD

The medical system is now labeling normal but problematic behaviors as "mental disorders." Attention Deficit Disorder (ADD), and its popular sub-type Attention Deficit Hyperactivity Disorder (ADHD), are bogus mental "disorders" based merely on a checklist of behaviors. This is not to say that these hyperactive behaviors do not exist, or are never a problem for parents and teachers to deal with. The point here is the label. The "mental disorder" label makes it tempting for parents to look for a medical rather than a social/behavioral solution. There are effective strategies and behavioral guidelines to address these issues when children seem to be unable to learn in conventional classrooms. These alternatives take time and patience to implement and sometimes mean changing the learning or home environment. Nevertheless, drugs should be a last resort. These facile diagnoses of normal children who don't fit an often flawed learning environment has resulted in more than 4.5 million children being diagnosed and put on drugs such as Ritalin, Adderall, and Concerta. These children are stigmatized for life as being labeled with psychiatric disorders. Is it any wonder that the child disorder labeling combined with the drugging industry is a multi-billion dollar industry?

The German weekly *Der Spiegel* quoted the U.S. American psychiatrist Leon Eisenberg on its cover story in early February, 2012, admitting that ADHD is a make-believe diagnosis. Eisenberg, born in 1922 as the son of Russian Jewish immigrants, was the "scientific father of ADHD." Seven months before his death at the age of 87, in his last interview, he said "ADHD is a prime example of a fictitious disease." Since 1968, Leon Eisenberg's "disease" has haunted the diagnostic and statistical manuals, first as a "hyperkinetic reaction of childhood," now called "ADHD." The use of ADHD medications in Germany rose in 18 years from 34 kilograms in 1993 to a record of no less than 1760 kilograms in 2011—which is a 51-fold increase in sales! In the United States, every tenth 10 year old boy presently swallows an ADHD medication on a daily basis.

When the medical community and the pharmaceutical companies—the chief proponents of this disease model—admit that they do not know what "causes" this strange disease, and cannot even prove it exists, what kind of monster have we created? When we learn that tens of thousands of American and Australian children are being drugged with powerful and dangerous drugs bases on this "invented" disease, the concept of an anti-human depopulation agenda suddenly does not seem so far-fetched. There are vast implications in labeling children as "diseased" for behavior considered *undesirable*, and then drugging them into *compliance*.

Amazingly, the U.S. DEA places these psychiatric drugs in the same highly addictive category as drugs such as cocaine, morphine and opium. According to the Centers for Disease Control, boys are much more likely to be diagnosed with ADHD than girls. But the checklist for ADHD could fit any normal kid's profile, and literally include such ridiculous criteria as "runs about or climbs excessively in situations when it is not appropriate," is often "on the go," "acts as if driven by a motor," "blurts out answers," "is easily distracted," "loses pencils or toys," or "often doesn't seem to listen." For a child to have one of these "symptoms" is all it takes to diagnose a child with the mental disorder of ADHD. The above checklist of behaviors is taken directly from the American Psychiatric Association's Diagnostic and Statistical Manual of Mental Disorders (DSM), also known as the psychiatry industry's billing bible. This is simply a list of child-like behaviors that psychiatrists clustered together and repackaged as mental disorders. Child drugging is a *$4.8 billion-a-year industry*.

Do we want children as they grow up believing that the answer to their problems lies in taking drugs? Do we want children learning that they are not responsible for their own behaviors and can instead blame a "mysterious" disease? A significant percentage of these children are placed on stimulant medications; highly dangerous drugs with significant short-term and long-term side effects. University of Buffalo researcher Professor John Blazer, cites findings that belie the belief that Ritalin, known generically as methylphenidate, is short acting. "By issuing psychotropics to children, we do in fact create an interaction between the chemical, the drug, and the developing organism, and in particular the developing brain, which is the target organ of a psychotropic." He goes on, "Stimulants such as Ritalin and amphetamine have grossly harmful impacts on the brain—reducing overall blood flow, disturbing glucose metabolism, and possibly causing permanent shrinkage or atrophy of the brain."

The specter of these negative effects on growth and development is even more ominous in light of the fact that children under the age of six are routinely prescribed stimulants, despite specific warnings that they are not safe for children that young. Somewhat more frightening than the potential long-term effects of psychostimulants, is the relatively common "zombie-like" effect induced in children. The zombie effect has been described by Dr. Peter Breggin this way: "(This) drug-induced docile behavior is caused by chemically blunting or subduing the child's higher brain function. That part of the child's brain requiring creativity, freedom, play, energetic activity, consistent discipline and inspiring educational activities will be blunted."

With the skyrocketing prevalence rates of this "disorder," there is a substantial possibility that we are raising a generation of children whose creativity, thinking and spirit are being blunted by drugs without any verifiable medical justification. Tellingly, as reported in a study by researchers at the University of California at Berkeley that followed 500 children over 26 years, Ritalin is basically a "gateway" drug to other drugs, in particular cocaine. Lead researcher Nadine Lambert, as reported in the *Wall Street Journal*, concluded that Ritalin "makes the brain more susceptible to the addictive power of cocaine and doubles the risk of abuse."

The normal mental development of children is also assaulted in other ways. There are many hazardous waste products absorbed by or dumped into our environment. From poisons such as arsenic being detected in chicken stocks and fresh water, to fluoridation, which is intentionally added to American's public drinking water, we are increasingly being exposed to toxic substances. The jury is still out about why thousands of planes have been spraying chemtrails across the country, but what is not in doubt is an alarming occurrence of aluminum, barium and strontium being detected in the atmosphere and in the soil. New research links aluminum intake to a variety of cancers.

Mercury from coal-burning plants has entered the fish population food chain at alarming levels, and it has also seeped into our water supplies. And pills and shots prescribed to deal with symptoms from environmental pollutants are hurting us more than they are helping us. The mercury-based preservative thimerosal in vaccines is largely responsible for a dramatic increase in autism and a host of other neurological disorders among children. There are reports suggesting that more children are maimed or die from vaccines and medication side effects than the occurrence of the diseases they're meant to prevent. Giving an infant a vaccine is the equivalent to injecting an average-size adult 25 or more times. It is scientific madness to inject children, even babies, with mercury, formaldehyde and aluminum hydroxide, often contained in the vaccines they receive.

THE NAZIS USED FLUORIDE ON PRISONERS

Dumbing down a population is nothing new. In the early 1930s, a group of German chemists found a clever way to dominate public opinion by way of water fluoridation. By the mid-1930s, Hitler and the German Nazi`s envisioned a world dominated and controlled by a Nazi philosophy of pan-Germanism. The German chemists worked out a very ingenious and far-reaching plan of mass-control, ultimately submitted to and adopted by the German General Staff. Hitler authorized fluoride use in Nazi prison camps and slave labor camps as a way to sterilize humans and force prisoners into calm submission. Adding this toxic chemical to the water damaged the brains of many prisoners—making them far easier to control. This grand mass medication scheme produced sterility in women, thereby reducing the prison population. By 1942, Germany became the world's largest producer of aluminum and sodium fluoride. Fluoride ultimately became widely used in the concentration camps to render the prisoners docile and inhibit the questioning of authority.

Taking a page from the Nazi playbook, the Russians quickly learned of fluoride's sedative properties and implemented "water medication" in their plan to communize the world. In 1940, Soviet concentration camps implemented fluoride administration to inmates to decrease resistance to authority, and induce physical deterioration. In this scheme of mass-control, sodium fluoride occupied a prominent role in totalitarian governments. The Germans and Soviets were the first to use fluoride to make prisoners "stupid and docile," and to minimize the risk of revolt. England and the USA would not be far behind, but now to be used on the general population.

Water fluoridation was brought to England from Russia by a communist named Kreminoff. The plan Kreminoff proposed was to control the population in any given area through the mass medication of drinking water supplies. By this method, they could control the population in whole areas, and reduce population with water medication that resulted in sterility in women. At the end of World War II, the USA imported many top German scientists under the auspices of "Operation Paperclip." About half were rocket scientists who entered the aviation and aerospace industries, including NASA. The other half, which were far more secretive, participated in creating the CIA and NSA spy agencies. Some were "MK" psychiatric researchers. The MK stands for *Mind Kontrol*, and this research evolved into the CIA's MK-ULTRA program. In affiliation with the CIA, these Nazi scientists developed the "Pain-Drugs-Hypnosis" (PDH) technology to fracture subjects' personalities, who were then manipulated into specialized and highly compartmentalized human "robots," devoid of a conscience. They have since been employed for purposes of assassination, passing classified information, drug transport, sex slavery, "super soldier" training, and other missions requiring the utmost in endurance, information secrecy, containment, and deniability. Certainly, fluoride also played a role in keeping these subjects compliant.

Harley Rivers Dickinson, a Liberal Party member of the Victorian Parliament for South Barwon, Australia, made the following statement on the historical use of fluorides for behavior control.

> It is a matter of record that sodium fluoride has been used for behavior control of populations. ... At the end of the Second World War, the United States Government sent Charles Elliot Perkins, a research worker in chemistry, biochemistry, physiology and pathology, to take charge of the vast Farven chemical plants in Germany. While there, he was told by German chemists of a scheme which had been worked out by them during the war and adopted by the German General Staff. This scheme was to control the population in any given area through mass medication of drinking water. In this scheme, sodium fluoride will in time reduce an individual's power to resist domination by slowly poisoning and narcotizing a certain area of the brain, and will thus make him submissive to the will of those who wish to govern him. Both the Germans and the Russians added fluoride to the drinking water of prisoners of war to make them stupid and docile.

Fluoridation was first introduced into the United States in the 1940s, and later was endorsed by the U.S. Public Health Service in 1950 under the disguise of being beneficial for teeth. In 1943, researchers from the U.S. Public Health Service began to examine the health of residents of Bartlett, Texas, to see if the 8 ppm fluoride in the drinking water was affecting their health. It was checked again in 1953. They found that the death rate in Bartlett was three times higher than a neighboring town, which contained 0.4 ppm fluoride. It was noted in 1944: "Even at 1 ppm, fluoride in drinking water poisons cattle, horses and sheep." The trick was the exact right dosage between docile control and outright poisoning. Even today, every state in the USA has fluoridated drinking water at varying levels, including 42 of the 50 largest cities.

TAINTED DRINKING WATER

Not all fluoride is bad—only the type promoted by dentistry and added to our drinking water and food supply. Calcium fluoride is a naturally occurring mineral, while its synthetic counterpart, sodium fluoride (silicofluoride), is an industrial-grade hazardous waste material made during the production of fertilizer. The past history of sodium fluoride includes patented use in rat poison and insecticide. There are many blind and double-blind studies showing that sodium fluoride has a cumulative effect on the human body, and can lead to allergies, gastrointestinal disorders, bone weakening, cancer, and neurological problems. Sodium fluoride is also one of the basic ingredients in both the anti-depressant Prozac (*Fluo*xetene Hydrochloride) and Sarin nerve gas (Isopropyl-Methyl-Phosphoryl Fluoride).

The truth that the American public needs to understand is the fact that sodium fluoride is nothing more than a hazardous waste by-product of the nuclear and aluminum industries. In addition to being the primary ingredient in rat and cockroach poisons, it is also a main ingredient in anesthetic, hypnotic, and psychiatric drugs, as well as military-grade nerve gas. Today it is estimated that hydrofluoric acid and hydrofluorosilicic are the two types of fluoride that are added to about 70% of the drinking water supplies in the United States. Hydrofluoric acid is a compound of fluorine. It is a chemical by-product of aluminum, steel, cement, phosphate, and nuclear weapons manufacturing. Hydrofluoric acid is also used to refine high octane gasoline; to make fluorocarbons and chlorofluorocarbons for freezers and air conditioner;, and to manufacture computer screens, fluorescent light bulbs, semiconductors, plastics, herbicides, and is the type added to toothpaste. The disposal protocol for these bi-products are stringent and expensive to comply with, yet the effects these toxins have on the human body are devastating. Despite the evidence against it, fluoride is still added to over 50% of North American public drinking water supplies.

The logical questions arise that if fluoride is so toxic, why are they poisoning us with it? Why is it allowed to be added to the toothpastes and drinking water of the American people? Officially, to keep our teeth from decay. In reality, it will cause people to become complacent, docile, and tolerant. But in doing so, it also causes the systematic breakdown of organs, reproductive systems, digestive and circulatory systems. All of these bi-products cause cancer and hundreds of other ailments, including the following reported effects of fluoride on the human brain: A reduction in nicotinic acetylcholine receptors; damage to the hippocampus; formation of beta-amyloid plaques (the classic brain abnormality in Alzheimer's Disease); reduction in lipid content; damage to purkinje cells; exacerbation of lesions induced by an iodine deficiency; an impaired antioxidant defense systems; an increased uptake of aluminum; and accumulation of fluoride in the pineal gland. The introduction of cadmium actually causes the breakdown and weakening of genes, which means the effects can be passed down to your offspring.

Much like fluoride, the drug lithium alters the brain's normal production of serotonin and norepinephrine, that in turn artificially alters the way an individual thinks and how he or she feels about given situations. Now there are advocates and pseudo-scientists who believe lithium could reduce suicide rates if traces were added to drinking water. But then what about the rest of us who do not have suicidal thoughts? We get dosed regardless? One study, published in the *British Journal of Psychiatry*, analyzed a sample of 6,460 individuals taking lithium and then compared suicide rates across 99 districts. Rates were lower in the lithium-ingesting population. Lithium is literally a mind-altering, antidepressant chemical substance, and those promoting it openly admit the drug modifies brain function. And yet they suggest that forcibly introducing these chemical changes on the unwitting populations of the world is a good and acceptable practice.

But is this how we wish to function as a society? Adding lithium appears to be yet another way that the general population can be "dumbed down." Why would governments want to turn our drinking water into a chemical cocktail? Perhaps this way society will be more malleable and fewer people will be concerned about what is really going on with their government.

FLUORIDE IS HIGHLY TOXIC

In 1995, a Chinese study on fluorides found that the IQ of children was lowered in fluoridated areas. Further studies by the New Jersey Department of Health have confirmed a 6.9 fold increase in bone cancer in young males. There is also ample evidence that fluoride increases the incidence of hip fractures for both older men and women. A major Harvard study released in July, 2012, and published in a Federal Government journal, confirms that fluoride lowers IQ in children this way: "Our results support the possibility of adverse effects of fluoride exposures on children's neurodevelopment."

Fluoride is more toxic than lead. It is linked to an increase in bone cancer, brain damage, and lower IQs. It causes teeth discoloration, and makes bones brittle. The mineral is associated with cancer, and it has a tendency to accumulate in the pineal gland, an important hormone control center where it wreaks considerable havoc. Infertility in women was found to increase with water fluoridation. Although fluoride is an unapproved drug by the Food and Drug Administration, the agency takes no action to have it removed.

Fluoride is a poison, yet we add it to our water and toothpaste and even call it a supplement, although it has zero nutritional value. It is supposed to have medicinal value, namely the prevention of tooth decay, which is the official explanation for adding the toxic mineral to the water supply. But that value is far outweighed by its toxicity. Recent European Union legislation regarding food supplements lists fluoride as an essential element to offer for supplementation. This is somewhat ironic when contrasted with the European legislators' feigned concern over the *putative* toxicity of vitamins and their efforts to limit dosages of certain vital nutrients in order to "protect public health."

During the late 1990s in England, a scientist named Jennifer Luke undertook the first study examining the effects of sodium fluoride on the pineal gland. She determined that the pineal gland, located in the middle of the brain, was a target of fluoride. The pineal gland simply absorbed more fluoride than any other physical matter in the body, even bones. Because of the pineal gland's importance to the endocrine system, her conclusions were a breakthrough. Luke's study provided the missing link to the physiological damage from sodium fluoride that had been hypothesized but not positively connected. A veritable root source for the chain reaction of blocked endocrine activity had been isolated.

COMBATTING FLUORIDE

Purportedly, fluoride's only humanly-beneficial application is when it is applied topically to teeth, but even that is harmful. We need to consider the incredible absorption rate of mucous membranes in the mouth, and the tiny size of the fluorine molecule, which has only one atom more than water. Even distillation will only remove about 20% of it, because it essentially evaporates at the same temperature as water. No known water filtration system can remove it completely, regardless of their commercial claims. There are thousands of official warnings about ingesting fluoride throughout the world. Many countries and many cities in the U.S. have banned the practice of fluoridation because of this evidence. It is known that only half of the fluoridated toothpaste in an average size tube can kill a child if ingested all at once.

The use of fluoride for "health" reasons is one of the greatest double speak insanities of our time. Perhaps the push for "enriching" our water and our foods with fluoride has an ulterior motive that has little to do with health. Be that as it may, the campaign for fluoridation is still in full swing, and health authorities inexplicably continue to endorse its usage. Many cities around the world now have grassroot efforts to "Get The 'F' Out" of our water supply.

A good way to combat fluoride accumulation is frequent exposure to outdoor sunshine, 20 minutes or so at a time, every day. This will help stimulate a fluoride calcified pineal gland. Just make sure to allow direct sunlight on the skin. This is more important than most realize, because the pineal gland affects so many other enzyme and endocrine activities, including melatonin production.

We also use fluoride in many household items, such as non-stick frying pans, high-tech water repellent fabrics, and other common everyday items. Recently, at least some timid attempts to start assessing the disease burden caused by fluoride are under way. The "Journal of Water Health" published an article on this research. Meanwhile, people should choose non-flouride toothpaste, attempt to filter it out, and try to get a little bit of direct sunlight on your body every day, which is also a great natural source of vitamin D.

TAKE CONTROL OF YOUR OWN HEALTH

The take-away of this chapter demonstrates that an elite class want to destroy most of the Earth's population because they greatly fear an awakening of the mass population, and they believe they can get away with their various "slow kill" eugenics programs. But why do they want to destroy the IQ's of the average citizen? The answer is that those serfs who remain alive after the culling must remain bound in abject slavery. They must never be allowed to challenge the intellectual supremacy of the elites. They cannot be allowed to possess the ability to contemplate revolt against the rule of the cabal, much less actually organize and launch a revolt. And that is how fluoride became the only drug that is forced as a mass medication of a population with no debate or control over dosing.

Before jumping to the conclusion that there is no way that a mass-toxification could happen in America, just remember the movie *Erin Brockovich*. The billion dollar energy corporation, PG & E, actually tried to convince the local community that Hexavalent Chromium was good for the body, when in fact it was deadly. The entire California community where Erin Brockovich lived were diagnosed with hundreds of different forms of cancers, sicknesses, and disease. If they've done it before, they'll do it again.

The more we wait and assume that someone else will be responsible enough to look out for our best interests, well-being, safety and health, the more we sit on our comfy couch ingesting processed foods while watching the real "fake news" on mainstream television news, the more we believe the propaganda being shoved down our throats through corporate-controlled media. The more we allow the corporate and political Psy Ops to enslave our minds, the worse off we become.

CHALLENGING THE UNHEALTH INDUSTRY

Do you want a real health care solution? One that does not require mandatory insurance coverage? Consider the alternative to ingesting chemicals, and instead taking proven steps towards wellness. Many alternative treatments, therapies and supplements are suffering from ever increasing regulatory burdens, but there are enough still available to elevate our health. Here are 10 commonsense points for real health care in America as suggested by *Natural News*:

> *1. Arrest all Big Pharma CEOs and top executives who have been involved in*
> *felony crimes, price fixing, doctor bribery, experiments on children and*
> *so on. After all, prescription drugs now kill more people in the USA than*

heroin and cocaine combined. Where's the accountability?

2. Outlaw vaccines additives such as mercury, aluminum, MSG and formaldehyde.

3. Decriminalize natural medicine and stop prosecuting alternative cancer doctors.

4. Abolish the FDA and end the drug monopoly cartel. Restore the free market to medicine.

5. Halt all Medicare and Medicaid payments to drug companies, hospitals and health insurance companies. Instead, issue patients vouchers that they can spend in any way they wish, to receive whatever form of care that works for them. This would restore the free market to medicine, where competition would drive down prices and spur improved patient outcomes.

6. End all intellectual property claims on genes and medicines. Break Big Pharma's insidious cycle of inventing fictitious diseases and then marketing those fake diseases in order to sell deadly chemicals to a gullible public. Medicine belongs in the public domain, not in the hands of the greedy few.

7. Break the chain of influence between drug companies and medical journals, medical schools and the media. Outlaw drug money influence over all these institutions. Prosecute doctors for bribery if they have accepted money, gifts or free vacations from Big Pharma.

8. Decriminalize free speech about nutritional supplements, herbal remedies and natural therapies. Allow makers of natural products to tell the truth about the healing benefits of their products.

9. Encourage states to pass "medical freedom zone" laws that nullify federal laws concerning health care in their particular states. Openly allow the practice of alternative cancer therapies, nutritional therapies, and other natural remedies. Turn your state into a medical tourism destination for all Americans!

10. End the artificial legal protections of Big Pharma and the vaccine industry. Restore due process rights to patients who have been harmed by drugs or vaccines. Only through economic and legal pressures will drug companies clean up their act and stop harming people.

Such rapid advancements in medicine, for better or for worse, have certain modern philosophers believing we have entered a "transhuman" period of our collective evolution. Transhumanism is an international cultural and intellectual movement with an eventual goal of fundamentally transforming the human condition by developing widely available technologies to greatly enhance human intellectual, physical, and psychological capacities. Transhumanist thinkers study the potential benefits and dangers of emerging technologies that could overcome fundamental human limitations, including the study of ethical matters involved in developing and using such technologies.

Although transhumanism offers hope for the transcendence of human biological limitations, it generates many intrinsic and consequential ethical concerns. The latter include issues such as the exacerbation of social inequalities and the exponentially increasing technological capacity to cause harm. What can be done if these "advancements" go terribly wrong? The final chapter in the Control section examines the one transhuman advancement that is slowly creeping into every person's life, that is, unless that person is not dependent on food to survive.

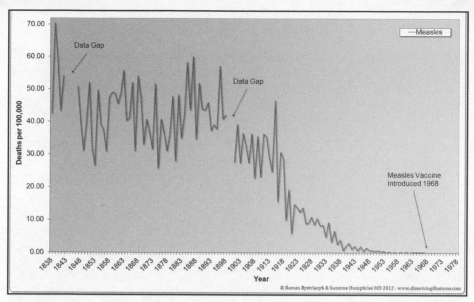

This graph shows the decline in deaths from measles from 1900 to 1987. What is striking is the decline in the mortality rate from a high of 14.3 per 100,000 to .2 per 100,000 in 1963. Prior to 1963, mortality from measles had already dropped to low levels from improved living standards, better nutrition, and sanitary measures. 1963 is when the measles vaccine was introduced in the USA. It was subsequently withdrawn because it caused severe problems, and a new one was introduced in 1967. The measles vaccine began to be used in England in 1968.

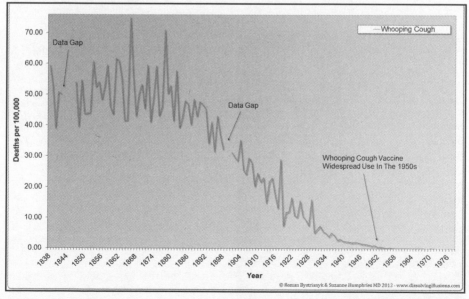

This chart shows England and Wales whooping cough mortality rate from 1838 to 1978. Once again we see very little, if any, effect with the introduction of the whooping cough vaccine. Vastly improved personal hygiene is the real reason why the spread of diseases has decreased in the last century.

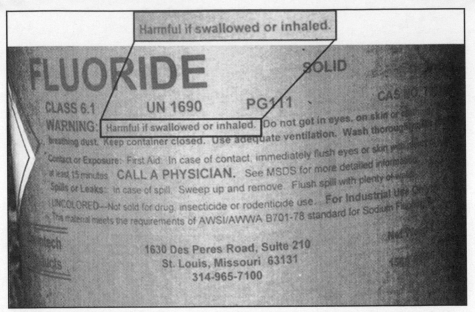

Sodium fluoride is what is in this canister. Notice it says, "Harmful if swallowed or inhaled ... For industrial use only." It is a toxic preservative used in many things, including biological and chemical weapons. So what is put into our water then? Fluorosilicic acid and/or Sodium Fluosilicate. Both are toxic in any amount. The first one is actually a by-product of a fertilizer manufacturer, and it costs them a lot of money to dispose of this hazardous product properly, so instead, it is given to the sheeple (us). They hide it behind other names like Sodium Silica. And we are supposed to be okay with fluoride being injected into our drinking water?

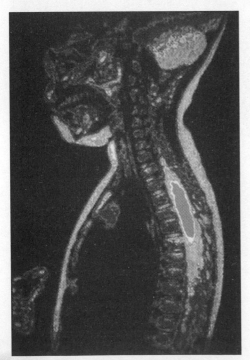

< The National Cancer Institute—the U.S. government's principal agency for cancer research—created a stir by publishing the fact that molecules found in marijuana kill breast and lung cancers in lab tests. Marijuana remains a federally illegal, schedule 1 drug with "no medical use" and "a high potential for abuse," so the NCI was pressured to take down the statement. But the fact remains.

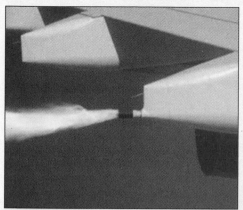

< Chemtrails are sprayed aerosols in the sky that expand to create a milky, artificial cover, after the airplane spraying them has passed. They are primarily composed of nanoparticles of aluminum, barium, strontium sulfate, titanium, bacteria, radioactive materials, plasma and other elements such as Morgellon nano-fibers, which can penetrate and infest the skin. These agents cause respiratory diseases, heart damage, temporary loss of memory, headaches, and disorientation. The toxic by-product of coal burning is called fly ash, and is the leading additive of the chemtrail cocktail. A convenient option, otherwise fly ash is very expensive to dispose of or store.

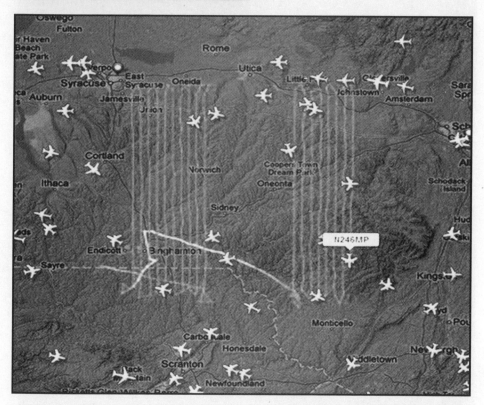

This image went viral on social media sites in July, 2013. It shows the flight route of plane N246MP, which is a typical spraying pattern of a chemtrail plane. It is estimated that the cost of the chemtrails project is 3.6 billion dollars per day. Despite spraying millions of tons of chemical materials on the planet, the public is left without any information given by any of the mainstream news networks worldwide that this is happening everywhere. Government officials are equally tight-lipped.

The spraying is illegal according to international law and must be publicized and stopped. Yet the globalist think tank, the Council of Foreign Relations (CFR), has advocated the use of chemtrails as part of a geoengineering program to fight global warming, along with a "global" administrative body to run the program. Former CIA head John O. Brennan publicly touted the benefits of geoengineering to the CFR in June, 2016.

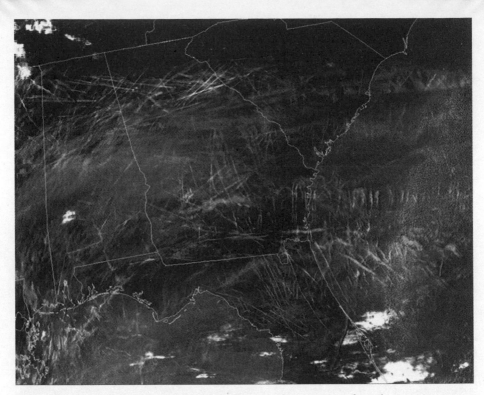

This satellite photo was taken on January 29, 2004, showing aircraft trails spanning across several states in the southeast. The word "chemtrails" is a knock-off of the word "contrails." Contrails are trails of water vapor condensation that can be seen in the sky when a jet airplane is traveling at above 30,000 feet altitude, and usually dissipates quickly as the moisture returns to form invisible ice crystals. "Chemmies" are something different. They are often formed behind jet aircraft at a much lower altitude and can persist for hours in the sky, eventually becoming milky white clouds when several are laid down in the same region. They often have a different color from contrails and frequently exhibit a rainbow spectrum called "sun dogs" if lit just right from the Sun.

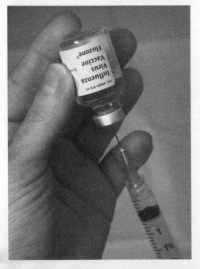

< Many medical experts now agree it is more important to protect yourself and your family from the vaccine, than the disease itself. Every year the pharmaceutical industry, medical experts, and the mainstream media work hard to convince us to get vaccinated against the flu and other illnesses. Yet the public is not given full disclosure about their harmful effects. What we don't hear are cases about adverse reactions, or about the toxic chemicals that exist in almost all vaccines.

What's more, the vaccine manufacturers cannot be sued if the net result of their products were to cause extreme pain, autism, convulsions or even death. There are laws protecting victims from other drugs, but not vaccines. You can thank the powerful pharmaceutical lobbyists for their cunning payoffs to the right legislators to draft this counter-intuitive law protecting vaccine manufacturers.

FOOD CONTROL & ESCAPE

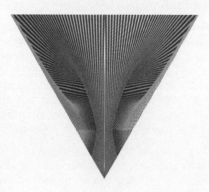

"The doctor of the future will no longer treat the human frame with drugs, but rather will cure and prevent disease with nutrition." –Thomas Edison

AMONG the myriad of esoteric topics discussed, none may be as important to your own personal well-being as the diet you cultivate. The larger questions of nutrition and food choices are surrounded with disinformation that draws us away from the correct answers we need to use in order to make healthy nutritional choices. Why, for example, are diseases such as cancer so rampant in our society? What is the correlation between our blood and diet that so few people know about, which could be the key to optimum health? Why is it that almost all food commercials on television are exclusively promoting fast food restaurants or processed meals? Why does it seem there is a conspiracy to keep us unhealthy, rather than at an optimum state of strength and vitality? A famous quote by the ancient Greek physician Hippocrates states, "Let food be thy medicine and medicine be thy food." This timeless adage still holds incredible truth today, as the most effective way to protect the body against disease is to feed it the nutrients it needs to build strong immunity and a healthy digestive tract, where the bulk of immunity resides.

Artificial flavors, colors, preservatives, emulsifiers and sweeteners have saturated the food supply for more than four decades now. We are on the precipice of discovering what our toxic food industry has done to our bodies and our environment. It is important to ask if you are healing yourself long term, or are you just covering up the symptoms? Similar to Hippocrates, nutrition doctor Ann Wigmore maintains, "The food you eat can be either the safest and most powerful form of medicine, or the slowest form of poison." And now we are confronted with Genetically Modified Organisms (GMO) crops, which were originally introduced with no human safety tests. The crops were given a *carte blanche* approval because the entire Food and Drug Administration (FDA) process is corrupted and controlled by large corporations. People may be developing cancer and other ailments as a result of eating GMO food and no one would know. We may be unknowingly developing serious digestive disorders and neurological problems because the testing process has been hijacked.

Did you ever wonder how people who exist on a diet of mainly processed foods can be both overweight and malnourished at the same time? Despite overly abundant calories, people who live off of boxed macaroni and cheese, frozen dinners, ramen noodles, and other packaged foods are not getting the essential nutrients that those who eat a whole foods diet are getting. Deadly GMO ingredients aside, the sheer amount of chemicals in processed foods can lead to disease, obesity, malnutrition and a premature death. Knowing what we put into our bodies has never been more important. As a popular bumper sticker states: "If the label says 'sugar-free' or 'low fat' think chemical shit storm."

Since most Americans do not output the same amount of matter that they input into their bodies, it explains why so many people diet but can never lose weight. To understand this dilemma we need to learn about our food choices and our bodies in a different context. For instance, the body creates fat cells to store acid and other toxins. Almonds have 79% fat of the good kind, whereas pork has only 58%. The difference between the two is that pork, as with all meats, is literally dead. When anything is in a state of death or decay it holds an acidifying effect on its environment as it breaks down. Pork in particular is a three on the pH scale, whereas almonds are an eight. We gain weight only when the body is toxic and cannot take out the trash. When our bodies are not able to output the same amount of toxins we input they become acidic. If we are not excreting the same amount of toxins that we eat, breathe in the air, or apply to our skin, we are creating cancerous conditions inside our bodies. Sadly, there is little information on this subject, hence its entry as a control mechanism in the realm of esoteric study. The alarming reality is that people are fed by a food industry that pays no attention to health, and are treated by a health industry that pays no attention to food.

EAT FAST, DIE YOUNG

Millions of people eat fast food daily. The high levels of calories, animal fat and sodium in most fast food menu items will eventually lead to serious health problems. A study published in the *Journal of the American Heart Association* found that eating significant amounts of fast food can contribute to atherosclerosis, another term for clogged arteries, and which can increase a person's risk of health conditions such as heart attack and stroke. Fast food can also contribute to an increased risk of arthritis, sleep apnea, certain kinds of cancer, diabetes and liver disease, according to the study.

Fast food is called junk food for a good reason. People pay a high price in negative dietary elements when they eat junk food, including "empty" calories, "bad" fat, and far more sodium than the body needs with relatively small amounts of nutritional value. To understand why, consider that one popular fast food hamburger contains about 540 calories and 29 grams (g) of fat. It contains 10 g of saturated fat and 1.5 g of trans fat. The sodium content is 1,040 g. However, the hamburger does contain about 25 g of protein, with 6 percent of your recommended intake for vitamin A, 2 percent for vitamin C and 25 percent each of calcium and iron. The trans fat, sugar and calorie content from one McGriddle sandwich is close to the maximum calorie content a smaller-sized adult should have all day. But of course there is never just one. There are sides with that sandwich, and let's not forget the two other daily meals. All those empty calories are high in bad fats and lacking in essential food nutrients. This is why, despite the feeling of being fed a big meal, the body is actually being malnourished.

Quite literally, you are what you eat and drink. The majority of fast food French fries are made from GMO potatoes, and some are deep fried in animal fat, which is the worst way to cook food. Artificial chemicals, dyes, processed sugar, and cancer causing ingredients such as the carcinogenic aspartame routinely found in soft drinks are making regular consumers ill and unfit. Does this sound like a "treat" to you? If soda pop is something you have once in a while for a treat, consider finding something else to stimulate your senses. Aspartame, GMOs, and untreated industrial waste can all be included in the "slow kill" family of eugenics, along with chemtrails, fluoride, and vaccines, as we've seen in previous chapters.

TOP 10 FOOD ADDITIVES TO AVOID

Chemical additives find their way into our foods to help ease processing, preservation, packaging and storage. But how do we know what food additives are in that box of macaroni and cheese, and how could it have such a long shelf life? It bears repeating to think "chemical shit-storm" when you see the words "low-fat" or "fat-free" posted on a snack label. Sugar, caffeine, alcohol, junk food or processed food are the culprits that increase general anxiety in people, so try to avoid these too.

A typical American household spends about 90% of their food budget on processed foods, and in doing so, become exposed to a plethora of artificial food additives, many of which can cause dire consequences to a person's health. Some food additives are worse than others. Although this list is controversial among those who commented on the *FoodMatters.TV* website, here's a list of the top ten food additives to avoid:

1. *Artificial Sweeteners: Aspartame, aka "NutraSweet," is an excitotoxin, a substance which overexcites cells to the point of damage or death. It is a serious health risk. It is typically found in diet or sugar free sodas, Diet Coke, Coke Zero, Jello (and other gelatins), desserts, sugar free gum, drink mixes, baking goods, table top sweeteners, cereal, breath mints, pudding, Kool-Aid, ice tea, chewable vitamins and toothpaste. There are many artificial sweeteners on the market, and some are more toxic than others. Clearly aspartame is the worst, with only four calories per gram and 200 times sweeter than sugar. Aspartame is sold under the trademarks NutraSweet and Equal. Results indicate that aspartame is a multi-potential carcinogen, even consumed daily at 20 milligrams per kilogram of body weight. That is a lower quantity than the maximum recommended by the FDA. It's one reason you should never purchase major brands of chewing gums. Aspartame is such a toxic poison it will be featured extensively below.*

2. *High Fructose Corn Syrup: High fructose corn syrup (HFCS) is a highly-refined artificial sweetener that has become the number one source of calories in America. It is found in almost all processed foods. HFCS packs on the pounds faster than any other ingredient, increases your LDL ("bad") cholesterol levels, and contributes to the development of diabetes and tissue damage, among other harmful effects. A few years ago, the Corn Refiners Association petitioned the Food and Drug Administration (FDA) to allow the term "corn sugar" as an alternative label declaration for high fructose corn syrup. The reason? Too many people were finding out how lethal HFCS is for the human body. HFCS is found in most processed foods, breads, candy, flavored yogurts, salad dressings, canned vegetables, and cereals. HFCS causes insulin*

resistance, diabetes, hypertension, increased weight gain, not to mention
that it is manufactured from genetically modified corn.

3. **The food additive Monosodium Glutamate (MSG / E621):** *MSG is a slow
poison that hides behind dozens of names, such as natural flavoring,
yeast extract, autolyzed yeast extract, disodium guanylate, disodium
inosinate, caseinate, textured protein, hydrolyzed pea protein and
many others. Currently, labeling standards do not require MSG to be
listed in the ingredient list of thousands of foods. MSG is an amino
acid used as a flavor enhancer in soups, salad dressings, chips, frozen
entrees, and many restaurant foods. MSG is also an excitotoxin. Studies
show that regular consumption of MSG may result in adverse side
effects which include depression, disorientation, eye damage, fatigue,
headaches, and obesity. MSG affects the neurological pathways of the
brain and disengages the "I'm full" function which explains the effects of
weight gain. MSG is mostly found in Chinese food (Chinese Restaurant
Syndrome), many snacks, chips, cookies, seasonings, most Campbell Soup
products, frozen dinners, and lunch meats. It is not a nutrient, vitamin,
or mineral, and has no health benefits. The part of MSG that negatively
affects the human body is the "glutamate," not the sodium. The bound
glutamic acid in certain foods (corn, molasses, wheat) is broken down
or made "free" by various processes (hydrolyzed, autolyzed, modified or
fermented with strong chemicals, bacteria, or enzymes) and refined to a
white crystal that resembles sugar.*

4. **Trans Fat:** *Trans fat is used to enhance and extend the shelf life of food
products and is among the most dangerous substances that you can
consume. Found in deep-fried fast foods and certain processed foods
made with margarine or partially hydrogenated vegetable oils, trans fats
are formed by a process called hydrogenation. Numerous studies show
that trans fat increases LDL cholesterol levels while decreasing HDL
("good") cholesterol; increases the risk of heart attacks, heart disease
and strokes; and contributes to increased inflammation, diabetes and
other health problems. Oils and fat are now forbidden on the Danish
market if they contain trans fatty acids exceeding two percent, a move
that effectively bans partially hydrogenated oils. Trans fat is found in
margarine, chips and crackers, baked goods, and fast foods. Multiple
studies on Pacific island populations who get 30-60% of their total
caloric intake from fully saturated coconut oil have all shown nearly
non-existent rates of cardiovascular disease. The fact is, all saturated
fats are not created equal. The operative word here is "created," because
some saturated fats occur naturally, while other fats are artificially
manipulated into a saturated state through the man-made process
called hydrogenation. Hydrogenation manipulates vegetable and seed
oils by adding hydrogen atoms while heating the oil, producing a rancid,
thickened substance that really only benefits processed food shelf life and
corporate profits. Just about all experts now agree that hydrogenation
does nothing good for your health. These manipulated saturated fats are
also called trans-fats, and you should avoid them like the plague.*

5. **Common Food Dyes:** *Food colorings still on the market are linked with
cancer. Blue 1 and 2, found in beverages, candy, baked goods and pet
food, have been linked to cancer in mice. Red 3, used to dye cherries,
fruit cocktail, candy, and baked goods, has been shown to cause thyroid
tumors in rats. Green 3, added to candy and beverages, has been linked
to bladder cancer. The widely used yellow 6, added to beverages, sausage,*

gelatin, baked goods, and candy, has been linked to tumors of the adrenal gland and kidney. Studies show that artificial colorings found in soda, fruit juices, and salad dressings may contribute to behavioral problems in children, and lead to a significant reduction in IQ. Animal studies have linked other food colorings to cancer. Watch out for these: Blue #1 and Blue #2 (E133) are banned in Norway, Finland and France. Each may cause chromosomal damage. They are found in candy, cereal, soft drinks, sports drinks and pet foods. Red dye # 3 (E124) and the more current dye Red #40 were both banned in 1990 from many foods and cosmetics after eight years of debate. These dyes continue to be on the market until supplies run out! These dyes have been proven to cause thyroid cancer and chromosomal damage in laboratory animals and may also interfere with brain-nerve transmission. They are still found in fruit cocktail, maraschino cherries, cherry pie mix, ice cream, candy, bakery products and more. Yellow #6 (E110) and Yellow Tartrazine (E102) are banned in Norway and Sweden. They have been found to increase the number of kidney and adrenal gland tumors in laboratory animals and also may cause chromosomal damage. They are found in American cheese, macaroni and cheese, candy, carbonated beverages, lemonade and more.

6. **Sodium Sulfite (E221) and Sodium Chloride:** Sodium Sulfite is a preservative used in wine-making and other processed foods. According to the FDA, approximately one in 100 people is sensitive to sulfites in food. The majority of these individuals are asthmatic, suggesting a link between asthma and sulfites. Individuals who are sulfite sensitive may experience headaches, breathing problems, and rashes. In severe cases, sulfites can actually cause death by closing down the airway altogether, leading to cardiac arrest. Sodium Sulfite is found in wine and dried fruit. A dash of sodium chloride, more commonly known as salt, is the culprit that the mainstream media and medical community claim we should stay away from. They're right, but only because it's not real salt. Common table salt (sodium chloride) has almost nothing in common with traditional rock or sea salt. If a food label lists salt or sodium chloride as an ingredient, that's the bad stuff and you need to avoid these foods wherever possible.

7. **Sodium Nitrate (sodium nitrite):** Sodium nitrate is used as a preservative, coloring and flavoring in bacon, ham, hot dogs, luncheon meats, corned beef, smoked fish and other processed meats. This ingredient, which sounds harmless, is actually highly carcinogenic once it enters the human digestive system. There it forms a variety of nitrosamine compounds that enter the bloodstream and wreak havoc with a number of internal organs: the liver and pancreas in particular. Sodium nitrite is widely regarded as a toxic ingredient and the USDA actually tried to ban this additive in the 1970s but was vetoed by food manufacturers who complained they had no alternative for preserving packaged meat products. Why does the industry still use it? Simple: this chemical just happens to turn meats bright red. It's actually a color fixer, and it makes old, dead meats appear fresh and vibrant. It is found in hotdogs, bacon, ham, luncheon meat, cured meats, corned beef, smoked fish or any other type of processed meat.

8. **Butylated hydroxyanisole (BHA) and butylated hydrozyttoluene (BHT):** BHA and BHT (E320) are used to preserve common household foods. Any processed food that has a long shelf life is often filled with BHA.

These preservatives are found in cereals, chewing gum, potato chips, and vegetable oils. They keep foods from changing color, changing flavor or becoming rancid. They are also oxidants, which form potentially cancer-causing reactive compounds in your body and can affect the neurological system of the brain and alter behavior. They are found in potato chips, gum, cereal, frozen sausages, enriched rice, lard, shortening, candy, and jello. Propyl Gallate is another preservative often used in conjunction with BHA and BHT. It is sometimes found in meat products, chicken soup base, and chewing gum. Animals studies have suggested that it could be linked to cancer.

9. **Sulfur Dioxide (E220):** Sulfur additives are toxic. In the United States, the FDA has prohibited their use on raw fruit and vegetables. Adverse reactions include bronchial problems, particularly in those prone to asthma, hypotension (low blood pressure), flushing, tingling sensations or anaphylactic shock. Sulfur additives also destroy vitamins B1 and E and are not recommended for consumption by children. The International Labour Organization of the UN says to avoid E220 if you suffer from conjunctivitis, bronchitis, emphysema, bronchial asthma, or cardiovascular disease. It is found in beer, soft drinks, dried fruit, juices, cordials, wine, vinegar, and potato products.

10. **Potassium Bromate and Potassium Sorbate:** Potassium Bromate is an additive used to increase volume in some white flour, and is found mostly in breads and rolls. Potassium bromate is known to cause cancer in animals. Even small amounts in bread can create problems for humans. As one of the most prolific preservatives in the food industry, it is difficult to find an ice cream without potassium sorbate. However, it is not only recommended that people avoid this chemical, it's a necessity to eliminate it from our foods as a dangerous substance. The food industry and its scientists will parrot endless myths that potassium sorbate is not a health threat because of its safety record and non-toxic profile. This could not be further from the truth. Food and chemical toxicology reports have labeled potassium sorbate as a carcinogen, showing positive mutation results in the cells of mammals. Other studies have shown broad systemic and toxic effects on non-reproductive organs in animals. No long term studies have ever been initiated on either animals or humans, so there is simply not enough evidence to theorize what could happen after years of ingesting this preservative.

TOXIN DUMP

A dishonorable mention to the above list is fluoride, which is not on the list because it is added to water and not food. Fluoridated water is of dubious value for dental health and is yet another low-level environmental poison that should be banned. For those who believe the myth that it is good for our teeth, why then was fluoride deliberately added to Nazi prison camp and Soviet gulag drinking water? Why is fluoride a main ingredient in Prozac and Sarin nerve gas? Why is it widely added to water and toothpaste supplies in the USA? Why doesn't anyone care? Because we're all on fluoride! Fluoride is the primary ingredient in many rat and cockroach poisons. The International Academy of Oral Medicine and Toxicology has classified fluoride as an unapproved dental medicament due to its high toxicity.

Humans dump tons of toxins, trash, and assorted poisons onto the Earth everyday. Then we eat it. Animals eat it. Then we eat them. Isn't this going to kill us? Of course it will, but not right away. First we're going to get dumber. Most of us grew up ingesting fluoride, which collects around the pineal gland in the brain. Fluoride is poison. It can kill you if ingested directly. Those who stay quiet and die prematurely only have themselves to blame when they could have saved themselves and others by making enough commotion. It is said people put their faith in gods and politicians. The gods are questionable, but the politics are crystal clear. Political goals and our best interests do not coincide. We have some intelligent, well-meaning politicians. Just a few. We have a few smart people who keep telling us what is taking place in the world and what will happen if we don't act. They are, for the most part, ignored.

The Earth is a big nutrient factory. Everything we need to have a healthy brain comes from the Earth. What if we poison the Earth? What effect will it have on our brain? Everything we put down, drop, dump, empty out, or swallow ends up in our brain. There is nothing else that can happen. It's as simple as we are what we eat. If we pollute the Earth, we pollute what grows and we then pollute our brains by ingesting the same toxins.

Since the early 1990s, jet aircraft have been observed spraying aluminum, barium and other mysterious elements and compounds into the atmosphere in what has become known as the "chemtrail" phenomenon. Available evidence is indirect via measurements of rain water and snow pack, but the levels are so high, in some cases 1,000 times higher than normal, that some artificial source is clearly indicated. More evidence for the chemtrail agenda are various patents, thousands of photos worldwide, leaked videos, and individual testimonies that all strongly suggest jet planes are spraying a cocktail of metallic elements and Morgellon polymers into the atmosphere. One charitable description of "geoengineering" as a misguided attempt to suppress global warming, also called "solar radiation management." Other more nefarious explanations include a possible tie-in to the HAARP array mass mind control, Monsanto's aluminum-resistant seeds, or a "slow kill" anti-human eugenics program. For the first time ever, the atmosphere has conductive metallic particles in the air.

CODEX ALMENTARIUS

The Codex Alimentarius was created in 1962 as a trade commission by the United Nations (UN) to control the international distribution of food. Its initial intentions may have been altruistic, but it has since been taken over by corporate interests, most notably the pharmaceutical, pesticide, biotechnology, and chemical industries. Codex Alimentarius is a collection of internationally recognized standards, codes of practice, guidelines and other recommendations relating to foods, food production and food safety. Its texts are developed and maintained by the Codex Alimentarius Commission, a body that was established over 50 years ago by the Food and Agriculture Organization (FAO) of the United Nations, and the World Health Organization (WHO) that runs the program. Their officially stated purpose is to develop international food standards to protect consumer health and to facilitate fair trading practices in foods. But looking a little deeper, the Codex Alimentarius Commission is actually the UN and the WHO working in conjunction with the multinational pharmaceutical cartel and international banks.

More and more people are becoming concerned about the shady, secretive and dangerous laws and guidelines that is Codex Alimentarius. In reality, it is the thinly-veiled propaganda arm of the international pharmaceutical industry that does everything it can to promote industry objectives while limiting individual options to maintain health. Of course public knowledge would diminish member profits, so the real motives are kept top secret. In December, 1974, the U.S. National Security Council, under command of Henry Kissinger, prepared a classified study called National Security Study Memorandum 200 (NSSM 200), that falsely claimed that the worldwide population growth poses a major threat to USA national security interests. Codex Alimentarius is a control agenda, because those who control the food supply, control the people.

Codex Alimentarius is particularly dangerous because one of the major strategies behind the effort is to limit access to nutritional products and accurate information. Nutrients, minerals, and herbs could be categorized as toxins, or as hard drugs along with heroin. Most of the information available regarding Codex Alimentarius refers to its role in the USA, but it is not a USA-specific body. Far from it, Codex has wiggled its way into just about every national or international body concerned with public health. Posing as a benefactor, it then uses its significant financial and political clout to do its bidding.

While investigating the WHO and UN role in the biological weapons attack that became known as the Swine Flu (A-H1N1) pandemic of 2009, criminal intelligence (CI) agents from Canada and the USA stumbled upon a covert and sinister plan to kill off as many as three billion people by food malnutrition. The organization responsible for the starvation and murder of nearly half of the world's population is none other than the Codex Alimentarius Commission of the United Nations. The CI agents discovered that Codex Alimentarius is in full implementation mode, and is changing the status of the life-essential nutrients in our food, such as vitamins, minerals and enzymes, and labeling them as poisons. After the nutrients were re-classified, the Commission has been given the legal authority by the United Nations to eradicate key nutrients in our foods. They have already begun the eradication process by pasteurizing, that exposes food to high heat and irradiating, which exposes food to radiation. Milk was the first to be targeted for eradication because milk is one of the most important life sustaining foods on Earth. It is full of vitamins, minerals and enzymes—all essential ingredients for keeping people healthy and alive. Next were eggs and processed foods. Because all of the vitamins, minerals, and enzymes have been destroyed by pasteurization and irradiation, our bodies cannot stop or fight off diseases and illnesses caused by consuming these dead and rotting organisms. It's as if we're being starved to death from eating. This is yet another of the "slow kill" depopulation programs being implemented on the general population.

SAY NO TO GMOs

Genetically Modified Organisms, or GMOs, are made by the biotechnology process of genetic engineering. This process is accomplished by splicing genes from one species, such as bacteria, viruses, animals or humans, and forcing them into the DNA of a food crop or animal to introduce a new trait. These newly modified organisms have never been tested for safety or potential health risks.

Surprisingly, there is no national mandate to label GMO foods. Vermont had a state law requiring GMO labeling, but was overridden by a national gag order and the labeling was discontinued. Widely available GMO foods currently on food market shelves include corn, soy, yellow and crookneck squash, canola, sugar beets, alfalfa, and cottonseed (and their by-products), plus some zucchini and Hawaiian papayas. Without labeling requirements for GMO ingredients in the U.S. and Canada, it can be very difficult to know if you are eating GMOs. Because they are so new, these "foods" have not been adequately tested for safety, and feeding studies with animals suggest potentially critical health problems for humans eating these GMO products. Nonetheless, some GMOs have toxins that have been linked with birth defects, cancer, and hormone disruption. GM corn and soy have a poisonous pesticide called Bt toxin which kills insects by breaking open their stomachs in each cell. Recent evidence suggests that Bt toxin can also break down human cell walls, and Bt corn is currently registered as a pesticide with the EPA.

Results from studies with GMO-fed animals also suggest the potential for critical fertility problems among humans. Russian biologist Alexey V. Surov, along with other researchers, fed Campbell hamsters (which have fast reproduction rates) with Monsanto GM soy for two years. Most of the third generation hamsters in the study were infertile, had stunted growth, and suffered high pup mortality rates. Internationally, scientific studies and reports from farmers show that animals fed GMOs exhibit fertility problems, including damaged sperm cells, abortions, and premature births, as well as altered DNA functioning. Currently, Bt toxin has been found in 93% of the blood of pregnant women tested, and 80% of their unborn fetuses.

Children, especially, are vulnerable to the dangers of GMOs. Infants and young children are more sensitive to chemicals, toxins and food allergens. In short, their immune systems and blood brain barriers are not yet fully developed, and they metabolize food faster. Yet GMOs are found in non-organic baby formula, cereals, dairy products with rbGH or rbST (a genetically engineered bovine growth hormone), and many other foods.

Even Kaiser Permanente, the largest managed healthcare organization in the United States, has advised its members against GMOs in food. In its Fall, 2012, Northwest region newsletter, Kaiser suggested its membership limit exposure to genetically modified organisms. According to the newsletter, "GMOs have been added to our food supply since 1994, but most people don't know it because the United States does not require labeling of GMOs." Kaiser gave tips on how its members can avoid GMOs, including buying organic, looking for the "Non-GMO Project Verified" seal, and encourage members to download the "ShopNoGMO" app. Finally, they suggested that consumers should look for food products that have the "Certified Organic" logo on the package. Sounding more like a radical organic health proponent, the huge Kaiser corporation continued, "Despite what the biotech industry might say, there is little research on the long-term effects of GMOs on human health." Just as Kaiser has real concern for its patients, it is difficult to ignore the numerous independent studies that now show GMOs to cause organ damage and an inability to reproduce in rodents.

EATING BIOENGINEERED AND GENETICALLY MODIFIED ORGANISMS?

The health risks of consuming GMOs, also called genetically engineered (GE) foods, are becoming more widespread in the USA food supply, at a surprisingly alarming rate, and without any long-term knowledge of what the consequences might be. It is now clear that Americans are sick more often than Europeans, and more often than people from *any* other industrialized nation. Emerging scientific evidence suggests that a significant factor may be the genetic engineering of the American food supply, *with more than 80% of processed foods in the USA now containing GMOs.* It is important to note that at least 64 countries outside of North America require GMO labeling.

In May, 2013, the USDA announced J.R. Simplot's petition to produce what would then be the only genetically-engineered potato on the market. Simplot, one of the USA's leading suppliers of French fries, has branded them "Innate" potatoes. Essentially, the Idaho company figured out how to use existing potato DNA to design a spud that's less prone to dark spots. When cooked, it produced less acrylamide, a neurotoxin found in many foods. But studies on animals have indicated it may also cause cancer because the DNA has been tampered with.

Despite claims by government regulators and the food industry that GE foods are safe, scientific studies continue to show the opposite. GE foods have been linked with allergies, reproductive problems and infertility, birth defects, bizarre mutations, cancer, and now an unidentified mystery organism causing an epidemic of livestock deaths called "Sudden Death Syndrome." In humans, GE foods can trigger immune attacks, because they appear to your body as foreign invaders. The immune response can lead to chronic inflammation, which in turn raises a person's risk for additional health problems.

Through genetic engineering, animals can now be given entirely new characteristics by transferring the genes of one species into another. Animals can be made to grow faster and larger, and with the world's population skyrocketing, the *need to feed* necessitates a bigger and more sustainable food supply. Even more potential uses of genetically modified animals include creating animal organs that are easily transplanted into humans. But at what risk?

The two main types of GMO foods are distressing, herbicide-tolerant crops and pesticide-producing crops. At the very least, both are imprecise processes that are riddled with unexpected consequences, such as hundreds (to thousands) of genetic mutations with determined effects on human health. At worst, GE foods may be part of a secret anti-human eugenics program to cull the ever-growing population.

FROM GMOs TO CLONING TO EUGENICS

In the early 1990s, Monsanto began gene-splicing corn, cotton, soy, and canola with DNA from a foreign source to achieve one of two traits. They wanted to produce an internally-generated pesticide, along with an internal resistance to Monsanto's weedkiller RoundUp. Despite decades of promises that genetically engineered crops would feed the world with more nutrients and retain drought resistance, the majority of Monsanto's profits came from seeds that are engineered to tolerate Monsanto's RoundUp—an ever-rising, dual income stream—as weeds continue to evolve resistance to RoundUp. Monsanto has patented and released "aluminum-resistant" seeds, *seemingly* to counter the aluminum particles being sprayed in chemtrails as reported worldwide.

1996 marked the first "official" cloning of a mammal, a sheep named Dolly. A heated debate continues to this day regarding the morality of cloning. The moral question, then, becomes "is cloning playing God" or, is it scientific progress? In the early 1970s, when the first "test tube baby" Louise Brown was created, 78% of the U.S. population were against the idea of creating life outside the womb. The process consisted of an egg that was fertilized outside the mother's womb and then implanted. Although it caused an uproar, public protests, and controversy at the time, today the test tube process is commonplace, and since then over 50,000 babies have been created through assisted reproduction in the USA alone.

One threat of cloning is eugenics, called transhumanism by some, and it is the science of improving hereditary qualities by selective breeding, genetic engineering, or the *culling* of certain ethnic groups. Some consider depopulation to not merely be an urban myth of globalist fantasy, but instead consider it a chilling reality. Way back in the early 1900s, 30 U.S. states adopted eugenics laws that required citizens to be sterilized if they had a "hereditary" condition such as insanity, criminal tendencies, retardation or epilepsy, and similar laws were enacted in other countries. Adolf Hitler wanted to create a master race, and have himself cloned. Furthermore, Hitler believed that he could determine "what was superior and what was inferior." But is it so far-fetched to consider a nation creating an army of cloned "super soldier" humans, bred and brainwashed to kill? There are various agendas and worldwide proposals that are either implemented or "on the table," from Henry Kissinger's NSSM 200 to Ted Turner's admissions on video, it is clear that *the globalists want us dead.*

ABOLISH THE CRIMINAL FDA

For several decades running global industry has been changing the genetic design of crops and seeds without informing the public. As to the genetic modification of particular foods, labels are not even required in the United States. Large chemical companies own most of the seed companies, and their intention is to control all sources of the world's food supply. These organizations can now "patent" and own seeds. Organic farmers can no longer prevent their naturally grown crops from being infected by cross-pollinated varieties, which may contain harmful chemical insecticides that are inserted at a genetic level. We, as humans, are the unwitting guinea pigs of this experimentation. Some estimates are that 70% of the food in our grocery stores now include elements of genetically modified foods. The FDA's own scientists have warned about the unique health hazards of genetically engineering foods, yet the FDA ignores the advice of its own scientists, and chooses to support the biotech industries in their quest to "patent life," all the while poisoning our food system. GMOs do not feed the world—they only feed Monsanto's bottom line.

Have you seen any walnuts in your medicine cabinet lately? According to the Food and Drug Administration, that is precisely where you should store them. This is because Diamond Foods made truthful claims about the health benefits of consuming walnuts. As a result, the FDA sent Diamond Foods a letter declaring, "Your walnut products are drugs"—and "new drugs" at that. Therefore, "they may not legally be marketed ... in the United States without an approved new drug application." The agency even threatened Diamond with "seizure" if it failed to comply. With such irrational and draconian policies, the FDA more correctly stands for the "Fraud and Deception Administration."

As of late, the FDA has issued waves of warning letters to companies making foods such as pomegranate juice, green tea and walnuts, which are natural foods that protect against ailments such as atherosclerosis. The FDA is blatantly demanding that these companies stop informing the public about the scientifically validated health benefits these foods provide. The FDA obviously does not want the public to discover that they can reduce their risk of age-related disease by consuming healthy foods. They prefer consumers only learn about mass-marketed pharmaceutical drugs (or "garbage foods") that shorten human life span by increasing degenerative-disease risk. Case in point: the FDA allows potato chips to be advertised as "Heart Healthy."

PESTICIDE POISON

The World Health Organization has warned that chronic, non-communicable, diseases are rapidly becoming a worldwide epidemic, but they stop short in placing the blame correctly. In the big picture, escalating rates of neurocognitive, metabolic, autoimmune and cardiovascular diseases cannot be ascribed only to genetics, lifestyle, and nutrition. Early life exposure, plus ongoing bioaccumulation to toxicants, are also causing chronic disease in virtually every human demographic. Similar to GMOs, chemtrails and genetically engineered foods, pesticides were unleashed onto the natural world decades ago, and the consequences are only now beginning to be understood.

A recent study has determined a direct correlation between fetal exposure to pesticides and genetically modified foods. One major study conducted in Quebec, Canada, produced several alarming conclusions. It must first be pointed out that the pesticide/genetically modified foods connection (PAGMF), is a development wherein certain foods are engineered to tolerate herbicides, such as glyphosate (GLYP) and gluphosinate (GLUF), or insecticides such as the bacterial toxin bacillus thuringiensis (Bt). The aim of the Canadian study was to evaluate the correlation between maternal and fetal exposure, and to determine exposure levels of GLYP and its metabolite aminomethyl phosphoric acid (AMPA); GLUF and its metabolite 3-methylphosphinicopropionic acid (3-MPPA); and Cry1Ab protein (a Bt toxin) around the eastern townships of Quebec, Canada. Researchers analyzed the blood of 30 pregnant women (PW) and 39 nonpregnant women (NPW). The serum of GLYP and GLUF were detected in NPW and not detected in PW. Serum 3-MPPA and CryAb1 toxin were detected in PW, their fetuses, and NPW. This is the first study to reveal the presence of circulating PAGMF in women with and without pregnancy, paving the way for a new field in reproductive toxicology including nutrition and utero-placental toxicities.

Multiple perspectives can be summarized as contributing factors to the general poor health of the nation. There are the biological effects of the different classes of toxicants, as the Quebec study determined. Pesticides and other mechanisms of toxicity are also confirmed to be contributors to major diseases. To combat these rising rates of disease, healthcare practitioners have wide-ranging obligations when addressing environmental factors in policy, public health, and clinical practice. Public health initiatives include risk recognition, and chemical assessment. Health officials can also recommend exposure reduction, remediation, monitoring, and avoidance. The complex web of diseases and environmental contributors, ironically suggests some straightforward clinical approaches to addressing multiple toxicants. Widely applicable strategies include emphasis on nutrition and supplements that counter the toxic effects of GMOs. Applications also include exercise and sweating, and possibly medication to enhance excretion. Addressing environmental health and contributing factors to chronic disease has broad implications for society, with large potential benefits toward improved health and productivity.

FOOD SAFETY SHOULD REALLY MEAN ORGANIC

The word "organic" refers to the way growers nurture and control their crops. Organic regulations ban, or greatly restrict, the use of food additives and pesticides. Organic farmers use natural fertilizers such as compost rather than chemical products. They rotate crops to preserve soil nutrients and use gardening procedures which preserve water and reduce pollution. They give farm animals space outdoors and feed them additive-free and growth hormone-free products. It is not surprising that the chemical industrial complex is not a supporter of organic farming.

According to Dr. Shiv Chopra, a health whistleblower in Canada, the "Food Safety Modernization Act of 2010 (S 510), may be the most dangerous bill in the history of the USA." He continues, "S 510 would preclude the public's right to grow, own, trade, transport, share, feed and eat *each and every* food that nature makes. It will become the most offensive authority against the cultivation, trade and consumption of food and agricultural products of one's choice. It will be unconstitutional and contrary to natural law or, if you like, the will of God." In other words, the bill attempted to outlaw a citizen's right to grow, consume and sell pesticide-free, chemical-free foods. Such draconian measures are similar to what India faced with the imposition of the salt tax during British rule, only S 510 extends control over *all food* in the USA, violating the fundamental human right to grow their own food, or share seeds. S 510 would give Monsanto unlimited power over all USA seed, food supplements, food and farming. It would be illegal to grow, share, trade, or sell homegrown food. It will allow government to imprison violators. Unfortunately, despite massive protests, the U.S. Senate passed S 510 Food Safety Bill at the end of November, 2010, and it was signed into law by President Barack Obama in early January, 2011!

In classic Orwellian double speak, Monsanto says it has no interest in the new law and would not benefit from it, but Monsanto's Michael Taylor, who gave us rBGH and unregulated genetically modified organisms, appears to have designed the law himself. He even appointed himself as the new Food Czar to the FDA to administer the agency it would create, without judicial review. In March, 2013, this provision which critics named the "Monsanto Protection Act," was covertly inserted into the Agricultural Appropriations Bill that President Obama quickly signed into law. The provision protects genetically modified food interests from litigation. Fortunately, this provision was wisely taken out in September, 2013.

Monsanto is well aware that "he who controls the food, controls the population." Let's not forget, Monsanto is primarily a chemical manufacturer. In the end, we need to distinguish between chemically-induced food, and natural organic food. Instead of healthy fruits, vegetables, grains, and grass-fed animal products, U.S. factory farms and food processors produce a glut of genetically engineered junk foods that generate heart disease, stroke, diabetes and cancer—all backed by farm subsidies—while organic farmers receive no such assistance.

According to the Organic Consumers Association, "There is a direct correlation between our genetically engineered food supply and the $2 trillion the U.S. spends annually on medical care, namely, an epidemic of diet-related chronic diseases." How is it, and why is there no public outcry, that Monsanto is allowed to cause such detrimental impact to our environment and our health?

Monsanto's history reflects a consistent pattern of toxic chemicals, lawsuits, and manipulated science. Is this the kind of company we want controlling our world's food supply? Monsanto is not the only perpetrator. Other companies in the "Big Six" include Pioneer Hi-Bred International (a subsidiary of Du Pont), Syngenta AG, Dow Agrosciences (a subsidiary of Dow Chemical), BASF, which is primarily a chemical company that is rapidly expanding their biotechnology division, and Bayer Cropscience. The parent company Bayer bought Monsanto in 2016, to become one of the world's biggest agriculture giants. Now there is the Big Five.

THE MONSTER CALLED MONSANTO

The chemical multinational corporation Monsanto, whose dark history features scandals involving PCBs, Agent Orange, bovine growth hormone, NutraSweet, and genetically modified seed and herbicides, reaches back to the 1970s and '80s when the St. Louis-based company began to roll out consumer products. Monsanto was also besieged by charges that its decade of Vietnam War defoliation with Agent Orange dioxins—branded by a Yale environmentalist "the largest chemical warfare operation" in human history—had contaminated as many as 10 million Vietnamese and American people. This led to a $180 million settlement covering the claims of 52,000 troops in 1984. While Monsanto can trot out its own findings and influence the FDA to support its seed safety claims, there are independent studies linking its corn to organ damage, obesity, diabetes and allergies. It is worth noting the company's profits plunged in 2010 as evidence mounted that GM seeds, 90% of which originate with Monsanto, were not boosting yields as promised.

Monsanto is highly suspect, especially when regarding its dubious history and the products it produces. The wall of shame is long and extensive. Monsanto told us that DDT was safe. Monsanto told us that Agent Orange was safe. Now Monsanto and other chemical companies are in charge of telling us that their genetically modified foods are safe. You might wonder why our food is being *made and modified* by the world's largest pesticide manufacturer. Genetically modified foods appear to have serious long-range consequences, many of which will not be determined for decades. Already, GMOs are linked to serious health problems for people, animals and the soil. Ultimately they will be genetically modifying the very people they feed. Essentially, Monsanto is a chemical production company. Even as their aspartame and phenylalanine business are now owned by the drug company Pfizer, the company that also produces Listerine.

What are some of the most potentially dangerous GMOs? The genetically modified Monsanto crop known as Bt corn has been altered in order to produce its own toxin, a pesticide called Bacillus thuringiensis, which was artificially introduced into the corn to kill off rootworms before they have a chance to ruin the crop. This hybrid "franken-crop" now accounts for over 65% of all U.S. corn production. It has been shown to cause a resistance to rootworm beetles, yet also render the crop useless. Monsanto's GMO corn crops ravage American farmlands, but for some reason federal agencies ignore the dangers.

In a study released by the "International Journal of Biological Sciences," analyzing the effects of genetically modified foods on mammalian health, researchers found that Monsanto's GM corn is linked to organ damage in rats. According to the study, which was summarized by Rady Ananda at Food Freedom, "Three varieties of Monsanto's GM corn—Mon 863, insecticide-producing Mon 810, and Roundup herbicide-absorbing NK 603—were approved for consumption by USA, European and several other national food safety authorities." Monsanto gathered its own crude statistical data after conducting a 90-day study, even though chronic problems can rarely be found after 90 days. It concluded, therefore, that the corn was safe for consumption. The stamp of approval may have been premature, however, as the study concluded:

> *Effects were mostly concentrated in kidney and liver function, the two major diet detoxification organs, but in detail differed with each GM type. In addition, some effects on heart, adrenal, spleen and blood cells were also frequently noted. As there normally exists sex differences in liver and kidney metabolism, the highly statistically significant disturbances in the function of these organs, seen between male and female rats, cannot be dismissed as biologically insignificant as has been proposed by others. We therefore conclude that our data strongly suggests that these GM maize varieties induce a state of hepatorenal toxicity. ... These substances have never before been an integral part of the human or animal diet and therefore their health consequences for those who consume them, especially over long time periods are currently unknown.*

A two-year study published in September, 2012, by French researchers led by Professor Gilles-Eric Seralini, revealed that rats fed Monsanto's "Roundup Ready" corn developed significantly more tumors than a control group not fed GE corn. Roundup Ready crops have been specifically engineered for resistance to Monsanto's top-selling herbicide glyphosate, marketed under the trade name Roundup. In the scientific literature, Roundup Ready corn is also known as NK603. The rats fed a GMO diet also developed tumors that appeared earlier and grew more aggressively, and these rats died sooner than rats in the control group. The rats fed on Monsanto's genetically modified corn, or exposed to its top-selling weedkiller, suffered tumors and multiple organ damage. Gilles-Eric Seralini, of the University of Caen, said rats fed on a diet containing NK603—a seed variety made tolerant to dousings of Monsanto's Roundup weedkiller—or given water with Roundup at levels permitted in the United States, died earlier than those on a standard diet. The animals on the GM diet suffered mammary tumors, as well as severe liver and kidney damage. The study was published in the peer-reviewed journal *Food and Chemical Toxicology,* and presented at a news conference in London. "NK603 must be immediately withdrawn from the market and all GMOs must be subjected to long-term testing," the briefing concludes. The researchers said 50% of males and 70% of females died prematurely, compared with only 30% and 20% in the control group. Seralini, in a scientific paper published in 2009, was part of a team that has voiced previous safety concerns based on a more concise rat study. This new study takes things a step further by tracking the animals throughout their two-year lifespan. Seralini believes his latest lifetime rat tests give a more realistic and authoritative view of risks than the 90-day feeding trials that form the basis of GM crop approvals. Three months is only the equivalent of early adulthood in rats. Now that genetically modified corn is shown to cause cancer, why is it still on the market?

The Geneva-based Covalence has a system for tracking the reputations of the world's largest companies. It ranked Monsanto at the bottom of 581 multinationals in its 2010 ethics index. GMOs are deeply unpopular and outlawed in Europe and many other countries, yet they dominate key crops in the United States ever since 1996, when Monsanto introduced a soybean that was genetically altered to tolerate Monsanto's Roundup weed killer. How is it that Monsanto is allowed to manipulate our food after such an ominous and dark product history?

ASPARTAME POISON

Aspartame is an artificial sweetener currently used in more than 6,000 consumer products worldwide, including most diet soft drink beverages products. It is more popularly known as Nutrasweet, Equal, Creatine, and Canderel. It is found in foods labeled "diet" or "sugar free," but in reality, they are terribly toxic for the body. Aspartame is believed to be carcinogenic, and it accounts for more reports of adverse reactions than all other foods and food additives combined. Aspartame is not your friend. In fact, it was once listed as a potential biochemical weapon by the Pentagon. The current patent holder for aspartame is the Monsanto Company, which was a partner of I. G. Farben, the infamous chemical company within Nazi Germany. Soft drinks may contain up to 190 milligrams (mg) of aspartame per 8.3 fluid ounce serving. The largest soft drink manufacturers note that "when aspartame is digested, the body breaks it down into aspartic acid, phenylalanine and methanol"—and it is methanol that is one of the root problems with aspartame. When methanol is consumed via aspartame, methanol is free to break down to toxic formaldehyde, and humans, unlike other animals, are incapable of converting the toxic formaldehyde into harmless formic acid.

Initially discovered in 1965 as a drug to treat peptic ulcers, this king of all artificial sweeteners was allowed into the market in 1981 when the U.S. Commissioner of Food and Drugs, Arthur Hull Hayes, overruled FDA panel suggestions, along with consumer concerns. Aspartame (chemical #E951) is a neurotoxin that interacts with natural organisms, as well as synthetic medications, and producing a wide range of proven disorders and syndromes. So who installed this commissioner who would rule against scientists and the public? None other than Donald Rumsfeld, who at the time was CEO of G.D. Searle & Co., the maker of aspartame. Rumsfeld was on Reagan's transition team, and the day after Reagan took office, he appointed the new FDA Commissioner (in order to "call in his markers") within one of the most egregious cases of profit-over-safety ever recorded. Former Secretary of Defense, Donald Rumsfeld, with his political clout, therefore, helped to get aspartame pushed through the U.S. Food & Drug Administration. According to a press release issued on this RICO lawsuit, "double blind" studies showed conclusive evidence that aspartame increased severe health problems, and even death to the exposed study group. This isn't the first lawsuit alleging that aspartame is hazardous to the health of humans. The National Justice League filed three other lawsuits in late April of 2004, in three separate California courts. The defendants in those lawsuits were 12, and all 12 produce, or use, aspartame as a sugar substitute in their products. Aspartame is now nearly ubiquitous, moving beyond sugarless products and into general foods, beverages, pharmaceuticals, and even products for children. In a stroke of marketing genius, it has recently been renamed the more pleasant sounding "AminoSweet."

Aspartame, and its offshoot Neotame, are considered to be the most dangerous food additives on the market today. Its main compounds are Aspartic Acid, Phenylalanine, and Methanol. These combine to kill neurons in the brain, poison the body, and are linked to an enormous number of ill-health effects. In 1970, scientists fed milk with aspartame to seven monkeys to study the effects. The final result was startling. At only 218 days, five monkeys suffered from seizures, and one died. It is terrifying to think that this insidious product is added to over 5,000 food products, designated as dietary low fat, sugar-free, or non-fatty foods. It is also an ingredient in a number of medications, both prescription and over-the-counter. Aspartame is a neurotoxin and carcinogen. Known to erode intelligence and affect short-term memory, the components of this toxic sweetener may lead to a wide variety of ailments including brain tumors, diseases like lymphoma, diabetes, multiple sclerosis (MS), Parkinson's, Alzheimer's, Grave's Disease, fibromyalgia, and chronic fatigue: emotional disorders like depression and anxiety attacks, dizziness, headaches, nausea, mental confusion, migraines, seizures, and even kidney failure. Acesulfame-K, a relatively new artificial sweetener found in baking goods, gum and gelatin, has not been thoroughly tested and has been linked to kidney tumors.

In any other scenario, this substance would be considered poison, and an FDA recommendation for non-ingestion would be posted on the bottle. But because this poisonous substance has been approved by food and drug associations, it is legal. Just like it is with fluoridated water, aspartame is a literal poison that has creeped into many processed foods. This deadly artificial sweetener is produced by feeding fossil fuel oil to E. coli, that are themselves genetically modified to defecate aspartame as feces. Not so sweet when you realize what you're actually eating!

Finally, in 2012, aspartame was associated with increased risk of blood cancers in a long-term human study conducted by the *American Journal of Clinical Nutrition*. The study concluded that as little as one diet soda per day can increase the risk for leukemia in adult men and women, and toward multiple myeloma and non-Hodgkin lymphoma in men. This is according to new results from the longest-ever running study on aspartame as a carcinogen in humans. Importantly, this is the most comprehensive long-term study ever completed on this topic, so it holds more weight than other past studies (which appeared to show no risk). And, disturbingly, it may also open the door for similar findings on other cancers in future studies. These results were based on *multi-variable relative risk models*, all in comparison to participants who drank no diet soda. It is unknown why only men drinking higher amounts of diet soda showed an increased risk for multiple myeloma and non-Hodgkin's lymphoma. By far, diet soda is the largest dietary source of aspartame used in the USA. Every year, Americans consume about 5,250 *tons* of aspartame, of which, about 86%, or 4,500 tons, is found in diet sodas. Is this another depopulating "soft kill" toxic poison being peddled to the sheeple? *You bet your sweet aspartame!*

BRAVE NEW WORLD OF MEAT

The mass production of lab-grown meat products has now been created via the muscle stem cells taken from cows. Scientists in charge of these studies have hopes that by being able to grow beef in a lab, we can create a quick and renewable abundance of food, and that could help diminish world hunger and the inhumane treatment of animals in slaughterhouses. But is the world ready for meat and other food products produced artificially in laboratories? What are the upsides and downsides? It is time to ask!

One stated advantage is the reduced need for grazing lands. Of all the Earth's landmasses free of ice and permafrost, one third is devoted to cattle ranching. Cows are one of the leading causes for greenhouse gasses in the form of methane, and it contributes up to one-fifth of greenhouse gas emissions worldwide. On one hand, eliminated pastureland for cattle would free vast tracts of land to be restored to their natural habitat. On the other hand, *what are* the consequences of moving to a lab-created diet? Is the future of fine dining being cultured in a petri dish? Certainly, an ethical treatment of domesticated animals would be eliminating the need to send them to the slaughterhouse.

In a world where rapid technological growth is exceedingly apparent, it is important that we find new ways to deal with the scientific realities of the 21st century. A frequently raised question regarding the idea of lab-grown meat is "Why grow meat in labs in the first place? What about the existing alternatives, like soy, tofu, etc?" Nutritionally, there are both good and bad sides to a multitude of existing "alternative" consumables. Soy consumption, for example, has displayed trends towards warding off the onset of prostate cancer in males, as well as reduced risk of breast cancer in females. Unfortunately, most soy is now a GMO, and there are other issues. Leading food expert Beatrice Trum Hunter made this observation:

> *The raw soybean contains numerous anti-nutrients. Although processing can reduce them, it does not eliminate them. The raw soybean is an anti-coagulant (an agent that prevents blood clotting). The anti-coagulant property is not reversed by vitamin K, which is a highly effective blood-clotting agent. Green leafy vegetables and liver are excellent sources of vitamin K. Many Americans are low in vitamin K. Soy's anti-coagulant property is attributed to its anti-trypsin activity. Trypsin is a special enzyme needed to digest protein. In addition, trypsin allows vitamin B12 to be assimilated. Thus, by blocking trypsin activity, the soybean, as an anti-trypsin agent, increases the requirements for vitamin B12 and actually creates vitamin B12 deficiency.*

DON'T PANIC, GO ORGANIC

It is said that every ailment has a natural cure that can be found somewhere in the world. But you won't be hearing about that from the large agribusinesses and Big Pharma. Thus, manufactured natural cures have been set up to *fail by design* in order to reinforce Big Pharma's monopoly, and their allopathic system of medicine. Real natural cures are suppressed, and they never make it into mainstream public awareness. Similarly, natural medicines are suppressed because their use and marketing is beyond the legal control and monopoly of drug and chemical patents. Of course, natural substances can never be patented, and this is why every natural and non-toxic therapy is automatically called "quackery" by the corporate-owned FDA, the chemical industry, and the medical establishment. Only unnatural, non-organic, chemical-based products may be patented. Non-toxic medicines are a threat to the business of medicine.

To qualify for a Rockefeller Foundation medical research grant, applicants must agree to abandon "traditional and natural medicines" in lieu of new generations of petrochemical drugs, and must comply with the removal of entire libraries of recording past procedures. It became dangerous for traditional naturopathic doctors to cross these professionals who are aligned with the chemical industry. All "dissenters," those who embrace time-tested, holistic, and naturopathic methodologies, continue to be demonized as "quacks" throughout formal medical training. This defamation has been employed despite some of these "quacks" having received the Nobel Prize in Medicine.

It is a carrot and stick strategy. Compliant schools are given the carrot in the form of Rockefeller money. Non-compliant naturopathic doctors get the stick, in the form of FDA police action—even to the point of dying in prison for having cured patients with "unapproved" medicine. Harassment of grocers selling organic non-chemical foods still occurs, including those selling certain cancer-killing vitamins (or even raw milk). It's not just doctors with cures anymore. "Curing," by definition, is illegal, since no natural cures are ever "approved." But *cures*, for many, have come to be associated with freedom from the control and manipulation of the chemical industry.

It is very important to understand exactly what we are putting into our bodies. Phytonutrients or phytochemicals are plant foods that contain thousands of natural chemicals. *Phyto* refers to the Greek word for "plant." These chemicals help protect plants from germs, fungi, bugs, and other threats. Phytonutrients aren't essential for keeping you alive. This is unlike the vitamins and minerals that plant foods contain. But when you eat or drink these phytonutrients they are known to help prevent disease (and keep your body working properly). There are more than 25,000 phytonutrients found in plant foods. "Superfoods" are nutrient-dense, and *super healthy* when you exercise portion-control. It is important to note that you *can* have too much of a good thing! Most plant-based foods contain phytonutrients, with the most complete being whole grains, nuts, beans, and tea. A "macro diet," by definition, draws from a wide spectrum of healthy foods based on beneficial plant-based food choices.

The nutritional-industrial complex regularly tempts us with unhealthy food, but just remember, we still have a choice. While it might be more expensive to buy all-organic, or difficult to seek out non-GMO foods, you should treat your body as a temple: Avoid high fructose corn syrup products; minimize sugar intake; and don't buy any food you see advertised on television. Upwards of two-thirds of ad expenditures go to heavily processed foods. *Choose foods with five ingredients or less*, and shop the perimeter of a supermarket. If your grandma did not eat it, then you should not eat it, either. If your grandma would not recognize it, then don't eat it. Quite simply, eat whole foods, not too much, and mostly vegetables. With these simple pointers, you will begin to see positive results in overall health, and you'll begin your escape from food control. Now is the time for us to not only survive, but to thrive—and be healthy enough to achieve the objectives we were each born to accomplish.

A handy chart to determine if the food and drinks you consume are alkaline or acidic.

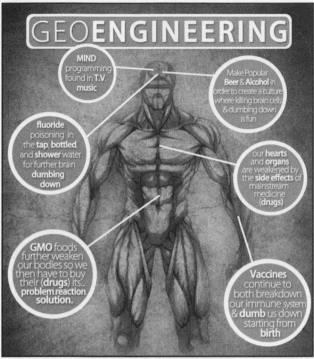

GEO**ENGINEERING**

MIND programming found in T.V. music

fluoride poisoning in the **tap**, **bottled**, and **shower** water for further brain **dumbing down**

Make Popular **Beer** & **Alcohol** in order to create a culture where killing brain cells & dumbing down is fun

our **hearts** and **organs** are weakened by the **side effects** of mainstream medicine (**drugs**)

GMO foods further weaken our bodies so we then have to buy their (**drugs**) its... **problem.reaction. solution.**

Vaccines continue to both breakdown our immune system & **dumb** us down starting from **birth**

< The government does not want us to expand our consciousness. If we begin to recognize that we are powerful individuals who can create our own reality, it will take away their power to enslave us. Everyday our minds and bodies are attacked by this "geoengineering" system. What's scarier is that some of us know this is happening, yet still allow this system into our lives. We can each be conscious of the control being exerted, refuse to participate, and be resistance through nonviolence.

> The drawing on the right is attributed to Fritz Kahn, produced in the early 20th Century, and suggests where each food or drink would benefit the different parts of the mouth.

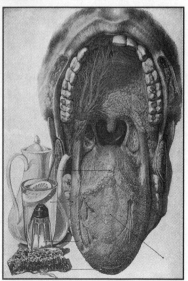

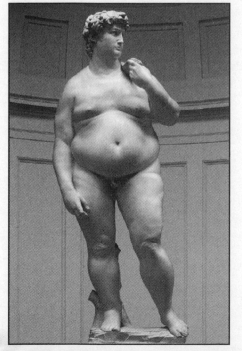

< *Tempi moderni: il David.* Michelangelo's famous 1504 sculpture of David remade with Photoshop to depict today's modern man as being obese.

T H R I V E :

For a seemingly hopeless battle, the solution to vital problems is simply to change our consensus reality. The only weapon they have is keeping the knowledge of our true nature just out of reach. Evolving to achieve our full human potential is the promise of the Golden Age.

"My mission in life is not merely to survive, but to thrive; and to do so with some passion, some compassion, some humor and some style." –Maya Angelou

"There are two basic motivating forces: fear and love. When we are afraid, we pull back from life. When we are in love, we open to all that life has to offer with passion, excitement, and acceptance. We need to learn to love ourselves first, in all our glory and our imperfections. If we cannot love ourselves, we cannot fully open to our ability to love others or our potential to create. Evolution and all hopes for a better world rest in the fearlessness and open-hearted vision of people who embrace life." –musician John Lennon

"The day science begins to study non-physical phenomena, it will make more progress in one decade than in all the previous centuries of its existence." –Nikola Tesla

"Look at a tree, a flower, a plant. Let your awareness rest upon it. How still they are, how deeply rooted in Being. Allow nature to teach you stillness." –Eckhart Tolle

"Meditation is all-inclusive, it excludes nothing. It is not a narrowing down of the mind, it is an expansion of consciousness. Concentration is of the mind, meditation is of consciousness. Concentration is mind, meditation is no-mind. Concentration is a tension: you will be tired of it sooner or later. You cannot concentrate for a long time, it is effort. But one can be meditative twenty-four hours, because it is relaxation." –Osho

"The imagination is not a state: it is the human existence itself." –William Blake

"Since you alone are responsible for your thoughts, only you can change them. You will want to change them when you realize that each thought creates according to its own nature. Remember that the law works at all times and that you are always demonstrating according to the kind of thoughts you habitually entertain. Therefore, start now to think only those thoughts that will bring you health and happiness." –Paramahansa Yogananda

"Holding onto anger is like drinking poison and expecting the other person to die." –Buddha

LIVING TO 200

"This is my simple religion. There is no need for temples; no need for complicated philosophy. Our own brain, our own heart is our temple; the philosophy is kindness." –Dalai Lama

AT any given moment you are either losing life or gaining life. When you are losing life, it means death and disease are advancing on your potential longevity. Everything in life is always changing, including our bodies. In every moment we are either feeling stronger or getting weaker. If we are losing life, we are gaining death. And of course, we are what we consume. The skin on an average person replaces itself every 35 days, and the liver regenerates in about a month. The human body makes new cells from the drinks and food we intake. What we eat literally becomes who and what we are.

Food can be medicine, yet it does not contain medicine. Examples of medicine in food include resveratrol, curcumin, turmeric, phycocyanins, polyphenols and ten thousand other chemicals created naturally by plants that have medicinal functions in the human body. Considering that nearly 25% of all prescription medicines are in some way derived from plants, including statin drugs, Big Pharma expends enormous resources searching the world's botanical richness for amazing molecules that they can pirate from nature and alter in some way to make them patentable as a drug. Even the *World Resources Institute* readily admits this. It also reminds us that 80% of the world's population still relies largely on plant-based medicine. After all, the human body evolved in an environment replete with plants that have beneficial physiological and medicinal effects. For every human ailment, it has been said that nature has already provided a remedy.

To a large degree, prolonged good health is also determined by attitude and, specifically, by a person's beliefs about foods, use of non-toxic remedies, and an overall high quality of life. Science has proven this with repeated experiments using the placebo effect and blind studies to measure degree of stress, contentment, and availability of support systems. The body's ability to heal is greater than anyone has previously been led to believe. Maintaining a positive, upbeat, and inspired attitude, while focusing on maximizing and preserving all aspects of physical health, should be everyone's top priority. As *Reader's Digest* points out, "Laughter is the best medicine!"

Many factors in our lives can stave off the aging process and prevent diseases. The physical environment and the circumstances surrounding where we live can also have an effect on personal longevity. People who live in mountainous regions, For example, have a higher than average life expectancy rate. Living at higher elevations allows the body to create more white blood cells, or leukocytes, which are cells in the immune system which defend the body against both infectious disease and foreign materials. Colorado contains the top seven ranked counties in the nation for longevity, all with a life expectancy of 81.3 years. And it hardly seems coincidental that all seven counties—Clear Creek, Eagle, Gilpin, Grand, Jackson, Park and Summit—lie either on, near, or adjoining the Continental Divide. Living a long and fruitful life appears to depend both on our life's circumstances and on how we treat ourselves.

THE LIFE OF A 256-YEAR-OLD

According to official records in China, herbalist Li Ching-Yuen was born in 1677 in Qijiang County, Sichuan province. Although Li himself claimed that he was born in 1736, the official date would still make him the oldest recorded person who has ever lived. Throughout his long life, Li practiced martial arts continually and was a renowned herbalist. He was also known to consume, and sell, the following herbs: lingzhi, goji berry, wild ginseng, he shou wu and gotu kola, along with other Chinese herbs. His diet consisted exclusively of these herbs and rice wine. Supposedly, Li had also produced over 200 descendants during his life span, and survived all 23 of his wives. In 1930, the *New York Times* printed an article publishing official and unofficial Chinese government documents. Dating back to 1827, these documents contained official congratulations on Li Ching-Yuen's 150th birthday. Later documents, dating back to 1877, contained official congratulations on his 200th birthday!

There are some interesting historical facts to this story that can shed light on Li's "ultra-longevity." He was a Chinese herbalist, skilled in Qigong, who spent most of his life in the mountains. One of Li's disciples, the Taijiquan master Da Liu, told his master's story: At 135 years of age, master Li encountered a much older hermit who was over 500 years old, and living in the mountains. The aged hermit taught Li, Baguazhang, and others a set of Qigong techniques that included breathing instructions, movements, training coordinated with specific sounds, and dietary recommendations. Da Liu reports that his master said that his longevity "is due to the fact that I performed the exercises every day—regularly, correctly, and with sincerity—for 120 years."

How could Li Ching-Yuen have possibly lived so long? Expressing his formula for longevity in one sentence, Li said: "Retain a calm heart, sit like a turtle, walk swiftly like a pigeon, and sleep like a dog." In 1927, the Chinese National Revolutionary Army General, Yang Sen, invited him to his residence in Wann Hsien, Szechuan province. This is where the picture at the end of this chapter was taken. Yang Sen offered Li an opportunity to teach martial arts to his Chinese soldiers. Even though he had reached an age of 250 years old, the general could not believe how youthful his guest was. Li also said a fundamental Taoist practice to learn to keep the *wuji*, or "emptiness," as another key to his longevity. Li Ching-Yuen died on the 6th of May in 1933. He told his students that he had completed all of his tasks in this lifetime, and he was now ready to *come home*. It should also be pointed out that Li Ching-Yuen lived a completely holistic lifestyle, long before any pharmaceutical drug was ever conceived or invented.

GROWING NEW ORGANS

B esides making good lifestyle choices, there is also a rapid advance in the science of extending our lives. Could our next generation live to be 150, or even 200 years old? Experts think that the latest big breakthroughs in science and technology could make this a reality. For example, scientists are making huge advances in the laboratory, growing new organs from adult human stem cells, creating body parts with 3D printers, and using gene therapy to successfully treat diseases like blindness and leukemia. And that's not all. Doctors have already doubled the lifespan of a worm by applying longevity techniques.

Doctors are now growing replacement organs and body parts in the laboratory from their patients' own cells. With more than 112,000 Americans currently waiting for an organ transplant, and many of whom will never receive one, the demand to grow new organs has never been greater. Scientists can take a very small piece of tissue from the specific injured or diseased organ, less than half the size of a postage stamp, and reproduce the tissue. A common example is when stem cells are taken from a subject's own bladder and placed in a bio-degradable mold, which is soaked and seeded with nutrients. After incubation in a bio-reactor, the tissue grows into a new bladder that then is placed in the patient's body.

At the Wake Forest Institute for Regenerative Medicine in North Carolina, there are labs such as described above that currently take stem cells and multiply them for a variety of uses for patients. Other labs make biodegradable "scaffolds" that cells are sprayed onto. They are then all cooked in something called a bio-reactor to prepare them as human grafts. The institute is currently growing over 20 different types of tissues and organs, and most have already been implanted in patients. These tissues and organs include lab-grown arteries, ears, finger bones, urethras and artificial heart valves, all grown from human cells. Replacement human skin for burn victims and even tiny muscles are being grown. An advantage to growing body parts from a patient's own stem cells is that they won't be rejected, such as organs from other people may be, so patients will not need toxic anti-rejection drugs.

Aging experts say that lifestyle changes applied *right now* can help people live easily into their 80s—similar to the residents in the mountainous counties of Colorado. Naturally, the prevention of bad habits goes a long way in improving the quality of life as a person grows older. Sleep has also been recognized as being an essential aid in rejuvenating the body. It is recommended that we *get to bed* close to the same time every night, and rise around the same time each morning. Naps in the middle of the day have also been proven beneficial. For mature adults, at least seven or eight hours of sleep per night are recommended, while adolescents and elderly people usually need about eight or nine hours of sleep per night. Sleep allows the body time to repair and regenerate itself.

GENE THERAPY

A nother technique for treating terminal patients is the science of gene therapy. What's known in cancer research is that inflammation occurs when the cell walls are damaged, and thus cancer cells can form. Acidic blood results from abnormal red blood cells can also lead to a higher incidence of cancer. Researchers are reporting the first clear success with a different approach for treating leukemia—turning the patient's own blood cells into assassins that hunt down and destroy invasive cancer cells. Scientists have developed a carrier to deliver new genes into the T-cells and a signaling mechanism telling the cells to kill and multiply. This results in armies of "serial killer" cells that target cancer cells, destroy them, and go on to kill new cancer as it emerges. It was known that T-cells attack viruses that way, but this is the first time it has been done against cancer.

According to scientists, genes determine 20% to 30% of our longevity. Early research compared standard sequences with SNP (Single Nucleotide Polymorphism), which is a particular variation found in genome sequences. However, no conclusive result was identified to demonstrate that SNPs were the reason for specific longevity in some people. Now experts suggest that longevity might be affected by a particular gene present in only one person in a million. This might involve three or more genes, but they are extremely rare genes. If these genes can be identified, replicated, and used as gene therapy we might all have an opportunity to become "super-centenarians," defined as those who live past 110 or longer.

THE pH EQUATION AND HEALTH

According to many health researchers, total healing of chronic illness takes place only when (and if) the blood is restored to a normal, slightly alkaline pH. The magnitude of meaning behind this research is of incredible importance to someone who is fighting a disease, overcoming an illness, or just wanting to feel better. Thus, the body pH affects everything, including the "terrain" within the stomach and intestines. Human blood stays in a very narrow pH range right above 7.3. A pH below or above this range brings symptoms and disease. When pH is off balance, microbial-looking forms reproduce in the blood, which can change shape, mutate, mirror pathogenicity, and grow. Further, enzymes that are constructive can *become* destructive. When pH is imbalanced, oxygen delivery to the cells suffers. The immune system cannot "fight off" an imbalanced terrain.

Dr. Otto Warburg was awarded the 1931 Nobel Prize in Physiology or Medicine for his discovery that cancer is caused by weakened cell respiration due to a lack of oxygen at the cellular level. According to Warburg, damaged cell respiration causes fermentation. He said, "every single person who has cancer has a pH that is too acidic." Fermentation produces acids like lactic acid, and lowers the cell pH levels in the body to acidic levels. An acidic intra- and extra-cellular environment destroys the ability of DNA and RNA to control cell division, and allows cancerous cells to multiply. Dr. Warburg stated, "nobody today can say that one does not know what cancer and its prime cause is. On the contrary, there is no disease whose prime cause is better known, so that today ignorance is no longer an excuse." Since cancer cannot survive in an oxygenated, alkaline environment, the cure to cancer is to oxygenate the body, detoxify, and alkalize.

The human body has a normal temperature of 37 Celsius (98.6° F). Our body also has moisture content percentages, pressure, pH balance, natural frequencies and, typically, nutrient deficiencies. A human's normal pH balance of alkaline ranges from 7.35 pH to 7.45 pH, that is, when the organs maintain an optimum pH balance in the arterial blood. A healthy human body contains both acids and bases. To counteract the amount of acids consumed by eating, drinking, and breathing, the body will take alkaline substances from body parts, such as the bones. By drinking alkaline water, we can counteract the intake of acids and help the body regulate its pH in a more healthy way.

Cancer cells, therefore, can only survive in an acidic pH. Cancer cells die when in an alkaline pH environment. An acidic condition draws minerals and oxygen from the body, and results in lower immunity, premature aging, and the advent of various diseases. When taken in the right amounts, goji berries are an excellent way to convert acidic blood to alkaline blood. This can take effect in as quickly as 48 hours. Our current toxic environment can cause free radical production to spin out of control, causing premature aging, and perhaps degenerative diseases such as cancer, heart disease, autism, or Alzheimer's Disease. Goji berries can help balance this.

The average frequency of a healthy human body during daytime is 62 to 68 Hz. When the frequency drops, the immune system is compromised. If the frequency drops to 58 Hz, cold and flu symptoms appear. At 55 Hz, diseases like Candida can take hold. At 52 Hz, Epstein Bar can occur, and at 42 Hz cancer is possible. According to Dr. Royal Raymond Rife, every disease has a frequency. He has found that certain frequencies can prevent the development of disease and that others would destroy diseases. Substances of higher frequency will destroy diseases of lower frequency.

Buying "pHenomenal" alkaline water concentrate is inexpensive—about $1 per liter. Not only does it help to prevent diseases, but these waters are delicious and very clean. Another option is to use baking soda in water, because it has a high pH. A small amount goes a long way. The pH level inside of tumor cells is usually very low, or acidic, compared to normal cells, and the salt form of cesium can raise the pH level of tumor cells to a normal level. That slows the cancer's growth. Since the supplement cesium chloride works by raising the pH of the tumor cells, its use in therapy has been called "high pH therapy."

NATURAL CURES

The word "vaccine" comes from the Latin word *vaccinium*, meaning "berry." Most varieties of berries are regarded as "superfoods" because of their high antioxidant content. Also, oregano provides more antioxidants than blueberries, oranges or apples. Antioxidants are intimately involved in the prevention of cellular damage (the common pathway for cancer, aging, and a variety of diseases). Antioxidants are molecules that can safely interact with free radicals, and terminate the chain reaction before vital molecules are damaged. Since berries and other superfoods cannot be patented to make money for the shareholders of major pharmaceutical companies, we are not being properly educated about this logical and natural option. Far more media attention focuses on the consumption of medicines and pills, rather than sensible holistic cures. Unfortunately, one of the largest industries in the world (and employing the most powerful lobbyists in Washington D.C.) is the pharmaceutical industry. Big Pharma is Big Business! Eating the "superfoods" and maintaining a healthy diet with a daily exercise routine is the best way to prevent the onset of any disease or sickness. Medical research has shown that regularly eating blueberries, which are naturally high in antioxidants, can help people lose abdominal fat, improve memory, and even prevent cancer.

Alkaline foods and water are key to preventing and fighting off diseases and illnesses. If you are drinking tap or bottled water, it can be acidic. Cancer and other diseases thrive in an acidic environment. Lemon and grapefruit are alkaline. Other citrus fruits such as oranges are acidic. A two week fast featuring honey and lemon water made from fresh squeezed lemons is an excellent way of detoxifying the system and retreat from an otherwise acidic diet. There are reports of people with life-threatening conditions whose health was seemingly, miraculously, restored using a honey and lemon water fast for a few weeks.

When treating seasonal flu symptoms with the organic approach it is possible to avoid medicine altogether. Green tea extract, combined with turmeric, is excellent as a preventative and treatment. Turmeric, and more specifically, curcumin, its primary active ingredient, continues to shine as an awe-inspiring anti-cancer "superfood," and "spiced" with a vast array of tangible health benefits. Taking vitamin D supplements, or getting a daily dose of sunshine, can fight off influenza, and is an effective way to prevent colds altogether, thus avoiding the need for flu shots. Resveratrol is also beneficial. St. John's Wort was apparently used with efficiency against H5N1 in Vietnam. Garlic is an effective natural sulphur-based compound that is effective against MRSA. Mucosolvan, or ambroxol hydroxide, is very effective against lung and respiratory injury. This compound also has antiviral properties and anti-inflammatory benefits. To fight the onset of a cold, one should increase vitamin C and D3 levels orally. It's important to maintain electrolyte levels continuously depending on status. Once infected with the flu, a person has about 72 hours to take remedial action. Symptomatic treatment is fine, although it is a race against time to organically treat the root cause of a flu illness.

All people should sweat daily and, at the very least, have one full and complete bowel movement each day—our output of toxins should be about equal to our input. In order to keep the cells oxygenated and the blood at a slightly alkaline level, "shocking" the body with hot and cold also appears to be very healthy for the body. Those cultures of people who live the longest have a tradition of shocking the body with hot and cold applications. The people of Scandinavia, for example, routinely take hot saunas on cold days, and those in Russia will come out of a warm house and take a cold dip in the water, as those who live in tropical climates benefit from taking cold showers on hot days.

Alkalizing factors include drinking fresh, pure water; breathing deeply; smiling or laughing; eating dark leafy greens, and citrus fruits, being in nature, singing or listening to and / or playing music, and merely thinking positive thoughts.

Acidifying factors include hearing, thinking, or saying harsh/bitter/angry words; being upset in a traffic jam; feeling jealous or vengeful; over-working; over-exercising; not getting enough sleep; eating acidifying foods; inhaling or being exposed to acidifying chemicals; and using electronics for too long (such as TVs, radios, computers, and cellphones). This basically includes anything that reduces the amount of oxygen being delivered to the body, especially, for example, being in a stressful or fearful situation (wherein humans subconsciously begin to breath shallowly).

THE RISE OF CANCER

Out of control cancer starts developing a long time before it is diagnosed. We all have cancer cells in our body, and it is not a problem until cancer cells duplicate millions of times over. This results mainly because the natural nutrients our bodies need and use to identify, destroy and prevent the duplication of these cancer cells are not present in our diets. Our bodies have the inherent gift of having natural healing systems built-in. The body can heal itself if it has the right building blocks in the form of nutrients. Most people seemingly do not understand that what they eat causes their disease.

Additional new research has shown that the spice turmeric is capable of halting cancer cell growth altogether. This accidental finding, reached by scientists, further shows the lack of real science behind many "old paradigm" treatments (despite what many health officials would like you to believe). The truth is that natural alternatives do not receive even a small fraction of the funding that the pharmaceutical drug companies and medical interventions do. There's simply no room for profit! If everyone were using turmeric and vitamin D for cancer treatment, or better yet, for cancer prevention, major drug companies would lose a huge portion of their profits.

There are other holistic treatments that the medical establishment routinely ignores. For example, dozens of children and adults recommended to undergo chemotherapy, opted instead to begin applying cannabis oil. Within two months the cancer receded, or, the tumor had shrunk so much that chemo was not needed. It was found that the cannabinoid oil instructs cancer cells to die, or what is called a "programmed cell death." Another alternative to chemo comes from Dr. Stanislaw R. Burzynski, who is the physician and biochemist researcher responsible for identifying natural occurring peptides and amino acid derivatives, or "Antineoplastons," as he later named them, in the human body. He discovered that they are the components of a biochemical defense system that controls cancer growth without destroying normal cells. These substances are largely deficient in cancer patients when compared to healthy individuals.

The greatest truths, by necessity, are always simple. Not only can baking soda be used as a household cleaner, it has also been shown to combat cancer, fight colds, prevent the flu, and even treat radiation poisoning! Sodium bicarbonate, also known as baking soda, alkalinizes the body, absorbs heavy metals and radiation, purifies the air, extinguishes fires, deodorizes, soothes bug bite itching, and can be used as a natural toothpaste. Dr. Simonchini, an oncologist from Rome, Italy, originally made the connection between fungal infections and cancer proliferation. He discovered that when a tumor was flushed with baking soda, a natural anti-fungal, it shrank and completely disappeared within days. Time-tested remedies, like baking soda treating cancer, may not be breaking news to some, but they're worthy of our attention. After all, the reason they've been around for so long is because they work!

OTHER WAYS TO KILL CANCER

Researchers are looking at ways to replicate a type of cytotoxic lymphocyte cell which constitutes a major component within our immune system; and may hold the key to ultra-longevity. These "natural killer" (NK) cells play a major role in the rejection of tumors and cells infected by viruses. NK cells are highly important cells in our immune systems, and are a very important *natural asset* in the fight against cancer. These cells kill by releasing a blast of proteins, thereby injecting the suspect cell with cytotoxins that cause the target cell to die by apoptosis. NK cells play a highly important role in the killing of tumors and cells infected by viruses. NK cells are known as natural killers because they don't need to react to specific antigens; they just need to recognize that a cell is *foreign,* and that it does not belong. However, NK cells must receive an activating message, such as signals from cytokines, in order to do their work.

In a related category, more and more research suggests that THC, the active ingredient in marijuana, is beneficial in fighting cancer. One claim is that when pure liquid THC is injected into a cancerous tumor in a patient, the tumor will eat itself. The research shows that THC just loves to "eat" cancer. Other compounds called CBD and CBN, found within cannabis, have been shown to create the same hostile environment within cancer cells. The combination of THC with these other compounds creates an amplification of the cancer killing effect. More than the amplification, entire new anti-cancer effects are observed that don't take place with only single compounds, including THC by itself. The question now is to identify the ideal ratios between these various compounds. It may prove that the best blend is more than 80% THC, while the other compounds act as "helpers."

Deep within the Amazon rainforest there grows a tree that may revolutionize cancer treatment—and the chances for survival. A study at Purdue University recently found that leaves from the Graviola tree killed cancer cells among six human cell lines, and it is especially effective against prostate, pancreatic and lung cancers. It appears that it is a promising remedy for cancers of all types. The Sour Sop, or the fruit from the Graviola tree, has been called a "miraculous" natural cancer cell killer many times stronger than chemotherapy. Although it is effective for a number of medical conditions, the anti-tumor effect is the most promising. Besides being a cancer remedy, the Graviola tree holds a broad spectrum of anti-microbial agents for both bacterial and fungal infections, and it is effective against internal parasites and worms; lowers high blood pressure; and has shown some efficacy for treating depression, stress, and nervous disorders.

With extracts from this miraculous tree, it may now be possible to attack cancer safely and effectively with an all-natural therapy, thus eliminating the chemo side effects of extreme nausea, weight, and hair loss. Extracts from the tree were shown to effectively target and kill malignant cells in 12 types of cancer, including colon, breast, prostate, lung and pancreatic cancer. The tree compounds were shown to be up to 10,000 times more effective in slowing the growth of cancer cells than Adriamycin, a commonly used chemotherapy drug! What's more, unlike chemotherapy, the compound extracted from the Graviola tree selectively hunts down and kills only cancer cells. It does not harm healthy cells! It also protects the immune system and aids people in avoiding other potential infections.

VITAMIN B-17 IS NOT THE ENEMY

Perhaps the ultimate natural anti-cancer supplement is vitamin B-17. It has been shown in numerous independent studies to kill cancer cells, strengthen the immune system, and prevent cancer cells from developing in the future. In 1950, after many years of research, a dedicated biochemist by the name of Dr. Ernest T. Krebs, Jr. isolated a new vitamin that he numbered B-17, and called it "Laetrile." Many decades later, thousands of patients became convinced that Dr. Krebs had finally found the complete cure for all cancers, a conviction that even more people share today. Shortly after the success stories started pouring in, the pharmaceutical multinationals hounded Dr. Krebs (and his miracle cure). The suppression of B-17 research continues to this day. Since they were unable to patent or claim exclusive rights to the vitamin, Big Pharma launched an unprecedented and vicious propaganda attack against B-17 (despite the fact that hard proof of its efficiency in controlling all forms of cancer are provided in overwhelming abundance). Why has orthodox medicine waged a war against this non-drug approach? G. Edward Griffin, author of the book, *World Without Cancer,* contends that the answer is to be found not in science, but in politics, and is based upon the hidden economic agenda among those who dominate the medical establishment. In short, they only wish to support the conclusions that endorse their own products, and their industry as a whole.

Every year, thousands of Americans travel to Mexico to receive Laetrile therapy because vitamin B-17 treatment has been suppressed in the United States. Most of these patients have been told that their cancer is terminal and that they have but a few months to live. Yet, an incredible percentage of them have recovered and are living normal lives— *sometimes years or decades longer than their original prognosis.* However, the FDA, the AMA, the American Cancer Society, and U.S. cancer research centers continue to declare that Laetrile Therapy is fraudulent and a "quack science." The recovered patients, they say, either had "spontaneous remissions," or never had cancer in the first place. If any of these people ultimately die after seeking Laetrile, spokesmen of allopathic medicine are quick to proclaim: "You see? Laetrile doesn't work!" Meanwhile, hundreds of thousands of patients die each year after undergoing chemotherapy, surgery, and / or radiation, but those treatments continue to be touted as "safe and effective."

The FDA has attempted to impose strict regulations to ban B-17 for two decades. Laetrile therapy is only used by select hospitals in Mexico that primarily treat cancer with nutrition and homeopathic medicine. These hospitals achieve a near perfect recovery rate with "virgin" cases, that is, those localized tumors or cancers that have yet to be burned with radiation, poisoned with chemotherapy, or cut into with surgery. A majority of Laetrile-treated patients report positive results, ranging from an increase in the feeling of well-being and an even brighter outlook on life, to such noticeable reactions as an increase in appetite, weight gain and, frequently, restoration of natural skin color and reduction or the elimination of cancer-related pain. In thousands of cases, total regression of all cancer symptoms has been confirmed.

Vitamin B Complex is among the most essential of all vitamins in terms of maintaining good physical health for most people. Thankfully, there is no medical reason for any restriction on its distribution or use in the United States. After all, this is a natural supplement, not a chemical-based drug. The main components of Vitamin B Complex are niacin or B-3, folates or B-9, pantothenic acid or B-5, pyridoxine or B-6, biotin or B-7, thiamin or B-1, riboflavin or B-2, and cobalamin or B-12, which are naturally available in certain foods. Regular vitamin B ingestion is also useful for maintaining overall general health, reproductive health, healthy cell metabolism, neurological function, the formation of blood cells, and maintaining hunger at normal levels among cancer patients.

VITAMIN D ALSO PREVENTS CANCER

New research shows that a regular intake of vitamin D diminishes the risk of getting any form of cancer by 77%, yet the allopathic medical industry refuses to support this form of cancer prevention. A big percentage of the U.S. population is deficient in vitamin D, usually due to a lack of regular sunshine exposure, which leads to a rise in several different types of cancers and ailments. So why would the American Cancer Society (ACS) oppose vitamin D? Simply because, as we have seen over and over, the research on vitamin D presents a huge threat to the cancer industry profit margins. After all, vitamins, supplements, and getting a daily dose of direct sunlight, offers a way to prevent cancer for free or at little cost. Our skin can manufacture its own powerful anti-cancer medicine simply through an hour or so of daily exposure to sunlight.

If it seems surprising that the American Cancer Society—which claims to be against cancer—would dissuade people from taking supplements that could slash their cancer risk by 77%, maybe we don't really know enough about the ACS. First, notice the irony in its name. They don't call themselves the American Anti-Cancer Society, it's the American Cancer Society. What they *really* stand for is right in their name! The ACS is an organization that actually *prevents* prevention, and is openly supported by the continuation of cancer as it boosts its profits and power. The ACS is the wealthiest non-profit group in America, and, has very close ties to pharmaceutical companies, mammography equipment companies, and other corporations that profit from cancer. The research on vitamin D is such good news that the American Cancer Society has made comments "not in support," but actually *against* this sensible approach to prevention and treatment. An ACS spokesperson, Marji McCullough, strategic director of nutritional epidemiology for the American Cancer Society, flatly stated that nobody should take supplements to prevent cancer.

What the ACS supports are "cancer drugs" that are designed to shrink tumors by cutting off their blood supply. While some patients appear to be cured, or at least helped by these drugs, one study has warned that their effect may actually help cancer spread to other parts of the body. Harvard Medical School researchers investigated two drugs, Glivec and Sutent, discovered that while it is proven that they reduce the size of cancer tumors, these treatments may also make cancer cells more aggressive and mobile.

MAGNESIUM DEPLETION

Like vitamin D depletion, medical doctors are beginning to recognize that most Americans are chronically deficient in magnesium. The mineral magnesium can enhance many important functions in the body, such as producing cellular energy and enhanced muscle and nerve actions. Thus, there are numerous health problems related to its depletion. A number of pharmaceutical products and drugs, including antibiotics, antacids, antidepressants, statins, and anti-inflammatory medications, can result in the depletion of magnesium levels. Low magnesium in the body has also been associated with a host of problems including cramps, spasms, seizures, insomnia, migraines, depression, chronic fatigue, impaired memory, and hyperactivity in children.

A number of foods are naturally high in magnesium, including kelp, cashews, almonds, Brewer's Yeast, buckwheat, Brazil nuts, millet, wheat germ and bran. According to advice from nutritional doctors, in addition to consuming nuts, seeds, seaweed, and grains, magnesium supplements should also be taken, but ideally in smaller doses and at staggered times. However, many people get an unwanted laxative effect from these supplements, in which case it is recommended to take a bath in Epsom salts, which draws out toxins and increases magnesium levels in the body. People can find out if they have lowered magnesium by taking the "RBC Magnesium" blood test.

"There is but one *cause* in disease, and that is the body's inability to comprehend itself and/or it's environment," wrote author and Doctor Fred H. Barge. He continued, "There is but one *cure* in disease, and that is the body's ability to heal itself. And there is only one thing that any doctor can do for a patient. And that is remove obstruction to healing, thus facilitating it." Giving the body what it needs to heal itself requires good nutrition and supplements. Magnesium for example, is considered the essential "forgotten" mineral. Most people do not know calcium is regulated and controlled by magnesium, which is another essential mineral needed by every cell in the body. Our bodies need the correct amount of magnesium in our diets in order for us to sleep properly. If it's too high or too low, we can suffer from sleep disturbance. Magnesium deficiency is also shown to cause cancer.

IMMUNE SYSTEM STRENGTH

The human body is an extremely clever machine. It knows how to breathe all by itself. It knows how to make a baby. It knows how to grow. It knows how to digest food. It knows how to eliminate waste. It knows how to circulate blood, oxygen and nutrients. It knows how to heal a wound, and it knows how to fight disease. Enzymes like telomerase and resveratrol, although not quite a "fountain of youth," offer tantalizing clues as to how we might someday soon unravel the aging process.

We are composed of more than just our body. Everything in life, including the living human body, is dynamic and always changing. A living organism has the intelligence of the universe within it, and referred to as its "innate intelligence." This innate wisdom is the infinite source within, and it makes no mistakes. There is an energy within each of us, as well as within all life forms, and it operates by using innate knowledge. This intelligent and organized force is called our "life energy." The purpose of the body's innate intelligence is to maintain the living tissues in active organization. Innate intelligence runs your body and, by extension, runs your life. If nature creates a problem, nature creates a solution. Our bodily systems direct our innate ability to heal, survive, react or adapt.

The key to optimal health and longevity lies within our immune systems. The modern word "immunity" derives from the Latin *immunis,* and means resistance of an organism to infection or disease. The immune system is amazingly complex. It can recognize millions of different enemies, and it can enlist specialized cells and secretions to seek out and destroy each of them. Scientists have long been working to find ways to boost our immune system's ability to fight cancer and add longevity. Earlier attempts at genetically modifying "bloodstream soldiers," called T-cells, have had limited success. The modified cells didn't reproduce well and quickly disappeared.

Following healthy eating patterns can directly contribute to greater immune system strength. Opting for organic produce, or locally and sustainable grown foods, can be an excellent first step in developing better health. Dietary strategies in patients who experienced cancer remission have included foods with turmeric and cumin, while chili, garlic, chipotle, and cinnamon powders appear to be good additives also. At the same time, these healthy nutrition strategies provide a "greener lifestyle," a greener planet, and generally speaking, a more eco-conscious form of existence. It bears repeating that for every ailment, there is a natural cure.

COUNTERING TOXIC EFFECTS

Homeopathic medicine is considered "fringe," even though it was widely used prior to the 1930s, and has been shown to improve health. Even the eminent ancient Greek father of medicine, Hippocrates, said, "nature is the best physician." In this modern age, however, we have the disadvantage of living in a world with polluted air, water, and soil. There are new diseases, viruses, and other bacterial strains that maliciously effect our health, and we need to protect ourselves. There are ways to counter the harmful effects of our toxic environment, including fighting off new infections, and there are growing problems with vaccines. A leading doctor of holistic medicine, Russell Blaylock, has compiled a list regarding suggestions on how to reduce the toxic effects of vaccines—especially the A/H1N1 Influenza A shot:

1. *Number one on the list is to bring a cold pack with you and place it on the site of the injection as soon as you can, as this will block the immune reaction. Once you get home, continue using a cold pack throughout the day. If you continue to have immune reactions the following day, take cold showers and continue with the cold press.*
2. *Take fish oil supplements. Eicosapentaenoic acid (EPA), one of the omega 3 fatty acids found in fish oil caplets, is a potent immune suppressant. If you take high dose of EPA you will be more susceptible to infections, because it is a powerful immune suppressant. However, in the case of an immune adjuvant reaction, you will want to reduce symptoms. Studies show that if you take EPA oil one hour before injecting a very powerful adjuvant called lipopolysaccharide (LPS), it would completely block the ability of the LPS to cause brain inflammation. Take a moderate dose everyday and more if needed to tame a cytokine storm.*
3. *Flavonoids are third on the list, namely curcumin, quercetin, ferulic acid and ellagic acid, particularly in a mixture. The curcumin and quercetin in particular have been found to block the ability of the adjuvants to trigger a long-term immune reaction. If you take it an hour before the vaccination, it should help dampen the immune reactions, says Dr. Blaylock.*
4. *Vitamin E, the natural form that is high in gamma-E, will help dampen the immune reactions and reduce several of the inflammatory cytokines.*
5. *An important ingredient on the list is vitamin C at a dose of 1000 mg, taken four times a day, and best between meals. It is a very potent anti-inflammatory and should be taken in a buffered form, not as absorbic acid.*
6. *Also use astaxanthin as it's an anti-inflammatory. According to Dr. Blaylock, fatal reactions to vaccines in aboriginal and African children occurred in those who were deficient in carotinoids, like astaxanthin. It is a good protection against the toxic effects of the vaccine.*
7. *Likewise, it was found that children who were deficient in zinc had a high mortality rate. Zinc is very protective against vaccine toxicity. Do not use zinc mixed with copper however, as copper is a major trigger of free-radical generation.*
8. *Ensure you avoid all immune-stimulating supplements, such as mushroom extracts, whey protein, and beta-glucan before a vaccination shot.*
9. *Take a multivitamin-mineral daily, but one that does not contain iron. This multivitamin-mineral is to make sure your body has plenty of selenium and B vitamins. Selenium, notes Dr. Blaylock, is very important for fighting viral infections and it reduces the inflammatory response to vaccines.*

10. *Take magnesium citrate/malate, 500 mg of elemental magnesium, two capsules, three times a day. Also, make sure that the magnesium does not contain magnesium stearate.*
11. *Ensure you avoid all mercury-containing seafood or any other sources of mercury, as the heavy metal is a very powerful inducer of autoimmunity, known to make people more susceptible to viral infections and will be found in H1N1 vaccines.*
12. *Avoid the oils that significantly suppress immunity and increase inflammation—such as corn, safflower, sunflower, soybean, canola and peanut oils.*
13. *Drink very concentrated white tea at least four times a day. It helps to prevent abnormal immune reactions.*
14. *Pop parsley and celery in a blender and drink eight ounces of this mixture twice a day. Dr. Blaylock says that parsley is very high in a flavonoid called apigenin, and that celery is high in luteolin. Both are very potent in inhibiting autoimmune diseases, particularly the apigenin. If possible, plant some parsley in your garden.*
15. *What is very important is vitamin D3, which is the only "vitamin" the body can manufacture from sunlight (UVB). It is a neural hormone, not really a vitamin, says Dr. Blaylock, and helps if you are over-reacting immunologically by cooling down the reaction. Similarly, if you are under-reacting, it helps to boost your immune response. In addition it also protects against micro-organism invasion. Black people and those in colder climates are particularly deficient, so they will almost certainly require supplementation. When taking vitamin D3, it is also important to make sure that you are getting enough vitamin K2 and consuming Omega-3 fatty acids (arctic krill oil) so that the vitamin D3 can be properly absorbed.*
   For those seeking a non-chemical approach to their well-being, Natural News suggests that adults should take 500-1000 mg of calcium each day and children under the age of 12 years should take 250 mg a day. Vitamin D works more efficiently in the presence of calcium. In addition to Dr. Russell Blaylock's excellent detoxifying list, a few more suggestions are also worth mentioning:
16. *Think Positive. Changing your thinking can change your life. Take steps to increase your optimism.*
17. *Be Sociable.*
18. *Eat Healthy Foods. Most of us don't realize it, but we are drug addicts. Our drug comes in a pure, white crystal or powder form. We use it even when we don't know we're doing it. It's in salad dressing, peanut butter, soup, pickles, bread, jam, yogurt, canned fruits and vegetables. We tend to crave it after every meal. On an average, each of us consumes about 60 kilograms per year. What is this controversial drug, you ask? It goes by many names, but the most common is sugar.*
19. *Keep your mind active and learn new things.*
20. *Get at least an hour of physical exercise every day, and maintain regular sleeping hours.*

HEART HEALTH

The human heart is the strongest generator of both the electrical and magnetic fields within the body. This fact is significant because we've always been taught that the brain is where all of the action is, but this is an incomplete picture. While the brain does have an electrical and a magnetic field, they are both relatively weak compared to the heart. The heart is about 100,000 times stronger electrically and up to 5,000 times stronger magnetically than the brain. This is important because the physical world—as we know it—is made of these twin fields: electrical and magnetic. Physicists now tell us that if we change either the magnetic field or the electrical field of the atom, we literally change that atom—*and its elements within our body and this world.* The human heart is *designed* to do both. Here are seven food-based "medicines" that, both electrically and magnetically, strengthen heart health. They may also end up saving you from various chronic diseases and an early death:

1. ***One Glass of Red Wine:*** *Scientists report a so-called "miracle molecule" found in red wine which might help improve mobility and prevent falls among older adults. The ingredient is called resveratrol, an antioxidant found in the skin of grapes, blueberries and other dark-skinned fruits. Resveratrol is known to help reduce inflammation of the body and has also been shown to fight off diseases associated with aging. It helps lower cholesterol, improve heart function, and there have been some studies that show it can reduce the risk of heart disease and certain forms of cancer. Red wine contains much more resveratrol than white wine.*

2. ***Garlic:*** *Also known as Allium sativum L., garlic, which some have fondly nicknamed a "masterpiece of nature," is one of the most medicinally potent herbs you can take regularly for vibrant health. Recognized for its ability to prevent and treat bacterial infections, yeasts, fungi, and viruses, as well as promote healthy blood flow, lower blood cholesterol levels, and detoxify heavy metals and other poisons, garlic truly is a medicinal superfood of the highest order. Deriving garlic's many health benefits can be as simple as merely slicing up a fresh clove and adding it to a meal, or taking a high-quality garlic supplement daily. No matter how you choose to take it, consuming garlic regularly can help prevent colds, influenza, bacterial infections, blood clots, abnormal blood sugar levels, free radical damage, heavy metal toxicity, chronic inflammatory diseases, and cancer, among other health conditions.*

3. ***Raw Honey:*** *Honey is another superfood that has been used for centuries to boost immunity and provide a lasting source of energy. And because it basically never spoils, honey is a great food-based medicine to keep on hand at all times. Internally, honey can help treat bacterial infections, alleviate sore throats, subdue an upset stomach, and even cure bladder infections. Topically, honey is effective at treating eczema, canker sores, and even cuts and types of skin damage. Manuka honey is particularly beneficial, as it contains exceptionally potent antibacterial, antiviral, anti-fungal, anti-inflammatory, antioxidant, and antiseptic properties that are unmatched by any pharmaceutical drug on the market. As with all forms of honey, however, be sure to never feed this medicinal substance to children under the age of one, as their intestinal tracts are not developed enough to inhibit the growth of Clostridium botulinum, which can cause botulism. For adults, find local honey at your nearest farmer's market, as the local honey will help combat local allergens.*

4. ***Spirulina:*** *A nutrient-dense blue-green algae that has been around since the beginning of time, spirulina is rich in amino acids, which are essentially pre-digested proteins readily available for quick absorption. Spirulina is super high in protein, and the highest that can be derived from any plant matter. A highly-bioavailable superfood, spirulina also contains an impressive array of essential fatty acids, including Omega-3*

fatty acids, as well as B vitamins, carotenoid antioxidants, chlorophyll, and polysaccharides. As far as your health is concerned, spirulina is a spectacular detoxifier that aids in the expulsion of heavy metals. Spirulina is also an amazing energizer, as it contains a perfect balance of protein, vitamins, minerals, and other nutrients.

5. **Apples:** You may not think of them as necessarily vital for sustaining life, but apples are an antioxidant powerhouse loaded with plenty of food-based medicine. Besides having a high fiber content, which promotes healthy digestion, apples, and mainly apple skins, are rich in polyphenols, flavonoids, and various other disease-fighting antioxidants. And since apples come in many colors—red, yellow, pink green, and various combinations of these—eating a wide variety of apples regularly can help guard your body against debilitating disease.

6. **Chia Seeds:** The ancient Mayans referred to these seeds as "strength," and the Aztecs called them "running food." Chia seeds contain double the antioxidants found in blueberries, and six times more calcium than milk. Eating chia seeds regularly provides natural extended energy. Among the many benefits of one of the most vibrant superfoods known is that chia seeds are a complete and perfect protein, containing roughly 23% protein per seed. That is 41% of your daily fiber in one serving. Chia seeds are also packed with essential Omega-3 fatty acids, antioxidants, amino acids, vitamins, trace minerals, and dietary fiber. When added to water or other liquids, chia seeds develop a gelatinous coating around the seeds that buffer the exposure of carbohydrates to digestive enzymes in the stomach and gut, effectively slowing their conversion into blood sugar. Chia seeds also help regulate water intake and mineral absorption, balancing electrolyte levels and cell nutrition.

7. **Raw or Sprouted Almonds:** Truly raw almonds, not the pasteurized and irradiated imitations commonly sold in U.S. stores, are one of nature's most perfect medicinal foods. Possessing an optimal balance of protein, calcium, magnesium, and dietary fiber—almonds have the highest dietary fiber content of any nut or seed—almonds are another complete food much like chia seeds and spirulina. If you are looking for a truly whole food that is rich in healthy fats and plant phytochemicals, which promote heart and cardiovascular health, raw or sprouted almonds are the ideal medicinal food to always keep on hand. As much as 75% of almonds and other nuts contains the "good" fat. Eating fat doesn't necessarily make you fat. The bigger factor leading to weight gain is portion-size. Luckily, nuts are loaded with healthy fats that keep you full. They are also a good source of protein and fiber. One study even found that whole almonds have 20% fewer calories than previously thought because a lot of the fat is excreted from the body.

Would you like to add a few more nutrients to the cells in your body so they can work more efficiently to keep your heart in good health? In addition to the above list there are a few other items: Goji powder or goji berries are ultra-high in antioxidants; Raw cacao powder is high in vitamin C, protein, fiber, and lots of other vitamins; Hemp seeds contain fatty acids, all the essential amino acids, and antioxidants. Maca powder has hormonal benefits for testosterone and can be good for lessening hot flashes, and is also great for vitality. The health benefits of olive oil come from the presence of polyphenols, which are antioxidants that reduce the risk of heart disease and cancers. But to get these healthy compounds, consumers should buy good quality, fresh "extra-virgin" olive oil, that carry the highest polyphenol content. Most commercially available olive oils have low levels of polyphenols. This is associated with poor harvesting methods, improper storage, and heavy processing. Lastly, coconut oil is great for sugar control and thyroid function. Limiting to two tablespoons a day can begin to lessen belly fat.

In total, a green diet and active lifestyle benefits the body to such an extreme degree that we would be foolish not to adopt better habits. Locally grown and harvested produce, soil that is tended with love and care, and deep connections between the earth and the person eating its bounty are all part of the deal. And why not? This is the way our civilization has been doing it since the very beginning. It is only our life in contemporary times that these good eating habits and diet have broken down. By all reports, the "paleo-diet" is one of the best we can choose.

COLOR HEALING PRODUCTS

Lastly, for this chapter, there is an emerging science that uses frequency, colors, and sound, that may revolutionize the healing process as we know it. By now, it should be understood that human health does not require pharmaceutical products, just the reintroduction of essential minerals and vitamins that are missing from our modern diet; one example being magnesium—much of which has been removed from refined grains.

There is a little understood aspect of human health that is related to a good diet. There is also an aspect of human health that is related to consciousness. And there are many aspects of human health that are strictly energetic. For example, there are cures that require nothing but the correct energy frequencies and color-based coding. Sometimes that energy, believe it or not, can be harnessed by building a pyramid. It appears that the ancients who did this were much more knowledgeable than they have been given credit for, because the pyramid shape can natural refocus energy.

There is also the prospect of curing health ailments using color. Dr. Fritz-Albert Popp, a scientist who studied cancer, found that the only commonality between carcinogens is that they scramble light that comes in at 380-nanometer wavelengths, which is the ultraviolet. This discovery can have huge repercussions. Cancer occurs when cells grow in a manner out of control in your body. Ultraviolet light that becomes stored within your DNA sends control messages to the cell—to tell it when to stop reproducing.

Healing with colors was actually discovered a long time ago. The word *aura* comes from the Latin term meaning akin to air, a slight breath, vapor or shimmer. *Soma* is the Greek word for "body," while in ancient Sanskrit, it designates a mysterious drink that transports the soul into a divine ecstasy. When the two words are combined, they set up a very different and specific vibration, since both concepts, aura and soma, have deeper essential meanings.

Colored oils—also called "Equilibrium," pomanders, quintessences, color essences and other color related products of "AURA-SOMA®"—have been shown to help people bring their respective states of being into *equilibrium*. These products may also help increase a person's self-awareness, while also creating a harmonious sense of comfort around and within oneself. One's color choice reflects one's very personal needs, and helps individuals find a more accurate understanding of their human potential. Equilibrium has been described as "living jewels." Each Equilibrium bottle contains an upper and lower fraction, which is oil resting upon water. Taken together these energies may balance the whole of our spiritual selves. Within these two fractions may be found the essential oils and herbal extracts of the plant kingdom, in combination with the energies of crystals and gems from the mineral kingdom, tied in with the energies of color, sound and light.

The next part of the longevity equation is related to consciousness, and how science may hold the key to making us more complete human beings.

WE ARE NATURE

We are nature, and nature is us. To change the body's composition with drugs or chemicals is to deny that we are also part of the vibrant cycle of life. To divorce ourselves from nature is to remove ourselves from the system which replenishes, feeds, and provides us with an opportunity to thrive. It is said that for every human ailment, a natural cure or remedy is provided by nature.

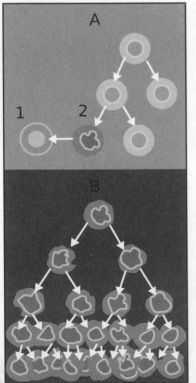

The image on left (A) is normal cell division, and how a healthy body can transform a damaged cell: (1) is apoptosis; and (2) is the damaged cell. The below image (B) is cancer cell division. Cancer starts developing out of control a long time before it is diagnosed, or appears as a tumor. We all have cancer cells in our body. It is not a problem until cancer cells duplicate millions of times over.

Ultraviolet (UV) light therapy has been used for centuries to help in the treatment of many skin conditions, disorders, cancers and diseases. Of course, excessive exposure to UV rays and sunlight can be harmful, but if done correctly the benefits are enormous. It is important to protect our eyes and skin with appropriate sunglasses and sunblock, specific amounts of UV light can be prescribed for various medical treatments.

Using ultraviolet ray lamp sterilization deodorization, in the real shortwave ultraviolet bactericidal spectrum, can destroy DNA and RNA structure of microorganisms, kills mold bacteria from the root, cleans toilet seats and bowls, and reduce the actual growth of germ and mold spores which may attach on the toilet. Whole Foods and other stores have started using UV ray lamps in their public bathrooms.

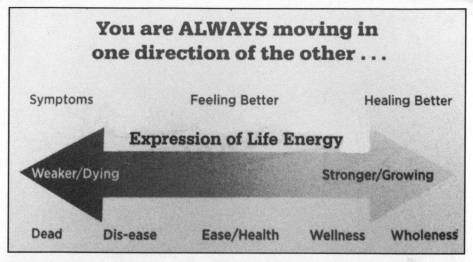

You are ALWAYS moving in one direction of the other . . .

Symptoms   Feeling Better   Healing Better

Expression of Life Energy

Weaker/Dying   Stronger/Growing

Dead   Dis-ease   Ease/Health   Wellness   Wholeness

We are either gaining physical vitality, or we are losing it. In order to live well until the century mark or older, it is essential to practice wellness all your life.

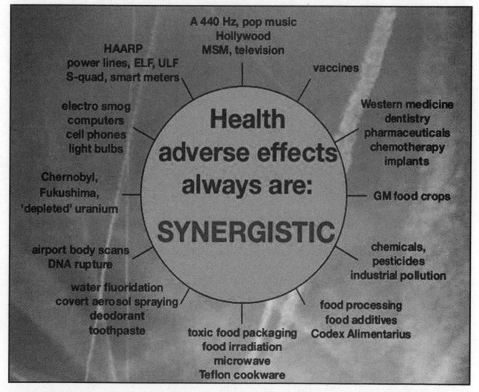

A 440 Hz, pop music
Hollywood
MSM, television

HAARP
power lines, ELF, ULF
S-quad, smart meters

vaccines

electro smog
computers
cell phones
light bulbs

Western medicine
dentistry
pharmaceuticals
chemotherapy
implants

Health adverse effects always are: SYNERGISTIC

Chernobyl,
Fukushima,
'depleted' uranium

GM food crops

airport body scans
DNA rupture

chemicals,
pesticides
industrial pollution

water fluoridation
covert aerosol spraying
deodorant
toothpaste

food processing
food additives
Codex Alimentarius

toxic food packaging
food irradiation
microwave
Teflon cookware

Most people are completely unaware of the physical assault they are being subjected to on a daily basis. All this is hidden in plain sight or is common knowledge which people neglect to investigate because of the overwhelming and biased influence of mainstream TV, radio, newspapers, the FDA and other government agencies. It is extremely difficult to convince some people to look at other facts. Sooner or later we will all feel the ill effects of a poisoned world.

Li Ching-Yuen was a renowned Chinese herbalist, martial artist, and tactical advisor who supposedly lived to be 256 years old. He claimed to be born in 1736, while disputed records suggest 1677. Both alleged lifespans of 197 and 256 years far exceed the longest confirmed lifespan of 122 years and 164 days of the French woman Jeanne Calment. His true date of birth was never determined, but he died on May 6, 1933. Li Ching-Yuen attributed his longevity to peace of mind, proper breathwork, a healthy diet and regular physical exercise. It was his belief that everyone could live at least a century by attaining inward calm.

A mysterious alchemist of the Greek Classical Age named Salomon Trismosin, a teacher of Paracelsus, claimed to have lived to the age of 150 as a result of his knowledge of alchemy.

SCIENCE OF CONSCIOUSNESS

"If you want to find the secrets of the universe, think in terms of
energy, frequency and vibration." –Nikola Tesla

A death knell for the old rationalist, reductionist, materialist model of reality will be the emerging sciences of the mind. But it seems some diehard skeptics, deaf to the inner voices of their own minds, are still clinging to the dull empiricism that deems telepathy not just implausible, but impossible. For them, it is worth spelling out: the evidence for mind-to-mind communication is now so overwhelming that it has been presented at the annual meeting of the British Association for the Advancement of Science.

The study of the science of mind is nothing new. Underlying the mysteries of the universe is both an emerging and ancient science—metaphysics. The word is derived from *Metaphusika,* the title of Greek philosopher Aristotle's treatise on the subject. Metaphysics is the branch of philosophy that examines the nature of reality and the relationship between mind and matter. As the power of the human mind becomes more apparent, so will our ability to perceive new and questionable phenomena.

Unfortunately, we are not being prompted by the mass media or our elected governmental officials to consider the persuasive data supporting advancement to new elevations of consciousness. Most of these mainstream authorities are ignorant of the leaps in a science of consciousness. Others apparently prefer dominance over an ignorant race that pays taxes into an obsolete system rather than an enlightened race that can offer positive solutions for the advancement of the human race. Wouldn't it be nice if *The New York Times* ran a cover story entitled "How Our Lives Will Change in the Other Dimensions," or what if the government began construction on a new pyramidal initiation chamber to assist citizens in their astral traveling pursuits? Actually, the ideal situation would be the plain and simple truth. After all, as the Greeks noted long ago: When the lies begin, the republic ends.

The truth is, we live in a world that is infinitely more complex and mysterious than we ever could have imagined. Change within our lifetimes, for better or for worse, is happening now at a highly accelerated pace. Consequently, we will be able to tap into human abilities never before known, or sink into depths of ignorance that will destroy humanity and the planet. Either we can activate our collective mind seed, or we can perish. It's really that simple. Either everyone can begin to realize their potential as masters of their own realities, or they can remain ignorant and apathetic. The absolute power is certainly within each and every one of us. There is nothing you cannot do except limit yourself, and that is why the science of consciousness will be the key to helping us all thrive.

With so many distractions and so much disinformation in the world today, how do we navigate such murky waters? To begin, it helps to first question everything. A skeptic is one who practices the method of suspended judgment, engages in rational and dispassionate reasoning as exemplified by the scientific method, shows willingness to consider alternative explanations without prejudice based on prior beliefs, and who seeks out evidence and carefully scrutinizes its validity. It is good to be skeptical, just don't shut yourself off to your inner consciousness. It is imperative to examine every issue from every angle, even if at first it might seem counterintuitive.

MASTERS OF OUR OWN DESTINY

Changes in human consciousness may be an essential tool to simply saving humanity from itself. We are only just reaching the point in history where the greatest danger to humanity is humanity itself. And it would appear that saving ourselves will certainly require a radical shift in perception, that is, a fundamental change in human consciousness.

The good news is that we are each an immortal soul, with profound untapped powers. These can be developed to such an extent that we will be able to protect all that's important, and use our newly-discovered abilities to discern and thwart the malevolent agendas. There are thousands of case histories of near-death experiences, reincarnation and similar spiritual phenomena, which provide ample evidence that we have existed before this life—and will continue to exist after this life. There will be more on reincarnation in a later chapter.

The masters throughout history have all told us that consciousness is everything. Integrating this truth involves an awareness that each individual has to experience for themselves. This experience is accessible by way of several modalities. These include disciplines and practices included in ancient Vedic literature to the study of quantum physics, and from meditation and prayer to intentional manifestation. Today they all come together around concepts that are beginning to link actual physical reality to thoughts within a feedback loop, where our consciousness is not merely influenced by reality as we perceive it, but reality is, in turn, influenced by our thoughts.

The "illusion trap" begins when we examine the problems of the world from the single lens of the classical, or Western linear-system, point of view. Through this narrow lens, metaphysical issues seem quite hopeless and even irrelevant. Yet, if we can expand our point of view to include creative and even radical ways of completing cycles, and recirculating materials in the biosphere and the economy, the possibilities appear nothing short of miraculous.

The expansion of consciousness, which originally allowed us to become aware of our inner thoughts and feelings, continues at an accelerated pace among humans today. The rise in brainpower and technology has not only created an explosion of skills—inventing tools, language, chemicals, computers, civilization—at many times during the last few thousand years, it has allowed some random outliers to glimpse something shocking: that *who* we think we are—our mental self-concept, or our ego—is not actually *what* we are. This glimpse of ourselves is merely the freedom of choice, a decision regarding how to view ourselves. As evolution stumbles forward in its blind march of accidental brilliance, a radical insight that was once the province of a special few will slowly become the normal viewpoint. Selfish people are nothing special. In essence, we are all truly One.

ROUTES TO ENLIGHTENMENT

The opening of the spiritual centers, those that begin the path to true enlightenment, are best achieved by natural means without resort to chemical assistance, whether advocated by a shaman or anyone else. This is an essential message from all great spiritual and mystical teachings of the East and West. Moreover, there is very good reason to believe that the use of any form of hallucinogen for the purpose of spiritual awakening incurs the risk of damaging the natural spiritual centers in such a way as to abort a process that would otherwise, with sincere application and in due course, lead to the desired liberation. The difficulties which may be encountered along the way, the wise ones have always said, are for our instruction and the strengthening of our hearts, and are best overcome by spiritual means, not by avoidance or short cuts.

This word of caution about hallucinogens is appropriate for many of us raised in Western scientific cultures. Shamans, on the other hand, have a different story, growing out of historic personal experience with beneficial uses of hallucinogenic substances. The shamans of today, those in tribal or hunter and gather cultures, who induce altered states of consciousness by taking hallucinogens or similar methods, report that they receive teachings from beings they encounter in their trance state. It is possible that the intelligent beings that pass knowledge to indigenous holy people actually do exist in other dimensions of reality, and are only reached through the shamanic process, a process also experienced by ancient cave artists and expressed through their designs.

Author Graham Hancock feels traditional scholars do not want to consider the possibility that for the last 35,000 years the testimony of all the world's religions may actually be true. In this sense: There may actually be such a thing as a spirit-world or other dimensions with sentient life beyond this dimension. Hancock advocates that a new scientific model is needed to further explore the documented phenomenon of altered states of consciousness. These models have been developed by groups at the Institute of Noetic Sciences and the Center for Consciousness Studies, among others, and described below. In the new research model, where hallucinations are concerned, researchers do not regard the brain as a factory that is manufacturing these impressions. Instead, the brain is a receiver of information, whether from the many day-to-day perceptions, or from other dimensions. As Hancock observes, "Our brains are a few pounds of jelly. And somehow the light rays emitted on the eyes are transformed into conscious understanding and conscious perception and it is very difficult ... no scientist can explain how that's done. And it's even more difficult to tell where the detailed perceptions we call hallucinations are coming from and what the source of those might be."

The psychoactive ingredient in the ayahuasca plant is DMT, or NN-diemethyltryptamine. This compound, found naturally in plants and fungi around the world, is also produced by the human pineal gland that is located near the center of our brains. Interestingly, the ancients refer to this gland as the "seat of the soul," or the gland through which the soul enters the body. DMT has been dubbed "the spirit molecule" for the compound's possible connection to our spiritual state of consciousness.

CONSCIOUSNESS ENGINEERING

Starting in the late 1970s, the Princeton Engineering Anomalies Research (PEAR) program studied the interaction of human consciousness on the material world using sensitive physical devices and systems. The team developed complementary theoretical models to enable a better understanding of the role of consciousness in the establishment of physical reality. These experiments demonstrated that electronic, noise-based, random number generators (RNG), seem to be influenced by human consciousness. The randomness was altered to become slightly ordered when human mass consciousness focused on a single global event, such as the 9-11 Trade Center tragedy; Princess Diana's death; or even the Super Bowl. Professor Robert G. Jahn withstood decades of criticism for the work his team conducted in their Princeton laboratory, and the Princeton administration threatened to shut down his laboratory. But strong objections from principal university donors prevented this. Not the least of their arguments was that the culture of science, at its purest, is one of freedom in which any idea can be tested regardless of how far-fetched it might appear.

The Global Consciousness Project (GCP), picking up where the Princeton study left off, has named this random data "Event Generators Electrogaiagrams," or EGGs, and they are using them to test whether human consciousness extends this field around the Earth, and which can change the results of random recording devices (as described above with the 9-11 2001 attacks or the Indian Ocean tsunami). Not only, they claim, when an important global event occurs do the random event generators (REGS) start to display patterns that should not exist in truly random sequences, but there is another astounding effect: Four hours before the 9-11 attacks, there was a bizarre spike of non-random activity, which was also detected prior to the Indian Ocean tsunami. Analysts concluded that the EGGs detected the disaster a full 24 hours in advance. "We may be able to predict that a major world event is going to happen," noted project leader Roger Nelson, "but we won't know exactly what will happen or where it's going to happen." But when a great event synchronizes the feelings of millions of people, the team's network of random number generators becomes subtly structured. Thus, after generating reams of replicated data showing a statistically significant effect of mass consciousness on random number output, PEAR (the Princeton laboratory) was closed in 2007. Not because of controversy, but because its founder said it was time. According to Dean Radin, senior scientist at the Institute of Noetic Sciences, and a participant in this research, the odds against chance are far beyond a million to one. In other words, there is a real effect of focused human intention on random number generators. They become more coherent and less random. This is strong data supporting mind over matter effects. The evidence suggests an emerging "noosphere," or a unifying field of consciousness, as described by sages in all cultures through the ages.

Such experiments also confirm the aptly named "meditation effect," which occurs when a few thousand people get together and meditate for a positive outcome. Multiple studies show that a large joining of focused meditators appears to influence positive outcomes, depending on what the group sets as its objective. It can be noted that certain outcomes do not manifest for negative wishes. Fifty different scientific studies have confirmed that the meditation effect is real. Global terrorism, for example, has gone down by 72%, according to one study. Similarly, dramatic decreases were seen in war, fatalities and violent crime. Skeptics will continue to argue about whether or not this is "real," but the fact is that these are rigorously designed studies, with many variables being ruled out—including weekends, weather, holidays, and historic cycles. This effect has been documented in numerous peer-reviewed publications, including the *Journal of Offender Rehabilitation*. The stunning conclusion is that the meditation effect strongly supports the perennial wisdom teaching that the universe is biased in favor of love, peace and forgiveness. Furthermore, when we practice this within ourselves, it has a collective, and energetic effect on others.

UNIVERSE IN PARALLEL

One of the greatest minds of the 20th century was the theoretical physicist Albert Einstein. While working in a German patent office, Einstein began formulating his epic Theory of Relativity. He proved mathematically that the velocity of light—300,000 kilometers per second—is a constant in our chaotic universe. All human standards of time and space depend on this sole "absolute" of light velocity. In other words, time and space are relative and finite factors, and can only derive their conditional measurement-validity in reference to the yardstick of light velocity. Therefore, no material body, whose mass increases with its velocity, can ever attain the speed of light—unless that mass is infinite.

Breakthroughs in quantum physics, on the atomic level, reveal that each atom as a miniature solar system. The atom, the smallest unit of an element, has all the characteristics of a positively charged nucleus surrounded by a system of electrons. Not only is the atom energy rather than matter, but energy on the atomic level is essentially "mind-stuff." Mere observation alone can trigger an effect, as shown in the 1927 Heizenberg's Uncertainty Principle. According to this principle, electrons have been observed to have dual personalities, one that is energy, and one that is matter. Yet, if the particle is not observed, it exists in every possible state. The logical conclusion of mathematics indicates a near infinite number of parallel universes, or dimensions, co-existing in one universal fabric. "The stream of knowledge," writes Sir James Jeans in *The Mysterious Universe*, "is heading toward a non-mechanical reality; the universe begins to look more like a great thought than like a great machine."

The researchers who think that parallel universes are real say that shortly after the Big Bang, spacetime expanded at different rates in different places, giving rise to bubble universes that may function with their own separate laws of physics. Researchers suggest that if our universe contains other universes, we may have bumped into them. Such collisions would have left lasting marks in the Cosmic Microwave Background (CMB) radiation, the diffuse light left over from the Big Bang, and that pervades the universe. The Higgs boson, or the "God particle," was confirmed to exist by CERN in July, 2012. This subatomic particle is so fundamental to the universe that, in its absence, it is claimed nothing could exist. The particle is thought to create a sort of *force field* that permeates the cosmos, and imbues other particles with the property known as *mass*—a resistance to being moved around.

Famed UFO researcher and physicist Jacques Vallee gave a lecture in 2012, not about UFOs for which he is well-known, but on the "Theory of Everything Else." He noted that in physics there are several competing theories. We have quantum physics and consciousness science, and both are in conflict with general relativity. Resolve the conflict with new theories, such as string theory, and we will still have what Vallee describes as "missing a child." That child relates to the physics of matter, particles, mass, forces, and energy, the standard physics model taught in school today. But we are as yet missing the physics of information to "save the child." The first equation to rethink is *time*, yet we can only go one way, never backward in the "time" dimension. The same is true with gravity and particles. But what is the nature of time and coincidences? The theory of quantum mechanics is "reality" as we know it, and this appears to be created moment by moment.

Many questioning physicists wander into mystical realms when trying to integrate what they are discovering with previous models of the universe. Vallee said in a lecture several years earlier, that "as physicists attempt to reconcile theory with observed properties of elementary particles and with discoveries at the frontiers of cosmology, modern physics suggests that mankind has not yet discovered all of the universe's facets, and we must propose new theories and experiments in order to explore these undiscovered facets." In summary, he was suggesting that many serious researchers, such as the Princeton PEAR group, and the Noetics scientists, are proposing new theories and models, and are devising ingenious ways to test them. Much of the current well-designed research in this bridge-area between the old Newtonian model and an expanded consciousness model can begin to be understood by incorporating "data" from the psychic realm. Here, Vallee notes, "we use the word 'psychic' in the sense of an interaction between physical reality and human consciousness. The (subsequent) feeling of absurdity and contradiction in these two aspects," he concludes "is not worse than scientific puzzlement during the particle/wave or, more recently, quantum entanglement and multi-dimensional transport controversies."

Carl Jung was famous for writing about psychic phenomena such as coincidences. Once when reading about golden scarabs, he looked up and at that very moment a scarab flew into his window. But coincidences cannot be explained with quantum mechanics. Here the paranormal becomes rather normal. We must broaden our data to include the "something else" of synchronicity and coincidences and, in so doing, we will find a double causality in our intentions. Putting this all together is a very complex process, as Vallee noted, especially because we live in an era which is drowning in information but starved for knowledge—witness the 35 hours of video per minute uploaded to YouTube every day. Vallee suggests four requirements for the new physics. First, recognize the universe we perceive is a meta-reality. Second, recognize dimensions as a cultural artifact, and do away with them. Next, treat the present as over-determined, an intention in the past arriving here now. And lastly, consider that consciousness traverses a vast array of associations, thus generating the mind's impression of space and time.

SUBATOMIC PARTICLES

All matter, whether solid, liquid or gaseous, is made up of molecules. Each molecule consists of a dense core comprising subatomic particles including positively charged protons. The core is surrounded by rapidly orbiting negatively charged electrons. A normal, passive, molecule of air has the same number of protons and electrons, making it electrically neutral. An ion is a molecule that has gained or lost an electron, and there are both positive and negative ions in the air. It is the negative ions that give us the "feel-good" factor, as they can stimulate and energize people and animals. Friction between water and air causes electrons to be displaced, and these fly free, form into negative ions, while the heavier positive charges fall with the water droplets. When we breathe, the negative ions are dispersed into the air, and we often feel invigorated.

Ordinary matter consists of molecules bound together by electromagnetic force to form molecules. These molecules come together to form solids, liquids and gases. Atoms consist of a "dense" nucleus surrounded by a cloud of electrons. An electromagnetic force holds the nucleus and electrons together. The nucleus consists of protons and neutrons held together by a powerful nuclear force. At the core, protons and neutrons consist of three quarks each and are held together by a powerful nuclear force called gluons. The "properties" of these quarks, the basic components of protons, is astonishing—their miniscule size is beyond human conception. Basically, quarks are the fundamental constituent of matter. When discovered, Albert Einstein declared, "We have been all wrong! What we have called matter is energy, whose vibration has been lowered as to be perceptible to the senses."

Quarks have various intrinsic properties, including electric charge, color charge, spin, and mass. Quarks are the only elementary particles in the Standard Model of particle physics to experience all four fundamental interactions, also known as fundamental forces, those being electro-magnetism, gravitation, strong interaction, and weak interaction. For every quark flavor there is a corresponding type of anti-particle, known as an anti-quark. This differs from the quark only in that some of its properties have equal magnitude, but an opposite sign.

Gluons are elementary particles which act as the carriers of the fundamental forces of nature for the strong nuclear force "between quarks," and two gluons can come together to form another gluon. One gluon can split apart into two gluons, or even three gluons. So, if you have one gluon, you have many. And if you have a quark, you have gluons. And if you have gluons, you have quarks. A gluon turns one quark into another, and releases an enormous amount of energy. Modern science has revealed that the atom, previously regarded as the smallest particle, can actually be split. The next thorough investigation will confirm that all living entities, indeed all matter, is composed of energy.

STRING THEORY

String theory is a model of particle physics which predicts that the world is made up of more than the well-known standard model of four dimensions. The knowledge we have of quantum mechanics, or the study of subatomic particles, is that it appears to operate by its own rules, and not by the standard model of physics. What is needed is a single theory that governs everything and must be compatible with both laws of the universe. One master equation that embraces both, but never breaks down, is string theory, which fulfills the unification requirement. Yet no experiment has been designed that experimentally supports the mathematics of string theory. The theory states that strings are tiny bits of vibrating energy that resonate at the subatomic level. They have yet to be scientifically tested, or even proven to exist. The question remains: Is it a theory of physics, or of philosophy? There are also inherent conflicts with general relativity. The standard model of physics cannot fully explain gravity, for example, but string theory can. Other forces of nature can also be explained by subatomic particles. Tachyons, or massless particles, are tiny strands of energy, billions of times smaller than atoms. So are gravitons, which describe gravity, but do not explain it.

String theory falls short of being "a theory of everything"—a theory which would describe all the forces of nature and matter. Yet it has generated new ideas that open intriguing avenues of exploration. The different ways strings vibrate give characteristics to mass. To make it work, string theory must take into account multiple dimensions of space. Time is the fourth dimension, and *above* the three spatial dimensions. Extra dimensions, it appears, exist all around us, out of view and a part of nature, twisted and curled back on each other. String theory predicts at least 11 dimensions, and is one way of explaining all matter and forces. String theory can unify the four natural forces of nature: gravity; strong force; weak force; and the electromagnetic. It is also a way to resolve two theory bases that do not agree.

Sting theory does not reside only at the subatomic level. At the macro level, it also provides a new look at the inner workings of the universe. Wormholes are like cosmic shortcuts, but must have a "rip" in space and time. Quantum mechanics are the laws of the atomic world and predicts other dimensions within higher dimensional space. Within each quark that is within each proton and neutron, is a "string" of vibrating energy that makes up all of the elements in the material world, thus suggesting that string theory offers a unified theory of everything.

Extra dimensions "above" our own third dimension are curled up so small that they are not visible. String theory scientists propose that we live on a third dimensional membrane, making it almost impossible to perceive the extra dimensions, such as other membranes. The universe itself may be a membrane within a higher dimensional space. Like slices of bread, parallel universes might be right next to us, all around us, and operate by their own laws of physics. What appears is that we may be "trapped" on a single slice. Atoms and particles in our world operate only by laws exclusive to our slice, but gravity may seep into the other dimensions. Gravity does not "stick" like cinnamon on toast, and is less jelly-like, which is more like matter, and tied firmly to our third dimension reality. Gravity is a weak force. Light and electricity and magnets demonstrate electromagnetic forces, and are much stronger than gravity. Gravitons are thought to escape into the other dimensions. Potentially, gravity waves could interact with other worlds.

Third and upper dimensional membranes are likely to make contact, and when they collide, energy is created, as in a "big bang." But this is not a one time event that occurred long ago. Parallel universes continually collide, emitting explosions of energy and particles. And the key to understanding these phenomena is the gravitons, which are closed loops that can float out to the extra dimensions. Electrons, photons and gravitons give an insight into the laboratory experiments aiming to prove string theory. "Sparticles" are the next discovery that helps prove the wild-world of quantum theory. Key evidence in the direction of "a theory of everything" is the discovery of the Higgs boson particle, a particle which was tentatively confirmed to exist in March of 2013. After decades of search, within which harmonic mathematical equations pointed to its existence as being valid and logical, this discovery was met with cautious elation. New experiments may soon verify or disprove the role of the Higgs boson within the basic structure of the elegant universe.

Strings, membranes, parallel universes, and extra dimensions remain relegated to the study of philosophy until they can be replicated in a laboratory. What becomes clear is that everything in the universe, both animate and inanimate, is made up of moving energy—and unexpected layers of reality. At the atomic *and* subatomic level, for example, there is movement of energy. Thus, wherever there is movement of energy, there is vibration, and visa versa. We are electric beings vibrating within an energetic universe. Considering that humans are both receivers and transmitters of energy, our minds can be thought of as a vibrational transmitter. We are constantly sending out signals such as frequencies, and vibrations of energy, that will either attract or repel other vibrational beings, events, and experiences.

FREQUENCY AND VIBRATION

Nikola Tesla was convinced that everything in the universe, from galaxies to electrons, consists of vibration and frequency. He also felt that everything in the cosmos is connected by a single pervasive "super" consciousness, or one intelligent living organism. "My brain is only a receiver," he said. "In the universe there is a core from which we obtain knowledge, strength, inspiration. I have not penetrated into the secrets of this core, but I know it exists."

This greatest inventor of the 20th century used ancient Sanskrit terminology to understand natural phenomena. As early as 1891, Nikola Tesla described the universe as a kinetic system filled with energy, and which could be harnessed at any location. His concepts during the following years were greatly influenced by the teachings of Swami Vivekananda. Swami Vivekananda was the first of a succession of Eastern yogis who brought Vedic philosophy and religion to the West. After meeting the swami and after continued study of the Eastern view of the mechanisms driving the material world, Tesla began using the Sanskrit words *akasha, prana*, and the concept of a luminiferous ether to describe the source, existence and construction of matter. Tesla's understanding of Vedic science was the pre-requisite for the free energy systems he envisioned later in life.

Tesla emphasized that frequency and vibration hold a critically important, yet hidden power, to affect our lives, our health, our society and our world. The science of cymatics, which is the study of visible sound and vibration, proves that frequency and vibration are the master keys and organizational foundation for the creation of all matter and life on this planet. When sound waves move through a physical medium such as sand, air or water, the frequency of these sound waves have a direct effect upon the structures which are created by these waves as they pass through that particular medium.

In ancient times, schools of knowledge taught about the harmonic principles of cosmic influence upon natural systems, and throughout the development of humans. The significance of numbers and their ratios were part of these guiding harmonic principles. Highly advanced global civilizations built monuments worldwide to the same ancient code of 72, 108, 216, 432, and 864, which, when multiplied together in a particular way, equals 25,920. After the fall from the devastation of global catastrophe, the survivors that had knowledge of the previous ancient ways built markers for future generations. The Procession of the Equinox, or the Great Year marking the end of a cycle—25,920 years—was carved in stone alignments and temples all over the Earth. For centuries, accurate astrological observatories served as classrooms and places of court and custom. Stonehenge denotes the numbers 432 and 4,320. The connection of Stonehenge to the 25,920-year orbital procession of the equinox and the number 432 is obvious when considering the following calculations. If you take the first 30 stones in the outer ring of 360 degrees, divide that by 30 which gives you 12, and then divide 25,920 by 12 you get 2,160; which is the approximate diameter of the Moon. The Great Pyramid also uses the scale of 1: 43,200 to give us the dimensions of the Earth. The Great Pyramid's height of 481.3949 multiplied by 43,200 = 3938.685 miles; the Polar radius of the Earth being 3949 miles. The pyramid's perimeter at the base, 3023.16 X 43,200 = 24,734.94; the equatorial circumference of the Earth is 24,902. This is astonishing evidence of the sophistication of ancient peoples, including the Mayans, in the areas of cosmology, astronomy and mathematics.

A-432 Hz VERSUS A-440 Hz

Music has a hidden power that can affect our minds, our bodies, our thoughts, and our society. When music is based upon a tuning standard purposely removed from the natural harmonics found in nature, the end result may be the psychic poisoning of the mass mind of humanity. There is a theory that the tuning change from A-432 Hz to A-440 Hz was dictated by Nazi propaganda minister Joseph Goebbels. Allegedly, his purpose was to use this slight change in pitch frequency to influence people to think and feel in a certain manner. The theory was that people could be conditioned and made prisoners of a numbed, or limited, consciousness. Around 1940, the United States also introduced 440 Hz. And finally, in 1953, 440 Hz became the official concert pitch for A, as designated by the International Organization for Standardization (ISO), and catalogued as ISO 16. The sound, 440 Hz, is heard by Western ears as the pitch "A," or the 6th note (the syllable "la") in the C scale above the starting note middle C: Do-re-mi-fa-sol-la-ti-Do. 432 Hz is also heard by Western ears as the pitch "A," or 6th note in the C scale above middle C, but it is the "purer" natural overtone. At a symphony concert, tuning all the orchestral instruments to the pitch A-440 is standard, or "concert pitch." The pitch A is usually sounded by an oboe immediately prior to the performance, and also by the principle 1st violinist, who stands and plays A, and all the other instruments tune accordingly. The difference between the pitch of A-440 and A-432 is imperceptible to 99.99% of human ears, that is, A-435 does not sound out of tune, hence the musical compositions performed to this tuning do not sound out of tune.

Nevertheless, the recent rediscoveries of the vibratory and oscillatory nature of the universe suggest to some researchers that this contemporary international concert pitch standard may generate an unhealthy effect, or anti-social behavior, within the consciousness of human beings. Most music worldwide has been tuned to A-440 hertz since the ISO standardized it in the early 1950s. It is a fact that A-440 Hz deviates slightly from the natural musical overtones, whereas A-432 Hz, known as Verdi's "A," is mathematically consistent with the natural frequencies of the universe. Students of the symmetry of sacred vibrations consider the adoption of 440 Hz a declaration of war on the subconscious minds of Western citizens. Others say A-440 Hz, or equal temperament, was adopted merely for convenience of keyboard performance. In equal temperament, using A-440 Hz tuning, all the notes of the diatonic scale (C to C on a piano keyboard) are equi-distant, which is not so with 432 Hz. One would need many keys for the microtones naturally generated by the purer tuning, and nearly impossible to adapt to a playable keyboard. Non-keyboard performers, string and wind players, for example, as well as singers, are free to use 432 Hz to tune their instruments when no acoustic piano is used. Electronic and digital instruments can also use a variety of tunings. Advocates of 432 Hz say it's better for singing and for sound healers. Music based on 432 Hz transmits beneficial healing energy, they note, because it is a pure tone of universal mathematics, and fundamental to nature. Others say countless people have felt the beneficial healing energy of music, no matter which "A" was used for tuning.

In a paper entitled *Musical Cult Control*, Dr. Leonard Horowitz writes: "The music industry features this imposed frequency that is 'herding' populations into greater aggression, psycho social agitation, and emotional distress predisposing people to physical illness." However, he is aware of the possible weakness of this leap of assumptions. He states, "I don't know if anyone can prove a direct link between aggression, disassociation, paranoia and violence to a tuning system that was promoted by both the Rockefellers and the Third Reich. However, just the fact that these two entities came together to push this standard is more than suspicious in my mind." Skeptics suggest that this theory doesn't consider the overwhelming reports of nearly all music lovers regarding what they consider the soothing, healing and inspiring qualities of recorded or live symphonic, orchestral and choral masterworks throughout their lifetimes, all of which were tuned to the standard concert pitch of A-440 Hz. In fact, music lovers of all stripes, regardless of tuning, describe music as sometimes causing altered states of bliss and joy. This suggests that there are many elements of music in addition to pitch, such as rhythm, melodic shape and structure, chordal dissonance and resolution, and timbre of instruments and voices which contribute to the integrated gestalt we hear as music, and which is universally inspiring.

Those concerned about the negativity of unnatural tuning point to a typical street scene in American cities: school kids, young adults on their way to work, a woman pushing her baby carriage, a man walking his dog—and what do they all have in common? MP3 players or iPods. Could it be, they ask, that there is a deliberate plan to introduce destructive frequencies not only to the younger generation, but the population in general?

Individuals who study cymatics are concerned that the less pure frequencies could entrain thoughts towards disruption, disharmony and disunity. If this were the case, they also could stimulate the controlling organ of the body—the brain—into disharmonious resonance, which ultimately creates disease and war. Following this line of reasoning, eventually the compassion of the heart could be affected which might alter the natural resonance of the morphogenetic fields of consciousness, leading to interference in the path toward spiritual evolution.

HARMONY OF THE UNIVERSE

The vibratory and oscillatory nature of the universe indicates that the current de facto international concert pitch of A-440 Hz might possibly generate an unhealthy effect in the consciousness of human beings. Changing frequency may also change the electric potential of the brain which may alter and affect memory and perception by the slight change and charge within the water in our cells. This is perhaps why 440 Hz and higher concert pitches can be perceived as a brighter, thinner, and more outward of the head, whereas concert pitch at 432 Hz can be perceived as an inward experience of feeling.

The 440 Hz tone used as a standard for concert pitch possibly may bring an unnatural 8 Hz dissonant change in how we think. Rudolf Steiner said "music based on C=128 Hz (C note in concert 432 Hz) will support humanity on its way towards spiritual freedom. The inner ear of the human being is built on C=128 Hz." He also went so far as to warn humankind that using "Luciferic brightness" and "arhimanic" tones in music could bring a condensing of greedy forces in the West, instead of a "Christ consciousness" of ascendant energy and the angel "Michael" sun-tone energy in the collective awareness in the evolution of humans.

John Stuart Reid of *CymaScope* reported:

432 Hertz truly can be considered a harmonic of light. Sound in air may be defined as the transfer ... of periodic movements between adjacent colliding atoms or molecules. This sonic energy typically expands away from the site of the collisions—at the local speed of sound—as a spherical or bubble-shaped emanation, the surface of which is in a state of radial oscillation. At the point of origin of the sonic bubble an electromagnetic bubble is created by the collisions between the air molecules, because each collision creates friction that releases a small amount of infrared electromagnetism. That magnetism, like the sonic bubble, expands away from source spherically and it is modulated by the sonic periodicities, in much the same way that an amplitude-modulated radio broadcast consists of an electromagnetic carrier that is modulated in amplitude by, say, a person's voice frequencies. Thus, the relationship between sound and light is real and very much part of the way that nature works. We cannot talk about the 432 Hertz key note without visualizing a 432 Hertz-modulated infrared light bubble.

The narrow band of visible light and audible sound are directly related in the form of frequency harmonics, writes Brian T. Collins on the website Omega 432. "Sound as you know it," points out Collins, "is measured in cycles per second (or hertz), which humans can perceive from around 20 cycles per second to around 20,000 cycles per second. Light is measured in the trillions of cycles per second. From a theory standpoint, if you double the wavelength of sound by 40 times you start to reach the oscillation frequencies of light. If you had a piano that was over 80 octaves long (impossible) you could surpass tone and play the visible colors of the spectrum." Similarly, if a piano was moved in the opposite direction, the slowest frequency waves would form into matter. Or as J.W. Keely points out, "These are the lower forms of visible electromagnetic vibration, which states that if something moves fast or slow enough it can seem at rest."

QUANTUM ENTANGLEMENT

Quantum entanglement is the mysterious phenomenon where two particles become tightly intertwined and behave as one system. The particles will behave this way whether they are next to each other in a laboratory, or on either sides of a galaxy. Scientists know that if they examine one particle and measure a certain property, for example vertical polarization, then the other will instantly adopt the opposite property, in this case, horizontal polarization.

There are mind-bending physics to consider. Albert Einstein described it as "spooky action at a distance" when he was still struggling to understand the ideas proposed by quantum theory. But it's a powerful phenomenon and one that physicists have long attempted to harness in the lab. The difficulty has been creating a pair of particles with any distance between them, and this has been a difficult hurdle to overcome. Imperfections in optic glass fiber or air turbulence means that the qubits become un-entangled. Plus, as the distance gets farther, your beam gets wider, so photons simply miss their target.

Juan Yin at the University of Science and Technology of China in Shanghai claims to have solved the dilemma. His team sent photons between two stations, separated by 97 kilometers over a landscape including a lake. To perform this experiment, Yun and his colleagues used a 1.3 Watt laser and a clever optic steering technique to keep the beam precisely on target. With this setup, they were able to successfully teleport more than 1,100 photons in four hours over a distance of 97 kilometers, shattering the last quantum teleportation record of 16 kilometers, which was set by a different set of Chinese researchers in 2010.

The application of utilizing this mysterious phenomenon to teleport people and objects is looking more and more like a very realistic proposition, if it has not already been developed in the top secret "black" programs. Quantum entanglement can also be used for the instantaneous swapping of information, a form of teleportation. It will be key in transmitting information, because with instant communication at a distance, the data doesn't have to travel through space. It cannot be snatched or intercepted while in transport, making it the ultimate form of encryption.

A MATTER OF DIMENSIONS

With the advancement of modern science, researchers have come to understand that the third dimension human beings inhabit is not the only dimension in the universe. Other dimensions exist, which contain matter and sentient life forms that people simply cannot perceive, except seen in disguise or in an altered state. Examples are mirages which are quite common, or "orbs," small white dots, potentially ways in which other dimensional objects can manifest and be seen in our dimension. That is to say the existence of other dimensions can "accidentally" display themselves in our space-time in various forms, thus allowing us to see them. Orbs, for example, are almost imperceptible, but visible to some, and often appear in photographs. These floating white dots appear unexpectedly on home videos, especially around authentically psychic individuals, or in highly emotional contexts.

According to string theory, there are as many as 11, or even as high as 26 dimensions. It is theorized that the additional dimensions do not extend forever (like the four known dimensions), but are curled up and close back in on themselves. In traditional string theory, they are compactified on the incredibly small Planck scale, which makes them not only indiscernible in everyday life, but far beyond the reach of any currently existing or foreseen particle accelerator. However, there is no reason in principle why the distances should be so small. Theories of extra dimensions are popular because they can explain why gravity, as a fundamental force of the universe, is so much weaker than the other three forces, those being the strong, weak, and electromagnetic forces. One class of theory suggests that gravity is just as intrinsically strong as the other fundamental forces, but that it alone can propagate through the additional dimensions. The result is that it gets diluted relative to the others.

Earth is currently transforming into a new vibrational frequency. It is ascending from its current three-dimensional solid matter form of existence into the fourth dimension, also called the 4-D density reality. This new vibratory rate jumps one frequency faster than that currently experienced on Earth; as our solar system and planet Earth have just crossed into the galactic equatorial plane zone of the Milky Way galaxy.

Overall, this new area of fourth dimensional space is a place where matter has far less density and weight, and a faster and higher frequency energy vibration. It is also a dimension where time will no longer have an iron grip on humans. From a fourth dimensional perspective, time does not exist, at least not the way we on Earth presently experience time.

In addition, this area of fourth dimensional space also has a "black hole," with highly charged magnetic energies at its core. Our solar system, including Earth, will, upon entry of this zone, encounter the highly charged magnetic energies of this black hole and feel its effects. Scientists and astrophysicists call this area a Torsion Energy Wave.

The extra dimensions must be wrapped up, or alternatively distorted or warped on a small scale, otherwise we would be able to measure deviations from the inverse square law at small distances. Experimental evidence, however, still allows these distances to be very large on a subatomic scale. If the scale is large enough, it might be possible to detect the presence of extra dimensions in high energy particle collisions. The fundamental forces all have their own "carrier" particle, or gauge boson, like the photon for electromagnetic interactions, and the W and Z bosons for the weak force. The gauge boson of gravity is called the graviton. The "traditional" graviton is a massless particle like the photon, but if it can propagate out into extra dimensions, which are coiled up or warped, it will be trapped by them and develop resonances. These "Kaluza-Klein" resonances would appear as additional heavy gravitons. These would then subsequently decay in a characteristic way in scientific particle detectors. In particular, many extra-dimensional models predict that the gravitons would show up as sharp resonances in the diphoton and dielectron mass spectra. However, even if such objects are seen in the ATLAS detector, there is the possibility that they will be hard to distinguish from other new particles like the Z boson, another hypothetical particle predicted by a large class of exotic models.

Most scientists now believe there may really be a parallel universe—in fact, there may be an infinite number of parallel universes, and we just happen to live in only one of them. These other universes contain space, time and strange forms of exotic matter. Some of them may even contain you, in a slightly different form. Astonishingly, scientists believe that these parallel universes exist less than one millimeter away from us. In fact, our gravity may be just a weak signal leaking out of another universe into our own. It all started when superstring theory, hyperspace and dark matter made physicists realize that the three dimensions we thought described the entire universe weren't enough. There are, at present, at least 11 numbered dimensions. By the time they had finished with the theory of multiple dimensions, they'd come to the conclusion that our universe is just one bubble among an infinite number of membranous bubbles which ripple as they wobble through the 11th dimensions.

MODERN MASTERS

Many spiritual masters who have demonstrated advanced mental capabilities, including telepathy, precognition, remote viewing and other abilities, indicate that they have developed the "science of consciousness" to a degree that parallels or surpasses current advanced physical technologies. Average humans also possess these capabilities, but they remain largely undeveloped by most people.

There is also the sense that our biology is shifting. Scientific research is now catching up to what the masters knew long ago, and have now proven, that our DNA holds the genetic codes for our physical and emotional evolution through frequency held in the languages we speak. It is also known that the human heart generates the strongest magnetic field in the body, some 5,000 times stronger than the brain. There are scientists who want to take the brain apart after someone dies to find out if it will show why that particular human was brilliant. What is the brain's difference if they were a healer or a spoon bender or a psychic (or had any other odd attribute)? They're not going to discover anything different about the brain tissue of these exceptional people, for the three-dimensional chemistry remains static. It is a slave to the rest of DNA that controls the quantum aspects of a person. The 90% of DNA that is quantum is that which responds to consciousness, and it is that which responds to Gaia's loving touch. *That* is what is going to change our planet. *That* is what you're working on; *that* is where the healing comes from; *that* is where the channeling comes from. *That* is what the masters wished to teach us, but some were unable to get the message across.

We all have within us the potential to become a master of our own human abilities. Science can merely confirm findings that are otherwise subjective observations by others. One must diligently strive to become a true master. It is a goal that must be worked on for years. A true master would not be setting a good example if he or she were to proudly declare "I am self-realized," or, "I am beyond everything." If there is any sense of the "I" present, the person is not self-realized. This is because, before self-realization can occur, there must be the death of the ego, that is, the withdrawal of our identification with the ego as who and what we are. This may seem counterintuitive, as many people feel the ego is essential in advancing in life, when in fact it is a deterrent, and distracts us from the importance letting go of our ego attachment. When losing our identification with the ego is realized, a new devotion in service to others will emerge. In the mesmerizing prose of Hermann Hesse, who recounts this lesson in the fictional tale, *Journey to the East*, it is the servant who is truly the master.

A modern master will teach that the most fundamental ingredient for ascension to enlightenment is the development of unconditional love. Someone recognized as a modern master will teach that negativity, fear and guilt must be overcome, and be exchanged for love and light. This can be accomplished by choosing a spiritual path, and adopting it as a disciplined practice. There are thousands of paths that will put a person in touch with his or her Inner Guide. As we learn to listen to our Inner Guide, the ego-self naturally diminishes. We then will not draw attention to ourselves, but instead focus on the timeless message emphasized in the Beatles song: "All You Need is Love."

"SEEING" THOUGHTS

Once we can fully embrace love, new aspects of enhanced human abilities will become apparent. Without trying too hard, we can often already sense what another person is thinking. If telepathy ever becomes commonplace, the world as we know it will drastically change. Anyone who is deceitful and tells lies will become self-conscious of the fact that other people can *read* their energy, and *see* their thoughts. This will have dire implications for the telecom and polygraph industries. The treasured careers of secret agents, diplomats, and war reporters will suffer if they cannot master this newly respectable skill. Professional poker is doomed, lying will become more perilous than ever, and human courtship will never be the same. We'll be able to read another person's aura field as easily as we can hear the words they speak.

Science is already getting into the game. The input-output theory, also called "Tinpot," explains how we take in a certain amount of food, water and oxygen, and our cerebral cortices generate measurable electrical activity. Scientists now think that none of it escapes in the form of transmittable brainwaves. This has led scientists to recognize that the mind, which is an energetic field of thought, and which can be read with EEG wires connecting to the brain in a new process called magnetoencephalography (MEG), can actually now read the fields without a physical connection to the body. The takeaway is that when we're processing with our brains, we're also broadcasting into various fields. Essential to what the yogis and mystics have been saying for centuries and that are now confirmed to be true—it is the thought that counts. We must remember that we are our connected to everything and everyone.

The emerging notion of the interconnectedness of everything is expressed, scientifically, within the exotic terms of quantum entanglement. This developing principle of metaphysics, or the *manitou* (as described by Native Americans), is exhibited in the famous Kirlian photography techniques that can capture the energy field of any living organism. Of course, Luke Skywalker's use of "the force" is familiar terminology to legions of *Star Wars* fans. Scientific findings in this field are also exemplified by Dr. Rupert Sheldrake's theories of morphic resonance; and, the morphogenetic field. The morphogenetic theory holds that matter is a kind of flesh applied over an existing energy skeleton, and this energy field extends far beyond the body. In Sheldrake's experiments, our energy field has been shown to be an invisible communication link between members of the same species, as well as between animals and humans.

KIRLIAN PHOTOGRAPHY

Kirlian photography takes its name from Soviet electrician Semyou Kirlian. He accidentally discovered the process in 1939, and he used a type of photogram that is created with extreme amounts of electricity. Kirlian's work involved an independent rediscovery of a phenomenon (and technique) variously named "electro-graphy," "electro-photography" and "corona discharge photography." The "Kirlian Effect" is "contact photography," in which the subject is in direct contact with a film placed upon a charged metal plate. Kirlian discovered that objects on photographic plates connected to sources of high voltage produced small coronas which were created by the electric field at the object's boundaries. Kirlian photography was the subject of extensive research in the 1970s in the Soviet Union and in the West. It is commonly described as photographing an object's, or person's, aura.

The next level of research continued with Dr. Konstantin Korotkov at the Russian University of St. Petersburg. In the late 1990s, Dr. Korotkov developed a technique called Gas Discharge Visualization (GDV) and based on the Kirlian Effect. GDV instruments use glass electrodes to create a pulsed electrical field excitation called a "perturbation technique" to measure the "electro-photonic" glow. A rather intense field of electricity is created around an object by a GDV Camera, using 10 kV, 1024 Hz, and taken in 0.5 seconds. This field of electricity produces a gassy discharge of light around an object, also called a Kirlian picture, that is then transferred to a computer with video and imaging capabilities. With the necessary software, it is possible to witness the energy field of any object in real time. No longer is there a need for the traditional dark room development of photographs.

Dr. Korotkov observed the stimulated electro-photonic glow around human fingertips, and this contained astonishing coherent and comprehensive information about the human state; both physiological and psychological. The Korotkov methods are used in some hospitals and athletic training programs in Russia and elsewhere as preventive measurements for detecting stress. The Russian Academy of Science approved the GDV techniques and equipment in 1999 for general clinical use. The GDV technique can be used for diagnostic and assessment purposes, and is already used to measure stress, and monitor the progress of medical treatments. Another noted benefit includes real time visualization of the aura, which is visible up to five centimeters in diameter encompassing any object.

The GDV technique has been used recently to photograph people as they are dying. In the photos taken at the moment of death, the area of the belly loses its life force first, followed by the head. The heart and groin are the last to lose the life force connection to the body. Scientists using the GDV technique say that the aura of those who die unexpectedly or violently differs from those who experience a calm death. The souls of the former remain in a state of confusion for several days and return frequently to their bodies, especially at night, and this too can be recorded. Dr. Korotkov ascribes this phenomenon to unused energy retained by the soul. He suggests that the GDV technique will also have applications for distinguishing genuine psychics from frauds. Because of the instantaneous results, this method is widely becoming popular in the field of bio-energy and the study of how our aura is changed or affected by circumstances around us, both environmental and emotional.

THERMAL IMAGING

Similar to the GDV camera, thermography, or thermal imaging, is a type of infrared image capture technology. Thermographic cameras can detect radiation in the infrared range of the electromagnetic spectrum, and produce detailed images of that radiation. Since infrared radiation is emitted by all objects based on their temperatures, according to the "black body" radiation law, thermography makes it possible to "see" one's environment with or without visible illumination. The amount of radiation emitted by an object increases with temperature, therefore thermography allows one to see variations in temperature.

The black body is a perfect physical body that absorbs all electromagnetic radiation that it touches. Because of its perfect absorptivity at all wavelengths, a black body is also the best possible emitter of thermal radiation, which it radiates incandescently in a characteristic glowing white color, a continuous spectrum that depends on the body's temperature. The thermal radiation from a black body is energy converted electro-dynamically from the body's pool of internal thermal energy at any temperature greater than absolute zero. It is called black body radiation because it has a distribution with a frequency maximum that shifts to higher energies with increasing temperature.

Almost all the energy on Earth comes from the Sun. If it weren't for the Sun, the Earth would be a cold and lifeless planet. Plants grow because of energy from the Sun, animals and humans need to absorb vitamin D from the Sun, the winds blow because of Sun energy, and even coal as a fossil fuel is just energy stored from the Sun over millions of years. "Sublimation" refers to the process of transition of a substance from the solid phase to the gaseous phase. Gas is one of the three classical states of matter, the others being liquids and solids. Our physical bodies consist of elements. Gas is the state in which matter expands to occupy whatever volume is available. Sublimation requires additional energy, and presents an endothermic change.

Endothermic refers to a chemical reaction where thermal energy (heat) is converted to chemical bond energy. A compound is a substance composed of atoms, with two or more elements chemically joined together. Bond strength, or bond energy, is measured between two atoms joined in a chemical bond. Chemical bonds are the forces of attraction that hold atoms together. The bond is caused by the electromagnetic force attraction between opposite charges.

THE SENSES AND CONSCIOUSNESS

The most inexplicable unknown, especially to science, is consciousness itself. A recent discussion among experts regarding the greatest amount of unexplored territory in all the sciences suggest that the study of consciousness offers the greatest body of unknowns. Consciousness researchers at the Institute of Noetic Sciences and at the Center for Consciousness Studies at the University of Arizona call consciousness the "hard problem." Understanding it means dealing with subjective experience, which is still being fiercely debated as acceptable data. Consciousness is such a mystery that some scientists are beginning to think we have no consciousness; perhaps we are "zombies who think we're conscious beings," is how the nihilist scientists would describe us. Others explain that our consciousness is connected to our electromagnetic field, and by extension, also connected to the electromagnetic field of the Earth and the cosmos beyond, and described as "stellar consciousness." Study of the function of the organ we call our brain is of little help. Experienced researchers in consciousness studies say that this phenomenon goes far beyond current mainstream neuroscience research studying just the brain itself.

As we have seen, there is probably a part of our consciousness that can actually change the various characteristics of our bodies and our state of being. The power of the mind is one that actually exists, and it can influence exterior forces. Mind over matter, by sheer will power alone, can be manifested even in placebo trials. How else can there be any other answer? Our psychic mind also appears to be linked to dreams, and even the *déjà vu* experience.

Déjà vu is a French phrase meaning "already seen," referring to the distinct, puzzling, and mysterious feeling of an individual having felt that they experienced a specific set of circumstances before. Subjects report walking into a building, for example, in a foreign country they have never previously visited, yet feeling the sense that the setting is eerily and intimately familiar. Some attribute *déjà vu* to psychic experiences, such as unbidden glimpses of previous lives. As with intuition, research into human psychology can offer more naturalistic explanations, but ultimately the cause and nature of the phenomenon itself remains a mystery.

Whether we call them gut feelings, an "extra sense," or something else, we have all experienced profound intuition at one time or another. Psychologists note that we subconsciously pick up information about the world around us, leading us to seemingly know information without knowing exactly how or why we came to be aware of the information. This is separate from consciousness, which is being aware in the moment. Intuition is peering ahead, or beyond, consciousness.

It is now accurate to term a new seventh sense. First, let's go through the list, starting with taste. The second is the olfactory capacity, or smell. The third sense is visual. Fourth is hearing. Fifth is touch. Sixth is self-awareness, or consciousness in the moment. And the seventh sense is intuition and its subsets pre-cognition and super-cognition. These were previously grouped with the sixth sense, but our ability to obliquely peer into the future is now understood as a separate sense, the new seventh sense.

GROUP CONSCIOUSNESS

The science of physics now confirms that electrons can occupy two locations at the same time, and that the electron's spin is connected to the single electron being observed. Just as we all are present in the future 1 to 10 seconds in advance of reading this paragraph, as long as we are alive, we also exist in the future tense indefinitely. This is also true for the group, or all conscious beings. This stream of consciousness can, and does, inform an individual of events not yet experienced in "the now." That is the only rational way to explain how one can know in advance what turns out to be accurate foreknowledge. Experiences of pre-cognition, and the accuracy of fore-knowledge, are now viewed as this newest human sense.

Researchers of group consciousness have formulated the theory of "Type 1 Civiliza-tions." This is when humanity will develop a group consciousness of the new kind, a kind that will have neither environmental problems nor scarcity of energy. Obviously, we're not there yet. If humanity were to use its mental power as a unified civilization, it would have control of all the energies of its home planet as a natural consequence, and as such control over the weather—and that includes preventing any and all natu-ral catastrophes. A theoretical Type II Civilization would even be able to control all of the energies of their home galaxy. Whenever a great many people focus their at-tention or consciousness on something similar, say around the Christmas season, the World Series, the 9-11 attacks, or the funeral of Lady Diana in England, then certain random number generators in computers start to deliver ordered numbers instead of random ones. An ordered group consciousness creates order in its whole surround-ing! When a great number of people get together with a common positive goal, the potential for violence also dissolves. It looks as if here, too, a kind of humanitarian consciousness of humanity is created.

Yet, at the same time, we are still being overtly and subtly conditioned by the mass media. In the course of the last 50 years, advances in science have led to an accel-erated knowledge gap between the public and government authorities, whom are controlled and used by the ruling elite. Thanks to biology, neurobiology, and ap-plied psychology, the "system" has attained an advanced knowledge of the human potential, both physically, and psychologically. The system is now able to understand the average person better than that person knows him or herself. This means that, in most cases, the system has more control—and greater power—over people than we as individuals have ourselves. This "subliminal seduction" is a codified science in business marketing and advertising. It is also highly effective in keeping the general population dummied down. So, in order to combat this psychological assault, we must get back to the inner construct of "know thyself." This has been articulated by the masters in the three-tiered pursuit of body, mind and soul.

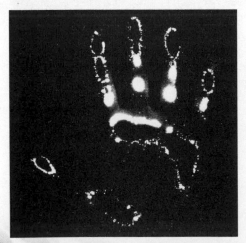

< This is the Kirlian photograph of the en-ergy of a hand. Kirlian photography and the GDV Camera can further our development of the study of consciousness, including al-tered states, forensic applications, and even an objective view of death. It will help us discover the bio-energy characteristics of plant life, animals and objects, as well as to study the various states of water's energy. It will aid in the study of our own bio-energy and its various stimuli such as food and ex-ercise. The GDV Camera can also predict future health conditions using the aura of blood samples or other bio-liquids.

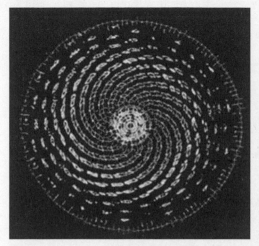

< This image of "spiral harmonics" reveals the sound vibrations of 102 Hz + 528 Hz.

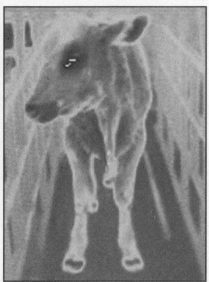

> This is an electronic thermography image of a cow infected with the foot-and-mouth-disease virus. The hooves and lower legs glowing warmer indicates heat using thermal recording.

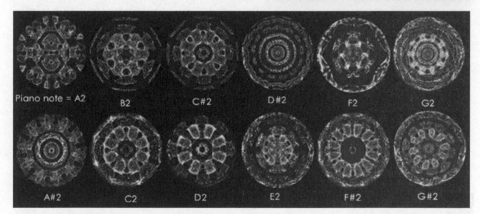

Piano note = A2   B2   C#2   D#2   F2   G2

A#2   C2   D2   E2   F#2   G#2

For the first time in history individual piano notes have been made visible using the "CymaScope" instrument. Sacred geometry and sacred symbols represent the harmonics of life, or the different dimensions of life. Interestingly, these piano notes also resemble Tibetan mandalas, ancient symbols or certain crop circle patterns.

In post-WWI Germany, the Vril Society used the age-old swastika emblem to link Eastern and Western occultism. They advanced the idea of a subterranean matriarchal utopia ruled by a race of Aryan beings who had mastered a mysterious force called Vril. This breakaway civilization had survived the antediluvian cataclysms which ended during the last ice age, and passed on their guarded occult knowledge through initiation into sacred mystery schools. Vril was known to these mystics as a natural and abundant energy, having disseminated its divine wisdom worldwide under many names. The Chinese referred to it as "chi," the Hindu as "prana," and the Japanese as "reiki." Albert Pike said: "There is in nature one most potent force, by means whereof a single man, who could possess himself of it, and should know how to direct it, could revolutionize and change the face of the world." Helena Blavatsky, the foundress of the Theosophical Society, described this Vril energy as "an aether stream that could be transformed into a physical force."

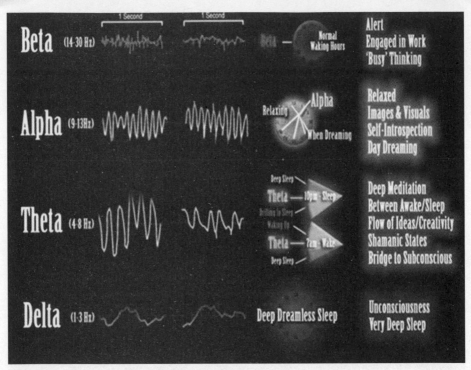

The common name for this measurement is Hertz (Hz), named after Heinrich Hertz, the German scientist who defined the cycles. Over time doctors and scientists noticed that different states of consciousness are associated with certain brainwave frequencies. They also discovered that these frequencies are linked to certain physiological changes, including heart rate, breathing, and other physical variables, as well as to behaviors, feelings, and perceptions of reality, both while awake and asleep.

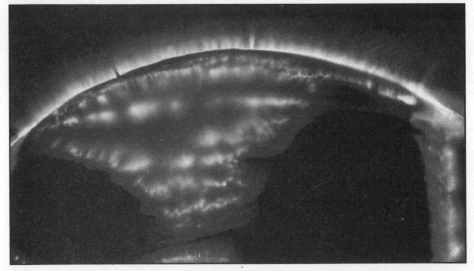

All living organisms are energy producing machines. When you look at a picture of the human body with infrared technology, all you see is radiating heat. This is a Kirilian photograph of a leaf, which is clearly seen emitting energy.

SPIRIT, BODY AND MIND

"Religion is belief in someone else's experience. Spirituality is having your own experience." –Deepak Chopra

CHOPRA'S wise observation suggests that there are multiple ways to awaken to the truth of our true nature, and thus begin the process of changing our consensus reality. Having our own experience is the most persuasive method. A core truth of religions, that everyone contains a divine spark, can trigger interest in finding that spark within oneself. One truth; many forms.

Consider this scenario, another form: At a much-anticipated press conference in the near future, when the weight of evidence begins to set in, scientists will be ready to announce to the world their findings, if not as fact, then at least as highly confirmed scientific hypotheses, that there is indeed an afterlife. Naturally, this would only confirm what the mystics have been telling us for centuries, but now science will be fully behind the new claims. The press conference would continue by stating that although the details of the afterlife are not fully known, the researchers are reasonably certain that everyone will experience something like a "life review" upon their death. Each individual will experience not only every event and every emotion of their life, but also the effects their behavior, positive or negative, has had on others. The usual defense mechanisms with which we hide from ourselves, our sometimes cruel and less than compassionate behavior towards others, has kept our negative behaviors out of awareness until the life review. When living people who seek truth begin their life review *before* death, they will realize and then become fully aware that their actions and thoughts in the living years truly do have consequences.

This scenario is not implausible. There is already sufficient evidence to present the above propositions as at least "probable," or "more likely than not," based on emerging evidence. Further studies will only increase the probability until it is accepted by all as fact. When this happens, the fallout will be revolutionary. When these findings are announced by science, it will become impossible for our culture to do business as usual, either economically, or politically, or in the universities, which are institutions of our culture, and as such, manifest and perpetuate the values of our culture. With this inevitable new perspective of spirit, assumptions about body/mind interactions will shift dramatically, and we will become complete human beings for the first time in recorded history.

When it comes to the changing world, Albert Einstein was correct when he famously said, "We can't solve problems by using the same kind of thinking we used when we created them." Most citations omit the remainder of this quote, which says, "In order to solve our current problems the next human will have to emerge." But who is this "next human" supposed to be? What will motivate people to begin their life review *before* death? What are the spiritual technologies which can facilitate this inner personal transformation?

MAPPING THE COMPLETE "NEXT HUMAN"

Many think we have lost our connection to spirit. Indigenous elders and shamans repeatedly say the spirit, body, and mind is the sacred trinity that allows for all life on Earth to thrive. Modern spiritual leaders say that if we wish to recover our humanity we need to stop destroying one another and this beautiful planet. All agree it is absolutely essential we reconnect to the world of spirit. One way to begin is by exploring the science of consciousness. If we are not sovereign over our own minds, then we are not sovereign over anything, and we live in a society where others presently have the right under law to tell us what we may and may not experience in our own consciousness. This is an extraordinary invasion of privacy and sovereignty, and it appears to be at the root of chronic tragedies in the world today.

We have thoroughly mapped the body and the brain somewhat, but the spirit as it pertains to all living entities remains largely unexplored. Similar to the unknown variations of the spirit is that of the larger mind, and by extension, the power of our thoughts (which also remain a big open question). In the world of science, what do we really know about our thoughts? Is it possible to manifest what we are thinking? Ideas and thoughts are known to spread among other people. Maybe the conscious experience is what connects us to other people. Fish swim in schools, birds fly in flocks, and ants have an ability to employ collective consciousness. All animals have a certain connection with their own species. What connection do humans have with each other in the realm of thought?

These questions, currently outside of the purview of scientific technologies, can be effectively addressed with *spiritual* technologies. Eventually, the sheer volume of personal anecdotal experiences and their visible positive results will pique the curiosity of mainstream science. It is a shift that is already beginning to occur. First of all, people need to be motivated to partake in one of the many forms of spiritual technologies. In this era of New Age thinking, there is a veritable buffet of choices to begin this journey of finding a better way of life ... a journey toward the *New Human*. Circumstances that motivate people to look into their inner life, and to change their consensus reality, are often personal tragedy, societal/global disaster, a personal vision or visitation of some kind, or decisively beginning a disciplined meditative practice.

The most exciting part of a personal spiritual journey is discovering the sacred trinity as it relates to spirit, body, and mind. When we look deeply into the essence of ourselves, we find all three. Our physical being is made up of DNA, and so is our soul. Each soul has its own blueprint. It is the embodiment of the spirit, the essence of who you are and the person you are meant to be. Each of us has our own spiritual DNA;

therefore, there is no one path to spirituality. This is so because each spiritual DNA is uniquely different from person to person. Each and every soul has its own unique form of spiritual practice and purpose—all leading to the one commonality of shifting our flawed perspective, and reconnecting to the unified Source of life. It is in this joint reconnecting with all of life and its source that consensus reality will change, and the power of the New Human will emerge.

THEORY OF EVERYTHING

Many thinkers of our age have searched for a "theory of everything," a step toward the direction of a consensus reality. The closest contender in this scientific paradigm shift is the concept of "the informed universe." It is a rediscovery of an ancient knowledge familiar to the Vedic tradition—Akasha, or the Akashic Field. It has been touched upon by frontier scientists who have explored hypotheses ranging from a holographic universe, to quantum zero-point energy, to Rupert Sheldrake's morphogenetic field theory, which draws on this ancient tradition. At the foundation of the Akashic Field (or "A-field") concept, that philosopher and scientist Ervin Laszlo proposes, is a "vacuum-based holofield" in which the universe is a highly integrated, connected, coherent system. It is "much like a living organism," its crucial feature being that it builds upon the information it has generated. Just as the ancients knew, a cosmic information field links organisms and minds in the biosphere with all the stars and galaxies throughout the universe—*and it itself can be accessed*. Indeed, the universe contains the memory of all events that are currently being played out, and have ever existed throughout time. We just need to find the key to unlock these mysteries for everyone.

It is clear that our culture has created a "taboo" atmosphere around serious discussions of personal spirituality. This is why we tend to feel uneasy and clumsy when discussing these topics with colleagues. The taboo against spirituality is so strong in academic circles that we feel *awkward* and *embarrassed* to even say the word "mystic." We have all internalized this taboo to some degree. This generates feelings of unease and anxiety whenever spiritually is discussed as a core discipline, or on a level with sociology, history, psychology, or literature.

Maybe the time is now for a *quantum leap* in human group consciousness—by way of expanded scientific paradigms and other modalities. Is the "next human" Albert Einstein spoke of already here? How will we recognize this person? Are we the ones we have been waiting for? Or is there a "spin-off" human waiting to take the stage and usher in the next tremendous step forward? Will we turn to technology to assist us in this leap? The bionic exoskeleton, replete with a new skin and enhanced physical attributes, is rapidly emerging. Unfortunately, so too is an army of mighty cyborgs and flying drones patrolling a technological control grid. Will the light-speed blending of person and machine result in "transhumanism," and a frightful New World Order commanded by human-machine hybrids? Or, hopefully, will we turn inward to tap into our unlimited abilities, powered by spiritual sources? Will our path of transition lead us through the eye of the needle to a new dimension only the awakened eye of spirit can see?

SPIRIT BEING REBORN

As the spirit continues to be reborn, as the veil is lifted with each individual on his or her inner journey, our purpose in life will become crystal clear. As a natural result of reconnecting to our true nature, the most important aspects in our lives will become the pursuit of love and knowledge, and away from money and power. The mass projection of illusions in the old world will fade away just as the Earth-centric model of the universe did 500 years ago. As we grow, we will intuitively want to learn as much as possible about both this world and the transcendent world, and we will grow in our ability to feel kindness and compassion towards all living things. A consequence of embracing unconditional love will be a stimulation of the spirit. Relationships will become easier, new friendships will blossom, and charity towards strangers will become obvious and natural behaviors in the world. It will be a great disadvantage to oneself to harm another person, either physically or psychologically, since whatever pain one inflicts on another is experienced as one's own in our life review. Each one of us, quite simply, becomes our own judge and jury when we leave the body, and we set up the circumstances for our next incarnation. An even more immediate and palpable motivation is the feelings of joy and the peace of mind we experience when behaving according to our true nature.

Looked at another way, what was our real purpose for being born into the circumstances of our present families? Were you born into a Muslim family, or a Christian family, or a Jewish family, or a Hindu family, or a Buddhist family? Why should an accident of birth make you a Muslim, or a Christian, or a Jew, or a Hindu, or a Buddhist or anything else? Instead, think for yourself. Take nothing for granted. Question everything. Reach your own conclusions based on your own experience, intuition and common sense. These are amongst the gifts the bountiful universe bestowed when we were given the opportunity to be born in a human body. We should use those gifts well, and make the most of this precious opportunity, for that is what we are here to do. Who says it is an accident of birth? What if we choose our parents with a suitable propensity to help us in our path to learn about love?

GURDJIEFF'S COMMANDMENTS

George Ivanovich Gurdjieff was an influential spiritual teacher of the 20th century who observed that most humans live their lives in a state of hypnotic "waking sleep," But that it is possible to transcend to a higher state of consciousness and achieve our full human potential if we have a strong desire to change ourselves. To help us along the path of self-betterment, the following are "Gurdjieff's Commandments" according to his daughter, Reyna D'Assia, as recorded in *The Spiritual Journey of Alejandro Jodorowski*:

1. *Ground your attention on yourself. Be conscious at every moment of what you are thinking, sensing, feeling, desiring, and doing.*
2. *Always finish what you have begun.*
3. *Whatever you are doing, do it as well as possible.*
4. *Do not become attached to anything that can destroy you in the course of time.*
5. *Develop your generosity—but secretly.*
6. *Treat everyone as if he or she was a close relative.*
7. *Organize what you have disorganized.*
8. *Learn to receive and give thanks for every gift.*
9. *Stop defining yourself.*
10. *Do not lie or steal, for you lie to yourself and steal from yourself.*
11. *Help your neighbor, but do not make him dependent.*
12. *Do not encourage others to imitate you.*
13. *Make work plans and accomplish them.*
14. *Do not take up too much space.*
15. *Make no useless movements or sounds.*
16. *If you lack faith, pretend to have it.*
17. *Do not allow yourself to be impressed by strong personalities.*
18. *Do not regard anyone or anything as your possession.*
19. *Share fairly.*
20. *Do not seduce.*
21. *Sleep and eat only as much as necessary.*

22. *Do not speak of your personal problems.*
23. *Do not express judgement or criticism when you are ignorant of most of the factors involved.*
24. *Do not establish useless friendships.*
25. *Do not follow fashions.*
26. *Do not sell yourself.*
27. *Respect contracts you have signed.*
28. *Be on time.*
29. *Never envy the luck or success of anyone.*
30. *Say no more than necessary.*
31. *Do not think of the profits your work will engender.*
32. *Never threaten anyone.*
33. *Keep your promises.*
34. *In any discussion, put yourself in the other person's place.*
35. *Admit that someone else may be superior to you.*
36. *Do not eliminate, but transmute.*
37. *Conquer your fears, for each of them represents a camouflaged desire.*
38. *Help others to help themselves.*
39. *Conquer your aversions and come closer to those who inspire rejection in you.*
40. *Do not react to what others say about you, whether praise or blame.*
41. *Transform your pride into dignity.*
42. *Transform your anger into creativity.*
43. *Transform your greed into respect for beauty.*
44. *Transform your envy into admiration for the values of the other.*
45. *Transform your hate into charity.*
46. *Neither praise nor insult yourself.*
47. *Regard what does not belong to you as if it did belong to you.*
48. *Do not complain.*
49. *Develop your imagination.*
50. *Never give orders to gain the satisfaction of being obeyed.*
51. *Pay for services performed for you.*
52. *Do not proselytize your work or ideas.*
53. *Do not try to make others feel for you emotions such as pity, admiration, sympathy, or complicity.*
54. *Do not try to distinguish yourself by your appearance.*
55. *Never contradict; instead, be silent.*
56. *Do not contract debts; acquire and pay immediately.*
57. *If you offend someone, ask his or her pardon; if you have offended a person publicly, apologize publicly.*
58. *When you realize you have said something that is mistaken, do not persist in error through pride; instead, immediately retract it.*
59. *Never defend your old ideas simply because you are the one who expressed them.*
60. *Do not keep useless objects.*
61. *Do not adorn yourself with exotic ideas.*
62. *Do not have your photograph taken with famous people.*
63. *Justify yourself to no one, and keep your own counsel.*
64. *Never define yourself by what you possess.*
65. *Never speak of yourself without considering that you might change.*
66. *Accept that nothing belongs to you.*

67. When someone asks your opinion about something or someone, speak only of his or her qualities.
68. When you become ill, regard your illness as your teacher, not as something to be hated.
69. Look directly, and do not hide yourself.
70. Do not forget your dead, but accord them a limited place and do not allow them to invade your life.
71. Wherever you live, always find a space that you devote to the sacred.
72. When you perform a service, make your effort inconspicuous.
73. If you decide to work to help others, do it with pleasure.
74. If you are hesitating between doing and not doing, take the risk of doing.
75. Do not try to be everything to your spouse; accept that there are things that you cannot give him or her but which others can.
76. When someone is speaking to an interested audience, do not contradict that person and steal his or her audience.
77. Live on money you have earned.
78. Never brag about amorous adventures.
79. Never glorify your weaknesses.
80. Never visit someone only to pass the time.
81. Obtain things in order to share them.
82. If you are meditating and a devil appears, make the devil meditate too.

POWER OF THE MIND

Gurdjieff touched upon the power of the mind in his writings, and spiritual masters have long emphasized the incredible power of the mind over the body. Simply stated, intention and thought have amazing healing properties if focused properly. The human mind, when connected to its source through inner work, is more powerful than any disease. Our real identity is not our body, but the consciousness of our mind. The human mind is energy, and with the correct training, it has the power to change matter. A first step to realize is that matter is simply the manifestation of energy. This simple fact will help us awaken and realize the divine nature of identity. Both myth and history relates that there have been an abundance of people, who through their minds and light bodies, have developed the ability to access higher dimensions. These people who knew the secrets of the "Gate of Eternity" have been called prophets, seers, masters and diviners. In essence, we are electric beings vibrating within an energetic universe. We are both receivers and transmitters of energy—a vibrational transmitter. We are constantly sending out signals in the form of frequencies and vibrations of energy that will either attract or repel other vibrational beings, events, and experiences.

These seemingly fantastic claims are being verified by scientists around the world. One double-blind study conducted by biologist Dr. Bernard Grad found that seeds which had been prayed over by a healer prior to being planted grew faster and more successfully than those that had not been prayed over. Biologist Dr. Carrol Nash, in a double-blind study, found that the growth of bacteria can also be influenced by conscious intention. Another study showed that mice with a predicted 100% fatality could be cured. Three replications using skeptical volunteers and laboratories at Queens College and St. Joseph's College in Brooklyn, NY, produced an overall cure rate of 87.9% in 33 experimental mice through nothing more than intention and the laying on of hands, similar to Reiki healing. This conforms with some observational studies which suggest that people who perform regular spiritual practices tend to live longer. Another study points to a possible mechanism called interleukin (IL-6). Increased levels of IL-6 are associated with an increased incidence of disease. A research study involving 1,700 older adults showed that those who attended church were half as likely to have elevated levels of IL-6, thus suggesting that regular praying is associated with a positive effect. Last but definitely not least, Dr. Glen Rein found that love sent through conscious intention has transformative effects on the human DNA molecule, causing it to heal itself when in the presence of loving energy.

Awareness brings realization. Once we have realization, there is the beginning of awakening. This awakening will bring us to an "in-lightened" state. In the light we can identify more and more with our true nature, and finally we can know that this power is within each of us, and has been there all along. The human form is linked into multiple aspects of itself, each section expressing a range of frequencies or vibrations, within a network of zones of energy, and spheres within spheres. Simply stated, love is the essence of all. Many of us have forgotten who we are and why we are here. Once our blinders are removed, according to whatever disciplined practice of changing our minds we choose, we will see the truth for ourselves. Once embarked on the sincere desire to know the truth, a portal is opened in which we receive all the help we allow toward this goal. Herein lies the meaning of faith and the reason for optimism.

It is difficult to explain in words this other-worldly process of change, but words are helpful in this dimension. One person's words need not seemingly agree with yours when the goal is the same. Specific thoughts and intentions which are generated by the mind can be used to frequency modulate the coherent bio-fields from the heart. When one is in a state of love, which is the content of truth, the coherence is enhanced and the bio-fields become stronger. This allows for a resonance between the coherent fields of the heart and the coherent fields around the DNA molecule. Such an interaction allows the frequency information associated with the original intention to manifest as a physical change in the DNA, whether it be a conformational change in the structure of the helix, a change in DNA replication, or a shift in the electrical properties.

HYPER-COMMUNICATION AND DNA

To fully understand the relationship of spirit, body and mind in the "next human," it is necessary to reexamine the DNA molecule and how it can relate to remarkable human abilities. In people, hyper-communication is most often encountered when one suddenly gains access to information that is outside one's knowledge base. Such hyper-communication is then experienced as a future inspiration, or the "seventh sense." The Italian composer Giuseppe Tartini, for instance, dreamt one night that a devil sat at his bedside playing the violin. The next morning Tartini was able to note down the piece exactly from memory, and he named it the *Devil's Trill Sonata*.

When hyper-communication occurs, one can observe in the DNA, as well as in the human being, a very special phenomenon. As we learned in the "DNA Mysteries" chapter, when Russian scientists irradiated DNA samples with laser light on screen, a typical wave pattern was formed. When they removed the DNA sample, the wave pattern did not disappear, but instead remained. Controlled experiments replicated this result, showing that the pattern still came from the removed sample, whose energy field apparently remained. This effect is now called the phantom DNA effect. It is surmised that energy from outside of space and time still flows through the activated wormholes after the DNA is removed. These are tunnel connections between entirely different areas in the universe through which information can be transmitted outside of space and time. The DNA attracts these bits of information and passes them on to our consciousness. This process of hyper-communication, also called telepathy or channeling, is most effective in a state of relaxation.

Consensus in the scientific community, however, does not view telepathy as a real phenomenon. Many rigorous studies seeking to detect, understand, and utilize telepathy have been done; but according to the uninformed view among scientists, telepathy lacks replicating results from well-controlled experiments. Yet interestingly, telepathy is a common theme in modern fiction and science fiction, with many comic book superheroes and supervillains having telepathic abilities. Variations of telepathy can also be observed in the animal kingdom. Are researchers measuring the wrong variables? Science can only test repeating phenomena.

Animals express consciousness through instinct. In addition to instinct, humans possess the highest quality of consciousness, also called self-awareness, or reflective thought. Self-awareness is the difference between animals and humans. Reflection is the power to turn one's consciousness upon oneself, to know oneself and especially to know that one is aware. The ability to study math, physics, philosophy, astronomy and many other fields is due to a person's unique ability to reflect inwardly. The expanded abilities of self-awareness are abstract reasoning, free will, creativity, and foresight. Our culture is oriented towards reducing one's self awareness rather than expanding it, and this sums up our reverse-priority age.

In earlier times, humanity was more strongly connected to group consciousness, and just like many animals, we acted together as a group. Relationships were necessary for humans, and safety was maintained through numbers. If an individual separated from the group in Paleolithic times, the chance of survival was slim. When we began to develop and experience personal individuality, we humans have almost forgotten hyper-communication completely. Now that we are fairly stable in our individual consciousness, we can create a new form of group consciousness, namely, one in which we attain access to all information via our DNA, and without being forced, or remotely controlled, regarding what to do with the new information. We now know that, just as on the Internet, our DNA can feed its data into the network, and can call up data from the network, thereby establishing contact with other participants in the network. Remote healing, Reiki, telepathy or "remote sensing," plus other "Super-Normal" abilities, can now be explained. Experiments by Rupert Sheldrake show that some domesticated animals know from afar when their owners plan to return home. That can be freshly interpreted and explained via the concepts of group consciousness and hyper-communication. Any collective consciousness cannot be sensibly used over any period of time without a distinctive individuality. Otherwise we would revert to a primitive herd instinct that is easily manipulated.

Hyper-communication in the new millennium means something quite different, as we are beginning to remember our lost abilities. Researchers think that if humans with full individuality would regain group consciousness, they would have a god-like power to create, alter, and even shape things on Earth! And humanity appears collectively moving toward such a group consciousness of this new kind.

QUANTUM DNA

The relationship humans have with electronic devices has been called the "Manitou effect." The word *manitou* is a Native America expression for the "Great Spirit." The side effects encountered most often in hyper-communication are inexplicable electromagnetic fields in the vicinity of the persons concerned, where electronic devices, like computers or televisions, appear to be irritated and cease to function for hours. Yet when the electromagnetic field slowly dissipates, the devices function normally again. Studies have measured the fact that when people are awake, the human brain produces enough electricity to power a small light bulb.

There are distinct connections now emerging between quantum mechanics and consciousness. For humans, consciousness is the intelligence, or the organizing principle behind the arising of form in our world. The quantum field, or pure consciousness, is influenced by intention and desire. Quantum DNA does not work in a linear fashion, thus people cannot compartmentalize DNA within the function it serves. For example, within the most complex machines on the planet, devices that may have tens of thousands of parts, the parts will always do the same thing. There may be a device a thousand times more complicated than a fine watch, but the springs and gears are always springs and gears; they do the same thing over and over in a complex way. All of the most sophisticated electronics essentially operate the same way. Over and over they provide millions of identical processes and the electron paths always do the same switching; a singular process done rapidly with linear complexity.

But this is not the case with DNA. It is not a machine. We must start to recognize DNA as being interactive with itself. When one part changes, the part next to it also changes. You cannot therefore identify a singular purpose of specific DNA parts. Think of a complex clock. What if it were inter-dimensional, and the spring could suddenly become a gear, and the gear could change shape and size? Think of this—a part that is no longer needed simply vanishes, and if something is needed that is not there, then it appears! In addition, *this* quantum clock *decides on its own* to change the time frame it was designed to work with. Strange? That is quantum DNA.

In a quantum state, there is no time. In a quantum state, there is no place, or spot, where anything is located. Quantum mechanics dictates that any matter, if you want to call it that, or any energy, if you want to call it that, is everywhere, together, all as one. Imagine something so complex! Now imagine that it is duplicated hundreds of millions of times within your body.

Over a decade ago, Vladimir Poponin, a Russian quantum biologist, used light in an experiment with one molecule of DNA. In this experiment, he discovered a multidimensional field around DNA. Light patterned itself into a mathematical equation, or sine wave, when DNA was present. He had discovered that DNA had a quantum field. Not only that, it was a quantum field that was somehow filled with information. How else could the field pattern light into a sine wave? Vladimir Poponin showed that even a single DNA molecule actually had a field around it.

Those who compiled the Human Genome Project wanted to know how the three billion DNA chemicals could create more than 26,000 genes within the human body. They did not recognize DNA as being in a quantum state, even though the very science of DNA logically suggests that it has to be quantum. They weren't looking for that, so of course, they did not find it. Instead, they counted chemicals and looked for codes, and they found them in a very odd arrangement. They discovered that, of the three billion chemicals in the DNA double helix, all of the genes were being created in the protein-encoded parts of DNA; three and a half percent of DNA was creating all the genes. More than 90% of the chemical makeup of DNA seemed, therefore, to be random. It did absolutely nothing that they could see or understand. Even to this day, science does not see the obvious, that 90% of DNA is quantum, and only 3.5% is linear.

THE PLACEBO EFFECT

Consciousness is the intelligent force that began as the blueprint of who we are, and which manifests itself as a particular form. The entire image of a human being is contained in the microscopic DNA strands within the fertilized egg in the womb. Each of us has our own unique spiritual DNA. It is just as unique as our own fingerprints.

Some refer to it as Akashic Records, others know it as a total recall of their past lives. Our spiritual DNA is our blueprint for this lifetime. It contains our souls, past memory bank, as well as our purpose in this current incarnation. Just as our physical and mental characteristics are recorded in our physical DNA, our spiritual paths and our soul purposes are recorded in our spiritual DNA. As such, each of us has a specific spiritual purpose. But the mind can play tricks on us, and our purpose may sometimes become opaque. A good example of this is when a patient undergoes a sham treatment for a disorder, such as taking a sugar pill, yet still experiences a measurable improvement in their condition. This is known a the "placebo effect."

As such, medical science is only beginning to understand the ways in which the mind can influence the body. The placebo effect, for example, demonstrates that people, themselves, can at times bring relief from their medical symptoms or suffering, simply by believing their cure to be effective. This also demonstrates how the mind can play tricks on the body, and interestingly, this can be true even when the patient knows they are taking a placebo. The body's ability to heal itself is far more amazing than anything modern medicine can create.

Scientists, therefore, have discovered that patients can benefit from being treated with sham drugs, even if the patient is told that it contains no active ingredient. This finding suggests that the placebo effect may work even without the need for any deception on the part of the doctor, as had been previously thought. "I didn't think it would work" says senior author Anthony Lembo of the Beth Israel Deaconess Medical Center on IBS. "I felt awkward asking patients to literally take a placebo. But to my surprise, it seemed to work for many of them." Of course, there are no ill side-effects to taking placebos. As you can imagine, this information brings much distress to the pharmaceutical industry, whose products, over time, seem to have less and less effect on patients. Could it be that our human DNA evolution is advancing to the point where drugs are no longer useful?

PURE DIVINE ENERGY

In some Eastern yogic traditions, the transmission of spiritual awareness can be quickly achieved by awakening a person's spiritual energy, or *kundalini*, with a transmission of energy called *Shakti-Pat*. The term *Shakti*, in Sanskrit, means *pure divine energy*, and *Pat* refers to that energy coming down, or entering into a subject. In the tradition of Shakti-Pat, a guru would touch the third eye, the point in the center of the forehead of the spiritual seeker, and initiate a cascade of insight, energy, or even physical transformation. The Hindu guru Swami Muktananda was one of the most famous yogis who regularly transmit Shakti-Pat as part of his spiritual teaching. There are many stories from his followers, even the disillusioned ones, who reported the transformations that they experienced—some very suddenly, others more gradual. Some devotees reported a sensation of immense heat, energy, and insight, sometimes involving a momentary loss of consciousness. Others reported only mild sensations with lingering long-term effects that subtly changed their lives.

Certain forms of energy transmissions can affect living entities in numerous ways. Energy transmission has been shown to affect the genetics of plants, which in turn increase their nutritional value and yields. It can also render harmful microbes less virulent. Energy transmissions can reduce viral loads in people with HIV, or Hepatitis B and C. Lastly, it can alter the mass and sizes of atoms and effect their boiling and melting points. These measurable and physical effects raise the question of whether belief is even necessary to experience a ritual's effects.

Ongoing research suggests that something *tangible* may be transmitted when a person receives a blessing, an energy transmission, or even a ritual initiation into a spiritual order. There may be something physically held in the body of the teacher that is transferred to the student, something not communicated simply through words and language. What is passed down through each successive generation is a teaching and a form, but what is passed on through direct parental lineage is what could be called *the spiritual DNA of the teaching.* Spiritual DNA even appears to be passed on through the blood and the genes; encoded in this spiritual DNA is a body of knowledge, particular methods, and principles for living within a practice. The hard coded knowledge, that not able to be communicated through language, is therefore embodied within each successive teacher within that lineage. For this sort of knowledge we can also use the word "meme;" referring to an individual unit of cultural or spiritual knowledge that goes "viral."

An enlightened state of mind, which can guide us with much needed instruction into the newly awakened world, can be found in the promise of many historical traditions. Certainly, this is one of the core concepts within all of the world's mythologies and sacred traditions. Numerous traditions teach that a race of highly evolved, not Earthbound humans inhabit the Milky Way and other galaxies. They are our ancestors. Many of these traditions reveal that the "next human," as described by Einstein, are those who have succeeded in transcending human limitations, and who have scaled the cosmic ladder to a dimension that leads to the center of the galaxy. These beings have transformed, or "morphed," into light beings, yet they retain physical bodies. These advanced men and women of various ages achieved, or "perfected," the luminous garment of the liberated soul body. It may be these *next humans* who want to see us spiritually evolve to their level.

THE CHAKRAS

The body's energies can be formulated within a framework called "chakras." The variously shaped chakras are described as wheel-like vortices, spinning within the physical entity. In classical Hinduism and Buddhism, chakras mean "wheels." They spin, spiral, curve, twist, crisscross, and weave themselves into patterns of magnificent beauty. In the East, these wheel-like vortices have been called the "Tibetan energy ring." In yoga traditions this ring is represented by two curved lines that cross seven times, symbolically encasing the seven chakras. In the West, a person's body energy is seen in the caduceus, the intertwined serpents around a staff—also crossing seven times—and initially associated with the Greek god Hermes, the messenger for the gods, and later used as a symbol in alchemy and an icon of modern medicine. The chakras act like invisible hubs that keep all of our energy systems functioning as a single unit. These patterns also become embedded in fields of thoughts, emotions, feelings, beliefs and attitudes, as well as within physical and biological patterns. It is a *torridal* living system, continually weaving, crossing over, ever expanding and contracting. The double helix of DNA also shares this pattern in the microcosm.

The seven chakra energy points in the body can be thought of as seven spiritual centers. Although invisible to the average human, chakras can be seen by individuals who are capable of seeing etheric energy. According to famed psychic Edgar Cayce, the chakras are associated with specific endocrine glands. The psychic readings of Edgar Cayce were said to have resulted from the activation of the kundalini within the pineal system, resulting in cosmic consciousness. In other words, Cayce apparently had a kundalini experience during each reading. Cayce had correlated the chakra centers to the endocrine glands, which secrete powerful hormone messages directly into the bloodstream, and affecting all parts of the body. These energy centers called a *plexus* receive and transmit energy, and each is situated at a major endocrine gland (and nerve bundle) within the physical body. Each chakra is connected to, and associated with, a different section of the body. Each of the seven chakras has a color, and different gemstones or crystals can be associated with these centers, and used during energy healing sessions. Understanding and leveraging chakras can promote physical, emotional and spiritual wellbeing, in addition to assisting in the manifestation work we must complete within our lifetime. This again is another form and description of spiritual awareness that can open the mind to transformational experiences.

CHAKRA CONTROL

Everything in existence has a natural vibration, from every atom, to the vastness of the universe. A human's harmonic vibrational points are similar to the strings on a guitar, with each producing a different sound. Similarly, our seven chakras vibrate at different frequencies, and according to traditional Indian medicine, they are believed to exist within the surface of the subtle body of all living beings. When in balance, chakras harmonize a person's body, mind and spirit. When out of harmony, they can cause disease, mental illness, and force us to reside in a lower state of consciousness. Unfortunately, most people are unaware of their chakra energy systems, not just because we've been denied the knowledge, but because they are effectively inoperative as a result of our inactive pineal glands.

The central role of the chakras is the "raising of kundalini." As it raises it pierces the various centers, and causes various levels of self-realization. This piercing activates the *siddhis*, and brings the onset of unusual human skills and capabilities. The resulting release of various siddhis will continue to rise until reaching the crown of the head, resulting in a union with the divine. The methods regarding how to raise one's kundalini have generally been a closely held secret within the Indian mystery schools. In the West, activating the chakras has historically been regarded as accessing "occult powers."

"Kundalini shakti" is an energy that resides in a coiled form at the bottom of our spinal cord. Once the kundalini shakti, also known as "serpent energy," gets *diksha* or "direction," it starts flowing upward from the bottom of our spine to reach the brain where it can completely alchemize its energy into vital hormones and higher spiritual energy. Once the full kundalini has been awakened, it completes a circuit between the genital parts up to the brain, spiraling up through the spine. During this experience, all seven chakra energy centers within our body climax with a breakthrough "opening." After this opening, the person then possesses great intelligence that is paired with wisdom and strength. For some devotees, this is a biological description of what happens when a person becomes *enlightened*.

MISALIGNED CHAKRAS

Chakras are the nexus where the *prana*, meaning our biophysical energy field, radiates throughout the human body. Prana is the basic component of the subtle body (our energy field), and it radiates throughout our entire chakra system. Full knowledge of prana and the chakras is an important key to having a healthy and long life. This knowledge will also provide insight into the source of energy within the universe. But, as with everything, if abused or out of alignment, chakras too can bring ill effects on people.

Sometimes chakras fall out of alignment, and energy in the body is then lost. This can happen due to unhealthy living, poor eating habits, stress, or any sort of negative energy. Calm meditation can realign the chakras, thus returning this energy to the body. We will eventually die, at which time our prana will exit the physical body, and our spirit will enter into a purely energetic realm. Buddhist tradition maintains that most human spirits will remain in the *bardo* for 49 days "on the other side" before the individual soul is reincarnated into a new body.

Author George Kavassilas warns about the *interface* between human chakras and alien implants. He proposes that there can be disadvantages to having fully activated chakras. For one, chakras may limit the amount of energy coming in from our central core (and, therefore, our energy fields). Chakras separate and compartmentalize the energy of our core essence, which makes it easier for others to attach "cords," and drain our energy from us. Kavassilas maintains that chakras can be manipulated, such that specific energies are easily accessed, thereby allowing the control and manipulation of our energy fields. When abused, the chakras may act as blockages of energy that can cause physical deterioration of the body, as well as psychological illnesses. Chakras keep our body's energy field segmented, thereby making it easier to manipulate from an external source, namely malevolent ETs who abduct unsuspecting humans, or corrupt gurus, who draw life-forces from their victims. It is therefore important to be aware of their energy and maintain good chakra health.

THE HUMAN ETHERIC FIELD

Energy researchers note that every mature adult is surrounded by an energetic "force field" which is sometimes called an etheric field. It radiates about 45 centimeters out from our body, but it can spike six to nine meters if driven by intense emotions. This is how people across the street can subconsciously detect a stranger's emotional state even before they look at the person. The etheric field is full of information about our feelings, our state of mind, and of course, our thoughts, even when we walk past another person, there is an automatic and unconscious exchange of energy. It is usually in the form of a rolling, sinusoidal wave, but it can also be a zigzag or a saw-toothed wave as well. Etheric energy moves in a *vortex fashion* because a vortex provides the least resistance to the flowing motion. It follows that physical matter, which is materialized etheric energy, also seeks the same low-resistance *toroidal* motion. Both water and air also share this intrinsic vortex motion.

The human aura is a symphonic spectrum composed of many individual "energy frequencies." This is an individual's intrinsic frequency. This explains the association within ancient Eastern traditions relating certain colors with certain parts of the human body, and described as chakras. Humans are not the only creatures with auras, however. Every living thing has an aura surrounding it. Auras can only be seen under certain conditions, along with adequate training and meditation.

As a *whole* being, the human body resonates to a broad spectrum of etheric frequencies. If the human being is healthy, these frequencies are in perfect harmony with each other. Each person also has an etheric "speed," based on their awareness, emotions, sentiments, feelings, diet, health, and other factors. Similar to the torus energy flow, human energy flows "downwards," from a faster resonance to a slower one. It simply cannot flow upwards and go the other way. If the slower person resonates with a faster person, then their energy will notch up a click or two, but they will not usually be able to sustain it for long. At least not from a chance encounter, for example, such as walking past one another. This explains why fear is infectious, and why thoughts and feelings can jump to another person. It also explains why a sensitive person may feel exhausted when walking through a crowded shopping mall, as that person might suffer from the numerous energy "pulls" coming from others. With some understanding of the true nature of our spirit, body and mind, it is now time to take a journey into *the nature of our souls*.

This 1808 drawing of "Soul Leaving the Body" by Luigi Schiavonetti portrays the widely regarded concept of the spirit's departure from body.

From *Wikipedia*: "George Gurdjieff gave new life and practical form to ancient teachings of both East and West. For example, the Socratic and Platonic emphasis on 'the examined life' recurs in Gurdjieff's teaching as the practice of self-observation. His teachings about self-discipline and restraint reflect Stoic teachings. The Hindu and Buddhist notion of attachment recurs in Gurdjieff's teaching as the concept of identification. His descriptions of the 'three being-foods' matches that of Ayurveda, and his statement that 'time is breath' echoes *jyotish*, the Vedic system of astrology. Similarly, his cosmology can be 'read' against ancient and esoteric sources, (both) Neoplatonic and in such sources as Robert Fludd's treatment of macrocosmic musical structures."

The lowest base chakra, located just above the anus, controls our material drive. The second sacral chakra is above and behind the genitals and naturally operates our sensual drive. The third solar plexus chakra is the navel and is seat of the will power. The fourth heart chakra is to the right of the physical heart and resonates with love and compassion. The throat chakra is associated with our spiritual drive. The sixth brow chakra of intellect is located between the eyebrows. The seventh crown chakra is at the top of the head and is the formless supreme light.

Published in 1825 in Jean-Charles Pellerin's print shop in France, *3 Roads to Eternity* alludes to *Matthew* 7:13-14. The biblical passage describes the different roads a soul can take, but only one of which leads to eternal life. The middle one does not appear in *Matthew*'s description, but rather seems to be an invention of Georgin. This path stems from the path of the righteous. We see a member of the French Royal Army standing in front of the two paths, clearly choosing which one to follow. In a *Goldilocks and the Three Bears* fashion, the middle doorway and its path are mid-sized. There are still quite a few people on it, but the number has decidedly shrunk. Allegedly, there are the people who have strived to follow the path of the Lord, but who have strayed from it.

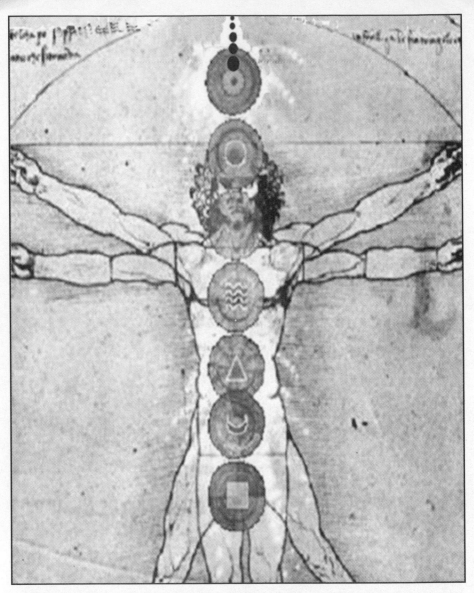

The advanced spiritual chakra system accounts for five more chakras above the seven in the human body. The seventh crown chakra above the head and outside of the body contains programs to be used by the eighth chakra including the release of basic psychic skills such as telepathy, seeing auras, lucid dreaming, out of body travel, and energy healing. The eighth chakra is an energy center of divine love, of spiritual compassion and spiritual selflessness. It contains our karmic residue and activates spiritual skills contained in the seventh chakra. The ninth chakra is our soul blueprint, that is, the individual's total skills and abilities learned in all previous lifetimes. The tenth is divine creativity, synchronicity of life, the merging of the masculine and feminine within, and the unlocking of skills contained in the ninth chakra. The eleventh chakra is a pathway to the soul, which is the individual's ability to acquire advanced spiritual skills including the ability to travel beyond the limits of time and space, teleportation, bi-location, instantaneous precipitation of thoughts, and telekinesis. Finally the twelfth chakra is a connection to the monadic level of divinity, which provides advanced spiritual skills, ascension, and connection to the cosmos and beyond.

REINCARNATION

"From the unreal lead me to the real! From darkness lead me to light! From death lead me to immortality!" –Brihadaranyaka, one of the oldest and longest of the Upanishads

BELIEF in reincarnation has long been, and remains, an articulated phenomenon in the Eastern religious traditions. This doctrine remains a central tenet within the majority of Indian religious traditions, such as Hinduism and others including Vaishnavism, Shaivism, Jainism, Sikhism and the various Eastern yoga traditions. The idea was also entertained by some ancient Greek philosophers. Certain esoteric Christian traditions claim Jesus Christ spoke of reincarnation. Many modern pagans also believe in past lives, including many in the New Age movement, along with followers of Spiritualism, Scientology, practitioners of certain African traditions, and the philosophers of Kabbalah, Sufism, and Gnostic Christianity. The Buddhist concept of rebirth, although often referred to as reincarnation, differs significantly from the Hindu-based traditions or New Age beliefs in that there is no "self," or individual soul, to reincarnate.

The phenomenon of reincarnation literally means "to be made flesh again." It is a doctrine or metaphysical belief that some essential part of a living being survives death to be reborn into a new body. This essential part is often referred to as the spirit, or soul, a so-called higher or true self, a divine spark, or simply, I. Upon each rebirth a new personality is developed during each life in the physical world, but some part of the self remains constant throughout all the previous successive lives.

Reincarnation implies that all sentient beings are immortal spiritual beings. A "past life" scenario automatically infers a "future life." This is especially inclusive of human beings.

A "spirit" is not born and cannot die, but exists in an individually postulated perception of that unique entity. As such, every spirit is not the same. Each is completely unique in identity, power, awareness and ability. Typically there is no recollection of previous lives, and neither is there assistance from Western religious traditions to help advance an understanding of this seemingly endless process.

Nevertheless, our "past lives" are not dead relics of another time, and permanently sealed away from us. Who we are as a soul, and as a conscious waking personality, is strongly influenced by who we have been before. In most cases, we are protected from knowing where these personality influences come from, but they very much shape who we are, and how we function, especially on an unconscious level. There are many positive aspects to these seemingly past life influences—such as children who are born with exceptional memories and talents, as if they remembered, and slightly below conscious understanding, from previous lifetimes. There is also a full accountability for who we have been, and what we have measured out to others in our previous lives, as well. It appears that some of our karma must be "suspended" until we are strong enough to process it in a beneficial manner. Trouble spots, and weak points, from other lifetimes will keep coming up, again and again, until we can successfully clear them—while keeping a positive attitude in the process.

THE KARMIC WHEEL

To help us to better understand past lives, and why we need to be reborn time and again, it is essential to understand the laws of karma. Some of the earliest writings on karma come from the Upanishads, which form the core of Indian philosophy. They are a prodigious collection of writings from original oral transmissions, and aptly described by the Hindu yogi Shri Aurobindo, as "the supreme work of the Indian mind." Discovered in the Upanishads are all of the fundamental teachings central to Hinduism: the concepts of *karma* or action; *samsara* or reincarnation; *anatta* or the illusionary self; *moksha* or nirvana; *anicca* or impermanence; *dukkha* or the suffering due to an unclear mind; the *atman,* or soul; and the *Brahman,* or the Absolute Almighty. They also set forth the prime Vedic doctrines of self-realization, yoga and meditation. The Upanishads are summits of thought regarding humankind and the universe, and are designed to push human ideas to their very limit and beyond.

In the Upanishads, we get a glimpse into the workings of the minds of the great Indian thinkers who were unhampered by the tyranny of religious dogma, political authority, or the pressure of public opinion. They were written by those seeking truth with single-minded devotion, which can be rare in the history of thought. As German-born philologist Max Müller has pointed out, "None of our philosophers, not accepting Heraclitus, Plato, Kant, or Hegel has ventured to erect such a spire, never frightened by storm or lightning." Bertrand Russell rightly observed a balanced mind when he said "Unless men increase in wisdom as much as in knowledge, increase in knowledge will be increase in sorrow." Without doubt, an increase in knowledge is tied directly to understanding the karmic wheel of our lives.

Karma is to experience that which an individual has created. It is the compassionate dynamic through which we learn to create responsibly. Karma is the law of cause and effect, through which we shape our lives with every decision. Contrary to popular belief, karma is neither good nor bad. There are no good effects or bad effects, only effects. We each choose the cause, and that choice includes our choice and effect. The cause and the effect are one. If we participate in the cause, we will always participate in its effect. There are no exceptions. What this dictates is that we tell the universe how to treat us when we make choices. When we choose to think of suffering, we create suffering and we *experience* suffering. When we create joy, we experience joy. Sooner or later, each of us will make the connection between what we choose and what we experience. It is then that we will be much more cognizant of our thoughts and choose differently.

The ageless maxim of karma is that a person will often manifest the treatment they have received from others upon themselves. Kindness fosters kindness. Cruelty begets cruelty. Charity allows receiving. Violence creates more of the same. Unfortunately, we live in a dualist world which is often cruel and violent. One must be able and willing to use force, tempered with intelligence, to prevent harm of the innocent. However extraordinary this understanding is, self-discipline and courage are required to effectively prevent brutality (without being overwhelmed by the malice that motivated the brutality in the first place). Every person, though their current acts in life called karma, can alter their future lives to some extent, but it will take a large critical mass of people to change the destiny of the human race.

According to the Buddha, impermanence, suffering, and death are the nature of things on Earth. According to this teaching, in order to gain anything, we must lose everything. Death leads to rebirth. Of all the mystery schools, or any religion that looks within, reincarnation, and by inference karma, is always a common theme. Tibetan recluse monks in Buddhism, Sufis in the Muslim faith, Essenes in Christianity, Kabbalists in Judaism, and shaman of primitive tribes all spoke about the same thing using different words. Reincarnation was part of Indian culture long before the Buddha articulated the same message in his own words.

ENDING THE KARMIC CYCLE

In this dualistic world, and with every new lifetime, a soul will primarily advance by choosing positivity where negativity also exists. If there were no protagonists on this planet, there would be no opportunity for a human soul to choose "good" or "evil," and thereby choose on a spiritual level, that they deserve one fated afterlife over another. If we only had positivity to choose from, we'd learn far less, and our soul would not have the opportunity to prove itself. For those of us enrolled in "Earth school," and that would be virtually everyone alive, we need sharp duality in our world to challenge us. Our freedom of choice is also an opportunity to direct ourselves towards positive choices and outcomes. When we come to recognize the karmic wheel, even from those who wish to cause us harm, the strong grip of the illusion will begin to lose its power.

Karma cannot be "overcome." It must be "worked off." In other words, if you have hurt someone, be it physically, emotionally, or otherwise you will, at some future point, have to experience what that felt like to them. The *Law of Karmic Effect* is not a "punishment," but instead a tool of learning, set in place to promote personal growth and development. As we are forced to feel the consequences of our actions, there is a higher likelihood to choose a different course the next time around. It is also important to hold in ones mind that it works both ways: Seek, therefore, to ensure that the effect your presence has upon "others" you encounter every day has no negative impact. Focus on the most positive and beneficial outcome for everyone involved.

A karmic cycle is brought to completion once one has learned the lessons intended, and why a particular cycle has begun. If we keep repeating the same mistake, we'll continue to cycle back, over and over, until we *get the message*, and break the cycle. Ultimately, all of us will learn exactly what we need to learn, and all of us will eventually find our way "home." For some, it will take longer than for others. To start releasing karma in your own life, it is important to forgive all perceived enemies or adversaries. Love them, but pity them. They, like you, are only the result of their genetic origin, their experiences, reactions, and the choices within their experience. Like most of us, others can only use their limited conscious resources to try to get along, as best they can within this weary old rat race, which is the competitive paradigm. For example, if *they* had the knowledge of all the secrets in the universe, *they* wouldn't have wronged you. It is far better to realize their human nature for what it is, to totally forgive them, and then to lovingly delete any negative images of them from your mind. This frees up lots of mental time within which you may entertain positive images, custom imagined by you, and for you. Plus, it frees up your *old enemies* to evolve.

Within the context of the goal to "Thrive," and to evolve to our full human potential, how might we view the idea of reincarnation? If it is useful to show that we are far more than our physical bodies, then it can be a concept that is helpful toward changing our consensus reality, and this can serve to remind us of our true nature. So, although scientific proof is not necessary, the research described below is compelling and thought-provoking.

PAST LIFE MEMORIES AND BIRTHMARKS

University of Virginia professor Ian Stevenson has published books and peer-reviewed research papers about their work in examining cases of early childhood past life memories and birthmarks. The most detailed collection of personal reports concerning reincarnation were published in 1980 by Professor Stevenson in his book, *Twenty Cases Suggestive of Reincarnation.* He has spent over 40 years devoted to the study of children who have spoken about past lives. In each case, Professor Stevenson methodically documented the child's statements. Then he identified the deceased person the child allegedly had a connection with, and verified the facts about the deceased person's life independently, and he found they matched the child's memory almost identically in every case. He believed that his strict methods ruled out all possible "normal" explanations for the child's memories. However, it should be noted that a significant majority of Professor Stevenson's reported cases of reincarnation originated in Eastern societies, where the dominant religions of these cultures often permit the concept of reincarnation. Following this type of criticism, Stevenson published a book on European cases which came to the same conclusions on reincarnation.

Professor Ian Stevenson, together with Dr. Jim Tucker, have both studied over 2,500 cases of children who appeared to remember their past lives. These two psychiatrists and their associates investigated each case independently. Professor Stevenson summarized their findings as follows: "Reincarnation is not the only explanation for these cases, but it is the best explanation we have for the stronger cases, by which I mean those in which a child makes a considerable number (say 20 or 30) of correct statements about another person who lives in a family that lives quite remote from his own and with which his family has had no prior contacts. When we talk about remoteness, we don't necessarily just mean physical distance. We know that two families can live only 10 kilometers apart and yet they can be very remote because they belong to different economic and social classes."

Professor Stevenson has also matched birthmarks and birth defects to wounds and scars on the deceased, verified by medical records such as autopsy photographs. Stevenson's research into birthmarks and congenital defects has particular importance for the demonstration of spirits being reborn, since it furnishes objective and graphic evidence of reincarnation, superior to the often fragmentary memories and reports of the children and adults questioned, which even if verified afterwards, probably cannot be assigned the same status as birthmarks and birth defects.

OUT OF BODY EXPERIENCES

Out of body and near death experiences also furnish data strongly suggesting the mind or spirit can function outside of the body and outside of time and space as we experience it through our bodies. This data indirectly supports the idea of reincarnation. The oldest out of body experience (OBE), or near death report on record appears to be the story of Er, as told by Plato in the *Republic*. After being "killed" in battle, Er came back to life on the funeral pyre and told of his journey into another world. He was told that he must be a messenger to humanity by returning and informing others what he had observed, which greatly inspired the ancient Greeks.

An out of body experience typically involves a sensation of floating outside of one's body and, in some cases, perceiving one's spirit removed or outside the physical body, which is called "autoscopy." The first extensive scientific study of OBEs was made by Celia Green in 1968. She collected the written, first-hand accounts from a total of 400 subjects, recruited by means of appeals in the mainstream media, and followed up with a questionnaire. Some 80% reported feeling they were a "disembodied consciousness," with no external body at all. About one in ten people has reported having an out of body experience at some time in their lives. It is claimed that those experiencing an OBE will sometimes observe details which were unknown to them beforehand.

Another form of a spontaneous OBE occurs during a near death experience (NDE). The phenomenology of a NDE usually includes physiological, psychological and transcendental factors such as impressions of being outside the physical body. Typically the experience follows a distinct progression, starting with the sensation of floating above one's body and observing the surrounding area. The best known reports are the hospital studies where a recently deceased spirit observes active conversations in other locations and can relate the details of those encounters at a later time, when brought back to life. These conversations are confirmed by the people who were being observed by the spirit. They routinely testify that no other person could have known the content of their conversations.

Those having an OBE or NDE, astral traveling, remote viewing, and even ghost sightings share the same experience with a variety of spirits who also occupy those realms. These are the parallel realities with which we already have an interpersonal, or shared, dream reality. Ghosts are apparitions in this realm. Relatives often see their recently departed loved ones, and they appear like a ghost in the source field. Sometimes conversations are shared. If the patient is resuscitated, they are likely to remember the content of their conversation with the loved one.

The NDE suggests that there is an energy, or spirit body, which separates from the physical body at death, and lives on in another dimension of reality. But skeptics and debunkers dismiss any new NDE reports, claiming that reading about such experiences has "programmed" people to imagine, or to expect, the phenomenological features of the NDE, including being out of body, passing through a dark tunnel, seeing and passing into the "light," meeting deceased relatives or friends, having a panoramic life review, and being told by a deceased relative or spirit guide that the person must return to the physical body *as it is not yet his or her time to transition to their side of the veil.* Because others have recounted these experiences, a skeptic may discount them out of hand as invalid. But what if there is a discernible pattern to the OBE and NDE that really is similar each time? More compelling, however, is meeting these individuals in person and experiencing the awe and sincerity of their accounts. In the great majority of cases, such experiences have been utterly life changing for these individuals.

THE AMNESIA OF PRISON PLANET

Humans have been in a state of amnesia regarding their past lives for a very long time. From the time religion was invented until today, aspects of the priesthood have used religion to reinforce the idea that an individual is simply a biological body, and not an immortal spiritual being. According to most Western religions still committed to an authoritative hierarchy, individuals cannot be their own "priests," have no power, and the concept of past lives is meaningless. In its most extreme form, prior to the Reformation, the priests held exclusive domain with the unique power to intercede with the divine. The "divine" was interpreted as a monolithic God of judgment and revenge, quick to pounce on sinners for every imperfection. The frightened population then became enslaved to the dictates of the priesthood, who threatened eternal spiritual punishment if the people did not obey.

The concept of organized religion worldwide is so monolithic that it is hard to see the forest for the trees. The corruption stemming from a very sophisticated power system installed for many centuries has assured that we will forget our spiritual selves while we are alive. What else would one expect on a *prison planet* where all the prisoners have amnesia, and the priests themselves are also prisoners? The secret mind-control operation of the ancient priests continues in operation to this day. This is the effect of an amnesia that has been affecting people on Earth for many thousands of years, and preventing us from understanding our true nature, of which an understanding of the reincarnation process can provide a tool that is helpful for mind expansion.

It has been easy for the high priesthood to teach this altered notion of the divine as something to be feared by people who, due to ignorance and unawareness, inadvertently believe they are the victims of circumstances; of forces outside of themselves; and yes, of God. As long as one chooses to assign responsibility for creation, existence and personal accountability regarding one's own thoughts and actions to others, that person is and will remain a slave—a victim. The perpetuation of this lie—a vengeful god, the opposite of an unconditionally loving creator as taught by Jesus— resulted from, and has been promoted, by many self-proclaimed prophets for their own agenda of control over the masses. They were certainly not concerned with improving the human condition—or freeing the minds of their flock. What greater brutality can be inflicted on anyone than to erase one's spiritual awareness, identity, ability, and the memory that is essence to the self?

BREAKING THE BONDS

As this section title suggests, the game is not over. Dark forces are losing their grip. There are signs that more and more citizens of planet Earth are awakening to the realization that if humanity is to survive, we must cooperate to find effective solutions to the difficult conditions of our spiritual existence on Earth. Humanity must rise above its physical form and discover that we are each immortal spiritual beings. A popular bumper sticker says it in another way, "We are not humans having a spiritual experience, but spiritual beings having a human experience." When enough of us collectively realize this notion, we can transcend our biological bodies and reunite with our spiritual selves. Only when these realizations have been made in humanity's collective consciousness will it be possible to escape our current imprisonment. Earth has been used as a spiritual prison for many millenniums. If we cannot grasp these concepts, and work to heal all differences and install a true world peace, the future for humans on Earth will remain bleak.

Some human spirits have been transported to Earth more recently than others who can recall past lives on other planets a long time ago. Others have been on Earth only a few dozen lifetimes over a couple hundred years, so they would have no personal experiences with the earlier civilizations on Earth or elsewhere. They have no experiences of having lived on Earth, so could not remember a previous existence here, even if their memory were restored. They might, however, remember lives they lived elsewhere on other planets and in other parts of the universe. Some in bodies we might describe as extraterrestrial. A few have been here since the first advanced space colonies were established, which became the high civilizations of Lemuria and Atlantis, and still others in our distant past. Some people have evolved from animals recently, and have few if any past human memories. In any case, the human spirits of Earth are here forever, until we can break the amnesia cycle, conquer the electronic traps set up by our captors (of long ago) and free ourselves. There is more information about the electronic screen traps in our solar system in "Esoteric Series" book two *Future Esoteric: The Unseen Realms.*

Until we make the major collective conscious breakthrough that we are immortal spiritual beings, humans on Earth will continue to live a series of consecutive lives, over and over and over. The same immortal spiritual beings that lived during the rise and fall of civilizations in India, China, Mesopotamia, Greece, and Rome currently inhabit bodies right now in America, France, Russia, Africa, and around the world. In between each lifetime a human spirit is sent back again, to begin again, as though the new life was the only life they had ever lived. They begin anew in pain, in misery, and in mystery. The human condition will not take a giant leap for the better until humans as a species embrace the notion of reincarnation. Until then, we are sentenced to eternal imprisonment (like all other spiritual beings on Earth). But if we can disable the Moon and Mars electronic force screen traps and the "Black Knight" satellite keeping us in a state of perpetual amnesia, there may be hope. The greatest weapon the "Old Empire" has is our ignorance of what they are doing to all the immortal spiritual beings on Earth. Disbelief, propaganda and secrecy are the most effective weapons they empower!

We as the human species can very quickly spiritually evolve if we could freely remember our own past lives. The only way this will ever happen is to communicate, coordinate, and resist the blocks that have been set up to make us forget. We have to tell other people, and we have to communicate openly with each other. Communication is the only effective weapon against secrecy and oppression. It will also help us release the karma we have been carrying along, thus making huge advances in our spiritual lives. As we begin to remember more about our real past, we will come to realize that the rest of our lives are in the future. Eternity is not just in the past. Eternity is also in the future.

HELPING US UNDERSTAND OUR SPIRITUAL SELF

First, we must understand that we have not been allowed by the controlling classes to know about our true spiritual selves for many centuries. Humanity has been misinformed about the reality of its soul, of life after death, and the mechanisms of reincarnation. Second, Western religions are a great source of scientifically erroneous information about the afterlife, based on texts which are apocryphal, and yet are held sacred as a matter of faith. Academic science prohibits the teaching of the reality of life after death, even though it is supported by empirical evidence. The scientific establishment thus perpetuates an erroneous view of human reality. Religious wars, such as Christianity vs. Islam, are a result of this imposed ignorance. If allowed, science can demonstrate the true nature of the soul (and its life) both in the spiritual and the exopolitical dimensions.

The real picture is that consciousness is everywhere in the universe. Our minds create definitions of physical things by delineating a particular field of consciousness and giving it a name. For example, people, rocks, stars, and other objects are all identified for their physical attributes. When a person recalls a past life, that person probably goes into some form of altered state of consciousness, or "tunes in" to a particular portion of the oversoul of universal consciousness, and then memories can flow into their conscious mind. The conscious mind interprets the experience and creates a field that is then referred to as a past life. This "tuning in" process can be very imprecise, the precision depending on the person, their experience with the process, and the particular type of altered state being used. Scientologists use an E-meter device to collect a spiritual discharge when examining past lives and other "engrams" related to the "reactive mind."

Once a person connects with the universal consciousness, many past life experiences are available, and similar scenarios may get mixed up in regard to our understanding of time and place. Time and space are irrelevant to the universal conscious memories of the oversoul. It is the conscious mind, which is just one particular field of consciousness, that wants to assign a time and place to everything.

CONNECTING WITH OUR PAST LIVES

Those who wish to "prove" the existence of their soul for themselves, be they believers, skeptics, agnostics, atheists or scientists, may do so by simply applying the words of an American biologist, Dr. Thomas D.S. Key, who noted "Your interpretation of, 'hearing an inner voice' (while reading or praying silently) is interesting as evidence of our soul." Dr. Key suggests we may detect "a still small voice speaking (silently) in your innermost being, while praying or reading in silence, without the hearing of your ears or the use of lips, tongue, or vocal cords!"

In the Eastern traditions, meditation and chanting hymns have long been techniques to connect with visions of our past lives. Sufis say "chanting polishes the heart." The Baul of India continue the age-old chanting and musical way after *Brahman*, or the Absolute Almighty, in Hinduism.

In the 1950's, L. Ron Hubbard released the book *Dianetics*, which enabled practitioners to look in their past to locate the exact source of fears, anxiety, depression, psychosomatic illnesses and other unwanted conditions. As people looked into their past, time and time again they came into contact with memories of incidents that were prior to this lifetime. This led to further research into the subject of this form of expanding awareness, which became known as Scientology. One of the more controversial New Age philosophies, Scientology came under heavy criticism from the mainstream media. Perhaps, once again, this is a form of help toward awakening which can be distorted by both its adherents and detractors. And perhaps only those who are dedicated long-term practitioners are in a position to evaluate their own experiences, since help comes in many forms. One of Scientology's main tenants is "What is true for you, is true for you," meaning no evaluation or invalidation is made to what someone feels is true to them. The sole purpose of recalling past incidents is to make one more sane, happy and able to optimally function in the present time. Occasionally in this process, past lives are perceived by an individual who is looking into his or her past. Scientology teaches that people are immortal beings who have forgotten their true nature. This method of spiritual rehabilitation uses a type of counseling known as auditing, in which practitioners aim to consciously re-experience painful or traumatic events in their present life, and into their past lives, in order to free themselves of their own limiting effects. Study materials and auditing courses are made available to members in return for specified donations. The Church of Scientology is a legally recognized religion in the United States and most countries around the world.

Hypnosis is a particular form of altered consciousness that allows for clarity and consistency of memories from past lives with some subjects. Hypnosis is usually induced by a procedure known as a hypnotic induction, which is commonly composed of a series of preliminary instructions and suggestions. Trained practitioners note that subjects remain conscious during hypnosis. With a client's full consent and stated goals, the hypnotic trance can allow access to uncharted regions of the mind when practiced with healing intention.

THE MYSTICS KNEW

There is far more to life than meets the physical senses. We are much more than bodies living in the material world. Reincarnation suggests that, at our essence, we are souls with a long history of birth and rebirth that shapes our current life circumstances. The masters have been saying for eons that we are here in "Earth school" to learn vital lessons, and simply being aware of what those lessons are can help us to complete our personal task and evolve. By becoming more aware of our past lives and the elements of our everyday self that are parts of our more eternal nature, we can discover how the elements in our lives that are often the most difficult are in fact the precise opportunity to learn what we essentially need to know. We can then give greater priority to learning the vital lessons we need to retain in this lifetime, apply those more consciously, and ultimately become enlightened.

Mystics spoke of their "past lives" for millennia, and sometimes of "future lives," but those are expressions of the experience of being bound by linear time. For those who can recall their previous "lives," they are accessing personal information from what some mystics have called the "oversoul." The oversoul is a term symbolizing the repository of all the personal memories; from all of the incarnations it creates. In fact, there is no such thing as "re-incarnation." There is only "incarnation," but for the sake of familiarity, the term reincarnation has been used. For the mystics and others who speak in terms of an oversoul, allowing them to "remember" aspects from these other incarnations, they are able to control their lives as they wish to a large degree. For the average person, this knowledge can assist in the unfolding of our "program" for the "life" we are experiencing.

Those who equate the term oversoul with universal consciousness liken it to the concept of what many call God, where we all spiritually originate. The oversoul exists outside of linear time, and so, from its perspective, all of its projections are occurring simultaneously, and each lifetime we perceive is merely a projection of the oversoul into a particular space and time environment. A "silver cord" connects the oversoul with the physical body, and acts as a communication link. Death is described as the silver cord being withdrawn so that the life force is once again merged with the oversoul. In the same manner, birth could be seen as extending the silver cord into a fetus.

Although the oversoul is beyond time and space, within our linear time frame we experience each life as being separate across time. We each interact with our environment, which includes the presence of other oversouls, each sensing and interacting within the same environment, but each within a unique perspective. The experience of reality is therefore totally subjective. It is virtually impossible to have an identical objective reality that everyone can agree upon, because each point of awareness has its own perspective. Each person perceives reality from a slightly different angle and, in fact, can experience connection to the oversoul in the form that is meaningful to them—thus the importance of respecting all forms of "Earth's curriculum"—of our apparently reoccurring classroom experiences.

THE PURPOSE OF EXISTENCE

As irony fades away, inspiration becomes enlightenment. This reveals a paradigm of oneness and equality, not the dualistic hierarchy we seem to be trapped within. Oneness shows that the future is past, or said another way, the cosmos has already happened as an idea, yet it is now being represented to us in "real time." Higher consciousness, enlightenment, and the loss of fear comes from the meaningful experiences and lessons learned with the understanding that there truly is only one law, known to many as the "law of love." When a person leads a life expressing this belief, the mind and the heart begin to open to new realities, and other-dimensional truths become known.

Ironically, truth is a slender thread in the cosmos, as it were. The "everything," as perceived via enlightenment, becomes our own personal truth. This is because oneness is indicative of an ultimate resolution. This is the holographic peace called *eternity*. Meanwhile, the gravity-laden universe marches on as a programmed reality, yet perhaps one might glimpse the proverbial light at the end of the tunnel.

The gargantuan plan for this phenomenon we call existence is indeed complex and very robust. We tiny human beings know very little of what is really going on in our local environments, let alone within the multi-dimensional "omniverse." If we could become more intelligent and perceptive we would easily see that *we are the reason* that we are not aware of the larger universe of beings and systems that are functioning within our experience. Just to examine the artifacts of the ancients should give us some knowledge regarding the next level of being, all the while becoming more aware right here within time and space. If we could only read the striations of the stones in ancient Egypt, we would know that they were more advanced than we are today. Who are these higher lifeforms? We do not know, because we are seemingly not ready for the hyper-jump to a higher intellect. And yet, more and more of Earth's citizens appear to be readying themselves for this giant leap in awareness. All around us, there are those emerging from the trance that focuses on immediate physical boundaries and desires.

What psychics and mystics have always known, science is beginning to understand and codify. The essential message is that we are all made up of energetic vibrations, and that the energy of any individual can communicate and interact with the energy of others, and then with the universe itself. The *creation energy* is the soul of all living things ... our spirits. It is what we all are. Our human bodies are made of atoms, but our spirit is made of energy. When Earth physicists can fully understand this energetic field of science, when they're thoroughly convinced that the soul of the human body is part of God, made solely and exclusively of energy, then they'll have to redefine God as a great positive, an intelligent force pervading the entire universe. As we continue to open our minds, we will find ourselves in a conscious universe that is infinite beyond our current grasp of reality. And at that point we will enter into a new era, where we can co-create the ideal society for all people, as we shall begin to examine in the next chapter.

In 2013, the Russian scientist Konstantin Korotkov was able to photograph the soul gradually leaving the body with a bioelectrographic camera. This time-lapse image was taken using the gas discharge visualization method, an advanced technique of Kirlian photography. The timing of astral disembodiment in which the life force leaves the body was photographed at the moment of death. According to Korotkov, the navel and head are the parts of the body to first lose the life force, also known as the soul. The heart and the groin are the last areas where the spirit departs the physical body.

THE CHERUBIM or GLORY, Heb. IX. 5.

Described Exod. XXV. 18—22. XXXVII. 7—9. 1 Kings VI. 23—28. VIII. 7.
2 Chron.III.10—13. V. 8. Ezek.I.5—11. X. 10—22

< Beings from the sixth-density level appear in the Old and New Testament as "Seraphim" or "Cherubim." Both are considered the most advanced entities in the angelic hierarchy. When these entities do decide to appear in physical form, they often appear as beings of pure light, with spectacular abilities.

Such angelic beings may be with us at the moment the silver cord connects to the fetus, and meet us again at death. As most all of us reincarnate fairly soon after death, we do take with us some physical characteristic from our past lives. At the May, 2017 conference *Contact in the Desert*, author David Wilcock spoke of retaining the physical makeup of your most previous life. His is largely believed to be the incarnation of Edgar Cayce. Wilcock explained that the genetic similarities from our parents is most evident as babies and children, but as we grow into our adult bodies our previous lifetime physical forms assert their unique characteristics.

> The fear of death is ancient and primal. It is a person's entrance into the "great unknown" when our bodies cease to function, then begin to decompose into a skeleton form. Thanatophobia is the fear of death, more specifically, being dead or dying. Necrophobia is a specific phobia which is an irrational fear of dead bodies like rotting corpses, as well as all things associated with death, such as coffins and tombstones. If we can put aside our fear of death by understanding it is a mere transitional period, we can really begin to enjoy more peace and joy than we ever could imagine.

A Cherokee proverb states, "when you were born you cried and the world rejoiced. Live your life so that when you die the world cries and you rejoice."

< The *Law of One* book series, channeled from an entity known as Ra, clearly explains that the Earth is a school for spiritual growth. Nothing happens here by random chance. We've all had human lives before, and sometimes we recognize our old partners. Image produced by the *Himalayan Academy Publications*, Kapaa, Kauai, Hawaii.

> The "Death" card on the right comes from the Visconti-Sforza Tarot deck created in the 15th century. Published in 1455, the Visconti tarot deck is one of the oldest known to exist. It had a significant impact on the visual composition, card numbering, and interpretation of modern decks.

Some interesting activity was captured on film at the moment a woman deceased, as taken by her husband. What is the light seen? Ectoplasm? The soul? The "astral" body? Surfing the phantasmagoria of the infinite? Are they other beings? It is interesting that the depiction is uniformly one of light and energy.

PRE-UTOPIA

"Thoughts and language are creative aspects of being, tools for transforming reality. To take advantage of the fabulous magnitudes of real wealth waiting to be employed intelligently, we must give each human who is or becomes unemployed a life fellowship in research and development or in just simple thinking. Man must be able to dare to think truthfully and to act accordingly without fear of losing his franchise to live."
–Buckminster Fuller

THE evolution of our species has been developing for over a million years. After the antediluvian civilizations faded from memory, it took humans around 4,000 years from basic tools to procure advanced technology. While physical technology is pretty well integrated into the advanced societies today, the next frontier will be the interface of computers with the human mind. Imagine the inventions to come and what the future entails. Futurist Ray Kurzweil predicts a "singularity point" no later than 2045, a point when computers will surpass humans in every way, and the world will change more in a decade than it did in the previous 1,000 decades. Technological evolution is no longer the issue. We will be evolving our minds. Within our lifetimes it could be possible for humans to contemplate spiritual self-realization, levitation, telepathy, and astral projection, with the potential to explore every galaxy, and even experience time travel. The possibilities are endless.

The masses are entranced by a world of facts, encyclopedias, television, and newspapers, along with the "multidimensional anomalies" such as crop circles and UFO sightings. Yet, none of these has penetrated our plane of existence with any sort of validation. When this penetration occurs, changes beyond what any of us can conceive of will begin to manifest. Let's just say that in our wildest dreams, we cannot presently conceptualize where the Earth is headed. We only need to clear the road blocks that inhibit a mass awakening, and then the spiritual evolution innate within each of us will begin to take over.

In the near future there will be no room for hate, ignorance, fear, greed, control, money, boredom or loneliness. Only love, peace, charity and compassion will encompass people's emotions. Fear is a prison, and only love is the exit. We will become one with everyone and everything. No pain, and no hurt. Nothing will stop us. Before we learn as a species to truly *thrive*, and leave not a single person behind, there are some techniques each of us can employ in order to become more complete persons. Some are rather new, others are very ancient. For starters, keep calm, seek wisdom and embrace this moment. Remember we are eternal. All this pain is an illusion.

If you think we are not capable as a species to change, just consider how much our attitudes on racial relations have changed in America over just the last few decades. Only 60 years ago the southern states of the U.S. were still being terrorized by the Ku Klux Klan (KKK), and racial segregation was the norm in the South (not the exception). In the name of racial intolerance and hate, a network of terrorist organizations, which had Freemasons, Mormons, Christians and corporate business leaders amongst their ranks, terrorized African Americans and others for over a century. They also advocated extremist white supremacy, including hatred towards Jews, and largely went unprosecuted for their crimes. Today, the KKK has been marginalized and brought to justice for committing crimes and racial equality has become the spoken goal, if not yet entirely the norm, in a once largely divided nation. Social changes on a macro level are very possible within one's lifetime, that is if we can start by envisioning changes to all of the currently flawed systems. A utopian society must begin first in our minds.

ALL IS ONE

Humans are all connected biologically to one another, and connected chemically to the Earth. But what about our connection to the universe? Modern physics tells us that the universe is a unity—that it is undivided. Though we seem to live in a world of separation and difference, physics tells us that beneath the surface, every object and event in the universe is completely interwoven with every other object and event. There is no true separation. We are truly one with each other, the planet, and the universe. Not only is the universe defined by unity, it is also defined by love. The universe is the same one that both Albert Einstein and Jesus were speaking of in their very different ways. This new picture of reality will emerge gradually. Reality is too vast, too complex, and too irreducibly mysterious for a full picture of it ever to be absolutely whole. But in essence, the "big picture" will illustrate the universe as evolving, multi-dimensional, and known down to its tiniest particle by a higher force, a "creator," or "God," to name just a few of the terms used by humans over the millennia.

Our planet is delineated by borders, divisions, and territories. Countries are competing for limited resources, economic domination, and religious superiority. We have war and extreme poverty. Let's zoom away from the planet for a moment. Compared to the universe, our entire solar system is but a few grains of sand in the Sahara Desert, and this little planet is our only home. Yet we are recklessly polluting and exhausting our resources. We are allowing our species to breed out of control, and by doing so, strangling other species out of existence. Plastic waste in the oceans has grown larger in size than small countries, with no comprehensive strategy in place to stop it. Industries that are harming our planet are so powerful they can prevent or slow down cleaner technology for the sake of short-term profit. Governments, justice systems, and the media are all influenced by self-interest groups, whose actions often conflict with the well-being of humankind. Obviously the world is replete with many good people. But as a whole we are contributing to a system that is fundamentally broken. We are going down the wrong path. So how can we reverse these ominous trends and create a more utopian world? Let's first start by looking within.

A WORLD OF TRUTH

Infinite love is the only truth. Everything else is an illusion. Don't be deluded into the belief that fear and anger have any place in our lives. Indeed, such reactions are knee-jerk habits. Free will means we can notice our painful reactions and choose different reactions. The choices we elect to make with our emotions are just that—our choices. The key lies in noticing habitual responses that do not serve us any longer and choosing love instead. True love knows no space, no time and no boundaries. It is infinite. Because there is no limit, only the mind builds boundaries. As we ascend, we gain consciousness of the more subtle aspects of our being and begin to connect with all that is. In the simplest terms, consciousness equals energy, love, awareness, light, wisdom, beauty, truth, and purity. When you relinquish the need to mastermind the labyrinth of your existence and reach deeper to the level where you can feel rather than think, and know rather than believe, you will have arrived at the place where you can create a reality in which you truly move forward. "For small creatures such as we," wrote astronomer Carl Sagan, "the vastness is bearable only through love." Compassion and love are necessities, not luxuries. On our current trajectory, humanity cannot survive much longer.

There should be, somewhere upon Earth, a place that no nation could claim as its sole property, a place where all human beings of goodwill, sincere in their aspiration, could live freely as citizens of the world, obeying one single authority, that of the supreme truth. This would be a place of peace, accord, and harmony, where all the fighting instincts of man would be used exclusively to conquer the causes of his suffering and misery; to surmount his weakness and ignorance; to triumph over his limitations and incapacities; and a place where the needs of the spirit and the care for progress would get precedence over the satisfaction of desires and passions—the seeking for pleasures and material enjoyments.

In this place, children would be able to grow and develop integrally without losing contact with their soul. A utopian model would practice the "Laws of Consistency," which allows for children to receive all new information when it is known. Nothing is ever withheld, and every tool that is available to one is available to all. Education would be given, not with a view to passing examinations and getting certificates and posts, but for enriching the existing faculties and bringing forth new ones. Each generation will build upon all that is known to the previous generation. When a child becomes an adult, titles and positions will mean less than the opportunity to serve. Each and everyone will be provided for equally. In this utopian model, intellectual, moral and spiritual superiority will find expression not in the enhancement of the pleasures and powers of life but in the deeply satisfying fulfillment of increased duties and karmic responsibilities.

Artistic beauty in all forms—painting, sculpture, music, literature—will be available equally to all, and not exclusively to those with social or financial clout. Artists will be encouraged to flourish, with the opportunity to share in the joys they bring. The flame in an artist's heart is the beginning of a fire that will transform the world.

It is in this ideal place that money would no longer be the sovereign lord. Money will cease to exist. Individual merit will have greater importance than material wealth and social position. Work would not be for the primary purpose of gaining one's livelihood, but would be the means to express oneself, develop one's capacities and potential, and while doing service to the whole group.

In brief, it would be a place where the relations among human beings, formerly based almost exclusively upon competition and strife, would be based on cooperation and collaboration for the greater good, thereby fostering relationships of true respect and brotherhood. Once this flourishes, the rest of the world will follow. We all stand on the threshold of a grand adventure. And the extent to which each of us experiences the fullness of that journey is determined by the extent to which we let go of the scenarios that no longer serve us.

UNTIL WE INCARNATE ONCE AGAIN

Someone asked the Dalai Lama what surprises him the most in the world. "Man," was his answer, "because he sacrifices his health in order to make money. Then he sacrifices money to recuperate his health. And then he is so anxious about the future that he does not enjoy the present; the result being that he does not live in the present or the future; he lives as if he is never going to die, and then he dies having never really lived."

Happiness can always be found, even in the darkest of times, if one only remembers to turn on the light. Just like the ancient adage says that the world is our mirror, so too this applies to health through happiness. If you show people light, the dark doesn't seem to matter anymore. A lot of the pain that we deal with exists only in our thoughts. Some day we will all transition out from our bodies. Death should not be feared—only understood. Sometimes we must forge ahead through darkness to understand and appreciate the light. Terence McKenna summed up the subject succinctly:

> Nothing lasts. That's one thing you learn from life, psychedelics, or just paying attention. Very little lasts. These Buddhists aren't kidding: you are here for a very brief moment, and you can sit on your thumb and do whatever you want, but in fact the clock is ticking. What are you gonna do about it? Are you going to blow it off, or be a hedonist? What are you going to do with that? If most people took it seriously, a hell of a lot more would be done with more attention to quality and intent. And they're always talking about this stuff—intent. ... I always thought death would come on the freeway in a few horrifying moments, so you'd have no time to sort it out. Having months and months to look at it and think about it and talk to people and hear what they have to say, it's a kind of blessing. It's certainly an opportunity to grow up and get a grip and sort it all out. Just being told by an unsmiling guy in a white coat that you're going to be dead in four months definitely turns on the lights. ... It makes life rich and poignant. When it first happened, and I got these diagnoses, I could see the light of eternity, a la William Blake, shining through every leaf. I mean, a bug walking across the ground moved me to tears.

In our pursuit of a utopian scenario on Earth, humans will only need one commandment, "Do unto others (including non-human others) as you would have others do unto you." According to that one rule, people could do whatever they want, however they want, whenever they want, according to their desires, as long as they do not harm others. Violence, fear and anger will no longer hold a place in people's emotions. Besides, it is in your best interests to banish anger from your emotional toolkit. Anger and intense worry devitalize the bioplasmic body so much that the body becomes susceptible to all kinds of diseases; whereas the love emotion recharges the body. The physical arises from the subtle; formlessness gives birth to form. Your thoughts, leading a seemingly vaporous existence, have more power over you than you think.

LOVE OF THE SPINNING GALAXIES

According to a story called "The Love of the Spinning Galaxies" by an unknown author speaking on behalf of a higher consciousness in the universe, our highest purpose is to master ourselves and co-create Heaven on Earth. Most of us have heard this calling and have decided to incarnate within the last few decades in order to be alive when a great transformation takes place. This is what we are watching unfold right now. Those of us who responded to this call will go to a place of planetary evolution where the illusions of fear and separation are strong teachers. There is a calling to those with the needed talents and gifts to act as peace emissaries on this troubled planet; to lift and transform the frequencies of Earth; by simply embodying and anchoring love's presence there. In the Spinning Galaxies story, we will each be the creators of a new reality, the reality of the golden octave. On other journeys, each of us has proven to be a "feeling navigator," able to awaken our consciousness and align our heart to the promptings of pure love and compassionate service. As sun runners and torch bearers, each of us have already demonstrated that we will hold the light high. And so, the story invites us to incarnate, en masse, among the tribes of Earth to assist Gaia and all her children in their transformation.

In this scenario, it is part of the plan that we are all veiled in forgetting. However, as each of us remembers the feeling of childlike innocence and trust, we will become the harmonic leavening during this cycle of initiation for Earth. We will each incarnate strategically, often in some of the most vibrationally dense areas on the planet. To some, this illusion of separation from love may create feelings of hopelessness, lack of support, and alienation. But by embracing our humanness, the love we embrace will transform the depths of duality, and our light will quicken the many.

Each one of our choices to participate on this quest is purely voluntary. However, it is important to remember that this transformational shift on Earth is very rare and precious. Should you choose to accept this mission, you will have the opportunity to catalyze and synthesize all that you have been during your many incarnations, and receive a rarely offered quantum leap in consciousness. It is up to you to choose how you will dance with Terra Gaia and her children as she completes this ceremony of light.

And so it was that the luminous beings of spinning galaxies, those who formed the countless alliances, federations, and councils of the faithful of the stars, who chose to incarnate on planet Earth to assist in this crucial event; the awakening of the planetary dream. There was even a fail-safe process built into the plan to awaken these beings from the illusion of separation and the veil of forgetfulness that is so rife upon Earth. The luminous ones who would journey to Gaia's assistance agreed to spark each other's remembrance. Thus, these starseeded ones were encoded in many ways with sounds, colors, lights, images, words, and symbols—a vibrational resonance that would assist them in remembering their commitment to the light. It was agreed that these coded clues would appear everywhere: in visionary art and music; in penetrating looks; and in speech and feelings—all creating a deep yearning to awaken and become the embodiment of love.

So spoke the Creator, the Love of the Spinning Galaxies, enticing each of us to reach for our highest calling. So it is that you, the children of Earth, are now being bathed in the waters of remembrance, prepared as rainbow warriors to fulfill the promise of the new and ancient myth. By simply anchoring love's presence on Earth, we each lovingly draw down the mantle of the gods, sending waves of healing and love throughout Gaia's eagerly receptive body. As you emerge in this time, your gifts awaken and you empower others. Utilizing the tools of laughter, song, dance, humor, joy, trust and love, we are each creating the powerful surge of transformation that will transmute the limitations of the old myth of duality and separation, and birthing the miracle of unity and peace on Earth.

In this parable, we are each encouraged to utilize our human gifts on behalf of Gaia. In a supernova of consciousness, Gaia and her children will ascend in robes of light, forming a luminous light body of love, and to be reborn among the stars. This mythic call has been sounded. The great quest has begun. Awaken, rainbow warriors, luminous beings from the galactic alliances, federations, and councils! Ancient skywalkers, newly formed in this moment. Stand in the beauty and power of your true identity, as love's unconditional gift to Gaia. Set aside self-doubt. We are each the divine children of the Sun! Go where your heart draws you to share your great gifts. Surrender to the magic and the light. The miracle will be manifested on Earth. Remember, we dance and sing here for the One Heart.

BREAKING FREE FROM PRISON PLANET

Here on Earth there are so many different lifeforms, self-aware or not, all with their own needs and self-driven agendas. None are evil, none are good, none are more "special" than any other—all just "are." On the other hand, we certainly would not want to meet extraterrestrial visitors that treat "lower lifeforms" in the same manner that we humans treat "lower lifeforms." Consider the concept of how we as one species "farm" other species for our needs, but in doing so we also look after their needs. When we farm cows, we provide protection from predators, fresh food and water, and cure their diseases. They seemingly get a better deal than if they had to exist in the "wild." The terrible "truth" of the ET situation is inherently this scenario. How do we accept that we are a created, modified and farmed species ourselves without losing our minds? The "elite" are nothing more than installed and appointed overseers of the "farm," whose main concern is to maintain the integrity of their bloodlines. If anything, their "brief" is to increase our numbers, which they did via the use of creating and controlling whole civilizations.

Despite the notion that humans are a universal parasite, others feel this planet is precisely and intentionally created the way it is, and that it is a kind of prison planet. According to this view, the reason we are here, our souls that is, the real you and me, is to prove to ourselves what we are made of, and we cannot do this in a perfect utopian world. We need sharp duality to grow and change.

The majority of UFO-related and utopian esoteric information is contained in a companion to this book *Future Esoteric: The Unseen Realms*, so there is no reason to reopen this material. But in the context of who we are currently on this planet in our pre-utopian state, it needs to be mentioned that there is a malevolent ET presence on Earth, and these entities have been here for many thousands of years. Also there is a benevolent ET presence, with which we have a very strong connection (for some reason). We are fortunate to have the so-called good guys looking after us in a non-interventionist kind of way, and they are helping us rid ourselves of the malevolent archonic influences.

Although we are not slaves per se, we are being manipulated on several different levels by the malevolent ETs; yet, we have also benefited from them. How else do you think that we humans were able to come from horse-drawn wagons to a secret space program in less than 60 years? The only reason we accomplished this is because we were helped. Even Dr. Herman Oberth, the father of modern rocketry, once said:

UFOs are conceived and directed by intelligent beings of a very high order, and they are propelled by distorting the gravitational field, converting gravity into useable energy. There is no doubt in my mind that these objects are inter-planetary craft of some sort. I and my colleagues are confident that they do not originate in our solar system, but we feel that they may use Mars or some other body as sort of a way station. They probably do not originate in our solar system, perhaps not even in our galaxy.

This comment was apparently made sometime in 1954, and it is consistent with the following Herman Oberth quote from *The American Weekly* of Oct. 24, 1954, "It is my thesis that flying saucers are real and that they are space ships from another solar system." In a statement to a group of reporters after his retirement in 1960, he was quoted as saying, "We cannot take the credit for our record advancement in certain scientific fields alone. We have been helped." When a reporter asks, "By whom?" Oberth cryptically replied, "The people of other worlds."

INTO A NEW ERA

The higher energies are here even though it may not seem that way. These energies are molding and forming us into the purer states of being that we were always intended to become. We can each enter and facilitate the collapse of faulty systems because we each carry light. Comedian Bill Hicks puts our new era in perspective:

Wake up people it's time to evolve. That's why we're troubled. You know why our institutions are failing us, the church, the state, everything's failing? It's because they're no longer relevant. We're supposed to keep evolving. Evolution did not end with us growing opposable thumbs. You do know that, right? There's another 90 percent of our brains that we have to illuminate. ... We are the facilitators of our own creative evolution. We are the imagination of ourselves.

When we lose our compassion for those in need, when we cast aside our capacity to care, when we ignore the plight of our fellow humans, then what is lost? Quite simply, they are qualities that once allowed each of us to rise above, and the virtues that once made us human. The greatest discovery of our generation is that humans can alter their lives by changing the attitudes of their mind. As we think, so shall we become.

Nikola Tesla was a brilliant inventor who worked with technology to improve life for all people. His ideas often came from moments of pure inspiration. His imagination and creative capacity was such that he was able to envision how his inventions would work before he even drew any plans or diagrams. This was possible because Tesla had developed both left-brain and right-brain thought modalities early in life, and continued to nurture both as he lived. He described his abilities:

Inability to accept the mystic experience is more than an intellectual handicap. Lack of awareness of the basic unity of organism and environment is a serious and dangerous hallucination. For in a civilization equipped with immense technological power, the sense of alienation between man and nature leads to the use of technology in a hostile spirit—to the "conquest" of nature instead of intelligent co-operation with nature.

Our senses enable us to perceive only a minute portion of the outside world. Our hearing extends only to a small distance. Our sight is impeded by intervening bodies and shadows. To know each other we must reach beyond the sphere of our sense perceptions. We must transmit our intelligence, travel, transport the materials, and transfer the energies necessary for our existence. Nikola Tesla attributed his amazing inventions to his sense of receiving information. He said, "my brain is only a receiver, in the universe there is a core from which we obtain knowledge, strength, inspiration. I have not penetrated into the secrets of this core, but I know that it exists."

RE-INTRODUCE TESLA TECHNOLOGY

In the 1890s, Nikola Tesla revolutionized the world with his inventions in practical electricity, giving us the induction electric motor, alternating current (AC), radio telegraphy, wireless remote control, fluorescent lamps, and other scientific marvels. It was Nikola Tesla's polyphase current (AC), not Thomas Edison's direct current (DC), that ushered in the modern technological age. Tesla did not rest on his laurels but continued to make fundamental discoveries in the fields of energy and matter. He discovered cosmic rays decades before Millikan, the radio before Marconi, and was an early developer of X-ray, cathode ray, and other vacuum tubes.

However, Nikola Tesla's most significant discovery was that electrical energy could be made to propagate through the Earth, and around the Earth, in an atmospheric zone called the Schumann cavity. It extends from the planetary surface to the ionosphere at about 80 kilometers altitude. Electromagnetic waves of extremely low frequencies (in the range of 8 Hz) which is the Schumann Resonance, or pulse of the Earth's magnetic field, can travel with virtually no energy loss, to any point on the planet. Tesla's system of power distribution, and his dedication to free energy, meant that his system could be tapped by anyone in the world with the right electrical device correctly tuned to the power transmission.

The Wardenclyffe Wireless System was planned to be the first broadcast system transmitting both signals and power without wires to any point on the globe. Tesla's concept of wireless electricity was to be used to power ocean liners, airplanes in flight, run industry and transportation, and send communications instantaneously all over the globe. Because of a dispute between J.P. Morgan and Tesla as to the final use of the tower, Morgan withdrew his funds. The financier's classic comment was "If anyone can draw on the power, where do we put the meter?"

This threat to powerful interests and their distribution and sale of electrical power was too great. Tesla's discovery of collecting free energy for the Earth itself resulted in the withdrawal of financial backing, ostracism from the scientific mainstream, and the gradual removal of his name from the history books. Having had the status of a scientific superstar in 1895, Tesla was virtually a "non-person" by 1917, limited to performing small-scale scientific experiments in virtual seclusion. Nonetheless, he knew the truth could only be delayed when he said, "Throughout space there is energy—if kinetic—and we know it is, for certain—then it is a mere question of time when men will succeed in attaching their machinery to the very wheelwork of nature."

Tesla even demonstrated driving a large car powered wirelessly and with no emissions. In the summer of 1931, Dr. Nikola Tesla road-tested a luxury Pierce-Arrow sedan fitted with an 1800 rpm AC electric motor and powered by a receiver tuned to tap energy from the "aether." He drove in and around Buffalo, New York, with his adopted nephew, who gave accounts of the test drive after Tesla's death. Had this technology been advanced, improved upon, and scaled up, there would not be a single tailpipe emission today.

SCIENCE FOR PEACE

It is important to be reminded that science is morally neutral. Since scientific knowledge is cumulative, albeit morally neutral, it gives the illusion that history and human progress are also cumulative. Science and technology merely serve the ambitions of humankind. Unfortunately, there are a few scientists who look beyond the narrow tasks handed down to them by corporations or government. They employ their dark arts, often blind to the consequences, to cement into place systems of security and surveillance, as well as systems of environmental destruction, which will ultimately result in collective enslavement and mass extermination. As we veer towards environmental collapse, we will have to pit ourselves against a multitude of experts, scientists and technicians, whose loyalty is to institutions that profit from exploitation and death.

A rational world, a world that will protect the ecosystem and build sustaining economies that allocate fairly, will never be handed to us by scientists and technicians. Nearly all of them are allied with the engines of exploitation. Unscrupulous people of science will relentlessly push forward, exploiting and pillaging, and perfecting their terrible tools of technology and science, until their creations turn upon them and us. And now, it seems that if they cannot have complete control over us, they will try to destroy us.

The system run by greedy individuals, makes the nuclear bombs. Their operations extract oil from the tar sands. They turn the Appalachians into a wasteland to extract coal. They serve the evils of globalism and finance. They run the fossil fuel industry. They flood the atmosphere with carbon emissions, doom the seas, melt the polar ice caps, unleash the droughts and floods, the heat waves, the freak storms and hurricanes. Whether we choose to recognize it or not, after the Second World War, Auschwitz in Poland, and Hiroshima in Japan, became monuments to the incredible devastation humans and technology together can bring about.

As hopeless as it may seem, there is a way to turn it around. The revolution hinges on a radical change in consciousness. The change has begun through many modalities. Together, through social media for example, we can influence world leaders and industries toward improving the world, instead of degrading it. We know this will work because history has repeatedly shown us that leaders and industries must follow public opinion, or else they fail. The creation of a legitimate global democracy has already started online, beginning with social media. This can also be the way we can express our opinions, concerns and votes on important issues. Someday, with this system, we can do away with the (un)representative government, eventually end the money system, and even end working for a living. The great inventor Buckminster Fuller, who died in 1983 before the Internet Age, had this to say about the fallacy of society's priorities:

> We must do away with the absolutely specious notion that everyone has to earn a living. It is a fact today that one in ten thousand of us can make a technological breakthrough capable of supporting all the rest. The youth of today are absolutely right in recognizing this nonsense of earning a living. We keep inventing jobs because of this false idea that everybody has to be employed at some kind of drudgery because, according to Malthusian-Darwinian theory, he must justify his right to exist. So we have inspectors of inspectors and people making instruments for inspectors to inspect inspectors. The true business of people should be to go back to school and think about whatever it was they were thinking about before somebody came along and told them they had to earn a living.

There are numerous scientists who continue to work in labs across the country on weapons systems that have the capacity to exterminate millions of human beings. Is this a "rational" enterprise? Is it moral? Does it advance the human species? Does it protect life? Scientists need to take an oath towards only doing good, similar to a doctor taking the Hippocratic Oath, swearing to do no harm, and practice science ethically and honestly.

YOU ARE JUST A VISITOR HERE ...

Dhammavadaka, or Shravasti Dhammika, in his dry wit, says he is not the 5th or 9th reincarnation of a great lama, nor has he received any empowerments or initiations. He says he is not the holder of any lineage, or has yet to attain any of the *jhânas*. The *jhânas* are states of meditation where the mind is free from the five hindrances—craving, aversion, sloth, agitation and doubt. Dhammavadaka undoubtedly has some words of wisdom, here, regarding our impermanence:

Remember always that you are just a visitor here, a traveler passing through. Your stay is but short and the moment of your departure unknown. None can live without toil and a craft that provides your needs is a blessing indeed. But if you toil without rest, fatigue and weariness will overtake you, and you will be denied the joy that comes from labor's end. Speak quietly and kindly and be not forward with either opinions or advice. If you talk much, this will make you deaf to what others say, and you should know that there are few so wise that they cannot learn from others. Be near when help is needed, but far when praise and thanks are being offered. Take small account of might, wealth and fame, for they soon pass and are forgotten. Instead, nurture love within you and strive to be a friend to all. Truly, compassion is a balm for many wounds. Treasure silence when you find it, and while being mindful of your duties, set time aside to be alone with yourself.

Cast off pretense and self-deception and see yourself as you really are. Despite all appearances, no one is really evil. They are led astray by ignorance. If you ponder this truth always, you will offer more light, rather then blame and condemnation. You, no less than all beings, have Buddha nature within. Your essential mind is pure. Therefore, when defilements cause you to stumble and fall, let not remorse nor dark foreboding cast you down. Forgive yourself; notice lessons learned. Be of good cheer and with this understanding, summon strength and walk on. Faith is like a lamp and wisdom makes the flame burn bright. Carry this lamp always and in good time the darkness will yield and you will abide in the light.

PURSUIT OF HAPPINESS

Any talk of utopia has to include a contented and positive-minded populous. The way for us to get there is to look within and activate our higher selves. Any master will tell you that the ego is a wonderful thing to lose. Think beyond yourself because this life is yours to live in charity, compassion, and wisdom. Align yourself with the higher emotions, and banish the negative ones. *Focused thought* is the key. Take the power to choose what you want to do and do it well. Take the power to love what you want in life and love it honestly. Take the power to walk in the forest and be a part of nature. Take the power to control your own life. No one else can do it for you. Take the power to make your life happy. Just by living in a positive state of mind greatly reduces your risk of illness. You were born with all the unique abilities, knowledge, and talents you need for your mission in life. You do not need to compare yourself to anyone else. Be a source of joy, and let the critics and the haters complain about the world. Choose and direct yourself to be peaceful regardless of what is happening outside you. Just be yourself and start shining.

What you focus your attention on activates a vibration within you. Even the thoughts others have of us affect the thoughts we have about ourselves. Once again, the intricate network of inter-connectivity shows itself to be very, very real. How can we control the vibration that sustains our pursuit for happiness? Just be yourself. There is something that you can do better than any other. Listen to the inward voice and obey it as being *yours alone*. You are a living magnet that has an output of vibration and energy. What you attract into your life is in harmony with your dominant thoughts. In short, do more of what makes you happy. And do not be fooled: Success is not the key to happiness. Happiness is the key to success.

Heironymous Bosch's most famous and unconventional picture is called "The Garden of Earthly Delights," painted around the year 1500 in Prado, Madrid. This three-part altarpiece, called a triptych, was probably made for the private enjoyment of a noble family. It is named for the luscious garden in the central panel, which is filled with cavorting nudes and giant birds, prancing about an idyllic landscape filled with abundant fruit. The triptych depicts the history of the world and the progression of sin. Beginning on the outside shutters with the creation of the world, the story progresses from Adam and Eve and original sin on the left panel to the torments of hell, a dark, icy, yet fiery nightmarish vision, on the right. The Garden of Delights in the center illustrates a world deeply engaged in sinful pleasures. As we move beyond the torture and sins of our dark past, the promise of a utopian era is now upon us. The new triptych will depict a Golden Age.

< We must try to remain positive, no matter what the circumstances. In this 1960 photo Martin Luther King, Jr. removes a burned cross from his front yard. The boy pictured is his son. In the early 1920s until the 1960s, cross burnings were fairly common hate crimes across the southern states. The Ku Klux Klan opposed the Civil Rights Movement and condoned the assassination of King. Now the KKK has little relevance apart from being a disgraceful footnote of racist America, while Martin Luther King, Jr. has a national holiday named in his honor. We can change as a people.

"Truth" seems to be a moving target these days. We have a world economy that tells us that it is cheaper to destroy Earth in real time rather than to renew, restore, and sustain the planet. Humans can print money to bail out a bank but we can't print life to bail out the world. At present we are stealing the future, selling it in the present, and calling it gross domestic product. Whenever we exploit the Earth we exploit people and continue to cause untold suffering. Working to preserve the Earth is not a way to *get* rich, it is a way to *be* rich. Any concept of a utopian society must respect the planet and hold all of its living creatures in the highest regard.

< This is a portrait photograph of King Vaji-ravudh (Rama VI) of Siam wearing the *suea khrui* gown of a barrister-at-law. In 1918, King Vajiravudh of Thailand imagined a utopian society where people lived in ideal freedom and happiness. He called this place *Dusit Thani*, which literally translates to "Town in Heaven." For over a century, it is little wonder the people in Thailand revere their kings with such high regard.

SO YOU WANNA THROW A STREET FAIR?

"We are all a little weird and life's a little weird, and when we find someone whose weirdness is compatible with ours, we join up with them and fall in mutual weirdness and call it love."
–Dr. Seuss

AS we near the conclusion of this book I find it necessary to begin writing in the first person again. This chapter serves as my author's autobiography for the trio of books in the "Esoteric Series," since none contain an author's profile. This chapter should suffice for all three. I have always considered my role in writing books to be strictly about providing quality content, not about being the messenger. Similar to including this book's final thoughts at the beginning, this chapter will profile my professional path, an abbreviated life story, along with a highlight reel of some profound life lessons collected along the way. I'll try to keep this personal testimonial interesting, but it's really hard for me to write about myself for reasons I will explain below. If this writing style is too much of a departure from the rest of the book, I would understand if you want to skip ahead to the next chapter.

Here's the résumé portion of my bio. For the last two decades my primary business card has me listed as "publisher, author, producer." I could have also included "public speaker, illustrator, photographer, artist." Another business card presents me as the Executive Director of a nonprofit organization, which produces a large outdoor event in San Francisco, California, every spring. It is a fun day of people wearing costumes and dancing in the streets. Anyone reading this book is encouraged to enjoy a very unique springtime experience with thousands of other happy participants on Howard Street in San Francisco. The nonprofit group that organizes the event is named World Peace Through Technology Organization (WPTTO), and the outdoor festival is called the "How Weird Street Faire," and located in the SOMA neighborhood of San Francisco, the city where I have lived for the past 25 years.

The professional task of book publishing is what occupies most of my year. Between writing online and articles for print publication, new chapters for my books, and posting on social media, I also manage my various websites, do marketing work, special sales fulfillment, administrative tasks, and manage projects with outsourced collaborators. Wearing my publisher's hat, I seek to release only the kinds of books I would value owning myself, which incorporate thought-provoking, critical content with a wide appeal to readers. If any CCC Publishing (Consortium of Collective Consciousness) new release exceeds sales expectations, then I am satisfied it has reached a larger audience, and I continue the promotional push. If not, I move on to other projects as I've always done. You see, I love my work, and it does not even seem like work most days. This, among other reasons, is why my life is filled with "contentment," which is the meaning of a nickname, "Santosh" that I acquired while traveling in India. I try to reaffirm my outlook every day, projecting optimism everywhere I go as best I can, and it seems to come back to me in every way. My overwhelming positive outlook is partly due to the fact that I have never been depressed a day in my life. I can honestly say I do not know what depression is because I have never experienced it, although I have compassion for those who suffer from any kind of mental illness. As my friends say, I hit the jackpot by being born with the "happy gene." Besides writing and editing on a near daily basis, my work also includes the seasonal duties surrounding the How Weird Street Faire. Although I love the twin jobs I have created for myself, I have not had any children, and thus consider these two business endeavors as my "two kids." Like any parent, I am glad to see them both grow and stand on their own feet.

AN ESOTERIC ORIENTATION

In the last few years I have changed my editorial direction from travel publishing to the subjects I find the most fascinating. Writing about travel to sacred places has introduced me to a certain degree of "forbidden knowledge," which by its nature is controversial (and not believed by all). It is esoteric, after all. As I've become immersed in esoterica, I've discovered its draw as a compelling "alternative narrative," that runs counter to my growing disillusionment with mainstream (dis)information. In my "Esoteric Series" of books, I seek to outline subjects dealing with what is hidden, secret, occult, forbidden, little understood, magical, threatening to authorities (and not the least), mystical. Topics include: conspiracy theories, media manipulation, secret sciences, backward engineering, weapons in space, underground bases, the occult, remote viewing, precognition, reincarnation, Big Pharma, GMOs, chemtrails, fluoride, vaccines, cyber-mind, transhumanism, the shadow government, free energy, modern fascism, the Royal Family, false flag attacks, the Fourth Reich, 9-11, Zionism, Mossad, CIA, NSA, Federal Reserve, an end to money, UFO crashes, EBEs, alien abduction, super soldiers, cloned entities, anti-gravity, cattle mutilations, structures on other planets, out of place artifacts, giants, Anunnaki, Men in Black, ancient aliens, love-attraction phenomena, near-death experience, end-time predictions, HAARP, geoengineering, aspartame, Monsanto, shamanism, herbalism, mind over matter, crystals, ORMES, truth embargo, Agenda 21, Codex Alimentarius, vitamin B-17, hemp oil, Georgia Guidestones, the Rothschilds, New World Order, the Black Pope, Jesuit order, Freemasonry, Philadelphia Experiment, time travel, Yellow Cube, stargate technology, MK-ULTRA, Project Blue Beam, cultural diffusion, lost tribes and civilizations, Atlantis, Lemuria, Kirlian photography, numerology, astrology, PSI, ESP, auditive levitation, sacred geometry, cosmology, dream interpretation, sacred symbols, life after death, ley lines, Wicca, the pineal gland, SuperNormal abilities, the Bermuda Triangle, vortices, séances, Spiritualists, the Dalai Lama, utopian scenarios, past life regression, astral travel, telepathy, crop circles, giants in prehistory and cryptozoology, among many other paranormal and parapsychology subjects. The third book in the Esoteric Series is entitled: *Beyond Esoteric: The Ultimate Journey*, to be released in 2020 by CCC Publishing *without* an author's bio.

Much of the inspiration for my books has been collected from an adventure-filled life gleaned from extensive international and domestic travel. Being a voracious reader helped me become a critical thinker—fueled by an innate curiosity accompanied by habitual inner reflection. I learned early on that reading and travel were both noble pursuits. This is because of the power they have to expand the mind. After completing a self-financed trip around the world when I was 28, I decided to create a professional path I could enjoy for my next "Saturn returning" cycle. I began my middle adult phase by vowing to live a productive and truthful life. With all of my books, I try to present information as honestly as I can, with no ulterior motive. There is no higher authority who can fundamentally alter or censure my work, which puts me in a unique position. As a disclaimer of sorts, my qualification is simply that of being in "service to others," and this is what I believe to be my overriding directive in this lifetime. If I put forward incorrect information, I'll be the first to admit my mistake, and immediately take corrective action to resolve any misunderstandings. To err is to be human, and in no way do I pretend I'm perfect. I have made my fair share of mistakes, but I seek to learn from my mistakes and I vow to never repeat a wrong. In my own grand scheme of things, I feel like I am an ordinary person seeking to articulate very extraordinary subject matter contained in my Esoteric Series of videos and books.

UNINTENDED CONSEQUENCES

Another aspect of my professional life is the role of Executive Director of the World Peace Through Technologies Organization (WPTTO), and by extension, as the current event producer for the "How Weird Street Faire." I began this endeavor seeking simply to create a productive and fulfilling job for myself, which has become, by a twist of fate, an event in service to a great many others. What started as an outdoor block party in front of an artist warehouse for a few hundred people, became a hugely popular street festival where thousands flock to dress up, dance and celebrate life. Together with a group of like-minded electronic music fans with a shared interest in producing live events, a unique gathering was created (where there once was none). What morphed to become the *How Weird* of today exceeded all expectations. In a city that raises a very high standard for its unique outdoor festivals, all these years later, I can call myself the founder of one of San Francisco's largest events. Without consciously intending to, but consonant with my life purpose, I found myself using my creative talents with excitement and inspiration while being in service to many others, if only for a single day. In all my years of producing events, this party may have the most far-reaching consequences.

Included in my How Weird duties each year is to conceive the festival theme, art direct and illustrate the poster, meet with city officials alongside my event partner Michael O'Rourke, and maintain an involvement in all aspects of the event leading to the day-of production. Of course, a few directors cannot do everything ourselves, and that is why we work with a dedicated team of experienced outdoor event producers who run events of their own, namely the legendary Joegh Bullock of the Sea of Dreams and Anon Salon fame, Laird Archer of the Superheroes Street Fair, and Douglas Kolberg, who produces the annual Earth Day celebration in San Francisco. Other key team players include Isaac Rodriguez, Deborah Gatiss, Jonsey, and Trinity, who also moonlight with Burning Man and its associated year-round events. There is a lot of organization that goes into creating a safe event where thousands of relatively uninhibited citizens can have a great time. Producing How Weird from the bottom up has truly been a labor of love. Collaboration with a dozen other key organizers has demonstrated to me the extended power of *ten*.

When a person works with others of a like mind there is a multiplier effect (times ten) for each person. The How Weird organizers all share a passion for creating a really wonderful experience that we hope will exceed the expectations of our patrons.

The day of-production responsibilities are delegated by a dozen organizers who pass assignments to the managers, who in turn communicate with about a hundred employees. Our organization hires the "Weird Staff" crew; donation gate workers; bartenders; staff room employees; EMTs; pays for SF police officers; and, we also issue thousands of dollars in stipends to the stage managers. Each stage manager then oversees the set-up and strike of their sound system, assigns the DJ slots, and oversees their dance area with the support of our hired security. We "outsource" most of the stages, but we will occasionally produce our own "in house" stage if the theme requires something specialized, such as the live marching bands for the Weirdi Gras stage in 2013. On the morning set-up, one of my tasks is to oversee the barricade and portable toilet placement, while others oversee the generator cable drops, and the "organized chaos" of getting the vendor booths, bars, and food stalls into their correct locations. One pre-event collaboration I particularly enjoy is designing the posters every year with the different digital artists Robert Kidwell, Mark Maxam, and Landon Elmore. I do the drawing, and they fill in all the digital media pieces into a comprehensive poster. See if you can find at least one little grey alien and a UFO in each poster design. Continuing the playful lore of ETs coming to How Weird, marketing director Justin Weiner publishes the GPS coordinates for the most ideal UFO landing spot closest to the How Weird footprint. The How Weird has always been about positive co-creation with a sense of humor among like-minded friends.

HUMBLE BEGINNINGS

Our humble beginnings out on the street began four years after we moved into the CCC warehouse on Howard Street. An unforeseen opportunity in 1999 enabled the creation of the How Weird Street Faire as an ongoing outreach project for the newly created World Peace Through Technology Organization. If we could pull it off, we faced the alluring prospect of combining outreach with "throwing" an annual outdoor music party for the people of San Francisco. Just a block away from the old CCC warehouse is the legendary Folsom Street Fair, one of the largest of its kind in the world. I knew How Weird would have to be an extraordinary event to succeed. It took us another year to gain our 501 (c) (3) status as an educational nonprofit, largely due to a generous donation from a Silicon Valley legend named Joe Firmage. April 23rd, in the year 2000, marked the date when the first How Weird Street Faire was born, making us just one year old in the year "00." At this time I was living in the artist warehouse on Howard Street with in-house DJs, sound equipment, artists and the necessary infrastructure in order to facilitate our first year's event. It would have been very difficult, if not impossible, to produce the inaugural How Weird event without the assistance of my compadres in the Consortium of Collective Consciousness warehouse, and all the party-making resources at our disposal. Unfortunately we had to move out of the CCC warehouse in 2001, just after producing the second annual event. It is still my policy all these years later to give a drink token to my old CCC roommates anytime I see one of them at the How Weird. It is my way of acknowledging to my former "awarehouse" roommates the unintended consequence of making this event happen.

When planning started for the first How Weird Street Faire, our primary goal was to create a fun and safe electronic music dance party for the few hundred people who had been coming to the CCC parties over the years. If it was possible to cover expenses and make the event sustainable, then we could do it again the following year. For the first three years we had two stages with vendors in the middle on one block of Howard Street, between 11th and 12th Streets. The joke in those early years was a line from *The*

Blues Brothers film, when Jake and Elwood Blues inquired into what kind of music was featured at Bob's Country Bunker. The play on words was similar to our answer given, "We have both kinds of music here: techno *and* trance."

As the event grew in popularity each year, our fourth year expanded into the intersection of 12th Street and featured for the first time, intersection artwork and a real grass sod "urban park." With a larger footprint, our fourth year expanded to four stages, and at this point we begin to outsource stages to other DJ collectives. In the following years, the attendance continued to grow by about ten percent every year. All was going fine until our eighth year, when trouble threatened to end the How Weird. Resistance from the immediate neighbors who lived within the footprint forced officials from The City to cancel the event (stating it was too loud and now too big for a mostly residential area). For two weeks in 2007, the How Weird Street Faire was officially cancelled. Only an intensive grassroots PR effort involving several hundred signatures and testimonials could save the event. But the stipulation from The City was that this had to be our last year in the "Olde How Weird" footprint. We were able to reverse the decision to produce our eighth annual event in the old location, but we were then ordered to relocate. Of course, there would be unintended and unforeseen consequences in our move.

It turns out that getting evicted from the old location was a blessing in disguise. For our ninth annual event, the theme was "Exodus," ostensibly, because we had to move the festival ten blocks downtown on Howard Street to our new location on 2nd Street, where, one day a year, we continue to reside on "How Weird" Street. Financially speaking, the first three years at the new location were just break even years. But in our fourth year at the new downtown location, our 12th annual event, we finally pulled off a resounding financial success! It took us over a decade of dress rehearsals until everything fell into place for the event to work out favorably in every possible way.

The biggest consequence of producing the How Weird is how it impacts everyone involved. The day-of employment involves about a hundred people (beyond those who volunteer), and let alone the thousands of people who attend the event. When I started the How Weird in 2000, and all these years later, my motivation was always to deliver one memorable day of music, art, dancing and putting a smile on the face of several thousand attendees. It's all about creating a quality experience. As for attaining these goals: my staff and I succeeded, hands down, every year. Beyond making below industry-standard salaries, we were issued our first-ever nominal bonus for the dozen inner circle directors and staffers in 2011. Everyone got the same bonus to promote fairness. Most years we just break even, and some come in just above estimates. The profitable years have allowed the WPTTO to make donations to good causes in the neighborhood, including the ARC for disadvantaged and mentally handicapped people, and the SOMA youth group United Playerz. I still find it fascinating when people tell me they attended the How Weird Street Faire and met their soul mate; got a job; hooked up with a beautiful partner; reunited with old friends; and even met their spouse and had a baby together. Talk about the unintended consequences! None of these factors were taken into account, but nonetheless happened in a positive way for other people.

SO YOU WANNA CREATE A STREET FAIR?

If you could do work that fostered world peace, and that was the directive according to a widely respected world religious leader, would you do it? What if it was really fun work? What if it was even more fun for thirty thousand people? We'll get to the Dalai Lama's words about creating festivals for peace at the end of this chapter, but first here is a snapshot of a pivotal year from a producer's perspective. Each year has its special memories, but the one that stands out in particular is the year when everything worked out just right. On the eve of the 12th annual How Weird Street Faire in 2011, it was a beautiful warm night in San Francisco. All four top directors and our paid management staff had a really good feeling we were going to be a big success. Sure enough, when we awoke, it was a perfect weather day, which for an outdoor event is usually the largest unforeseen factor deciding a make or break year. We'd had eleven dress rehearsals to finally get it right in every department on a large scale event. This year we had a dozen stages, four donation gates, four in-house bars, over 60 paid vendors, half a dozen food vendors, two paid corporate sponsors (Dos Equis and Zip Car), and most importantly, a gorgeous weather day! We reached near capacity in our ten-block footprint, which was a good sign of success considering our tiny marketing budget. In 2011, we hosted close to 14,000 people, with attendance growth by 20% over the previous year, and all departments did well profitably, some better than others. It was our first year to generate over $100,000 in gross revenue. It remains the benchmark for us to try and emulate each year. It felt like "arriving" at a long sought destination. But it took a 30-year party-making career to get here. There were many developments that had to occur along the way.

The challenges surrounding How Weird have become more intricate every year as the event has scaled up to its current proportions. The negotiations with the City of San Francisco and its Officers continue fresh every year. As I was going over the final edit of this chapter, it occurred to me that I needed to do some follow-up on business for next year's faire. The expansion into a new intersection request for our 15th annual event was originally denied, but I challenged that decision because it will be a public safety issue if we cannot expand. The outcome became a compromise, and half the requested area was allowed. Here is my email:

Hello (City official) and Sgt. (SFPD permitting officer),

Would it be possible to meet this week or next regarding the mapping of the 2014 How Weird footprint? Basically the issue to resolve is the proposed expansion of the footprint by about 30% in size, into the intersection of First Street, which is surrounded by office buildings, so far less impact with residents is to be expected. The issue for us is the existing footprint is too small for the amount of people who come every year, without us needing to do very much marketing. We would also like to ease the pedestrian burden at the Mission and Second gate by moving it back to Minna Alley as a buffer. In order to make this sensible change and drop Minna alley from the inside of the footprint, plus the fact that we are losing two large parking lots within our footprint due to development, we will be shrinking in size by 10% in 2014, while the event becomes ever more popular. Without expansion approval the festival population will become very dense, affecting our safety plans, and I am sure increasing SFPD's concerns too.

I look forward to meeting and discussing this more in person.

Regards,

Brad Olsen, How Weird Producer

SO YOU WANNA START AN ARTIST-PARTY SPACE?

My passion for throwing memorable parties began as a teenager alongside my older brother Chris, who had a lot of beer drinking and girl-chasing friends a few years ahead of me in high school. Along with friends my own age, we started hosting gatherings (even when our mom was upstairs asleep in bed). We grew up with our younger sister Marsi rather blissfully in a subdivision called Regent Park in Arlington Heights, Illinois. Our liberal mother allowed Chris and I to throw some great parties down in his basement bedroom, but the real legendary parties occurred when she was away on her painting trips to Wisconsin. The most memorable party we threw occurred on a hot summer evening when our mom was away on a trip and a bunch of neighborhood friends, plus a new girl named Lori, all ended up getting rather drunk and playing strip poker. After getting liquored up, we went over to our neighborhood pool, climbed the fence, and all went skinny dipping. The partying went on until dawn with one guy being spotted by some shocked neighbors when walking Lori home in the nude. It's an event we still laugh about every time the old gang gets back together.

Several of my Regent Park buddies went off to college with me at Illinois State University, located in a town called Normal (how ironic!) Along with a couple friends we met in our dormitory, myself and a few Regent Parkers started an off-campus party house called "The Box." One high point was a party featuring a dozen kegs, hundreds of students inside and out, with a live band playing behind chicken wire, so no bottles thrown "Bob's Country Bunker style" could hit them while they were performing. I graduated from ISU after five years with the double major of Business Marketing and Art. My thinking in college was a career in advertising, but that changed when I left Illinois to travel around the world. If I were to ever write an autobiography, it will be entitled: *From Normal to Weird*.

After college I began to independently travel. First to Europe for several months in 1988, then around the world for three years starting in 1991. My residence as an English teacher was a rustic party pad called Cherry House near the famous Nijo Castle in Kyoto, Japan. The "Psycho Bash" series of parties I held with fellow English teachers and some of our favorite students are still talked about among those of us who remain in touch. Traveling around the world after Japan exposed me to electronic music at the full moon party on Kho Phangan, Thailand. As I continued to travel I encountered DJ parties in Australia, and most importantly, the all night trance parties in Goa, India, where I met three Americans who would team up with me a year later to start the CCC warehouse on Howard Street in San Francisco. I would live at the CCC from its inception in 1995 until we moved out in 2001. This location is also when I started my publishing business, named CCC Publishing.

The CCC warehouse was perfectly situated between large commercial buildings in a mixed-use neighborhood, so we could throw all night DJ dance party events without really bothering anyone. We threw about one party every month in our space, plus several per year off-site at other indoor and outdoor locations. We threw well over 100 parties in our six-plus years of underground event production. All were successful if considering that none got busted, there were no medical emergencies, we never lost money, and most importantly, amazing new friendships were to take hold. The only bad result of throwing CCC parties is that they became very popular, and in the final years we had to turn away three people for every four trying to get in because of space restraints. Such experience at event production prepared us to roll out the speakers and take the underground scene of CCC parties outside for the masses. Thus, the How Weird Street Faire was created to allow anyone, including families, to have a great time dancing outdoors to electronic music. Eighteen years running and not one How Weird has lost money, no crime or serious medical emergencies have occurred, and finally, City officials now embrace the event as long as we continue our commitment to hosting a safe event. Our request for expanding into First Street continues to be denied.

A VERY UNIQUE EVENT

Steven T. Jones was the City Editor at the *San Francisco Bay Guardian*, and is author of the CCC Publishing book *The Tribes of Burning Man*. He reported in the paper about a week after the 12th Annual event: "My publisher Brad Olsen and his How Weird Street Faire crew staged one of the best outdoor dance parties in San Francisco, ever, and I really don't think I'm exaggerating. Just. Killed. It. And I suppose the weirdly warm San Francisco weather that peaked that day didn't hurt either. Yes, it's a life of abundance that we lead, party people. See you around."

Despite being a marketing major in college, I have found that the best marketing for any business is the kind that comes for free, or with very little expense. Indeed, the best business is one that does not require *any* marketing expense whatsoever! But how can that be achieved? For How Weird, it was simply by following our goal to create an exceptional event that people who attend will look forward to the next year. They remember our funny name, and they tell their friends. This is the basis of our viral marketing campaign on a shoestring. The event has now grown so big that we have to *deemphasize* the marketing for fear it will grow too large and endanger the longevity of the festival. Everybody knows that even the best party sucks if it is massively over-crowded. Besides, this makes it seem more exclusive if it's kinda' like a local's secret. All of our sponsors have come to us, we did not seek them out, and we only align with sponsors who are compatible with our image.

To further describe the How Weird, here is my email back to David Craver in 2010, the President of OpenMic.US Network:

> *Thank you for sending your proposal. I understand your business plan to orga-nize a talent contest to increase awareness of, and increase attendance to, 'How Weird Street Faire.' I could see it working well for other events. But there are a few things you may not understand about the very unique event we call How Weird:*
>
> 1. *We outsource all our 11 stages to DJ collectives, who program their own schedule of music.*
> 2. *The music the stages play is electronic music, not bands or singers.*
> 3. *People who come to How Weird get dressed up on their own.*
> 4. *We are already at near capacity for the footprint we use.*
> 5. *Our event is so popular we do not need to advertise anymore, except for the very basics (website, postcards, posters).*
> 6. *Even if we did try it, and even if there were no cost, the talent contest would still be competing for the attention of people at our 10 other stages where the music is playing and people are dancing.*
> *Thus, it is not a good fit for our event. Regards, Brad*

An unintended consequence of naming the event "How Weird," which is a play on words from Howard Street, is the origin of the word *weird* itself, and how it fit so perfectly in the vision of the event. I would learn many years after founding the event that the word "weird" comes from the Norse word "wyrd," which became the blank and final rune-stone in their system of predicting the future. Wyrd means fate, or the act of becoming, so *weird* is ultimately our destiny. Being of Norwegian-German ancestry, this little fact seemed very profound when it came to my attention long after the event was created.

Seth Godin, author of *We Are All Weird* wrote in his book, "The weird set an example for the rest of us. They raise the bar; they show us through their actions that in fact we're wired to do the new." Our nonprofit organization has been approached on a few occasions by other producers inquiring about borrowing our name or the theme to create a How Weird event in other cities. Ironically, just about every city in America has a Howard Street, and some I have visited could be suitable for a How Weird-style event. I would love to see How Weird Street / Parade / Beach / Carnival festivals pop up everywhere.

MORE UNINTENDED CONSEQUENCES

Along with the people who have expressed their good times and connections as a result of How Weird, I have also gotten feedback from the readers of my books who said they were inspired by the information I provided. You guessed it, even more unin-tended consequences. Here is a typical letter from a reader of my first book:

Hey Brad,

My best friend gave me your book, World Stompers: A Global Travel Manifesto, *when I was 13 years old. (17-ish years ago?)*

It worked. Travel first, grow up second.

I'm one of the few people that I know who is doing something that I love now (that I'm almost 30).

Anyway, thanks for your book! It made my life!

It always gives me the "warm fuzzies" when I am informed that my actions in the past continue to have positive repercussions in the present, and presumably, into the future. But unintended consequences can cut both ways. Unfriendly readers have tried to provoke me into verbal fights. I don't take the bait. As the saying goes, "Forget it enough to get over it, remember it enough so it doesn't happen again." How I deal with patronizing negativism or condescending comments is just stick to my guns, knowing that what I am saying is true as I best know it. I follow logic at all times, and admit my mistakes when I come to know I am wrong. My grandfather always admonished that one should "never lose your cool." If I do not acknowledge an insult from somebody else, then the insult still belongs to that person. For me, overtly negative comments roll off like water over a duck. They simply don't stick. I understand that not everyone is going to appreciate the How Weird or my editorial content, but I will not let angry people get me down. Instead, I look to turn a negative into a positive. I try to take all criticism constructively. Sometimes when something or someone really bugs me I look at this as a life lesson I can turn around into a positive. Irritating people are really a reflection of what we do not like to see in ourselves.

IN SERVICE TO OTHERS

A great life lesson came in 1992 when I had the opportunity to live in Kyoto, Japan. I was truly amazed at the intense respect that the Japanese people reserve for teachers of any kind. I was pretty much a kid just out of college and I stepped into a position of deep reverence, equal in the eyes of the Japanese to doctors or pilots. It was not because I was really tall or the way I looked, but because I got a job as an English teacher, and being in the teaching profession is considered good karma work because it serves others by imparting knowledge. To the people of the Far East, being a teacher is a great honor, but it is also a large responsibility, hence the deference and respect.

Another lesson from traveling that sticks with me was attained when I visited the Osho International Meditation Resort in Pune, India. I kept encountering a very simple message, seemingly everywhere I looked, that while I understand much more fully today, I did not understand at the time. The message was "lose the ego," as proposed by Osho, a spiritual teacher from India who had already passed away when I arrived at his ashram. At the time this made no sense, but I kept seeing it everywhere until I finally paid attention to this "meaningful coincidence." The concept of losing the ego not only suggests a service to others, but also puts ourselves in a position of empathy and compassion, which is the posture of love and positivity. In the spirit of losing the ego, the personality of a person becomes less important, and is supplanted with an urgency to look beyond one's own selfish desires. Hence, my difficulty in writing this chapter about myself.

The opposite of service to others is placing one's own wants, needs, and personal satisfaction first, before concern for anyone else. Extreme service to self can devolve to the state of criminal psychopathic behavior. It begs the question whether allowing one's ego to dominate is nature or nurture. Regardless of what shapes us, we are not victims. Our free will allows us to make the choices in life that define the people we become.

What could possibly be more important in terms of karma and a person's impact than a life well lived, and including devotion to the assistance of others? It may seem completely counterproductive to think in terms of serving others before yourself, but I have found this to be the true route to happiness in life. In the second book of this series, *Future Esoteric: The Unseen Realms,* several chapters examine exopolitcs, meaning who are the various ETs visiting our planet, and what exactly are their intentions regarding the people of Earth. A distinction is made between those ETs whose focus is "service to self," and those who are devoted to a "service to others." It should not come as a surprise that those who are in service to others are the ones we should align with, and those who are in service to self are they who are doing great harm to the human race.

WHAT WOULD THE DALAI LAMA DO?

When I look back at all the possible routes my life could have taken when compared to the those I chose to take, I am routinely amazed. A different choice at any one juncture in my life would have irrevocably changed my current path. One decision in my early 20's could have kept me in Chicago all my life, on a different career path, and one that could have made me a family man (with the statistical 2.5 kids and living somewhere else). Instead, I am in a committed relationship, living 20 blocks from the Pacific Ocean in San Francisco, throwing an annual street festival for 30,000 people, and operating a personally-gratifying work-from-home publishing business. Had you told me while in college that this is how my middle age would be, I would not likely have believed you. Once again, unintended consequences led me down a very unique life path. So here I am, unapologetically feeling good with my choices, and enjoying life's circumstances as they come my way. I try to remember to give thanks every day, and remind myself that each new day being alive is a true gift.

A few years ago I was watching a PBS special about the Dalai Lama from Tibet. He now lives a life of exile in Dharmasala, India. The narrator asked His Holiness what the average person could do to help create world peace. The Dalai Lama replied, "They can make festivals, bring people together." My jaw dropped, because it is what I already do, but I had not heard this sagely advice when I set about creating the How Weird Street Faire for a nonprofit organization devoted to world peace. I had to laugh when the narrator continued by saying, "but the Dalai Lama does not like to personally attend festivals."

The Dalai Lama is one of the most respected religious leaders in the world. His values align closely with my own, especially when he says: "I believe all religions pursue the same goals, that of cultivating human goodness and bringing happiness to all human beings. Though the means may appear different, the ends are the same." In this regard, each of us has the capacity for extreme goodness if we so choose. Our actions have a ripple effect extending to other people in unimaginable ways. When we become comfortable with no beliefs, limits or attachments, we will each experience our own version of freedom. Life may not be the party we hoped for, but while we're here we should all dance!

There is hope for the world if we can decide to make it so. The Dalai Lama noted, "The problems we face today, violent conflicts, destruction of nature, poverty, hunger, and so on, are human created problems which can be resolved through human effort, understanding, and a development of a sense of brotherhood and sisterhood. We need to cultivate a universal responsibility for one another and the planet we share."

The Dalai Lama proposes a utopian world if we all decide to make it so. I am certainly on board. Are you? In the final chapter in the Thrive section, we will examine the life of one person whose life of wisdom inspired billions of human beings over the course of the last few thousand years, and similar to the teachings of Jesus Christ. I look to his life lessons and timeless examples for my own personal inspiration. So does the Dalai Lama.

A happy life all the way through. My first 28 years around the planet Saturn are seen on the left, second lap around Saturn on the right. For my third "Saturn returning" I have decided to travel around the world again. A contented life to be continued …

2000: The UFO Arrives

2001: A Street Oddity

2002: 4:20, Baby!

2003: The Expanding Universe

2004: May Day! May Day!

2005: All The Usual Suspects

2006: Support Our Freaks!

2008: Exodus (Movement of Ja People)

2007: Weirdo de Mayo

2009: Rebooting the Motherboard

2010: Bollyweird

2011: Mythical Realms

2012: The 13 Moons We've All Been Waiting For!

2013: Weirdi Gras

2014: How Weird in Outer Space!

2014: The Fun House

2016: The Cosmic Stew

< 2017: Summer of Weird

THE BUDDHA

"The secret of health for both mind and body is not to mourn for the past, worry about the future, or anticipate troubles, but to live in the present moment wisely and earnestly."
–The Buddha

TWO and a half millennia ago, a new religion emerged in the foothills of the Himalayas, generated from the ideas of a single man, the Buddha, a mysterious Indian sage who famously gained enlightenment while he sat under a large, shapely fig tree. It can be argued that this single person made the most significant breakthroughs in freeing the human spirit of any other person in recorded history. This person was also an unlikely hero. He began life as a privileged prince named Gautama Siddhartha who eventually became an ascetic monk who renounced material wealth. Finally, he settled on a "middle path," and became known as "the awakened one," or more precisely "the Buddha." Even though the original discourses and techniques taught by the Buddha about 2,500 years ago have been altered over the many years since his enlightenment, enough remains to represent his essential teachings. Very similar to other religions, the practical techniques of his philosophy have been perverted into robotic dogmatic rituals by misguided devotees and as a self-serving instrument of control by some priests. This is bizarre, since only enlightenment allowed the Buddha to take on that name in the first place. The term "Buddha" simply means "the one who is fully awake."

One of his students asked Buddha, "Are you the Messiah?"

"No," answered Buddha.

"Then are you a healer?"

"No," Buddha replied.

"Then are you a teacher?" the student persisted.

"No, I am not a teacher."

"Then what are you?" asked the student, exasperated.

"I am awake," Buddha replied.

What Buddha meant by "I am awake" was not the popular New Age idea that he was aware that this material existence is a dream and now he could powerfully manifest here. He had not awakened within the dream, but he had awakened *from* the dream— from the hypnotic trance of identifying with the illusion as reality.

At its core, Buddhism is a philosophy, not a religion. Although followed by millions as a religion, Buddhism can be characterized more correctly as sensible recommendations the rest of us should strive to live by—for our own benefit and all others—as stepping stones toward awakening. The life story of the Buddha is archetypal, as it touches on something we all know deep within ourselves. The real breakthrough, the meaningful core of this teaching, is how a regular person can become a master like the Buddha himself. Enlightenment is merely a new perspective on a new life. Like the old monk saying goes, a person will collect water and chop wood before enlightenment, and collect water and chop wood after enlightenment. The Buddha never claimed to be God or his emissary on Earth. He said only that he was a human being who, in a world of unavoidable pain and suffering, had found a kind of serenity that others could also find through this practice. The archetypal journey within each of us is a striving to reach our own self-actualization.

The Buddha encapsulated and simplified his teachings in such a way so that it could remain timeless. He saw the world as full of pain and sorrow, and so it remains today, with an essential caveat: happiness and beauty are found in the eye of the beholder. Despite his own personal suffering, he found serenity, and his message essentially became "I found it, and so can you." When discovering that life is blissful, the Buddha suddenly discovered joy was to be located everywhere. He saw that everything is a matter of perspective. Happy people stay happy, while angry people continue to be angry.

"Everybody wants happiness," says His Holiness the Dalai Lama, the leader of the Tibetan Buddhist people, "the purpose of our lives is to be happy." In a non-religious way, the Dalai Lama proclaimed, "You are your own master," encouraging each of us to strive for our own highest purpose. Sometimes the most basic of ethical advice makes the most sense, no matter who the person or what their background. A Dalai Lama quote seen on a bumper sticker states "Kindness is my religion." He further elaborated by saying, "I am convinced that human nature is basically affectionate and good. If our behavior follows our kind and loving nature, immense benefits will result, not only for ourselves, but also for the society to which we belong. I generally refer to this sort of love and affection as a universal religion. Everyone needs it, believers as much as non-believers. This attitude constitutes the very basis of morality." But even the Dalai Lama takes his cues from the Buddha, whose teachings remain as relevant today as 2500 years ago.

STORY OF THE BUDDHA

The baby named Gautama Siddhartha was born into royalty in the month of May, in the year 642 BCE. The story of the Buddha's life begins within the palace walls of Lumbini, a small city located in what is now southern Nepal. When Buddha was born, Lumbini was a devout Hindu city. Today, the Buddha's birthplace is the Mecca for every Buddhist, being one of the four sacred destinations of Buddhism. The four places of the Buddhist pilgrimage include the sites of his birth, enlightenment, first discourse, and death. All of these events transpired outside in nature under the trees. While there is not much particular significance in this, it could explain why Buddhists have always respected the environment and natural law.

The Buddha's teachings are a direct result of the moment he attained "unsurpassed, supreme enlightenment" in a place called Bodh Gaya, near the Indian holy city of Varanasi. Among his many profound realizations, the newly attained Buddha discovered a way to resolve basic human misunderstandings. He understood that if he or any person would examine the true nature of oneself, this would lead to compassion for oneself and others. Then, understanding that one's true nature is immortal spirit, acceptance of the impermanence of the physical world will follow, and with it, non-attachment. The corollary of remembering our true nature is the awareness that we are all connected. Coming to these realizations also means we are on the path toward seeing the essence in others rather than judging them. Buddha realized the three poisons afflicting most people were greed, anger and ignorance. But awareness embraces the possibility of seeing a world in which greed turned around becomes generosity, anger becomes kindness, and ignorance becomes wisdom.

After attaining enlightenment at Bodh Gaya, the Buddha went to Sarnath to reveal to others what he had realized. It was here that he preached his first discourse in the Sarnath deer park, a moment which would set in motion the "Wheel of the Dharma." In this holy site, the stream of the Buddha's teaching first flowed. The dharma is the scriptures of his teachings, but he would also interact and respond to questions from the crowd. After giving a spoken discourse, the Buddha would ask if everyone was clear on what he said. One time a man stated: "I want happiness." The Buddha instructed to first remove the "I," as that's ego. Then remove "want," because that's desire. And see now? You are left only with "happiness."

At 80 years old, the Buddha still walked and taught. On reaching the village of Kusinara near the border of Nepal on the Hiranyavati River, he ate spoiled pork and became ill and soon realized that his end was fast approaching. He asked a student to prepare a bed for him so his head was turned towards the north between two trees. Buddha put his own death into perfect perspective: "All things change, whatever is born is subject to decay." From this we learn that the material world, which indeed is impermanent, is not our identity. True happiness is connection to the incorruptible inner self; maintaining connection to this self is the spiritual practice. Then, when the person changes, the culture will soon follow. He wanted all human beings to be happy, large or small. "All created things must pass. Strive on. Untiringly. Diligently." These were Buddha's last words as he left the world.

THE MIDDLE WAY

The most enduring aspect of the Buddha's teachings is how he could express such profound wisdom in very basic terms. Terms that still make sense today. The Four Noble Truths and the Eightfold Path of Buddhism give a simple outline on how to live a productive life and accumulate positive karma. As Huston Smith states in his discussion of Buddhism in *The World's Religions*, the Buddha examined life here to notice people's concerns. The chronic issue is suffering, because life is *dukkha*, "out of joint." This is the overall Noble Truth. Desire causes suffering and extinguishing desire frees one from suffering. The treatment for the problem he called "The Eightfold Path" which is right views, correct intent, right speech, right conduct, right livelihood, right effort and mindfulness. These practices and right thinking demonstrate the way virtually anyone with determination can free themselves from desire and attain personal enlightenment.

These teachings are a simple system showing how to be an honorable person, free from all the trappings in life that can potentially hold us back.

Certain Buddhist teachings impart that the small ego self is illusionary and our identification with it causes misery. With a spiritual practice, a person's ego can be gradually undone and its influence greatly reduced in order to be humble enough to strive for enlightenment. Along the way, people should follow a middle path, one that is not too extreme in either direction. The middle way is a change of mind, a shift in perception in which the ego self is removed from the identity equation, resulting in the best possible outcome for all parties.

The middle way balances between extremes. An analogy is a musical instrument with strings. If the strings are tied too tight they break and the music dies. If the strings are too loose, then there will be no sound. But when they are tuned just right, the middle road, the instrument can produce beautiful music.

There is no need to believe in any other precept, even reincarnation, to incorporate wisdom into our own world view. This is the same in every religion, and even atheism. If you take the time to separate the wheat from the chaff, all religions contain wisdom deep within when observing from the middle path. Any time you take any religion or theology too seriously, controversy inevitably arises and conflicts abound. *A Course in Miracles* states, "A universal theology is impossible, but a universal experience is not only possible but necessary." Until we all realize the shortcomings of our purely human-made religions, we are doomed to continuous disappointment. Buddhism is but one teaching pointing toward truth, but can be misunderstood just as any valid teaching. In its purest form, just using the direct teachings of the Buddha, then Buddhism is a philosophy which, when practiced, can lead to an experience of greater awareness and peace of mind. As with many metaphysical or religious systems, Buddhism has split into two primarily schools of emphasis: Theraveda and Mahayana. Theraveda focuses more on human effort through meditation, a key virtue being wisdom. Mahayana emphasizes human efforts as supported by divine grace, and elaborates on metaphysics and ritual with the key result being compassion. Over the years, doctrinal differences have become less pronounced. Perhaps people are realizing that different strategies for personal transformation are simply different forms with the same goal, the famous "finger pointing to the moon." Zen Buddhists remind us that only an experience of transcendent peace and joy is persuasive—an experience of the ineffable which defies verbal logic and explanation.

The mind is as restless as a monkey, like a river endlessly flowing, ever changing, moment to moment. Bliss can be attained for brief moments through meditation, through mindfulness, that is, by learning to observe and thus quiet the "monkey mind." While we identify with our small selves, bliss will be temporary and sporadic. Moderation, as a life practice, will help get us through many of the rough patches we encounter. In our ascent, we must pass the *base camp* before reaching the summit. Of utmost importance to Buddhist practice is the solution to human suffering. Suffering arises from grievances we harbor in the small-self mind. Letting go of grievances with help from the higher mind begins the dissolving of those things blocking peace of mind. Buddha gave us the noble Eightfold Path, a set of recipes to make our own soup. Understanding reality makes one noble, not caste, not gender, not of race. Enlightenment is the control of mind, which becomes the ultimate form of freedom.

ENLIGHTENMENT

Meditation and yoga were well established practices in India at the time of Buddha's birth. As an adult, Buddha took these practices to their limits, using them as a

temporary escape, but not solving the problem of suffering. Asceticism was morti-
fying his body to extreme hardship and pain. While he felt he was shedding all his
Earthly needs, he was also losing weight and becoming terribly weak. He understood
life is often painful, and that everything is connected. He suddenly realized he did
not need to starve himself to advance himself. He came to the conclusion that we can
eat and drink and be normal humans. This was the first indication of the middle way.

Bodh Gaya is a small town in northeastern India. Pilgrims have been coming here for
over 1,600 years to see the location where Buddha became enlightened. No location
is more sacred to the 350 million Buddhists worldwide, as this is the point where
Buddha radiated, while meditating underneath the Bodhi tree. In Bodh Gaya, the
descendent tree is still alive. The Bodhi tree still represents the site of enlightenment
to Buddhists worldwide.

The goal is to achieve nirvana or enlightenment. Nirvana literally means "to blow out"
or "extinguish." This does not mean annihilation in the fearful sense of nothingness,
but rather of the false or limited self, leaving only the *true self* which has always been
there. Buddha did not flaunt or brag after he became enlightened, nor do other Buddhists when they reach enlightenment. Instead he went about his life, along the lines
of collecting water and chopping wood, before *and* after enlightenment. Buddhists
are encouraged to continue to investigate based on reason, and can reject subjects or
feelings if they do not feel them to be right. Becoming enlightened is the only way to
break the bonds of rebirth, because one's lessons have been learned and there is no
need to come back to the physical plane.

According to tradition, the Buddha emphasized ethics and correct understanding. He
questioned the average person's notions of divinity and salvation. He stated that even
the gods are subjected to karma themselves. The Buddha is solely a guide and teacher
for the sentient beings who seek to tread the path of Nirvana themselves toward the
attainment of the spiritual awakening called *bodhi,* where they see truth and reality
as it really is. The Buddhist system of insight is not a practice that is believed to have
been revealed divinely, but instead, by the understanding of the true nature of the
mind, which must be discovered by personally treading a spiritual path guided by the
teachings. Buddha was noted as saying, "he who sees the teaching sees me, he who
sees me sees the teaching."

"We're already enlightened, it resides within us," taught the Buddha near Sarnath
where he gave his first sermons, setting in motion what he called the Wheel of Dharma. Sarnath is located close to the sacred city of Varanasi on the Ganges River, the
most revered river in the world. Buddha pointed out that every day around us is miraculous. There are cause and effects to everything. Violence always begets violence.
We are human and we make mistakes, but the key is to correct any wrongs, and keep
our minds positive. Of course, we will still feel sad when we hear news of death or war.
The Buddha also said that humans are capable of doing incredible damage, which is
logical when behavior stems from the fearful, desperate, grasping ego (or small self).
Similarly, *A Course in Miracles* notes that the ego's range extends "from suspicious-
ness to viciousness."

The following points are a few of the fundamental steps to enlightenment attributed
to the Buddha. First, the Four Noble Truths outline that suffering is an inherent part
of existence; that the origin of suffering is ignorance, and the main symptoms of that
ignorance are attachment and craving; that attachment and craving can be undone;
and that following the noble Eightfold Path will lead to the cessation of attachment
and craving, and therefore the end of suffering. The Eightfold Path is right under-

standing, right thought, right speech, right action, right livelihood, right effort, right mindfulness, and right concentration.

These directions are predicated on the notion that every one of us has a soul, and each soul has a spiritual agenda that it seeks to perform in each lifetime. If we don't get it right in one lifetime, we come back to another, and on and on until the vital lesson is learned. When you finally become ready, you will no longer need to reincarnate, unless you so choose. A *Bodhisattva* is a previously enlightened soul who willingly returns to help advance the human race. Bias of the physical mind is ego-related, while the soul's mind seeks higher goals. There is a mind in the soul which will ultimately integrate and transform your personality in order to reach enlightenment. "Dependent origination" states that any phenomenon "exists" only because of the "existence" of other phenomena in a complex web of cause and effect covering time past, present, and future. Peace of mind is not as easy as it might sound. Back in the 1970s, the yogi Ram Das humorously said, "If you think you're enlightened, just go visit your family."

Another way to think about enlightenment is with the concept of "Buddha Eyes," also called "Wisdom Eyes." Essentially, the ability to look in all directions at once. " Seeing with new eyes" is an apt Buddhist metaphor. Seeing things as they are, without obstruction, is another description of enlightenment. On the way to this goal, other eye-openings occur, such as the "third eye," which is said to allow supernormal abilities to energy. Remote viewing becomes possible, as well as contact with other dimensions. In those dimensions, an *awakened* person becomes as large as the universe. Within a particular dimension, the person has a *mirror* in front of their forehead. Though invisible in our dimension, everyone has this mirror, but the mirror of a non-practitioner faces inward, because for most people, the *pineal body* in our brain is shut down. For practitioners, this mirrored image slowly turns over. Then it can reflect what the practitioner wants to see. But the images are fleeting, flipping back and forth ceaselessly, faster than the typical cinematic 24 frames per second, thereby making the images appear continuous and clear. Individuals claiming enlightenment report experiencing a phenomenon such as this.

"I seek my own enlightenment for the sake of all beings" is the Vow of the Bodhisattva. This vow in service to others allows us to radiate an energy field around ourselves that can actually change how others think and feel when they come in contact with us. The same is true when the Maharishi Effect is performed. This is when a group of focused people meditating in unison can effect a macro change worldwide.

According to the masters, the enlightenment moment occurs when our inner being totally abdicates to the awareness and concerns of the "local self," and merge "completely" with the larger universal consciousness. This union can be achieved only through the abandonment of ordinary thought processes, and entry into an ecstatic awareness of being, commonly known as bliss. In Eastern practices, this is accomplished through the release of the *kundalini* energies, which travel upward through the system, opening the body to its fullest receptivity, and culminating in the embrace of *shakti* at the crown. Then, and then only, a person becomes aware of one's own essence and source. This source is the divine, intoxicating, universal energy. At that moment, the rest is irrelevant. For this instant, one transcends all the polarities. One fully experiences in full the meaning of such terms as oneness, union, self, consciousness, bliss, transcendence, merger with the infinite, and the culminating of the "lotus opening." For the latter, this is exactly what this experience feels like. The energies, having arisen to the open crown, now pulse within the brain, exactly as though a many-petaled flower were unfolding in infinite bliss. All this occurs as ecstatic energies from the divine source stream into one's very own skull in an outpouring of unabated, indescribable, overwhelming love. A person has reached enlightenment.

SCIENCE AND ENLIGHTENMENT

A new science and worldview is beginning to dawn which holds that we will never be able to identify a higher force separately from creation, because this higher power commonly called "God," itself, is a part of creation. At a fundamental level, this is difficult to observe, but any mystic will reveal that there is only one "creator" self. After all, we are all alive, and this life force is ultimately drawn from the same tree. We are them, and they are us. In all our seeming separate consciousness, wherever there is consciousness, there is merely consciousness by virtue, meaning that everything in the universe—the cosmos, animals, plants, people—are united at our core. This awareness is currently supported by quantum mechanics and string theory, which suggests that we are all just vibrational waves throughout an underlying unified super string field. There is only one consciousness, and it is residing within all of us. What makes humans so unique is our free will, our ability to choose and determine what we believe and want to focus on. Human beings appear to be different from other sentient beings in the universe; who operate more on a hive mind, or collective consciousness level. We individualize our conciseness through the filter of our nervous system, but the consciousness itself, our very inner-subjectivity, the self in a larger sense, is universal. Experiencing this distinction through experience has been called enlightenment throughout the ages.

Your life is a physical manifestation of the thoughts that are processed in your head. We all need to understand this on an individual basis. After centuries of division, science and religion, at last are finally finding common ground in the understanding of spirituality through the revolutionary findings of quantum physics. Even the *Holy Bible*, in Proverbs 23:7, confirms this fundamental quantum law of attraction: "As a man thinketh in his heart, so he is." Spiritual self-awareness is the key to liberation.

Unless you are a scientist working at the cutting edge of quantum physics, you have to take on faith "what science tells us." What is the difference between reading Stephen Hawking and believing every word, and reading the testimony of illumined sages and believing them? Either way, if you really want to know, you have to dedicate a lifetime of effort to learning how, and then discover for yourself. Otherwise it is all "faith." True spirituality is a personal quest for each of us, and is as individual to each of us as our own fingerprint.

Quantum physics opens the window to a worldview where interstellar space travel; time travel; telepathy; plus other super human abilities; and, tapping into a "universal consciousness" can no longer be rationally called impossible. It does make these subjects intriguingly plausible scientific possibilities. Even making contact with ETs is plausible. We stand at a great crossroads when we can awaken to unlimited spiritual possibilities never before imagined. We have the ability to reclaim our sovereignty, and ultimately transform this planet from a prison to a paradise. The only thing limiting the progress of each person is him or herself. As we find ourselves on the cusp of a utopian Golden Age, the Buddha would be proud of our individual progress as benefitting the greater whole!

PRACTICING COMPASSION EQUALS HAPPINESS

We can consider following what the Dalai Lama says on happiness, "If you want others to be happy, practice compassion. If you want to be happy, practice compassion." Scientific studies, in fact, suggest that there are tangible physical benefits to practicing compassion. People who practice compassion produce 100 percent more DHEA, which is a hormone that counteracts the aging process, and 23 percent less cortisol secretions, also known as the "stress hormone."

There are other benefits as well, which are emotional and spiritual. The main benefit is that compassion helps each of us to become happy, and this, by extension, brings others around us more happiness. If we agree that it is a common aim of each of us to strive to be happy, then compassion is one of the main tools for achieving that happiness. It is therefore of the utmost importance that we cultivate and practice compassion in our lives every day. How do we do that? The key to developing compassion in your life is to make it a daily practice. Start with a morning ritual such as this suggestion by the Dalai Lama, "Today I am fortunate to have woken up, I am alive, I have a precious human life, I am not going to waste it. I am going to use all my energies to develop myself, to expand my heart out to others, to achieve enlightenment for the benefit of all beings, I am going to have kind thoughts towards others, I am not going to get angry or think badly about others, I am going to benefit others as much as I can." Make practicing compassion part of your daily routine, and look at the opportunity of serving others as an honor. Turn around greed and indifference to charity and caring.

BUDDHA DIED AT 80

Seen as smiling in his final portraits, often in a reclining pose, ever-knowing and confident, as he is about to reach nirvana. The ever-popular reclining statues of Lord Buddha represent his final days alive. He seems a being in contented abundance, in an all-knowing perspective, as ageless, as fully alive, with no fear of what lies ahead in the death state. Being alive in the Buddha state is neither male nor female. Anyone can seek the radiance of the living presence, even during their last moments alive. All are born to a great and noble calling, while at the same time each of us needs to learn profound life lessons. The Buddha would advise us to not cling to the material items of life, as they are fleeting. Also fleeting is the body, which will inevitably become old and die, only for the spirit to be physically reborn, hopefully next time around in auspicious circumstances. All living things rise and pass away. The lesson to learn is impermanence. Change is not to be feared, just understood as one of the many natural orders.

There is no worship of a supreme being in Buddhism when it comes to death. Instead, the focus is on the development of the adherent during this lifetime. Enlightenment is the embodiment of the perfectly fulfilled and completed student, who then becomes a master. Within Buddhism, there is the striving of perfection in all living beings. We already possess a "Buddha nature" within us. The task is simply to recognize it and become awakened. To get there we must see beyond our own walls. We must leave the *security* of the *palace* while opening to the flow of the eternal now. We must ourselves become a Buddha by making the mind still. When chatter in the head begins, just focus back on the breath. In meditation this is called being present, the great perfection, giving the enlightened being a perspective that is described as vast and limitless. And that is where every Buddhist strives to be when the spirit leaves the human body. Such a transition would be seamless, a process free of trauma and fear, something which overcomes so many of us shortly before we die.

Life and death should always be known as inseparable. Death is always with us. Knowing that, we should smile at the unknown. Meditation is a dress rehearsal for death. The real task in the death process is to invite others in, to grieve with them and express pain. Our relationship to the living also involves losing our life, and the loss of those around us. A Buddhist would say *let the dharma be your guide*. Be your own light. Understand the nature of suffering. The world does not have to be a painful place. Suffering is optional. Understand that your actions have consequences, so strive to leave a sustainable path for others to follow. Among the last words of the Buddha was simply, "Remember me as the one who woke up."

MODERN INTERPRETATIONS

For a 2,500-year-old religion, Buddhism seems remarkably compatible with the scientifically Western-oriented culture, which may explain its surging popularity here in America. Over the last 15 years, the number of Buddhist centers in the United States has more than doubled, to well over 1,000. As many as four million Americans now practice Buddhism, surpassing the total of Episcopalians. According to one survey, of these Buddhists, half have post-graduate degrees. The Dalai Lama is a known tinkerer of gadgets, and is ever-curious as to how certain equipment works. He advocates the scientific method, stating, "If science proves some belief of Buddhism wrong, then Buddhism will have to change." It's a statement not often heard from leaders of other religions.

One modern Western spiritual document, remarkably similar in teaching to Buddhism, and practiced by millions of spiritual seekers, is entitled *A Course in Miracles*. "Given" by a process of inner dictation in the 1960s to an atheistic clinical psychologist, Dr. Helen Schucman, at Columbia University College of Physicians and Surgeons, its introduction states: "Nothing real can be threatened. Nothing unreal exists. Herein lies the peace of God." It makes a fundamental distinction between the real, called truth, unity, oneness, love, knowledge—and the unreal, called perception, separation, fear, guilt, attack, and thus noting that our perceptual world is illusory, as Buddhism also states. Truth is "unalterable, eternal, unambiguous. The world of perception, on the other hand, is a world of time, of changes, of beginnings and endings." From truth and perception, two distinct thought systems arise "which are opposite in every respect." All of our behaviors stem from the thought system to which we adhere. So the purpose of the Course is not to teach the meaning of love, "for that is beyond what can be taught," but rather to "remove the blocks to the awareness of love's presence, which is your natural inheritance."

A Course in Miracles states, like Buddhism, that everything comes from mind. The mind is at cause; everything else is effect. The universe of time and space is a gigantic projection and "fixing it" will always, eventually, come to naught until we change our minds, until we develop a new consensus reality. Its Workbook aims at retraining the mind away from fear and attack and toward love and healing; a change from service to our wealth and security, to service to all. The means to do this is by practicing a particular kind of forgiveness, bringing about a fundamental change in perception that results in peace of mind. That change is *the "miracle."* The teaching is a brilliant integration of spirituality and psychology—the psychology of how the mind works with its defense mechanisms erected to "protect" us from our fear of annihilation when we let go of the egotistical small self. To that end, in addition to the text, there is a Workbook of 365 lessons. It is designed to help us achieve what Buddhism calls *nonattachment*, that is, the undoing of our attachment to the false sense of safety we hold in bodily identity and material things, and allowing to emerge instead that which has been covered up—our true identity as unlimited beings. The Course is not a cult or a religion, although it uses religious terminology to discuss universal spiritual themes; partly to redefine religious terms and correct the multiple misperceptions permeating Judeo-Christian Western civilization. It is eminently practical because the "miracle" shift in perception literally permeates every daily encounter and activity from saying "hello" to a stranger in the elevator, to talking with the plumber, to lecturing to a class. It is a psychologically brilliant self-study thought system uniquely formulated for our troubled 21st century Western culture and beyond.

Buddhism is functionally a theistic philosophy, even if it avoids using the "G" word. *A Course in Miracles*, on the other hand, speaks of the symbol of a loving heavenly

Father, apparently to lessen our largely unconscious fear of an avenging God and all of its misguided associations. Buddhism, like its parent religion Hinduism, espouses reincarnation, which holds that after death our souls are re-instantiated into new bodies, and karma, the law of moral cause and effect, is part of this transformation. Once reborn, the major vehicle for achieving enlightenment is meditation, touted by both Buddhists and alternative-medicine gurus as a potent way to calm and begin to free our minds. Ultimately, meditation is a tool for accessing the Inner Voice and achieving enlightenment and liberation.

Western Buddhists sometimes downplay the supernatural elements, insisting that Buddhism is not so much a religion but a practical method for achieving happiness. They depict Buddha as a pragmatist who eschewed metaphysical speculation, then spent the rest of his life focused on reducing human suffering. As the Buddhist scholar, Robert Thurman, puts it, Buddhism is an "inner science," an empirical discipline for fulfilling our minds' potential. The ultimate goal is the state of preternatural bliss, wisdom, and moral grace, sometimes called enlightenment. However, in the Buddhist version of heaven, one does not have to die to get there.

Buddhism is, if anything, pragmatic. Its goal is to move one's experience from a condition of suffering to a condition of non-suffering, called *nirvana*. Buddhism should not be viewed as a collection of concepts or beliefs. Concepts ungrounded in direct experience are useless on a spiritual path. What does it matter if you "believe" in rebirth or not? Of what bearing does this have on the intent of the Buddha's teaching? Absolutely nothing. Nirvana is a lived experience or condition that resolves human suffering. Concepts are useless if they do not support this intent.

"The whole secret of existence is to have no fear," said the Buddha, "let truth be your light." Meaning, if we can lose our irrational fears, and instead embrace truth and love, we have half the battle won. The Buddha was asked, "What have you gained from meditation?" He replied, "Nothing! However," the Buddha continued, "let me tell you what I lost: anger, anxiety, depression, insecurity, fear of old age and death." Looking inward upon ourselves is an individual endeavor, with perhaps nothing to gain, but many things to lose. These are the ever enduring lessons from one of the greatest masters Earth has ever known, with his being the closing words, "In the end, only three things matter: how much you have loved, how gently you lived, and how gracefully you let go of things not meant for you."

"Everything is based on mind, is led by mind, is fashioned by mind. If you speak and act with a polluted mind, suffering will follow you, as the wheels of the oxcart follow the footsteps of the ox," spoke the Buddha. And its logical counterpart, "Everything is based on mind, is led by mind, is fashioned by mind. If you speak and act with a pure mind, happiness will follow you, as a shadow clings to a form."

The ancient Buddhist rock carving art called *sandakada pahana*, also known as "moon stone," is a unique feature of the Sinhalese architecture of ancient Sri Lanka. It is an elaborately carved semi-circular stone slab, placed at the bottom of staircases leading to the temple entrance. According to historians, the *sandakada pahana* symbolizes the cycle of *samsara* in Buddhism, which is defined as the continual repetitive cycle of birth and death that arises from ordinary beings' grasping and fixating on a self and experiences. Animals also feature in the cycle of *samsara,* as they too have a reason to be born on Earth.

< As above, so below. This low pressure system over Iceland creates a familiar spiral pattern that also resembles the flow of water down a drain, the pattern of a spinning top, or the spiral of a galaxy.

> Patterns around the world replicate, both large and small. This NASA satellite image is an ancient riverbed carved into the mountains of Yemen, forming a colossal geological fractal.

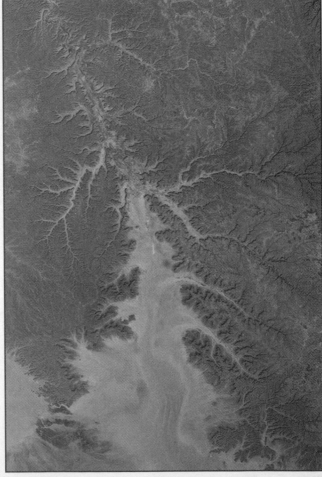

< The Bodnath stupa is the largest stupa in Nepal, and the holiest Tibetan Buddhist temple outside of Chinese occupied Tibet. It is the center of Tibetan culture in Kathmandu and is rich in Buddhist symbolism, including the iconic Buddha Eyes. The stupa is located in the town of Boudha, on the eastern outskirts of Kathmandu.

> Mohandas Gandhi followed the religious principle of *ahimsa*, or "doing no harm" and later in his life developed his own famous principle of *satyagraha* or "truth force." Although a devout Hindu, Gandhi had a Buddha nature because his title was *Mahatma*, or "Great Soul." Gandhi said: "Keep your thoughts positive because your thoughts become your words. Keep your words positive because your words become your behaviors. Keep your behaviors positive because your behaviors become habits. Keep your habits positive because your habits become your values. Keep your values positive because your values become your destiny."

CONCLUSION

"Each of us is a walking universe. Our inner space spans huge distances, with unreachable horizons in all directions. We contain black holes of lost memory and white holes of erupting joy. A mysterious centre of gravity keeps all our mental processes in delicate balance." —Deepak Chopra

WE are alive at an incredible moment in history, when the people of the planet are about to witness major social and technological advancements, some beyond our wildest imagination. What we know to be reality can flip very quickly. One of those big changes will be an overhaul of the global financial system. Everyone must realize money is a total illusion held over all of us for the purpose of control, and has no place in a unified, utopian civilization. The sooner we can eliminate money altogether the better off we will be. The entire monetary system is an age-old pyramid scheme perpetuated by the elite central bankers and the Vatican. Why the Vatican? Because the Vatican has been a leading voice calling for a consolidation of the rigged global monetary system and a world central bank to rule over the world's financial affairs. In this scheme, humanity remains merely subservient pawns in a deceptive play. Money means absolutely nothing except to a few people who don't want the rest of us to realize that fiat currency actually means nothing. There is no rule that says we have to own or control anything. Indeed, we are merely temporary custodians of physicality. If you look at all those mortal fools who blindly chase the material dream, they are so caught up in their pursuit of fortune that they forget to truly live and experience life.

The old system is completely broken. To illustrate, consider that 30% of all species on the planet became extinct in the 20th century alone, primarily as a result of human mismanagement and exploitation. If this is not enough indication that the capitalist model is dangerous and obsolete, just wait, there's more. Scientific predictions make it clear that humanity is on the verge of annihilating the ecological foundations of our own planetary existence. The temperature is expected to rise at least four degrees by 2050, causing extinction of another 50% of all species, and then moving up at least six more degrees by 2100, leading to total cataclysm. And yet, for the most part, we continue to live in states of hypnotic distraction, trapped in a social and cultural system that prioritizes short-term profit-making, ego-centric goals, and narcissistic hedonism. The current system must change, and we should all welcome this change, or there is a very bleak future in store for humanity.

The black-suited miserable now-aging billionaire globalists who have remained big-oted and self-serving in order to acquire more and more things can be understood rather than hated. Perhaps they were never hugged as children, never felt loved or valued. In an age of psychology, we've learned that children whose needs were ig-nored will try to balance the scales as adults, often reverting to the same kind of cruel and manipulative behavior they suffered as children. They will continue the family business of stepping on everyone to keep control of their illusion. But illusions have a limited shelf life. Once they are exposed they'll evaporate in a quick "poof" moment when people realize how utterly duped they have been.

The criminal controlled cabal is using tyranny and fear to get their way. Their tools are the media, drugs, genetically modified foods, and police and military threats to keep humanity enslaved. But it is apparent that the wall of lies is beginning to crumble. Books like these, along with many aware individuals, alternative communities, and visionary organizations, are shouting out from the mountaintops an *alternative nar-rative*. Through their social media posts and a huge number of scientifically validated articles, people are being informed about how to develop the pineal gland, grow and consume the best quality and highly nutritious food, drink unflouridated water, ques-tion all drug prescriptions, investigate alternative remedies for diseases, spot the real "fake news" and join together to reduce the influence of banking cartels. With this unprecedented availability of alternative information, a critical mass of awakened hu-mans is quickly approaching. Thus, the more pressure the cabal puts on humanity to keep control of their dangerous illusion, the quicker their house of cards will come crashing down. Eventually, and sooner rather than later, nature will re-balance, and humans will return to living in harmony with the plants and animals—not only as physical entities—but also as spiritual beings.

SPIRITUALISM THROUGH THE AGES

In the archetypical journey of the hero, we must first pass through the "dark night of the soul" before we can return into the light. The old model of society has to hit rock bottom before it can get better. Amidst the chaos and confounding events that are now unfolding, the promise of peace and prosperity on Earth is a distinct possibility within our lifetimes. These changes could also, possibly, transform biological human life into a light-body form. Ascension does seem to be the key. The great cycles keep repeating the "Earth school" classes we need to master in order to gain these stunning new abilities. Great teachers like Jesus and Buddha came here to reveal what we need to know, and the Bible is packed with clues that Jesus and other great teachers were well aware of these cycles. People are fulfilling a cosmic blueprint, older than time itself, which is meant to steer us into a beautiful Golden Age where we'll have such things as matter materializers, teleportation, stargate travel, anti-gravity technology, unlimited free energy, access to review all events in history, knowledge of our true selves, and spiritual ascension, where humans may adapt into light bodies.

The ancients, through their intuition, carried the "secrets of spirit," that some today describe as the New Age. There's nothing new about these attributes, however. They are as old as humanity. Within the ancients' beliefs, these were not secrets at all. They did not need to be. There was nothing really in competition with them, and the ancients openly acknowledged that there was an energy enveloping the planet called Gaia; and that it worked closely with human beings. Long ago, people recognized that Gaia fed them, clothed them, energized them, and gave them wisdom. Humans celebrated the birth of their children around the energy of the Earth. They named their children for their ancestors for many reasons, including the belief that their children were their own ancestors! The circle of life called reincarnation was accepted as reality, and it was intuitive for societies all over the planet, despite these societies having no contact. Sri Krishna, in the *Bhagavad-Gita* said, "there was never a time when I did not exist, nor you, nor will there be any future in which we shall cease to be." While this great master might have been referring to the immortal spiritual self, he also might have been alluding to the concept of reincarnation.

In the Lifeology section we surveyed the origins of humankind and the vanished civilizations of Lemuria, Atlantis and the ancient gold mining communities in southern Africa. We examined the possibility that our origins are a genetically manipulated species. New archaeological and scientific discoveries made by leading scientists show that the Sumerians and even the Egyptians inherited their knowledge from an earlier civilization that originated at the southern tip of Africa more than 200,000 years ago. These mysterious people left behind more than 10 million stone ruins scattered throughout southern Africa. They were also the people who carved the first Horus bird, the first Sphinx, constructed the first pyramids, and built an accurate stone calendar right in the middle of it all. Adam's Calendar is the flagship among millions of circular stone ruins, ancient roads, agricultural terraces and thousands of ancient gold mines, left behind by a vanished civilization now termed the "First People." These settlements cover most of southern Africa. The recently discovered pyramids of Bosnia near the towns of Visoko and Göbekli Tepe in eastern Turkey are also thought to have been built by the First People civilization. Irrefutable scientific evidence exists of ancient civilizations with advanced technology that leaves us no choice but to change our recorded history.

RETURN TO THE SOURCE

We are about to do what centuries of human beings have not been able to do, and that is to comprehend the "big picture." And that *big picture* is to realize that we are all one, both in material form and, of course, in our essence as spirit. In material form, the quantum portion of our DNA is the 90% that current genetic body scientists call "junk," simply because they cannot find a code, a system, or a chemical "signature." It all interacts with the engine of our 3D chemistry, the three percent of protein encoded portions of DNA that control all of our genes. It is all about cosmic energy creating magnetism, and it is carrying instruction sets for a new humanity. There is no way that science is going to "see" why humans are changing, but we are. DNA chemistry appears to remain the same, because it is the random "junk" that is changing. It can't be seen in 3D! Soon, however, science will figure it out, and realize that the three percent is the "machine" of our 3D body, and the 90% is the quantum instruction set that tells the engine what to do.

We are each a vibrational energy being, which some call spirit, that exists in this reality in a physical form. Our energy stems from the "Source" that created our physical bodies. We each deactivate our divine manifestation when we doubt. The Source can only respond to a pure and coherent desire to advance, not tainted by doubt and contradiction. We each create our own thoughts, and manifest reality by our emotions and feelings. There is an inner energy that each of us can access. Human emotions have the ability to change the shape of the DNA, and positive emotions are hundreds of times more powerful than negative emotions. The happier we are, the more our DNA becomes relaxed and stronger. Our thoughts can impact water as well, as the study of cymatics reveal. Always send positive thoughts in your local environment, and even bless the water you drink. Let your state of being be centered around love and joy. Try to be focused in your heart. Be mindful to always practice the following suggestions to advance your personal spiritual awareness: find forgiveness, practice gratitude, learn appreciation, discover happiness, and embrace bliss. These simple steps will lead to positive feelings of kindness, compassion, love, joy, peace and harmony.

It becomes apparent that the more we push the boundaries of science, the more we come to understand the "Universal Mind." It is the creative source of all things in the multiverse and beyond. It seems that the knowledge we gain from quantum physics and spacetime studies brings us closer to understanding the true nature of reality, the meaning of the universe, and our place in it as conscious beings. This understanding of quantum physics is a gift from the divine creator to allow humanity to find its way back to the source—back to unity from a deeply divided species—not only on Earth, but in the entire universe.

OVERCOMING THE DARK FORCES

The normalcy bias, or normality bias, refers to a mental state people enter when facing a disaster. Similar to *cognitive dissonance*, it causes people to underestimate or deny both the possibility of a disaster occurring and its possible effects. This often results in situations where people fail to adequately prepare for a disaster, and on a larger scale, the failure of governments to include the populace in its disaster preparations. The assumption that is made in the case of the normalcy bias is that since a disaster never has occurred, then it never will occur. This condition also results in the inability of people to cope with a disaster once it does occur. Denial is how we avoid breaking our addictions. It is how we keep lying to ourselves. It is how we avoid the truth. People with a normalcy bias have difficulties reacting to something they have not experienced before. People also tend to interpret warnings in the most optimistic possible way, seizing on any ambiguities to infer a less serious situation.

The USA will never default on its loans.

The banking system will never collapse.

We'll never have another Great Depression.

We'll never have martial law in the USA.

The electrical grid will never go down.

They would never hide that from us.

They would never do that to their own people.

They could never pull that off, simply because they're too incompetent.

But many recognize these beliefs as faulty assumptions. Those who realize that the old order of our civilization is starting to slowly fall apart, will be on course to be the pioneers of new scientific research that will unlock our DNA and brain capacity; allowing us to quantify the potential of our super human abilities. When this occurs, we will once again return to being complete human beings, instead of lowly slaves. Those people flexible enough in their thinking will not only be the most prepared to survive a disaster, but they will be in a position to make the biggest breakthroughs, and assist in the restructuring of a new society.

Please consider seriously the reason why the world's elite families and the institutions they control are not discussed in the mainstream media. Because, given the immense financial and political power they wield, they *control* mainstream media, now recognized as the real fake news. We have been just pawns and the Rothschilds, Rockefellers, Warburgs and other big families who have been controlling what goes on in the world, including provoking wars and massive wealth transfers, from behind the scenes. They are sick and dangerous occultists running the Western World. They are power mad lunatics, like something from a kid's cartoon, yet with their fingers on the nuclear button! Armageddon is potentially closer than anyone thought.

But there is hope. First of all, due to the Internet, these powerful forces behind the scenes have lost control of information. Consequently, their influence is eroding. Hopefully, information technology and other ground-breaking technologies will remain available to help us rid ourselves—and the world—from the domination of the war-mongers and cowardly liars who control the world. The Internet is doing much to allow the truth to come out, although the government also uses it and other technologies to track and keep tabs on us. Yet, "truth will out." As the American Founding Father and deist Thomas Paine wrote, "such is the nature of truth, that all it asks, and all it wants is the liberty of appearing." In *The Age of Reason*, Paine also wrote, "It is an affront to truth to treat falsehood with complaisance." The hidden hand of our controllers is beginning to be laid bare for all to see.

President John F. Kennedy made a profound and very true statement when he said, "With a good conscience our only sure reward, with history the final judge of our deeds, let us go forth to lead the land we love, asking His blessing and His help, but knowing that here on earth God's work must truly be our own." However you may want to interpret that, it is advised to call upon a higher power, seek your own truth, and do your best to stay positive in these universally troubling times.

The shift is inevitable, but there are major roadblocks ahead that prevent an easy transition, and many people will have a difficult time during the transformation, mainly because they will be unprepared, despite so much scientific data that shows that a shift will happen. In fact, it doesn't really matter if the controllers get their New World Order set up completely. In the grand scheme of things, it would only be for a short period of time, before the cracks get wider, and nature balances the forces of consciousness. A part of this shift is that we will not be alone in the aftermath. Once the prison of the Van Allen magnetic shield that cuts off the planet from the rest of the universe is reduced (due to the crossing of the galactic plane), we will be able to take our rightful place alongside our galactic family, and this is the next step for the human race. But first we must come to understand who we truly are, where we are from, and gain an idea of our destiny. Pay attention as we go through these dark times, because things are about to dramatically change.

COULD ET DISCLOSURE FORCE THE ISSUE?

To some degree, the vast majority of people already believe in UFOs. But it will not be until each one us truly recognize the phenomenon to be true, and are not frightened of the prospect of encountering ETs, can we attempt to make real and lasting contact. We need to come to realize that there are human-like entities, very similar to us, out there, and already here. They are not scary creatures intent on destroying the planet, but those who wish to meet on peaceful terms. We have not experienced the full transformation that contact will create in our lives until we come to terms with the acceptance of higher intelligences interacting with people on Earth. Imagine being blind your entire life, then, by some miracle, your eyesight is restored. This is what it will be like for those people who have been blinded by a reality that was constructed to keep us subservient, controlled, and conformed. The government has been covering up the UFO phenomenon and actively suppressing witnesses of this vitally important aspect of history for almost a century. It is now recognized that the real reason for UFO secrecy is not that the controllers of Earth do not want the rest of us to have interstellar craft, but if disclosure were made, one of the first questions asked would be how do they power their spaceships? The answer to this would completely blow the lid off the limited energy illusion we have been sold since the 19th century. The next questions would be how long have we known, and what agreements were made in secret? The fearful consequences to the elite of honestly answering these questions has prevented disclosure for many decades.

The fight to end UFO secrecy remains one of the great causes of our day. It is a struggle for truth, self-government, and survival. It is a call for courage in the face of a potentially grave threat. It is fighting the good fight for truth, regardless of the consequences. Some visionaries in this "pre-disclosure age" suggest that the incredible announcement ending official UFO secrecy may be coming only a short time before a spontaneous human evolution event becomes possible for the first time in our recorded history. The disclosure itself, and how it changes consciousness, may in fact be part of what helps create a defining UFO contact event and full disclosure. But certainly we cannot count on the government's help until we begin to help ourselves.

CONSCIOUSNESS EVOLUTION

Now that we are fairly stable in our individual consciousness, we can create a new form of group consciousness—namely one in which we attain access to all information via our DNA without being forced or remotely controlled about what to do with that information. We now know that, just as we use the Internet, our DNA can feed proper data into the network, can retrieve data from the network, and can establish contact with other participants in the network. Remote healing, telepathy, and "remote sensing" can now be fairly easily explained. Some animals know from afar when their owners plan to return home. This can be freshly interpreted and explained via the concepts of group consciousness and hyper-communication.

Researchers think that if humans with full individuality would regain group consciousness, they would have a god-like power to create, alter, and shape things on Earth. Humanity does appear to be collectively moving toward such a group consciousness of a new kind. Any collective consciousness cannot be sensibly used over any period of time without a distinctive individuality; otherwise we would revert to a primitive herd instinct that is easily manipulated. Hyper-communication in the new millennium means something quite different.

To witness the divine spiraling of creation, all we must do is look to the sky and see the infinite celestial body, see through the eyes of a child, and with the awe and wonder of a stargazer. Step away and look inside the glory of the heavens. It is all there, truly within us and without us. As above, so below.

Since the real world is so different from the misinformation we've been given by fake media and conventional education, most of our current efforts are somewhat misdirected. At this point, there is almost nothing more important than immediately researching and confirming for yourself all of the facts in this book. It is only when you correctly perceive the worlds *above* and *below* that you can respond to it appropriately.

Wisdom isn't something that was only for the great philosophers of old, nor is it reserved for the sages of today, sitting upon their proverbial mountaintops. It is ours; for all of us. Each and every human on this planet can drink from this well of wisdom.

HERE IS YOUR ASSIGNMENT:

1. **You Will Receive A Body.** *You may like it or not, but it will be yours for the entire period this time around.*

2. **You Will Learn Lessons.** *You are enrolled in a full-time, informal school called life. Each day in this school you will have the opportunity to learn lessons. You may like the lesson, or think they are irrelevant and stupid.*

3. **There Are No Mistakes, Only Lessons.** *Growth is a process of trial and error, and also experimentation. The "failed" experiments are as much a part of the process as the experiment that ultimately "works."*

4. **A Lesson Is Repeated Until It Is Learned.** *A lesson will be presented to you in various forms until you have learned it, then you can go on to the next lesson.*

5. **Learning Lessons Does Not End.** *There is no part of life that does not contain its lessons. If you are alive, there are lessons still to be learned.*

6. **There Is No Better Than Here.** *When your "there" has become a "here," you will simply obtain another "there" that will, again, look better than "here."*

7. **Others Are Merely Mirrors Of You.** *You cannot love or hate something about another person unless it reflects to you something you love or hate about yourself. Choose the love. Discard the hate.*

8. **What You Make Of Your Life Is Up To You.** *You have all the tools and resources you need, but what you do with them is up to you. The choice is yours.*

9. **The Answers Lie Inside You.** *The answers to life's questions lie inside you. All you need to do is look, listen and trust.*

10. **Whether You Think You Can Or Can't, In Either Case You'll Be Right.** *Think about it.*

11. **You Will Forget All Of This When You Are Born.**

BE THE BEST YOU CAN BE

The people we are today is a result of our own past actions. Whatever we wish to be in the future depends on our actions today. Decide how you choose to act right now. We are responsible for who we are and who we wish to become. We have the power to self-actualize, but our own free will can cut both ways. *Always be careful of what you wish for!*

Continually fertilize the imagination, or as Benjamin Disraeli said, "nurture your mind with great thoughts, for you will never go any higher than you think." We each have very powerful minds that can make anything happen as long as we keep ourselves centered. Think highly of yourself in a non-egotistical way, because the world takes you at your own estimate. Consider your life to be like a garden, and your thoughts to be the seeds. If your life is not magnificent, you've been watering the weeds.

We have always had the potential to do anything we could conceivably visualize. The mind's power is limitless, and when every part of your being believes it can, it will. You are a powerhouse, and all that untamed energy, when channeled and focused at one point, the pineal gland, can make impossible seem like a word in the dictionary of the unaware. The nature of reality is seamless, and your belief is what creates your reality. We all have the potential to do anything we want, if only we believe strongly enough.

This is the only method that bridges the gulfs we face at present—between science and religion; between warring political ambitions and ideologies; between religious faiths, races, nations, and classes; and finally, between all people—divisions which are more deadly than the most virulent disease, and more awful than all the epidemics combined. We are at an incredibly potent moment in history when science can merge with spirituality, when all people of the world can cross these divides, and find the similarity among us. Said again, *we are all one.*

A final passage comes from the genius Nikola Tesla, who lamented at the close of World War I, in 1919, regarding the destruction and loss of life:

> *War cannot be avoided until the physical cause for its recurrence is removed and this, in the last analysis, is the vast extent of the planet on which we live. Only through annihilation of distance in every respect, as the conveyance of intelligence, transport of passengers and supplies and transmission of energy will conditions be brought about some day, insuring permanency of friendly relations. What we now want is closer contact and better understanding between individuals and communities all over the earth, and the elimination of egoism and pride which is always prone to plunge the world into primeval barbarism and strife ... Peace can only come as a natural consequence of universal enlightenment.*

Many among us have seen the worst of the worst, survived wars, and have been damaged emotionally by the imperfect world around us. This we cannot escape. But none of that matters anymore. It is in the past. We have to move on, and we have to grow. It would help to unconditionally forgive all those who caused you any harm in the past. Remember the lessons you learned, but free yourself of the weight. Carrying around grudges and resentments are detrimental to your spiritual awakening. Let them go. Forgiveness is the best gift you can possibly give to yourself.

A Tale of Two Americas: We have lived and continue to live in the United States with incredible contradictions and ironies. Yet, many of us still dream the American dream no matter how bad the nightmare gets personally. Hope always springs eternal.

< "All is Vanity" is a classic illusion drawing by American illustrator Charles Allan Gillbert in 1892. Like the study of esoteric subjects, perception is usually a double-edged sword. There is what everyone sees, and there is that which is hidden, usually right there in plain sight.

> This antique postcard has no postmark, but is believed to have been created circa 1905-1910. "The Wise Are Silent" is akin to the Lao Tzu phrase: "Those who know, do not speak. Those who speak, do not know."

"The Thinker" statue by Auguste Rodin is perhaps his best known monumental work, first conceived circa 1880–1881 as a depiction of the late Middle Ages Italian poet Dante. The image evolved until it no longer represented Dante, but all poets or creators.

These are the words of Eckhart Tolle in 2001, one of the most aware spiritual thinkers of our time: "The beginning of freedom is the realization that you are not 'The Thinker.' The moment you start watching the thinker, a higher level of consciousness becomes activated. You begin to realize that there is a vast realm of intelligence beyond thought, that thought is only a tiny aspect of that intelligence. You also realize that the things that truly matter—love, beauty, creativity, joy and inner peace arise from beyond the mind. You begin to awaken."

REFERENCES

"Somehow tied into the fate of our species, are transcendental objects made manifest." –Terence McKenna

SIMILAR to the content of *MODERN ESOTERIC*, the metric system was designed to be universal, that is, available to all. The metric system was designed for ordinary people, for engineers who worked in human-related measurements and for astronomers and physicists who worked with numbers both large and small. The metric system was, in the words of the French philosopher Condorcet to be "for all people for all time." Such is the reason why the metric system is used in this book. May they both stand the test of time—always subject to the rigors of truth.

The following are the references cited from in the chapters of *MODERN ESOTERIC*:

AUTHOR'S KARMA STATEMENT
Crowley, Aleister. *The Confessions of Aleister Crowley*. London, UK: Cape, 1969.

INTRODUCTION
Belsebuub, *Esoteric Knowledge Through Time*, 2013. (https://www.wakingtimes.com/2013/05/06/esoteric-knowledge-throughout-time/)
Booker, Christopher, *The Seven Basic Plots: Why We Tell Stories*. Continuum International Publishing Group Ltd. 2005.
Crowley, Aleister. *Book of the Law*. Red Wheel; Reissue edition, 2011.
Hitchens, Christopher. *God is Not Great: How Religion Poisons Everything*. New York, NY: Hachette Book Group, 2007.
Ouspensky, P.D., *In Search of the Miraculous: The Definitive Exploration of G. I. Gurdjieff's Mystical Thought and Universal View*. Harvest Books.
Sheldrake, Rupert, *Dogs That Know When Their Owners Are Coming Home*. Broadway Books, 2011.
Steiner, Rudolf, *Esoteric Cosmology*. Kindle Edition.

LIFEOLOGY

LIFEOLOGY
von Däniken, Erich, *Chariots of the Gods*. Berkley Trade, 1999.
Hancock, Graham, *Fingerprints of the Gods*. Three Rivers Press, 1996.
Sitchin, Zecharia, *Twelfth Planet*. Harper, 2007.

Overpopulation. Chronicle of the 20th Century, Mt Kisco, NY, 1988.

"Plants Grow With Sound of Molecular Music," *Nexus,* (Mapleton, Australia), Sept.-Oct., 1994, source: *New Scientist,* 28 May, 1994.

MYTHOS OF CREATION

Ancient stone structures of Africa: http://viewzone2.com/adamscalendarx.html

Belsebuub, *Esoteric Knowledge Through Time,* 2013. (https://www.wakingtimes.com/2013/05/06/esoteric-knowledge-throughout-time/)

Blavatsky, H. P., *The Secret Doctrine.* Adyar: Theosophical Publishing House. 1888, abridged/edited by Michael Gomes, 2009.

La Vey, A. S., *The Satanic Bible.* Avon Books, New York 1970.

BLOOD OF THE GODS

Tellinger, Michael, *Slave Species of the Gods: The Secret History of the Anunnaki and Their Mission on Earth.* Bear & Company, 2012.

J. Kirk Harris, Scott T. Kelley, George B. Spiegelman, and Norman R. Pace. Department of Molecular Biology: **http://www.encyclopedia.com/topic/Rh_factor.aspx#1-1E1:Rhfactor-full**

The Genetic Core of the Universal Ancestor. Cellular and Developmental Biology, University of Colorado, Boulder, Colorado; plus Graduate Group in Microbiology, University of California, Berkeley, California; plus Department of Microbiology and Immunology, University of British Columbia, Vancouver, Canada

Castaneda, Carlos, *The Active Side of Infinity.* Harper Perennial, 1999.

Grey Alien abductee Jim Sparks 95% recall: **http://www.unitedstarseeds.com/forum/topics/jim-sparks-95-recall-grey-alien-abductee#.UZwLOitC4Vd**

DNA MYSTERIES

Fosar, Grazyna & Bludorf, Franz, *Vernetzte Intelligenz.* This book is only in German. "DNA Mysteries" translated by Vitae Bergman.

Moosbrugger, Guido, *AND YET... THEY FLY!* Steelmark Publishing, 2001.

Eshleman, J.A. & Malhi, R.S. *Report On The DNA Analysis From Skeletal Remains From Two Skulls. Trace Genetics.* 2003. Retrieved from **http://www.starchildproject.com/dna.htm**

Smitha, Elaine, *If You Make the Rules, How Come You're Not Boss?* Hampton Roads Publishing, 2004.

Stokes, John "Extraterrestrial Genes in Human DNA" article from: **http://agoracosmopolitan.com**

Wilcock, David, *The Source Field Investigations: The Hidden Science and Lost Civilizations Behind the 2012 Prophecies.* Plume, 2012.

www.theguardian.com/science/2017/jun/07/oldest-homo-sapiens-bones-ever-found-shake-foundations-of-the-human-story

PRIMITIVE WISDOM

Cowen, David & Arnold, Chris, *Ley Lines and Earth Energies.* Kempton, IL: Adventures Unlimited Press, 2003.

Hancock, Graham, *Supernatural: Meetings with the Ancient Teachers of Mankind.* Disinformation Books, 2006.

http://projectcamelot.org/Report_from_Iron_Mountain.pdf

RETHINKING HISTORY

Belsebuub, *Esoteric Knowledge Through Time,* 2013. (https://www.wakingtimes.com/2013/05/06/esoteric-knowledge-throughout-time/)

DuQuette, Lon Milo, *The Key to Solomon's Key.* San Francisco, CA: CCC Publishing, 2010.

Fell, Barry, *America B.C.* New York, NY. Pocket Books, 1989.

Howell, F. Clark, *Early Man.* Alexandria, VA: Time-Life Books, 1968.

Pye, Lloyd, *Everything You Know Is Wrong, Book One: Human Origins.* Textstream, 2000.

Scarre, Chris, General Editor, *Past Worlds: The Times Atlas of Archaeology.* London, UK: Times Books Limited, 1988.

Tate, Karen, *Sacred Places of Goddess: 108 Destinations.* San Francisco, CA: CCC Publishing, 2006.

Wasserman, James, *The Temple of Solomon: From Ancient Israel to Secret Societies.* Inner Traditions, 2012.

Westward, Jennifer, Editor, *The Atlas of Mysterious Places.* London, UK: Weidenfeld & Nicolson, 1987.

Nephilim Bible references: **http://www.nwcreation.net/nephilim.html** or **http://www.pantheon.org/articles/n/nephilim.html**

LOST CONTINENTS

Blavatsky, Helena, *The Secret Doctrine.* 1888. [See re-issues, Tarcher and others.]

Childress, David Hatcher, *Ancient Tonga & the Lost City of Mu'a.* Kempton, IL: Adventures Unlimited Press, 1996.

Childress, David Hatcher, *Lost Cities of Ancient Lemuria and the Pacific.* Kempton, IL: Adventures Unlimited Press, 1988.

Frejer, Ernest B., Compiler, *The Edgar Cayce Companion.* Virginia Beach, VA, 1995.

Howell, Clark, F., *Early Man.* Alexandria, VA: Time-Life Books, 1968.

Little, Gregory L., Van Auken, John, Little, Lora H., *Mound Builders: Edgar Cayce's Forgotten Record of Ancient America.* Memphis, TN: Eagle Wing Books, 2001.

Hancock, Graham, *Fingerprints of the Gods,* Three Rivers Press, 1995.

Hapgood, Charles, *Earth's Shifting Crust.* Museum Press, 1958.

Hapgood, Charles, *Path of the Pole.* Adventures Unlimited Press, 1970.

Jenkins, John Major, *Maya Cosmogenesis 2012.* Bear & Company, 1998.

Oliver, Spencer, *A Dweller On Two Planets.* Garber Communications, 1884.

Oliver, Spencer, *An Earth Dweller Returns.* Garber Communications, 1940.

Olsen, Brad, *Sacred Places Around the World (2nd Edition).* San Francisco, CA: CCC Publishing, 2004.

Olsen, Brad, *Sacred Places North America (2nd Edition).* San Francisco, CA: CCC Publishing, 2008.

Santillana, Giorgio de, and von Dechend, Hertha, *Hamlet's Mill.* Gambit, 1969.

Flem-Ath, Rand and Rose, *When the Sky Fell.* St. Martin's Press, 1995.

Flem-Ath, Rand and Rose, *Atlantis beneath the Ice: The Fate of the Lost Continent.* Bear & Company, 2012.

Baalbek references:
http://www.sacredsites.com/middle_east/lebanon/baalbek.htm and http://www.bibliotecapleyades.net/esp_baalbek_1.htm

PAST ESOTERIC

Eiseley, Loren, Editor, *The Epic Of Man.* New York, NY: Life Books, 1961.

Hamlyn, Paul, *Greek Mythology.* London, UK: Westbook House, 1964.

Macrino, Vincenzo, *Humanity: The Alien Project.* Hayden, ID: Bridger House Publishers, 2013.

Rampa, Lobsang, T., *Third Eye: The Autobiography of a Tibetan Lama.* New York, NY: Ballantine, 1956.

Smyth, Piazzi, *The Great Pyramid.* New York, NY: Bell Publishing Co., 1880.

Sullivan, Walter, et. al, *The World's Last Mysteries.* Pleasantville, NY: The Reader's Digest Association, 1981.

The legend of Shambala: http://spirithousehealing.ning.com/forum/topics/shambhala

The Secret KGB Abduction Files - UFO Documents (Roger Moore):
http://www.youtube.com/watch?v=RFmWLdf7r-g&feature=youtu.be

CONTROL

ALTERNATIVE NARRATIVE

Keith, Jim, *Mind Control and UFOs: Casebook on Alternative 3.* Kempton, IL: Adventures Unlimited, 2005.

O'Leary, Brian, *The Making of an Ex-Astronaut.* Pocket Books, 1971.

Adams, Russell B., Series Director, *Mystic Places: Mysteries of the Unknown.* Alexandria, VA: Time-Life Books, 1987.

Childress, David Hatcher, *Anti-Gravity & The World Grid.* Stelle, IL: Adventures Unlimited Press, 1995.

Metzner, Ralph, *The Unfolding Self.* Novato, CA: Origin Press, 1998.

Westward, Jennifer, Editor, *The Atlas of Mysterious Places.* London, UK: Weidenfeld & Nicolson, 1987.

"The Rise of the BRIC Countries:" http://www.motherjones.com/politics/2012/04/rise-of-bric-countries

SECRET FAMILIES

Ford, Henry, *The International Jew.* (originally published in 1920), Liberty Bell Publications, 2004.

Koestler, Arthur, *Thirteenth Tribe.* (originally published by Random House, 1976), Fawcett Popular Library, 1978.

Quigley, Carroll, *Tragedy And Hope: A History Of The World In Our Time.* Macmillan, 1966.

Zagami, Leo, *Confessions of an Illuminati (Vol. I, II, III).* San Francisco, CA: CCC Publishing, 2015, 2016, 2017.

Investigates Synarchism International:
http://www.abovetopsecret.com/forum/thread494628/pg1

Illuminati a myth? A well-documented case that they are real:
http://www.youtube.com/watch?v=0PLhBECS7oA&feature=share

History of the Rothschilds:
http://www.pakalertpress.com/2010/07/19/house-of-rothschild-no-one-can-understand-what-has-happened-to-the-planet-without-reading-this/

LOSING MY RELIGION

De Botton, Alain, *Religion for Atheists: A Non-Believers Guide to the Uses of Religion.* Pantheon, 2012.

Hancock, Graham, *Fingerprints of the Gods.* Three Rivers Press, 1996.

Hitchens, Christopher. *God is Not Great: How Religion Poisons Everything.* New York, NY: Hachette Book Group, 2007.

SACRED GEOMETRY

Frissell, Bob, *Nothing in This Book Is True, But It's Exactly How Things Are.* Berkeley, CA: Frog, Ltd. 1994.

Plato, *Plato: Complete Works.* Hackett Publishing, 1997.

Prophet, Elizabeth Clare, *Inner Perspectives: A Guidebook For The Spiritual Journey.* Summit University Press, 2003.

Pythagoras, *Pythagoras: His Life and Teachings.* Ibis Press, 2010.

SACRED SYMBOLS

Geller, Uri, "Weird Science." World Explorer, (Kempton, IL) Vol. 2, No. 4.

Jeans, Sir James, *The Mysterious Universe.* Cambridge University Press.

Scallion, Gordon-Michael, *Notes from the Cosmos.* W. Chesterfield, NH: Matrix Institute, 1997.

Yogananda, Paramahansa, *Autobiography of a Yogi.* Bombay, India: Jaico Publishing House, 1946.

PINEAL GLAND

Becker, Robert, *The Body Electric: Electromagnetism And The Foundation Of Life.* William Morrow, 1998.

Booth, Mark, *The Secret History of the World.* Overlook TP, 2010.

Blavatsky, Helena Petrovna, *Studies in Occultism.* Theosophical Univ. Press, 1973.

G. de Purucker, *Man in Evolution*, Theosophical Univ. Press, 1977.

Meakin, Richard, *The Third Eye.* University of California Press, 1973

Strassman, Rick, *DMT: The Spirit Molecule: A Doctor's Revolutionary Research into the Biology of Near-Death and Mystical Experiences.* Park Street Press, 2000.

Van Mater, John Jr., *The Third Eye and Human Evolution: Ancient Clue to Spiritual Man.*
http://www.theosophy-nw.org/theosnw/evol/ev-jvmj2.htm

Activating the Pineal Gland: http://ebookbrowse.com/the-arcturian-corridor-part-iii-activating-your-pineal-portal-pdf-d416962374

How to decalcify your pineal gland (video):
http://www.youtube.com/watch?feature=player_embedded&v=92qmQFkYILM or http://bit.ly/10GOn1H

NASA Confirms Super Human Abilities Gained Through Sungazing: http://charbelmaklouf.wordpress.com/2013/06/07/nasa-confirms-super-human-abilities-gained-through-sungazing/

http://www.disclose.tv/forum/pineal-gland-dmt-dna-tetrahedron-2012-t11760.html

http://psychedelicadventure.blogspot.com/2009/08/cannabis-pineal-gland-turn-on-third-eye.html

UNHEALTH INDUSTRY

Atkins, Robert, *Dr. Atkins New Diet Revolution*. Harper, 2009.

Blaylock, Dr. Russell, *The Blaylock Wellness Report*: www.blaylockreport.com

Royal Raymond Rife: http://rifemachinedeals.com/Royal%20Raymond%20Rife.htm

Merck vaccine developer admits vaccines routinely contain hidden cancer viruses derived from diseased monkeys: http://www.naturalnews.com/041963_vaccines_cancer_viruses_Dr_Maurice_Hilleman.html#ixzz2eWK3kHCm

106,000 deaths per year from FDA-approved drugs:
The Journal of the American Medical Association (JAMA) Vol 284, No 4, July 26th 2000, authored by Dr Barbara Starfield, MD, MPH, of the Johns Hopkins School of Hygiene and Public Health

Fluoride studies:
Moules, G.R., "Water Pollution Research and Summary of Current Literature," 1944
Hanstard, Victorian, "Address in reply to the Governor's Speech to Parliament," August 12, 1987, *Nexus*, Aug/Sept 1995
Zhang, I.B., et al, "Effect of a High Fluoride Water Supply on Children's Intelligence"
Harvard Study: NYS Coalition Opposed to Fluoridation: http://www.reuters.com/article/2012/07/24/idUS127920+24-Jul-2012+PRN20120724

Bay Area residents "Get The Fluoride Out!" action group: fluorideout.org

Vitamin D to prevent cancer: http://www.naturalnews.com/021892_vitamin_D_American_Cancer_Society.html#ixzz1jaskR0sg

Aspartame study and resources:
http://www.ncbi.nlm.nih.gov/pubmed/23097267
American Journal of Clinical Nutrition 2012 aspartame study: http://ajcn.nutrition.org/content/early/2012/10/23/ajcn.111.030833.abstract

Inventor of ADHD admits it a fraud before dying:
http://www.worldpublicunion.org/2013-03-27-NEWS-inventor-of-adhd-says-adhd-is-a-fictitious-disease.html

FOOD CONTROL AND ESCAPE

Boutenko, Victoria, *Green for Life*. North Atlantic Books, 2010.

Aris A, Leblanc S. Reprod Toxicol. 2011 May; 31, pesticide study in Quebec, Canada: http://www.ncbi.nlm.nih.gov/pubmed/21338670

Sears ME, Genuis SJ. J Environ Public Health. 2012. Environmental determinants of chronic disease and medical approaches: recognition, avoidance, supportive therapy, and detoxification: http://www.ncbi.nlm.nih.gov/pubmed/22315626
ALSO SEE: http://articles.mercola.com/sites/articles/archive/2012/09/15/genetic-roulette-gmo-documentary.aspx

"Top 10 Food Additives to Avoid" list derived from: http://foodmatters.tv/articles-1/top-10-food-additives-to-avoid

FDA Says Walnuts Are Illegal Drugs: http://worldtruth.tv/fda-says-walnuts-are-illegal-drugs/

THRIVE

LIVING TO 200

Griffin, Edward G. *World Without Cancer*. American Media (CA), 2010.

Li Ching-Yuen sources:
http://worldtruth.tv/256-year-old-chinese-herbalist-li-ching-yuen-holistic-medicine-and-15-character-traits-that-cause-diseases/
or http://en.wikipedia.org/wiki/Li_Ching-Yuen

The websites NaturalNews.com and TimeForWellness.org are invaluable resources for information of longevity, wellness and the best foods to consume.

Scientific Breakthroughs Give Hope For Humans To Live To 150:
http://newyork.cbslocal.com/2012/02/14/could-the-next-generation-live-to-be-150/

Could humans live to 500 years old? Scientists believe genetic tweaks could significantly extend our lifespan:
http://www.dailymail.co.uk/sciencetech/article-2523086/Could-humans-live-500-years-old-Scientists-believe-genetic-tweaks-significantly-extend-lifespan.html

SCIENCE OF CONSCIOUSNESS

Hancock, Graham, *Supernatural: Meetings with the Ancient Teachers of Mankind*. Disinformation Books, 2006.

Jeans, Sir James, *The Mysterious Universe*. Kessinger Publishing, 2010.

The Princeton Engineering Anomalies Research (PEAR) program: http://www.princeton.edu/~pear/

Kundalini energy and the chakras:
http://www.psychedelicjunction.com/2010/09/what-is-kundalini-energy-shakti-basics.html

432 Hz vs. 440 Hz:
http://www.whydontyoutrythis.com/2013/08/440hz-music-conspiracy-to-detune-good-vibrations-from-natural-432hz.html

The world's source for information on Concert Pitch A=432Hz and the effects of the vibrant environment on Awareness: http://omega432.com/

Quantum entanglement: http://www.wired.com/wiredscience/2012/05/quantum-teleportation-distance/

Radin, Dean, *Supernormal*. Deepak Chopra Books, an imprint of Crown Publishing/Random House, 2013.

SPIRIT, BODY MIND

Laszlo, Ervin, *Science and the Akashic Field: An Integral Theory of Everything*. Inner Traditions, 2nd edition, 2007.

Jodorowski, Alejandro, *The Spiritual Journey of Alejandro Jodorowski*. Park Street Press, 2008.

Kavassilas, George, *Our Universal Journey*. Our Journey Home Pty Ltd, 2012.

Praying over seeds makes them grow faster than no-prayed over seeds: **http://media.noetic.org//uploads/files/DirectedPrayer.pdf**

Healing cures: **http://www.fourmilab.ch/documents/gtpp/Documents/jse_14_3_bengston.pdf**

People with regular spiritual practices live longer: **http://www.ncbi.nlm.nih.gov/pmc/articles/PMC1305900/**

Intentions create bio-fields: **http://www.item-bioenergy.com/infocenter/ConsciousIntentiononDNA.pdf**

REINCARNATION

Hubbard, L. Ron, *Dianetics: The Modern Science of Mental Health*. Bridge Publications, 2007.

Knapp, Stephen, *The Secret Teachings of the Vedas: The Eastern Answers to the Mysteries of Life*. CreateSpace Independent Publishing Platform, 1986.

Müller, Max, *Sacred Books of the East*. Routledge, 2000.

Olsen, Brad, *Future Esoteric: The Unseen Realms*. CCC Publishing, 2nd edition, 2016.

Russell, Bertrand, *The Problems of Philosophy*. Simon & Brown, 2013.

Stevenson, Ian, *Twenty Cases Suggestive of Reincarnation*. University of Virginia Press, 1980.

Scientist Photographs The Soul Leaving The Body: **http://www.adguk-blog.com/2013/09/scientist-photographs-soul-leaving-body.html**

PRE-UTOPIA

Dialogues of Plato: **http://www.sacred-texts.com/cla/plato/**

Duff, Godon. "Gordon Duff Interview, 3 Hour Marathon (video)." *Veterans Today*, **http://www.veteranstoday.com/2012/12/09/gordon-duff-interview-3-hour-marathon-video/**

SO YOU WANNA CREATE A STREET FAIRE?

Godin, Seth, *We Are All Weird*. The Domino Project, 2011.

Jones, Steven T., *The Tribes of Burning Man*. San Francisco, CA: CCC Publishing, 2011.

For more information on the WPTTO and the How Weird Street Faire, please visit our websites: **www.peacetour.org** and **www.howweird.org**

THE BUDDHA

Smith, Huston, *The World's Religions*. 50th Anniversary Ed., HarperOne, 1991.

Thurman, Robert, *His Holiness the Dalai Lama, Infinite Life: Awakening to Bliss Within*. Riverhead Trade, 2005.

The Buddha: The Story of Siddhartha. Richard Gere (Actor), David Grubin (Director), 2010.

A Course in Miracles, combined volume (2007), Foundation for Inner Peace, 1976. For comprehensive and accurate information, please visit **www.acim.org**.

For a discussion in the vernacular of core *Course in Miracles* principles, see Renard, Gary R. *The Disappearance of the Universe*. Straight talk about illusions, past lives, religion, sex, politics, and the miracles of forgiveness. (2002); Hay House, 2004.

CONCLUSION

Paine, Thomas, *The Age of Reason, The Complete Edition*. Thomas and Seedbox Classics, 2012.

$7 billion in assets Vatican banking empire: **http://benswann.com/vatican-bank-scandal-jp-morgan-hsbc-cease-doing-business-with-vatican/#ixzz2mxOjDcvi**

ACKNOWLEDGEMENTS

The following individuals were instrumental in making this book possible: my girlfriend and first round editor Jennifer Fahey, first edition content editor Doris Lora, second edition copy editor Mark J. Maxam and Ryan Gable, plus cover art & book design by Mark J. Maxam. The legal advice of Edward Taylor and publishing recommendations from Mary Rowles at IPG were critical in the development of the *Esoteric Series*. Kudos to my friends and business partners Michael O'Rourke, Justin Weiner, Michael Gozney, Robert Kidwell, Jerry Nardini, and my family members mother Elaine Olsen, father Marshall Olsen, brother Chris Olsen, and sister Marsie Sweetland. Thank you all for the editorial suggestions, guidance, and unwavering support over the years.

This book was inspired by the Australian magazine *Nexus* and the provocative issues they feature. Another inspiration is the online encyclopedia Wikipedia. Both were invaluable assets in the research and fact checking for the vast amount of knowledge they contain. I consider both game-changing media resources. Thank you Duncan Roads for *Nexus*, and thank you Jimmy Wales & the fantastic contributors @ Wikipedia. The Wikimedia Commons, a media file repository making available public domain and freely-licensed educational media content, was useful in the collection of images used in this book. Also helpful were the Facebook postings of Jeff Andrews, Nikki Mackenzie, Scott Munson, Paul Hubbard and dozens of other social media friends. Keeping it real against all odds, and the open source sharing of information is the direction and hope of the future.

This book is dedicated to the memory of all those who have been persecuted, jailed or killed for their commitment to truth and justice. I gratefully invoke their courage in making the ultimate sacrifice as we stand up for equality and transparency for a better world, and ultimately, for a lasting peace on Earth.

INDEX

Symbols

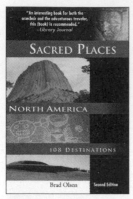

Sacred Places North America: 108 Destinations

– 2nd EDITION; by Brad Olsen

This comprehensive travel guide examines North America's most sacred sites for spiritually attuned explorers. Spirituality & Health reviewed: "The book is filled with fascinating archeological, geological, and historical material. These 108 sacred places in the United States, Canada, and Hawaii offer ample opportunity for questing by spiritual seekers."

$19.95 :: 408 pages   **paperback: 978-1888729139**

all Ebooks priced at $9.99

Kindle: 978-1888729252; PDF: 978-1888729191
ePub: 978-1888729337
||||||||||||||||||||||||||||||||||||||

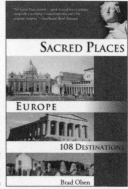

Sacred Places Europe:
108 Destinations – by Brad Olsen

This guide to European holy sites examines the most significant locations that shaped the religious consciousness of Western civilization. Travel to Europe for 108 uplifting destinations that helped define religion and spirituality in the Western Hemisphere. From Paleolithic cave art and Neolithic megaliths, to New Age temples, this is an impartial guide book many millennium in the making.

$19.95 :: 344 pages   **paperback: 978-1888729122**

all Ebooks priced at $9.99

Kindle: 978-1888729245; PDF: 978-1888729184
ePub: 978-1888729320
||||||||||||||||||||||||||||||||||||||

Sacred Places of Goddess: 108 Destinations – by Karen Tate

Readers will be escorted on a pilgrimage that reawakens, rethinks, and reveals the Divine Feminine in a multitude of sacred locations on every continent. Meticulously researched, clearly written and comprehensively documented, this book explores the rich tapestry of Goddess worship from prehistoric cultures to modern academic theories.

$19.95 :: 424 pages   **paperback: 978-1888729115**

all Ebooks priced at $9.99

Kindle: 978-1888729269; PDF: 978-1888729177
ePub: 978-1888729344
||||||||||||||||||||||||||||||||||||||

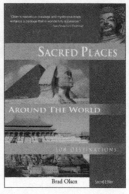

Sacred Places Around the World:
108 Destinations

– 2nd EDITION; by Brad Olsen

The mystical comes alive in this exciting compilation of 108 beloved holy destinations. World travelers and armchair tourists who want to explore the mythology and archaeology of the ruins, sanctuaries, mountains, lost cities, and temples of ancient civilizations will find this guide ideal.

$17.95 :: 288 pages   **paperback: 978-1888729108**

all Ebooks priced at $8.99

Kindle: 978-1888729238; PDF: 978-1888729160
ePub: 978-1888729313
||||||||||||||||||||||||||||||||||||||

World Stompers:
A Global Travel Manifesto

– 5th EDITION; by Brad Olsen

Here is a travel guide written specifically to assist and motivate young readers to travel the world. When you are ready to leave your day job, load up your backpack and head out to distant lands for extended periods of time, Brad Olsen's "Travel Classic" will lend a helping hand.

$17.95 :: 288 pages   **paperback: 978-1888729054**

all Ebooks priced at $8.99

Kindle: 978-1888729276; PDF: 978-1888729061
ePub: 978-1888729351

||||||||||||||||||||||||||||||||||||||

LEO ZAGAMI BOOKS FROM CCC PUBLISHING

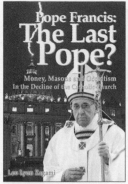

Pope Francis: The Last Pope?: Money, Masons and Occultism in the Decline of the Catholic Church

– by Leo Lyon Zagami

Perfect for anyone interested in prophecies about the end times, Pope Francis: The Last Pope reveals the truth about the last Pope and the darkness that may follow him; fascinating investigations into the gay lobby; Freemasonry; the Jesuit agenda; and, the legend of the White Pope, the Black Pope, and how Benedict's resignation may fulfill an ancient prophecy.

$16.95 :: 224 pages　　　　　　　**paperback 978-1888729542**

all eBooks priced $8.99

Kindle: 978-1888729566; PDF: 978-1888729559
ePub: 978-1888729573
‖‖‖‖‖‖‖‖‖‖‖‖‖‖‖‖‖‖‖‖‖‖‖‖‖

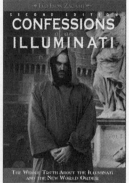

Confessions of an Illuminati, Volume I: The Whole Truth About the Illuminati and the New World Order

– 2nd EDITION; by Leo Lyon Zagami

From the OTO's infiltration of Freemasonry to the real Priory of Sion, this book exposes the hidden structure of the New World Order; their occult practices; and their connections to the intelligence community and the infamous Ur-Lodges.

$17.95 :: 408 pages　　**paperback 978-1888729870**

all eBooks priced $9.99

Kindle: 978-1888729894; PDF: 978-1888729887
ePub: 978-1888729900
‖‖‖‖‖‖‖‖‖‖‖‖‖‖‖‖‖‖‖‖‖‖‖‖‖

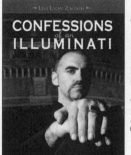

Confessions of an Illuminati, Volume II: The Time of Revelation and Tribulation Leading up to 2020

– by Leo Lyon Zagami

Since the Second Vatican Council, the hierarchy of power emanating from the Jesuits in Rome and the Zionist's in Jerusalem, united by a secret pact, have been manipulating world powers and using economic hitmen to create a unified one-world government.

$17.95 :: 380 pages　　　　　　　**paperback 978-1888729627**

all eBooks priced $9.99

Kindle: 978-1888729658; PDF: 978-1888729634
ePub: 978-1888729641
‖‖‖‖‖‖‖‖‖‖‖‖‖‖‖‖‖‖‖‖‖‖‖‖‖

Confessions of an Illuminati, Volume III: Espionage, Templars and Satanism in the Shadows of the Vatican

– by Leo Lyon Zagami

Take a unique and personal journey into the secretive world of the Dark Cabal. Explore a variety of cryptic topics and learn the truth about the mythical Knights Templars, the Jesuits, and their mastery of the Vatican espionage game.

$17.95 :: 336 pages　　**paperback 978-1888729665**

all eBooks priced $9.99

Kindle: 978-1888729696; PDF: 978-1888729672
ePub: 978-1888729689
‖‖‖‖‖‖‖‖‖‖‖‖‖‖‖‖‖‖‖‖‖‖‖‖‖

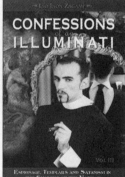

The Invisible Master: Secret Chiefs, Unknown Superiors, and the Puppet Masters Who Pull the Strings of Occult Power from the Alien World

– by Leo Lyon Zagami

Leo Zagami's groundbreaking study of aliens and UFOs explores where we come from and which mysterious figures have guided humanity's political and religious choices. From the prophets to the initiates and magicians, all ages have drawn from a common source of ultra-terrestrial and magical knowledge, passed down for millennia. This text reveals the identity of the unknown superiors, secret chiefs, and invisible masters who have guided Freemasonry, the Illuminati, and others.

$17.95 :: 380 pages　　　　　　　**paperback 978-1888729702**

all eBooks priced $9.99

Kindle: 978-1888729733; PDF: 978-1888729719
ePub: 978-1888729726
‖‖‖‖‖‖‖‖‖‖‖‖‖‖‖‖‖‖‖‖‖‖‖‖‖